For Jim on Fathers' Day, 1994
Roswell, Georgia
with love from
Barb.

The Autobiography of Henry Merrell

Henry

The Autobiography of

HENRY MERRELL

Industrial Missionary

to the South

Edited by James L. Skinner III

The University of Georgia Press   Athens and London

© 1991 by James L. Skinner III
Athens, Georgia 30602
Published by the University of Georgia Press
All rights reserved

Designed by Sandra Strother Hudson
Set in Janson by Tseng Information Systems, Inc.
Printed and bound by Thomson-Shore
The paper in this book meets the guidelines
for permanence and durability of the Committee on
Production Guidelines for Book Longevity of
the Council on Library Resources.

Printed in the United States of America
95   94   93   92   91   C   5   4   3   2   1

Library of Congress Cataloging in Publication Data

Merrell, Henry, 1816–1883.
    The autobiography of Henry Merrell : industrial missionary to the
South / edited by James L. Skinner, III.
        p.   cm.
    Includes bibliographical references.
    ISBN 0-8203-1253-3
    1. Merrell, Henry, 1816–1883.   2. Industrialists–Southern States–
Biography.   3. Textile industry–Southern States–History–19th
century.   I. Skinner, James L., date.   II. Title.
HC102.5.M46A3   1991
338.4'7677'0092–dc20
[B]   90-10919
                                                              CIP
British Library Cataloging in Publication Data available

Title page illustration: Henry Merrell (1816–1883)

For

JOSEPHINE NORVELL FRY SKINNER

Qui transtulit sustinet

Contents

Acknowledgments

It is a pleasure to acknowledge the support that my college has given me in my research and travel. Two summer grants from the Faculty Development Committee of Presbyterian College have enabled me to do research in New York, Georgia, and Arkansas. Teresa Inman and Jane Presseau of the Thomason Library staff have helped me acquire many of the primary and secondary sources that I needed to annotate Henry Merrell's memoirs. Other librarians and archivists who have been exceptionally helpful have been Robert Quist and Barbara Brooks of the Utica Public Library, Utica, New York; Boyd Reese of the Office of History of the Presbyterian Church, U.S.A.; Sheila Garske of the Camden and Ouachita County, Arkansas, Library; Mary Medearis of the Southwest Arkansas Regional Archives; and Russell Baker of the Arkansas History Commission. I received frequent and welcome help from the staff of the Georgia Department of Archives and History, Atlanta, and from the staff of the University of Georgia Libraries, Athens.

One of the pleasures in tracking Henry Merrell has been attempting to locate the factory sites that he built or helped to build in the early and middle years of the nineteenth century. Archaeologists in Georgia have been very helpful to me, especially David Hally of the University of Georgia and Dean and Kay Wood of Southeastern Archaeological Associates, who are currently engaged in a dig for the original Roswell Manufacturing Company, a project under the sponsorship of the Roswell Historical Society.

Local historians and historical societies in New York, Georgia, and Arkansas have helped me to track many of Merrell's references. I am particularly grateful to Douglas Preston and Richard Manzelmann of the Oneida County Historical Society; to Larry Morrison of the Ouachita County Historical Society; and to E. H. Armor of the Greene County Historical Society, who drove me through much of his part of Georgia and charted my course to two of Merrell's factories. Michael Hitt of Sugar Hill, Georgia, and Louise Westbrook of Nashville, Arkansas, provided valuable help at key points in my search for the original Roswell mill in Georgia and the Royston mill in Arkansas. Martha Stovall, Shirley

Deuchler, and Darlene Walsh of the Historic Roswell Preservation Commission helped me sift through records at Bulloch Hall concerning the Roswell Manufacturing Company. Ruby Ezzard showed me the historical records of the Roswell Presbyterian Church, and Clarece Martin shared with me her copies of the minutes of the Roswell Manufacturing Company. Sam Dickinson of Prescott, Arkansas, was kind enough to offer suggestions concerning Merrell's account of the Camden Campaign in Civil War Arkansas, and Bruce Murph of El Dorado, Arkansas, helped to trace old deeds. Louise DeLong of the Roswell Historical Society has been most helpful and encouraging.

I have received invaluable background material on the Merrell and Camp families from Chester Talcott Park of Tulsa, Oklahoma; from George H. Keeler of Marietta, Georgia; from Edith Caldwell of Watertown, New York; from Robert Brennan of Sackets Harbor, New York; from Clifton Paisley of Tallahassee, Florida; and from Elizabeth Huckaby of Little Rock, Arkansas. People who have stepped forward at key points to help me fill in crucial gaps in Arkansas have been my brother Wirt Skinner, Sam D. Dickinson, Dewayne Gray, Jan McGalliard, and Bobbie Hendrix. The same aid was provided in other states by Caroline Hunt of Madison, Georgia, and Linda Stuard of Palestine, Texas. Robert McMath, Theodore Rosengarten, and Jack McLaughlin gave me advice and encouragement. My colleague David Needham offered background and counsel in American history. Morris Galloway and Patricia Lynn provided me with computer resources.

My good friend John Idol of Clemson University provided encouragement and good advice, and my wife, Ramona, and son, Jimmy, gave me help, patience, and understanding when I needed them most. My father, James L. Skinner, Jr., gave me the publishing rights to Merrell's papers and much, much more.

But most of all I thank my brother Arthur, not only for his help in proofreading and in making four of the maps that illustrate this volume, but also for the tireless energy and determination that he brought to the task of finding and cataloging the Smith family papers, of which Merrell's papers are a part. Had he not spent a sabbatical year combing and sifting through what was often the literal trash of the past, virtually all of the supporting material from the Smith House would have been unavailable to me at a critical stage and would perhaps still be packed or scattered in a dark, squirrel-fouled attic in Roswell, Georgia.

Note on the Text

In preparing his manuscript for publication, I have let Henry Merrell speak for himself. His dedication to his profession, his keen eye for detail, his off-hand humor, his Victorian earnestness, his boundless energy, his religious zeal, his racial prejudices, and his rich but always fluid style will all be immediately apparent. I have divided his work into three sections — New York, Georgia, and Arkansas — and have provided an introduction to each section.

Whenever possible, I have transcribed Merrell's hand exactly as it appears. But much editorial work had to be done. Merrell's punctuation, for example, is highly irregular. He uses what looks like a semicolon for most of his commas, and he apparently has no logical system for using commas. He ignores them, especially, in writing nonrestrictive phrases and clauses, yet he often uses them to set off a restrictive phrase or clause or puts them in other awkward places. I have therefore regularized and modernized most of Merrell's uses of the semicolon and comma. Where the reader may be confused by his usage, I have followed the same procedure with Merrell's hyphens and apostrophes, which he rarely uses where the modern eye expects them.

Merrell is also an unorthodox and inconsistent speller, and here I have taken a divided approach. I leave most of his rare British spellings intact, but I have silently corrected and modernized unusual and old-fashioned spellings that might distract the reader. His inconsistent spelling is particularly troublesome with proper names. "Southhampton" is soon followed by "Southampton," "Seneca" by "Senaca," "Scyler" by Scuyler," "Bullock" by "Bulloch," "Altimaha" by "Altamaha," "Green" by "Greene," "Kenion" by "Kenyon" and "Beattie" by "Beatty." He once has "Seaward" and "Seward" on the same line of manuscript, and he spells a Dutch name three separate ways: Van Rensaalier, Van Renslaer, and Van Rensalier, never using the correct spelling, Van Rensselaer. I have regularized and modernized such spellings.

As he notes, Merrell's memory occasionally plays him false with many proper names: Bishop Hobert of New York was actually named Hobart; a Utica brewer whom he names Matthew Cobb was named Codd; a circus that he names Eldridge's was actually Eldred's; a prominent family that he names Wetmon was named Wetmore; the Ellison brothers in Greene County, Georgia, were actually the Allison brothers; his General McLearned of Arkansas Post fame was actually General McClernand; his teacher in Utica, David Prentiss, was known as David Prentice. Sometimes these errors can be taken as spelling problems: for example, his Fort Sumpter was South Carolina's Fort Sumter; Governor Flannigan of Arkansas was actually Governor Flanagin; his Colonel Miltonbuger who accompanied him through Texas and Mexico to Havana was actually a Colonel Miltenberger; and the Union general whom he calls Solomons was named Salomon. His spellings of French and Spanish names seem to be phonetic. I have corrected all such errors without noting them.

It should be noted that, although others frequently spelled his name "Merrill," he always used "Merrell," as did everyone of his generation of the family.

Few of Merrell's errors were impossible to find and correct, but there were some. In speaking of the horse that he rode on his two-thousand-mile journey in 1838 (chapters 21–23), he keeps changing its sex from male to female. Because the horse was so cantankerous, I have arbitrarily made it male.

I have let stand many of his cavalier capitalizations and his every use of the ampersand, but whenever Merrell's verb tense or usage might puzzle a modern reader — as it would with "strown" instead of "strewn," "glozed" instead of "glossed," or "wrot" instead of "wrought" — I have made silent corrections.

Whenever his memory clearly fails him in the matter of dates, I place the correct date in brackets following the one that Merrell actually wrote. Occasionally I follow this practice with proper and place names; however, as I noted above, most of the time such corrections are silent. An empty bracket [   ] will mark words that Merrell left out or that were impossible to decipher. I have occasionally inserted words in brackets where I believe they are necessary to clarify Merrell's meaning. I do not use *sic*.

Finally, Merrell is not consistent in numbering his chapters. There are two chapter twenty-one's, for example, which I have brought together by merging the first chapter 21 into chapter 20. Also, he begins renumbering his chapters with the later, smaller volume. Once, he changes from roman numeral IV to arabic number 5 in the next chapter. I have preserved his system of numbering chapters. He asks his reader to move chapter 34 forward between chapters 8 and 9. I have done so.

Introduction

On the second floor landing of the Smith House in Roswell, Georgia, I found, in the top drawer of an old chest, a record book that was bound in marbled boards. As soon as I read the opening words, I was hooked:

> My name is Henry Merrell. No middle name. Never had one. Have always got on without one. I don't know if I have not observed all my life that the most substantial, steady-going men as a rule have but the one christened name; for instance "George Washington, Henry Clay, Andrew Jackson," & so on down to such as myself. One reason, perhaps, is that a mother who has at the outset hard sense enough to be content with a plain, unromantic name for her boy will probably be free from nonsense in other respects, & for that reason all the more competent to train up that boy to be a substantial man.

My parents, who had recently inherited the Smith House from my mother's aunt, Mary Norvell Smith, were sitting on the couch across the hallway as I read, and I asked them, "Who was Henry Merrell? Did Arthur ever mention him?" Arthur William Smith (1881–1960), my great-aunt's husband, had been the grandson of Archibald Smith (1801–86), the builder of the house and one of the founders of Roswell. Arthur often spoke of his historic family, but that day neither my parents nor I could remember his ever mentioning a Henry Merrell.

My curiosity about him increased as I read on into the afternoon and later found, in the same drawer, a Civil War commission signed by General Edmund Kirby Smith on December 22, 1864, for Henry Merrell "to leave these shores" for England "to purchase and forward . . . certain machinery required by the clothing bureau." My questions were rapidly multiplying. In what I had already read, Merrell had told me that he was a Yankee, born in Utica, New York, in 1816. Yet he was commissioned by a Confederate general in Louisiana to travel to England on behalf of the Department of the Trans-Mississippi at the end of the Civil War. And both the journal and the commission had been resting in a drawer in an antebellum house in Georgia whose owner had no apparent connection with the author of the volume and the subject of the commission.

In the ten years since I opened that drawer, I have been able to answer these and other questions. The answers, inevitably, have led to further

The Smith House (1845), Roswell, Georgia. In 1841 Merrell married into the Smith family, one of the six founding families of Roswell. His manuscripts were discovered in this house in 1981. This photograph was taken around 1940.

questions. It turned out that the record book in the drawer, in which Merrell had begun writing in 1873, was the companion to a larger one, also found among the Smith papers, which he had begun writing even earlier, in 1863, in Pike County, Arkansas. This larger and earlier volume he wrote in the end sheets and margins of his copy of David Dale Owen's *Report of a Geological Survey of Wisconsin, Iowa, and Minnesota* (Philadelphia, 1852), for the Federal blockade had left him with no other supply of paper. At the beginning of this volume, he notes that, owing to the insurmountable pressures brought upon him by the war and the effects of his northern birth on his southern neighbors, he has just sold the mill and village that he had created in the Arkansas wilderness and had named Royston. He tells us later that he sold the mill to John Matlock of Camden, Arkansas, in February 1863. In a letter that she wrote on June 10, 1863, Merrell's wife, Elizabeth Magill Merrell, told William Seagrove Smith (1834–65), the son of the builder of the Smith House where the letter was found, that she and her husband had moved away from the factory village across the Little Missouri River to a place that he called "The Retreat." There, according to his memoir, Merrell says that he has exhausted himself in his

Archibald and Anne Magill Smith, Merrell's brother-in-law and sister-in-law. The Merrells, after maintaining a lifelong relationship with the Smiths and their children, made them their heirs.

The Merrell Family
of New Hartford and Utica, New York

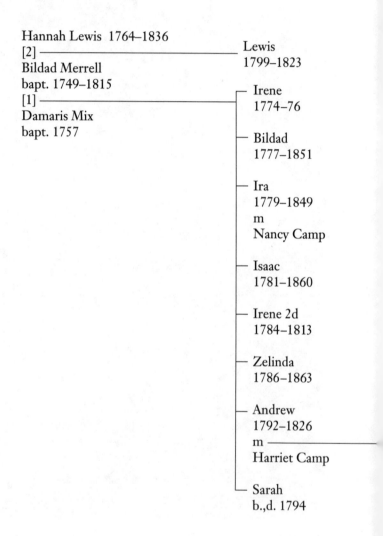

Hannah Lewis 1764–1836
[2] ——————————————— Lewis
Bildad Merrell   1799–1823
bapt. 1749–1815
[1] ———————————————— Irene
Damaris Mix   1774–76
bapt. 1757
                                     — Bildad
                                       1777–1851

                                     — Ira
                                       1779–1849
                                       m
                                       Nancy Camp

                                     — Isaac
                                       1781–1860

                                     — Irene 2d
                                       1784–1813

                                     — Zelinda
                                       1786–1863

                                     — Andrew
                                       1792–1826
                                       m ——————
                                       Harriet Camp

                                     — Sarah
                                       b.,d. 1794

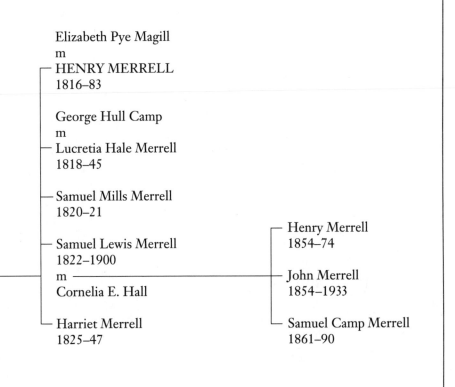

Elizabeth Pye Magill
m
HENRY MERRELL
1816–83

George Hull Camp
m
Lucretia Hale Merrell
1818–45

Samuel Mills Merrell
1820–21

Samuel Lewis Merrell
1822–1900
m
Cornelia E. Hall

Harriet Merrell
1825–47

Henry Merrell
1854–74

John Merrell
1854–1933

Samuel Camp Merrell
1861–90

The Camp Family of Utica and Sackets Harbor, New York

Elnathan Camp
b. 1/24/1734
m ——————————————— Talcott Camp
Eunice Talcott   1762–1832
1736–1804   m ————————————
                                 Nancy Hale
                                 1758–1806

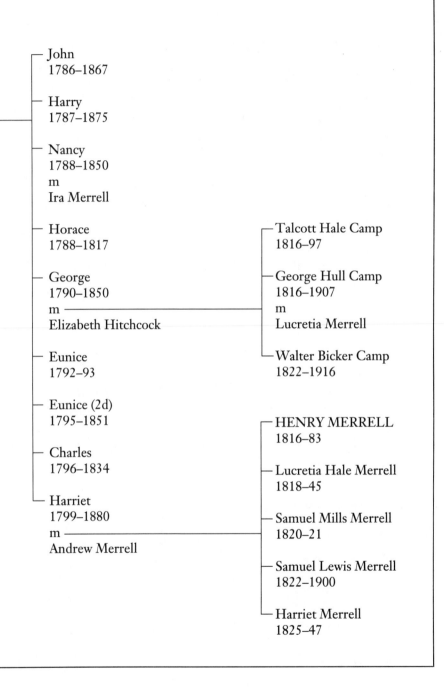

John
1786–1867

Harry
1787–1875

Nancy
1788–1850
m
Ira Merrell

Horace
1788–1817

George
1790–1850
m
Elizabeth Hitchcock

Eunice
1792–93

Eunice (2d)
1795–1851

Charles
1796–1834

Harriet
1799–1880
m
Andrew Merrell

Talcott Hale Camp
1816–97

George Hull Camp
1816–1907
m
Lucretia Merrell

Walter Bicker Camp
1822–1916

HENRY MERRELL
1816–83

Lucretia Hale Merrell
1818–45

Samuel Mills Merrell
1820–21

Samuel Lewis Merrell
1822–1900

Harriet Merrell
1825–47

The Smith Family of Roswell, Georgia

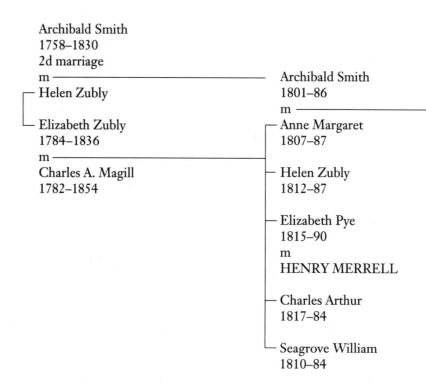

Archibald Smith
1758–1830
2d marriage
m ———————————————— Archibald Smith
Helen Zubly   1801–86
                                              m ————————————
Elizabeth Zubly   Anne Margaret
1784–1836   1807–87
m ————————————————
Charles A. Magill   Helen Zubly
1782–1854   1812–87

                                   Elizabeth Pye
                                   1815–90
                                   m
                                   HENRY MERRELL

                                   Charles Arthur
                                   1817–84

                                   Seagrove William
                                   1810–84

Elizabeth Anne
"Lizzie"
1831–1915

William Seagrove
"Willie"
1834–65

Helen Zubly
"Helena"
1841–96

Archibald
"Archie"
1844–1923
m
Gulielma Riley
1846–1921

Archibald
1874–1947

Frances Maner
1875–1939

Arthur William
1881–1960
m
Mary Norvell
1890–1981

venture and in keeping it going during a war, that he has read everything in his library, and that he is now going to write an account of his life. The date on the first page is August 1863.

In the same letter, Mrs. Merrell tells Willie Smith that her husband has been called to military duty to block the Arkansas River to impede the possible capture of Little Rock by Federal forces. Although a copy of his actual orders has not survived, Merrell preserved in his papers a letter that he wrote on April 27, 1863, to Lieutenant General Theophilus H. Holmes, containing his requirements in order "to begin the Obstructions in the Arkansas River." He signs this letter "Henry Merrell, Major in Charge of the Work."[1] Merrell says that he reported to headquarters in Little Rock in May and that he shifted the location of his obstruction downriver near the White River cutoff. Merrell kept documents and receipts from his work on the river that are dated as late as June 26, 1863, and he writes that he received informal leave to return home following the "miserable business" of the battle of Helena, which took place on July 4. So he began his memoir that August, immediately following his first military efforts on behalf of the Confederacy.

It is reasonable to assume, therefore, that Merrell, in the light of his northern birth and upbringing, felt the need to justify to someone what he had done and what he had become. He began writing in the Owen volume at "The Retreat" on the Little Missouri River in Pike County in August of 1863, took it with him when he moved to Camden in October, following the Federal advance on Fort Smith and toward Pike County that took place in early September, and stopped writing in it in late September of 1864, when, according to documents he kept, he was ordered to Shreveport, Louisiana, to attend General Kirby Smith, the Commander of the Trans-Mississippi Department. At the end of this volume, in a note added in 1873, Merrell says, "my narrative was interrupted by military duty."

The smaller, later volume he began in Camden, Arkansas, in early November 1873. Thinking the earlier volume had been lost, he began his life story over again, but he discovered the Owen volume after writing a few pages. He then changed the direction of this later account to pick up where he had left off nine years before. The two volumes together, therefore, cover his life from his birth in New York through his trip to England on behalf of the Confederacy in 1864–65.

Henry Merrell (1816–83), clearly one of the manufacturing pioneers of the South, was the son of a Utica bookseller and publisher. He learned the textile trade in nearby Whitesboro under William Walcott of the Oneida Mills; then, worrying about his weak lungs if he remained in the North and considering himself to be following a call, he left Utica in the fall of 1838. He wanted to begin a "Southern Manufacturing System." "I felt a call to make it the special object of my life," he writes. "I believed it practicable, and I thought it a patriotic calling to try and inaugurate a line of things tending to reconcile unhappy differences between the North and the South. This idea may be regarded as the key to my motives during the next twenty years of my life."

On the lookout for a place and an opportunity, he traveled from Utica by rail and horseback through Virginia to Lexington, Kentucky, where a close friend of his mother and former resident of Utica, the Reverend Marvin Winston, told Merrell that, while living in Georgia, he had heard that a group of planter families from the Georgia coast near Darien were beginning a manufacturing community in the part of northern Georgia that had recently been cleared of the Cherokee Indians. The fact that these settlers were, like him, Presbyterians, certainly added to Merrell's interest in what Marvin Winston told him, and Merrell wrote from Lexington to the chief agent of the new Roswell Manufacturing Company, Barrington King, son of the founder of the colony, Roswell King, for whom it had been named.

Although the fall of 1838 was long advanced by this time, Henry Merrell then returned to Utica on horseback to await Barrington King's reply. This turned out to be a harrowing trip through snow and icy wind, not the thing for a man who had been warned from his youth to care for his lungs. By the time he had returned to Utica, he was ill from the effects of his two-thousand-mile journey, and he must have decided to accept any offer that came from Roswell, Georgia.

While he was recovering from his illness, King's offer arrived. The terms were favorable, and in the early spring of 1839, "with a stout heart and the best of resolutions," Merrell left his mother, brother, sister, and friends, "bending my steps Southward, while my school-mates generally sought to establish their fortunes in the West." He went by way of Paterson, New Jersey, where he picked up machinery for the Roswell mill. Traveling by sea to Savannah, by stage to Augusta, by rail to Greensboro, and by stage to Decatur, he arrived on horseback in Roswell in May 1839.

There he began work as Barrington King's "Assistant Agent," resetting the foundation of the first mill, supervising the installation of its machinery, and handling the daily operations of both the mill and its store. After overcoming a challenge to his authority by winning a fist fight with a surly English stonemason named Atkinson, Merrell was invited to the residence of Archibald Smith, where he met and in 1841 married Smith's sister-in-law, Elizabeth Pye Magill (1815–90). His marriage into the Smith family brought this self-made Yankee manufacturer into intimate contact with southern ladies and gentlemen who had been born into the coastal planter class. The Smiths, although participants in the manufacturing experiment at Roswell, were still farmers, and their beautiful farmhouse is a certain symbolic distance from the central cluster of Greek Revival mansions of the Kings and Bullochs. Merrell's reflections on the differences between the values and manners of his native North and his adopted South constitute some of the most memorable passages in his memoirs.

During his stay in Roswell, Merrell invited several Utica friends to come South to help him in work for the Roswell Manufacturing Company. Merrell was crushed by the early death of one of them, William Smith, whose arrival, hopes, illness, and death among strangers he painfully recounts. Later Merrell called upon his brother-in-law, George Hull Camp (1816–1907), to become the manager of the mill store. Camp's wife was Henry Merrell's sister, Lucretia Hale Merrell Camp, and one of the most poignant sections of the memoirs concerns his riding seventy miles from Athens to Roswell in a storm when he received word that she had died in childbirth, March 22, 1845. He could not get to Roswell in time for her burial.

He had been in the Athens area looking after an investment, an investment prompted by his feeling that his contributions to the Roswell Manufacturing Company had not been properly rewarded. He knew that he was "over-working [himself] in the service of the Roswell Manufacturing Company." "My unlucky position in the business required it," he says, adding, "my responsibilities begat work, & my industry begat promotion, & promotion begat work again until my place became untenable even to myself." Looking for a way to improve his independence and his status, Merrell in 1844 had invested in a textile factory called Mars Hill, then in Clarke County about seven miles southwest of Athens on Barber's Creek.

A historian of the industrial development of Georgia has called the Mars Hill factory "the chief factory at Athens."[2] Merrell was able to quadruple (although he maintains that he doubled) his investment in this factory in six months,[3] and he must have impressed the investors in the Curtright Manufacturing Company to whom he sold it, for they invited him to remove to Greene County, Georgia, to operate the Curtright Mills on the banks of the Oconee River. Merrell accepted, and leaving his cousin George Camp in his place as Barrington King's assistant agent, he and his wife moved to Greene County (apparently in October 1845), subsequently built another mill for the Curtright concern, and was so successful in his work for them that several early maps of Georgia have the name "Merrell" or "Merrell's Mill" at that point on the Oconee where the Curtright mills were located.

In what was later to him a dark hour, Merrell's directors persuaded him to establish a steam-powered textile mill in the town of Greensboro, a mill that was eventually to compete with the mills on the Oconee owned by many of these same directors, a mill into which Merrell poured his own capital when he could not get authorization from the directors for money to make planned improvements. This mill eventually failed, and Merrell bitterly assails the directors for the failure. Yet he manfully accepts "failure" as a label for himself. Borrowing from his wife and others, scorning any attempt at compromise with his directors, he charts a new course for himself and his wife in 1856, a course which will certainly strike modern readers either as a model of Victorian enterprise or as a species of Victorian insanity.

Using an 1847 map of the United States, along with data which he had extracted from its 1850 census, and incorporating criteria that would form the basis of a modern computer program—rainfall, population growth, income, watercourses, proximity to crops, number of churches and schools, and so on—Merrell selected a five-county area of southwestern Arkansas, where he would begin life anew. How he selected the site for his mill in the wilderness of Pike County, Arkansas; how he moved himself and his family the hundreds of miles to their new home in this wilderness; how he built his dam and mills and maintained them in the face of truly incredible difficulties that ranged from hostile natives to civil war; how he made from nothing a profitable industry which by the end of the Civil War was the only operating textile mill in Arkansas, one on which the Department of the Trans-Mississippi heavily depended; and how he later served the Confederacy as an engineer and strategist will constitute what for the modern reader will surely be the most gripping part of Merrell's story. In this section of his account, he twice compares himself with Robinson Crusoe, and his reader will be loath to disagree with the comparison. The final pages of his memoirs are filled with accounts of challenges faced and difficulties overcome, of battles fought and occupations witnessed, and of the heroic but futile attempts of the Confederate states west of the Mississippi to maintain their cause in the face of attack from without and anarchy from within.

Having traveled from Havana via Matamoros in Mexico, and having arrived dirty and disheveled in the harbor at Southampton, England, on his commission from General Kirby Smith, Merrell notes a German steamer going out, "black swarming with emigrants . . . bound to reinforce the Federal power." For the only time, his boundless energy and optimism fail him. He says, "I felt then, all over me, that it was a hopeless case."

As it stands, Merrell's narrative breaks off abruptly in London in April 1865. However incomplete it is, his work is a moving testimony to one man's odyssey and accomplishments and is a remarkable testimony to early- and mid-nineteenth-century American life, especially in regard to the cultural differences between the industrial North and the nonindustrial South.

But why were these memoirs in a drawer in the Smith House? Because the Merrells had no children, the Smiths eventually became their heirs. It is possible that Mrs. Merrell—"Betsey" to him, "Aunt Bet" or "Ambet" to the Smiths—could have sent or brought the volumes from Camden to the Smith House, probably between her husband's death in 1883 and the deaths in 1887 of her two sisters who had lived there: Anne Margaret Magill Smith, Archibald senior's wife (1807–87), and Helen Zubly Magill (1812–87).

In some pages that she did not record with her will ("there are too many little things in it"), pages dated July 22, 1887, and re-signed January 8, 1889, Mrs. Merrell effectively disposes of her every possession to family members and servants. She details carefully her wishes about her clothing, tablespoons, saucers, and the like, but never mentions the memoirs, either in these notes or in her will.[4] And she certainly knew of the memoirs, for two of her "corrections," written on small slips of paper, are pinned into the larger volume. I conclude, therefore, that when she wrote these pages, the volumes were already in Roswell. She names Archibald ("Archie") Smith, Jr., as one of her executors, and, if they were not already at the Smith House when she died in 1890, it is possible that he could have brought the volumes back to Roswell with him from the trip that he made to Camden the same year, or that they could have been sent to him by her co-executor, her Camden neighbor G. H. Stinson, a local jeweler.

If the volumes were in the Smith House as early as 1886, they could have been read by Archibald Smith, Sr., who died that year. Merrell would certainly have wanted the paterfamilias, his wife's original trustee, to read his apologia. Following Archibald senior's death and the deaths of Archibald senior's wife and her sister during the next year, the younger Archibald moved from Roswell to LaGrange, Georgia, leaving the house in the possession of his sister Elizabeth Anne ("Lizzie") Smith (1831–1915) and Helen Zubly Smith (1841–96), the two girls who had accompanied the Merrells on a tour of Europe in 1866. Their brother, William Seagrove

("Willie") Smith, who had followed Merrell to Greensboro, who had accompanied him on his first trip to explore the possible site for his Arkansas factory, who had worked for him at the Royston mill, who had traveled with him and his wife on an 1860 trip to the North, and who had always been especially close to Merrell, had died in tragic circumstances as a Confederate soldier in Raleigh, North Carolina, at the very end of the Civil War.

Because they knew and loved the Merrells, these two women would have understood the importance of the volumes, and certainly their preservation must owe something to their care. But it would appear that they did not communicate the whereabouts or possible importance of Merrell's memoirs to the next generation of Smiths: Archibald (1874–1947), Frances Maner (1875–1939), and Arthur William (1881–1960). Following Helen's death in 1896 and Lizzie's in 1915, their brother Archie, who had himself visited the Merrells in 1860, 1867, and 1869, never took up residence in his father's house.[5] It remained shut up, with a caretaker living in only two rooms, from 1915 to 1940, although Arthur Smith, who was thirty-four when Lizzie died and who was a frequent visitor to the house, noted the record book in an inventory that he conducted in 1938. In that inventory he describes the volume as "Henry Merrell war history, scenes in the Western theater," indicating both that he had read some of the volume and that he apparently was not aware of the other volume.[6] It may have been he who placed the record book and the commission in the drawer where I found them in 1981.

Henry Merrell was obviously writing "these memoirs" for family and friends, but the possibility of his having in mind a larger audience must be maintained. Although the early pages contain a wealth of family matters, the intended audience of the later sections certainly seems at times wider than his circle of family and friends, and we are entitled to imagine that his memoirs may have been written for us.

Chronology

1791	September 8	Merrell's grandfather Bildad moves to New Hartford, N.Y., from Hartford, Conn.
1797		Merrell's maternal grandfather, Talcott Camp, settles in Utica, N.Y.
1816	December 8	Henry Merrell born in Utica, N.Y.
1826	January 25	Merrell's father dies.
1828–1829?		Merrell sent to school in Paris Hill, eight miles from Utica.
1829?–1830		Attends the Oneida Institute, Whitesboro, N.Y.
1830		Begins working at the Oneida Factory, Whitesboro, N.Y.
1838		Archibald Smith family moves to Roswell, Ga. Merrell's two-thousand-mile journey looking for opportunity. Accepts offer from Barrington King to work for Roswell Manufacturing Company.
1839	Spring	Merrell travels to Roswell, Ga., via Paterson, N.J., and Savannah, Ga. Travels to Tennessee before taking up his duties.
1841	July 7	Merrell marries Elizabeth Pye Magill, sister-in-law of Archibald Smith.
1842		His sister Lucretia comes to Roswell with her husband and cousin George Camp.
1844	April 23	Merrell allowed to purchase stock in the Roswell Manufacturing Company.

	December	Buys the Mars Hill Factory, Clarke County (now Oconee County), Georgia.
1845	January 23	Merrell leaves the employment of the Roswell Manufacturing Company. Smith House is completed during this year.
	March 22	Merrell's sister Lucretia dies in childbirth.
	May 31	He sells the Mars Hill Factory to the Curtright Manufacturing Company.
	June	Merrells move to Greene County, Ga.
1846	May 26	Long Shoals Factory named "Merrell" by U.S. Post Office.
1847	March–April	He writes four articles on Georgia manufacturing for the *Milledgeville (Southern) Recorder*.
	December	Merrell is planning "a steam factory for fine work" in Greensboro.
1848	January	Smith family visits the Merrells in Greensboro. *DeBow's Review* refers to Merrell as "one of the shrewdest Yankee manufacturers."
1849	July	Merrell may no longer be active manager of the Curtright Manufacturing Company.
	July 26	He sells the Greensboro Manufacturing Company the land for its factory.
1851	June 23	Merrell is no longer agent for Curtright Manufacturing Company.
1854	February 18	Merrell, Ga., is changed to "Curtright" by U.S. Post Office.
1855	August–September	Merrell writes four articles that appear in the *New York Journal of Commerce*.
1856	January 8	Breakup and arbitration of Greensboro Manufacturing Company.
	January	Merrell leaves Georgia with his nephew Willie Smith to "prospect" in Arkansas.
	February 23	He buys land for his new manufacturing village in Pike County, Arkansas.

	After August	His "famous dam" on the Little Missouri River is completed.
1857	January 14	State legislature issues charter to the "Arkansas Manufacturing Company."
1858	February	Factory crippled by flood waters.
	September	The Merrells' first house burns. Merrell suffers an almost fatal attack of diphtheria.
1859	April	Willie Smith rejoins Merrell to act as his clerk.
1860	From June	Merrells and Willie Smith travel in the northern states.
	December 29	Merrell helps draft resolution from Pike County to the state legislature arguing against secession.
1861	May 6	Arkansas becomes the eighth state to secede from the Union.
1862	May 31	Thomas Carmichael Hindman assumes command of Trans-Mississippi Department.
	July 7	Theophilus Hunter Holmes assumes command of the Trans-Mississippi Department. Merrell commissioned captain in partisan rangers by Theophilus Holmes in order to defend Royston from raiders.
	Winter	After being threatened with arrest by Confederate authorities for discounting Confederate money, Merrell gains his point and pushes several recommendations on Trans-Mississippi Headquarters which seem to have led to the establishment of the Clothing Bureau.
	December	Merrell assists in a military review after the battle of Prairie Grove.
1863	January 11	Surrender of Arkansas Post.
	February	Merrell sells Royston to his partner, John Matlock.

	March 3	Edmund Kirby Smith assumes command of Trans-Mississippi Department.
	April–June	Theophilus Holmes commissions Merrell a major in engineering department of the District of Arkansas, which he now commands, and orders him to obstruct the Arkansas River to help prevent the capture of Little Rock.
	August	Merrell begins writing his autobiography at the "Retreat" in Pike County.
	October	Merrells and Magills move to Camden, Arkansas.
	November	Confederate states buy Royston mill and begin to move it to Mound Prairie, Texas.
1864	March	Theophilus Holmes urges Merrell to help with building manufactory in Mound Prairie, Texas.
	March 23	Federal General Steele begins Camden Expedition.
	April 15–26	Steele occupies Camden. Merrell remains in the town.
	April 27	Steele begins his retreat from Camden in early morning hours.
	July 3	Merrell has not left for Texas. He is probably working on Camden fortifications.
	July 6	Federal troops in Georgia burn the Roswell Manufacturing Company.
	September 12	Merrell leaves Camden to report to Kirby Smith's headquarters in Shreveport. He probably writes no more of his autobiography after this date until 1873.
	September 27	Kirby Smith orders Merrell to England to buy machinery for Mound Prairie.
	October 8	Merrell leaves for Texas.
	December 1	Kirby Smith orders him to depart for England. Delays until December 25.
1865	January 12	Merrell gets final instructions and leaves for Matamoros, Mexico, accompanied by, among others, General Polignac.

	March 8	Merrell departs from Havana, Cuba.
	April 1	He arrives at Southampton, England.
	June 2	Kirby Smith officially surrenders the Trans-Mississippi Department.
	June	Merrell leaves England for France.
	July 7	Willie Smith dies in Raleigh, North Carolina.
	August	Merrell returns to England.
	September	Merrell returns to the United States.
	October 26	He applies for pardon in Washington, D.C. (filed Nov. 2; granted Nov. 3).
1866	April	Merrells visit Smiths in Valdosta, Ga.
	April 7	Merrell, his wife, his nieces Lizzie and Helen Smith depart from Savannah on trip to Europe. Smiths return to Roswell after their departure.
	November	Merrells and Smith girls return from Europe.
1867		Merrell and Magill enter mercantile business in Camden.
1868	November 18	Merrell is behind movement in Camden to establish "manufactory" there.
1869	January 15	Merrell and Magill are the most active cotton buyers in Camden.
	July	Merrell and Magill wool-carding factory begins operation in Camden (1869–86).
1870		John Merrell (1854–1933), the son of Merrell's brother, Samuel, comes to work for Merrell in Camden.
1872	April	Merrell is very ill. He perhaps has tuberculosis or "brown lung."
1873	February	His illness worsens.
	November	Thinking he is dying, and thinking that his earlier volume has been lost, Merrell takes up his autobiography again.
	November 5	Finds older volume and incorporates it into his writing plan.

1874?		He breaks off his memoirs to begin a work of fiction based on his experiences. He calls it *The Refugees*.
1875	August 14	Merrell's work is noted and his photograph appears in the *Camden Beacon*.
1877	June 21	On trip to represent Southern Presbyterian church at "Pan Presbyterian Council" in Edinburgh, Merrell has "the first hemorrhage I have had in several years" while getting aboard his ship in New York.
	December 27	*The Refugees* begins running in the *South-Western Presbyterian*.
1883	January 19	Henry Merrell dies in Camden, Arkansas.
1884	November 14	Charles Arthur Magill, his brother-in-law and business partner, dies.
1886		Archibald Smith, Sr., dies.
1888	May 27	Destruction of Royston, Arkansas, by rampaging waters of Little Missouri River.
1890		Merrell's wife, Elizabeth Pye Magill Merrell (b. 1815), dies in Camden.
1915		After death of Lizzie Smith during this year, the Smith House is closed up, with a caretaker living in two rooms, until 1940.
1940		The Smith House is reopened and renovation begun by Arthur William Smith and his new bride, Mary Norvell Smith.
1960		Arthur William Smith dies.
1974–75; 1978		Archaeological surveys and excavations of Curtright Manufacturing Company undertaken by University of Georgia archaeologists under sponsorship of Georgia Power Company.
1981	January 1	Mary Norvell Smith dies and leaves the Smith House to Mr. and Mrs. James L. Skinner, Jr., of Decatur, Georgia.

March	One volume of Henry Merrell's memoirs is discovered during an inventory of the Smith House.
1989	Archaeological excavations of the original site of Roswell Manufacturing Company begin under the sponsorship of the Roswell Historical Society.

The Autobiography of

HENRY MERRELL

New York

ALTHOUGH MANY MAY FIND the Georgia and Arkansas sections of Merrell's memoirs more immediate and energetic, his recollections of his native Utica have an appealing vigor and freshness. He is more prone to anecdotes in this section, but he is also less likely to become distracted by his problems in business or by accounts of Civil War battles. In addition, this section is colored by the understandable warmth and nostalgia that a man in his late forties and living in a wilderness would have for the lively town of his youth. Therefore, "New York" could well stand alone on its qualities as a memoir.

The Utica that Merrell describes was making the transition from a frontier village built on the Mohawk River around Old Fort Schuyler to a prosperous trading and industrial town on the Erie Canal and what would become the New York Central Railroad. When Utica was incorporated in 1798 as a village of under three hundred in the town of Whitestown, it was smaller than nearby New Hartford, but it broke off from Whitestown to form an independent township in 1817, at which time it had a population of three thousand.[1] Henry Merrell had been born the year before in what the Utica historian Moses M. Bagg calls the "pent up" village of Utica in 1816, with 420 dwellings and stores and 2,861 inhabitants.[2] The month after Merrell left Utica for the South in 1839, the first train to connect Syracuse with Albany would pass through the city of Utica, with its population of almost 12,000.[3]

If "a single quite extraordinary town can, like a biography writ large, illuminate, enliven, and give a human dimension to our understanding of general social conditions and developments," then Henry Merrell's memoirs can illuminate, enliven, and give a human dimension to that quite extraordinary town. The quotation is from Mary M. Ryan's study of Utica, *The Cradle of the Middle Class*, which traces the way "Oneida County was one medium through which a variety of changes in the family and society made their way into the broader channels of American history."[4] She sees mirrored in Utica the transition from agriculture to commerce and industry that was occurring not only in the northeastern United States but any place in the world where a community was moving from a frontier to a town and from a town to a city.

This community and Merrell's account of it also demonstrate that the new industrial order, as Jonathan Prude has stated, "was not *only* a process by which economies moved from 'old' to 'new.' " As the new order emerged, it interacted with traditional structures such as the family and the church. The coming of the industrial order "was also a process by which old and new were bound together, by which old and new proceeded in one another's shadow." We have in Merrell's Whitestown, as in Prude's Dudley, Oxford, and Webster, Massachusetts, "an advancing market economy still constrained by widely held, traditional community norms."[5]

This industrial order had begun in 1789 with Samuel Slater's introduction of textile manufacturing in Pawtucket, Rhode Island. By 1809 there were more than fifty mills in New England, most of them grouped in an area extending from Providence and Pawtucket, Rhode Island, into the nearby townships in Massachusetts and Connecticut, but by that time cotton was being spun as far north as New Hampshire, as far south as Baltimore, and as far west as Oneida County.[6] In this early phase of the industrial order, America was spared the shock that the English underwent with the sudden emergence of sooty cities such as Manchester, for these early factories were water-powered and built in largely rural districts.[7] Merrell makes distinctions between the British and American industrial experience, and his memoirs largely concern his work in rural areas with water power.

Merrell was taught by the early industrialists to attempt to link the characteristics of good workers—sobriety, punctuality, steadiness, diligence, and discipline—with traditional Protestant morality. He learned from the Walcotts, who had learned from such as the Slaters and the Lowells, that the entrepreneur should be the head of a large "family" whose function was to reform his workers and the world.[8] Many manufacturers saw industrialization itself as a "civilizing mission." They believed that in making good workers of their hands, "they were rescuing them from barbarism and granting them the benefits of Christian discipline."[9] Later, in recounting what he brought to Arkansas, Merrell will proudly point to the improved food, clothing, religion, prosperity, and habits of his hands and their world. Although Merrell was himself not a member of the "orderly and closed community" of wealthy northern industrial families, he was trained to be one of their agents, and the Protestant paternalism that he learned in Oneida County would be with him through his manufacturing career.[10] He viewed himself literally as a missionary, an industrial missionary to the South.

Not only does Merrell's account depict the larger economic changes of his time, but he makes clear what Ryan so abundantly demonstrates in *The Cradle of the Middle Class:* that economic changes occurred in connection with changes in the religious and social values among the people of Oneida County. Ryan's book, as will be noted, frequently refers to the Merrells and the Camps as representative county families. Henry Merrell's memoirs would have added even more strength to her case.

Even for those readers who are not interested in the larger patterns, Merrell's account of revival and reform will provide remarkable insight into the social dynamics of a community that is moving away from its New England and Puritan roots toward a more modern and progressive condition. If, as Milton Sernett maintains, Oneida County was "another little New England," then Whitney Cross is equally correct in saying that "the New York descendants of the Puritans were a more quarrelsome, argumentative, experimenting brood than their parents and stay-at-home cousins."[11] After surveying the Oneida County that Henry Merrell depicts, his reader will be fully prepared for the shock that this Connecticut-rooted, hard-working, middle-class, individualistic representative of industry feels when he has a head-on collision with Georgia.

Many of the early settlers whom Merrell mentions had passed through upstate New York while serving with Benedict Arnold, John Sullivan, George Clinton, and other generals in the Indian and Revolutionary wars. They "had observed the pleasant nature of the county,"[12] had noted the economic possibilities of the Mohawk valley, and had moved to Whitestown and New Hartford from their homes in New England. Douglas Preston and David Ellis have estimated that almost half of the 84,776 inhabitants of Utica in 1845 could trace their origins to New England.[13]

As Merrell himself was to be transplanted by choice and opportunity from Oneida County to Georgia and Arkansas, so had his Merrell and Camp ancestors been transplanted from Connecticut to Oneida County. Because so many early settlers of the Utica area had come from Hartford, Connecticut, they gave the name New Hartford to their 1788 settlement a few miles south of Utica. Among them were the Merrells. The Camps moved directly to Utica. Many Merrells and Camps are mentioned prominently in Moses M. Bagg's *The Pioneers of Utica* (1877), the major historical source for the area and the period. The two families frequently intermarried. Both Merrell's father, Andrew, and his father's brother, Ira, married daughters of Talcott Camp. Merrell's sister Lucretia was later to marry a grandson of Talcott Camp, George Hull Camp, her mother's nephew by her brother George.

Merrell understands and makes abundantly clear how the religious fires of the "Second Great Awakening" in "the Burned-over District" of upstate New York formed the values that he carried with him, even as he moved farther from home and family.[14] The years of this "Second Great Awakening" in Utica and Oneida County, says Mary Ryan, mark a "busy intersection of American history," a "pivotal turn" in American identity from one molded around "domestic values and family practices" to one that would "trespass beyond" the family in establishing more complex relationships.[15] Furthermore, this spiritual movement "helped to determine the great reform movements of the 19th century and influenced dramatically the great debate on slavery which ended in the Civil War."[16]

In a penetrating study of the area, Whitney R. Cross maintains that here congregated "a people extraordinarily given to unusual religious beliefs" and to a "moral intensity which was their most striking attribute." Cross traces that attribute to their New England spiritual inheritance and, in a statement that is significant in relation to Merrell's own family and roots, notes that "Oneida was the new Connecticut."[17]

In Merrell's own family and in his separation from it, one can observe how evangelical religion and the new industrialism worked together to create a reformed order. Merrell's father, for example, played a leading role in bringing revivals to Utica. He was a printer and a churchgoing master whose apprentices learned from him not only the printing trade but also religious doctrine and moral habits. As Paul Johnson discovered in his study of Rochester, New York, during this period, "churchgoing merchants and masters tended to be the proprietors of family firms." The converts in the revivals were often "the most firmly rooted men in town." Further, merchants, masters, clerks, and apprentices "had grown up in communities in which labor relations and family life were structurally and emotionally inseparable." But by the 1820s the bonds had begun to break, and "subtle estrangement" occurred all over Rochester until workmen began to leave the homes of their employers.[18] The death of his father forced such a break on Henry Merrell; yet what was forced on him came naturally to other young workmen who, touched by the new reform spirit, moved out of the small shops and family firms. Many of them, like Merrell himself, moved into the new factories, which ironically attempted to maintain the old patriarchal intimacies.

Merrell's analytic mind probes the objections to evangelical fervor, even as it submits to that fervor; but the political applications of evangelicalism, at least as they concern the abolition of slavery, he never submitted to, and it will pain the modern reader to survey the racial prejudices that fill his memoirs. His reflections on both Indians and blacks do not do him much credit, but his accounts of the appearances of Indians in Utica, of their teaching him and his friends the use of the bow, and of the early racial relations in the town are certainly valuable eyewitness accounts, especially the account that he gives of the area called "Hayti," where his father rented some tenements to blacks, and of "Negro Independence Day" in 1827, the day slavery became illegal in New York. Merrell thinks that the hanging of an Indian named John Tuhi marked a point of departure in town affairs, for never before had white men executed an Indian for a crime committed against another Indian.

A significant part of Merrell's account of his days in Utica concerns his education in a town that had thirty-three schools when it had only eight thousand citizens.[19] This education at a series of private schools and academies, judged by its success in producing a literate, cultivated, and brilliant engineer such as Merrell, must have been a substantial one.

But the most important part of Merrell's education took place a few miles west of Utica, in Whitesboro. After he was removed from the famous Oneida Institute in Whitesboro, the first institution of higher education in the country to admit blacks,[20] he was placed in one of New York's earliest cotton factories to learn the textile trade. He dwells long and affectionately over his initiation into the industry under Benjamin Walcott's son William Walcott at the Oneida Factory, his "old home," a sketch of which he made and later pasted into his memoir.

About a mile from this mill lay what he called the "ancient & aristocratic village of Whitesboro," and in it Merrell's education was to be completed by his introduction into the elegant and literary society of the Berrys. Of this "Maeonian Circle," Henry Merrell was elected president in 1835, when it was over two years old, and he carefully preserved among his papers both his "inaugural" and "valedictory" addresses to the group. The wit, the humor, the literary aspirations, and the facility with English syntax which always belonged to Merrell were surely born with or developed in this select society of Whitesboro young people whom he never forgot. After his death in 1883, Merrell's friend and pastor in Camden, Arkansas, was to write of this New York literary circle: "Here it was, in all probability, that he acquired that taste for reading and for intellectual conversation which was so manifest in all his subsequent life."[21]

Merrell was not apprenticed to Walcott, or he would never have been admitted as the social equal of the Berrys of Whitesboro. "I was to learn to be a scientific manufacturer and machinist," he says, and his family's intention in placing him under Walcott was apparently to prepare him to take over a mill that was under the control of his uncle John Camp.

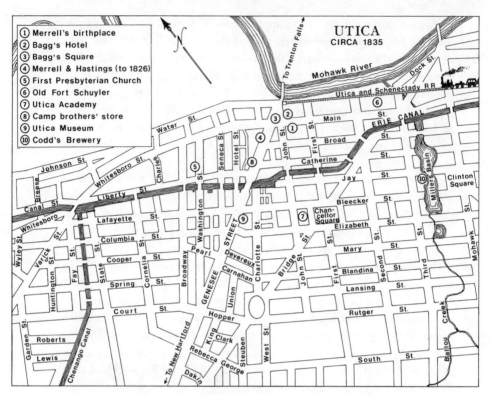

1. Merrell's birthplace
2. Bagg's Hotel
3. Bagg's Square
4. Merrell & Hastings (to 1826)
5. First Presbyterian Church
6. Old Fort Schuyler
7. Utica Academy
8. Camp brothers' store
9. Utica Museum
10. Codd's Brewery

UTICA
CIRCA 1835

Merrell's native town of Utica, New York, as it looked about 1835 when Merrell was learning the business of textile manufacturing. Based on an 1836 miniature map by M. M. Peabody.

Merrell was even paid a small stipend for his services, and he was on such terms with Walcott that he seemed to view him as a father.

We see in his account of factory life, with its practical jokes during work and good times after work, something of the patriarchal atmosphere that the founders of the American textile industry attempted to create. In 1790 Samuel Slater's first successful spinning mill in Pawtucket, Rhode Island, integrated the new industrial system with older systems of value, belief, and authority: the family, the church, and the town.[22] So did the Walcotts of New York make of their mills "little more than a paternalistic update of the New England textile village." Their workers were paid in kind (food, shelter, cloth, etc.) until Merrell's day.[23] As he took with him to the South and West his family, his church, and his town, Merrell also brought the habits of the heart that he learned in the Oneida Factory, even to preferring water power, the company store, and a barter economy as long as he remained in the manufacturing business.

For all its rich detail, Merrell's portrait of Utica may also be interesting for what it leaves out. Unrecorded are such dramatic events as the cyclone that hit Utica on August 14, 1834; the famous riots of October 31, 1835, protesting a meeting to organize a state abolition society; a sensational robbery of the Oneida Bank in March of 1836; and the destructive fire of March 31, 1837, which destroyed everything in a block bordered by Genesee, Broad, John, and Main streets.[24] But he was remembering his home city in the middle of an Arkansas wilderness and a war that he always deplores. In these circumstances he recalled especially those events of his childhood and early manhood that concerned him personally. We are well-rewarded with the many attractions of his birthplace that caught the wandering eye of the bright, intelligent, and inquisitive young Mr. Henry Merrell.

Introduction

*M*y name is Henry Merrell. No middle name. Never had one. Have always got on without one. I don't know if I have not observed all my life that the most substantial, steady-going men as a rule have but the one christened name; for instance, "George Washington, Henry Clay, Andrew Jackson," & so on down to such as myself. One reason, perhaps, is that a mother who has at the outset hard sense enough to be content with a plain, unromantic name for her boy will probably be free from nonsense in other respects, & for that reason all the more competent to train up that boy to be a substantial man.

During this winter of the year of our Lord 1873/4, a good deal confined to my sick room, some days quite sick & conscious of ailments enough to cut short my days (how speedily I know not!), I have conceived the intention to review my life pen in hand. Possibly I may live to finish the record — nearly; possibly I may be cut short in the midst; all that rests with God my maker. But in either case I must be brief, for it is not a wise biographer who, in his own narration or in revising that of another, divulges too much of the inner life. Let all that which needs to be repented of remain secret & confidential between myself & my Lord, who alone is to be my judge.

The remainder is fairly the property of those among my kindred who feel interest enough in me to read what I shall write; & I hope my pen will be guided to record nothing unfit for them to know, but rather much that shall be for their good example & instruction.

Supposing no one cares to read it, even then I have had my own humor in the writing; for it is my vent for all that the ill-natured might call "garrulity" if inflicted on unwilling ears.

Autobiography.

CH. I

*M*y native place was what is now the city of Utica in the State of New York. The date of my birth was the 8th December 1816, so that at this writing I am about 57 years old.

The nervous character of my hand-writing, at an age so little advanced beyond the prime of life, is occasioned by the nature of my complaints. In common with the entire generation to which I belong, I have had over-work and worry enough to account twice over for so early a breaking up of a good constitution.

During my early days, the situation in public affairs was about this. In religion all Protestant denominations were pretty well of one accord, interchanging pulpits, communing together, free in social intercourse & often occupying the same house of worship jointly. This last was the case with the Episcopal and Presbyterian orders in Utica, at which time Bishop Hobart was over that Diocese.[1]

Those asperities, which later on drove all this wide apart, socially & in respect to public worship, were after-thoughts, to which I have never yet found myself quite reconciled. I see no good that had come of it; but have in my time seen some who thought those alienations to be quite matters of practical utility. As to politics, they always did run high & always will— at least in a Republic. At the time I refer to, James Monroe was President of the United States with not much to do, and Danl. D. Tompkins was Governor of the State of New York.[2]

Public opinion was in the transition state from the doctrine of the Old Federal or Centralizer's party having spent their force. A more Democratic state of things came gradually along, while at the same time the new

Whig party increased apace. We had John Quincy Adams for President and De Witt Clinton for Governor & the Erie Canal to begin & finish. Then came Genl. Jackson & the Democratic party & party proscription for opinion's sake: — & "after that the deluge."

So much for Politics! I had not alluded to them at all, only it is impossible in this free country to escape from them; & I especially wish to make this point: that my life-time has just been equal to the life-time of the boasted Liberty & Freedom, Happiness, & Economy of American Independence. I consider that the span of my years has just bridged over all that was worth living for in American affairs. I can remember when the best talent of the country & men of the very highest standing & character were available in the public service. Once in a place of public trust, such men could then reasonably expect to hold their positions, subject to no change of party or loss of popularity. Impeachment for mal-administration, or retirement through old age or incapacity were all that any appointed officials had to fear, from the Judge on his Bench down to the smallest clerkship. The country was then economically governed. Those in office had the advantage of long training & peace of mind. Fraud, defalcations, malfeasance in office were extremely rare; & no one for a moment suspected the impartiality of the Judiciary.

Alas! I have lived to see the reverse of all that become the standard of party rule, for the town, county, state & national Governments. Every office, from the meanest to the most lofty, & as many more offices & sub-offices as could possibly be put upon an overtaxed people; all — all bestowed upon men for no other qualifications but that they labor & spend & be spent to perpetuate their party in power.

And now that I have given vent to my feelings on this subject, I may hope to get on with my story without recurring to the subject of Politics, at least not until we reach the miserable times of Secession & the Civil War.

My native place first took its location as a strategic point in the War of the Revolution; — or secession from British rule. As early as the "French and Indian" War, the Mohawk river had become a thoroughfare for canoes of the Indians and batteaux of the French carrying to & fro between the Dutch colony & the great Lakes.

During the war of 1776 the Dutch settlements were advanced up that fertile valley as high as Herkimer & Frankfort. This same line of water carriage via Fish Creek, Oneida Lake, & the Oswego River into Ontario Lake, became of increased value as our probable lines of approach to the enemy. The other military line to and from the Canadies was that by Lake Champlain, Lake George & the head-waters of Hudson River. This latter was the route attempted by Genl. Burgoyne with an army of British & Hessians, the former took the invasion of Genl. St. Leger whose army consisted of British soldiers & Indians. In order to block this last thorough-fare, two forts were constructed at & near the head-waters of the Mohawk river: one called "Fort Stanwix" [Schuyler], where the city of Utica now stands; and another twelve miles higher up stream, which was called "Fort Schuyler" [Stanwix], where the town of Rome now stands.[3] This last was an earth-work of scientific construction with ditch & covered way.

It withstood Genl. St. Leger a notable siege, holding out unto starvation, & was at last relieved, not by the relieving army of Genl. Herkimer, for that was defeated & turned back eight miles away at the Battle of Oriskany; but the garrison relieved themselves by a sortie, capturing the British camp & taking possession of their supplies while they were absent in force looking after Herkimer.[4] I have heard the old people say that one of their first public duties after the War, when they came from New England to settle these lands adjacent to the forts, was to go in a body, upon a day appointed, & inter the bones left bleaching on the field of Oriskany. Genl. St. Leger abandoned the siege & went back the way he came; more fortunate in that respect than Genl. Burgoyne at Saratoga, whose army did not enjoy the privilege of going back at all.

In my boy days, the best guns that could be had for shooting at the billions of wild pigeons that annually in their season visited us was the old "Queen Anne's" musket captured from Burgoyne; — or Burgine as it was then pronounced. They were really a perfect gun of their kind. Heavier than a soldier could carry through the rapid evolution of more modern warfare, the bore was made to carry a round ball of fully double the present regulation weight; & as to pigeons shot, I should be afraid to tell how many of those birds have been destroyed at one explosion of a Queen Anne piece! But O! the lock of that gun! Was there ever a boy that could bring it to full cock with his thumb alone. Have not I seen them do it with the foot & the whole weight of the body? Have not I seen them load with a handful of powder & a double handful of shot & then shooting from a rest? Would not the gun assert itself by kicking the boy like a mule & giving him a swelled face besides?

Those were great times for us boys to be sure!

We scarcely knew the meaning of the word gymnastics, but I think we shot better, swam stronger, & paddled the canoe longer than the more scientific fellows of present times. But, having thus boasted of our youthful accomplishments, a spirit of candor prompts me to admit that we could not in those days & in a mixed frontier population learn to know so much, without learning at the same time to know some things that were better unlearned.

The men and boys who made the forest & the river afford them a means of livelihood in those days, were rather a low class, & in their language & manners they were not fit associates for young men & boys of Christian training. It is all very well, perhaps, for Mr. Cooper in his novels to represent his "Natti Bumpow" as such a simple-hearted, good man by nature, with a natural religion quite satisfactory to Mr. Cooper, but there is not a word of real truth in it so far as I remember the characters peculiar to frontier life; at least not when those characters commingled with the men & the habits of the settlements.[5] They had some natural powers of mind peculiar to themselves. They were cunning & wise in their own way; but their code of morals was not fit to be our code, & their language was not worth repeating.

The same might be said of the Indians (or nearly the same) by whom we were surrounded & annoyed at the first settlement of that country. But more of that, perhaps, by & by.

N.B.

At intervals during the war, I had noted passing events. For want of paper it was done on the margins of a folio volume to the extent of nearly 700 pages.

When ordered away on military duty I concealed the book, & finally gave it up for lost. Today it has been found unexpectedly. This recovery does away with the necessity to go back & re-write from the beginning.

So let the recovered book [1863] stand for Vol. I, this [1873] for Vol. 2 & Chapter 2 [II] is really the beginning of this [1873] volume.

My Autobiography

Begun in August AD 1863
Finished in [   ] AD

reface. Sick in body, doubtful whether I have days enough of my life left in me to finish what I begin, sick at heart for the woes of my country, and doubtful whether the events of this dreadful war will leave me what remains of life and health unmolested, I begin to write my Autobiography. I do it for the reason that I have nothing better to do. I have had occasion to remark several times in conversation that the memoirs of almost any man who has flourished during the last forty years and in America — stirring and eventful America! — must be interesting if well told, and this I desire to illustrate in my own case, at some risk of a failure, not so much in the life, as in the telling of it.

The blockade cuts off our supply of writing paper, which sufficiently explains why these notes are jotted down at some inconvenience upon the fly leaves of a printed book. Out of business, quite too much broken in health to take an active part in passing events, wife and I have a temporary residence on the banks of the Little Missouri River of Arkansas in the County of Pike. Chills and fever pervade the atmosphere. Every dismal noise known to the forest with no sound that is musical, vibrates on the air. Two little niggers hold triumphant possession of the yard, disputed only by the occasional chastisement of their grandma, whose violence never fails to end in submission to their ways. Barn yard fowls range cackling through the house, the roosters crow in mutual defiance of the head of this family; the cat puts up a plaintive cry for "more" when it can no longer eat what is before it, and late at night the stranger, "Helloá, can we get to stay all night?" Amidst all this confusion, let not the reader be surprised if a nervous man, writing as he feels, should at times write distractedly.

I have no plan in my writing, only to be truthful if not accurate. Relying altogether upon memory, I may err sometimes in dates; and most particularly am I conscious of a bad memory for names; but this need not lead me to give wrong dates or wrong names — it will simply be the occasion of my omitting those, particularly in cases when I am not quite certain. I shall make no attempt to write a romance; there will be no occasion. If at all successful in my authorship I hope to be able, without romancing, to make good the proposition with which I set out above: at least so far as to make out a life that shall be interesting to my friends. Beyond that I have no care to please. It scarcely seems possible for one to narrate the events of his own life without an exhibition of more or less vanity. Since I am writing only for the eyes of those who have known me personally, I shall not spoil my story out of any *mauvaise honte* on the score of vanity. I will try and tell it as I would sit down in confidence among my kin, after returning from a long journey, & telling my adventure without restraint or fear of criticism.

Henry Merrell

CHAPTER 1

Genealogy

Of decidedly Protestant succession, and Calvinistic at that. "As far back as the memory of man runneth," my progenitors have been always members and generally officers of the Presbyterian or Congregational churches.

My father was.
Andrew Merrell. Elder in the Pres. Church (1st) of Utica, N. York. He was born May 6th, 1792, & was raised in the town of New Hartford, Oneida Co., N. York. He died at Utica 25 January 1826, after a short but eminently useful life

My mother. God bless her! was *Harriet Camp* Born in Utica, N. York, May 14th, 1799, and still living when last heard from her.

Family Record. Merrell side

Bildad Merrel & *Damoris Mix*. Were married at New Hartford, Connecticut, Jan. 16, 1774. 24th & 17th years of their lives.[1] To them were born.

Irene born Dec. 30, 1774; died
        Sept. 28, 1776.
Bildad   " Sep. 9, 1777 died [   ][4]
Ira   " Oct. 29, 1779 died [   ][5]
Isaac   " Dec. 8, 1781 died 1860[6]
Irene 2d   " Jan. 8, 1784 died
        Oct. 12, 1813
Zelinda
(Hurlbut) " June 16, 1786[9]
Andrew
(father)   " May 6, 1792 died
        Jan. 25, 1826
Sarah   " April 7 — died Apl. 12, 1794
By second marriage to *Hanna Lewis*
Lewis born Aug. 23rd, 1799 died April 27, 1823. Lewis was engaged to be married to Amanda Winston (sister of F. S. Winston of N.Y.) when he died. She never married another.

Family Record. Camp side.

Talcott Camp born Mar. 4, 1762. died Sept. 5, 1832.
Nancy Hale " July 24, 1758
        " Aug. 31, 1806.
These married & then were born of them
John Camp born 11 Feb. 1786.[2]
Harry Camp " 20 June 1787.[3]
Nancy)   " 11 Nov. 1788
     } twins died June 1850
Horace)   " died 1817[7]
George Camp " 8 Aug. 1790
        died Dec. 1850[8]
Eunice Camp " 10 Sep. 1792 "[10]
Eunice 2d   " 16 Mar. 1795
        died June 2d, 1851
Charles   " 22 Dec. 1796 died 1834
Harriet
(mother)   " 14 May 1799[11]

Hartford Records, Connecticut
New Hartford Ct.

Thomas Merrells son of Thos.
Meeriels Nov. 1646
John Merrills son of John Jr. & Sarah
his wife. Sarah born Jy. 13, 1696 . . .
Ebenezer, Nathan, Anne,
Caleb, Lydia.[12]
Boston Record. Boston Mass.
Pedigree probably from *Nathaniel*
Merrell Newburn Ipswich
Records, 1638.[13]
Note. New Hartford in N. York State
was settled from N. Hartford in Ct.
soon after the old Revolution. N.
Hartford in Connecticut was settled
from the vicinity of Boston. In all
these migrations I find the Merrells; &
always I think respectable in a plain
way. Record of Freeman Cambridge &
Newbury, Mass. 1640 John Merrell.
1682. Danl. Merrell.[18]

The Camp family, in like manner
colonized from the vicinity of Boston
to Hartford Ct. thence to Durham Ct
& finally from thence soon after the
old Revolution. My grandfather
Talcott Camp became one of the early
settlers of Utica in N. York state.

Beginning with *John Camp* Sr., who
died by the Hartford Records 1710.[14] A
long lived family.
Lt. *John Camp* died 1795. aged 84.
(5 wives)[15]
He was son of [   ] Camp who
died Jan. 16, 1767 aged 80 years.[16]
Lt. John Camp's son Elnathen Born
1734[17] built the family house still
standing in Durham, Ct. Built it on
the same lot near the old house about
the year 1785. The old homestead is
still owned by Henry Camp of
Hartford, Ct., whose father Dennis
Camp lived in that house and died in
1857 aged 82 years.

Under the American Constitution of Society, it may not be safe to affirm the quality of "Respectable" in favor of any family connexion or descent. But as it respects my own progenitors, I will venture to assert that if in the records of more than two hundred years to find no stain of crime, no public defalcation & no private fraud; — if to be found on the muster roll of every war with no mark of discredit; — if to be uniformly of the same church & in good standing, sometimes holding offices of honor & trust, though never seeming to aspire after them; — if to register intermarriages honorable and wealthy; — if to be esteemed of old as a temperate, long-lived folk, industrious & useful members of community always, though never in affluence long at a time, liberal to give; — if to increase & multiply abundantly a stock of people who are never found begging bread; — if this is to be *respectable*, then we are quite respectable, and come of a good stock, and have nothing to be ashamed of on that score. If we have given to our country no heroes in the field or the church or the state to lord it over other men, we have for that same reason no public crimes or mistakes to stand against us in the History of our Country. And the crowning mistake, blunder, crime of all, this present civil war, tearing up the foundations of every thing we have been taught to venerate, lies not, thank God! at our door, any of us. I have not at present the means of knowing the views of all my kin; but reasoning from the antecedents of the family, & from what I do know of conservative views among the living, I venture to congratulate myself that no drop of the sea of bloodshed in this hopeless war is in our skirts as authors before hand or causes of the same. At the same time, our country once at war, however unfortunate, we should not be true to the traditions of our family did we not "stand in our lot," & do our duty against the public enemy.

None of us have ever, to my knowledge, attempted to trace our lineage across the Atlantic. I believe we have generally been content to rest our claims upon a pure descent from the Pilgrim fathers, and a good name on the right side of the Revolution of 1776. The names Camp (or Kemp), Hale, and Mix are plainly old English names. Nothing Scotch, Irish, or Welsh there. Merrell is perhaps as clearly a name of French origin. It may be from *Merelle* a game (hop scotch).[19] I have met the name occasionally in my reading of modern English affairs chiefly in and about London, and I find in British heraldry a coat of arms assigned to some of that name, which likewise indicates French origin (see the fleurs de lis) — viz. *Coat of arms* on a pale engr. gee voided of the fields betw. two fleurs de lis az. *Crest* a peacock's head erased ppr. — (Glad it is not a peacock's tail in place of the head!)

A traveller once told me that he had made a friendly acquaintance in the Italian Alps up on the borders of Switzerland, with a substantial citizen of my name "Henry Merrell." This traveller was a Protestant clergyman, & to the best of my recollection, he said my namesake was Protestant likewise. I cannot remember all the particulars of the investigation; but the conclusion long ago arrived at in my own mind was that the Merrells came away from France under some early persecution, long before the revoking of the Edict of Nantes, and settled as many did in and about the City of London. And I have fancied that to this day there is something Frenchy in the Merrell features, & the family traits of character.

When I was little I remember a coat of arms of the Hale family. It was a stag and two rafters denoting fleetness and strength. What besides I don't remember, neither the motto. It belonged to our grand-aunt Lucretia (Irvine) Hale who, in very reduced circumstances at the time, parted with it for the value of the silver in order to meet the expenses of a surgical operation for her son. If there is anything in "blood" to produce a higher physical development, the Camps have it in preference to the Hales

& Merrells. Of the Mix family I have not seen much. What I have seen [is] not very favorable.[20] They were an honest folk. The Camps I have seen of four generations. They are generally portly, dignified gentlemen, of correct deportment & graceful manner; taking good care of themselves but not fast enough for these times. So much the better for them! My grandfather's mother was, I believe, a Talcott of a family described among Connecticut folk as "no account gentle people who stayed about Middle-town."[21] The only Talcott I ever knew was a Saml. Talcott, a lawyer of Utica eminent in his profession about the year 1828.[22]

CHAPTER 2.

"Before I was Born"

*N*o American need care to run his family history further back than the Revolution of 1776, and alas for my poor country, it may be that none will care to bring it down later than the Revolution of 1860! Who knows? Perhaps I am wrong. Perhaps those 76 years were years of education & growth "under tutors & governors"; this present war a time to "sow the wild oats" & waste the patrimony; and yet there may be the lifetime of a nation before us. No more of growth, no more expansion, but vigor, strength, and the wisdom of sad experience. Reduced in circumstances, may we yet be a happy nation whose God is the Lord!

My forefathers bore their parts in the Old War of Independence. I have heard my grandmother Merrell tell how the men came to church meeting armed as minute men, the service to be broken up at any moment [if] the express rider from some out-post announced the coming of the Cow-boys or Britishers.[1] Grandfather Talcott Camp was a freshman in Yale College at New Haven when the British captured that town, after some resistance on the part of the students, who were headed on that occasion, as students are not often led in a fight, by their learned President, Ezra Stiles. The Prex refused downright to surrender, and a platoon of soldiers aimed to fire upon him, when a British officer recognized him and saved his valu-able life.[2] That event put an end to grandfather's collegiate career, & from that time, although very young, he served the Continental Congress as a soldier and before the close of the war arrived at the rank of Lieutenant.[3] In his old age by the chimney corner, I have listened to his stories of the Old War, my hair on end at the shock of battle & the hairs-breadth escape;

little thinking that in my own lifetime there would arise a war among ourselves, one month, yes, one week of which should cause more blood to
flow than all seven of those irksome years, the war of the Old Revolution.
At another time I would fill a chapter with his adventures as I heard them
from his lips; but now they would not seem worth recording. Any weary
soldier who now comes home from the war can tell us a better story and
think nothing of it. Men did not fight in those days as men fight now. They
did not come together with such a shock. Our skirmishes are equal to their
pitched battles of the olden time. Our arms are more deadly. Men hate
each other worse than they did, and when once engaged do not part so
easily. This is improvement in the art of war to the disadvantage, I think,
of all concerned.

For my part I had rather go clean back to the time of mailed knights
and do my military duty safely cased in armor in which I could cut and
slash all round, or hack the armor of some other knight with little risk of
damage either way.

Grandfather finally married into the Hale family, but that was after the
war.[4] His intimacy in that family began long before, for I have heard him
say that David Hale of N. Haven, a man of wealth who unfortunately
was a Tory, when about to embark for Halifax a refugee, presented to
him his valuable library. The present was of no avail, for the library was
confiscated. By this marriage he became connected to Capt. Nathan Hale
of the Continental Army who was executed by the British at Wall-About
Bay, now the Navy Yard at Brooklyn, N. York. The last words of Capt.
Hale were, "My only regret in dying is that I have but one life to lay
down for my country." This execution of Capt. Hale rendered it impossible for Genl. Washington to spare the life of Major André. (See André's
last speech before his Court Martial, in which he pays an exalted tribute
to the memory of Hale).[5] Capt. Hale was a graduate of Yale. His memory
was very dear to the old people of our family. They had some anecdotes
of him not published. His camp equipage, or a part of it, is now in the
Historical Soc. room at Hartford, Ct. One basket, with compartments for
bottles, indicates that those old heroes took a little liquor into camp for
the stomach's sake.[6]

The war of the Old Revolution ended; the old folk found themselves
in reduced circumstances. No wonder! I have heard grandfather say that,
reduced by hunger and in the presence of the enemy, he once paid a Hundred Dollars for a pound of cheese & in his hunger ate it all at once.
The immediate effect upon his digestive organs and his dreams may be
imagined. But I was saying they were all impoverished, or nearly so, by

the war; hence the emigration which followed. They had not far to go. At that early day, the emigrant and his wagon, after departing from the western boundary line of the New England states had no more than about one hundred miles that he could travel due west without trespassing upon the hunting grounds of the wild Indians. True to the hereditary instincts which of old had led their forefathers from England to Boston Colony, thence westward to Hartford & again by the same point of the compass to other colonies in the same state; true indeed to the occidental genius of the Yankee nation, the Camps & Merrells crossed the Hudson now and rolled on up the valley of the Mohawk. That region of country had then recently been the scene of fierce warfare. The Mohawk tribe of Indians—led by British commissioned officers and backed by British Tories, Canadians, & regulars—had struggled hard and cruelly for the possession of that rich valley. Forts Schuyler and Stanwix on the head waters of the Mohawk river, projected by the Continentals, were built and defended with success by the Dutch settlers from the German Flats, who in their blundering, stubborn way lost well-nigh every battle, but made it a victory as to results. The Mohawk found themselves, before the close of the Revolution, expelled from their lands & banished to the British possessions in the Canadas. The new settlers found the bloody field of Oriskany strewn with the bones of our own men. They gathered & gave them a burial, and thereabouts located their future homes.

The Oneida tribe of Indians, friendly in the late war, retained their hunting grounds, near neighbors to the whites. Hard by, the Stockbridge and Brotherton Indians, few in numbers, had colonized from N. England (I believe); westward, in something like the order of their names, roamed the Onendagas, Senecas, Cayugas & Tonawanda tribes, the last holding lands upon the Niagara river and the great lakes. Slender encouragement to new settlers! All west of them held by warlike tribes of Indians, whose friendship might be the most uncertain of all reliances. No land at all belonging to Government and rightly surveyed as in our own times. The whole region was shingled over with Indians with Indian titles unextinguished, Indian grants doubtfully recognized by the late British Government, and old Dutch Government grants and "Manors" vested in Holland land companies, or in the Patroons of Dutch families, who held the fee simple in the land, with certain rights of seniorage—inalienably & in contravention of the existing laws against entail and primogeniture. How these conflicting titles gave rise to great law cases, I may have occasion hereafter to narrate. How they wound up sixty years afterwards in the "Anti-rent Rebellion" of N. York State is well-known history of later times. Other discouragements

there were. The valley of the Mohawk had been settled at the first intention by the Dutch. Not very enterprising certainly, but very tenacious of
their ways. They had no use for the English language. It was not for the
interest of their proprietors, any more than it was the inclination of the
people, that they should learn anything. Sometimes one member of each
family learned to speak the English in order to transact business; but swallow up every other prejudice, they entertained a thorough hatred of the
"Yankees." Not in the least daunted by these discouragements, the Yankees
came and over-ran the Dutch on their own ground, until a Dutchman
in any position whatever could scarcely be found. The New Englanders
repaid the scorn of the Dutch with ridicule. Every wag had his story to
tell on the Dutch. Their honest mistakes, their tenacity of the old way,
their clothing bequeathed from father to son, their double Irish blunders
in language and affairs, their awkward and unwieldy wealth served daily
to "point a moral or adorn a tale."[7] The Yankees seldom mingled with
their sturdy neighbors, & still more rarely intermarried. They taught the
schools and academies and founded colleges; they brought forward all the
improvements, and took the lead in trade. They published newspapers and
books, built churches, sent missionaries to the Indians and even to foreign
parts, and erected houses fronting the streets. They introduced cookery
more tolerable than sauerkraut and dough-nuts. Gradually, but not very
slowly, the face of things was changed. Finally, in a whole country you
should scarcely see one house standing gable end to the street, scarcely ten
men to be distinguished for Dutchmen by their dress. Among ten churches
in our town, you might not find one of the "Dutch Reformed" &, when
found, there would probably be a Yankee preacher in the pulpit.

So prejudices will ever wear away. It is the old story of a dominant race.
Pity the same race should over-reach itself, and over-reach its own genius
so far as to expect to dominate over its own flesh and blood of the Southern
States! Hence come these "wars and fightings."[8]

The Merrells settled in New Hartford, Oneida Co. N.Y. (They came
from New Hartford in Ct.). One of the first undertakings — probably the
first after providing homes for their families, was to build a house of
worship. And it is commendable of their faith as well as their zeal that,
although they had it to do with their own hands — the very nails to make in
the black-smith shop and, for want of a sawmill, the planks to rive out of
the trunks of trees, dressing them with the axe and drawing knife — they &
their neighbors erected a house so large and so substantial, steeple and all,
as to meet the wants of an increasing population to this day. The steeple
was shingled all over the outside, a man being hoisted in a basket for that

purpose. In 1860 I visited the spot and found the building modernized, & the ancient weather-boarding renewed. The house where my father was born is no longer standing. The place where it stood may be seen next to Mr. Dickerson's old farm on the hill road from New Hartford to the town of Paris. N. Hartford is a village yet.[9]

The Camps, more fortunate in their location, settled at Fort Stanwix [Schuyler], afterwards named Utica and in our time containing 20,000 perhaps 25,000 inhabitants.[10] But for all that, it was once, & for a long time, a village. Its chief magistrate was styled the President, of which post Grandfather Camp was some time the incumbent.[11] The Church was then called a "Society." In 1786 public worship was commenced. In 1805 the "Congregation" was incorporated. The first pastor was Revd. James Carnahan D.D., subsequently President of Nassau Hall College, Princeton, N.J.[12] The first house of worship, used until 1803, was a school house still standing in the rear of the Old Camp House on Main Street & used as a wood house. Among the *Elders* of that church the following were of our family connexion: Stephen Potter, Ira Merrell, Flavel Gaylord, John Bradish and my father, Andrew Merrell. *Deacons* Bildad Merrell. *Trustees* Talcott Camp (Grandfather), Benj. Plant, Bildad Merrell, Andrew Merrell, John Camp.

The Old Camp house, now modernized, is No. 44 Main Street. There my mother was born. There the Camp "boys" (as they called each other until they reached the ages allotted to men) were raised, & were well-thrashed doubtless. Otherwise they had not been such excellent men. There their mother died, a great loss to her growing family. And there at the kitchen door was a rock upon which Uncle George, righteously no doubt, dashed out the brains of Mother's cat when she was a little girl. A memorable event to my mother, the justice of which she never could understand.

In those days merchandise was transported in poled boats on the Mohawk River, which was then a more reliable stream of water than it has been since the timber lands and swamps have been cleared up and drained round about its sources. Its headwaters in the boating season are now diverted at Rome to supply the Erie Canal. Utica was the head of that navigation, hence its first importance. I remember the last of the river boats. Its hull lay a long time at the foot of 1st Street, after the Erie Canal commenced carrying freight. By "1st Street" I mean the street at right angles to the Canal, & running from Chancellor Square to the river past Trinity Church and Abram Varick's house. I may be wrong in the name.[13] During the war of 1812 with Gt. Britn., Utica was a depot of stores and men, to radiate for any desired point on the lake frontiers. The military and naval operations of those times then extended from Lake Vincent and Sackets Harbor to Erie in Pennsylvania, and all put together would at this time be compared to a "Tempest in a tea-pot." Great events they were, however, in those days and much talked of in after times when I was a boy with listening ears. I verily thought that war must be a fine thing! Alas! I fear the present generation will so talk before their children, forgetting the horrors, dwelling upon the glorious actions, as to ripen another generation for another war. My own parents were more thoughtful, but I would tease somebody to tell me stories about the war, and I read [about] it in the books with pictures.

But this chapter was to tell of "what happened before I was born." The military spirit was high; but when it came to "drafting" men to go, the war became irksome. I have heard Uncle Harry Camp say that he was drafted to go, & sent a substitute to whom he paid, say, a hundred dollars. The substitute was killed, upon which Uncle H. reflected often very profoundly that he would have been killed if he had gone, which indifferent Calvinism I finally put out of his head by telling him I thought not, for if he had been there he would have run away and lived to fight another day.[14]

When I came into the world soon after the close of that war, I found the martial spirit running high, and some of my kin quite valiant on parade days. Almost the first I remember of my father, he was in gauntlets & chapeau & plume with a sabre at his side & big brass pistols in his holsters. He was adjutant to Genl. Sill.

This war spirit generally died out in after years, & the prospect of another war became more and more remote. At last the millennium came to be a good deal talked of in religious circles, & the "Peace Society" came into existence, & finally it came to be taught to the rising generation that, among other bad things, self-defense was almost a crime; and so I was partly taught and at one time believed, but could never quite divest myself of the early impression that this is bound to be a great military nation, like any other Republic. Has not the event justified that idea? When my neighbors talked of "peaceable secession" in 1860, and a short feeble war in 1861, I felt that they were certainly mistaken. The whole people North and South were, by tradition and by virtue of the race from which they sprang, at heart a military people. United against any foreign foe, invincible. Divided, a heavy Civil War must be the consequence, and the fortunes of such a war uncertain.

Alas! those fanatics goaded the brave people at the South until they lost sight of reason. The deed was done. We are in the third year of the war that followed, yet are further and further from practicable results. After what has passed, no one thinks re-union desirable if it could be effected. No one understands how the final separation can be adjusted. And what then? Two generations of peace will scarcely efface the memory of these times. Two generations of industry cannot pay the debt and repair the damages of the War. How much better would it have been if that enterprising, zealous, inquisitive, industrious and religious temperament of the New England race could have been restricted within bounds. So they might simply have minded their own business, "fretting not themselves about evil-doers," for whose alleged transgressions they could have no responsibility.[15] I blame them primarily for this War. I blame especially their pulpit. In the progress of this narrative, I may throw some light upon this censure & make it seem more just. That pulpit, so far as it has published Jesus Christ the Son of God and him Crucified, is beyond all blame; but in so far as it has preached, over and above the teachings of Christ and his apostles, anti-slavery or any other politics, it may be as guilty of blood as any other institution.

Well, the institution of Slavery is fairly at stake in this War. If after the super-human efforts on the part of the Northern Government to subju-gate us; & the sub-human, devilish, fiendish methods it has adopted to "affright and desolate the land," they should fail, as they most certainly will, for God will not prosper such courses, will it not be demonstrated that the Negro slaves are where God designed them to be? God grant it!

But this is "by the way," as pious old Plutarch was wont to write. I set out to tell what was said and done before I was born, and end the chapter in speculations upon events that may not transpire until I have long lain in the grave.

CHAPTER 3

"About the time when I was born"

*W*hat event of great importance at the time, and to my mother before me, took place on the 8th December 1816. Mother being then only in her 18th year, of course I was the first born. My mother entertained a very high opinion of me from the first, and I continued to retain that good will in my own favor until another child was born. Upon that occasion, for some reason never explained to me, I lost my popularity in the house, & from thence forward flourished as "second best," continuing to decline in importance, I thought, at each successive increase of the family; and not unfrequently as I came to years, I came also to grief by means of the rod.

The house in which I first saw the light was still standing & belonged to my mother in 1860, the date of my last visit. I will be a little particular in designating the place, in case a grateful country should hereafter take a notion to secure it, or the curiosity vendors should ever find it for their interest to work it up into tooth picks and walking-sticks. This not for any deeds I have yet done but for something I may yet do, that "the world will not willingly let die."

I forget the number, but it is a two-story white house on Main Street, standing nearly opposite the Camp house referred to in the preceding chapter. Setting all humor aside, without a doubt, that old house has been the scene of mightier joys and sorrows than many a more notable place could boast.

There have died in many lands, and there still live Christian heroes, and men of renown, as well as sweet faithful women many, whose brightest memories have clustered around that old house. Men have died in the full fruition of their earthly ambitions, whose sweetest and last lingering recollections were of hours spent around that domestic hearth; for the Merrells were hospitable always, whatever their circumstances.

My father was a book publisher. He had an interest and was the active man in a house which consisted of a Book store with a circulating Library, a printing office, and a book-bindery.[1] At that early day, the publishing of books had not, neither had trade generally, centralized in the great cities, as in our time. Facilities for travel and transportation have made the difference. Before the days of steam, labor and subsistence were cheaper in the rural districts, and the trades for that reason flourished best in the country towns, and better as it was, I doubt not. It will be found some day that we have lost in public safety all we thought to have gained in political economy by the maelstrom of public conveyances, drawing population into the vortices of great cities. At my earliest recollection the firm had been styled "Camp, Merrell & Camp" of Utica, N.Y.[2] I remember seeing only one book published by them, and that had an engraved frontispiece in the highest style of wood cut of that day. Grandfather made a journey to Albany expressly to superintend that great work, the engraving; but when finished, nothing short of a printed explanation at the bottom could give any idea of what the engraving was intended to represent. I was told in my innocence that it was a fond mother teaching her child from a book at her knee. I believed it on trust, & would have believed it all the same to be a she bear & her cub. Nothing has improved more in my time than the art of wood-cut engravings. (See Harper's Monthly Magazine—not the shabby "weekly") contrasted with such performances as the above. Subsequently, and for a long time, the firm was well known as "Merrell & Hastings of Utica," publishers of many books, but only one periodical, the "Western Recorder," a religious newspaper. The first religious newspaper except one published in America, or in the World. The first was the "Boston Recorder." From these small beginnings grew up that influential family of religious publications in the available form of newspapers, which circulate the world over. At the time I refer to, forty years ago, the whole thing was an experiment at much risk of loss; hence the merit I claim for our house.

This paper finally died out, like all the rest, under the overshadowing influence of City publications. I think its lifetime was about ten years; but they proved to be eventful years in the Christian world, years of more moment than twenty years over again.[3] During that time the foundations were laid and the working principles established of perhaps every Christian Enterprise of real utility in the land.

Subsequently little else was added but to run those same Christian enterprises "into the ground." All that was substantial, I think, was laid down by the really good and simple-hearted Christian men of my father's day. A brief day! After that, disintegration.

My mother was very young at my birth, and beautiful I have no doubt, for she was a handsome & "dear old lady" when I saw her last in 1860—61 years of age. My father was seven years older at the time of their marriage but died in 1826 at the age of 34 years nearly. To the best of my recollection he was a tall, genteel figure of a man with black hair and eyes. Good looking enough, I judge, for they say I look like him, or did at his age. It was a love-match between these two, I think ripening into profound respect as they grew older. At least I never saw anything to the contrary while father lived, and after his death mother never married again, although she was still young—27 years of age, comely to look at, & considerably sought after as I believe. If I had been a girl, doubtless my mother would, some day, have told me all about her courtship and love; but as I was not a girl, only one item under that head has ever come within my knowledge. Freeman Parmaler Esq. formerly of N. Orleans, now dead, whose story would make a chapter by itself, once told me that he was an apprentice boy in the publishing house. One night—staying out after the house was closed (he lodged at grandfather's & the household regulations were strict), he clambered in by the pantry window, and in making his way without noise though the sitting room to his apartment, he came unexpectedly upon my father and mother, sitting close together & enjoying their courtship as best they might in all the decorum of those times & a Connecticut household. They were shortly married, and I believe commenced housekeeping forthwith — perhaps the same day. In the Main Street house.

I do not remember any particulars of my early infancy in the Old House. I was Baptized by the Revd. Henry Dwight, then pastor of that church. His voice failing, he afterwards retired from the ministry and became a Banker & a man of wealth. His residence was in Geneva, N. York. I believe he never lost sight of his Christian ministry. I last saw him in the desk trying to lecture on Scripture subjects to his neighbors.[4]

When I first remember, we were living in a house on Genesee street, East side, at the head of what is now Franklin Square (being no square at all, but a triangle) and next door to Mr. Bradish. That house is no longer standing, at least not in that position. Subsequently we moved back into the old homestead on Main St., & there we lived when father died and years afterwards. I never understood those moves.

True to the traditions of my family, at the age of two years I set out upon my travels. Started for the town of New Hartford four miles distant, & was found & brought back probably in a high state of rebellion by somebody. This was perhaps the first outbreak of genius on my part. The next was the result of local investigation and an inquiring mind. I toddled into the garden one day, & was feeling with my fingers around the beets and onions in order to satisfy my doubts about their growth and expansion. Unluckily, I had left open the garden gate & let in the cow, who took a queer fancy to toss me on her horns, giving me a wound in the cheek of which I carry the scar to this day. I had trouble with that wound until fifteen years afterwards. My next attempt to travel was to cry after my father and beg him to carry me along with him to "Little Falls," twenty miles distant, whither he was going to the paper-mills. He refused, telling me the "Yonces" might catch me among those rocks. Remembering that he was a grown man and a man of truth, especially to his children, I have concluded that there must have been some such danger at that time. Who could the "Yonces" have been? Were they not a tribe of Gipsys, or gipsy-like people, inhabiting that wild region in those days?

Speaking of travels, I remember once my father carrying me on his back through the streets from the Store home; he wore at the time a sealskin fur cap, very curly, for I examined it as we went. I mention this to illustrate the simplicity of those times. Utica was a village then. Father was a dignified man and would not have carried me thus through the streets of a City. In those days the streets were not paved; at least Main Street was not. The citizens took it turn about to do patrol duty at night, thereby saving to the Corporation the Expense of watchmen or police. The fire Engine was a mere squirt. All the bells tolled when a child was lost; and in the Country—not in town, the age of the deceased was tolled by the Church bell immediately the breath had left the body! Inconvenient that to the ladies! An old maid's life-long secret made public before she was cold in death. It is not to be supposed that the wrong age could be *Told* by the church bell, after the venerable maidens had departed, & were no longer at hand to deny the fact.

> My boast is not that I deduce my birth
> From loins enthroned, & rulers of the Earth;
> But higher far my proud pretensions rise
> The son of parents pass'd into the skies.
>
> Cowper[5]

CHAPTER 4

Early Religious Training

I thank God! the first ten years of my life were spent altogether among religious people. I have often heard it remarked, but never by good people, that it is always so much the worse afterwards for young men to have been shut up in early life to a strict religious training. I do not think so. It is not reasonable that it should be so. Although I have myself seen the sons of the best of men sometimes go astray in early manhood, I have likewise observed that wicked men take more pains to lead them astray because they are the sons of good men, and make the greatest parade of their errors. For all that, such cases are few compared with the aggregate of young men strictly and religiously brought up. And it is not always true that the sons of good men are rightly trained. Parents are sometimes very weak in their government of children. Fathers, especially distinguished ministers, are a great deal over-worked, to the neglect of their domestic life. In such cases, & in almost any case, it is the mother who educates. I will venture to say that it will never be affirmed of the children of good *mothers* that they are most likely to go astray.

My father died when I was little over eight years of age, but I enjoyed the training of the best of mothers & the example of a strictly religious circle of family friends. Not that I enjoyed it much, for my natural heart rebelled sadly against the catechism and the rod. Tight as it seemed to me at the time, Grandfather often told me that I was having an easy time compared with when he was a boy. "When I was a boy," he would say, "the Connecticut Blue Laws were in force. And in respect to parents, why boys now-a-days know nothing about it. I had to take off my hat and make a bow every time, no matter how many times a day, I entered the front door of my father's house. And again as often as I left by the same port, I had to turn square round, off hat, & make the bow again. What do you think of that? The fact is we have no boys now-a-days. All men! All men!"

The first ten years after the close of the War of 1812–15 were decidedly years of expansion. No "isms" then. Nothing was "anti"; all the Elements of Society seemed to work in together for the advancement of Christ's Kingdom. After War, Peace & good will. Nothing more natural than that the woes engendered by years of war should recommend the religion of Peace, and bring on a re-action in favor of all that is quiet and lovely in Society. So I think it was in those times. So I hope it may be in our own day. My father's years were drawing to a close. He was consumptive. His position as a publisher and a ruling elder in the leading Church of these parts, and above all, his reputation as a good man, secured to him the intimacy of the leading men of town in every good work of that day. I saw a great deal of them, and watched them, as boys will, much more closely than older persons suppose. And now after nearly fifty years experience with human nature, running through every shade and degree of right and wrong, I record my testimony in favor of the men of that day. They were in earnest about everything, and about religion especially. They laid down deep and strong the foundations of their temporal affairs and the education of their children. They felt the importance because they had themselves been restricted in education & reduced in Estate by the misfortunes of two wars. As I hinted in another chapter, they established the working principles of all the Boards and religious Societies worth preserving to future times.

They suffered no nonsense about them. Temperate in all things, they did not understand that "If a little is good, a good deal must be better." They did not reason from the abuse of a good thing against the use of it. Look at my Grandfather Camp's portrait hanging before me as I write. No brains there cultivated at the expense of all the rest of the frame! Rather a small head with no great "frontal development" but compact, such a head as you shall see at the time of Cromwell: erect & manly upon shoulders and chest for a man of two hundred pounds weight. And I remembered well his dignified carriage, exacting courtesy from all he met on the street. Not a speck upon his shoes or clothing. Clean off his head he lifted his hat with a gesture inimitable. Such as he had a right to speak slightingly concerning the manners of their grandchildren! The religion of those men was as substantial as their manners and as muscular as their brains. I saw men come and go at my father's store and his house who were as much in earnest for the faith, every day in the year, as St. Paul ever was, barring his inspiration.

Their conversation [was] as rich as their preaching and their works. These men were believers. They believed in a local Heaven and Hell. They believed in a personal God and Jesus Christ the Son of God, and in the Holy Spirit of whose direct influences, they enjoyed personal experience. They believed in the new birth. They believed in the Devil and his works, and renounced them heartily, and they had no trouble with the contradictions of science "falsely so called." Their lives were governed according to their belief, conscientiously. My father was pre-eminent among this high style of men, not for mental ability, but for simple fidelity. So I have been often told by his contemporaries, so his correspondence indicates, and I remember nothing to the contrary, but much to verify that estimate of the man.

I have been told that my father never would be many minutes in the company of any man without making himself known as a religious man, introducing some topic for profitable religious conversation. In order to sustain such a character & lead in conversation, he must have possessed a certain kind of ability. I imagine that he possessed a mind saturated and overflowing with Christian experience, & more or less Christian knowledge, sanctified by prayer, & commending itself to the most obdurate by evident sincerity. The result was that everything about him, not only in his lifetime but for years afterwards, assumed the type of religious usefulness. At that time the most heroic form of Christian enterprise was to be a foreign missionary. Next to that an Evangelist or a domestic Missionary, and after that a Minister in charge of a congregation.[1]

Let us see how many such went out from under my father's hand, remembering that he had but ten years to work in, before he died. Gerrit Judd, M.D. – who went a missionary to the Sandwich Islands, became a leading man in the Civilization of those isles, & finally for many years acted as prime minister there – was first a clerk in my father's store.[2] James O. Rockwell the poet, author of the "Iceberg" & some other poems which have ranked as American Classics, was once a printer in father's office.[3] So likewise were [   ] Sampson and Alfred North, afterwards printers to the mission at Singapore.[4] There was in the office a [   ] Fisk, brother of Pliny Fisk, the first missionary to Jerusalem.[5] I have understood that he also became a missionary. Freeman Parmaler, before referred to, from a washer-woman's son, became apprentice in the bookbinding of our house, afterwards a stylish young merchant & married into the high life of those times, because of his good figure and address. Finally he became a merchant of N. Orleans but never lost sight of his early training. First an useful superintendent of the largest Sabbath School in Utica and author of "Parmaler's questions" for Sabbath Schools; afterwards in N. Orleans, having first secured a popular preacher (Sylvester Larned I think it was) and a room for the purpose, he every Sabbath managed to assemble the first Protestant congregations in that Roman Catholic City by standing at the corners of the streets and handing printed cards of invitation to the passers by.[6] Those congregations were the nucleus of the first Presbyterian church of that city. This I have understood from others. My father had something to do with Revd. H. G. O. Dwight, missionary to Constantinople, and with Revd. Marvin Winston an eloquent Presn. preacher, first in Georgia and afterwards in Kentucky.[7]

This is as far as my memory serves me at this time. The young men generally from that establishment were superior to the mechanics of that day, and generally succeeded in after life. I don't remember an exception. One good thing he did for all who came, as apprentices, under his control. He whaled them well with the old-fashioned birchen rod when they went astray: which, being according to scripture, I set down as a most important part of their religious training.

I need not say that Prayer was the "vital breath" of those good people. They had but few of the poor to care for, yet in giving they were liberal abundantly, which is attested by the noble church and school buildings and the foundations of liberal & religious institutions laid down faithfully in their time. Religious correspondence by letter was another means of mutual improvement, at least I have seen evidence that my father was a pains-taking letter-writer on subjects interesting to the church. Sacred music, both vocal and instrumental, was cultivated in a very high degree. I believe I have since heard the best music of the later schools, native and imported, but remember no finer voices, no more thorough training, and certainly nothing more classical than the musical society of that time could bring to the performance of the "Creation," the "Messiah," and the great works of Mozart and Pleyel. Neither did they lack genius for Musical Composition among themselves. The editor of the *Western Recorder* was no less a musician than Mr. Thomas Hastings, no mean poet by the way, but a musical composer and author of such renown that he had then already received from London in England a diploma as Doctor of Music.[8]

Mr. Dutton was the organist & keeper of the musical store. Among the female voices I remember a Miss Emily Gould, Mrs. Blake, & Mary Merrell (now Mrs. Platt of N.Y.). My own mother's voice always seemed to me the sweetest of all & the best cultivated. I have heard that my Aunt Zelinda was gifted with an extraordinary alto voice, but do not remember ever to have heard it.[9]

Their method of cultivating the voice was simply to sing hymns of prayer and praise all the time while engaged about their ordinary avocations; and, when two or more happened together, then the duet, the trio, and the quartet.

All in those times were near enough of equal rank in society to participate in those enjoyments, and take it all in all I think the people of Utica were a long way happier than they have ever been since they arrived at greater refinement of manners, education and wealth. The influence of such people does not die with them. To this day, I will venture to say, the citizens of Utica, although it is a city now, have a quiet sabbath and a church-going people. No theatre, assembly rooms, gambling houses, saloons have flourished there as in other cities; and yet it has not been a dull place by any means.

CHAPTER 5

Boyhood

Infant schools had not yet been invented when I was little. Fortunately for me, I think, unless it is fortunate (perhaps it is) for one to die young of a precocious intellect. All that I learned in early life I had to take in the natural way. I think I know practically all that boys generally know of entomology, for I tortured insects, and the insects tortured me. And so on of zoology in general. I translated frogs & pelted them with stones. Never passed a snake harmless if I could help it. Had my pet squirrels, woodchuck, rabbits, and puppy-dogs. From the young Indians who were then in town on all high days, I learned to use the bow and arrow, by which means a bird now and then came to be dissected; but not often, for the white boys could never equal the young Indians in the use of that weapon. Every fish hole worth knowing in the Mohawk and its affluents, not too far away, was known to me and my comrades.

I could paddle a canoe, row a skiff, swim, skate, get up a kite & even a paper balloon, run a race round a square, or if there were "new boys" to run, send them round, and we go home leaving them to come back out of breath and find us gone. I could even ride a horse, for my uncle Bildad had a Livery Stable and a line of Mail stages, & I sometimes could ride the horses to water.[1] As to a jack-knife, could not I tell a mean one when I saw it? "Buck horn on the handle and Barlow on the blade" for me.

But none of these things could I do as well as some other boys. I had been very ill about the time Uncle Lewis died, in 1823, and was puny after that.[2] Very ambitious to keep up with the boys in everything, I often overworked myself at play, and remember lying down in the street to sleep from sheer exhaustion while others went on with the fun. Fist-fighting and rough-and-tumble plays were tolerated amongst the boys. Of course I could not hold my own at these, which put me upon the study of strategy in those matters, sometimes with brilliant success, and quite as often ending in my getting the worst of both the strategy & the fight. I had a cousin Horace Merrell, a little younger than myself but robust in health; a noble fellow, constitutionally above any caution or fear, or strategy. He was a double cousin, & we were like brothers seldom apart, though as unlike each other in many respects as we could be.[3] If a boy dared me to knock a chip off his shoulder, I might safely do it, for if I got the worst in the fight, Horace was sure to come in as champion. Boys carried no deadly weapons in those days. I never knew a knife, or stick, or stone to be used in a fight, among boys; or if attempted, the foul play was instantly punished by the spectators. No gouging. A fair fist fight was all that they allowed. Under these regulations, that school for boys was perhaps beneficial. They acquired, that difficult thing to acquire, the power to control the temper, and the ability to think and act quickly with self possession, in spite of surprise, pain & sudden violence. Some first rate men have been raised in that way. Grandfather Camp used to say that boys had nothing to go through in our time. When he was Freshman in Yale College, he was compelled by the regulations to act as "fag" to a senior, and take all the beatings he chose to give, without the privilege of resentment. His senior, he said, for want of something better for him to do, would send him all the way from the college to Long Wharf with a clam-shell to bring it full of sea water; the distance a mile more or less. Fagging was done away with before my time. Probably that institution had its uses and benefits. I have lived to learn that the abolishing of old-time usages is not the best line of things.

The best of our skaters was "Kip's Nigger." (Slavery was not abolished in N.Y. state until 1825.)[4] And after him John Van Rensselaer. The Negro was a great favourite among the boys, being a slave, which he would not have been as a free Negro. He was drowned in a foolish display of skill at skating backward around an airhole in the ice. That took place above the Mohawk river bridge at the foot of Genesee St. and near the "Old Brick Ware House." His body, afterwards recovered & duly interred, was subsequently found in the dissecting room of a Doctor Lattle, who came to grief about that deed, & among other penalties had to leave the town, his brother doctors being very much surprised, no doubt, at his courses!

John Van Rensselaer, being a Van Rensselaer, of course flourished in high life and took good care of himself; if not, somebody took good care of him, for the last I saw of him was in Washington City holding, as I understood, some position there.[5] The best swimmer was Tom Long; he was a printer & died early. For a wonder, he was not drowned. The best fisherman was Morgan Brown. I have lost sight of him. He took things so quietly and systematically that we called him "the deacon." Without an accident, he is probably living somewhere at this time & quite to his own satisfaction. He was a boy of great system with his fish pole and lines. I loved to be with him. His father, Nehemiah Brown was not a good man by any means. Much the reverse; but he revered the memory of my father and I respected him for that sentiment.[6]

But what a liar he was! One day a fencing master came to town and advertised to give lessons in his art. Meeting him before a crowd, Nehemiah Brown, as he was wont to do, began talking anecdotes of his own prowess in fencing, of which, all the time, he knew just nothing at all. The fencing master of course asked him to his exhibition room for a mutual trial of skill. Brown, in due time, made his appearance armed with a huge cleaver, for by the way, though wealthy at that time, he was a butcher and had a meat stall in Haymarket Square. At sight of the cleaver, the fencing master had no more to say, & Nehemiah Brown was free to boast of himself more than ever. I have heard him tell, and he appeared to believe it himself, that in the late war with England, he was captain of a gun in battery somewhere on Lake Ontario. "The Enemy" said he "were coming on in a solid column, nearer and nearer. I seen my men was impatient to fire. Steady men! says I, don't fire until I give the word. The gun was loaded to the muzzle. But the men could not wait. No sooner was my back turned than fire met the priming. I knew what was coming, and quicker than the powder itself, I clapped my hand over the muzzle and stopped the whole charge, powder and all. There now, do that again will ye! Now run that charge back, and let me see one of you dare to touch it off again until I tell you!"

In the fisticuffs I cannot undertake to point out the victors. The fortunes of war are ever uncertain. Sometimes one gained the day, sometimes another.

The meanest thing I ever did in my life was in connexion with a general engagement. I crawl all over with self-conscious meanness whenever I think of it to this day. It was at the "Academy." Mr. Prentice was principal.[7] He was passionate & unreasonable sometimes, though generally all that could be desired. We boys of the school had labored until we had erected on the "Common," now "Chancellor Square," a fort of snow, large enough to engage the whole force of the school in a sham siege. Saturday, the half holy day, was the time fixed upon. For some reason, the principal took a notion to forbid the battle. The boys did not think he had any right to interfere, since Saturday afternoon was their own time. Any way, they determined to have the fight since they had prepared for it; and fight we did. The projectiles were snow-balls. I will not stop to describe the battle. It came to blows at last, of course it did, whenever the storming parties surmounted the parapet. How many were pitched out neck and heels, after covering themselves with glory by getting us, I don't remember. Finally the fort was taken, as forts always are, & we departed. But all looked forward to school hours with apprehension of another affair in which the blows must be all on one side.

Sure enough, the old man's wrath was very great. There was never any doubt about it when that white spot appeared in his cheek. "All who were engaged in that fight stand up in a row. I shall flog every one of you." At the word of command many went up, some stayed behind. *I stayed at my desk*, miserable wretch that I was! I avoided my whipping & deserved a whipping for that. Although I probably satisfied my own reason, if not my conscience, at the time, by some casuistry. I have always thought less of myself for it. Talking of Fighting, Montgomery Hunt, afterwards a Lieut. in the U.S. Navy, ought to have been the bully, for his father encouraged it.[8]

The old gentleman wore a powerful ruffle to his shirt & was for many years cashier of the Utica Bank. The boys said—I never saw it myself—that the old gentleman used to get country boys in his yard and give them money if they could thrash his son in a fair fight, he sitting in the shady piazza as the umpire. I remember once being well-beaten by Gum Hunt and Josh Penton jointly. The Pentons were a large family of newcomers direct from Ireland, but genteel in their ways, and for some reason they were admitted on arrival into the best of Society. The boys were disposed to question the titles of the Penton family, and Josh at school bore on a little hard in asserting the same. He was telling us about a house they lived in in the Old Country, very grand with white marble steps in front. So fine indeed that we wondered why they ever left it. "And what was the house made of Josh?" said I. "Of wood, and two stories high," was his reply. "I don't believe there ever was a wooden house with white marble steps." So

I had given the lie to an Irish gentleman, & must take what comes next, which got somehow so mixed up that I was to fight both Josh & his friend Gum Hunt. It did not make much difference to me, for either one of them could whip me, & I preferred to, or I had to, fight them both at once. So after school I placed myself in position, back to a high fence, front covered by a drain as wide as they could well leap. They came up struggling, and I had a good chance at them in detail as they took the flying leap & scrambled up the bank. After that, it was all over with me. But after all, I was no better convinced than before about the marble steps.

Concerning the subsequent careers of my play-mates and school-mates, upon reflection I find I know less than I thought I did. Ever since my schoolboy days, I have been only an occasional visitor in my native town, and living far away, off the lines of Western Emigration, I have lost sight of them. At the rate Northern people work and excite themselves, probably half my comrades are in their graves ere this; and of the remainder no doubt the better part are those who have been content not to emigrate but remain where they were best known, in the city of their birth. Doubtless a brief history of each one of those who were adventurous might be as good as a novel to read, and of those who remained where they were would, on the contrary, seem very hum-drum; nevertheless, commend me to the innocent life of one who lives in one place and follows one honest round of duties all his life.

CHAPTER 6

Several Celebrations and Some Excitement

*T*he general emancipation of Negroes in N. York was consummated, I think, in the year 1825.[1] On the 5th of July was the Negro Independence day. I witnessed the first celebration of that day, & to the best of my recollection it was also the last enthusiastic commemoration of the event. On that occasion the town was in an uproar. The Negroes felt as if they "had the world in a string," but before the close of their first day, many had quite enough of sweet freedom. For one thing they discovered that they had to fight their own battles, & look no longer to their masters for protection.

Towards evening on that day, I happened to be returning from school with my books in my hand. Suddenly at the crossing of Catherine & John Streets, a mob of Irish laborers encountered a procession of Negroes with

*The intersection of Washington and Genesee Streets, Utica, New York, in 1838,
the year before Merrell came to the South. Lithograph by E. N. Clark after
W. H. Bartlett. Courtesy Oneida County Historical Society, Utica, New York.*

a flag. I ran with others upstairs to the platform of a carriage-maker's shop
& so had a view of the battle. I can give no account of the plan of the
battle, only that it was a terrific row in which the blows and cursing were
chiefly on the part of the Irish, and the tumbling over was in the Negro
ranks. I did not understand that the Negroes were freed at that time in
the spirit of abolitionists in our day. Probably there were so few slaves in
proportion to the free blacks, & those few so nearly free, that there was
little or no violence done to any man's interest. If I mistake not, there was a
remuneration to the owners.[2] It very soon appeared that the Negroes were
no better, but rather worse, for their freedom. To them it was freedom to
run down lower and lower in self-respect and in social position.

I was knowing to this because my father had some tenements to rent
in that part of Main Street at that time called "Hayti" because it was the
Negro quarter. Indeed they finally so infested that vicinity that our homestead was nearly ruined in value as a respectable residence. Freedom to
those Negroes was freedom to be paupers in their old age, and vicious in
their prime. A more filthy, slovenly, squalid crew I never saw. The excep-

tion were Negroes who had been raised neat and orderly house servants as slaves, and cherished the memories of Old Master & Mistress, proud to assume their names.

This tendency to relapse at once on becoming free into barbarism, I have been told by abolitionists, was because of the ignorance they had been kept in as slaves; but that was not true in the case referred to. The emancipation had been gradual, & the preparation unrestricted; moreover, it was the Negroes already free who proved to be the worst. I especially marked their cruelty to animals, and to their own kind. And however this may be glossed over at the North, in the Abolition interest, and the Negro put forward in fine clothes, neither fine clothing, or jewelry, or swaggering airs will render the free Negro of the North equal to the slave of the South in point of usefulness in political Economy, or of simplicity & innocence in Morals and religion. The outward display of Negro finery in the free states ought not for a moment to be (yet it is) mistaken for material improvement in their condition, any more than the same display would indicate a useful laboring class of whites, & not so much so.[3] Look at their flimsy clothing and hands covered with finger rings; are those dandies fit laborers to enrich the commonwealth, and have they any better heads or hearts for all that? Look at their complexions, & answer me as to their morals! I have heard something about their education. They may have educations enough given them at the North to make them smarter rascals than before, but further than that I doubt. Sure I am that any corn-field Negro on Port Royal Island in Carolina can tell them more about the Catechism, & the Prayer book, and the religion of Jesus than they will ever consent to learn as free Negroes—and further, they can tell more about religion and good morals than the Abolition officers themselves ever knew.

In the summer of 1860, I was at Sackets Harbor in N. York State where my mother resides at present. As I walked the street, I beheld in a barber shop window this inscription. "Close Clend Hear Sizzurs Grownd Hear—" permanently painted on a sign board. I inquired, "Is that barber of yours a free Negro?" "Of course he is. Why?" "How long has he lived in your village?" "About fifteen years." "So I supposed, and I suppose that sign board illustrates the amount of education you vouchsafe to a free Negro in the North! You have had him among you fifteen years. You have had scarcely another Negro but him to educate, & that is all you have done for him! And yet you talk to me of the sin of keeping Southern Negroes in ignorance."

The fact is, the Negro needs a master if he is to be a producer in the political economy of any country. And some white people would be better for a good master. There is more freedom abroad in the land than is good for us. At least that is what Grandfather Camp would have said about it. "No one walks in the happy valley of humiliation in these days," he would have said.

Talking of Irishmen reminds me of the Erie Canal excavated by the labor of immigrants, and completed at about this date.

Three hundred miles long, connecting the Hudson river (and the sea board) with the Western lakes, it was regarded at the commencement as a stupendous work & by the old Dutch settlers as a folly. The ground was first broken not far from Utica, and the first section completed was the extraordinary level of sixty-nine miles from Syracuse to Frankfort, passing through Utica, so that long before freight and passengers could be transported from Lake Erie to the Hudson river, boats were running and business very brisk at Utica. This first gave Utica its rise from a village towards the stature of a city.[4]

The first boat built expressly for carrying passengers was named the "Montezuma." My father and uncles either owned her or had stock in the concern, a clumsy model, I dare say, compared with elegant packet boats of later days.[5] I judge so, for it required a good many horses to haul it. I remember the trial trip. Friends were invited. Music of course, and I doubt not prayer on board. The Erie Canal was declared a success; and those old fogies who had vowed at the start that they would not ask to live longer than until it was finished quite forgot they had ever entertained such views. It was a saying that "Every man wanted the canal to go by his own door." Another error in foresight; for in after years when this great artery pulsated with business, teemed with immigration, swarmed with mosquitoes — its tide reeking with offal and the air round about blue with curses — the most impassioned admirer of Venice and the Bridge of Sighs would not have desired the Erie Canal on his premises at home, nor a bridge of any size.

At last one day it was announced that the great work was completed and De Witt Clinton its founder well-nigh a demi-god. I believe he earned the reputation he enjoyed, for although greater works have since been undertaken and carried through without the aid of Government, his undertaking has the merit of being the father of all internal improvement, begun and ended by the same man under many discouragements and against great opposition. A great man was De Witt Clinton. I have heard my Uncle John Camp say that he was great even in private conversation.

As I was saying, the announcement came that the meeting of the waters, the marriage of the Great Lakes to the ocean would be celebrated along the route all the way from Buffalo to the City of N. York.[6] And a great time it was for us boys! First came along a boat loaded with the greatest cannon that ever were seen. No telegraph wires in those days, and the opening of the gates at Buffalo was to be signalled by sound of cannon all the way to N. York City. Our gun was a twenty-four pounder rolled off on the ground near Judge Miller's residence. It was expected to smash all the glass windows in those parts & carry dismay among the women and children. Finally it exploded at the right time, but to our disgust, much more quietly than we had supposed. The day of celebration was not at the firing of the signal but a few days afterwards when Gov. Clinton in person came from Buffalo in a decorated barge drawn by six white horses. The day was fine. The town was thronged with country people in their finery.

Flags flying, ladies gaily dressed; bonnets were then worn so large as to require the opening of both doors of a store admitting a customer. We boys endeavored to express our emotions on the great occasion. The military were sublime; never more so except on the one other occasion when Lafayette came our way. The field artillery were planted on the common ready-loaded and primed. George Merrell was Colonel of the Militia.[7] He told me to stand at Thornware House near the present market and watch the Genesee Street Bridge, and when I saw him ride onto the bridge and do "so" with his sword, I must wave my handkerchief towards the cannon; for then the Governor would be in sight, and they must shoot and keep shooting. So I took my stand, but of course I summoned other boys to witness my official greatness. In order to gain a better view, I mounted on the head of a barrel, contents unknown. It proved to be Tar. The head of the barrel caved in with me. To the best of my recollection, my mother was vexed when I presented myself at home for a change of trousers; and I quite forget how many months it was before my skin outgrew the coat of tar. That night the town was illuminated, but I was stiff in my lower limbs. And so the Erie Canal was finished, and the future pre-eminence of N. York City placed beyond a doubt.

But the Academy boys had not enough of the celebration yet. There was a brook which took its rise on the old turnpike road and, running in the rear of Jas. Van Rensselaer's house, crossed the common diagonally, emptying into the canal at First Street bridge. With much labor the boys converted this running stream into a canal, with locks and bridges, if my memory serves me right. And when it was done, there came our "celebration." Didn't we have a good time! Our cannon (the largest the size of a horse pistol) we planted at intervals along the line of our canal; mine, I remember, was at the junction, and my cannon kicked into the big canal. I cannot undertake to reproduce the speeches made on that occasion. I was still stiff in my legs with that tar.

CHAPTER 7

"Before the Indian was hung," *and after that event*

*I*f called upon to name the most memorable epoch in the history of Utica, I should unhesitatingly say, "When the Indian was hung." Other events of far greater importance there were, but none that I remember from which the people during so many years dated back or forward. A hanging was not so important an event in itself, although I believe finally there was never but that one execution in our town. It was not the County town.

The Indian referred to was John Tuhi or Jontui and was hung for killing his brother.[1] I know of no reason why the hanging of such a villain should become an important event. I don't know, unless it was that the hanging of an Indian at all in that early day might have been a dangerous experiment, so near to his own people. This is probably the true explanation, for I remember hearing about the armed guard employed on that occasion. As a test whether the white man's laws could be extended over an Indian tribe, and that too for the killing of an Indian and not a White Man, I can understand that this might have been an event of absorbing interest to the early settlers. This explains perhaps why the Execution took place in Utica, the larger town, and not at Whitesboro, the County town and nearer to the Indians. The gallows was erected near the head of John Street on the grounds of Judge Miller, the site of that family mansion built subsequently.[2]

There was once a noted rock, since broken up, for it came in the way of a street. It lay nearly in front of the gate leading into the Miller grounds. Huge rock! It was at least as large as a sugar hogshead! but in that alluvial valley rocks were so scarce, before the canal brought stone quarries into town, that it was thought quite worthwhile for boys and girls to make a Saturday afternoon of it, going to play on "The Rock." Poor me! The writer has had enough to do with rocks in after life, to wish he might never see another while he lives!

I was an infant in my mother's arms at the time "the Indian was hung."

One young man, our neighbor, named Hull, the son of Dr. Hull, a wild youth, volunteered on that occasion as one of the guard. In less than a year afterwards (if my memory is right as to the time) he was hanged himself. He went off from his father and, getting into bad company, was executed near Baltimore for robbing the mail. Much sympathy was felt in our community, for the father; and a prayer meeting was held in his house at the hour of execution, although nearly five hundred miles distant.

Dr. Hull lived in a brick house on Main Street, north side near the Hinmans. The house had a doctor's office and shelves for drugs in the basement. The same house was subsequently occupied for many years by Dr. Pomeroy, afterwards by Mr. Curran, and the last time I was in Utica, Bill Duner the drayman told me that he owned it.[3]

One day I was walking down Genesee St. leisurely. The sky appeared to me cloudless overhead. Suddenly everyone was startled by a crash of thunder that seemed to each person as though a building close at hand had fallen down. The lightning had struck that house, passed down the tin conductor, and killed a servant girl who was washing clothes under the back piazza. At another time I was in front of our own house, assisting my grandfather, who was endeavoring to set upright a hitching post that still remained in the same position when I last saw it thirty years afterwards. The same post planted in Arkansas would have rotted at the ground in five years! Well, as we stood there, it was in the spring or "January thaw" when the street was partly bare pavement, and partly snow enough for sleighing. A reckless driver, hauling bricks in our sight ran over an aged man. A crowd collected and bore the wounded man to Dr. Pomeroy's office hard by under that same brick house. I ran there and found our respectable next door neighbor, old Mr. Jones, lying dead or dying. He was a Welshman and very deaf. He was reputed to have money laid by, and had a right good-looking daughter named "Ellena," who no doubt did well afterwards. The Welsh can take care of themselves.

Dr. Hull soon after removed to N. York City, probably for change of scene, and afterwards became distinguished in his profession. He was inventor of the Truss. He was one of the few who persisted to the last in the by-gone fashion of knee-britches and stockings. Of course that was because he had limbs he was vain enough to display in that manner.

I never have heard that any of my schoolmates came to the gallows or to prison for crime. There was one boy across the way named Sam Hooker, whom I don't remember at school but knew him in the street. He was a bad boy, and I was afterward told he became a pirate, and when taken starved himself to death. He had a good-looking sister named Mary [who] afterward flourished in N. York City and turned out badly. I think their mother was a Fleming by name, & there was something bad about the blood.

They seldom hear such loud thunder at the North as we hear in any storm at the South; moreover, they have not as many thunderstorms. But that is rather a common-place remark upon the differences of climate.

In my early days the Oneida Indians had their Council House at a place called "Oneida Castle" about fifteen miles from Utica. I saw first and last a good deal of those Indians as a boy, but never much that was very good or very bad — certainly nothing romantic. Their costume, on high days when they came to town in crowds, was picturesque but not cleanly. They seemed to me rather stupid, or sulky. They brought Indian wares to sell, also wild berries, but we were careful to wash them before eating. The men were generally drunk when the time came to start for home. The women, seldom intoxicated, had all the labor to perform. Besides their infants lashed to a board and swung down their backs by a strap across the forehead, they brought prodigious loads of baskets and other articles of their rude but fanciful manufacture. When trading in the stores, they would try and make the change themselves, which was a good idea. I never heard much harm, nor any good those Indians ever did. They were simply of no use in the world, according to American ideas of usefulness. They claimed great breadths of land to hunt over, next to none of which would they till. If then came a partial failure of crop, they had to be fed out of the labor of white people. Pressed on all hands by the inevitable tide of immigration, they had either to conform to the economy of the white settlements, or get away. They preferred to go, and always will prefer to keep going, under like circumstances. It is their destiny. I know it is more sentimental to say "Alas the poor Indian" and so on. Alas! the poor white man if he had remained crowded in the old countries of Europe, instead of peopling the waste lands of the new world. I never could see any general hardship in the westward removal of Indian tribes. Hard it may have been in a few particular cases of educated Indians, but I presume such would generally have been welcome to remain and be absorbed into White Society. Some did remain. The DeForests of N. York are of Indian blood, intermarried with French.

But I was saying, where is the hardship of their removal, admitting the right of immigration at all? The Indians were miserable drunken wretches when hemmed in by white settlers. They wanted room to hunt and fish for subsistence. They were averse to tilling the soil. Mere soil had no intrinsic value for them, and they sold out partly for money, partly for wild lands in the far west. The Oneidas removed to the shores of Green Bay beyond Lake Michigan, as good a country as they left, and had more money besides than their old lands in N. York state were worth *to them*. Of course not so much as the same lands were worth to the buyers. And is not that the correct principle in every trade? But, it is said, the Indians decrease in numbers; they are disappearing; by and by there will be no more of them left. That is bad for them, or not, as the case may be, and is owing no doubt to the fact that they do not take good care of themselves and have no one to care for them. It is their own choice. They simply are not born as fast as they die, & I see no necessity for their being born any faster or living any longer. So likewise will it be with the Negro race, should the abolition crusade overrun the South. The first generation of free Negroes, having the advantage of an industrious raising on the plantations, may possibly make a living, but I doubt it. After that, idleness and filth, then anarchy & war among themselves & infanticide; then depredations upon their neighbors, and massacres in self-defense by the same whites who freed them. By and by each decennial census will make more and more manifest that the colored race, which increases to a proverb in slavery, dwindles in freedom; and what is worse, relapses into native barbarism. Unless indeed laws should be extended over them and enforced, tenfold more severe than the institution of slavery itself.

CHAPTER 8

Go back and try it again

The first school I went to was Miss or Mrs. Bowen's in a small brown house which then stood on the S.W. corner at the crossing of John and Broad streets.[1] I remember that I was dressed for the occasion of my first entrance into this school in an ample, checked apron with sleeves, the same covering me before & behind, from the throat to the knees. Stuke Shearman laughed at me, and I vainly petitioned the authorities at home against the apron. It was to be some time yet before I could flourish at school in three rows of bright buttons like the larger boys. My next school was Miss Clarke's over the engine house then on the west side of Franklin Street. Miss C. was sister of Capt. Clarke, architect and keeper of a Lottery and Exchange office. She was a very high style of old maiden lady. Her memory is worthy of much respect. At her little school I first learned, bashfully, the art of public speaking in a small way. Anson Upson, her nephew, is now or recently was professor of Elocution in Hamilton College.[2] I suppose I heard his first public effort in that school. The words were, "You'd scarce expect one of my age &c." or words to that effect, if my memory serves me right. I desire not to be too positive about the verbal accuracy of such an important quotation as that. Outgrowing the schools kept by ladies, I attended Mr. Dorchester's school, and finally arrived at the dignity of an Academy boy.

It seems to me that for some reason I took a turn at Mr. Dorchester's between whiles at the Academy. Mr. D. was a capital teacher.[3] A man of robust constitution himself, he bore onto the boys very hard, and I some-times thought he was vindictive towards us. At the time I refer to, he was building a house for himself partly or altogether with his own hands. When he was digging the cellar, he would come to school late and very savage, with his trousers soiled with clay. I heard afterwards that he had become a preacher, a calling in which I should have thought him likely to fail.

The Utica Academy was kept in the Jury rooms of the Court House on the Common, now Chancellor's Square. As Utica was not the County town, Courts were not so frequent but that the Academy could flourish in the same building, giving the boys a vacation during Court Weeks.

I don't remember the names of the Courts held there, but I remember that Judge Williams was on the bench with one or two sleepy-looking old gentlemen seated each side of him, to whom he now and then made the motions of a consultation, but the old Judge himself never looked to me like a man who could be much moved by the opinions of other men.[4] Among the lawyers of that Court were Thos. E. Clark, who seldom argued; James Beardsley, who in his manner of speaking was dignified and forcible; he afterwards arose in my memory when I came to look upon John C. Calhoun. Hiram Dennis, a very strong man, who in his line of duty as prosecuting attorney seemed to me as though he persecuted the prisoner at the bar, thirsting for his blood as though he had slain his own brother. It was something very frightful to see, but all professional, as I afterwards understood, for when he became a Judge he was not a "hanging Judge," as many thought he would be. Mr. Dennis was an extraordinary man. Joshua Spencer pleased me better than other men as a public speaker, and he possessed a gift in the Examination of Witnesses. I remember as lawyers Erastus Clark, Senr., and Judge Maynard, but that was when I was too young to form an opinion of their powers. I have understood that they were both distinguished men. There was a younger lawyer named Noyes, who I thought promised to become eminent in his profession, but that was ten years later than my school days.[5]

A Session at Court was a grand affair in those times. John E. Hinman was Sheriff and threw into the office all the dignity in his power. He was a tall, erect, and fine-looking man. He dressed on those occasions in black from head to foot, and carried at his side a dress sword with a black scabbard.[6] The Court started in the morning in procession from Bagg's tavern, headed by the Sheriff with his sword drawn.[7] After him Judge Williams and the assistant judges, & in the rear the members of the bar. All stern and silent, two and two they walked to the Court House. The parade was impressive to my young mind. I forget whether this ceremony was every morning or only at the opening of the Court on the first day. So long as Sheriff Hinman continued in that office, there was a dignity about official proceedings that I suppose belonged to the old regime. With the incoming of the great Democratic party (the period was distinctly marked), that dignity all fell through. The change was sudden and unmistakable to my mind. I thought then and still think that forms and ceremony had better been maintained. I could give good reasons for this opinion.

There was one little Episode in my school days that I came near passing by unnoticed. There were two young men in College in whom our church took deep interest. H. G. O. Dwight, afterwards missionary to Constantinople, and Marvin Winston, who became a distinguished preacher in Georgia (State). They were, I think, just through College, and needing funds to proceed at Andover Theological Seminary. They started a school for boys in a music room over Mr. Butler's saddler shop, which was a rickety wooden building then standing on the North corner of Broad and Genesee streets.[8]

The Presbyterian influence was immediately cast in favor of that school, and a crowd of us boys went, not at all satisfied to be separated from our comrades, with a change of text books and all that. The school flourished only a few days and broke up in a row. The Dana boys were at the head of it, which surprised me, for Mr. Dwight was their uncle.

I don't think the oldest of the Dana boys was there at the time. I refer to Jas. Dana, who afterwards married the daughter of Prof. Silliman at N. Haven, finished his education abroad, went round the world on Wilkes' Expedition, and has since been a celebrity in the scientific world.[9] He belonged to an older set of boys, quite as rough in their own time, I've no doubt. Mr. Butler the saddler went blind, and after that kept the Utica Museum.[10]

The Utica Academy consisted of two departments, the English and the

Classical. The former, always much the largest, was under instruction of a succession of young men from College and on their way to fame. They changed frequently. Trustees managed all that, I suppose. There was one teacher named Barber that I should be glad to know more about. If he lived, he probably distinguished himself. He was one of Nature's Noblemen in stature and mien, and used to practice public speaking on the boys. We became very tired of it sometimes.[11]

Both departments of the Academy were under one Principal, who took charge of the Classical instruction. During all my time this position was filled, and well filled, by Mr. Prentice, a fine scholar and a gentleman. Afterwards he was professor of languages in the College at Geneva, N.Y.[12] He reported favorably of me, to my mother, but I never could see the justice of it. There were so many smarter boys in school than I that I felt myself to be stupid. I must have provoked my teacher greatly.

I never could learn anything as other boys learned, by repetition of the same idea until the memory retains it. On the contrary, any point that struck my mind favorably and arrested my attention was quickly mastered and stored away in the memory forever. I think I had excellent parts, but lacked the power of attention. Hence in the Latin or English languages I never succeeded in mastering a rule, although I went on with the classes many a weary month. In mathematics I had to make my own rules and sometimes my own demonstrations. I never could even master by rote the multiplication table, but had a process of my own. Yet I seemed to get on very well, and took prizes now and then.

I imagine that for the want of attention I was compensated by a power of concentrating the ideas that did strike me favorably, and reflected upon them at leisure, so as to make tolerable sense at last. My mother tells me that I had long fits of thinking in those days. I would not have so much to say about this if it had been a thing to boast of on my part. At the time, in school, it was a source of much grief that I could never memorize lessons like other boys. I do not now think that a scholar or his parents need be disheartened greatly should he lack the power of committing to memory. Observation and reflection may be made to compensate for the deficiency.

At that time, or a portion of the time, the Utica Academy was a Military School. We were drilled every evening by a sergeant of the U.S. Army. Our uniform was white pants and a blue roundabout with three rows of silver-plated bell buttons. I was never able to get as many buttons on my coat as some of the other boys. Now I think of it, the military character was first bestowed upon that institution by Charles Stuart, who preceded Mr. Prentice as head master of the Academy. A queer man was he every way. He was a Scotchman, who for ten or fifteen years came and went. Sometimes he crossed the ocean, as it was said, to realize his income. He appeared to have money at his disposal and was liberal in making presents when he had accepted any favors. He had been an officer in the East India Company's service, a Colonel, I think. He always wore a plaid surtout with a cape, until he became a preacher. After that, the coat was of the same pattern but made of black worsted. With a fine, tall, & very erect figure, curling hair, his eyes turned upwards with a rapt expression, he walked the street apparently unconscious that he was gazed at by all who were unacquainted with his ways. He was beloved by those who knew him intimately, and he was himself a great lover of children, frolicking with them sometimes in a very grotesque manner.

About this time he published a religious novel. I forget the name, but the scenes were laid in Hindostan. He finally became a preacher, and I do not know what became of him after that. The last time I saw him was about the year 1830. I met him on foot, on the Yorkville bridge, dressed as usual. To my confusion he ran and embraced me and kissed me, as he said, for my resemblance to my dear father.[13]

CHAPTER 34

A chapter of Digressions

Reading an old number of *Putnam's Magazine* the other day, I found an article on Rifles and Rifle-practice, by which it appears the most accurate shooting in the world has been done with the rifle-guns manufactured by Morgan James of Utica, N. York.[1] Morgan James and I were boys together, & I advert to the circumstances in order that I may here give my testimony in favor of that skill and excellence which the artisan attains, and can only attain, by a life-long application and industry in his own department.

Morgan James was a poor boy, & having no school education early in life, if he has derived any aid from science, it has probably been through the suggestions of gentlemen from time to time visiting his shop. Morg. James suffered unusual disadvantages, even for a poor boy. His father was a Welshman, a maker of shoe-lasts and boot-trees by trade, & that was un-usual for a Welshman. He was not a thrifty man, or even a man of steady habits. His mother, I think, was not a Welsh-woman. At least she could scold in very good English. I thought she was always scolding, & yet she looked complacently upon me when I spent my Saturday afternoons with "Morg" in his little work shop that he kept in one corner of the woodshed. I could tell him what I learned at school of natural philosophy, & he could help me to make kites that would outfly, and cross bows that would out-shoot, the rest of the boys. The cross-bow especially he brought to great perfection. He made them with a wooden barrel like a gun, to shoot a bolt of cat-tail or a slug of lead with considerable force and accuracy. Finally he came into possession of a shot-gun barrel. It was a very poor one, I remember, but he worked on it until he had him a fowling piece, with a white pine stock stained with the juice of the Cokeberry, or some other bright red stain. It seems to me that I furnished the ammunition. Let that be as it will, together we repaired to the common south of the town, now covered with houses, but at that time the resort of wild fowls. There he stood patiently waiting for a flock of plover to come within range. By and by he got a fair shot on the wing, & down came his bird. Great was the joy on that occasion! Morg was not the boy to get excited at a great excess, throw down his gun, and run for the bird. O no! He could wait. I might bog for the wounded bird, but he, sportsmanlike, would stand & re-load. After that I lost sight of James for twenty years. One day while visiting my native city, I found him the proprietor of a noted gun-smith shop & went in to see him. He had been plodding at that trade from his boyhood up, and he told me that his reputation brought him orders for more guns than he could possibly turn off and maintain his reputation for excellence. He did not increase his works, but was at that time, I think, content to enjoy his reputation without growing rich upon it.[2]

Then there was a family of boys in my time, raised up as gun-smiths, who never arrived at so high a reputation. Their name was Rogers, the family of Riley Rogers, who had a gun-smith shop on Main Street in Utica upon the same lot where Andrews afterwards made silver spoons, or was understood to be thus employed, for he (Andrews) was seldom or never seen beyond his own door-sill.[3] Old Riley Rogers had longings to possess a farm & quit his trade, which I believe he finally did, & probably was never as contented or so useful afterwards. Two of his sons followed the gun-smith trade in Georgia. One in Augusta and another in Macon. They were good workmen, but the one I knew in Augusta had more reputation for promising work that he could not execute than he had for his work when done. They never gained the reputation that James arrived at, without their advantages.

Horatio Seymour, the present Governor of the State of N. York, is a native of my native town.[4] His home is, I believe, still there. He was a big boy when I was a small one, & when I was at the Academy, he had gone away to West Point. Occasionally at home, he was even then a young man of marked distinction among his fellows.

There [was] a dignity & propriety about everything he said or did, a certain air of refinement and good breeding rare in those times. Perhaps I have mentioned him before in the course of these memoirs; if so, the repetition may be set down to the score of a garrulous old age. When first Governor of N. York, Miss Murray, who had been a maid of honor to Queen Victoria, pronounced him a very fine gentleman, & she ought to have been a good judge. He lost his re-election upon the Maine liquor law, which he vetoed, but was afterwards re-elected in the Conservative interests upon the issues growing out of this War.[5] During the interval of time between his first and second Governorship, he retired to private life, and my mother told me that he received from Prest. Buchanan the offer of an appointment as U.S. Minister to the Court of St. James; but although that position must have been equal to his highest ambition at that time, he declined because of the illness of his mother, whose life was drawing to a close, & he would not be absent from her at such a time. Although this is what any good son might be expected to do towards his mother, I mention it as a singular instance of self-control and filial piety in a politician of these times.

The play-actor Mr. Hackett resided in Utica when I was a boy, but he was not a native of the place.[6] He came there to mechandise, but was more of a good fellow than a merchant & of course made a failure in his business & returned to the stage. He lived on the North side of Broad St. near Genesee St. in a brick building that had pilasters and arches of brick, intended for an ornamental front. The Circulating Library was afterwards in the same building when Mr. Rathbone was librarian. Mrs. Hackett had been an actress and sang very loudly, sitting in her window. No doubt she and her friends thought it very fine, but the religious people of Utica said it was theatrical, and enjoyed the joke very much when a Negro living opposite, unconsciously or otherwise, acquired her style of singing, but with a much louder voice, [and] squalled concerts across the street until the actress was silenced. Mr. Hackett's own voice in speaking was something remarkable, even in private conversation. Someone told me that he had heard what he said in a private conversation across Wall St. in N. York City, above the noise of that crowded thoroughfare.

Note: Chap. 34. Should have come in here

CHAPTER 9

In which it turns out that this "Autobiography"
is after all nothing more than rambling Memoirs
about all sorts of men and things.

*A*t that early day, the confines of the village of Utica were of course limited, compared with the extent of the present city. Bounded on the West at Potter's bridge, South by Fayette Street, and East by "the Gulf," which has since been flooded with water from the Canal and is or was called Miller's Basin. La Fayette Street was built up suddenly when I was at the Academy. That Street has a more remarkably rapid and unanimous growth than any other. All beyond Chancellor Square to the South East, and beyond Hart's Foundry to the North West, were suburbs. I remember Lorenzo Dow preaching in Cooper's Woods far enough from town then, but not far from the present site of a brewery just beyond the Cotton Factory.[1] At Nail Creek there lived a German, maker of wrought nails, very expert. Made them all one by one on his anvil, and had a dog in a wheel like a squirrel cage to blow his bellows.[2] It was not until about that time that cut nails, now so common and so cheap, came into very general use. The invention of machinery for making nails was a necessity of the time, before ever cities, towns, and villages could possibly be erected fast enough to meet the advance of immigration, which came in like a flood soon after the completion of the Erie Canal.

I have never heard who was the successful inventor. I remember seeing one model of such a machine that was a failure, by one of the Walcotts; possibly he may have succeeded upon another trial, but that is not likely. Probably the cheap nail being a necessity of the time, many inventive minds were upon it, and, as is usual in such cases, several good inventors claimed precedence at about the same date.

The Gulf, where Miller's basin now is, was then a ravine, in the bottom of which on Broad Street were the Slaughter House and dwelling of Nehemiah Brown and the Tannery of Mr. DeLong.[3] The latter was a stone building two stories high. Higher up the ravine was the distillery of an Irishman named Codd, who also claimed to have been a gentleman in the "Ould" Country, whatever he might be now. I think the ladies of that house were visited by good society, & I have heard tell that there was a display of plate and perhaps other signs of wealth inside their house, but outwardly saw nothing genteel; and the mean house stood right in the fumes of the distillery. It seems to me that Mrs. Bradstreet was a Codd.[4] Utica should never forget Mrs. Bradstreet, lest the good citizens might ever settle down in the belief that anything they have, or ever had, belongs to them. Mrs. B. claimed to inherit from Col. Bradstreet of the Indian Wars, who, she alleged, had some grant of land, older than all the rest, and covering perhaps all the present area of the City and I don't know how much besides. In furtherance of this claim, she had suits in court which continued through a series of years, and then she disappeared. During weeks preceding a court, Sheriff Hinman, mounted on the Church steps after the service, might be seen and heard reading in a loud voice sheet after sheet of law documents of which the key note, ever ringing on the ear, was the name of Bradstreet. No one stopped to listen except a group of boys.

This long suit, it may be supposed, was nuts to the lawyers. Not a bit of it, so far as she was concerned. A stout, vulgar-looking woman, theatrically dressed for the occasion in scarlet satin, with a wheel-barrow load of books and papers, would present herself in the court and conduct her own case. That was Mrs. Bradstreet. Finally one suit she gained and there was great excitement in Utica. How it was all finally adjusted, I don't know that I ever heard.[5]

Eastward and beyond the DeLong tannery lived Col. Walker, who had been in the old Revolution on the staff of Baron Steuben, & the Baron stopped at his place whenever he came to Utica; but that was before my recollection.[6] That Walker family had a beautiful place, but finally, I understood left and turned up in France, at least some of them, for a daughter was married to a Col. Coombs, one of Napoleon's officers and very much of a gentleman. Leaving his country, he came and built him a brick cottage near the Walker place but on the opposite side [of] the road. It is possible that he married a Walker in this country; but he was as old as forty-five years at the time I speak of. He lived genteelly but not apparently in affluence. On his place he cultivated the finest fruit trees, and seemed to be pleased when the boys on Saturday afternoon would sometimes visit him and taste his fruit, with his consent.

At the Revolution of 1830 in France, Col. Coombs returned to his native city and had some position on the staff of a Royal Duke (Duke de Nemours I think) who was Commander in Chief of the French in the first of the Algerian War. At the siege or storming of Constantine in Algiers he was killed, & I was sorry to hear it. The Col. Walker place was subsequently occupied by Mr. Seward, & after him by David Wager, Esq., a retired lawyer. Seward [and] Williams [of] Utica was the name of the rival publishing house, and more extensive than Merrell & Hastings. Same Mr. Seward, father of Alex. Seward, my school fellow.[7]

The exact site of Old Fort Stanwix [Schuyler] was on the bluff in front of Judge Morris Miller's old residence at the extreme East end of Main Street. A creek ran by the fort, which, draining the "Gulf" above referred to, passed under the Canal, and discharged itself into the Mohawk river at a gravelly point called Kip's Landing. Below that, on the river bank was fine pasture land. Above, as far up as the bridge at the foot of Genesee Street, was a swamp with flags or bul-rushes. The "Cat-tails" from that swamp supplied us boys with arrows for our bows. Across the river to the right of the bridge was a mill dam of about six feet fall.

The old bridge was a covered bridge, painted of a Spanish brown color, and overhead a sign board painted in large letters "Five dollars fine for crossing this bridge faster than a walk." To the right and close at hand on the City side was a mill painted same color as the bridge, which carried on a great stroke of business, until the river farmers of Whitesboro, the next township above, established a law suit against the Utica dam as a nuisance to them, backing water in high times over their bottom lands. The suit was a hard one to determine; for it is always difficult to make any but practicable mill-wrights and engineers understand how a dam of six feet head, with a pond not half a mile long, could back water ten miles up stream against a strong current and an intermediate fall of perhaps twenty feet. But it is even so. Water is an imperfect fluid, & in flowing down an inclined surface, it piles more than would be supposed. I have always had much more land to purchase for the head of factory ponds, than the leveling instrument indicated. Very properly the law-suit went against the Utica City Mill, and the dam finally had to be removed. Probably in an early stage of the suit the whole might have been compromised for a small sum, whereby a valuable water-privilege would have been secured to the City, which otherwise had none at that time.[8]

The meadow lands below the City were owned or rented by a farmer named Mitchell, who in place of hired hands worked apprentice boys taken from the town and bound to him by written Indentures.[9] Those boys, like some Negroes, whenever dissatisfied with their treatment, ran away and were advertised. They were often bad boys who "cared for nobody & nobody cared for them."

I remembered distinctly the countenance of one of Mr. Mitchell's apprentices who ran away with a circus & never was recovered. Twenty years afterwards I met him in Georgia, and subsequently heard of him in other

Southern States. He was flourishing as one of the proprietors of Robinson and Eldred's Circus and Menagerie. His name was Robinson; he had not changed it. He had still the same daring mien with which those boys used to jump off the river bridge twenty feet high, and rising to the surface with a yell, go over the mill dam head first. I have seen them do it many a time.[10]

I was much interested listening to Robinson's adventurous story. A better story he could make of it by far than Barnum's wretched book about himself.[11] When I saw Robinson, he had been performing over Georgia in hot haste ahead of another Circus Co. who had extraordinary fine hand-bills posted a long time in advance. *Robinson had been playing to their hand bills*, altering the time only. He regarded it as a good professional joke, and satisfied his conscience, if indeed he had any conscience left, by the fact that he had not only as good a circus, but a menagerie of wild beasts "throwed in" as he said "to draw the church going people."

Walking up the Whitesboro Street, on the North Side, holding my little brother Samuel by the hand, on our way to visit our cousins, the Potter boys, I must look sharp when I get opposite Seneca Street, and not fall into the hands of old Mr. Parker.[12] We will know him by his decrepit age and by his always wearing a Spencer (roundabout) over his coat.[13] His house stands opposite his stables at the foot of Seneca St.

If he catches us, he will tickle us under our ribs until we kick & scream again; but he will make it all up to us again, by presents of nuts, raisins, and candy that he will bring forth from those capacious pockets of his.

Jason Parker in his prime must have been a very energetic man. At the time I speak of he was an aged man, but then he sat in the front porch of his house (front stoop it was called) overlooking the multifarious outgoings and incomings of his stables across the way. Not that he had need to do so. Theodore Faxton, his head man, would see to all that; but habit was strong in the old man. Mr. Parker was the head proprietor of all the mail staging in those parts, and it was immense until the day of Canal packets and even after that, until the railroads carried the day. It seems to me that this Mr. Parker or his family took the lead in Canal packets as well as stages, and after that, Mr. Faxton's name was great among railroads and Telegraph wires.[14] The specialty of that family was, for two generations at least, to carry strangers where they wanted to go, with baggage in reason, and all for a consideration in money. No credit system in that trade. All this was from very small beginnings. When all the mail from Albany to Utica could be carried in one pair of saddle bags (I think I have seen those saddle bags at Mr. Parker's), Jason Parker carried it on horseback for a consideration, and saved the money until he could purchase a wagon, and so carry a passenger now and then. That wagon was the father of all the stages that afterwards thundered over the paved streets of the future City of Utica, which finally became the radiating point for travel by means of this same individual enterprise. "Bagg's Tavern" was their halting place.

And what about "Bagg's Tavern"? Well I might write a chapter about that, but will not try it. That far-famed stopping place long afterwards got up in the world and was called a Hotel; but that, like many another dignity, added nothing at all to, but rather damaged the reputation of the recipient. Only three very striking events occur to my mind just now in connexion with that noted stopping place. The reception of Lafayette. He stood at the curb-stone near the old entrance on the Square. There he shook hands with many & said charming things which French gentlemen so well know how to do. Among other things he told Grandfather Camp that he remembered seeing him at Genl. Washington's quarters. Whereat Grandfather was delighted; but I had my doubts.[15]

Next was the coming and going of Joseph Bonaparte, late King of Spain & co. with his suite, filling several of Jason Parker's stages with French people. They were on the grand tour, and stopped at Utica until they could visit Trenton Falls. Ate with their own knives, forks, & spoons. The latter of gold. Had they waited for the rail-road and "lightning train," they might have seen Niagara Falls at less inconvenience, but at that same time had they waited so long, they took a risk of not seeing them at all; for they were living very fast, and probably all died without hearing a steam whistle.[16]

The last event referred to was the death of Miss Suydam, in a fashionable tour from N. York City to the Falls, & was drowned at the Falls of Trenton. I looked upon her dead face in one of the rooms of that hotel, black and blue with bruises against the cruel rocks.[17] Her monument is in the old graveyard at Utica. Yes, in connexion with Trenton Falls and Bagg's Hotel there is one other incident illustrating the refined sensibilities of overly refined people. A Mr. Thorne, American citizen resident in Paris, France, came one day, his party filling several stages. They visited Trenton Falls. There the nurse, by accident, dropped the infant child of Mr. Thorne into the water, and it was lost. Without loss of time to the gay party, they came away, advertising a handsome reward for the recovery of the body! The amount of the reward offered was highly respectable; but if they only could have waited a few hours & taken some interest in the search, how much better it would have seemed![18] I have since read of Mr. Thorne, the American gentleman in Paris who quite outshone the

King of the French in his equipage and escort; but I never could quite forget that little dead baby. I had no pride in Mr. Thorne, the great American. I may be mistaken about Mr. Thorne in particular. He may not have been a gentleman of refinement—he may have been a parvenu; his ostentation indicates that he was; but he doubtless aimed to imitate the refinement he had witnessed in the society of Paris; and that is what I complain of.

CHAPTER 10

Sunday Reading

*T*he state of Religious feeling and principle, alluded to in a former Chapter as predominant in Utica during the first decade of my life, was too good to last long. We were a progressive people. Very ingenious. Could invent anything. Could invent you a new principle in morals, or a new doctrine in Theology. Any thing so it savored of progress and development.

I have often wondered how my father would have stood, had he lived, in relation to the novelties of my own day; for as he would have gone, so should I have been glad to go. While he lived, and for some time after his death, the Church was watching out, with much prayer and anxious solicitude, for some great event. Young as I was, I could see that, and some written memoranda left by my father indicate the same great expectation. "Why are his chariot wheels so long in coming?" was the ejaculation of many a prayer. The burthen of every petition was for a revival of religion.[1] Reports came in of a great work, and distinguished champions of religious reformation, at other places round about, and drawing nearer and nearer. One of the last official acts of my father's life, as appears in a journal or memorandum book in his handwriting, was to negotiate for the more speedy arrival and secure the services of Revd. Jedediah Burchard as a revival preacher.[2]

Grave misgivings there were, and many a discussion about the "new-measures," but so strong was the evidence that the Holy Spirit was influencing the hearts and minds of multitudes, if not by means of excitement and of extraordinary measures, at least in spite of them, that no good man dared take the responsibility of objecting, while the greater part enjoyed the excitement, and courted its exhilarating influences. The most prudent looked on with solemnity, content to say, "If this work be of men, it will come to nought; but if it be of God, ye cannot overthrow it." Some there were who sneered and reviled, but they were persons known to be infidels at heart, wishing no good to the Church in any way and not a few even of those changed their minds. The writer himself has always had a rebellious feeling that the excitements, and public displays of emotion, and the use of different measures by different revival preachers, sometimes almost whimsical, were not in good taste; but there is no accounting for tastes, and I would not long suffer my judgment upon a vital religious question to be led astray by a consideration of mere taste. For my taste is not my conscience. My taste may have been wrongly cultivated; it may have been decidedly irreligious and need mending. Examine myself, and I find my taste approving many things that my conscience condemns; read the life of my Savior, & I find things about him that I would fain have had otherwise. It was not to my taste that my Savior was a poor man in this world, that he was a Carpenter by trade, that he did not resent the blows of his persecutors. Therefore, I would not trust so blind a guide as taste to lead me in a matter of religion.

Moreover, those revival scenes, so repugnant to my taste, were exactly suited to the tastes of far the greater number whose souls were to [be] saved or lost, according to their courses in this life. I always had sense enough to admit the force of these considerations, and never to withdraw myself from, or refrain from, placing myself under the influences of a Revival of Religion, let it be conducted never so badly.

Nor would I now dare to suffer my influence, by look or word, to go counter to such a work, in any denomination of Christians, for one moment. I have received too many profound religious impressions myself on such occasions, and I have witnessed too often the power of the Holy Spirit, changing bad men into good under their influence, to risk my soul against them. When men came to sneer and revile and went away asking what they must do to be saved, as many did, I was dumb, and prayed God to bestow upon me the same blessed spirit.

I would not, by any means, undertake to explain the operations of the Holy Spirit philosophically, for they are over and above all philosophy, falsely so called; but, admitting that the Agency of the Spirit was manifest in those early revivals, I could explain very reasonably the various and sometimes grotesque effects of the same upon a multitude comprising every degree of temperament, education, and refinement.

What about the leading men of those great revival times, the Evangelists or Revival preachers? There have been many hard stories told on them. They were agents, or instruments only—leaders, not the authors, of the work. It was true that *apparently* no revival began until one or more of these arrived, and the same appeared to cease soon after they left; yet it may have been equally true that they did not arrive until it had become evident that men's souls were already deep stirred within them; and they went away when the religious interest began to decline, leaving them alone responsible for the "measures," and the excitement.

As to the revival preachers being bad men, any of them, I don't believe a word of it. I saw and heard most of them & knew rather intimately some of them. They were men of great power as preachers and could stir the hearts of men deeply. They were not illiterate, as many suppose. They believed what they preached. No one who would give them a hearing could doubt that they were happy and honest in their work, and the pure unction of their preaching could have been poured upon them nowhere but at the Throne of Grace. Several of them were a little eccentric in mind, the more as they were men of genius. Overworking themselves in times of religious excitement, they doubtless had periods of nervous re-action, during which they were not agreeable companions. If any of them turned out badly afterwards, which I don't believe, that circumstance need throw no discredit upon the works of revivals in which they were only instruments in the hands of God. The results of those revivals are matters of statistics not within my reach. Doubtless they were not all that could be desired, but I have heard the wisest & most conservative in the church of those times speak of them as satisfactory in the main.

These remarks refer back to the revivals of 1826 to 1830, during which the revivals, then at their first, reaped a golden harvest which had been cultivated beforehand by a generation of faithful Christians. During that time my opinions were formed and my character, so I trust. I am not fitted to be the historian of revivals, for I was very young at the first, and subsequently failed to make more than general observations; my own mind was made up. My impression is that during the ten years after 1830 the churches (of those parts) continued to enjoy the fruits of those early revivals and did not willingly suffer them to die out. After that came in by degrees a new set, aiming to lead in the Church first, and through that in politics. They were partly ignorant, partly fanatical, partly designing men; and all tolerably sincere in their way. I shall have to treat of this school in another chapter. Reformers they esteemed themselves to be; censors they were, self-appointed of other people's affairs; the public listened to them, & in so doing, "sowed the wind to reap the whirlwind."[3]

CHAPTER 11

In which the story makes an effort to progress

At the age of about twelve years, I was sent away by myself to a village called Paris Hill, nine miles distant from Utica, and placed in a school of some note kept by the Rev. Mr. Weeks, D.D.[1] There, among other things, I studied navigation. I had a notion of my own to become a Midshipman in the Navy. I never was a Midshipman in the Navy but have been at sea several times. I thought, before I tried it, that I had a natural love for the sea, but discovered that the sensation of sea sickness was stronger than any natural disposition whatsoever.

Dr. Weeks was a very learned man of an original turn. Noah Webster thought enough of his learning to consult him in person about words. I have known the two to be closeted together long and imagined there must be hard words passing between them. The old Doctor was small of stature, poor in circumstances, but contented, supporting, without debt I think, a family of twenty-odd children, his own and some orphan kin, upon a salary of Three Hundred Dollars a year for preaching and the proceeds of a school of bad boys, of whom fully half were of his own family.

The whole family of boys (I think there was but one girl) were uniformed in summer with clothing of striped bed-ticking throughout and hats of simple paste-board. Bad as we boys were, we never had the heart to remark upon the poverty of their appearance. They were well-disposed boys, the Weeks boys, and knew a great deal more of books than we did. I boarded first with a village Doctor who was a passionate admirer of Dr. Weeks, that is to say, he flew into a great passion whenever the dominie was evil spoken of, which sometimes happened, for, as I stated before, he had an original turn of mind. He did not preach exactly the standard doctrines, being styled a Hopkinsian, whatever that may be.[2] I afterwards boarded with a gentleman named Steele, who had property enough but was embarrassed with a chronic law-suit which swallowed up all his other considerations and quite soured his temper. He wrote his own law documents with great care, at least in the penmanship, and when he was absent at court, his wife was as unhappy as he. They had only one child, a daughter named Harriet. She was absent most of the time at school in Utica but when at home was quite the toast among the boys, only we drank no toasts.

Dr. Weeks had one white horse, apparently as old as he, which he rode occasionally to Utica when he generally had something in process of publication. He wrote for the periodicals, and I have heard printers say they never knew an error or a word amiss in his "copy." Instead of writing like other men, a running hand, he made printing letters like type, and very beautifully done. He published books also. Only one bad habit he had, and that was the taking of snuff, which he did to excess. He carried two handkerchiefs, which he laid carefully across the desk, one on either side of him, whether preaching or teaching. One was the snuffy handkerchief, and the other was understood to be clean. His boys I lost sight of in after life, but they must have become valuable men, if they lived. Good engineers if nothing else, for they had from their father that kind of training for both mind and body.

As for me, the old gentleman had me learn whatever I chose and changed my studies at my request. He was differently to other scholars. Why the difference I did not know, unless he had been advised that it was about the only way to do with me. I took a prize at his school. Don't think I remained there exceeding one or two terms. I remember both warm weather and cold weather while I was there.

I never re-visited Paris Hill but once after I left that school, and that was under the following circumstances. It was in the summer of 1832. The cholera was then for the first time in Utica, causing more alarm than was necessary. The citizens, all who could, fled with their families to the country for miles around, carrying the panic with them to their country cousins, who perhaps had been ignored until that event.

I was then learning my business at the Oneida Factory. Old Mr. Mix died, but not of cholera. A distant family connexion,[3] I volunteered to carry notice of the funeral to another still more remote family connexion who lived in Sangerfield, twenty miles away. I went and came 40 miles in the same hot day in August, on horse back, and long unused to riding. I thought I should have died of fatigue. On that trip I passed through the town of Paris Hill. There I remember seeing William Backus, the Exchange broker, known in Utica as the "Black Prince" because of his whiskers. Always carried a large & white pocket tooth brush to match his teeth, which were very large and white and perfect. He was rusticating like the rest. Probably had found some country cousins.[4]

There I learned that my old schoolmate Henry Steele Clark was sick of cholera at the house of his uncle Mr. Hopkins or Hotchkiss, who had already died of the same & was buried by his neighbors in a cowardly manner, with long poles. I could not think of passing my comrade so and got off my horse to go in and see him. I found him convalescent and right glad to see me. The skin appeared to be peeling off his face in spots.

He recovered and afterwards became a minister of the gospel and a D.D. resident, the last I heard, in Philadelphia.

Grandfather Camp died of cholera in Utica in the month following. The whole family had, like others fled at the first alarm; for we had country cousins to go to as well as others. But a little out of town, the axle of the over-loaded carriage gave way, which was looked upon as an indication of Providence that they were to remain. They did remain. I was written to not to venture into town. A bulletin was printed daily of the cases, naming the dead, and sent to the country. Tired of the suspense, and anxious about my kin, I went to town in the dark. The streets were silent and almost deserted, few lights in the windows. Even the free Negroes in the quarter called Hayti had ceased to drink and howl.

At home I was gently chided by my mother for coming. She was in bed with a slight attack of cholera. Grandfather had died. Uncle Charles Camp had been sick, but was recovering.[5] A sad visit I had of it and returned the same night to my business. No cases of cholera occurred in the Factories. We ate as usual the fruits of the season. Epidemics seldom or never reach factory people, although crowded more than others. The general health of factory people is as good as the health of other people. It is all nonsense to be scrutinized about the health or the treatment of Factory folk. They know how to take care of themselves as well as others and thank no one to pity them. There is no danger of anybody tyrannizing over them in a free country; far more danger they will tyrannize over their employers.

Wrong views on that subject have obtained by reading English books prose and verse. Factories [are] quite a different system there, compared with this land of larger liberty, and yet villainously traduced are English Factories in English books. Political pamphleteering the whole of it. The manufacturing towns of Great Britain belonged to the Anti-Corn-Law League. It was for their interest, and they made the most of it. The land-owners, embracing the Aristocracy, were for many years arrayed on the other side. "Their craft was in danger." They had the large incomes & no expense on their side, & plenty of leisure; the education and (with the money, of course) the Literature was with them; and they likewise made the most of it. The press teemed with savage attacks, and sorrowful stories, and pathos in verse, upon the manufacturing System and its effects, which all the while was doing too much better than its revilers, and did come out at last uppermost in the struggle of British politics.

So likewise has it been in the political crusade against the institution of Slavery, only reverse the parties. The people of New England and their offspring preferred making their living by their wits. It suited their genius.

If they invested their money, it would be in the manufacture or invention of something to be done by machinery, on the top of which they must sit & manage it with a lever or a crank or a screw. Anything to get round the original curse of living by labor. It was for their interest that they should not have foreign competition. No matter that three-fourths, at least, of their fellow citizens in the United States preferred to till the soil and demanded free trade, whereby they could sell their products to foreigners at the highest rates, and in return purchase what they had to consume at the lowest. The New England interest enjoyed a closed corporation of six small states, all put together not exceeding in area or in population a single state, sending twelve Senators where others could send but two; likewise an undue proportion of Representatives to the Federal Congress. They had shrewdly made the most of these advantages for their own interests during three-quarters of a century and thereby made themselves wealthy with ease, while all the rest had labored with the sweat of the brow.

Their descendants teemed everywhere. They taught the schools and colleges. They wrote the Class books on Ethics and Political Economy and History. We must even spell our words and pronounce them by rules laid down there. They had the literature in their hands, both verse and prose, without much opposition. And, like Jews, they controlled the ready money. The Great West was, by interests, as much the antagonist of the New England system as the South could be; but the West was mortgaged three-deep to them, and their offspring had the lead in public matters. Their generation owned the rail-roads and held a lien upon well-nigh everything beside. Until the New England Capital and New England influence had grown to be a dark cloud hanging over the whole western sky. Men's hearts were hardened by it. They brooded over it. A few years more and the great west would be arrayed in open repudiation against New England pressure.

With rare sagacity, what did New England do? A long way off, foreseeing that the South and West united would rule the country against their interests, that people massed their forces against the South alone, hoping thereby to cripple the one before its junction of the other. The institution of Slavery was the raw place in the Southern Economy. It was an institution liable to abuse, though established by God himself and never revoked by our Savior. Like the Sabbath or the institution of Marriage, or any other good thing, it was subject to abuses, and from those abuses they could falsely argue for the abolishment of the Institution itself.

Not that they cared for the welfare of the Negro or for anything else but their own interests. They had found a sore place in the Southern interest, quite as raw to the touch as the Tariff question was to them, and they went to work irritating the same to inflammation. In so doing they were sure of abundant sympathy in foreign parts. They had only to abolitionize the Western mind; then all that remained was to irritate the Southern people past endurance, and the work was done.

To effect such a purpose as this, the New England influence was precisely the most fitting method. From their loins had gone forth schoolteachers, and from their brains school books, that permeated Western society everywhere. In like manner preachers of New England descent were in almost every pulpit, and lectures and books and periodicals ran to and fro up and down in the land. At the same time, with a thrift characteristic of that people, they managed to make their dupes pay as they went for the teachings that led them astray. More than that, they made it another source of profit to themselves of N. England.

Even the Education and Religious training of Southern people was, to a certain extent, in the same hands. Wm. H. Seward himself was once a School-teacher in the State of Georgia.[6] I can remember at one time, about the year 1840, many good people had read and listened until they had come to doubt whether the holding of Negro slaves was not a sin. As to the sin of abusing the slave, no one ever doubted that. About that time it was popular in the State of Georgia, with many, to free their Negroes and outfit them back again to Africa. A miserable shuffling off of responsibility, which did not stand the test of experiment.

Just in the nick of time, the abolitionizing of the whole West was completed, and simultaneously the mass of Southern people were wrought up by a sense of wrongs done them, and still greater wrongs threatened, to a state of mind fit for war.

Another four years, another stormy discussion of the tariff question, and it would have been all over and past with the New England system, falsely called "the American System." Another Congress, and the West and the South would have been of necessity leagued together in self-defense against that aggressive system of a few against the many, which had its roots in New England and its branches everywhere.

The Abolition movement then was a timely success, in the hands of its authors and in their own interests. Not that it abolished slavery, or ever will in any sense to benefit the Negro race, but it drove the South into a declaration of independence, and a War.

This War New England foresaw with complacency, trusting the genius of her sons to make the most of that also. But they counted on a short and decisive war—an easy subjugation, and the spoils of a conquered people. More than that, they counted upon the future use and benefit of Negro labor, without the guaranty and responsibilities of ownership.

That War is a problem yet to be solved. The fortunes of war are uncertain to a proverb. With every physical advantage on their side, and a million of men under arms, I wonder they have accomplished no more in two years' time. They do not lack the quality requisite for good soldiers. Those who have fought them say it is no child's play but "Greek against Greek." They are very persevering, very ingenious to fix up tricks, and as industrious as so many ants. They can fly over in a balloon. They can dig under and blow you up, and a point gained by cunning has more praise with them than a Heroic deed.

They have succeeded no better because they are not fitted by genius or education for a dominant race, in the higher and better sense of the term. They are smart; they have genius, but they are not talented — not great. In all their eighty years of success, the New England people have brought forward the smallest number of great men. The generalship of this war illustrates the same thing. They have not the ability to manage the elements they invoke. Should they succeed in this war, they will not know how to control its results, but they will have inaugurated a condition of things that will swallow them up politically. Let the war turn out as it may, they will make a good thing out of it somehow, as it respects the money making. That much can be relied upon.

When I was last at the North, I had occasion for information which could only be obtained in the library of Yale College. I asked a leading man among them if the Librarian would be too high-minded to receive a remuneration for his aid in the matter. Would I insult him if I offered money? "Don't give yourself the least concern," he said, & he was not joking either. "There is not a gentleman in N. England whose feelings can be hurt by the offer of money under such circumstances."

Money is the end of all obligations between man and man amongst them.

CHAPTER 12

In which the story makes no effort to progress

In the preceding chapter I adverted to Wm. H. Seward's early residence in Georgia as a school teacher. He is now Secretary of State in the administration of Abraham Lincoln, Prest. of the United States. He was a native of the State of New York. At the age of about twenty years, he took charge of a neighborhood school in the North Eastern part of Putnam County in Georgia, the Ward settlement, & in sight of the Oconee River. He lived in the family of Mr. Ward, & was understood by the family to be engaged for marriage to a daughter of theirs who died.[1] He went away. Years afterwards he was heard of in the political world as Governor of the State of N. York, and as Senator in Congress.

About that time the Abolition question opened a promising vista to a politician aspiring after the Presidency—nothing less. Hard pressed for a sensation case to begin on, we find Mr. Seward making a speech of several day's duration on behalf of a Negro man named Freeman, a free Negro of their own raising, who had murdered a whole family of Whites. All that took place in the State of N. York. No question who did the deed, but the plea was insanity. Anything so it was a Negro. The worse the deed, the more pure and simple his love of the Negro, who could undertake the defense.[2]

Not long after that, Mr. Seward had occasion to visit New Orleans upon professional business; and on his way back he got off the cars at Greensboro in Georgia, and made himself known to the Hon. Wm. C. Dawson, afterwards U.S. Senator from Georgia, signifying his wish to revisit the scenes of his early life.[3] Judge Dawson forwarded him. He visited the Wards. Many changes had taken place. Mr. Seward was sentimental. Talked very touchingly to the old lady. Asked to be allowed to sleep in his old room. Revisited his former haunts; and I doubt not the grave of his first love. There he probably shed a tear; and then he came away and returned to his political career.

Months afterwards came by mail to Rowan H. Ward, the son of his old friend, a letter enclosing his, Mr. Seward's, ugly picture in a morocco case.[4] The letter accompanying the picture was long, and closely written in so crabbed a hand that I was called in one day to help make it out.

It was quite refreshing to read a latter containing so much fine feeling, and so much good advice to Rowan Ward, who aspired to be a politician himself. And now for the moral of all this.

Judge Dawson asked Mr. Seward how he could think of being an abolition leader, with so strong a local attachment & so many friends in the South. Judge D. said his reply was, "You are politician enough yourself to know that, in order to gain an object, we must take all such chances."

Years after that, in Arkansas, in 1862, came to my place Cullen Reed, who married a daughter of the same Ward family. By the way, they were of the Pocahontas descent, and thought a good deal of themselves. Reed's wife had died, leaving him but one child, a boy named Cullen. Reed was at my house, as I said. We were speaking of old times, and, among other things, of Mr. Seward's visit. "Yes," said Mr. Reed, "and when he was at my house, he took my little Cullen between his knees and petted him, and said, "Cullen, my lad, you will be just about old enough for a soldier in time for the War that is coming."

It was even so. Young Cullen was of just the age when the war did come, and he died. Now was that sagacity and clear foresight in Mr. Seward? Or was it a foregone, cold-blooded determination of mind? I will not record my own opinion, lest Mr. Seward should some day catch the writer.

CHAPTER 13

The Oneida Institute, a School of Fanatics

*A*t the time when I was in the Paris Hill School, my mother's circumstances were reduced. I never understood it. There was something about closing up the affairs of the publishing house at a loss. No man's estate ever did close out, I suppose, as well as persons the most interested expected. Widow ladies generally consider themselves imposed upon in their affairs. Their lady friends agree with them that the man of business is a brute. I don't know any reason why my own mother, at her time of life, should have been an exception to this rule. Upon these observations, made long ago, I have through life so far kept myself clear of administrations, and executorships upon estates. In the choice of a College for me, my mother, governed by her reduced circumstances, placed me in a new, low-priced institution at Whitesboro, which went partly upon the manual labor system; but it turned out that the labor did not amount to much. The original intention of the founder of that College was no doubt good. The Rev. Mr. Gale was a good pioneer in such matters, but he did not preside long enough in this instance to give a permanent character to his school.[1] He went westward to Illinois, then the *terra incognita*, and founded a place called Galesboro, which I understand has succeeded better. His Oneida Institute, the College to which I was sent, proved to be a miserable failure.[2] Always in need of funds. Its President and leading professors were a great part of the time away from their posts, begging for the Institute from town to town. For a blind, they had to appear before the public as preachers and lecturers upon some novel or exciting subject.[3] The current topics were "New School & Old School" in the church, in which they were of course for the new; and with the multitude anti-masonry, anti-liquor, anti-slavery, Graham bread and the Peace Society (Abolition and Peace!), of course they were for the

Antis throughout.[4] Wherever they appeared, pretty soon the church would be split and an opposition started which made a new pulpit for some half-educated protégé of theirs. With them the doctrines of Peace were to drive society into as many pieces as there were hobbies to go upon.

They noted well the times and seasons. All winter when the evenings were long, and the farming people free to drive about from town to town, no dancing, no theatres to amuse them otherwise, and keep them out of worse mischief. No pure revival of religion to elevate the public mind above the want of amusement: then you would see the placards posted that Beriah Green, D.D., Pres. or Theodore Weld, A.M., Professor of Elocution in the Oneida Institute would lecture upon anti something, or maintain a discussion of the same question with all comers.[5] Then the roads leading into Utica would be seen blackened with long sleigh-riding parties coming in to the excitement, bringing their own supplies, and bent upon being excited and stirred up about something. All that was nothing more than the popular craving for amusement or a row. In a Roman Catholic country the same people would be running after a new popular miracle, or the sham relic of a saint. In our own country, free and enlightened, it must be something new as opposed to something reverend and old; and the faculty of our college knew just where to take them. They were men of striking power in language, and having made polemics their study, they came before the public always prepared, and therefore with all the advantages of the unexpected assailant on their side. It is easier to oppose than to support. It is easier, always, to destroy than to build up. No wonder then that the steady-going gospel ministry and the lawyers were no match for the Anti's in a popular discussion. It is just what might be expected: that in the lapse of twenty years of "perpetual rub a dub," as Danl. Webster styled it, the conservative element should subside, and acquiesce for the sake of peace; Politicians, of course, falling in on the popular side. It is in vain to regret these things, & perhaps not worth while to look for explanations.

All this is doubtless just what was to be expected. The people came, at last, "to think of themselves much more highly than they ought to think"; and finally War was the only remedy. After War, I calculate there will be Peace, and not before; and then perhaps one generation of my own people may be willing to go softly and mind their own affairs.

Beriah Green finally got to be twenty years too fast for his backers and was dropped.[6] The last I heard of him, he pronounced a funeral address for the burial of an ancient kinsman of ours named Phineas Camp, who died at the advanced age of I think ninety-nine years.[7] He had a son of the same name who was a preacher, and wrote queer verses which he published and called them poetry. A good man for all that. Should he live to the age of his venerable father, he may yet be a poet by dint of long practice.[8] At the funeral of the father Dr. Green had his say. True to his idiosyncrasy, he gave in his dissent at the old gentleman dying so young. Had he pursued the course of living that he ought to have done, and that everyman's duty requires him to do, he would have at least lived a century & perhaps he never would have exactly died, but dried up just so!

I did not hear it, but Uncle John Camp, who was there, told me all about it. He was grieved to hear that the deceased was so much to blame, and had no further use for Beriah Green and his ultraism.[9] And yet that, ridiculous as it reads, is about the logic of all that school of "Anti's," whose teachings have culminated in this present War.

Theodore Weld was a son of thunder. If he was a good man, it went mightily against him. In his prime he was master of the powers of oratory and the tricks of logic. I knew him as a young man first "sowing his wild oats." He was a tough double-jointed boy, who could swim further, skate faster, and endure more than others, and did well what he undertook. Especially he had a prodigious voice. When I first knew him, he was clerk in Warner and Harvey's drug store.[10] At that time there was open war in the streets between the Clerks and the Apprentices. I don't remember any question at issue, but only that they would fight when they met, either singly or in mobs. Probably the Apprentices, in their shirt sleeves, took exceptions to the fine clothes and superior airs of the Clerks. In this war Theodore Weld was a champion on behalf of the Clerks. One night, defeated as usual, Weld retreated fighting to his master's drug store, pursued by a mob of Apprentices. Barring himself in, he filled a syringe with *aqua fortis*, and by squirting it upon the crowd, effectually raised the siege. Whether he had to fly for that, I never heard, but that was the last I knew of him, until I came under his tuition years afterwards as Professor of Elocution in the Oneida Institute. And the last of him was that he had married a Quaker lady of wealth, and an exhorter or lecturer and an abolitionist named Grimké, formerly of Charleston So. Ca.[11] I ought to add that Weld was of a very respectable family connexion. He lost his voice, big as it was, one night. It seems he was fording a stream somewhere in Ohio; it was past his depth, and he was carried away and had to swim for his life with his big boots on. It was a winter night, and far from any habitation, but his extraordinary voice served him that last good turn. He was heard and relieved, but he never spoke in public much afterwards. His voice was broken. The orator's occupation was gone. I never heard that he wrote and published anything.

Other professors there were in our college, of lesser note but more attentive to their duties; but no officer of a well-balanced mind could stay there long. The school depreciated in such hands. The standard of education went down lower and lower, and finally logical consistency compelled them to admit Negro students, whereupon the whole thing went to ruin; but that was after my time.

I had no business there. I had no one idea in common with that school. I was full of fun and mischief, & so were others, my comrades. There were many clever fellows among the students known to each other, and several really good men, I have no doubt; but the greater part were "Indigent young men of talents," so esteemed by their friends and patrons, but who turned out to be young men of indigent talents. What they lacked in sense they made up by extravagances, and ultraisms the most consummate. Some were ascetic until they perished away to skin and bones. Some would eat no flesh because it was sinful to take life. One I remember, and he was a tutor or professor, would sometimes pray in a very loud voice, way in the dead of night, if not all night, disturbing the sleep of the whole house. Several would indulge themselves in no sleep except on a hard board and a blanket. Professor Weld practiced that. And the whole school was desired to eschew the use or consumption of all products of slave labor. Some of them appeared to go without any cotton shirt or any shirt at all, buttoning their jackets up to their chins. The use of wine at the sacrament was forbidden unless it could be proven to be the pure juice of the grape and not intoxicating. So they made wine, such as it was, of dried raisins and water.

Another's conscience would be so tender that in common conversation he could not be sure of the simplest matter of fact, for fear of a falsehood. And yet it is wonderful sometimes to see what such tender consciences and soft hearts can go through! They will persist in a false doctrine ten times refuted; — they could look upon an *auto da fé* without winking.

Such half-educated fanatics were turned loose by scores from my *alma mater*, to go to and fro in the land as teachers and preachers! Other institutions there were in different states, of the same character or worse, perhaps twenty in all. As might have been expected, such blind leaders of half-educated and crack-brained population unsettled the very foundation of society; for such as they worked with the tide in their favor, while sound and conservative teachers had to labor against the current of popular inclination.

I did not stay to graduate at the Oneida Institute. I always thought I had been taken away at the request of the faculty. I thought so probably because I knew that I deserved it for my pranks. My mother has told me since, that I was mistaken about the cause of my withdrawal. It had become necessary that I should be learning some business, which in the mean time would afford me a support, so that my younger brother and two sisters might have better opportunities. I had a young brother, Saml. Lewis Merrell who, if he is living, is a minister of the Presbyterian Church.[12] Also two sisters Lucretia Hale, and Harriet, since both deceased to my great grief.[13] Harriet was the youngest and never married. Lucretia at the time of her death was the wife of our cousin George H. Camp, who was an excellent husband to her while she lived.[14]

CHAPTER 14

I go to work and work goes against me

At the time of this writing, a family council would find no difficulty in deciding what to do with a growing boy. The War would find use and consumption for all such; but at that time of my life (the year 1830) the choice of a business for life, and the way to go about it when chosen, were matters of great solicitude in all well-regulated families. As for me, a learned profession was out of the question for several reasons. Trade, for nearly the same reasons, was impracticable. My choice lay between Civil Engineering and Mechanical Engineering. The only fresh opening for a young man at that time seemed to be in those directions. Subsequently, Architecture and ship building would have come under consideration, but I came on too early for that. I was shut in to a choice between internal improvements and Manufacturing. So far as we could see at that time, all the outcome of the country was in those directions.

My uncle Charles Camp had begun the world with the surveyors and engineers of the Erie Canal; and the hardships he then had to encounter with a feeble frame like mine, were believed to have laid the foundation for that disease which had brought him to an early grave, and that circumstance probably decided the question in favor of in-door employment for me.[1] At the same time, doubtless my dear mother made the whole matter the subject of much prayer to God. My own views were taken into consideration likewise. It was finally decided that I should enter as a sort of cadet in a manufacturing establishment until I should reach the age of twenty-one years. There were to be no Indentures of Apprenticeship, but I was free to go and come. I was to learn to be a scientific manufacturer and machinist, if I proved to be competent. It was difficult to tell how such an arrangement could be for the advantage of the Employer, without I paid for the tuition; but nothing of the kind was expected, and I was even allowed a support and spending money as much as was good for me.

Wm. Walcott Esq. Agent of the Oneida Factory in the town of Whitesboro, three miles from Utica, very generously gave me the excellent opportunities above described, in the Cotton Factory & Machine Shop at that time under his control.[2] The handsome manner in which he put me forward caused me afterwards to feel myself under an obligation to bring forward promising young men in like manner; and I trust that those I have assisted will in their time, in their own day of prosperity, remember and do the same to others. I have, it may be, taught young men all I knew of my profession, and they afterwards went into competition against me; but for all that I have no regret, provided they will do the same good turn for their successors.[3]

Manufacturing in general was at that time under a protective Tariff, quite profitable, rapidly improving by new inventions, and thought to be promising for the future.[4] Cotton Manufacturing was my first choice, because my Uncle John Camp had, or intended to have, a controlling interest in a certain establishment of that branch, which in time I might hope to manage.[5] So at it I went with all my heart, but with a feeble body, to learn the art and mysteries of machinery in general and Cotton machinery in particular, with the advantage of a fair mathematical education, which I was expected to improve as I went along. Another cadet was my comrade at the outset, but took a dislike before long and went home. His name was Charles Hurlbert. His family owned a Cotton Factory, and he was to learn under Mr. Walcott, who enjoyed a high reputation at that time. Charles had better have persevered I think. With no practical manufacturer in the family, they were always at a disadvantage owning a Factory. A factory, in order to succeed in all times of tariff or free trade, should be owned and carried on by a manufacturing family, propagating the same from father to son and as much as possible intermarrying with the same end in view. That is the only sure manufacturing system that I know, for a permanency. Witness the tradition of the Benj. Walcott family. If they do not succeed, it will be in vain for others to try.

The rudiments of my new business were formidable, I thought. And inasmuch as I had all the branches to learn in succession, I had the rudiments of a new trade to go through almost every year. The whole was more laborious then, by far, than it is now; the improvements all aiming to save labor have come on gradually. Our Mr. Walcott was more of an inventor than he was a money-making manufacturer, and we had many trials to make which proved to be unsuccessful after much worry and fatigue. I was never fond of work. I had not physical strength to make it a pleasure to me as it was to some; but I desired to excel, not only in the labors of the Factory but in the games and sports of the men.

After spinning with the hand mule all day, walking on the heated floors bare-footed, for my raw feet would not endure shoes and stockings, I would in the summer join the workmen at their game of quoits, or in the winter evenings carry my part in a glee or band of instrumental music, as long as I could stand at all. Boxing and singlestick were too rough for me; yet I learned enough of those, as well as fencing, to take care of myself, & nothing more. The English workmen I never liked. The Scotchmen I took kindly to, and in return they were fond of me, and the liking continues to this day wherever I find a Scot. I could understand their conversation, could sing their songs, and was well-read in their history, poetry, and novels. They would sometimes have me drink too much, but I never was in danger of becoming a hard drinker. I could not like liquor or its effects. That innate love of spirituous liquors, which carries a man into excess, I suppose to be hereditary, a disease.

O! the times I have had with the Scotch Weavers at their musical gatherings and their anniversaries of Robert Burns. I cannot think they led me much astray for a young man; I think they rather kept me from running into worse associations. They were not profane or vulgar in their conversation, only quarrelsome, which was rather amusing in the way they went on. As to their religious views, I think they generally based their future hopes upon the virtues of their forefathers, which, seeing it was likely their forefathers were as themselves, but more so, quarrelsome in their cups, was not a theology to lead me astray. We never undertook theatricals, but occasionally a recitation would be received with applause in place of a song or story. We never played at games of chance. I learned whist, and of course chess and back-gammon, but that was afterwards and in other society. That was as far as I ever went in that direction. Smoking never agreed with me. I never formed the habit of using Tobacco in any form, but never on the other hand felt that repugnance to the use of it by others, which is sometimes so offensive and uppish in itself. I deserve no praise for all this abstinence; it was constitutional with me. Had I been in full health and vigor, I might have indulged like many others.

CHAPTER 15

Bad Boys!

$\mathcal{I}$ could always endure anything about Factory regulations better than getting up in the morning and going to work before day. The recollection of this put me afterwards upon the plan of starting Factories at day-light, which answered quite as well, I think, and has become the rule in Georgia & Arkansas where I have, in my time, had some lead in such matters. My only time for reading and amusement was at night after the labors of the day, and both amusement and reading were often prolonged far into the "stilly night." [1] Indeed, it was one of our social amusements, as will appear by and by.

I had also to learn the keeping of accounts in the Factory offices, but double-Entry Book-Keeping I never knew anything about until I came under the instruction of Barrington King, Esq., in Georgia; from him I learned, I thought, to be quite the master of that art, of which I will here take occasion to say I think very highly, notwithstanding the maledictions of Lawyers, juries, and administrators who have sometimes to investigate the affairs of real business men, without themselves possessing the first qualification for such a duty. [2]

The head Clerk in the Office was Lewis Berry. Under stature, short neck, round shoulders, elegantly turned hands, feet and limbs, and at that time a confirmed old bachelor, it was thought, but has since married. A truer man to me it has never been my lot to know. Like others of his particular conformation, he had his "quips and quirks," and might have been called eccentric, but was not. No one could know him and love him as I did, except his own family. He came of a family respectable by descent and, in our time, noted in the literary world. Of the family I shall have more to tell hereafter. My friend Lewis would annoy us by his singularities and his practical jokes. He would at one time have his finger nails grow until they were as long as the claws of a bird, but he would keep them clean. He was scrupulously clean in his person always. When it was the fashion to wear short hair, his must be long down to his shoulders. When all chins were shaven close, he would have his beard grow. He was a small eater, but an enormous dresser, and had a passion for accumulating articles years ahead for future use or wear, as remote from the prevailing fashion as they might be.

His assortment of walking sticks alone would have set up a peddler in that line. Some straight and some as crooked as saplings ever grow. Some of wood and some of materials one would little suspect. Some of his own making, others presents from his friends or won on "a trade," at which he was most adroit.

He had a chest of tools of his own construction, and with those tools he was both ingenious and industrious to make anything of wood or iron that he thought he wanted. Never read in a book or wrote a letter if he could avoid it. Kept a learned dog which he sheared to look like a lion. Had not an idea of music but was the most violent performer I ever knew on any instrument of music that came to his hand, whereat his dog would howl in harmony equal to the music. He had a pew in church where he and his dog were quite regular in attendance, and might be seen always sound asleep, both of them, except during the time of singing and prayers. In the singing he would carry a dismal bass of his own, at which his dog could scarcely refrain from howling again in the church itself.

The Berry family held some blood relation to our Mr. Walcott or his lady. He had been the factory clerk & book-keeper time out of mind, and no one ever thought of his leaving that post, except to die at some very distant future day.

Practical jokes were his study, whereat he never smiled or moved a muscle of his upper lip until it was consummated, and then he would roll on the counter and on the benches and roar with laughter until he disturbed the neighbors. He would work secretly and in silence for weeks to consummate a trick that was to produce some great result. Public meetings were especially obnoxious to his practical jokes. His dwarfish size protected him against personal chastisement in revenge for his tricks; indeed we all would have fought for him, let the cause be just or unjust. Yet he was a brave man and never backed down from a position he had taken in earnest. I have seen his pluck tried several times. One night he and I were dressed for company and walking to town (a mile distant) on the side-walk. It was in the spring season, and the snow had nearly melted & was worn out from the road so that the temptation was, especially in the night, for strangers to drive their sleighs upon the side-walks, in spite of a corporation fine against the trespass.

It was after dark, and as we walked along, nicely dressed in blackened boots and kid gloves, and smelling of perfumes fit for ladies' society, suddenly ahead of us we saw a cutter coming down the side-walk and two men on board. No time to lose; instantly we should meet. The sleigh filled the side-walk, and we could not pass without jumping to one side and into the ditch, which we dandies had no idea of doing. "Halt there," said I. "Get off the side-walk with your cutter." Instead of stopping, crack went the whip, and the horse was urged to run over us. With a violent effort, I seized the horse by the bit and turned him over into the ditch, cutter and men and all, whereupon it appeared that we had ruffians to deal with. Fortunately for us, one had to stay and hold the horse. The other came up out of the mud in a dreadful state of mind, judging by the language he used. He was plucky and armed with a black leather whip, of which the head was leaded. We were unarmed. The first assault gave me new ideas of astronomy, for he hit me hard on the head, and I saw no end of stars. The man looked to me like a very large and strong man, and, not expecting any help from Lewis, I commenced a retreat; but not so with Berry. The blood of the Crawfords was up in him. I had not gone ten steps away before I glanced back & saw him making a stand with his feeble strength. He was like a boy in the hands of such a man, armed as he was with formidable weapons.

I will state here, once for all, that I never was possessed of that kind of courage which carries a man into a danger and through it, reckless of consequences. At the same time, I do not think I ever lacked pluck or fortitude to execute a dangerous thing which reason beforehand told me was either necessary to be done or promising of success.

In the present instance, I saw at a glance that my little friend must be backed at any risk, and at the second glance, that we two together could probably give a good account of the big fellow in the end of a fight, provided it could be all over before the enemy's reserve secured his horse and came into action. In less time than it takes to tell it, the plan was conceived and executed with entire success. The fist proved to be a better weapon than the loaded whip, for once inside the fellow's guard, I had it all my own way. The damage to our antagonist turned out greater than could have been expected. Berry was not hurt at all, and I only had a bloody head, for which I was compensated by the applause of the young bucks, my comrades, who were proud whenever one of the swell mob came to grief at our hands.

As usual in such cases at the North, the beaten man, whose name turned out to be Loomis, took his satisfaction by means of a law-suit for assault and battery at, to, and upon his person with sundry sticks, stones, and bludgeons, out of which the pettifogging lawyers made a little, but the plaintiff was a loser and carried a patch over one eye a long time after.

I never knew Lewis Berry to do a malicious thing, although he appeared to be a strong hater and was sometimes very vindictive in his language. Many of his tricks studied out with seeming malice aforethought savored more of the cunning which the weaker party always feels constrained to use against the stronger.

Giles Mix, the drayman, was a very large and strong young man, with hair curling closely to his head. He owned a famous squirrel gun, which Berry fancied, although he had no use for a gun, and had tried many ways to effect the trade. Mix was obdurate, although the trade once made, he might have had the gun back at a sacrifice. So it went on until one day Mix, who was lazy when off duty, lay at full length on the counter fast asleep. On tip-toe Berry goes for the ram-rod of the gun, which had a wormer on the end. This he softly twisted into the curly hair of the sleeping man until it was quite secure, and then the pain awoke him; but he could not turn his head or attempt to rise, for the ram-rod which Berry held at arm's length, twisted him down firmly, with no relief of the pain except on condition of remaining quiet.

In this situation he held the huge man between his thumb and finger until he had traded him out of his gun and several other articles, including, I suppose, his watch; and then, before letting him up, made him promise before competent witnesses, never to rue his trades, nor thrash him ever afterwards for the trick. I have often thought that was rather an extortion; but, under the circumstances, it did not seem so to us at the time.

Did an unwelcome visitor at the office bore us by offering to stay through a long winter evening, Lewis would soon be rid of him. Closing all doors, he would fill the stove full of the smallest and best fire wood. Shortly it would be red and the heat of the room intolerable. Those in the secret would off coat, cravat, and waistcoat; and, if necessary, we would strip to the shirt and drawers, but do it all the time with an air as though it was our custom every evening. No matter if the heat of the room became sufficient to cook a beef-steak very rare done, we would stand it cheerfully, sure to be rid of the intruder at last.

If loungers sat or lay upon the counter by day and leaned over the writing desk, Berry would have a spring and sharp needle, or several of them under the counter, with a string in reach of his hand, which he would jerk at the right time. Even if Mr. Walcott was writing by his side. The unhappy lounger would of course jump off the counter in haste and shake his trousers, expecting to see a dead wasp or hornet come away.

There was a way of throwing bird-shot from a quill fastened on one end of a stiff whale bone, which would sting a person at distance, provided his pantaloons fitted closely to the skin. There was no trick of this kind unknown to Berry, although he must have been at that time thirty years of age at least. I never could learn his age, and when I last saw him in 1860, he did not seem as old to me as he did in 1830.

This love of mischief in the office of course set a rather bad example to the factory boys, which they improved upon when they dared, in face of the regulations which we in the office might to a certain extent violate with impunity.

There was an old overseer, a genuine Yankee. For although we were some of us of N. England descent ourselves, we felt as strong a dislike to the real Yankee characteristics as if we had been raised Dutchmen or Southerners.

This overseer had control of one of our rooms in the Factory. He did not affiliate with others as he ought for his own good and kept himself aloof by living across the creek at considerable distance away. He had one saying which he uttered many times a day with a peculiar accent: "B-a-d Boys!" In winter, early in the morning before day, he would come from his house at a dog trot, and crossing the dark-flowing creek on a plank which he kept there for his own use, be at his post by times. One night some of the boys sawed that plank on the under side nearly through and then lay in wait next morning to see the fun. At the usual time came along the "boss" at his jog trot. The plank gave way gently as it was intended to do, and the old fellow had a cold bath. "B-a-d boys!" were his last words as he plunged into the flood; but the bad boys waited long enough, concealed, to make sure that he did not drown. I never knew who played that trick, and still further, I venture to say the overseer never found it out himself.

At another time some of them on a winter night took down the Factory bell from the cupola and, mounting it on a sleigh, visited at midnight the factories round about for several miles, ringing up the hands to go to their work.

At another time somebody's two-horse wagon was to be seen in the morning, in perfect running order, astride the ridge of the Factory, perhaps sixty feet from the ground, and such weights must have been carried up by ladders in the dark at great personal risk and, if unknown to the watchman, with extraordinary secrecy.

One more story on my friend Lewis Berry, and I will be done with him for the present. On a certain day the boarding-house keepers round about the Factory village combined to raise the price of board and appointed to hold a public meeting for that purpose one evening at the brick school-house. Berry, and the rest of us as well, did not approve the object of that meeting, and he laid his plans accordingly. The hour for meeting arrived. The attendance was large. Silence prevailed. Berry rose with perfect gravity and nominated one of us for Chairman. It was passed. Another of us for Secretary. That also passed. Then he asked leave to offer the following Resolutions: "Resolved, that the price of board in future remain as it has been and that the fare be improved." "Resolved, that this meeting does now adjourn." All of which was passed, and the house cleared, before the original callers of the meeting had presence of mind to understand what was going on. We heard little more about advancing the price of board at that time.

CHAPTER 16

A Friendship

One other office comrade I had, but he was of a different style. John D. Wells. He was a kinsman of Mr. Wm. Walcott, who was a Curtenius, descended from Peter I. Curtenius, an old-time N. York merchant of note. He was also a cousin of the N. York Primes (Ireneus); thus my friend John was of the best Dutch relationship, and the Dutch, I suppose, consider themselves the best blood in that State.[1] Wells was no discredit to the best of them. I knew him as a young man very intimately, and never knew anything low about him.

He had evidently enjoyed a careful training at the hands of his widowed mother, and there were unmistakable signs of "breeding" in his whole deportment. Younger than either Berry or myself, he was a check and restraint upon the Exuberance of our fun. It must never degenerate into wickedness in his presence. Only one trick or practical joke, I ever knew him to perpetrate, and that was on the side of Mercy. One day a man rode up on horse-back and asked permission to visit the Factory. John had noticed as the man dismounted that his horse's sides were bleeding from the unreasonable use of spurs; and glancing from thence at the rider's heels, he saw the rowels unreasonably large and sharp. "You can visit the Factory," said John, "but you had not better wear those spurs among the machinery." So the stranger unbuckled the spurs and left them in the office. Immediately he was gone, John ran for a file, and long before the man returned, he had every sharp point of the rowels filed off short and smooth, and then fell back to his desk to await the result. It all passed off well. The man never noticed his spurs as he put them on again, and rode off apparently quite pleased at his visit to the factory.

Wells improved his time by study, and I think he never neglected the duties of religion, although the situation was unfavorable for that.

I forget how long this went on, but it was, I think, several years; when one day he announced that he should leave us and enter upon a course of study in order to become a minister of the gospel. A determination once deliberately formed, he was not likely ever to change. No one of us dared dissuade him from so laudable a determination as this. When he left us, I went part of the way with him, and we separated with mutual promises not to forget and write often. Some famous letters passed between us at first; but like all such promises to correspond, this one died out gradually. Yet I never quite lost sight of my friend.

Once I visited him at Sing Sing in the State of N. York, where he was studying under the tuition of Dr. Prime, the father of all the "Primes." They took me to see the State Prison, and across the Tappan Zee to visit the Rockland Lake, a delightful trip, made in delightful company.

Years afterward, I again visited my old friend John. He then had charge of a neat church near the Croton reservoir, which was at that time "missionary ground."[2] Being too far away from population to support a Presbyterian Church, several benevolent ladies of the family of Jas. Lenox, Esq. had purchased the ground, erected a church building of brick large enough for the present church and small enough for a future lecture room, supported the Rev. John D. Wells as missionary pastor, neatly furnished him house and library, and looked kindly after his health and comfort.[3]

I understood it was a systematic thing with those excellent ladies, thus to establish churches for N. York City and nurse them, in advance of population. At the same time bringing forward deserving young men. I also understood that while they were about it, they purchased land enough to ensure in each case the future building of a large church edifice upon the advance in the value of real estate. John's mother was his house-keeper at the time I speak of, and at the same time was an active "visitor" in one or more of the leading public charities. Poor fellow! he had taken the small-pox and was badly marked. He was a dyspeptic, and at times unreasonably low-spirited. In those times he would doubt his own interest in the Great Salvation, which he nevertheless labored earnestly to preach to others. His pock-marked face was a sorrow to him, and he must needs find himself a pock-marked wife, which he did; and a good wife she was. When I last saw him, ten years or more after that, the marks had sufficiently disappeared from both their faces, and two happier faces I never saw.[4] He [was] no longer dyspeptic, satisfied in his own mind, and successful in his work of winning souls to Christ; she [was] charming at the head of her little family. It always did me good to visit him. I last saw him in 1860. He was then pastor of a large Church in Williamsburg, (a suburb of N. York City), and evidently a growing man. As a preacher he deserves some day to stand very high. He always was, as a boy, an uncommonly good reader, a gift which he took care to improve afterwards; and his powers for extemporaneous speaking were far above mediocrity. I never knew a person in whose sincerity I had more confidence.[5]

I have never seen his name in print as an author but once, and that was a little work entitled the "Last week in the life of David Johnson, Jr.," not an ordinary book. God bless my old friend to the end of his days!

CHAPTER 17

Novercalis, and the "Faculty"

*O*ther friends I had, each in their degree, who did me more good while learning my business than I can ever repay.[1] The least I can do is to record their names. Ira Hand, superintendent of the Factory. Raised to the business from boyhood, with a family connexion in the same business, he knew all that could be known of his duties as a manufacturer without any science or even education more than what a thoughtful man will always pick up in the progress of affairs. Mr. Hand had thus acquired a great deal more useful knowledge than many educated men ever remember.

And I may as well here say, once for all, that factory folk, raised to their business, as distinct from those taken from the plow or dairy for an occasion, are a very sharp folk. I have heard a distinguished preacher, now a D.D., in one of the larger cities say that he owed his renown as a preacher mainly to the fact that in early life he had to preach in a Factory village, where his intellect was stimulated to a high degree in keeping up with the mental activity of his people.

Mr. Hand was naturally a gentleman in figure, deportment, and in feelings. He could have had little sympathy with us wild fellows; but he did by me, in the line of his duty, all that I had a right to expect, with much more forbearance than I had a right to expect. When last at the North, I failed to see him, but understood that he held an honorable position in the same business of manufacturing.

Speaking of Factory people as a class. At the North, a sense of justice constrains me to give my testimony that they are, so far as I was ever able to find out, distinguished for morality. Enjoying a daily income, though it may be small, and in the main provided with the necessaries of life by their employers, they generally find no difficulty in gauging their wants according to their income; & there is the least possible temptation to dishon-

Merrell's own sketch of the Oneida factory in Whitesboro, N.Y., where he learned his craft. He pasted this sketch into his manuscript.

esty. Numerous among themselves and fully employed, they have society enough, and do not much aspire after admission into higher circles. As to the intercourse among the sexes, I never found it otherwise than pure. This is contrary to the generally received opinion of communities where the sexes have employment together, but my observation was that the working together, in grease and dirt, and seeing each other daily under the most unfavorable circumstances is rather a cure and a preventive against evil inclinations. At any rate, in all my seven years' stay among them, I never knew or heard of but one *faux pas* between the sexes, in any well-regulated factory. The one case referred to arose from an intrusion from high life among factory folk.

The lives of factory people, under good regulations, are quite as innocent as the lives of other people, and since idleness and want engender sin, & not industrious poverty, I conclude that the Factory laborers are entitled to a better social standing than has ever yet been accorded to them. — All of which time will bring about.

Others of my friends there were. Deacon Wood and his sons John and Leander. The old deacon was a fixture, and a long way behind the times. Had charge of the weaving department, but his sons did the work, while the old man would wear out several pairs of trousers sitting down to every one pair of shoes walking. He was a good man, I believe; talked as long as he could get a listener, and when he was not talking, he purred like a cat. He was very strong in the doctrines of our religion, and did all he could to check and restrain all wildness. He was one of the most ill-favored men I ever knew, and how he came to get so fair a woman as he had for a wife I never could understand; & having a good-looking wife, how he could have got such ungainly boys was another mystery to me. I received nothing at their hands but what was well-intended towards me, although I often rebelled against their influence. I thought the boys very opinionated, but they made me a thorough weaver. John studied for the ministry and afterwards became a preacher, I have understood. The old father, although subject to severe epileptic fits, was living recently, and when I last saw him, he did not appear to have aged a great deal.

Deacon Wood was the father of Power Loom weaving in our parts.[2] Not that he ever invented anything, but he came on with the improvements. He came from Rhode Island. During the war of 1812 he flourished in Utica, N.Y., as a hand-loom weaver, or master of hand-loom weavers. The fly shuttle was the first improvement. I have heard him say that the first power loom was built on rockers like a cradle, rocking at each stroke of the lathe, so the shuttle might slide down hill. This clumsy invention was so much thought of that the weavers mounted it on a car, and paraded it in triumph through the streets of Utica.

William White, a Scotchman, was an honest man. I have heard him sing a Scotch song in a style that left nothing to be desired.

His brother-in-law, William Ballantine, a younger man, came from Scotland about the year 1832. They were both natives of Paisley, and Ballantine had been raised in the Works of the Clarks, whose spool Thread was there what "Coats" has been since: the very best.[3]

A year or two afterwards came all the way from Scotland Ballantine's Sweet-heart, and they were married. He was an uncommonly fine singer, even for a Scotchman. Years afterward, he sought employment from me in Georgia. I gave it to him, and to a son of his. I suppose they are all there at this time.

There were some Beckers, Dutchmen by birth and raising, who were not factory folk by nature. They came from the plough & went back to it.

There were also some Divines, also from the plough. I could never locate them as to their birth and raising. They were not an ordinary family. Had no front teeth, but double teeth all round. One of them was a great pedestrian. Another would let you put a pin to the head into his muscle, with apparent pleasure. Another, who was an absentee, was publicly known as the "Fire King," perhaps under an assumed name. He would stay in a heated oven until a beef-steak was cooked in his hand. He said it was done by sheer endurance, with no great art, and he felt it was injuring him. Should think likely. All the boys enjoyed the initials D.D., being named Dennis Divine, Davis Divine & so on. All of them, I think, had each some particular thing in which he excelled; and [all] were well-disposed. I have lost sight of them.

In the machine shop were at one time John Puffer, an ingenious man of the Yankee school, who one day lost an arm in the machinery, which put him upon ingenious contrivances to do without the arm. At another time David Shapley, a clever man, who also lost two middle fingers of one hand in machinery. Both were men of character, and doubtless rose in the world.

Another Scotchman there was, named Manville, who could neither sing a song or tell a story; but he could laugh. He always seemed pale, like many other factory folk, because he worked always in the shade, and he in particular had the dressing room which was kept at a high temperature by steam. I had fallen in with the notion that such an employment must be unwholesome, but was undeceived by seeing him in 1860, looking as well as he ever did, and laughing all the same.

Factory business, in general, is not unhealthy, but the contrary. I have had the best opportunities to judge both in the North and South, and at the West. Even Negroes taken from the field thrive better in the Factory. There is dust flying, but they soon learn to breathe through the nose, and no dust reaches the lungs.

The popular idea that Factory folk sicken and die comes partly of political antagonism as set forth in a former chapter, and partly from the pale complexions and thin skins which are caused by working in the shade.

Those I have named were our sterling men of the manufacturing trade. Others there were, coming and going, of whom I make no note. But one only that now I remember was anything to me. He was a Wetmore of the well-known Wetmore family, original settlers of Whitesboro.[4] Theodore I think was his name, a clever young man in the English sense of that word. Whatever he did, he did it well. He had no love for the Factory. Machinery was not to his taste. He was raised a farmer, and his highest aspiration was for 160 acres of Prairie land somewhere in the state of Illinois, then just coming into market. In reduced circumstances, he forced himself to be a manufacturer long enough to lay by a fund sufficient for his darling object; and then he went. I never have heard of him since, but doubt not he took care to do well.

Wetmore was specially skillful in spearing fish by torch light. Touching the butt end of his spear to the ground, it was wonderful to see the leaps he would take from one bank of the creek to the other, in pursuit of a hapless fish. He was, I suppose, the only one among us at the time who could fire a gun without winking. None of us cared much for a gun. Game was scarce. The pursuit of it would not pay. To be a gunner was synonymous with being an idle fellow.

Our head master, Wm. Walcott, deserves, and shall have, a Chapter by himself in connexion with the distinguished Walcott family.

CHAPTER 18

The "Walcotts"

Here is what may be called, consistently with the genius of things in Yankeeland, a "Distinguished Family." Manufacturers always, they took their start with the rise of manufacturing in the days of Saml. Slater in the State of Rhode Island.[1] About the time of the Embargo which preceded the War of 1812, or during that war, the father of all the Walcotts, by name of Benjamin Sen. established a Cotton Factory, under a joint Stock Company, in the town of Whitesboro, Oneida County, State of N. York.[2] It stood on the site of the present Oneida Factory, and was the nucleus in all that neighborhood of Factories, of all styles, radiating from that centre all over that region of country wherever water power could be found. That region was at that early day the "far west." Water-power was more permanent then than it has proved to be since the country round about the sources of the streams has been cleared up, drained, and exposed to evaporation. There were no canals or rail-roads and no foreign commerce to bring in manufactured articles from abroad; and the relations of our Government towards foreigners were a guarantee against free trade and foreign competition for many years to come. Steam power was not then much thought of. Hence all things considered, the choice of time and location made by Old Mr. Walcott was judicious; and although Rail Roads, Canals, Steam power, and foreign competition have since come in one by one to disturb the original calculations, yet so deep and strong did those old pioneers lay down the foundations of their undertakings, that although their prospects may have been over and over again ruined, apparently, by untoward events, and even by bad management itself, there they stand to this day, more like a permanent institution than almost anything else in the land.

When I last visited the North, there were, I think, as many as fifty Cotton and Woolen Factories in that one county, and some of them were as large as Factories ever ought to be. All this Wealth originated at the Old Oneida Factory, erected in a poor way by the Elder Walcott. I do not mean literally that the dollars came from there, though I might almost say that; but I do mean to say that the example, the personal influence, the skillful laborers, [were] colonized from or to that original stock. And yet the Walcotts were not always themselves successful. Reverses were necessary, reverses were good for them. Nothing genuine in the arts or manufactures ever succeeds at the first intention. Experience is necessary, and experience comes by defeats, and by trying again.

I heard this best illustrated in a speech by Alex. H. Stephens, at this time the Vice Pres. of the Confederate States. He said that in the up country of Georgia a father and son for the first time in their lives undertook to butcher a beef, and as might have been expected they did it badly. When they had done, and the quarters of beef, sadly mangled, were hanging on a tree, the boy stood off and took a look at it.

At length he said, "Dad, we've mummucked it, let's kill another & try again."

The Walcotts each one, no doubt, had to "kill another & try again" many times.

Benj. Walcott, Sen., had several sons, who all were trained to his business, and had the genius for it in different degrees. I never saw the old gentleman; he died before my time. His sons Benjamin Jr. of the N. York Mills I knew and admired, and William, as I have before stated, was my master for seven years. Other sons there were, whom I knew only by reputation, seeing them occasionally. Benjamin and William were a different style of men, the one from the other. Benjamin was the Elder, a man of talent rather than genius, of dignity and no smartness, of strict discipline and sound maxims; he invented nothing, affected the old style of doing things, laid down his work for permanency, and waited for others to try experiments at their own expense and prove what was genuine before he would have anything to do with it; and therein he was right as a practical man, taking care always to avail himself of improvements as fast as their economy was demonstrated.

William, my master, was the opposite of Benjamin in all those particulars which I have enumerated. A man of genius rather than talent. He was an inventor, and as such had many experiments to try. Indeed he was more of an experimenter on the inventions of others, & of course he had to father many failures.

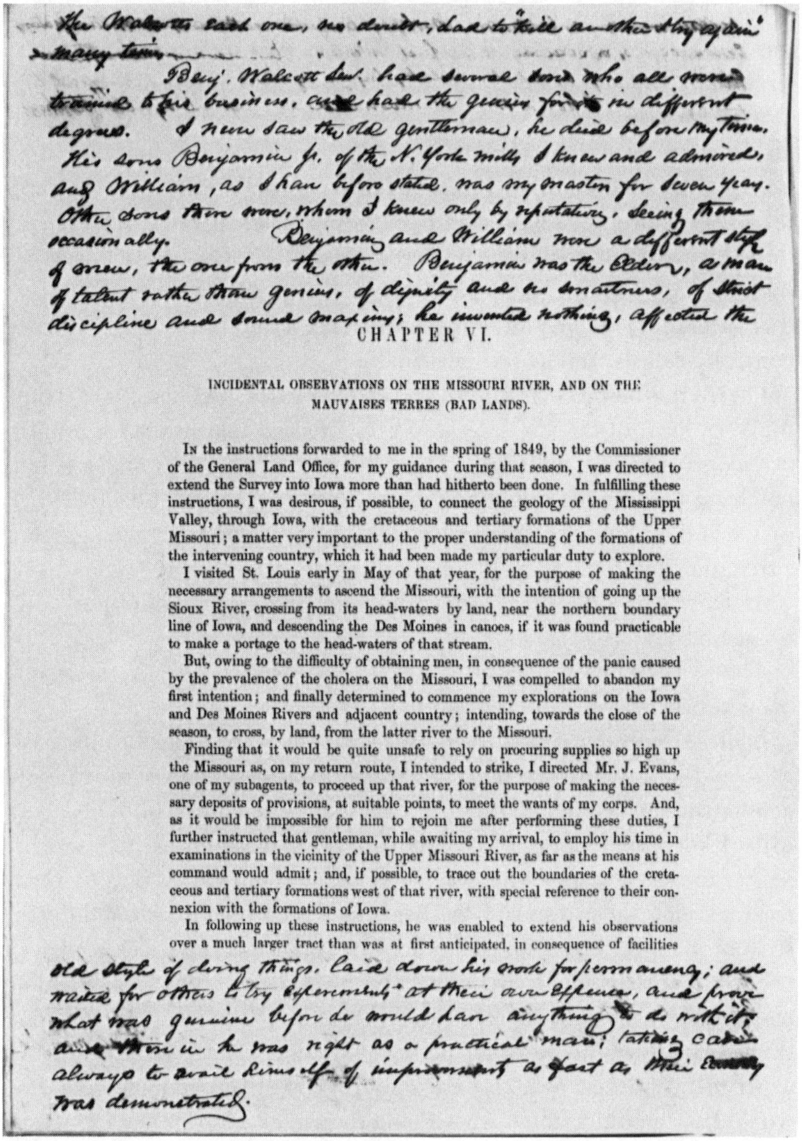

the Walcotts each one, no doubt, had to kill another & try again many times.

Benj. Walcott Senr. had several sons who all were trained to his business, and had the genius for it in different degrees. I never saw the old gentleman, he died before my time. His sons Benjamin Jr. of the N. York mills I knew and admired, and William, as I have before stated, was my master for seven years. Other sons there were, whom I knew only by reputation, seeing them occasionally. Benjamin and William were a different style of men, the one from the other. Benjamin was the Elder, a man of talent rather than genius, of dignity and no smartness, of strict discipline and sound maxims; he invented nothing, affected the

CHAPTER VI.

INCIDENTAL OBSERVATIONS ON THE MISSOURI RIVER, AND ON THE MAUVAISES TERRES (BAD LANDS).

In the instructions forwarded to me in the spring of 1849, by the Commissioner of the General Land Office, for my guidance during that season, I was directed to extend the Survey into Iowa more than had hitherto been done. In fulfilling these instructions, I was desirous, if possible, to connect the geology of the Mississippi Valley, through Iowa, with the cretaceous and tertiary formations of the Upper Missouri; a matter very important to the proper understanding of the formations of the intervening country, which it had been made my particular duty to explore.

I visited St. Louis early in May of that year, for the purpose of making the necessary arrangements to ascend the Missouri, with the intention of going up the Sioux River, crossing from its head-waters by land, near the northern boundary line of Iowa, and descending the Des Moines in canoes, if it was found practicable to make a portage to the head-waters of that stream.

But, owing to the difficulty of obtaining men, in consequence of the panic caused by the prevalence of the cholera on the Missouri, I was compelled to abandon my first intention; and finally determined to commence my explorations on the Iowa and Des Moines Rivers and adjacent country; intending, towards the close of the season, to cross, by land, from the latter river to the Missouri.

Finding that it would be quite unsafe to rely on procuring supplies so high up the Missouri as, on my return route, I intended to strike, I directed Mr. J. Evans, one of my subagents, to proceed up that river, for the purpose of making the necessary deposits of provisions, at suitable points, to meet the wants of my corps. And, as it would be impossible for him to rejoin me after performing these duties, I further instructed that gentleman, while awaiting my arrival, to employ his time in examinations in the vicinity of the Upper Missouri River, as far as the means at his command would admit; and, if possible, to trace out the boundaries of the cretaceous and tertiary formations west of that river, with special reference to their connexion with the formations of Iowa.

In following up these instructions, he was enabled to extend his observations over a much larger tract than was at first anticipated, in consequence of facilities

old style of doing things, laid down his work for permanency; and waited for others to try experiments at their own expense, and prove what was genuine before he would have anything to do with it, and therein he was right as a practical man; taking care always to avail himself of improvements as fast as their utility was demonstrated.

A manuscript page from Merrell's autobiography, written in 1863. Merrell resorted to writing in the margins of a published geological survey after the Union blockade had shut off the Confederacy's supply of paper.

As a business man—a man of results, of course—Benjamin was the man far the most likely to succeed in the end; William the most likely to please a company of fancy stock holders who knew nothing about it, but thought they knew it all.

As men of business to deal with, and as gentlemen, they were equally men to be respected and beloved. All the Walcotts that I ever knew were so. I never knew one of them to do a mean thing. As for myself, living under the immediate influence of William, and studying his very uncertain results, I came to regard the maxims of Benj. Walcott as the best, and determined to adopt them as the rule of my business life. But I erred, as imitators will, in going over too far to his side. Although I possessed a decided genius for inventions, & had the peculiar gift of elaborating an improvement in my brain, and bringing it to perfection without much experiment, I went so far as to conceive that I had an aversion to improvement in general, which finally led me into one or two memorable failures in the State of Georgia, by using old-time machinery at a conjuncture when I should have adopted every genuine improvement, and taken all the chances for success. Hence it was that in Georgia, my own pupils, in their turn, profiting by my errors, out-ranked me in my own profession, and made their fortunes while I was losing mine. I learned wisdom at last, and in Arkansas, I have tried to hit the proper medium, and I have had success.

I have in my possession the pictures of both the Walcotts, Benj. and William, and their personal appearance accords with the outlines of mental character that I have given them.[3] Benjamin: a large frame, ample chest and muscle, and an old time head, with simply an honest countenance; William: a slender figure, flat chest, stooping shoulders, & large brain projecting forward. I am constrained to say that neither of them appear ever to have been handsome men; but they looked like men to be relied upon. Benjamin was a plain man in dress and equipage. William loved a little style, and especially a fine horse and neat gloves and boots.

At the time I speak of William was the wealthiest man, having married a lady of property; but in the end, Benjamin a long way outstripped his brother, both in wealth and in distinction as a successful manufacturer. William deservedly had great praise for the building of the steam Factory in West Utica; but I have understood that he ran down, and after his death his estate would scarcely pay out. William had no family. I am therefore in my chapter on the Walcott family narrowed down to the recollections of Benjamin & his noble family.

The War of 1812 was of short duration, giving citizens barely time to adjust their affairs to the new economy before it ended and left all in status quo. While the return of Peace was hailed with joy, many were ruined in their affairs. A Factory establishment gotten up at war prices, could not go on at peace prices against foreign competition.

Under these circumstances, I have understood that Benj. Walcott Sr. found himself in the year 1817 to 1822 reduced to the necessity of beginning the world over again. Accordingly we find him first a builder of spinning machinery for others. After that he altered a flouring mill, called the "Burr Stone Mill," into a small cotton Factory which always after went by the same name. That flouring mill, I believe, was owned by the Doolittles, from which family (Genl. Doolittle) Mr. Walcott had taken to himself a wife who was the mother of all the children that were on the stage in my time. I always understood that the "Burr Stone Factory" was owned by a co-partnership of the Directors and Benj. Walcott, the latter having control.

The "Burr Stone Factory," though a poor concern to look at, was under Mr. Benj. Walcott's hands a model Factory. No other establishment had so fine a reputation for its products. Those maxims which distinguished him afterwards above all other manufacturers in the United States, were then and there verified by Benj. Walcott. He would have only the best of mechanics about him, and such an one once in his service settled down for life. He would have about him only the best of operators, & those of unblemished moral character; and those in like manner, once in his service, felt themselves settled, father and son, with a fair prospect of rising in the business. Dignity on his own part must be met with high respect on the part of his Employees, and severe discipline maintained.

He would have the best of machinery, and that must be in order, even if it had to be re-built outright. The best of oil; and above all good cotton and no other. Nothing mean or low-priced about him. The result was, as might be expected, the goods he manufactured were, for those times, perfect. He was after reputation, and he won it. He might not have made so much money in a flush time as others who slighted their work, but when a hard time came, his manufactures would be sought after, and others neglected.

The special emulation of the time was to cheapen the cost of goods so as to drive out foreign competition; his aim was to improve the character of his above the reach of foreign competition, and he did so finally, until foreigners themselves were fain to counterfeit his brand. I never saw him exhibit strong resentment, except upon that occasion.

This thing went on until, I think it was, the year 1822. There had been in N. York City a wealthy importing house of Englishmen, *Benj. Marshall* and his brother Joseph. The high protective Tariff of 1822 put an end to their importing trade, and they found themselves in funds to the amount of several hundred thousand dollars with no use for it. Benjamin was the man of that house also. By some means he satisfied himself that the next season would bring with it a speculation in Raw Cotton; whereupon, for lack of something better to do, he took up a temporary residence in the town of Augusta in Georgia, until he had invested his money in cotton to please him, shipping the same to Liverpool, whither he followed it in person during the spring of the year. In Liverpool, when the speculative time arrived, as he expected, he managed his own sales. That is to say, he would appear in the market, not as a seller at all, but as an excited buyer. He would buy some, but at the same time his agent was selling more, until he had sold clean out, at a profit which nearly doubled his capital. Depositing that in good hands to draw upon, he returned to N. York City and sold his exchange at a profit, and then "what next" was the question.

By this time Benj. Marshall had satisfied his own mind that under the protective Tariff, manufacturing would be highly profitable in the United States, and he determined to invest the bulk of his funds in a Cotton Factory of the largest and highest style.[4]

Having decided upon this, the next thing was to find the man. Benj. Marshall, though an Englishman himself, had sense enough to know that he need not bring a pig-headed English Cotton Spinner, of one idea, to build up an American institution and control American hands. Like a sensible man as he was, he simply went through the N. York Market and satisfied himself as to which style of goods of American Manufacture had the best reputation, and who made them. The man was Benj. Walcott, of course. His further inquiries about Mr. Walcott satisfied him that in all respects he was the man for him, & he went to see him.

Here I will remark lest this should read too much like a romance, that part of this story I had from Mr. Marshall's own lips, once when I fell into his company in a journey, and part I learned otherwise; but none at all from any of the Walcotts, for they seldom talk of themselves or their affairs.

Now Benj. Marshall was a great pedestrian. He would not ride when he could walk. He was at that time a very tall, erect, hale-looking Englishman, and his presence was commanding. I do not remember about his feet, but judge that like most Englishmen he could make very large tracks as he went along. About his shoes he was extremely particular. He would procure, all the way from England, a supply of the best leather tanned under the Royal seal, enough at one time for himself and friends. Then he would take his share to the shoe-maker, and sit down by him, watching the fidelity of every stitch, until the shoes were completed to his notion, and then in due time he would put on those shoes and outwalk the mail as it was carried in those days.

One day, say in the year 1823, Benj. Marshall walked into and walked over the little Burr Stone factory, four miles from Utica and 250 miles from N. York. How much of that distance he had walked, I cannot tell; probably he came as far as Utica on the Water Craft of the times, and walked up and down the deck in his seven-league shoes twice as fast as the vessel itself went through the water. And finally he walked into the affections of Benjamin Walcott. Never were two men better calculated to meet each other's views. They were as much alike, and yet as happily different in their temperaments and powers, as two brothers could well be. The partnership which ensued was rather a brotherhood and a family arrangement.[5]

Quietly, the Burr Stone factory was purchased, the lands and water power over a great circle round were purchased, in order to secure to themselves the benefits of any advance in the value of real estate that might accrue, upon the erection of extensive works with their own money. As usual in all such cases, there were some sharp ones who knew better than to sell under such circumstances; but in the main, enough location was secured to warrant the erection of extensive works, with a good deal of outcome for the future; and the foundations were forthwith laid for that great establishment the "New York Mills." The date inscribed on the cap stone over the door is 1824. In such hands, it was bound to be a success. From that beginning sprang a business, apparently as permanent as anything can be under American institutions.

How much wealth was divided out of the profits of the business during nearly forty years, I have no means of knowing. Mr. Marshall afterwards built up extensive works elsewhere, besides being able to purchase the interest of his brother Joseph. Out of the whole he made a present, or consideration for services, of one quarter of the whole to Benj. Walcott, besides at other times Ten Thousand Dollars to build him a house, and other gifts, as I have understood. Finally Benjamin Walcott was able to purchase the whole at say Half a Million of Dollars, giving to his own family a share, as Mr. Marshall had done by him. This is a rambling history of that property, as it has come to my ears from time to time. I cannot vouch for its accuracy in financial matters.

When I last visited the place in 1860, it had the air of great prosperity and improvement. It had absorbed adjacent property to a large amount.

Among other things, it had bought in the Oneida Factory, my old home.[6] The premises made one continuous village, say a mile and a half in length. On this occasion I was shown the premises by William D., the son of Benjamin, who merits a separate notice.

Quite ten years before the date of this visit, Benjamin Walcott, feeling old age coming upon him, had turned over the business to his son William as head man, and under him certain subordinate managers who had risen from the ranks. William was every way well calculated to fill his father's place.[7] Indeed he possessed educational advantages over his father, and was strictly trained up to the business in all its details. A more valuable man in his place there could not well be. Moreover he was, as nearly as possible in business life, a perfect character. As a boy, he was known as "little Bill," his uncle Wm. Walcott being the Big Bill. I have understood that in school, Little Bill was scarcely a boy, but always like a little man. One day the master punished him, to which he submitted like a man, but carried home his own statement. His father received William's statement in place of that of the teacher, saying that his son had never deceived him; and he withdrew William from the school, saying moreover that any teacher who could not get on with William without whipping, was not fit to be a teacher. It afterwards turned out that William and his father were correct. This transaction was characteristic of both the man and the boy.

Wm. D. was working in the N. York Mills to learn his business at the same time I was the same way engaged at the Oneida Factory hard by. I had not the opportunity to be intimate with him but was well acquainted, and I regarded his character as a model for my own imitation; but, alas for me! My temperament was not such as to qualify for such an imitation. I tried it, when I afterwards commenced life in earnest in the State of Georgia. I tried to be a steady old man at the age of twenty-two; but it was a restraint, and at this writing, though nearly fifty years of age, I feel younger than I did then, trying my best to be such a man as Little William Walcott. I think that he in his time liked some things about me. He once told me that he liked me to be with him when there was any amusement or recreation in hand, for I seemed to enter into the spirit of it. That was him exactly. I had a way of throwing my whole force and energy into whatever was on hand to be done. Whether it was work or play, and too often mixing the two, while he, sedate as a judge, was glad to see others enjoying themselves, and was always wanting to pay the bill.

I never knew how much I loved that young man until one time, away in Georgia I dreamed one of those life-like dreams that he died and I mourned at his funeral. My grief, sleeping and waking, seemed to me almost inconsolable. I might have been Jonathan to his David, had we been thrown more together. Possibly I possessed some qualities as a manufacturer that he lacked, & might have been of great service to him could I have remained and gone on with the old established business instead of pioneering in new countries as I have done. A much more agreeable and more innocent life certainly.

Young William Walcott visited me once in Georgia. So did his father, Benj. S. Walcott, and likewise my old master William Walcott the uncle, all at different times.[8] I was proud indeed to think that they felt so much interest in my affairs, but I was not making money at the time, and felt humble that they should see it. I was contending against great difficulties then, and they were men to see through that at a glance. They did not withhold their good advice from me. Good advice could not save me then, as will appear in the sequel of my Georgia career.

Benj. S. Walcott probably is no longer living. He was very feeble in 1860, and travelling for change of scene. I did not see him. I fear the events of the last two years have broken his mighty heart. He loved to travel much in his old age. Without that kind of education which is generally thought necessary for an accomplished traveler, he nevertheless possessed a thoughtful and observing habit, tempered by native shrewdness and dry humor, which made his letters, by the way, highly amusing and instructive. He went over Europe and visited Egypt and the Holy Land. His observations upon the state of Manufacturing, wherever he went, were curious indeed.

William Walcott the older became mixed up with Rail Road and land speculations at the West. Dying at a bad time for closing up such affairs, his Estate, as I have before said, did not turn out well.

Little William has yet, I hope, a long and prosperous career to view. God Bless him!

There was a younger brother, Charles D. Walcott, who also learned the Manufacturing business, but broke down in health and died.[9] Poor fellow! He had a habit of saying, "It is hard, is it not?" when he intended to speak deprecatingly of any thing. Those were his last words as he died, so young. "It is hard!" I enjoyed more intimacy with him than I did with his brother William.

There was also a Sister named Elizabeth who was of exactly my age, having been born on the same day. She was room-mate of my poor sister Lucretia at a Boarding School. I had a notion one time that I loved her; but a sober second thought showed me it was nonsense, for she was already marriageable, while I had yet my mark to make. So I said nothing about it, and I suppose it was "puppy love." Imagine my pangs when I saw her courted with great assiduity by the only son and heir of the great Benj. Marshall. The young fellow was little short of an idiot at the time, and I believe went that way finally, having not far to go. He had, however, a good enough person, and was dressed to the best advantage by City Tailors. What he ever found to say to her I could only fancy. He seemed to me to be thinking he loved the ground she trod upon, walking single file behind her, looking down, and carefully stepping in her tracks, putting his foot down when she took up hers. His courtship did not prosper. Had old Mr. Marshall himself addressed her on his own behalf, the noble old man might possibly have succeeded. At least the arrangement would not have been quite so preposterous.

I had my thoughts & admired the girl's spirit; but in fact it was none of my business.

In 1860 young William showed me with pride a young married son of his, working in the Factory as his father had done before him.[10]

But I must close this chapter on "The Walcotts." They were not men to write anecdotes about. Such steady men furnish no staple in a whole life time for many anecdotes. Their works and their results must illustrate their characters. May their affairs prosper a thousand years!

Speaking of anecdotes, allow me to tell one. Marvin Winston, referred to in a former chapter, afterwards arrived in due time at the dignity of minister of the gospel.[11] He had married in Georgia a Southern lady of good family — a McIntosh. Returned to the North, & stopping at my mother's house, he was asked one day to drive over to the N. York Mills & preach. His wife put some things in his valise, and he went. This was on a Saturday. He was entertained at Mr. Walcott's house. Sabbath morning came, but instead of a clean shirt he found in his valise another garment belonging to his wife! In this dilemma, of course, he had nothing that he could do but submit his trials to the master of the house, which he did & received all the sympathy the case required, Mr. Walcott's shirts being large enough certainly.

CHAPTER 19

Whitesboro Village & round about

It is a wonder to me that any boys are successfully raised up from infancy, or being safely through the risks and dangers of infancy, that they ever arrive at manhood. As it respects the raising up of girls, I have nothing to say. There is that shirt-tail nigger Jo, mischievous as a monkey, rampaging in the yard as I write. See him pulling the carriage horses by their tails! What on earth is the reason the horses do not kick his brains out? Then hear his grand-mother, as she pulls his shirt over his head, whips him roundly in spite of his outcry for going under the horse's heels, and in ten minutes he is balancing himself on the top stick of a precarious pile of wood. What possible chance is there that he can go within an inch of his life five times every day, and finally grow up to reimburse me for the anxiety I have looking after him, to say nothing of his destroying more food & making more noise than a hound or a Shanghai fowl and tearing all the clothing that can be put on him?

Think what I have gone through myself. I was drowned once, so that the water ran out of me like a cask with the spigot turned. Charley DeLong trod water and told me that he was on the bottom. "Come along." I tried to follow, and went under. He stopped not to save me, but ran for help, leaving me to drown. Once I fell from an elevation onto the pavement, and was insensible until the day following; and again nearly the same thing happened to me swinging on a gate. At another time my poor cousin Horace accidentally cut my head open with an ax. The scar is on my bald head now. In the factory among swift running belts and gearing, before modern improvements had covered them with safety, what hair-breadth escapes! Once I remember I jumped on top of Deacon Wood's work bench to take down a heavy roll of wire. It turned in my hand, and over my head like a huge collar. The upright shaft and heavy gearing were roaring close by. The roll of wire was caught in the gearing and whirled into fifty shapes, at the very instant that I had dodged my head out of the mortal coil. It did not seem to me that I had half a second of time to spare. Twice I understand I have been shot at with rifle and pistol deliberately, and O! what threats have I outlived, and seen the threateners pass on harmless. How many times in the power of fractious horses. Once my clothes torn into ribbons by a runaway horse in my buggy. In sickness often, often; and sometimes very sick. Cut with knives, chawed by mill gearing, stung by great venomous insects, hardly escaping the deadly spring of the rattle snake, stubbed my toes until amputation might have followed had the doctor's views prevailed, wrecked once on salt water; and above all high-strung with the nervous excitement of pressing and unfortunate business long continued, and failing at last. Surely there is a hand unseen that guides us through!

Turning from these dangers merely physical in their character, what moral risks and exposures have we to go through! I remember as distinctly as though it was a year ago, the first irreligious doubt infused into my mind. We boys were playing in the Street—in Main Street in front of the old house. Jim Comstock, who lived across the way, suddenly and abruptly asked me how I knew "but what the Bible was all a story book, and not a word of truth in it?" The idea went through me like a pang. I could not answer him, and I have no doubt I gave my mother equal pain when I reported the question to her.

But during my stay at the Oneida Factory (which was about seven years) I had one safe-guard against the evils of bad company. That was the Society of young ladies, and some of them literary ladies at that. The ancient and aristocratic village of Whitesboro, shaded with old elms, lay only a mile off.[1] It was in sight across the meadows from the Factory windows, & a more pleasant landscape I have rarely seen. The society of that village was very select and exclusive. It had need to be so, for the neighborhood of that college, called the "Oneida Institute," exposed it to the intrusion of Students, who thought no better of themselves than to associate with Negroes. At the very head of Society in Whitesboro were the Berrys, one brother and several sisters of my friend Lewis Berry. They were all and all a distinguished family. Some called them "singular," but that was because they did not know them intimately as I did. The Mother of all that family I seldom saw. She was a very retiring homebody and never appeared in Company. I think she was a Wells, same family with John D. Wells. She must have been no ordinary woman, judging by the family she raised. Humor she had, but conscientious in her humor. I remember Lewis once telling me that when he was a little boy, he got possession of some bird shot. He had witnessed the effects of bird shot when fired from a gun, but did not know rightly whether it was caused by the powder or the shot. Appealing to his mother, she told him to find out by experiment, at the same time to be very careful that the shot should not blow him up. So Lewis, after much preparation, at arm's length with the tongs and a fire coal, winking, touched off the shot. As might have been expected, they did not explode, and Lewis found himself the butt for the family to laugh at.

Years afterward, that good mother continued to grieve and asked forgiveness of her son for having that once, the first and the last time, deceived him.

The father [was] a tall, fine-looking old man, erect, venerable, and of the old school; told a good anecdote with the driest humor, and was famous for his skill in carving at the table, and in arranging the fuel in the chimney fire. No one who knew him sitting by his hearth would ever venture to touch the tongs to punch the fire, or alter the position of a stick of maple wood. I do not know that I would myself have ventured so far as to pick up a burning brand that had rolled out on the floor.[2]

The oldest son, Morris Berry, was his father over again, but considerably a younger man, of course. Skilled in languages, an adept at whist and chess, capital at sketching, he suffered the gift to run fearfully into caricature. He was no mean poet, and as a prose writer he excelled. At the time when I first knew him, he wrote, I think, for "The Casket" and afterwards for the "N. York Mirror."

The sisters with whom I was acquainted were Elizabeth, who never wrote anything that I knew of, but was an elegant lady & conversed well. She married Olivar Barber, afterwards L.L.D., a young lawyer at that time, and nephew of Chancellor Walworth. His residence was at Saratoga, where he distinguished himself & earned his Diploma by his "Reports" in the Chancery Court.[3]

Miriam Berry was superior to Morris in all the gifts. She wrote likewise for "The Casket" and the "N. York Mirror." She possessed very decided genius, & as to rhyming, it seemed to be more natural to her than prose. I have now in my possession, in her hand-writing, addressed to me, rhyming notes reading like a ballad, and sometimes quite epigrammatical. She finally married an Episcopal clergyman (I forget his name) & died.[4]

Since her death, I have seen published the first volume from her hands, styled "Widow Bedott Papers." Very popular, I believe. Intensely interesting to me, but not up to my idea of her genius. She was a great mimic (and so were also Morris & Kate), and such composition as the Bedott Papers I have heard them run off in conversation for mere sport, taking parts and mimicking all the characters to the very life. O, those times! How I have laughed until my sides ached!

Kate Berry was a prose writer for the periodicals. I never knew her to attempt poetry. She was a sweet girl, and the youngest of them all. I sometimes thought she liked me. I know I was fond enough of her, but, not in circumstances to marry a stylish girl, I never said anything about it. The last time I saw her was at Saratoga, & we had a good cry over the happy old times.[5]

The society of Whitesboro village, in which the Berrys had controlling influence, was in the main literary because of that influence; but at the same time it was enlivened by other amusements a-plenty; and in respect to good manners, I have never witnessed more, scarcely as much, polish and refinement in any society where I have since had the pleasure to move. I myself never cared much for mere "Society." I always felt, after an evening of small talk, that I could have spent the same time more profitably at home with a book; but they had in Whitesboro a literary society for reading original compositions which interested me more than all the rest. I could fill many pages with reminiscences of those meetings. I have thought that the memoirs of that society, edited by one of the Berrys, would have been very well worthy of publication. I had, for my part, a manuscript periodical or newspaper to keep up, which was received with applause at the time; but some numbers that I still have among my papers seem to me now to possess little merit except originality. That Society was called "The Maeonean Circle." It is no doubt remembered with pleasure by many whose paths in life have since radiated widely apart.[6]

Note. I here insert a specimen of "The Cotton Bug." The letter from a correspondent was written by myself, & the rhyming epistle was from Miriam Berry.[7] It appears that the young Lawyers & Doctors of our circle had made an attempt to excavate & explore a certain Indian Mound in sight of Whitesboro village. Some said they were scared away from their undertaking, others that, unaccustomed to labor with shovel & pick, their wind gave out. Whatever the reason, their attempt was a failure, & the object of this article was to make the most of their failure.

The ladies of Whitesboro village were all that could be desired: lady-like, & intelligent generally, but none of them were "pretty." I doubt if there was one among them who would have felt pleased at being called so.

The gentlemen, as well as I can recollect, were much inferior to the ladies of the same village. The young doctors, I thought, would amputate the limb of a man that was sure to die any way; and they would go in a crowd rejoicing to do it. The young lawyers pettifogged altogether. They were already seedy, and wore the same clothes until the young ladies were tired of seeing them and made remarks about them, from all which I judged that the students of law & medicine were generally in straitened circumstances. I could, now & then, detect them in doing mean things that we at the factory would have scorned, & I thought the young ladies were sometimes of our opinion.

Yet, as they were professional gentlemen, they went in and out easily in society, & the young ladies made much of them with more or less sincerity. In after years some of the same young men became famous, as I have since learned, but by what means they acquired renown, I am unable to say. Doubtless they had as much merit as others, but I question if any one of them ever added greatly to the general wealth, or caused two blades of grass to grow where there was but one before.

The Geological indications of that region were that the Mohawk River had at some remote period been dammed by a barrier at the place now called Little Falls, twenty miles below Utica, creating a lake of probably thirty miles in length by four or five miles wide, which covered the whole valley where Utica, Whitesboro, and Rome now stand. This story brings forward an Indian who is imagined to have lived before these geological events.

I was not happy at this period of my life. I had to work beyond my strength. I had, unhappily, aspirations above my business; and I was not satisfied with myself on the subject of Religion. As to recreation, we all took that occasionally, but always strictly subordinate to the business of the Factory. Once little William Walcott and Gambia and I made an expedition to fish for speckled Trout in the Salmon River, which flows into Lake Ontario. We had a good time, a complete success. Carried ice to preserve our fish. I remember that wading all day, sometimes up to the middle in trout streams as cold nearly as spring water, produced no bad effects upon me, although I was not then in sound health, but subject to the tooth ache. Gambia was an unhappy character at that time. He was part Indian. His features were ugly, except his eyes; but in all other respects his person was elegant. Exquisite teeth and feet and hands. Extraordinary breadth of chest, and a gait in walking the street as though he had been born a King. The ladies said that the other young bucks about town made fools of themselves trying to walk like Gambia. He was a man of some genius, at least in drawing and painting, but was very unhappy because of a jealous disposition. I never saw any other person so bad in that way. I remember once he had prepared an article with great care for the "Circle." While reading it himself to the society, some giddy young lady laughed, but not at him; but he thought it was at him or his article. Whereupon he stopped reading, gnashed his teeth, and with flashing eyes, his face blue with rage, strode to the fire place, tore his article in pieces, and committed it to the flames. The effect of all this upon the audience was very painful, and it made known to the ladies what his intimate friends already knew about his disposition. The consequence was that, although he was a favorite with ladies, they were afraid of him, and he did not marry in that set. Years afterward, when I lived in Georgia, I met Gambia by accident in N. York City. The fine figure and noble gait were gone, but his disposition seemed to have changed for the better; his countenance indicated a contented mind. He said he was doing well in some Western town, and the change in his appearance had been caused by a tree, which falling upon him, had broken both his legs and otherwise injured his body.

Once, during this period, I visited N. York City & spent all my money, besides $50.00 borrowed from Berry in Sight Seeing. It was that time that I visited my old friend John Wells at Sing Sing. At another time I visited the beautiful village of Geneva in N. York State to attend the final examination of my sister Lucretia and bring her home from a boarding school, which was kept by a very Frenchy lady named Ricord, who was much thought of because she had a son gone soldiering in Texas, then struggling with Mexico for Independence. The lady had fits about her son, done in a style to bring her school into notice.

This mythical son, who if he lived was probably not worth the powder it would take to kill him, was, nevertheless, a hero in the imagination of boarding school girls, and an occasional reference to him, with pathos and a swoon, never failed to bring down the sympathies of the school, which answered in place of dignity, discipline, scholarship, & all that on the part of the principal. I may be unjust in these remarks, but that is the impression made upon me. At that examination I made a *faux pas* myself. I took it upon myself to re-write and correct my sister's innocent little composition. A grand affair I made of it! Of course it failed in the public reading. The working teacher in that school was Miss Thurston. A missionary of that name was her relative, & it seems to me that this Miss T. became distinguished afterward for something. I think it was in Authorship.

Returning from this trip, I visited some distant connexions of ours then living in the village of Syracuse, named Edwards. Mr. Edwards was clerk of Court. Mrs. Edwards had been the widow of my uncle Horace Camp, who died in 1817. Uncle Horace had been connected with Saml. Stocking, Esq., of Utica in the trade by which Mr. Stocking laid the foundation of his large fortune. Dying young, Mr. Stocking held his memory in high esteem, and my Cousin Horace, for his name's sake, always had a new hat free of charge, at Mr. Stocking's store, whenever he chose to call for it.

One little trip I took to Sackets Harbor, cousining, because I had a boil under my arm & could not work.[8]

Further than I have mentioned, I do not recollect that in the seven (7) years of hard work learning my business I ever took any recreation to carry me away from the Factory further than a sleigh-ride now and then, or a visit to Trenton Falls with the ladies.

Talking of sleigh-riding. One evening little William Walcott called for me in his father's sleigh to go and hear a lecture in Utica. Lectures were beginning to come into fashion. Two of Walcott's sisters made up the Company, & very good company too; at least so thought I. We heard the lecture and had our little difference of opinion about it as we rode along coming back. Now I think of it, I believe the lecture was a debate, & we continued the debate. As I was saying, we were getting on finely towards home. The snow was very deep, nearly as high as the fences. There was only one hard-beaten track in the middle of the road. In a few places only was the track wide enough to admit of two sleighs passing each other. All the rest was soft, treacherous snow, sparkling in the bright moonlight. We came along delightfully, without a care in the world, until we were over against the "Obier house," which was opposite the old rope walk & near the bridge half way to Whitesboro, where, alas! we met another sleigh. Crowding us off the track, over we went, pitching us young gentlemen clear from the sleigh into the soft, yielding snow. As for me, I went head first, stretching forth my arms like a swimmer. Of course, my head being down, my heels were in the air, and there I was, fast. Not so the ladies. Their part of the sleigh being covered, they did not fall into such a predicament. The end of it was that the young ladies, laughing all the time, had to extricate me the best way they could, Walcott holding the horse. You can "phancy my pheelinks," when you remember what I before stated, that I was quite in love with one of the same young ladies, and wished to appear to advantage when she was present.

CHAPTER 20

An Episode

The exact day of this writing corresponds with the date of the fall of Little Rock and the events hastily following that event. This day is the 15th September, 1863.[1] I am writing this, as stated in the Preface, at my temporary home in Pike County Ark. near the Factory which I erected seven years ago, more than half of the interest belonging to my family. This unhappy war placed me before the public, as a Northern man in their midst, with a factory necessary to their pressing wants & making money by means of these necessities. Hence followed a persecution which well nigh cost me my life; indeed I may be said to have done business with a halter about my neck. I literally had to work with gun, pistol, and cutlass by my side. I stood this until February last when an opprty. offered to sell out to a Southern man, & I did so, because I considered the place to be a false position & quite untenable for any Northern person.[2] Pecuniarily it seemed to be a bad arrangement for me, but the parties will know more about that when they get through.

I moved my family to a house away from the Factory, in a retired place among romantic scenery, hoping to be allowed to live in peace until the close of the war. Here I have read well nigh all the books to be had, and among other recreations these memoirs have interested me. But it seems like there is to be no rest for me.

On the 4th Instant, came fugitives (deserters) from Brig. General Cabell's army reporting the fall of Fort Smith, and the battle of "Back Bone" (if it can be called a battle) between Genl. Cabell and a portion of the Federal army under Genl. Blunt. That affair took place on the 1st Sep. in Scott County about fifteen miles north of Waldron, and was followed by the rapid retreat of Cabell's Brigade to the Caddo Gap, & from thence to Centre Point, at which place a courier brought him orders to re-inforce Maj. Genl. Price, who was then on the Bayou Meto, defending Little Rock against the advance of the Federal Army from Helena, under General Steele.[3]

In the meantime it appears that the Federal General had reconnoitered in force until he had discovered a ford across the Arkansas River about twelve miles below Little Rock. It appears then, that after maneuvering some time to make Genl. Price believe that he intended to advance upon the City by the Old Batesville Road, considerably to the left of the Confederate Army, on the 10th instant Thursday, he threw his cavalry across that ford twelve miles to the right and in rear of the city.[4] Of course the city fell, and Genl. Price did well to cross the Arkansas River and get away at all, in the presence of a superior force, his own army all the time scarcely in a state of mind to fight. So the Capital of Arkansas is at last in the hands of the U.S. troops.

While all these events were transpiring so rapidly, I felt called upon to get away from my mountain home. My interests are no longer here. I have many personal enemies in these parts, for no better reason than because I would not suffer them to lay violent hands on me, because of my Northern birth, when I was standing in my right as a manufacturer, and because I resisted the action of their public meetings which threatened to take the Factory away from me. From the presence of these I must fly, because they will be likely to take advantage of the inter-regnum between the Confederate and Federal authorities in order to "do what seems the best in their own eyes," and among other things they would, some of them, take pleasure in hanging me to a tree, and plundering my house.

For these reasons I have been, ever since the news of Cabell's retreat, removing my things the best way I could, and expect soon to follow them.

It is hard (is it not?) to be thus broken up by a war which I would have given all I had in the world to prevent. I told my Southern friends and kin, who talked of "peaceable secession," that such a thing was impossible.

Such great violence as Secession could not be done, under the Existing State of men's minds, without a Civil War, a War the results of which, to say the least, would be very uncertain.

The Federal army, we understand, entered Little Rock on Thursday last and followed the retreat of Genl. Price to Genl. Rust's place and the stone fence several miles this side the Rock, on the military road.[5] We hear today that Genl. Price arrived last night, or was to arrive, with his army at Arkadelphia, whether to make a stand there or not, I cannot learn. Some fugitives who travelled all night last night, report that they heard firing at Arkadelphia and think there was a battle there last evening. If so, the Federals have a better General than common, & they are making a thorough campaign of this state. The results are in the hands of God.

There are many deserters from the army passing, and some that I can see going forward to reinforce Genl. Price. As near as I can learn, the poor class of men are satisfied that the War should come to an end so. They say it is the rich man's war, & they have no interest in it. This impression on their minds seems to have been made first by that law of the Confederate Congress which exempted the owners of twenty Negroes from Military duty, and finally the reluctance of planters to have their Negroes assist the Army in laborious military operations, as evinced by the last law of the Confederate Congress on that subject.[6]

These observations I record in passing, as I receive them.

The Federal authorities, as they come in, will, it seems to me, be likely to fall into errors of politics equally as great. We learn by their newspapers that they intend a general confiscation. Any general law they can make will sweep the property of nearly every man, for the pressure of this war has been such that well-nigh every person is implicated, whether in favor of the War or not. We will suppose this confiscation to have arrived. There is a Highland Scotch proverb, "Burn a man's house, and you make him a soldier." In the present instance, Confiscate, and they leave a man nothing that he can do, & nothing he feels like doing but to fight, and that with desperation. Then would come *a poor man's war*, and another sort of War it would be from this.

Note. The month of Oct., 1863, finds me with our family & servants removed to our new home in Camden.

Camden is my home. When we sold the Factory in February last, we received in part payment some real estate in & about the City of Camden, & among other property a dwelling suitable for myself & one for Dr. Magill.[7] Those dwellings were rented until 1st Oct.; otherwise we should have moved here before so that our Hegira did not much violence to our plans after all.

At length I arrived at the age of twenty-one years. A very knowing age. I thought I understood my business, and concluded that I had "the world in a string." Yet my prospects were not as good as they had been seven or eight years before, for in the meantime South Carolina nullification and the political compromise which followed on the tariff question had reduced the profits of manufacturing below what was then considered fair investment of money.[8] My uncle John sold his interest in the Factory intended for me, & I was left to rely upon my own resources. I therefore continued at my work, laying by some money & improving my mind a little, until the summer & fall of the year 1838, when a strong desire to see something of the world impelled me to convert my little patrimony into a very little ready cash, and start upon my travels.

Very good letters of introduction were placed in my hand, and I set out. My general plan was to go southward and find a climate favorable to my lungs, which would at the same time be favorable to my business of manufacturing. The recent discussions upon the "Tariff question," had started the very pertinent inquiry, "Why could not Southern people make the Tariff as good for them, as it was understood or alleged to be for the Northern people, by simply manufacturing for themselves?"

And as I advanced further into the Southern country, and was led to converse freely with intelligent people, into whose society I was admitted upon my letters of introduction, I gradually found myself becoming a warm advocate of a Southern manufacturing System. I felt a call to make it the special object of my life. I believed it practicable, and I thought it a patriotic calling to try and inaugurate a line of things tending to reconcile unhappy differences between the North and the South. This idea may be regarded as the key to my motives during the next twenty years of my life, & will explain to my friends some movements and undertakings that otherwise could not be understood.

I am writing now in confidence, for the perusal of my *friends*, and by that I mean those who will believe what I tell them, & be willing to admit cheerfully the favorable construction. To those who profess themselves friendly but regard my acts as "*So* Singular," I have no explanation.

I assert that during the first twenty years of my manufacturing life at the South, I was a public-spirited man, without even ordinary regard for my own private interests. I wrote for the public prints. I lectured a little, & I talked a great deal, in favor of a Southern Manufacturing System, when it would have been much more to my interest had I discouraged others from going into competition against me.

I put myself to inconvenience in training the sons of gentlemen & others who were not gentlemen & teaching them the art & mysteries of my profession, who before they were half-taught would go off into direct opposition to my interests. They "stole my thunder." They enticed away my best hands; they seduced my customers. I even went on building more factories, when there were already too many, until at last I was reduced to poverty, when at the same time many a protégé of mine was growing rich. I had given them a stick to break my own head, and I had to leave Georgia because of it. What wonder then that in my subsequent career I have been no longer a public-spirited man when so doing would be against my private interests, or that I should no longer feel disposed to be the patron of young men? If I have at last secured a competency against old age, it is because I have had my views changed in these particulars. In a word, I have learned to look out for myself, and study my own interests. And I am now satisfied that so doing is the best public economy, as well as the best private economy; for if every man would strictly mind his own business and nothing else, would it not be better all round?

I advert to this in order to explain the fact that there are two distinct periods in my business life: first, the public-spirited era, and then the contrary, so that my maxims at one period of my life ought not to be quoted against my maxims at another time. Probably at either time I thus ran into the one extreme, & afterwards into the other. It had been better, doubtless, if I could have struck a general average; but it is too late now for regret.

I was saying, before I made this digression, that I had set out upon my travels. I had seen Niagara Falls and the lakes, and if I remember rightly, I had once spent a week in N. York City, which was at that time, of course, a smaller city than it now is, "Union Square" being at the period of my first visit, the outside limit of the dense population. Even then it was thought to have grown prodigiously, for at the opening of the Erie Canal, fifteen or twenty years before, the City Hall was in the outskirts. When it was first erected, I remember it was much talked of; that and the Tontine, & finally Holt's Hotel became the rage.[9] The City Hall was deservedly popular for its architectural beauty. Its resemblance was re-produced in every form familiar to the arts at that time. The City Hall & the battle of Navarino were thought to be excellent illuminations on a printed cotton handkerchief.[10] My mother had for a long time a bonnet box with the "City Hall" imprinted on its sides; such is the power of early associations that to this day I regard that edifice as the finest in N. York City.

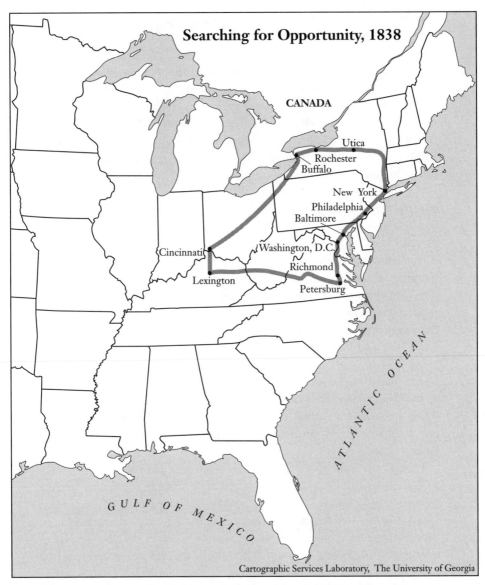

Searching for Opportunity, 1838

CANADA

Utica
Rochester
Buffalo

New York
Philadelphia
Baltimore

Cincinnati
Washington, D.C.
Richmond
Lexington
Petersburg

ATLANTIC OCEAN

GULF OF MEXICO

Cartographic Services Laboratory, The University of Georgia

Merrell's two-thousand-mile journey by rail and horseback from Utica, New York, through Virginia, Kentucky, and Ohio and then back to Utica.

Behold me started on my travels, with hopes large enough to carry me over the whole world, but with very little money in my pockets. My delight as a mechanic was great in flying over the little piece of Rail Road then finished west of Albany, so great indeed that I repeated the pleasure until I had gone the whole length of every such road then completed in the United States, which was not a great undertaking, at that time, even to my limited means. There was a Rail Road from N. York to Paterson in N. Jersey, one from Albany to Schenectady, and one from Schenectady to Saratoga Springs. Beside these there were no others. But Stop! I am too fast. This was the case upon my former excursion to N. York City, but at the time I now report the progress of Rail Roading had been so rapid that the Great Central road of N. York State was in a forward condition, & I was able to travel as far as Petersburg in Virginia almost altogether by rail.[11]

At Richmond in Virginia my letters introduced me to a merchant named Fleming James & his brother James Shippen James, both living elegantly. The former a brusque, overbearing man with a beautiful wife, the latter a refined gentleman in delicate health, & a bachelor widower. They entertained me finely & gave me letters to their brother Edward James at Petersburg, Va., also to gentlemen in Western Virginia.[12] For at that time my views did not range further south than that latitude. About ten years afterward, I had to spend a week again in Richmond as a delegate from Georgia to the General Assembly of the Presbyterian Church in the United States. Again I received attention from Fleming James, but he was no longer a merchant Prince. His brother Jas. S. had died, all of which was about as I had expected.

I found the business of Cotton Manufacturing already well under way at Richmond and Petersburg, but heard of new beginnings going on further up the Country. I therefore travelled by stage from Richmond to Charlottesville in Albermarle County, Va., having letters in my pocket to the Timberlakes (John and Robert), who were laying the foundations of a large manufacturing business at Shadwell, a water power formerly the property of Thos. Jefferson, and lying within sight of his residence near Charlottesville. They treated me well enough, but thought they knew so much that I could be of no service to them, & I soon found myself associating and associated with the Young Timberlakes, John & Ned. Good fellows enough they were, but rather hard cases.[13]

At that time, the tide of emigration from Virginia ran to Missouri, but no further. A horse-back journey into Missouri was, to a young Virginian fresh from the University, what a whaling voyage "round the horn" is supposed to be to a native of Cape Cod: the necessary probation before marriage. My new friends Jack and Ned happened to be making their arrangements for this grand tour when I was introduced to their acquaintance. I decided to go with them. And while they are looking out for me a good horse, saddle, bridle, and saddle bags, I will tell what happened in the stage as I came from Richmond.

It was in the night when the stage left Richmond & very dark. The coach seemed to be full, we stopping at several places to take on passengers. During one of those stoppages, a female voice on the back seat broke out in quite a rage, "Let me alone, Sir! Keep your hands off me! Is there no gentleman present who will protect a lady from insult?" etc., etc. Of course there were several such gentlemen at hand, & I myself felt very much like being one of them; but in the dark who should we pitch upon? Whom should we protect? The offender might be one of us, indeed very likely would be the most officious in trying to discover himself. As might be expected, nothing at all was done, and the offense, whatever it may have been, was not repeated. When daylight came, we passengers examined each other's countenances critically, & the opinion of our little community settled down upon a flash gentleman on the back seat, who appeared to be well-known along the road. He was a very patronizing gentleman, and carried in his broad-brimmed white hat a sample of tobacco, which he exhibited as a very fine article, the product of his own plantation. I afterwards learned that he had no plantation, but very much the reverse. I had not been accustomed to witness so much polish of manners & language in gentlemen, & probably showed the greenness of my admiration in my looks; for he evidently took a fancy to me, & we became quite conversable together. Finally, when I made known my destination on the road, it turned out that he happened to be going to the very same place. We arrived (at Evansville) in the night and were put to sleep in a room together. I thought the landlord inquired of me in a very pointed manner if we were to room together; &, if I remember rightly, my companion answered for me, "Yes." Whereupon mine host took me aside & warned me that my roommate was a noted sharper, for which I thanked him & governed myself accordingly. The next arrival of the Richmond Stage brought a police officer in hot pursuit of my new friend, by name Volney Peyton, for the crime of carrying away the wrong trunk from a Baltimore Hotel. My landlord afterwards said that he did not look for a charge of that character to come against Volney Peyton, Esq., for he was one of the F.F.V.'s (First families in Va.), but he did know him capable of fleecing such an innocent young man as I appeared to be.[14] I acknowledged my obligations to Mr. Timberlake (for that was his name, he being a kinsman of the gentlemen to whom I brought letters), but since I have had more experience with the world. I rather think that Mr. Peyton would not have made much of me, even if I had been left without warning of his designs. I never have been much the victim of sharpers, pick-pockets, or any of that class who live by their adroitness. To begin with, I had not much to lose. Then again I did not play cards, or billiards, or drink; and perhaps had as little the look of Moses in the *Vicar of Wakefield*, as any young man ever had.[15]

Although I have travelled a great deal, & by all means of conveyances, & in all sorts of country, & among all sorts of people, it has never been my lot to be any where robbed of any thing about my person. I could always be prudent enough for any kind of sharpers except first, N. York City salesmen in Wholesale stores; second, clerks and others under me handling money & other property of mine; & third, since this war has made it a virtue with some to plunder a man of Northern birth and habits, openly and boastingly, I have had not much I could do in the way of preventive.

This same Volney Peyton was of the Thos. Jefferson family connexion, of whom there was still living at that time, in that vicinity, a Mrs. Randolph, who was the daughter of Mr. Jefferson. She was in reduced circumstances & kept a school for a livelihood.[16] I did not visit the Jefferson mansion, which was on a very high hill, said to be going to decay & was owned by one Levy, a Navy officer, & judging by his name, probably a Jew. If he purchased that place with a view to social position in the vicinity, he threw away his money, for it was the fashion to speak of him with contempt; probably for that very reason, that he had by means of purchase money alone come into possession, & society was determined to grant him no more than just that which could be bought with money, and not the good will, which went to the Jefferson family, although in poor circumstances. It was the old story over again of the ancient family and the parvenu, & I need not have so many words on the subject.

These remarks apply to the social position of the Jefferson family, partly, but not altogether then springing from his eminence as a statesman, &c.; but the personal reputation of Mr. Jefferson in his own neighborhood was not very highly cherished. As a citizen, he was thought to have done much harm by the establishment and maintenance of the Virginia University in religious infidelity, or something akin to that. His want of common sense was familiarly illustrated by the "wind mill story" and by the general decay of his property. And finally, he was said, by those who knew him best, to be a corrupt & a corrupting man. The Rev. Dr. Bowman of Georgia told me that when he was a young minister of the Gospel, he was for a while stationed at Charlottesville, in sight of Mr. Jefferson's seat.[17] Being a young gentleman of good appearance, very conversable, and withal a good knife and fork at any genteel table, Mr. Jefferson had him up at Monticello occasionally to dine when he had distinguished company, of which, by the way, he saw a good deal, not only American, but strangers from foreign parts.

It was not very long before Mr. Bowman thought he discovered on the part of Mr. Jefferson more pointed attentions to himself than their relations called for. Mr. Jefferson could be very fascinating in conversation when he pleased, & he was pleased to lavish his blandishments for a time upon the young Presbyterian minister, towards whose order it was all the while understood he entertained unmitigated hostility.

Mr. Bowman, though not very cunning himself, knew very well how to deal with a cunning man. He saw that Mr. Jefferson had some ulterior design, & he gave him his time. So finally one day, out it came in a deep private and confidential way. The great man's idea was this. Mr. Bowman was a young man &, of course, ambitious in his profession. He would do well to listen to the advice of an old experienced head. Unitarian doctrines were bound to prevail all over this great country, to the downfall of other creeds. He could see it with his prophetic eye. All the out-come in religion was bound to be in that direction. It could be no other way. Jews and Gentiles could find a home in that one unanimous Church, and all was to come round as he predicted in the life-time of Mr. Bowman. And now Mr. Jefferson's profound advice to him was to take this tide of good fortune in the flood, and find himself great at the head of a prodigious movement!!

This was Mr. Jefferson's estimate of men. He had been accustomed to influence politicians by such motions; & he thought a minister of Christ might be turned in the same way! I scarcely need add that Mr. Bowman was not carried away by this advice; but, on the contrary, as long as I sat under his preaching, he taught the Divinity of Christ and the Trinity of the Godhead in well-nigh every sermon, until the question arose among his hearers whether that was not his one idea.

CHAPTER 21

I think it was in the month of September, 1838, that Ned and Jack Timberlake and I left Charlottesville in Virginia upon our horseback journey towards Missouri. In order to condense my trunk full of clothing into a pair of saddle-bags, I had to lose a part: that is to say, I left my trunk and part of its contents behind, & never saw them again; for I have never returned to claim them.

Soon after leaving Charlottesville, we passed the University, undergoing such criticism as the students, lounging under the colonnades, saw fit in their rudeness to bestow upon our appearance. That night, we lodged at the Rock Fish gap in a public house which was the resort of rusticated students.

The next morning we got up to see the sun rise from the summit of the Blue-ridge, and then we passed a tree which was understood to be the corner of three adjoining counties. According to the usage, we had to go through the ceremony of riding, one following the other, round that tree, thereby making the tour into those counties in as many seconds of time. We debated whether or not we should leave our direct course to visit Weyer's Cave and other natural curiosities in the vicinity of Staunton, and concluded not to do so, but proceeded on our journey by the way of Lexington, passing next day the military school, where Lt. Genl. "Stonewall Jackson" was long afterwards the Prest. or professor of Military Science.[1] This day I witnessed a novel exploit of chasing a snake. My travelling companions on horse-back pursued the snake through all his windings, and whipped him to death, or nearly so, with the lashes of their riding whips. I looked upon it then as a display of great skill, both with the horse & with the whip, but have seen surpassing horsemanship many times since.

The next night we spent at the public house of a Dutchman named Kiser, who lived in the gap through which James River flows. Near his house we had the pleasure to see the "natural arches" mentioned by Mr. Jefferson in his Notes. They are not arches overhead, under which the spectator can pass and look up, but they are upheavings of the strata showing a vertical section delineated on the perpendicular face of the bluff, in form nearly like the rainbow. The river flows by the spring of the arches, and they appear as though painted on the face of the rock. These are several, thus [⌒⌒] in the base of one mountain. A Geological curiosity I take it to be. I remember seeing only one other place like it, and that is on the Little Missouri River in Pike Co., Ark., about three miles above the Factory. In that case also there are a series of such up-heavings of the lower strata, complicated by a lateral pressure; but in this latter case, forming a pointed arch or rather sharp angles thus [⋀⋀].

In this vicinity we visited the Natural Bridge over Cedar Creek, which impressed me as well worth going a long way to see. Standing on the bank of the stream below and looking up gave me a momentary sensation of the sublime that I long remembered, for I have not many times in my life been able to realize that grand emotion, as others claim to enjoy it. I have thought less of myself for it, but at Niagara Falls, and under the mighty cliffs of the Saguenay, I could only realize my own littleness, not the grandeur of the scene.[2]

From Buchanan in Botetourt County, we passed over the Purgatory Mountain, part of the way by a new-made turnpike road which rendered the passage quite easy, even for our loaded teams. At the very summit was a peak said to be the highest point of land in the United States, on which was a flag staff & the stars and stripes, not "fluttering in the breeze," but tugging and pulling and snapping themselves into ribbons in the gale of wind always, or nearly always blowing on that lonesome place among the clouds. We were told that Mr. Van Buren, at that time President of the United States, had passed by that way a few weeks before and directed that the National flag should be planted there.

Mr. Van Buren was, like ourselves, on his way to the White Sulphur springs of Virginia.

We were late in the season & saw but little fashionable company at the Springs. None of us were sick, or cared much about the place. So we tasted the water, saw the Old Proprietor (Caldwell by name) with his queue of hair behind, and went on our way. At this place I made a still further reduction of my wardrobe. I had no over-coat, but a large broadcloth cloak. What was called a Spanish Cloak, I think. At any rate, it was much too bulky to be strapped behind my saddle, & not sufficient protection against the Mountain air. So I swapped it away, even for a stout overcoat which I wore a long time afterward. I exchanged with the landlord at our Hotel, & he had a good bargain, for my coat was very rough & very remarkable in appearance. He said he had it from a gambler who could not pay his bill. Whatever became of that old coat, I quite forget now. I know that in its time I wore it through rude and stormy scenes. There is no garment which so much endears itself to a man as his old overcoat. Everyone had read about Napoleon's gray *surtout*. How often have I seen a man with an emergency before him get on his old overcoat & then, but not until then, feel equal to the undertaking! My old coat resembled one I afterwards saw worn on all occasions by Edward Dunscomb, Esq., a cousin of my wife. Wear it he would in the streets of N. York City and at Church, the stiff-standing collar keeping his ears quite warm. I asked him about that remarkable coat, & he told me that he had well-earned it. Once returning a passenger in a brig or schooner from some West Indian port to N. York, the Yellow Fever made its appearance on board. All were sick at one time except himself and the cabin boy, with whose aid alone he managed to navigate the vessel and nurse the sick. Fortunately, the weather was favorable, & he knew enough of navigation to get the vessel safe into the harbor of Beaufort in N. Carolina.

A fellow passenger died in his (Dunscomb's) hammock, & thus he was buried in the sea, sewed up in the hammock and hoisted on deck with a block and tackle. To compensate himself for the loss of his hammock, Dunscomb appropriated the overcoat in question, which belonged to the deceased. And if the truth were known, I suppose it would appear that he ever after wore it in order that he might be questioned about it & have his story to tell. Edward Dunscomb, still living when I last heard from him, has since passed through many scenes well-calculated to illustrate the times he lives in, if I had space to record them. But that would be writing his memoirs & not my own; so I will refrain.

From the White Sulphur Springs of Virginia we shaped our course across the country to the Valley of the Kanawha River. We first saw that river from the "Crow's Nest," a beetling cliff from which we looked several hundred feet downward, I believe they said five hundred feet perpendicular to the water. What may be the true name for the Emotion one suffers looking down from such an Elevation, with large birds of prey so far below him in the air as to seem like insects, I am unable to tell. Certainly it has nothing of the sublime. I never ascended in a balloon but believe I have been in almost every other situation. The precise sensation like that I have referred to at the Crow's Nest, I have felt at one other place, and that was on the Lookout rock, the point of Lookout Mountain, overhanging Chattanooga in Tennessee. It is a sensation to be experienced once in a life time but not worth seeking after again. I have had such emotions often in dreams, but was glad when I awoke.

Near the "Crow's Nest" we stopped with a well-known character in those parts, a Col. Hamilton or Hammond, who talked very loud & was, I presume, influential in proportion as he was loud in his talk. He was a brave advocate of duelling, would have nothing shorter than a long rifle in a duel of his. He showed us a copy of the Koran which he seemed to admire and explained to us, as an important point, that "Al Koran," being translated, means *the* Koran. This style of man was at the time quite new to me, but I have known many of them since; and the estimate I put upon Col. H. at the time on his own showing, I have found subsequently to stand good for all that class. My estimate was this. As to fighting, he would be a coward; in religion not sense enough to be even a dangerous infidel;

and in learning an ass. This present war, which is raging while I write, has brought out all such men in their true colors. There are many of them, and their patriotism proves to be like all the rest of their good qualities, decidedly in the negative.

The same day we left the Crow's Nest brought us to Charleston & the Kanawha Salt Works. The local conveniences for making salt, & the facilities for shipping the same, were even at that early day very great; but at that time the salt was tinged with the color of Iron. The process of purification, which came into use about that time, was invented by one [   ], a Polish exile, a scientific man, and of course a nobleman in his own country. Unfortunately for him, he became entangled with the "Patriot War" in Canada & was taken prisoner and hanged at Fort Henry near Kingston in Canada West. I thought he "died as the fool dieth." The Canadians already had more Liberty than was good for them; and if they had not, whose business was it but their own? What call for an intrusion from the States?

My entry into the town of Charleston, on that occasion, was not so dignified as I could have wished it to be. My horse had proven to be a vicious fellow & had doubtless been sold to me for that fault. No amount of fatigue, no low condition in flesh ever made much impression on his spirits. I carried a heavy-loaded riding whip, at one end a leash, and at the other a ball of lead. As we entered the long street of Charleston, my horse commenced his antics, and by some means in giving it the lash behind, that portion of the whip became wrapped round its tail. Instantly the ears were laid back, the tail drawn in, the heavy whip jerked from my hand, & away we went at full speed through the town, at every jump the loaded end of the whip going up in the air & coming down with violence against his heels. I managed somehow to keep my seat, but cannot under those circumstances be expected to tell much about the statistics of the town.

We left the Kanawha River below Charleston and crossed the Big Sandy River or Creek at its mouth where it empties into the Ohio River.

The Water courses were all very low. We forded the Big Sandy and at the same time saw a female on horse-back fording the Ohio River, where Steam Boats were wont to pass. From this point we took the nearest route, through the Wilderness of Eastern Kentucky, towards Lexington. Nothing worthy of Note occurred on the route, except at the Crossing of the Licking River, my horse was sick over night. I sat up & nursed him, & felt very lonesome. I remember that the frogs and other "Voices of the Night" had an unusual melancholy sound to me.

Soon after, we entered the noble country which surrounds Lexington, the "Garden of the West." I do not know that it is any finer land than the country round about Nashville in Tennessee, but at [that] time it was more highly improved.

Immediately upon our arrival at Lexington, we were waited upon by several gentlemen in black coats, who tendered us cards of invitation to attend certain lectures at the Medical College. As we did not come there for that purpose, we did not ask whether any money was expected in payment for the lectures, but judging from the affability of the gentlemen, perhaps the whole was free of cost. However, I may be mistaken, & they might have been very dear lectures. I have heard of such things.

At Lexington I parted company with my comrades. I had no sufficient motive for going as far as Missouri. That country was too new to invest surplus capital in Manufacturing. Round about Lexington something of the kind might be done. Moreover, I had a friend living near by, at whose house I knew I should be welcome, and I resolved to hunt him out and gain the desired information from him.

Rev. Marvin Winston. I have mentioned him several times before.[3] I found him located near Lexington & glad to see me.

CHAPTER 22. — *1838*

Revd. Marvin Winston had become an eloquent preacher of the gospel.[1] Indeed, all that family had talents for something. He had married in the State of Georgia a Miss McIntosh, of a family descended from Genl. Lachlan McIntosh.[2] His wife brought him some property, as is very apt to be the case when ministers from the North marry at the South, and still further, as usual, the property added nothing to his happiness, and diminished his usefulness.

Winston, in common with many others in Georgia at that period, had doubts about the innocence of the relation of a master to his servants. He desired to set his Negroes free, in the absence of any law by which he could effect that purpose in Georgia, the property being vested in Trustees for the use & benefit of his wife and her heirs.

The Revd. Joseph Stiles, now Dr. Stiles, though a Native Georgian by birth, was of the same mind as Mr. Winston, and they were intimate friends.[3] They decided to remove with their Negroes into the State of Kentucky, which was then expected to become a free State; and so their Negroes become free by the laws under which they lived.

It was at this conjuncture that I visited Mr. Winston at his home in Kentucky. I also saw Mr. Stiles at that time in Lexington. They had their Negroes with them. Mr. Stiles had built one hemp-spinning Factory in order to employ his Negroes, & they had burned it to the ground by carelessness or design. He had erected another Factory, & they were waiting for the good time to come that was to rid them of their Negroes. That time never came. All their plans failed. Abolition interference at the North turned the Southern mind against emancipation in any form. The Trustees of Mrs. Stiles and Mrs. Winston, who lived in Georgia, sent and carried their Negroes back to their native state. Mrs. Winston died just before the date of my visit and, shortly after I left them, Mr. Winston died also, leaving three orphan children named Frederick, Susan, and Lucy. Of whom more hereafter.

Mr. Winston was favorable to the project of starting a Cotton Factory, but his own funds were not in readiness, and after riding over the country, I satisfied myself that the locations were not favorable. That idea dropped, Mr. W. told me about a new colony in the State of Georgia that would suit my views exactly. He said that the attention of Georgia people was at that time a good deal turned to the Cherokee Country which the Indians were then vacating, under a military escort of United States troops.[4] It was looked upon as a healthy region to serve as a refuge from the Low Country fevers. A colony of Presbyterian families, whose plantations were near the sea-board, had decided to settle in this mountainous region which they called "Roswell." It was before their time called Lebanon. There they were to erect a Church and a school for their children, and finding a good water power on the place, they had determined to have a cotton Factory, and their arrangements for the Factory were already in a forward state.[5]

Here was a schedule which came nearer to my own views than anything I had yet heard of, and Mr. Winston's offering to back my letter with his introduction, I wrote to Barrington King Esq., who was the business man of the Colony; and having mailed the letter, I pursued my journey as before, not knowing, of course, that anything would grow out of the Georgia business; it was my duty to take all the chances. I therefore wrote to my uncle John Camp at Utica an explanation of the prospects, such as they were, in Kentucky. He told me afterwards that he had thought well enough of the opening for my business in Kentucky to write me by mail that he would invest money in company with Mr. Winston and Mr. Stiles to establish a Cotton Factory there. But I did not stay long enough near Lexington to receive that letter; it was probably well for all parties that I did not, for I had not then experience to start a new business by myself.

Kentucky was not the best location for the enterprise, & Messrs. Stiles & Winston were, as I have before stated, on the eve of great changes in their own affairs.

At Mr. Winston's parsonage I found his Mother and his only sister, Amanda, on a visit, the melancholy occasion of which was the death of Mr. W.'s wife & the necessity of a provision for the children. There was nobody in the World, after my own mother & sisters, that I knew better than old Mrs. Winston & Amanda.

Amanda was a maiden lady. She had been engaged for marriage to my uncle Lewis, who died in 1823. Subsequently, Amanda lived a great deal with my mother, and they were like sisters. Her mother was a dear old lady. She also was a good deal at our house, & much beloved by us all, though I thought her a good deal too severe upon my errors and the sins of my youth. Mrs. Winston had evidently been bred a lady, & her children were well-bred in like manner. I never could get any items of her history, except that she had originally come from Virginia, or at least that her deceased husband was a Virginian by birth, & that they had spent a painful period of their married life at and near Balston Springs, which, by the way, were in my early days more talked of than Saratoga. "Winston" being one of the Virginia family names, that is doubtless the way the children of our Mr. W. came to have so much of "blood" in their personal appearance, genius, and temperament. There must have been something very unhappy about their early days. They were at one time very poor. I do not recollect that I ever saw the old lady smile; and, although a member of the Episcopal Church, she was more ascetic, I thought, than any Presbyterian. Her children were Marvin, a Presbyterian minister, and an eloquent man, as before stated; Amanda; and Frederick S., afterwards a distinguished merchant of N. York City, & when I last saw him, President of a famous insurance company.[6]

The Grandchildren have also a little history, for I love to trace out the lives of the "children of the righteous"; they are "never found begging bread." One of the girls, Susan, was raised by Mrs. Barrington King of Georgia. The other, Lucy, lived with F. S. Winston, Esq., in N. York City & had the advantages of a city education, by which I understood she profited to the highest degree.

Frederick finally came to me. Soon after his father's death, he went to one of his guardians, a Mr. Blackburn at or near Frankfort, and was put at school. Fred was a queer fellow. When I first saw him a boy, he was more dignified than most men. He walked into Church with a lofty air, & placing his hat on the table in front of the pulpit, he turned and walked up the middle aisle to his seat, as though he was one of the dignitaries of the Church newly appointed.

Afterwards, about the year 1846 or '47, I was living in Greensboro, Ga., and had two Cotton Factories on my hands. One day I was sitting at the desk in my office, and lifting up my eyes, saw a tall, well-made young man drawing nigh, with an air of the most determined dignity. It was Fred Winston, all the way from Kentucky, who said he wanted business. Had come from Kentucky in a drove of mules determined to find work. Was tired of School & did not ask any favors from his guardian.

"But," said I, "Fred, I am no kin to you. There is your uncle, Mr. King at Roswell. You should have tried him first." "I did. He does not approve of my quitting my guardian & wants me to go back. I am not going back, & I came to you." "Well, Fred," said I, "you are welcome to the best my house affords as long as you can make it convenient, but I cannot take you under my care without the consent of your family. I will write to Mr. King at Roswell, also to your other guardian, Dr. Stiles at N. York; & you shall be my guest until we get their answers." In due time letters came from them, consenting that Fred should learn the Manufacturing business under me. So I put him to hard work, having no idea that he should learn the business any easier than I did. But I soon found that he must work with gloves on his hands. Ere long, I heard of his making a Fourth of July Oration in the country, and heading a debating school in which he acquitted himself in such a style that I concluded the genius of his family. Winston & McIntosh combined was irrepressible, and he had missed his calling in the Manufacturing business, & had better try and be a lawyer. If so, he had no time to lose. I told him so, & he thought so too. Whereat I wrote once more to his guardians. This time, I did not gain their consent so readily. They did not like so many changes of plan. There were too many Lawyers already, & it was not always an innocent calling; but they consented if I still thought best, & Dr. Stiles concluded by tendering him his law library, for he had been a lawyer before he was a minister.

I do not think that Fred worked for five minutes in the Factory after his future course was decided. He read law sixteen hours a day. The weather was hot, and to counteract the relaxation of body & mind, at night before retiring he would have a Negro go with him to the spring and pour a bucket of cold water over his naked body. By such means, and with an excellent constitution, he sustained himself at a high rate of scholarship, not only in the law office, but, as I afterwards understood, all through the law school at Cambridge, and there I lost sight of him. He repaid some money that I advanced him, but no correspondence ensued. I heard well of him from time to time & learned that he had settled down in Chicago, Ill., & was partner in the law-office of Mr. Judd, a distinguished man of those parts.

In the summer of the year 1860, I happened to be in the City of Chicago. I had heard that Fred had become much of a "swell head," & would probably ignore an old friend who had contributed towards his rise in the world. So I let him know I was in town. I wanted to try him.

He seemed glad enough to see me & was in fine constitution of body. He told me that he had been entirely successful. Had chosen Illinois because he had a stake in that country, his father having long ago invested in lands "lying and being" in that state. He had sold those lands at the right time & re-invested the proceeds in Chicago city lots, and again selling out while others were buying, he had become rich independent of his profession. Was married also & had a family. I did not see his wife; she was absent on a visit to Kentucky. I understand that she was a daughter of Dr. Dudley of Lexington, whose lectures I had so good an oprt. to sit under in 1838.

I afterwards saw Fred a few moments accidentally at Niagara Falls, & since then, while looking over my father's papers, came across some documents concerning his father, and his relations to my father, many years ago, which I thought he ought to preserve; so I sent them to him by mail & received the proper acknowledgement, except that, lawyer-like in all this, he was very careful, so far as I remember, to make no reference to any obligations on his part towards me, or on the part of his father towards my father. This was just as it should be, according to the ways of the world, as I understand them.

CHAPTER 23

(1838)

*T*he fall season of the year was now far advanced, and although the weather in that latitude was still comfortable, it was not reasonable for me to expect much longer to travel on horse-back, for I had been taught from childhood to take care of my lungs;—indeed I had been raised to be daily familiar with the unpleasant idea of dying young with consumption, until that one idea caused me to be a quite melancholy young man, when by myself, not in company.

Upon reflection I concluded not to travel any further west at that time but to return to Utica and during the winter to follow up my plans by correspondence upon the information I had already collected. I had no idea of going all that distance on horse-back, but thought I would ride as far as Cincinnati and there dispose of my horse and equipment, and from thence proceeding by public conveyance.

My first view of Cincinnati was from the heights opposite the city, and although that remarkable town was not then so great as it has since become, I was sufficiently impressed with its importance at first sight. Moreover, my feelings were enlisted. I had been looking forward with pleasure to the time when I should meet my cousin Horace, who lived in Cincinnati, and I anticipated in his society once more a renewal of the feelings of those days when we were boys together, and he was my champion at school and on the play ground. He was my double cousin: our fathers were brothers and our mothers were sisters.[1] We had been near neighbors and school mates as children, so that his home & his bed had been as often mine as his, or nearly so; & we loved each other with the love that "passeth the love of woman." And I was to see this my favorite cousin in an hour! The ferry was too slow for my impatience! Alas! when I inquired for Horace Merrell at his office, I was told that he had died less than a week before. This was the first heavy bereavement of my life. The death of my father had not touched me so nearly, for I was very young and thoughtless at the time. This stunned me like a blow. I cannot tell by what means I found my way back to the Hotel.

I roused myself to call upon the widow, whom I had never seen. There was no child, & I was not pleased with the widow. I imparted such consolation as I had to bestow, but at the same time had more need of consolation myself.

I did not stay in Cincinnati long after that. I had no heart for it, and ever since, it has been a disagreeable place to me. And, as though there was some fatality about it, my subsequent visit was attended by sickness, and nearly all my business transactions in that city have turned out badly; until I am disposed to avoid the place in future. I can add that I have never had any satisfaction on board any Cincinnati steamboat.

I tried to sell my horse in that unhappy city, & what do you suppose was the highest offer I got? Twenty-five dollars! I was a stranger, & they thought I was on expense and obliged to sell. I was in no humor to submit to such wrong. My horse was in fine condition, and in spite of the cold, I determined to ride it home.

I should have mentioned that I wrote from Cincinnati to the parents of my cousin, giving an account of his death and burial. I afterwards learned that they wrote me to bring his remains, but I never got the letter. This omission occasioned my aunt (his mother) great grief, and being a sickly person, she took a strange fancy that the body of her son had been dissected by surgeons. What put that notion in her head, I cannot tell; but it was a very disagreeable one for her to entertain & one that made her quite miserable, as I could see.

My travels in Kentucky brought me into contact only with refined people generally. Only twice I met with specimens of the "Hunter of Kentucky," and they were old men. Long before this writing, I suppose the whole race have passed away. The first I saw was at the Factory of Messrs. Crozier & Hill near Versailles. He had come in from what was then called the "wilderness" in the Western part of the State. Instead of his buckskin hunting shirt & leggings, he had, in the worst possible taste, dressed himself specially for a visit to the settlements. His coat was a blue coat with brass buttons, which glittered high up on his back. Swallow-tailed with the great rolling collar of a fashion ten years gone by. His hat of what might have been a fashionable shape some day, but had never enjoyed the shelter of an umbrella; and such was his style from head to foot, in which he appeared ill-at-ease, sitting on the edge of a chair, quite bashful in the presence of ladies. Mr. Hill talked to him of religion and the Bible, but he had not use for either.

The other I found living in a secret valley among the hills, & I stayed at his house overnight. It was somewhere between Cynthiana & Covington.

The old man was in comfortable circumstances and had long since turned his attention to his farm and his stock of cattle. He told me all about the battle of the Thames in Canada. He was present & saw Tecumseh when he fell or soon after. He said they turned the dead Warrior on his face & stripped the skin from his back in pieces of which they made razor straps to remember him by. I have carried the idea that he showed me a razor strap made of Tecumseh's hide, but I am not quite sure of that.

In those days, the first question put to every stranger visiting Kentucky was, "Have you seen Henry Clay?" I did not go to see him (for I never was a man-worshiper), and when I answered "No," I could see by a look of chagrin that I had lost ground in the speaker's good opinion. It has been to be a thing almost incredible, the enthusiasm with which Mr. Clay inspired large masses of men not only in Kentucky but often elsewhere. With some that I have seen, it amounted to enthusiasm in the very bad sense of ascribing to its object superhuman powers.

I have seen a strong, healthy man, not in liquor, weep & blow his nose like a woman, and declare that he loved Mr. Clay & would come nigh giving his life or even his money all to him, if he stood in need of it.

By the time I could leave Cincinnati, the weather had become quite too cold for travelling on horse-back. Ice is a bad footing for a horse with the weight of man and baggage upon him, and damp snow, balling in his feet, is even worse than smooth ice. Nevertheless, I persevered in my journey, passing through the entire length of the State diagonally, from Cincinnati to Erie in Pennsylvania. The principal towns that I passed through were Xenia, London, Columbus, Mt. Vernon, Wooster, Akron, & Ashtabula. After passing Mt. Vernon, which was at nearly the dividing watershed between Lake Erie and the Ohio River, I came upon a newer-settled and richer soil called the "Western Reserve" or "New Connecticut," where the characteristics of the people were as widely different, the Northern from the Southern, as though they had belonged to different States. The Southern part was first settled by immigrants from Pennsylvania, among whom were many Dutch, with their own style of building and their ways of doing things. The Northern part called the "Western Reserve" was then settling and growing and teeming with immigrants from Connecticut. The townships were laid off five miles square, the town in the centre, with its church steeple. The main roads ran everywhere at right angles, intersecting each other in the centre of the town. Everything was going up by the square rule. The music of hammer and nail floated on every breeze. I could not get out of sight or hearing of "improvements." But, O the mud! Muddy roads are a penalty we pay for rich lands in a new settlement; and, judging from appearances, I should say that fever and ague was another of the compensations in that promising region, destined some day to support a dense population.

Upon reaching Ashtabula, which stands on the lake shore, I found the people a good deal exercised about a vessel which had been wrecked the night before. The navigation of Lake Erie is peculiarly dangerous. It had become late in the season for sail vessels to be out of port. I myself suffered greatly through all my clothing, riding along the lake shore, with the cold north wind blowing fresh across the expanse of water and with a crash and roar, heaping great cakes and fields of new-made ice upon the beach. What must have been the sufferings of ship-wrecked sailors! Such were my reflections as I rode along.

I made a halt with some distant relations named Mix, who had made a new settlement about seven miles south from Erie.[2] I did not think well of their prospects. Indeed, the Mixes are by generations an easy-going folk, not calculated to secure their own fortunes in the general scramble of our times. I doubt not they were the happier & more innocent for all that.

I had a very cold ride indeed along the lake shore from Erie to Buffalo in N. York State. Under such exposure, all my hereditary care about my lungs could not save me from taking violent colds, which brought me to a halt on my arrival near Rochester. By the time I reached the village of Penfield, seven or four miles from Rochester, where dwelled some distant cousins named Ely, I was quite unfit to proceed farther by any means of conveyance & found that I was equally welcome at the house of my kin. O! the kindness of womankind when we are sick! Did not I spend a happy Christmas time after my lonely rides nursed and pampered by my sweet cousins, the Ely girls?

Here my horse-back journey of two thousand miles came to an end. When I had a little recruited my health at Penfield, I journeyed home to Utica in the stage which went on sleigh runners over the snow. In due time my horse was forwarded by kindness of the Elys, but that was not until after the breaking up of winter, when the bland weather of early spring enabled me to leave the house and ride out on horse-back. But the vicious brute, made more impatient by rest, was of such a temper that no one cared to ride him but myself. One of his first exploits was to jump off a canal bridge with me. It was quick over, & I had little time enough to save myself. It was by the goodness of God that I had presence of mind to spring from the saddle & let go all holds, so that I found myself standing high and dry on the bridge, while he fell on his back into the water below. After that exploit I thought it best to sell him for what I could get. A tougher and more enduring animal for a long journey I never knew, and at the same time it never was my fortune to meet with a more worthless beast for any other useful purpose whatever.

CHAPTER 24

*C*omparing myself with myself, I did not find that my morals had been improved by my travels, whatever benefit the tour may have conferred upon my manners. I had learned to drink a little when others asked me & had the habit of swearing; but both these vices I acquired in a poor milk-&-water fashion, purely for want of moral courage to resist them in company.

I never loved drink, or ever derived any satisfaction from expletives. I consider that pure language is strong enough to express any ideas I am ever likely to have.

Mere common sense, to say nothing of the fear of God, before my eyes was sufficient to cure me of the habit of profane swearing; and, independently of these considerations, the sweet Christian influences of Home were sufficient to guide me back into right ways, for at that time I had a mother and two sisters living.

In due time I received from Georgia, by mail, an answer to the letter I had written from Kentucky to Barrington King Esq. Agent of the Roswell Colony. It contained an invitation for me to go and take charge of their manufacturing business as "Superintendent." The salary was satisfactory, and I accepted the appointment, most especially because the recent attack of cold upon my lungs seemed to indicate that my only hope of escaping early death, must be in a permanent removal to a Southern climate, and the substitution of bilious diseases for those of the lungs, all of which cogged in with my idea of a Southern manufacturing system. This negotiation (for mails were then comparatively slow) brought me to the end of the winter months, & I did not get off on my journey to Georgia until spring.

I consider that I cannot better fill up this period of inactivity than by devoting a page or two to the Good Genius of Our family, "Uncle John." God bless him and his!

Uncle John Camp was, at the time I refer to, a bachelor, fifty-three years of age.[1] He was a retired merchant &, having been successful, he still preserved his regular business habits, went and came to and from his counting room with the old punctuality, going through all the motions of a strict businessman, though it did not appear that he had anything in the world to do much more than to recognize his old customers with a kind word for each and a kindly interest in their prosperity. Many said that he was wealthy, but he blushed at the idea. If he had wealth, he never suffered it to appear in personal display, or in his words, or in the ostentation of giving, although he did give away more in his quiet way than any man I ever knew. His wealth, let it be more or less, did not appear in his counting room, where the windows were never washed, or the cobwebs brushed away. Two old-time solid mahogany writing desks served, one for himself & one for "Harry," his brother, also a bachelor, who laboriously and affectionately assisted him in doing nothing, with painful accuracy and an honesty like that the Quakers have been supposed to enjoy.[2] The furniture of "John's" desk corresponded with the plainness and solidity of the venerable desk itself. A goose-quill pen; no steel pens there. A heavy ink stand, and all around great blotches of ink, for no housekeeper had ever invaded those precincts to rub and scrub and scold. There was nothing else except the round ruler, perhaps a barlow knife and, yes, I remember a lump of excellent rhubarb, once the size of my fist, which represented the entire pharmacy of the brothers. The same root of rhubarb, not perceptibly reduced from year to year, indicating the consumption of their one remedy. That lump of rhubarb! I fancy I should know it now, if I should see it, after a lapse of thirty years.

While the old gentleman is re-plenishing the fire, we will take a look around the room. No new-fangled stove or grate there, but a good fire place for burning wood, & andirons of wrought iron & a fender as high as your knees. Tongs that might hold a fire brand tight or they might shut over and let it fly just as it happened. Leather firebuckets. An iron safe of the old style, which under an outward display of great strength, might have been good security against honest men, certainly none against professional thieves. Grandfather's old gun and his walking stick carved to represent a corn stalk, with a spring sword or dagger in the end. A framed adver-tisement of the regular line of pole boats on the Mohawk River long ago with a picture of the same. And near the door a map of London printed on a handkerchief. That map of London I never could account for, but it was cherished and often referred to by Uncle Harry as the very highest authority in determining disputed questions, which no one "raised" but himself, concerning the topography of the great metropolis. The map itself was calculated to create more differences of opinion than it settled, for it was blindly printed in the first place, & had grown dim with dust and age, while at the same time the city itself had doubled its population & extended itself miles in every direction. Nevertheless, Uncle Harry would try and hunt out upon his map the exact site of every street or location in & about London that he met with in the reading of their news papers, which was, as might be suspected, no other than the "Journal of Commerce." What other paper could it be, unless it had been the "National Intelligencer"? No other journal of those times could be called "the gentleman's paper," & since their day, perhaps there are none left like unto them.

To this description, already too long, I can add only certain pieces of pine shingles conspicuously stuck in chinks where friends who dropped in could find each his own shingle as he left it ready to whittle, instead of whittling the furniture as they certainly would otherwise have done.

This place of the shingles was the nightly rendezvous of all the respect-able old bachelors about town, and with them as many of their ancient society as had been led away into matrimony & yet could get leave of absence occasionally to rejoin their old associates. It was no club. It had no organization. No one remembered its origin, or ever contemplated its termination. It had no name. After tea one and another would drop in or depart without salutations, quietly & as a matter of course; and again, they were all in their beds by nine or ten o'clock. During that time all the news was discussed. Every important purchase or sale of city lots or Bank Stock made known, & the propriety of subscribing to the new stock or loan settled & determined, and there was no little gossip about marriages, births, deaths and failures, past and present and to come.

The presence of a new face among them would impose a respectful silence, but among themselves alone a great proportion of the finances of the town would be adjusted over-night, or at least ideas exchanged, which after a night's sleep would mature into sound policy for the next day. Here was the nucleus of a Merchant's Exchange, with the advantage of sleeping on it overnight, and at the head of this was John Camp, never saying much, not forward to give his opinion, but thinking profoundly, or at least prudently & honestly upon all passing events.

Among the old bachelors, and those who had been old bachelors but married late in life, there was not one who had not a strongly marked character. Charles Broadhead always came in scolding about something, got laughed at, & went away in a huff. Charles Doolittle, a kind and gentle man. Harry Camp (Uncle Henry), who would dispute you any proposition you could make, all in good humor, but very pertinacious.

Wm. Backus ("the Black Prince") a money-broker & auctioneer who always seemed to me out of place there. Shubel Storrs, who seldom or ever had anything to say. Honicle Smith, who had a great deal to say & was a very quotable man for a joke to go current in the town, but always at his own expense. Fred. Potter, who could read a newspaper in the morning and recite it correctly in the evening. Alfred Hitchcock, who could narrate his last journey to N. York and back, with all the particulars, down to the condition of the napkins and bed linen, with comical mimicry of what each man and woman said & how they looked. Occasionally an important event would come in Moses Bagg, James Platt, James Van Rensselaer, Childs, Faxton, R. R. Lansing, Munn, Jesse Doolittle, James Dana, and many others.[3] There was a class of capitalists who, more dignified or genteel, met only at the banks and counting rooms during the day, but a great deal of the solid unostentatious wealth of the city made up its mind in the Circle that I have described.

Uncle Harry never married, unless he has done so since 1860. Uncle John would have blushed at the idea, until one day, when he was about fifty-five years of age, his friend Charles Doolittle died, leaving a widow who had been a Belle within my recollection; & now with a family of several girls was, I believe, as good as she had been beautiful. Uncle John had to act as executor or administrator upon the Estate. This by necessity brought him to speak with the Young Widow occasionally, a risk he never would have taken but from sense of duty. Of course, he became interested in the lady. It was the most natural thing in the world. How could he help it with his great heart? And she, how could she fail to reciprocate the love of such a man? They were married.

I have several times visited at their happy home. In 1860 I found them with one girl the fruit of this union, Harriet Camp. The maiden name of my mother.

I know not if Uncle John is still living. I should not wonder if the sad events of this war had killed him, for he loved his country, not as politicians love, but with the old-fashioned patriotism. But whether living or dead, I can have but one absorbing emotion of love and gratitude towards him for his good deeds to me & my mother's family. I shall love his child & regard her happiness as though she were my own.

"Lovely in their lives" were Uncle John & Uncle Harry! I have no idea that an unkind word ever passed between them, whatever may have been their humor at times towards others. Grandfather called them "the boys" as long as he lived, and so they were boys to each other & to my mother, their sister, even in their old age.

In the summer of 1860 I found the old store modernized and John Camp's office transposed to a dried up block of brick buildings in Liberty Street. All inanimate things remained the same, except that the lump of rhubarb & the map of London had disappeared, and in the absence of the old-fashioned fireplace, the iron safe stood in the middle of the floor, & around it sat the brothers with such old friends as still dropped in to make a call. Their chairs all turned back & their feet all in a row round the top of the safe. Many of the old set had long since been followed in long procession to their graves, and those who remained were grown old, old and told the same anecdotes, and exercised among themselves the same old censorship on passing events; but in my eyes John & Harry seemed not older or much, if any, older than they had always been. I myself have grown old faster than they, and all our feelings had been mellowed by time and sorrows. My visit was brief, but delightful to me.

With Uncle John, happy in his married home, I thought all the asperities he ever had when a bachelor had disappeared. He was still the same princely giver of timely and acceptable presents that he ever was, as my wife can testify. Uncle Harry remained the old bachelor, intensified more & more.

The same readiness to dispute you any proposition whatsoever. The same anxiety about fire on the premises. The same affected indifference about things, which, it was all the time easy to see stirred up depth of his affections. Still they were "the boys" to all intents & purposes; & if still living, may they long live to enjoy the esteem of those who have the privilege to know them intimately!

Georgia

HENRY MERRELL left a flourishing Utica in 1839 and came south to build, between 1839 and 1855, what were at the time three of the largest textile factories in Georgia: the Roswell Manufacturing Company in Roswell, the Curtright Manufacturing Company at Long Shoals on the Oconee River in Greene County, and the steam-powered Greensboro Manufacturing Company in the town of Greensboro. During a six-month period in 1844 and 1845 he also reconstructed an older mill called the Mars Hill Factory on Barber's Creek in what was then Clarke County, about seven miles southwest of the town of Athens.

Merrell says that there were only "ten or twelve" cotton or woolen factories in Georgia when he arrived in the state and that they were small-scale operations. According to a contemporary source, there were thirteen cotton factories in Georgia in 1837; a modern source estimates "about fifteen" factories in 1837, "small affairs" that were near the fall line on rivers or in such towns as Athens, Augusta, or Columbus.[1] There seem to have been nineteen mills in Georgia by 1840, and this number, according to Merrell himself, had increased to thirty-one by 1847, though a more modern source says that the number that year was thirty-two. A correspondent in the influential *DeBow's Review* stated that there were thirty-two cotton factories in Georgia by 1848.[2] A modern source says that the number was forty by 1850 and that Georgia had become by that time the chief manufacturing state south of Pennsylvania.[3] Merrell says that there were fifty before he left in 1855. In that year Georgia had almost double the number of textile workers of runner-up Virginia and was already being called "the New England of the South."[4] By 1860 Georgia had sixty cotton mills, and "southern industry had so challenged New England that southern mills produced 25 percent of the textile products made of cotton."[5]

Henry Merrell was thus a true pioneer of southern manufacturing. But according to Victor Clark and other historians of southern industry, explanations are required to show why "with idle white labor, abundant raw materials, and ever present water power, more manufactures did not arise."[6] After a book-length study of this question, Fred Bateman and

Thomas Weiss conclude that "the South could have done better than it did" and that it did not attain "its full industrial and economic potential." Merrell often makes this same observation, and it would seem that his reasons for the failure are exactly those of Bateman and Weiss, who conclude: "That there was not more industry reflects the decisions of planters, acting individually and without legal constraints, to shun manufacturing opportunities." [7]

He was a pioneer in other respects. The Roswell into which he rode in May 1839 had been settled by white men and women for only a few years. It was located in the area of northwest Georgia that had belonged to the Cherokee Indians until December 1831 and that had been cleared of them as recently as 1838. The area had been opened up to settlers by means of a land lottery held in October 1832, and pioneers had begun to arrive in a steady stream by early 1833.[8]

Roswell itself, then in Cobb County but now a part of Fulton County, was begun by Roswell King (1765–1844), yet another person in Merrell's history who traced his roots to Connecticut, for King had been born in Windsor. He had come to Georgia in 1789 with his father and later had managed the estates of Pierce Butler in Glynn County.[9] It seems that in the early 1830s Roswell King was asked by officials of the bank in Darien, Georgia, to investigate the possibilities for mining gold in Cherokee country and that, while on this assignment, he had become interested in the industrial possibilities of Cedar (Vickery) Creek, which dropped quickly before emptying into the nearby Chattahoochee River.[10] By 1837 he and his son Barrington (1798–1866) had established the village of Lebanon, where they built flour mills.[11] Merrell disputes what has come to be a common view of the reason for Roswell King's leading his group of friends from the coast of Georgia into its foothills. Merrell indicates that the primary reason for the move was to find a cool retreat away from the heat and sickness of the Georgia coastal summers, and that the industrial development of Roswell was a secondary, even later concern.

In any event, Roswell King brought to the village that would be named for him the friends and their families who helped him to form what was called "the colony." The Archibald Smiths were one of the six founding families who built Roswell. These families began arriving in 1838 and by the 1840s had built houses that still stand, most of them Greek Revival mansions which rival some of the best in the South. Roswell King and his daughter Eliza Hand built Primrose Cottage; Barrington King built Barrington Hall; the Bullochs built Bulloch Hall; the Dunwodys built

Mimosa Hall; and the Pratts built Great Oaks. Archibald Smith, who held to his agricultural ways longer than did his friends, built his house, which he had completed by 1845, a good distance away from these.

Readers who are familiar with Roswell today will be interested in Merrell's account and sketch of the Kings' living in what is known in Roswell tradition as "the Castle," but which Merrell calls "the Labyrinth." They lived in this bungalow, which expanded with the arrival of each resident, before Barrington Hall was completed. Merrell knew and commented on the founders of the colony, and, as a member of the Roswell Presbyterian Church, seemed especially respectful of the Reverend Nathaniel Alpheus Pratt, who had been the pastor of the Darien Presbyterian Church before he followed his friends to Roswell.

It is one of the ironies of Merrell's life and times that much of what he brought to Georgia and found in Georgia had originated in New England. Roswell King, remembering the towns of Connecticut, had his new village of Roswell laid out in the manner of a New England town square, with the residential area to the west and the business area to the east. To the south of the square, Barrington Hall had a captain's walk like that of many New England houses, and the Presbyterian Church was built in the style of a New England meetinghouse. The claim is often made that a New England carpenter built several of the stately Roswell homes,[12] and the name of the Connecticut carpenter Willis Ball does appear in the 1840 census of Roswell. Several houses associated with the mill village, as well as the Smith House itself, have the New England "salt box" design.

Very soon after Roswell was settled, work began on the cotton mill at which Merrell would be the Assistant Agent to Roswell King's son Barrington. Work on building the mill began in 1836 or 1837, and it was still in progress when Merrell arrived in May 1839.[13] Merrell says that the building was there when he came, but that he had to help resettle the foundation. Therefore, there was little for him to do until the building was finished and the machinery, most of which he had brought with him from New Jersey to Savannah, was installed. The factory building was completed in November 1839, and it may be that Merrell was the man who actually got the operation going. The Roswell Manufacturing Company was chartered in December 1839.[14]

Merrell preserved among his papers a document dated February 1840, addressed to his uncle John Camp of Utica, "with reference to an application for insurance," a document that describes the mill rather completely: "The basement is closed & contains no machinery except the driving drum. The first story is designed for the weaving room & also contains no machinery but the refulator. Second story is the Spinning Room. Third story the Carding rooms & Picking & the attic intended for mules is yet empty of machinery."[15]

As Barrington King's "Assistant Agent" at the Roswell Manufacturing Company, Henry Merrell attended the stockholders' meetings, along with such shareholders as Roswell and Barrington King, John Dunwody, James Bulloch, and Archibald Smith. According to the minutes of the company, Henry Merrell was allowed to purchase one share of stock for $750 on April 23, 1844. That he took an active role in these meetings is indicated by the adoption of his motion to declare a 22 percent dividend in 1844. He attended these meetings until he left the employment of the company in 1845, "having removed on the twenty third January."[16] It would seem that Henry Merrell was the first middle-class man in Roswell and the first of many. The conflict between his "mission" as a manager and his role as the husband of a woman from the planter class is demonstrated in the tension between them over his being seen to work with his hands.

A brief and painful account of his ten years in Greene County, Georgia, concludes this section. During that time Merrell built and managed the Curtright Manufacturing Company at Long Shoals on the Oconee River and the steam-powered Greensboro (officially, "Greenesborough") Manufacturing Company in the town of Greensboro. The Curtright site, whose postal address was officially "Merrell" between 1846 and 1854,[17] was capitalized at $100,000. Merrell built for the company a substantial brick building with stone foundations, three stories high and 150 feet long. The Curtright Manufacturing Company was authorized in 1851 to increase its capital by selling stock to the value of $500,000.[18]

Henry Merrell put his best efforts into Curtright. He wrote, "In everything relating to the Long Shoals Factory I have aimed at permanence. I have been at extra expense to make it so. The works are substantial." He even imported "humble, decent, Protestant" Irish immigrants to labor in this factory, thinking that they would work for "more reasonable wages than the corresponding class of native Georgians." His operation was so successful that he had dug a six-by-sixty foot canal one thousand feet long "for the increase of our works," and he had the mill lighted so that work could continue until eight or nine o'clock at night.[19] While he managed Curtright he was awarded two national prizes for the quality of work that the mill produced. He won "best and finest in the Fair" for "a very beautiful specimen of Cotton Twist" at a national fair in "Washington City" in 1846. In November 1846 he won the prize for "best specimen of Cotton Yarn" at the fair of the American Institute in New York City.[20]

But the location on the river at "Merrell" was unhealthy, and the Merrells moved into Greensboro, sixteen miles from the factory, in December 1846. Although he found it difficult to manage at a long distance, Merrell was called by *DeBow's Review* in 1848 "one of the shrewdest northern manufacturers." The periodical quoted him as saying that with the present duties he was making a large profit and that "he expected to retire with a fortune before competition could bring it down to 12 per cent." [21]

But times had changed by 1851, when he was no longer agent of the Curtright Factory and was president of the Greensboro Manufacturing Company. One of his contemporaries, again writing in *DeBow's Review*, commented in 1852 on the current depression in textile manufacturing. Dr. A. W. Ely maintained that "these suspensions and depressions of our cotton manufacturing operations" were "undoubtedly attributable" to the low tariff, the high price of cotton, and the manufacture of coarse goods rather than fine cotton fabrics. [22]

Merrell had already complained in print, in a series of articles that he wrote in 1847 for the *Milledgeville (Southern) Recorder*, about the effects of low tariffs and overproduction on manufacturing in the South. He would mourn more deeply in a series of articles written for the *New York Journal Of Commerce* in 1855. [23] The Curtright Manufacturing Company failed after he left Georgia for Arkansas, but Merrell had to preside over the ruin of the Greensboro company.

Although this section of his memoirs does contain such colorful and humorous incidents as his fight with a British stonemason who had challenged his authority, his account of a wedding party held at the Dunwodys', his delightful picture of the elegant Roswell ladies having to scratch their red-bug bites, and his portraits of Yankee peddlers who gouged Georgia backwoodsmen, his account of his time in Georgia is dominated by his work. Even when he stops writing of his work, the subject is not far beneath the surface, as in the event of his being overtaken at dusk by a man who he thinks is going to rob him of the company accounts; in his story of going to court his future bride but falling from his horse, asleep from exhaustion, onto a spot recently vacated by pigs; and in the statement that he was busy at his working desk the morning after their marriage.

Even when he writes of his own highly developed imagination, which was apparently so keen that he could "when wakeful, call up visions to walk round my bed, as real to my senses as flesh and blood," he mentions that what we would call the repression or rechanneling of this faculty has made him a better engineer, for "it enables me to master a machine or a puzzle without the use of drawings or specifications." "In business & affairs it forecasts events," he adds, and it "has kept alive in me the principle of Hope, when all around me have been in despair."

There were in Georgia many causes for him to despair: the deaths of his sister and of his Utica friends who had followed him to Roswell; the fact that he had to run both the mill and the mill store in Roswell, wearing out a pair of shoes every two weeks in doing so; the lack of reliable currency and the necessity for barter trade; the problems with incompetent or dishonest subordinates and storekeepers under his supervision; the personal and professional problems that he faced because the sons of gentlemen looked upon his kind of labor with contempt; the economic depressions of 1840 and 1842; the rapid expansion of manufacturing in Georgia, which, together with the tariff acts of 1846 and 1850, decreased the profits of the concerns that he managed; the bad machinery that he was forced to buy to operate his last two factories in Georgia; and, finally, the failure of the Greensboro Manufacturing Company.

"And yet," he says, "I have worried through. I had to 'make out' with mill wrights who denied the first principles of hydraulics & hydrostatics, or the strength of materials. With engineers who treated steam as a mystery. . . . With hands who looked upon their employer as their natural enemy." From the other end of the spectrum came problems "with managers who expected me to execute their private revenge against each other & against the hands." After reading the professional difficulties that Henry Merrell faced in nineteenth-century Georgia, even the most overtaxed modern businessman must sympathize with his complaint: "Truly he who sets out to be leader in new enterprises running counter to the genius, & cutting across the prejudices of a people — and that twenty years ahead of his time — has an arduous life!"

Merrell does not complain much in the New York and Arkansas sections of his memoir, but there breathes through this Georgia section a sense of weariness with the amount of work that he had to do, a sense of injustice about how little he was rewarded for that work, and a sense of frustration with the people in Georgia who would not listen to him, profit from his instruction, follow his lead, or express gratitude for his help. After the stockholders of the Greensboro mill did not support him in his management of that concern, nor value his sacrifices on their behalf, a fiery self-righteousness burns through Merrell's account of how he spurned them and their offers of reconciliation, even after they had cleared him of any wrongdoing in the affairs of the company. He seems to glory in the name "failure" and to shake the dust of the town from his feet as he makes bold plans to begin his life over again on borrowed money in the Arkansas wilderness.

Having returned to Roswell on a visit in 1860, Merrell noted that many managers were then doing the work which he had had to accomplish by himself fifteen years before. The tone of much of this section of his memoir is captured in the mournful repetition, "Not so in my time. Not so in my time." Henry Merrell came to Georgia as a pioneer, and he left it as a pioneer.

CHAPTER 25

*W*ith the early spring of the year 1839 came round the time for me to depart for Georgia and enter upon my first appointment. I felt that the course of my future life was now determined, & I mentally resolved to be a man. I dispensed with all jewelry, and every fleshly article of dress. I dropped a habit I had acquired of punning and joking, & otherwise trying to be witty in conversation, aiming in [the] future at more perfect accuracy in all my statements. And I endeavored most especially to cultivate the power of applying myself with assiduity to whatever I had in hand. Without a tithe of Franklin's ability, I think I was quite as much in earnest with my maxims as he ever was at my time of life with his maxims; and it may be that I persevered in the same as long as he, although that may not have been long enough; for with this artificial character, differing from my natural disposition, I soon found myself falling short of my own standard of excellence.

So with a stout heart, and the best of resolutions, I parted from my mother, and Sisters, and brother Sam, and "all inquiring friends," bending my steps Southward, while my school-mates generally sought to establish their fortunes in the West. Not many young men in those days were content to plod through life in the places where they were born and raised. Some to mend their fortunes, some for a better position in society, & a few for health, emigrated. It was said to be the Genius of the American people. Whatever the causes, I am sure that the few who remained behind and took up affairs where their fathers laid them down, enjoyed the more innocent lives, and longer lives, & had more comfort if not more wealth in the long run.

I was to proceed to Paterson, N. Jersey, and for a while look after the building of machinery for the new Factory in Georgia. There I learned a great deal more about my business, than I was able to impart, for Mr. Rogers (Rogers, Ketchum & Grosvenor) was a great mechanic.[1] True to my own maxims, I attended strictly to business. So much so indeed that I made no acquaintance outside the shop. My landlady notified me that a certain young lady(?) wished me to know that she was in love with me. I had just curiosity enough to take one good look at her in the street in order to see what sort of a somebody it might be, & she was indeed good looking enough, with jewelry in her ears and all that; but positively upon my honor I never spoke to her. I wondered a little if she saw "anything green about me," & that was all the thought I bestowed upon her. Had I been idle, it might have been otherwise, which shows advantage of active employment, "Satan finds some mischief still for idle hands to do."

When the machinery was safe on board the good ship "Milledgeville" bound from N. York to the port of Savannah, I went on board, the only passenger. In those days there were no sea-going steamers. The experiment had been tried in the coasting trade; but the art of building suitable craft had not yet arrived at sufficient perfection, and the losses of the steamers "Home" & the "Pulaski," on the Southern coast, had caused a strong prejudice against any more experiments in that line on this side of the ocean. And nothing further was attempted until after the success of the British ship the "Great Western," had demonstrated the practicability of sea-going steamers.[2] After that, ocean navigations by steam increased and multiplied rapidly enough, but no coasting steamer gained the confidence of the Southern folk until the appearance in those waters of the "Southerner," Capt. Berry, & even then it was as much confidence in the man as in the ship.

The traveling public of Georgia and Carolina, after the heart-rending tragedies of the "Pulaski" and the "Home," was very sore on that subject. Scarcely an extensive family among them that had not lost some friend or kin by those events, and their minds were greatly embittered towards those Northern ship-owners who offered inducements for them to risk all they held dear on board half-built steamers that were already or would have been condemned in their own waters. However, in the course of ten or fifteen years afterwards, all that was reconciled, and finally a noble line of steamers plied from New York to Philadelphia and Baltimore to the ports of Charleston and Savannah, and there was no longer any question as to their sea going qualities.

I was ten days at sea on board the "Milledgeville," & arrived at Savannah

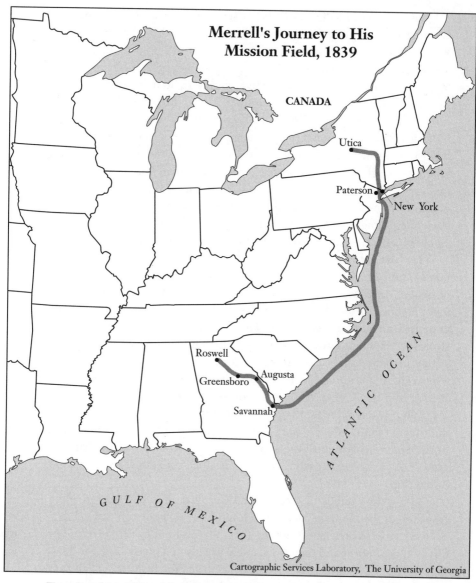

**Merrell's Journey to His
Mission Field, 1839**

CANADA

Utica

Paterson

New York

Roswell

Greensboro

Augusta

Savannah

ATLANTIC OCEAN

GULF OF MEXICO

Cartographic Services Laboratory, The University of Georgia

*Traveling from Utica, Merrell stops in Paterson, New Jersey, to pick up
machinery for the Roswell Manufacturing Company, then proceeds by water,
rail, and horseback to Roswell, Georgia.*

early in May. This was my first sea voyage. I have been [on] many voyages since, but never across the ocean; and let me say once for all that I am not fond of the Sea, because I suffer a great deal from sea-sickness. But for that, sea-going would be my delight, and I apprehend that sea-sickness is a wise provision to prevent everybody going to sea. As it is, few go upon salt water unless they have business there.

The scenery below Savannah on the river, with rice plantations on either hand, as seen from the City, is said to resemble no little the banks of the river Nile as seen from the City of Cairo.

Immediately upon my arrival at Savannah, my zeal prompted me to spend my time on the deck of the ship superintending the careful unloading of the machinery, but I soon found the heat of the Sun, under the bluff, almost intolerable; and was glad directly to fall into the Southern way about that thing at last, and leave the hauling of the machinery, for better or worse, to the stevedore and his Negro men, while I consulted my own comfort over such iced refreshments as were tendered me for "a bit" by the old Negro woman in a man's hat, who expected me to address her as "Momma."

The Hotel of that time in Savannah was the City Hotel, kept by Wiltberger, who was not so old as he came to be fifteen years later at the Pulaski House, but was then a portly, fine-looking man & the very perfection of a landlord. I had been consigned with my cargo to the firm of Ralph & William King. In order to avoid the entanglements of a Hotel, I asked for a private boarding house, and was directed to Mrs. Hardee's in Broughton St. She was kind and motherly to me, looking upon me as a very feeble young man who stood in need of a mother's care. I found her out to be a native of my own native valley of the Mohawk. Her maiden name Henry, she had been raised in the old house still standing near Johnstown, N.Y., where Sir William Johnston lived & plotted & fought during the old revolutionary war. When I knew her, she was the widow of a brother of him who is now Major (or Lt.) General Hardee in the Confederate army.[3] Whoever takes the trouble to read what I write may think all this very unimportant, but it seems not so to me; therefore, I record it all. A motherly lady in reduced circumstances keeping a boarding house for young men has a position of great influence for good or evil. A successful boarding-house keeper with Negro servants cannot be an ordinary woman. Her business daily calls for extraordinary energy, firmness, & tact. Her influence over the young men in her house is bound to be considerable, & whether it shall be for good or bad is the question. That any woman's influence could be otherwise than good, a young man would be inclined to doubt, & therein

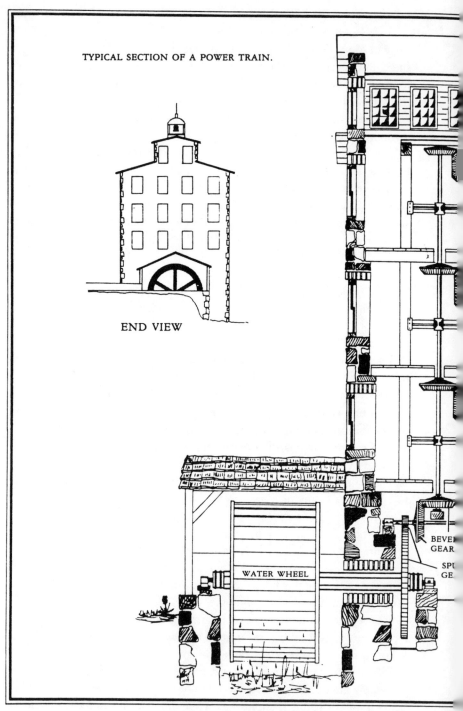

TYPICAL SECTION OF A POWER TRAIN.

END VIEW

WATER WHEEL

BEVE
GEAR

SPU
GE

An early nineteenth-century textile mill, typical of the ones that Merrell worked in and built. From Rockdale *by Anthony F. C. Wallace (illustrations by Robert*

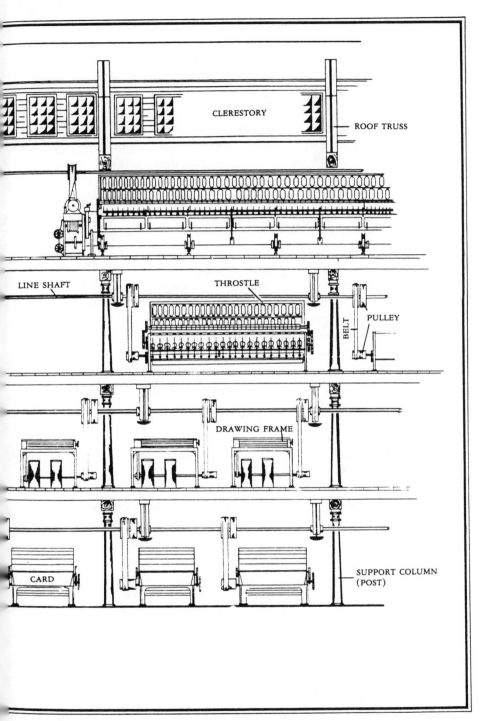

Howard). Copyright © 1972, 1978 by Anthony F. C. Wallace. Reprinted by
permission of Alfred A. Knopf, Inc.

lies the danger. That her influence, under such circumstances, might be bad, witness the attempt of my landlady at Paterson to set me in the wrong way; then contrast her with the good Mrs. Hardee, who was a mother to me in a strange city.

Mrs. Hardee gave me a good room up stairs, the window of which was over the front door of her house. When she ushered me into it, she remarked that it had last been occupied by two young ladies of her acquaintance who had left a few curl papers & one or two little tanglements of hair, such as they will take from the comb & wind round the finger into a little nubbin before casting it into the fire place. It so turned out that one of those same young ladies was to become my wife. She was then from the confines of Florida (her native town being St. Mary's), & I from the borders of Canada at the North, both of us finding our way to the "Roswell Colony," there to become two years afterwards husband and wife; but at the time I refer to, unknown to each other, we had thus accidentally upon the same journey occupied the same room. It is not much of a coincidence to be recorded, but it made an impression upon me.

From Savannah I journeyed all the way to Augusta by stage, & very hot I found it toiling through the sand. From Augusta to Greensboro in Georgia was rail road; again from Greensboro to Decatur by stage & from thence to Roswell on horse-back.[4]

CHAPTER 26

*A*rrived at Roswell in Cobb County Georgia in the month of May 1839. I met a cordial reception literally at the hands of Mr. King and as many of the future colonists as were already on the grounds;[1] for they shook hands not only at introductions, but upon meeting in the road every day and as many times a day as they happened to see each other. I had been accustomed to the flying recognition, a nod, or a jerk of the hand on the street to gentlemen, & a touch or lifting of the hat to ladies, which is all the time a busy population at the North could afford to bestow upon politeness every day; and the elaborate manners of Southern gentlemen seemed very stupid to me until I at last became satisfied that to me at least they were as kind and cordial as they seemed.

I found the Roswell colonists living in the woods & in such rude buildings as they found already upon the lands they had purchased from the original settlers. Major Bulloch was at a farm five miles distant on the

Lawrenceville road. John Dunwody had his temporary residence one mile nearer on the hill beyond Howell's mill. Arch. Smith at his farm on the Altoona Road, and Barrington King with his numerous family of children marooned at the place afterwards called the "Labyrinth" because of successive additions. At that time it consisted of a double log cabin & a few outhouses only.[2]

Besides those I have named, with their families, I do not remember any of the numerous colony who had yet arrived; except the father of B. King, Esq, Mr. Roswell King. He had been there from the first, and a mill he had erected was the nucleus of the place.[3] From him the town took its present name "Roswell." The idea of the Colony was to have a Summer resort of their own, entirely under Presbyterian influence, & in a healthy mountainous location, to which they could retire during the sickly seasons; and at the same time have the advantages of schools and public worship. It had been for many years fashionable, but not convenient for low country planters to spend their summers at the North. The manifest inconvenience, to say nothing of the expense, of those yearly migrations away from the servants, with large families of children, suggested the plan, and the hard times that set in about those days reduced it to a necessity,[4] that they should spend the hot season among the mountains of their own state. Such was the rationale of the Roswell Colony. It was an experiment, the success whereof was questioned by many. The business of manufacturing, which finally made itself the distinguishing characteristic of the place, was at the outset of secondary importance and more questionable success than the other objects of the Colony; but, as it turned out, the manufacturing became a success at the very crisis, when the hard times of 1840 to '42 caused the other resources of the Colonists to fail. There was business, new to them, which grew fat upon that which impoverished the planter: to wit the low price of cotton. It supported their families through a period of depression when their plantations would barely support themselves; and the consequence was that finally they turned their capital more largely into the business than they had at first intended; and they did not lose sight of the moral, educational & religious designs of the original settlement; their town came to be known mainly as a manufacturing town, the most successful if not the most important in Georgia. Of this manufacturing town I was not the founder; that honor was due to old Mr. Roswell King the father of Barrington King. I was not the responsible agent; that office belonged to Barrington King Esq. who filled it with great firmness, & probably retains it for life. I finally arrived at the dignity of assistant Agent, & so shared in that responsibility, but my part in the building up of that place was limited to the Engineering & Mechanical departments & the organizing & discipline of the hands: no light undertaking, I now think, for a very young man, considering the rough population that I had to deal with, & the remoteness of the place from mechanical facilities. But I had a strong will then, & I must say of Mr. King that he never weakened my hands, but "backed" me at every emergency.

Upon my arrival at the place I found the first factory building of brick completed according to drawings furnished by Mr. Rogers of Paterson, N.J.[5] The superstructure had been erected with remarkable fidelity under the eye of Mr. B. King; but unfortunately the foundation, which had been laid by his father before his arrival, had proved to be insufficient to support so great a weight: the building was cracking and giving away. After due consultation it was agreed upon to adopt the bold measure of shoring up the brick building, three stories high, & after removing the old foundation, so far as it was defective, to replace it with one of hewn granite.

Like bold measures generally, this was attended with entire success, but it was a work requiring time.[6] This gave me leisure to look about me. The machinery had not yet arrived, & I resolved to execute a little plan I had agreed upon, conditionally, before leaving home.

I have before spoken of Wm. Backus of Utica, N.Y. The "Black Prince," he was called.[7] He was a money broker and auctioneer of that city & traded in real estate. It appeared that he had come into possession of one or more of those square Leagues (more or less) of lands in Texas, which more than likely was shingled over three deep with Spanish Claims. This Texas land he had exchanged with somebody in N. York City, Wall Street, named Smith (for I desire to be particular) for 12,000 acres of land in East Tennessee in Bledsoe County. He had desired me, as I was to be located within a hundred and fifty miles of his land, to ride over some day on horse-back and, after viewing this property, to make him a written report. Of course he wanted a favorable report to sell by. In order to defray my expenses, he had handed me some bank notes which I afterwards had reason to think must have been bad stock, even in his broker office. As I was saying, the delay caused by new under-pinning the Factory gave me a little leisure to try and carry out the views of Mr. Backus.

Mr. King kindly mounted me on his blooded mare "Clara," and I found myself once more journeying in my old way, with the beast under me. The first day I reach Altoona Mountain & had time to view the old Indian gold-diggings & the preparations for the deep cut of the State road through that place, before retiring to rest at "Dawson's." He was a brother of Wm. C. Dawson, afterwards U.S. Senator from Georgia. Roomed with a

View of Merrell's Roswell Manufacturing Company (in the foreground). This sketch was made by Charles Holyland of the Chicago Board of Trade Battery shortly after he helped to burn the mills in July of 1864. Courtesy of the Roswell Historical Society.

very young man named Nelson, who was son or some other near kin to Genl. Nelson of the Florida War. He was on his way to visit another kinsman at his plantation at Farish Carter's on the Oostanaula River, & we concluded to ride together.[8]

He was rather a wicked young man, but I became interested in him, for he gave promise of considerable ability. He was afterwards sufficiently distinguished so that I never lost sight of him long at a time.

At the breaking out of the Mexican War, he volunteered, was elected Captain, & served through the War in the Georgia Regt. under Col. Henry Jackson.[9] Next I heard that he had married somebody to his advantage. Then in due time that he was Mayor of the City of Atlanta, Ga. And finally in this present war, one day came along a Texas Regt. of Infantry that for a wonder was distinguished for good order and discipline. It was ably commanded by Col. Nelson, my old acquaintance. Not long after, I heard that he had been promoted to be a Brig. General, & very soon after that he had died, much lamented in the Army.

Parting with young Nelson at the crossing of the Oostanaula River, I pursued my journey alone through the "Cherokee Nation," *i.e.*, the country which the Cherokee Indians had left the year before on their removal to Arkansas. And crossing the Tennessee River at the mouth of the Hiawassee, arrived in due time at Pikeville. the capital of Bledsoe County, near unto which the domains of the "Black Prince" were supposed to lie.

In the County book of Records I found Mr. Backus' deed or deeds duly recorded just as he had described them to me, and I had only to visit said lands, wherever they might be, and after viewing them to make, if possible, a glowing report upon the same. Soil, climate, water courses, & mineral resources. As to that, there was one thing I had resolved upon, that probably he did not understand or he would not have sent me there. I would never be party to an imposition. I was incapable of making out for his benefit, or my own, a "bogus" report. Just as I should find things, so I intended to describe them, for better or worse. At the outset it struck me as singular that near so old and worn out & noted a country as the Seqautchee Valley, there could be 12,000 acres of vacant land in one body.

Upon further inquiry, I found that the lands I was in search of lay on the top of "Walden's Ridge," which was a high mountain bounding Bledsoe County on the East; but on the top of the ridge there was a table land four or five miles in width of very good country for raising grain, fruit, and live stock. And I was told that if my friend's title was all right, it was probable that his lands were well worth looking after.

So I went onto the mountain by a gap to which there was a turnpike gate kept by a man named Beatty, & was by him directed to the house of a hunter named Callahan. Old man Callahan, although he lived precariously, as hunters are prone to do, made me welcome to the best he had, and what he had was nice and clean.

He had some fine strapping, healthy girls dressed in homespun, & all neat and clean, who seemed to look upon me as worthy of their admiration, but I did not trifle with them. I took enough interest in them, however, to enquire about them years afterwards and found that they had married & done well. There I first learned that wild honey is excellent to sweeten coffee in place of sugar. It has this advantage, that other sweets in the mouth at the same time do not impart to the Coffee a bitter taste, as is the case with sugar. At the old man's there was little to eat besides venison for meat, and for bread, corn meal with butter and honey, and milk when the cows condescended to "come up."

But at all times, cost what it would, the hunter must have his Rio Coffee — the real green seed-tick Coffee — whether or not he could garnish the same with cream and honey. As to the honey, that was found wild in the woods; and from Mr. Beatty's house he showed me high up on the face of the perpendicular bluff, inaccessible to man, a fissure in the rock which actually ran down with surplus honey so that it glistened in the sun's rays.

Among these people I first learned something of Bee Hunting, but it was always too slow a business for my taste.

I found upon the mountain a Methodist preacher named Thurman, who had carried chain for the surveyors in running out the very land in question. He agreed, after the next Sabbath, to act as my guide at the rate of One Dollar per day, & I was fortunate in my selection, for he was able not only to show me the lands, but to put me in the way to know all about the titles, which were wild enough. I attended preaching at a log meeting house in the forest so as to be on hand for an early start in the morning. The preacher had his rifle by him in the desk, and a full-grown pet deer with a bell & collar on its neck, browsing and ringing round the house during service. What he said, I do not remember; probably it was not of much consequence. Next morning we were early at our work. My guide was an excellent woodsman, & went to the corner we wanted to find, as straight as a bee to a bee-tree; and that, you know, is a perfect air line.

I had been told a great deal about the rattle-snakes in those parts, and having never encountered one, felt no little dread of them. I had been told there were enough rattle-snakes in those mountains to fence the land. I did not quite believe that, but reflected that making due allowance for exaggeration, there must be a great many of those venomous reptiles against whom I ought to take precautions. My guide laughed at my apprehensions & told me what is true, that the woodsmen & their families live and die among them, and in a whole life time scarcely hear of one to their own knowledge bitten at all, certainly not bitten to death. But I told my guide that he might keep ten steps ahead on the trail. I would let him deal with the snakes, while I looked on and learned his art.

It turned out that this was the worst thing I could have done. Passing on before, he roused up the snakes in the grass & left them in a fit temper to bite me as I came along. I had not followed in his trail a quarter of a mile before I was brought to a halt by a rattle-snake of the very largest kind. It was at least as large round as my thigh & the maddest-looking animal I ever saw. The rain which fell that morning had soaked his rattles so that he made no startling noise, although his tail vibrated too rapidly to be seen distinctly; but he tainted the air with a sickening smell resembling a green cucumber, but far more fetid. Such an attitude of rage and hate I never imagined before. He was in a coil about to strike, but it was a spiral coil with his tail for the base and the head erect and thrown back, with a mouth apparently as large as my hand, the upper jaw thrown back showing two white fangs hooked downward. How red his mouth looked and the fire that shot from his eyes! So full of spring was his coil that it seemed to quiver! I had no time to lose, & yet I seemed to make these observations as distinctly in an instant as I could have done at another time at my leisure.

Quick as thought, quicker than I could think, if I had not been sensible of great danger — that is to say, scared — my gun was at my shoulder and fired. I did not think to run; that would have been the better course. I fired, but fired an inch too low, tearing up the ground until it left a hole in the ground under the belly of the snake. So near was it that the flame of the gun must have done execution as well as the lead. The gravel wounded my snake mortally, & the explosion blew him into the air. He had finished his career, & I was victorious. Affecting to re-load my gun with great in-difference, but quivering all over with suppressed excitement, I stood over my dying game, awaiting the approbation of the guide, who soon returned to me. He pronounced my snake a fine specimen of the "dimented" rattle snake of the very largest kind and a female. "When you have done loaded up again," said he, "we will soon meet up with the old he one, who can't be far away; and then don't you fire, but call to me, & I will show you some sport." I need not say that I did not walk ten paces in the rear of my guide after that.

We had gone but a few yards again before, sure enough, we saw the male rattle-snake. He was not so large, but much longer than the female.

My guide told me to stand & keep my eye on the snake while he would go and return shortly. Directly he came back with a long stick like a fishing rod, on the end of which was a tuft of green leaves. It was some kind of ash wood, he told me, very offensive to the rattle-snake. With this he tormented the snake into a very great rage, causing him to strike at the pole and go through hideous contortions, besides smelling very badly, which the hunter called "sport," the end of all which was that he killed the snake without wasting his charge of powder & lead, as I had done. I observed that wherever the snake struck its fangs into the back of the ash pole, they left two little globules of venom of a pale green color, and at each successive bite the quantity of venom became less until it appeared that his stock of poison had become exhausted.

We saw no more rattle-snakes, & only one of any other kind of snake during our whole trip. Doubtless many snakes saw us and kept out of our way. I have since seen a good deal of the rattle-snake & have learned neither to fear or respect it. It is a cowardly reptile, flying always when it can & fighting only in ambuscade or at other advantage. As to its giving a magnanimous warning by its rattle, I don't believe it had any such intention. Wait for its rattle, & you are too late generally to escape its blow. The fetid scent it emits is a better warning. The common cure for a bite of any snake is to pour down whiskey or other strong liquor, which is said not to intoxicate so long as the poison remains in the system. At any rate, it is the cure nearest at hand in most cases, & by many thought to be not bad to take.

Speaking of snakes, Jack Magill, who was consul at some port in South America,[10] told me that he was once in nearly at the death of an Anaconda, and that he tried his whole strength with a new Collins axe, very sharp, to cut into its flesh, but so tough and elastic were the fibers of the muscles that the axe did bound back, making no gash in the meat! This being so, I can understand how the coils of the Anaconda might crush a bullock, as I have read, provided the snake was large enough & the ox not too strong. In snake stories I have sometimes been asked if I could not "fall a snake or two," but these I have told for true stories.

Note. These rattle-snakes were white underneath their bellies, golden yellow up their sides, shaded darker on the back, and marked down the back with beautiful diamonds of black.

I have seen in the woods one rattlesnake quite black, but only one in my life of that color, or any other but that first described.

I found much good land on Mr. Backus' claim, although it was, as I have said, on the top of a mountain; but alas! it had been settled many years, &

the sale to him had been a swindle. I do not mean that the land was thickly settled, for the proportion of arable land was small, but there were as many settlers as felt disposed to neighbor with each other and make an amicable divide of the range for their cattle. And I soon got word to be off with my bogus claim to their land, or I would get a rifle bullet for my pains. I had already lived long enough to know that people who threaten are not very dangerous & did not give myself much uneasiness on that score. I remained until I had found out all I wanted to know. It appeared that I was by no means the first to visit the same land on the strength of sales made in Wall St. They told me that one purchaser had come with his wife and daughters and a piano all the way from N. York City to take possession of their extensive domain and had to go back the way they came.

The land in question was what was called "School-lands." No government survey having ever been made, any one who chose to hire the county surveyor a few days could have a plot made out of any shape or quantity he saw fit, & such surveys might run over and into each other to any amount. I was also told what I scarcely could believe: that by paying the price into the school fund, quit claim titles from the state could be obtained to the same land over & over again. Let that be as it might, the swindlers managed to obtain or fabricate entry papers, with which they went into the land market of N. York City & made sales to the unwary, of whom my friend Backus was one. He had promised me, for my trouble, 250 acres of wherever I chose to locate it on his land, but I never had the heart to press the demand on him. The possession of it would have been to me only the possession of a law-suit, and it was one of my maxims never to buy a law-suit nor even to take one as a gift.

I returned from this fruitless journey & arrived at Roswell the day before the 4th July 1839. That day was celebrated by a grand dinner party at Mr. King's. He had during my absence removed his family to the buildings which now serve as kitchens to his fine residence.

At that dinner I first was introduced to the ladies of the Colony in high dress. I there first became slightly acquainted with my future wife. I thought the ladies, generally very polite, a good deal too much so to be quite sincere; but as in the case of gentlemen's manners, I found it all right at last. The fault was in my own want of manner, & not their excess. At the same time I was quite up to fair good breeding in the North where I came from. Northern people, as I said before have not the spare time to bestow on the genuflecting of very polite society. At least not when I was young. I have seen very well-bred men in Northern society during my later visits.

One thing I observed. The Roswell ladies scratched themselves a great deal, & by common consent it seemed they waived Southern etiquette, whatever that might be, concerning the bites of insects. The truth was, the future thriving town of Roswell, was at that early day in the bushes and very stumpy. One could lose himself in the cow-path where the main street now is. And there was an insect generated of rotten wood and swarming on the leaves of underbrush; and the name by which it went was "red-bug." At whose bite no human could resist the temptation to scratch, wherever that bite might happen to take effect.

CHAPTER 27

*M*y first measure after entering upon the duties of my Superintendency was to obtain suitable overseers to act under me. My own success depending upon a judicious choice of subordinate officers, I resolved to have them from the North, and to have them selected from among my own comrades, whose qualifications were known to me & I to them. The correspondence on that subject resulted in the engagement of two first-rate young men, raised in the Oneida Factory, who joined me in the best spirit of personal good-will, and came on from the North without loss of time; but unhappily one of them contracted the seeds of Yellow Fever in Charleston, S.C. on their way, and died in a few days after his arrival. The name of this unfortunate young man was William Smith. He was a nephew of Mr. Ira Hand, the Supt. of the Oneida Facty. This was my second heavy bereavement.[1] Smith and I had been good friends of old, & his coming so far to give me a successful start in business had endeared him to me still more. My feelings as I followed him to his grave were those of utter desolation and lonesomeness. Eric Parker, his comrade, wept mournfully and could give me no comfort. The suddenness of the event, the violence of the disease, the necessity for immediate interment; two lone mourners among so many strangers following our comrade to the grave dejected and bowed down with grief, the long weepers, strange to us, that they gave us to wear on our hats, all combined to make a lasting impression upon my memory. These circumstances drew Parker and myself closer together, and until the day of his death, which was several years afterwards, not a shadow passed over our mutual good understanding, although he, the older, had to act in a position subordinate to me, the younger and, in some things, a pupil of his.

We erected a granite monument over the grave of Smith, which was

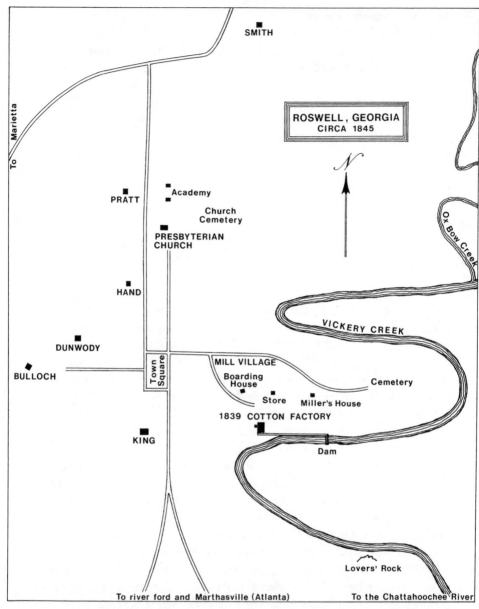

Roswell, Georgia, about the time that Henry Merrell left it. The "colony," as it was called, founded in 1838 by planters from the Georgia coast, was modeled on the New England village and was intended to be a manufacturing settlement. The location of the Smith House one mile to the north indicates that this founding family intended to continue its agricultural ways apart from the town.

in good repair when I last visited Roswell. This same monument finally served for both Smith & Parker, for the latter was laid by the side of his comrade.

Parker's early death I had anticipated. He was consumptive, and during several winters before his removal to the south, he had been confined to his chambers, shut in from the cold air. His coming South was a boon to him, & apparently prolonged his life. He finally died, not of any lung attack, but with a very sudden & high bilious fever, resembling the case of Smith. In his case I had, besides the hardship of losing so good a friend, nothing to regret, except that pressure of business in his absence, & ignorance of his danger prevented me from conversing with & praying for him on his death bed as I ought to have done. However, his religious views had been adopted long before, and upon mature reading and reflection. In the case of Smith it was otherwise. I had to regret deeply the circumstances of his untimely death. He was younger than I. We had been boys together. His mother had placed confidence in me. For many years I felt unpleasantly whenever my mind reverted to the subject, because I felt that I might fairly be chargeable with inducing him to follow my fortunes until he died. I believe this because somebody had written [a] letter putting the case in that way, & I had those regrets until the time of this writing; but, looking over some old papers, I came across the correspondence by which I negotiated the engagement with both Smith & Parker; and I find that correspondence happily free from anything of the kind on my part. On the other hand, I had left the whole negotiation with third parties who engaged whomsoever they saw fit; I only expressing my preferences.

Smith, poor fellow, "was brave and loyal." Almost his first word to me on arriving at Roswell was to ask me if there was any fighting that I wanted done, or something to that effect. "Because," said he, "Parker and I heard along the road as we came, that you had fighting to do, & we agreed together that we would stand by you." His father, an Englishman, had been a boxer in his time, & William had learned from him the art of self defense, which he in turn had taught to me. But I never had the "scientific" skill at Boxing that Smith possessed or his father before him. I had not the strength or wind to hold out long, though I was at that time quick & could take pretty good care of myself in sparring with my comrades. The circumstances which called forth the above tender of alliance, offensive & defensive, on the part of Smith & Parker, were these.

Returning from Tennessee, & entering upon my duties in July, I soon found that Mr. King, ignorant of mechanics and their ways, had about him a bad-set kind from among the adventurers lying about the city of Savannah. They drew large pay &, in return, idled away a great deal of time, drank at their work, & were disorderly in their conduct. They were headed by an old one-eyed sinner from N. York City—an Englishman named Hagg & well named. He was a mill wright by trade. This gang were disposed to dictate unreasonable terms to their employers, & they were not at all disposed to accept me, a very young man, as their Superintendent.

Seeing my engagement was permanent, & theirs temporary & drawing to a close as fast as the factory buildings and millwright work drew near completion, I was disposed to waive the dignity of my office & worry through with that banditti until we could get the work so far along as to dispense with them altogether.

But it soon became manifest that they had no intention of bringing their lucrative engagement to a close, so long as they could "put in time" & make no progress. I gained no credit by forbearance. They evidently thought I was afraid of them. Matters grew worse until it became evident that without a change for the better, the funds of the company would be exhausted upon them & there would be no factory at last—the whole thing resulting, so far as I was personally concerned, in the commercial failure of the first factory committed to my management & the consequent loss of reputation to me. I reflected deeply upon this. Mr. King had little means of knowing which party to sustain. Me alone, a very young man, just arrived; or they, older men and several of them, who had been there from the first and could conspire to tell him what they pleased. Things grew worse and worse. I was insulted in a ruffianly manner in my place at the head of the public table; & I resolved to bring matters to a crisis, caring but little about the result. If Mr. King had the spirit and the sagacity to side with me, I would gladly stay on with the work under strict order & discipline. If he thought me in the wrong and temporized with the workman, I would as gladly quit and leave him & the business to go the wrong way.

So I told the men, one and all, that I was determined to stand it no longer. They knew as well as I what was due from a workman to his employer, & I should exact from them their whole duty. And to begin with, the factory bell would in future ring the hours of work; & any man idle any part of that time should submit to a reduction of his pay in proportion. I selected this among their many offenses, as the one most available for any determined purpose to have a sharp collision & soon over with.

The head stone mason on the new foundations was a stout fellow named Atkinson. I think he was an Englishman. Him they put forward as the bully.

By long wielding the heavy stone-hammer, he had acquired great strength in his arms, as I had great reason to know from the weight of his fist; but he was a heavy, inactive man; & I had little to fear from him in a fair fist fight.

He forthwith set himself, with twenty or thirty Negro men under his command, to lose more time than ever. Prompt to my word, when dinner time came round, & all were assembled at the door of the Boarding House, I said looking at my watch in a matter of course way, "Mr. Atkinson, you have lost say one quarter of a day's time already to-day. You will be 'docked' that amount on the time book." The words were scarcely out of my mouth before I was rolling over and over down the steep hill. He had planted a blow in one of my eyes, so heavy as to stun me quite. I did not parry, because I had both hands at the moment engaged in returning my watch, which was fat, to the fob of my linen trousers, which were sweaty. Once on my feet, I was maddened at the sight of all my enemies in a crowd backing my antagonist with pleasure in their faces at what they considered my defeat. So I made a rash charge up the hill, all the time fumbling at the watch, expecting to have it secured in time to use my fists; but Atkinson charged down the hill to meet me, & again I went over backwards with his fist in my other eye. I had now no time to spare. Soon both eyes would be swelled past seeing. What became of the watch I forget, but think I left it swinging by the guard chain. It was easy to see that Atkinson, big as he was, knew nothing of boxing. I knew a trick with the left fist from the shoulder straight out & then up the lip & nose, which done quickly, neatly and accurately, with strength such as nervous people alone can put into a single blow, so as nearly to break one's own arm. Such a blow I calculated would quite satisfy him. My having the under side the hill was an advantage in this case. I was active in those days. Running quickly under his guard, if he struck me again in his awkward way, I did not know it. I got in my one blow just as I intended & as I expected, he did not fight any more.

I never had any more trouble with those men. Mr. King had the good sense to take my side promptly & firmly. Atkinson was discharged & a better man named Patten put in his place. One by one, the conspirators intimated to me slyly that they had always believed in me; & what was best of all, I never had to fight again so long as I remained in that part of the country.

This trick with the left fist I had learned from poor Smith, but in all my life, only on one other occasion, I never had to put it in practice except in sports. It was this skirmish that I have described, that Smith & Parker heard of on the way, magnified into a battle Royal, that drew from him the words with which he met me on arrival, & which were nearly his last words to me.

Strangely enough, my two black eyes of which I was heartily ashamed, introduced me into polite society more favorably than if I had done several good things. Such is society! Mr. King finally gave it as his opinion that I would fight a duel if occasion required it, & fighting a duel, you know, is the grand entree among the better class of people at the South. Even Christian people cannot, or do not, divest themselves of their partiality for a man who will fight. Especially did my black eye first bring me more intimately to know the lady who was to become my wife. Arch. Smith Esq, at whose house she was a sister-in-law—the most conscientious Christian man I ever knew—reported to the ladies (so my wife tells me) that I had shown a Christian Spirit, & he wished to invite me to his house.[2] What on Earth he could discover that was Christian-like in a rough and tumble fight, I never could understand, but I availed myself of the invitation, nevertheless, to enjoy the society of ladies, & finally to secure me a good wife. I tell them that they courted me in that family. Wife says it is no such thing, but intolerable vanity in me to think so. She says I courted her, & she married me to put an end to my importunity.

Talking of the Southern practice of Duelling: brother Charley says he once heard a celebrated beauty, who belonged to the Church, inveighing against it & declaring she would never marry a gentleman who had fought a duel.[3] "Would you," he asked, "ever associate with a gentleman who had declined to fight in a duel?" "No I would not." There it was, the whole history of duelling in a few words. The ladies are at the bottom of it. Gentlemen are averse to it, as is evinced by their extreme politeness & regard for the feelings of others, in all circles where a duel is the penalty for an offense.

CHAPTER 28

(1839 or 1840)

*B*ehold me then confirmed in my office, easy about my future in society, and rapidly bringing my machinery & my wild Arab hands into a state of organization to produce returns of profits in place of the heavy outlay that had been going on.

Here I first discovered that my genius for mechanical improvements and invention was no kind of benefit, but rather a hindrance to a practical businessman who has money to make for his employers. Accordingly, I suppressed every aspiration of the kind in my own breast, and tolerated no contrivances among my hands until I found myself at last inclined entirely the other way—a conservative in the bad sense, positively averse to all improvements & consequently opposed to progress in the mechanical arts. However, I erred, & the error cost me dearly at a subsequent period of my career. At the time I speak of, it was well enough. My first business at Roswell was to make the most of the machinery that had been placed under my management, and get money out of it for my company, and I did so.[1]

The business during several years proved to be a perfect "Teel Mill."[2] Labor and Cotton were cheap, because the "times were hard." Cotton we often got a cent to a cent and a half a pound in the seed, and four cents a pound for the "lint."[3] Labor of able-bodied men was abundant at Eight Dollars per month, they feeding and clothing themselves, which they could afford to do because provisions were low in proportion. Bacon four cents a pound. Flour One and a half to Two Dollars per hundred pounds. Fowls five cents each. Eggs five cents a dozen, &c. All this time our manufactured products bore all the price, nearly, that we had the conscience to ask, the only drawback as to profit being the fact that there was no currency.

The reasons for the state of things I have represented were as follows. The country was new, having been but recently wrested from the Indians. The population were new-comers from all points of the compass, to better their conditions. The mass of these men were what were called "forty acre people," having means & force only equal to that quantity of land. Many were disappointed gold hunters, for that was the famous "Gold region" of Georgia, about which there had been overly much excitement and intrusion.[4]

The region thus rapidly filling up was without navigable rivers, remote from rail-roads, and without a convenient market. The increase of population—which came into the "Cherokee Nation," upon the removal of the Indians, from all sides, as air rushes in to fill a vacuum—was a pre-mature immigration, which had yet several years of hardships to undergo, awaiting approval of public improvements to carry off their products for a market. Those public improvements were the Georgia Rail Road, which beginning at Augusta had during this time reached first Greensboro then Buck Head & finally Madison. The Central Railroad commencing at Savannah had reached a point somewhere in Jefferson County. The Monroe Rail Road intended to ply from Macon to Atlanta.[5] Atlanta was then no place at all. I have been over the ground on horse back, feeling very lonesome, for there was then only one old house in that vicinity. And finally the State Road, swallowing money like a sand heap takes water, was to connect all the above rail roads with the Tennessee River at Ross Landing, now called Chattanooga. This State road seemed to me at the time to be a terrible nest of barnacles on the good ship of State. Money voted by Legislature for that purpose, was like pouring water into a rat-hole. There had to be a revolution in its management, which took place when Col. Garnett from Virginia superseded Col. Long as Superintendent. I wonder if that Col. Garnett was not afterwards the Genl. Garnett who was killed early in this war, at some ford, attempting to resist Genl. McClellan's advance into Western Virginia?[6]

In all these new Rail roads rested the outcome of the up Country of Georgia, at the time I refer to, say 1840. The hope of the Country was in their completion, but the most sanguine had begun to despair of that event. The bridges & crossties seemed to rot on the ground before iron could be purchased, and iron had to lie and rust away for want of rolling stock to fetch it away.

Did I say that these public enterprises swallowed up a great deal of money? There was no money for them to swallow. The Rail Road companies were endowed with banking privileges. The state itself had a Bank (called the Central Bank) and, in addition, issued scrip, which was convertible into Bonds drawing 8 percent Interest.[7] So low down did the credit of this paper currency go that for a long time the State Scrip was at 44 to 50 cents on the Dollar. Central Bank money 25 cents, & Monroe Rail Road Bank 12½ cents on the Dollar and finally to nothing. So that in the daily transaction of business, one had to be his own money-broker and, in making change, go into all the vulgar fractions of discount & premium. At last the public wanted to fall back upon private credit & responsibility, making a circulating medium of private promises to pay, which were called "Shin-plasters." The Roswell Manufacturing Co., like others, issued Shin-plasters, & I had to sign them until I have fallen asleep over the irksome task. A rapid penman can sign his name about 4,000 times in a day of 12 hours, or at that rate for an hour or two. I have heard old Jacob Barker, the Banker, say that in his prime, he had under pressure signed bank notes about twenty-four hours continuously, keeping himself awake by an occasional douche of cold water. It is not a very intellectual employment, but I found it in hot weather very tiresome. We did not keep it up long. We became satisfied that to men who had something other to do, it was a poor business. As to the popular notion that the issuers of change bills have large profits, we found it very much the reverse. Besides the risk of counterfeits, there was the first cost of engraved plates, paper, printing, filling out, sign-ing, & cutting neatly bills of denominations as low as a dime! And then how limited is the full amount at any one time of the largest circulation of such trash. I refer, of course, to the issues of men who redeem their notes when presented. It is a poor business [for] an honest man who does not in-tend to run away. It is borrowing money without interest from an exacting public who call for their pay every hour. We found it so, and I once heard a sound banker of Georgia say that, even in the larger issues of a Bank, the net profit on the circulation part of the business was a problem. It was not legitimate Banking, & in the end I believe it is that which is at the bottom of bank-failures generally.

I have noticed that the great Bankers often prefer to make their pay-ments with the notes of other banks, calling in their own, if indeed they have any out.

I remember that in the case of the Roswell Co., shin plasters, redeem-able in Cotton yarns, [were] among other vexations. True to the public idea of the duties of a Bank, it was a few days only before we had a customer wanting a loan of only a few thousands, upon the security of somebody else, who in his turn would shortly have demanded a timeless loan on the security of it. To all of which Mr. King had the satisfaction of saying, "in the affirmative, no." If I was a poet, I would sing the praises of that King of all words, "no." It is the business man's safe anchor. He may pay out with it as much chain cable of talk as he likes, but to be safe, at the end of his talk must be the word "no."

But I have wandered a little. I was speaking of the hard times in Georgia in the years 1840 to 1841. The currency was one cause or one effect, I don't know which; probably it was both cause and effect.

Those hard times for others were good times for our manufacturing enterprise, & might have been made much more so could we have known which part of the currency to put off again and which to lay by as profits.

Very cautious persons often arrive at the wrong conclusion. As it turned out, the State Bond & Scrip were the paper we should have laid by, but we had little confidence in the politicians & stood in fear of public repudia-tion. So we passed off the 8% obligations of the State & put our trust in private responsibility.

I believe we had on hand about $4,000 or $5,000 of the Monroe Rail Road Bank bills when that institution broke flat, but generally speaking, we kept ourselves in the situation of the man who, when he heard of a Bank failure, went home in great distress of mind, but when he found after a general search that he had no money at all of that Bank *or of any other*, he felt relieved & happy.

The State of Georgia had no idea of repudiation, although there was an issue of scrip to which there was no way of getting at a knowledge of the amount except to wait the developments of time. For, according to the testimony of Col. [   ], one of the Commissioners, there was no registry of the amounts signed & issued, and, said he with great naivete, "with little or no pay for our time, how could we be expected to trouble ourselves about that?" Under such circumstances, it was almost a miracle of novelty that the State was not ruined. If there was any party in the State that ever longed for repudiation, I never knew it. Yet one had it to fear.

Had we placed our confidence in the public credit and laid by the 8% Bonds that cost us fifty cents on the Dollar, we should have made a good thing of it, as others did. Those who did secure their fortunes in that way had a controlling influence in the politics of the State, about all of which we knew nothing. I have been told that the whole thing was managed by capitalists in Augusta & perhaps in Savannah, who first purchased all they could get of the State Scrip & Bonds, & then becoming the Electors of Gov. Crawford, backed him with financial advice and money to pay this interest until the public works were completed & the State Bonds went up in price.[8] But for those self-seeking financiers, it is possible our fears of repudiation might have been realized; for that reason had we to look for more honesty among politicians in Georgia than in Mississippi or in Pennsylvania?

In the meantime, what did we do for profit? I had little to do with the finances, but I know we had a great many outstanding debts due us in notes in the usual forms of notes & book accounts. We had semi-annual Dividends to make to the Stock Holders, which generally went to the support of their extensive families; for whatever their wealth, all their other resources dried up, or nearly so in that time of commercial distress.

Besides all I have mentioned, we increased the Works every year, more or less, by the addition of new machinery, for which we paid in part by the shipment of such produce as we picked up in the way of trade. As I said before, I never was familiar with the original finances of the Company, although I might have been, for the books were often in my possession, & at times I was myself their keeper.

I never was of a prying disposition & am averse to others prying into my affairs. What my original disposition may have been in this respect, I do not remember. When first setting out in the World, Mr. F. S. Winston gave as a secret of success the advice "to keep my own council."[9] I remembered the advice, & for that became rather secretive of my own affairs, and I came at last to believe in respect to the affairs of others that I could manage my own quite as well without knowing their secrets. I have heard an expert and successful gambler say that he could play his own game best, without knowing the cards of his antagonist; and never failed to defeat one of those swindlers who have the art of knowing his hand by the backs of cards, or by signals of a confederate, because so much knowledge, all at once, of both sides [of] the question will perplex and mislead the rapid judgment of any man. Accordingly, I have never read even a letter of my wife's except at her request; and, as to the organic affairs of the Roswell Co., I doubt if ever I traced back anything in their books, unless I had a call to do so. My impression is that Mr. King had no secrets from me or from the stock holders of the Company. He was a very honest and high-minded man, easy to understand through and through.

I do not know why I retard my narrative to discuss the Profit & Loss of that business, except that it is an interesting reminiscence to me.

My impression is that there was not a large capital of cash paid into the first Factory owned by the Roswell Co., but the profits were turned inward from time to time to Dividends of Stock, supplementary to the cash Dividends. Enough for me to say is that, under my management, the profits were very satisfactory to the owners.[10]

CHAPTER 29

(1840 to 1841)

*T*he want of a reliable currency suggested the idea of a barter-trade with the country for our supplies at the Factory, and that exchange of commodities, once begun, grew and spread in a circle round us until we had the best of the "wagon-trade" from a radius of at least a hundred miles from North round to the West and twenty-five miles in all other directions. I do not think we made the most of it. It had not been contemplated in the original plan of the company, and although the trade of the place did finally make considerable sales of general merchandise from the Store, in addition to the sales of our own manufactures, that branch (the general merchandising) did not expand as it might have done. I speak of this knowingly, since I have re-produced the same system in Arkansas with such improvements as experience suggested.[1]

The original Store for selling goods at Roswell was a small building standing on the point of one of the three ridges of rock and gravel. On the first point next the big road was the Boarding house kept by Mrs. Green.[2] On the next point the Store as I have said, & upon the next point of the ridge a loghouse occupied by the miller Tom Fee & afterwards by his successor Mr. Langley.[3] By the way, I once met a sister of Tom Fee living in Arkansas near the Indian Line. I inquired after Tom, and she said he had made himself rich & lived at some place this side of California. I forget the name of the place, but his making himself rich I did not doubt. It is such men as he was that get riches and hold them in this world. This original store had, in the beginning, about a back-load of calico, marked 40 cents a yard & some Rio Coffee at four pounds to the Dollar. The key of this store was generally in the pocket of Mr. Fraser, whose attention was about equally divided between the store, the work bench, and his duties as an exhorter. Mr. F. was very much of a Scotchman in appearance and in temper. He was angry, I think, every day. He would go into a rage with you for doing a thing and for not doing the same thing, but was a good & honest man for all that.[4]

I remember one night my light went out &, not being able to lay my hand on the matches, I went to his door for permission to walk in & light my candle. He was at prayers with his children (they had no mother living), & I suppose must just have kneeled down. I thought he asked me to walk in, & in I went, but he was on his knees. I retired. I never shall forget the rage he went into. He seemed to consider himself the most outraged man living. What for was hard to tell. He prayed in public often & was not bashful about it. His prayers with his little family were heard and much respected by his neighbors. Somehow the Devil possessed him that I had insulted him, & it is a wonder I did not get into another fisticuffs right then and there. I scarcely think Mr. Fraser ever forgave me that fancied insult. There was never any cordiality between us afterwards &, if I remember rightly, it ended in me having to keep the key of the store and climb the hill to wait upon customers as they came. A bad arrangement certainly, for I had more important business; but it was no longer safe for me to have to go to him for the key of the Store.

The trade of the Store increased, and it was determined to erect for it a more commodious building, send and get a professional store-keeper, expand that branch of the trade, & use the old store for an office. When I was last at Roswell in 1860, the Office was nearly or quite in the same spot, built of Brick and Mud layers. The new store, I laid off myself, fifty yards higher up the hill and quite as far away, I thought, as the business of the place would ever warrant, certainly as far as I felt disposed to walk to and from the Factory. One had to be considerable of a goat to get about that business place. At that time it was very rocky, & from the lower room of the Factory to the upper room of the new store, and from thence round by the gin to the Wool Factory (all of which & more came within my beat), was the means of wearing out a great many pairs of shoes for me. As nearly as I can remember, a pair of shoes such as Boston then made exclusively for Southern trade lasted me on an average about two weeks. At my last visit, still another store of brick had been built three hundred yards further up town, & the late store was converted into a dwelling.

The officials had become numerous, and quite able to ride about the works on horse-back. Not so in my time. Not so in my time. The improvement is for the better, for I worked too hard for my own good & for the good of the business in the long run.

The first regular Store Keeper was David Howell, a Welshman from Utica in N. York. Saving, as they will, quite all he made, he accumulated enough money to go back to Utica & marry a Welsh girl after his own heart, and set up a family grocery store in Utica, expecting the exclusive trade of the Welsh population. Several years afterwards, I found him at the same place, talking the Welsh violently with his customers, but making no money by it. He told me he found that closeness on a trade, which was so good for himself, to be very disagreeable in his customers. He was exactly throwing away his time, neither making or losing by doing business with his fellow countrymen the "Ancient Britains," as they called themselves; & he wanted me again to give him a situation as storekeeper. This I did, and was glad to do at the time. I gave him the situation of Store Keeper at the Curtright Factory in Greene County Georgia, but the engagement did not turn out well for him or for me. I will not go into particulars, at least not in this connexion. It ended in his superseding me as Agent of the Company, and making a complete fizzle of the business. I don't say it was his fault. Probably he was hampered with an ignorant and meddlesome Directory. A machinery I would never be troubled with. I would always take the responsibility of my own measures, right or wrong.[5]

The successor of Mr. Howell as Store Keeper of the Works at Roswell was my Cousin Geo. H. Camp who had married my sister Lucretia. His lungs were in a bad way, so that he wore counter-irritants of Croton Oil, i.e., upon his breasts;[6] and it was thought best by his friends (& I was one of them) that he should settle at the South. I have understood himself to say it was all against his wishes, & he considered himself wronged in the transaction. Consumptive persons seldom understand their own case so as to approve of the resolute measures for their recovery.

If this should ever meet the eye of my Cousin George, whom I esteem for many excellent qualities & love for his kindness to my poor Sister, his wife, I desire to say to him that he wronged me once, at least, in questioning my veracity. He said I had written him, as an inducement for him to come, that figs grew in Georgia, & when he got there he found there were no figs. I did not dispute his statement at the time, but wondered to myself how I came to write to him anything about figs. Probably I was writing playfully, & having seen figs growing somewhere in Georgia mentioned it, & he expected to find them in Roswell. Long ere this he has seen figs in great perfection grown in Georgia, & perhaps in his own garden.

Once for all, about this question of veracity which has several times been raised against me, not only by George but by other matter-of-fact friends of mine. I am a truthful man. I am truthful in these writings, and have always, since they have known me, labored to be truthful; and at times, under the pressure of a morbid conscience, I have been so fanatically veracious that I could not be sure enough & accurate enough in language to meet my own views, & have kept silence when I ought to speak. At other times, I have found myself making statements as Uncle John sometimes would do. "100 acres. 75. 50. 15. 20. 150 or 250 acres some-where along there." The truth is, whatever I may have of intellect, more or less, the imagination predominates, as any man will see by reading the copy of the "Cotton Bug" which I have affixed seq. p. 226 of this volume.[7] I might have been a tolerable poet, had I cultivated that power of the mind, but I did not cultivate it. I suppressed it, because it was unbusinesslike. For all that, I can to this day, by giving way to the imagination, conjure up wonderful sights and sounds. I have read an account of a battle which interested me until I could hear the outcry, see the combatants rush upon each other through the smoke and dust, & could even hear the orders of the general above the roar of cannon and the roll of musketry.

For days and nights after being in a fox-hunt, I could hear the cry of the hounds, sweeter than the music of a fiddle, ringing in my ears. In the silence of the night, I can, when wakeful, call up visions to walk round my bed, as real to my senses as flesh and blood; but thank God! except in times of sickness, I can control all that, & even in sickness & great weakness can distinguish the real from the imaginary, and hold my good sense master of it all. Knowing this weakness or strength of my imagination, I have many years studied to keep it under control. It has served me for good purposes sometimes. In mechanics, it enables me to master a machine or a puzzle without the use of drawings or specifications. In business & affairs it forecasts events, and by holding it down firmly to contemplate the future, instead of lingering over what is past, it has kept alive in me the principle of Hope, when all around me have been in despair; and, if I have when I chose been a leader of other men, it is because of this forecast and buoyancy of my mind, independently of my physical condition.

If any friend, upon reading this, takes up the idea that these memoirs may be partly imaginative likewise, I have to say that he errs as the rest of my friends have often done. He does not understand me. He questions my veracity against logic. It is precisely because I am writing truthfully and intend to hold myself to it, that I make these developments. The hourly language of any man who does not, or any ordinary man who does, labor to express himself with philosophical accuracy may be picked at past unraveling by a very stupid critic or, what is worse, by a friend who has the bad habit of arriving at his knowledge, not by observation & reflection, but by asking questions. When asked questions by a friend (?) that I could see were leading to entangle my veracity, my rule has been to keep silence & let the party make the most of it. A case of this kind I remember.

Soon after my marriage, a temporary coldness arose on the part of Mr. King towards me, about which I gave myself no concern until my brother-in-law Archd. Smith told me it concerned my honor to make some explanations; otherwise, he himself could not be my friend. Now my idea of a "friend" is one who will not assume it to be possible that I can have done a dishonorable thing, & take the responsibility of denying everything of the kind right and left, and against evidence, until my case can be heard. I understood Bro. Archd. to say distinctly that I was in the wrong and would have to repent. He talked to me about religion in the premises. I was nettled. I said nothing. I never made any explanation because it involved the veracity of my young wife, who had simply misunderstood my meaning & said too much about it, as ladies will.

The case was this. We were about setting up house-keeping. Mr. King was going to Savannah & took our commission to make certain purchases. Knives, forks, dishes, & spoons, I suppose. He failed to get all the things called for. My wife, asking the reason why, I told her I did not know; it was certainly not for want of funds of mine in his hands, or words to that effect. She went off with the idea that Mr. King had used my funds for his own purposes, while she had to begin house-keeping lacking things that she had set her heart upon. Soon the story got cross-ways between the families & made a coldness. I never explained it away & was too proud to do so. Bro. Archd. never afterwards had the same confidence in my word, & I returned his bad opinion of me with coldness. It was the beginning of a series of misunderstandings that determined me finally to remove from Roswell.

Had I seen fit to explain, the simple story would have been this, to the best of my recollection. I had an open account on the books of the company, with a large balance due me generally drawing interest.

The times were hard, & Mr. King, not finding it convenient to pay up largely just then, took the liberty of an old & near friend to razor my wife's memorandum of things for the house. As a house-keeper himself, he probably thought he knew what was good for me better than I knew myself. My wife understood me to say that I had actually placed money in Mr. King's hands for the specific purpose of paying for those things & went off with the natural inference that he had done us a wrong, when doubtless he intended to do us a benefit. Certainly, my own vivid imagination had nothing to do in all that matter, nor with Cousin George's figs, nor ever shall get the better of my veracity if I can help it.

Once for all, concerning veracity. I will never stoop to explanations, however easy, with a friend or foe whose foregone conclusion it appears to be that I have erred.[8]

My sister Lucretia Hale, next in age to me, as I before stated, was married to cousin George H. Camp and with him removed to Roswell. She died in childbirth or by premature confinement. The child died also. She was buried in the Roswell burial ground. I do not like to dwell upon that event. It was my third great bereavement, & I bore it badly enough. I was at Mars Hill in Clarke Co., Ga., at the time. The Roswell boys at College in Athens were spending the night at my house. In the night a messenger arrived from Roswell with the sad & unexpected news of my sister's death. The messenger was Cicero Tippens.[9] In order to be at the funeral, I had seventy (70) miles to ride in the cold rain. It was in the month of March, 1845. A wretched, miserable, disconsolate ride which I accomplished, by changing horses, in about 18 hours through the mud, arriving at Bro. Archd. Smith's late before bed time & ready to fall down with fatigue and anxiety. I was too late. My sister had been buried. My interview with Bro. George on that occasion, was a most painful scene. Sister Anne (Mrs. Smith) and Sister Helen endeared themselves to me by their delicate kindness on that occasion. Brother George succeeded me in the office of Asst. Agent of the Roswell Manufacturing Co. In due time he married again. His second wife was a daughter of Henry Atwood Esq. of McIntosh Co. Ga. and he married well for his future happiness in this life.

May he be happy also in the life that is to come! He was a kind husband to my poor sister while she lived.[10]

The administrations, first of Mr. Howell and then of Cousin George Camp in the Store Keeping department of the Roswell Company, lasted out my time; and, as I said before, Cousin George succeeded me in the office of Asst. Agent.

During the same period there were, under my control, several successive superintendents in the Factory. Enos Parker was the first and best.[11] I forget the date of his death. That event left me with both offices on my hands: that of Asst. Agent & Supt. Not disposed to go backwards in the grade of promotion, I worked so much the harder, keeping up as I best could with the duties of both offices until I could get from the North a man capable of filling Mr. Parker's place. Such a man never was found, & would still be hard to find any where. He had set up a standard of Excellence in his department beyond the reach of any other man I could get.

My friends employed & sent to me a man named Cheever. He was a veteran manufacturer. At least I had often heard of him in my early days as making a stir among manufacturing operatives; but whether it was for good or bad, for ability or the reverse of that, I had no clear idea; neither had any one else. He was one of those who can obtain good papers from their late employers, given to get rid of them, which, when carefully read, are found to be so worded as to bear two distinct and opposite meanings.

Upon his first arrival, we thought, judging from his fluent conversation, that in spite of his one eye, & the drop at the end of his nose, we had a fine specimen of the live Yankee. Thin as a June Shad, he seemed to be all springs and wires inside of him, with a motive power somewhere in his frame equal to a small Steam Engine. Up stairs & down stairs would he go as if to his speed he had wings. He was wild with surplus energy & talking. But alas! a perfect fizzle. I stood it, until one morning before day, he set the factory on fire by his own heedlessness, & I never forgave him the fright he gave us, although he extinguished the fire himself with his usual quickness and energy. Cheever was brimful of ingenuity, which imparted itself even to his forms of speech and the stories he told; but he had not one practical or practicable bone in his body.

One other man I got from the North, but not to act as Superintendent, & that was William Ballantine. I have mentioned his name before.[12] He came in the subordinate capacity of Weaver & Dresser. I thought he did very well, & kept up with his own department so long as I remained at Roswell; but years after, when he sought Employment from me at the Long Shoals Factory, I found that he had gone a long way on the road to be a drunkard. The fate, too often, of those who add to a convivial disposition, the gift of singing well in company, as he did.[13] Other Northern men and foreigners I hired and discharged from time to time, but the above are all that I drew from my original acquaintance and connexion in Oneida County. The deaths of Smith & Parker deterred me and my old friends from making overtures either way. It seemed to them that the climate or something else made it dangerous to follow me, & it seemed to me that I ought to look upon that source of Supply for overseers and mechanics as dried up, to make room for the young men of Southern birth who had grown up in the factories, & ought by that time to be able to carry them on.

I had foreseen this state of things, & done what I could to provide against it. There were two sources from which to draw this future supply of Southern manufacturers and mechanics. *First*, the sons of gentlemen rich & poor, & *Second* the factory boys themselves as they grew up under my own eye and developed the qualifications of which I was in quest. I might have added a *Third* class: to wit the Negroes themselves, but at that time prejudices barred my way in that direction, & I will not say whether they were my own prejudices or those of others; perhaps we shared them all around.

First then, the sons of gentlemen rich and poor, educated and ignorant. For them to labor was disreputable. That was the miserable *Esprit de corps* of their class. I have been told by young gentlemen from the low country of Georgia that, until they saw me, they had never seen a white man do a hand's turn of work. Even the overseers and Negro drivers rode on horseback, & were exempt from labor. To such my practical answer was to take off my coat, roll up my sleeves, & go at doing something useful, although I had no occasion to do so. The duties of my post did not require it. When I saw young gentlemen escorting young ladies down the hill to visit the works, I would off jacket in like manner, to show my contempt for their one maxim & standard of gentility. That was before I married. After that event, my wife rather exacted from me more dignity, & I had no right to go counter to all her Southern prejudices.

But bravely as I played the blunt mechanic, when I was a young fellow, it was sometimes a bitter pill to feel that I was looked upon with contempt by young gentlemen & ladies to whom I was conscious of being quite equal in point of birth, education and refinement. I did it, however, from a sense of duty. I did it to vindicate the fashion of my native town, where every young man of every station is forced by public opinion to "hang out his shingle"—*i.e.*, to have some visible means of livelihood in case of future reverses of fortune. I was too proud to sink the shop in order to go into polite society. I was resolved that Southern society should receive me on equal terms as a scientific mechanic, or not at all. And if not at all, so much the better for me; it would leave me the more leisure to improve my mind.

Moreover, I considered that I had "a calling to fulfill" & that was, as I have before stated, to promote a system of Southern Manufactures, which I hoped would, in the course of time, reconcile Southern with Northern interests, & neutralize the efforts of mad and ultra politicians on both sides to use the general government as a tool to legislate for a class, or for a section against the interests of the whole, and I thought if I could induce the sons of gentlemen to accept my views of the dignity of labor, so much the better for them; if not, I must bring forward the low class of white people & make men of them.[14]

With this in view, as before stated, I labored with my own hands, on such occasions as I thought called for an example. I wrote articles for the public prints over a *nom de plume*, & I was an attentive correspondent with all who wrote me on the subject of Manufacturing, imparting freely, without remuneration, information it had cost me time & money to obtain. In all this I am quite sure I had no aspirations except to be useful. I had not an idea as yet of ever leaving Roswell to push my fortunes elsewhere, and in my relations to the Roswell Co. never put myself in the posture of demanding a more full remuneration for my services. Whether I performed the full duties of one, two, three, or four offices, as was always the case more or less, it was all the same as to pay. During my first year at Roswell, that Company had, upon the motion of old Mr. Roswell King, who was not my friend (at least he did not speak to me when we met), advanced my salary to $1,000 a year besides my board. After that, so long as I remained, my warm friends did not voluntarily add to that, & I was too proud to ask it. One gift I had from Mr. Barrington King in person, & that was a building lot, which at my leaving I returned to him at the nominal price of $100.00. I am not a man of small grievances. I despise the character. But I have to reveal things as they were in order to account for me finally leaving Roswell, when my friends thought I had better stayed, and perhaps I had. I will tell things as they occur to my mind, in order that when, in the progress of my story, the time arrives for me to leave Roswell, the reader may know as much as I did, about my reasons for so doing.

I was speaking of my rather Quixotic attempt to break down by example, by writing for the public, & by private correspondence, the Southern prejudice against labor. And here let me remark, as a paradox of civilization, that, ungenteel as it may have been for the Southern gentleman to labor with his hands, the Southern ladies of Roswell were the most laborious housekeepers I had ever known. The more servants they had, the greater their Augean labors of housekeeping seemed to be. No slavery equal to the bondage of a faithful mistress of many faithful servants. O! the life long agony of house-keeping! That basket of jingling keys, & that scolding tongue!

Whether it was through my influence and example, or owing to the force of circumstances, I will not undertake to say, but finally several of the sons of Barrington King, Esq., adopted my views. Charles, the oldest, would come to me as soon as school had closed for the day, & work in the factory. He was a very gentlemanly boy, and had a natural turn for mechanics. I was for a time in hopes I had found a disciple, but he went away to college, forgot the Factory, & concluded to study Theology & become a minister of the Presbyterian Church. Of course if I had possessed the right to a voice in the matter, I should not have taken the responsibility to oppose the course he pursued, but I always thought, and still think, that in him a first rate manufacturer was spoiled. And when I reflect upon the field of usefulness that a manufacturer, who is a religious man, has all round him every day, I more than doubt whether Chas. B. King would not have done more good as a manufacturer than as a preacher of the Gospel. He possessed a firmness & determination which would have served an excellent purpose as master of many hands, but could not be acceptable in the pastor of a Church.[15] James King went away and learned the Manufacturing business at the fountain head of our style of spinning, Paterson, N.J. Tom King learned affairs in the office & subsequently became partner with his brother James in a new Woolen factory at Roswell.[16]

Young Barrington King went North to learn ship-building. Others of that large family of boys finally learned different departments of trade and affairs, so that by this time I doubt not there are enough of them in case of need to continue all the business of that place without any professional aid from outside the concern.[17]

Rev. Mr. Pratt, our beloved pastor, whose picture hangs before me as I write, raised his boys to work, all of them, & himself set the example. He was like myself a Northern man married to a Southern lady, & the greater portion of his life resident at the South.[18] This is, I think the very best cross of the *Genus Americanus* yet discovered. Nearly all that noble race, the original colonists of Roswell, were of that kind of stock. Barrington King was of Northern descent by his father's side. All the wires & energy in him came that way. Old Mr. Dunwody told me that his ancestors came out with the Dorchester Colony first to Carolina and then to Liberty

County. And even those gentlemen who would have spurned the idea of N. England descent, could not run their lineage far back without coming up with the imported stock, and generally of the Puritan order at that.[19]

Several of the Dunwody boys turned their attention to trade and mechanical affairs, and without knowing all the particulars, I venture to say that it is alone those young men in all this colony who deviated from the traditions of their class and went to work, and persevered in the same, who now are most useful in the commonwealth, & the most comfortable in their private circumstances.[20]

Besides those I have named, I remember only two young gentlemen from any part of Georgia who turned their attentions seriously to mechanical pursuits. One was a son of Benj. Stiles Esq. of Savannah & the other a son of the Hon. Andrew J. Miller of Augusta. But all these aimed to be leaders themselves, & I, as a manager, could not reasonably hope to make any of them available in any subordinate relation to me, or that they would submit to an apprenticeship of seven years, as I had done.

I had therefore to look among the rank and file of my own operatives for young men to be my future mechanics and overseers. I never failed to make a good workman of a smart Negro, first having a care to select my man. Negroes have the manipulation for anything the most difficult. They barberize & they fiddle better than white people with the same opportunities, but they are, the smartest of them, puzzle-headed, & must have their orders given to them one at a time. The whole secret of getting along with Negroes, even those who have the reputation of being unmanageable, is to give orders of but one idea at a time & make sure that they understand them. Never, never get into a rage; be strictly just to them and do as you have promised, being careful, of course, of what you promise. I have never failed to get on well with Negro men about the works, and I have had them sent to me who were given over as unmanageable on the plantation. Whipping I do not believe in, & should never be inflicted upon a Negro except for offenses that would send a white man to prison. But Negro men, however efficient, could not be placed in situations of responsibility, even among Negro hands.

Looking for trustworthy men among the lower class of white people at the South, I have been only tolerably successful. Ability enough I have found—practicable ability of the very highest style. I could find men & boys in the ranks whose natural powers of mind made me ashamed of myself. But the lack of early education & religious training diluted and vitiated the whole. I had been raised to look for gratitude and fidelity in return for favors shown. I found that I must not even look for a "thank you, sir." I had been accustomed to see a working man, once in my debt, stay with me certainly & work it out; I found the sure way to lose a valuable man forever was to loan him money. A difference between men I had been used to see settled by logic, or an arbitration, or a law-suit, or a fair fist-fight, & then shake hands and be better friends than ever. But I found that a man, once offended, must take the sulks and never forgive. If it came to blows, I must look out for a knife between my ribs. If it was a debate, the everlasting sharp, long devilish knife was ready open under pretense of picking the teeth or whittling a stick. If not a knife, then it was a "Derringer" or a "Colt" pistol. As to ever making an ignorant man understand anything against his interests or against his fore-gone determination, it was a hopeless case. I found not a little of all this among the Gold-digging, dirt-eating crackers in Georgia; and what I did not encounter in those early days in Georgia, I learned to a certainty during these latter days in Arkansas.

And yet I have worried through. I had to "make out" with mill wrights who denied the first principles of hydraulics & hydrostatics, or the strength of materials. With engineers who treated steam as a mystery. With managers who expected me to execute their private revenge against each other & against the hands. With hands who looked upon their employer as their natural enemy, & no kindness could ever satisfy them to the contrary, and all this in communities sympathizing always, & rendering their verdict for the employed against the employer: — the poor against the rich. Truly he who sets out to be leader in new enterprises running counter to the genius, & cutting across the prejudices of a people — and that twenty years ahead of his time — has an arduous life!

I said I had worried through. Alas! No man knows about that until he gets clean through. Here have I struggled through reverses & prosperity, often against hope, looking forward to the time when I could retire from active life with a competency sufficient for old age. And here am I let down in the midst of this dreadful war, shut out from intercourse with my kindred, & threatened with the loss of all that is valuable except honor, and all for no fault of mine, at least for no sin against my fellow man or against the State. Such is life.

CHAPTER 30

1842 to 1845

*T*he first Cotton Factory erected in the State of Georgia was during the Embargo or War of 1812 erected by the father of Wm. Gregg of Charleston So. Ca. who himself, carrying out the tradition of his family, has in late years become the distinguished founder of the extensive works at Graniteville in South Carolina.[1]

I think Mr. Wm. Gregg himself told me that his father's factory was a small affair, on the Towallagee River in Henry County, not far from the town of McDonough.[2] When I purchased the Mars Hill Factory in Clarke County, Ga., I was told that some of the irons about the place had formed part of the running gear of that old Factory. If I mistake not, the water-wheel shaft of white oak, with the wing-gudgions and bands firmly secured, & sound as they ever were, Mr. Garwood told me he had recovered from the site of that old factory.[3] If so, Mr. Gregg's father was a thoroughgoing man with his mill-wright work, & a good judge of materials.

This reminds me that I have recently read in some engineering book directions for obtaining durable oak timber. The writer says go to low grounds & rich lands to select your timber. His advice does not accord with my experience in the Southern climate. The most durable white-oak timbers will be found growing on an elevation in an old field of poor and worn out soil.

When I arrived in Georgia, there were about ten & perhaps twelve manufactories of Cotton & Wool in all the State.[4] These were on a small scale generally, and far behind the times in the style of their machinery. Under the old protective Tariffs, that small and slow way of doing things might remunerate the owners, but not benefit the public. Since the violent discussions of the question of Protection, duties on foreign goods had been reduced, with the prospect of still further reduction; so that, in order to live, the American manufacturer had to cast about him for means to increase his works & improve his machinery. In this race for improvement (which in manufacturing parlance means anything that tends to reduce the cost of production), the Northern men, especially those of N. England, were ahead of all others. Improvements traveled slowly from the North to the South. The Southerner is the best manager of manual labor in the World. The Northern man aims to arrive at his results by means of contrivances and machinery. In the matter of manufacturing, which as yet formed no part of the Southern System of things, it seemed that those who had embarked their capital in that line at the South had a mind to lose what they had invested & give it up.

Free trade would be their ruin, and free trade, was the manifest tendency of things. In a few years, the great West, given to agriculture & not a manufacturing Country, might be expected to cast its influence in favor of free-trade. Many Southern politicians glowered menacingly upon the infant manufacturers at the South as a small cloud that might some day overcast the sky and call on them for *protection*, and protection was a hateful word to them.

Such was the state of things when I arrived in Georgia. The Erection at that conjuncture of the New Factory at Roswell, its size larger than any built before, its machinery of the latest improvements, its management on humane and Christian principles, and its great success, formed an era from which others took a fresh start. In a few years new Factories were erected of constantly increasing size, larger capital & improved machinery, until about the year 1850 I was able to count on my fingers fifty manufacturing establishments of Cotton & Wool in the State of Georgia, some of which were of the very largest capacity for business.[5] Another reduction of the Tariff came. I believe it was in 1846.[6] The demand for improvements in machinery, in order to meet the reduction of prices and drive back the invasion of British goods, stimulated to the highest degree the inventive powers of Northern machinists. With this view a fair was held in Washington City, under the eye of government but at the Expense of American Manufacturers. If the object of that fair was to obtain the sympathy and the protection of the politicians in Congress, it signally failed & produced the opposite effect. They came to the dry conclusion that so much smartness, stimulated by adversity, could not fail in the long run to outstrip the artisans of the old world at an even race, with no protection. And a Tariff for revenue only was decided upon, with this mental reservation among New England men: that they would bide their time and ride into power again on the Abolition question, which was invented as an antidote against the Western proclivity to affiliate with the South on the question of Free Trade.

In the mean time, mechanical improvements came in like a yearly revolution. Sometimes it became a positive benefit to the owners of a Factory if their old works burned to the ground, making room for something new. There were not wanting cases under partial Insurance where there were well-grounded suspicions of foul play on the part of owners. Our original

Roswell Factory, ere five years were past, found itself growing old, and plodding on in the old way with profits yearly becoming less, in spite of hard work & increasing economy. The Rail Roads had been completed, bringing in cheap goods, & carrying the farmer a pleasant ride to a market on the Seaboard.[7] Factories had been erected between us and the frontier, cutting off our wagon trade. We had no longer any local advantages whatever, & we had nothing we could do with our surplus products but throw them upon the large markets to be sold on their merits in comparison with the greatest and the best of domestic manufactures, and foreign importation.

Note: About this time I received from the American Institute at N. York City, the Silver Medal for the best specimen of cotton yarn.[8]

Right here we ought to have stopped and re-juvenated the old Roswell factory; or, what would have been better, we ought to have gradually adopted genuine improvements as they appeared, so keeping our Works up with the times. We did from time to time increase our works, which is one way, but not always the best way, to diminish the cost of production; but all we did was over & over again in the old way. Herein I erred. My practical objection to ingenious men had gradually & imperceptibly taken in my head against ingenious things, finally amounting to a chronic aversion against things new and improved, & a love for what was older. In a word, my usefulness as a manufacturer was drawing to an end, until such time as I should be brought by reverses and losses to set myself right by a review of the causes leading thereto. Of course I did not see all this at the time. Neither did my employers see it, but it was not intended by Providence that the cost of my future education would fall upon the Roswell Company. So I was led, by ways imperceptible, to purchase a small factory in Clarke Co. Ga. which was made up of scraps of machinery picked up here and there, & some of it, as I before stated, so very old as to have belonged to the first factory ever started in the state, so far back as 1812. Here was a perfect museum of old things for me to flourish among, at my own private cost! And one would have supposed it must have been my ruin. But no, such is the virtue of hard work, and close attention to business that in less than six months I had so raised the reputation of that establishment, that I was able to sell it for twice what I gave for it, and with the Sale came proposals to erect extensive works for a wealthy company in the adjoining county.[9]

Here then I had a new start. With a handsome fortune of my own obtained by honest means, a reputation of my own with not a stain. I could grasp in all the improvements of machinery; I could add to my own reputation & secure the fortunes of my company. The tide of fortune was with me. Did I profit by it? We shall see.

But in the lapse of those five or six years past, many things took place which will carry me back in my story to pick them up. I will change this worn out steel pen for a new one, in order to announce the important event of my marriage, which deserves also to begin a new chapter of this manuscript.

CHAPTER 31

I was married in July 1841 to Miss Elizabeth Pye Magill and a good wife she has been for me. Under all the circumstances a very good wife indeed for me.[1]

She was born in the town of St. Mary's, the South Eastern corner of Georgia & on the confines of Florida. Her father was a native of Middletown in the State of Connecticut, so that her ancestors and mine, at least by her father's side, came from within a few miles of each other in the same N. England state. Her mother was named Zubly—Eliza Zubly. She was a native of the Spanish possession, having been born at St. Augustine, before the territory of Florida was ceded by Spain to the United States.

Her father, David Zubly, was a planter on one of the Bahama Islands (Cat Island or San Salvador, the same that Columbus first discovered), & she was partly schooled at Nassau in the Island of New Providence, partly at Savannah, where her sister, who had married the father of Archd. Smith (by name Arch. Smith) resided.[2] At Savannah she was married to the father of my wife.[3]

Her Grandfather, the great-grandfather of my wife, was John Joachim Zubly, D.D., of the University of Halle in Germany. He was a native of Appenzell in Switzerland on the confines of Austria. Fitted by sympathy and education to be useful among the Saltzburgers who immigrated under the auspices of the Georgia Company, he came and was the founder of the Independent Church in Savannah.

The mixed character of that early population in and about Savannah required that he should preach in three different languages: *viz.*, the English, German, and French, which he did, as his manuscripts in possession of the family show. Early in the American Revolution, he was sent, much against his own judgment, to represent the Colony in the Continental Congress. There he found himself out of place, and retired under some unpleasantness, which however did not touch his integrity as a preacher of the gospel. He died and was buried in Savannah.[4] A street in the city of Savannah is named for him, and his descendants have always been respectably & even highly connected. I married one of them myself! We two have had no children, whereat we are content when we reflect that our children, if we had any, would now be of ages to be involved in this dreadful war.[5]

CHAPTER 32

Intended to be rather Anecdotical

Old Mr. Roswell King died within two or three years after I began at Roswell, at a very advanced age, considering his vigor.[1] When I first knew him, he was still quite an active man, had a great many good ideas, & was youthful in his feelings. He had been an adventurous man, bore marks of old wounds about his person, and his face was spotted with blue powder marks. He had been blown up by a blast in a gold mine. For a long time he did not speak to me because I had differed from him in some opinion. He was opinionated, & perhaps I myself was no less so. I had reason, all the time, to think he bore me no ill will—but the contrary. He was by no means a Christian man, at that time, but he was possessed of generous impulses. Of Northern birth & education, he told me that he was, I think, super-cargo of a vessel lying in some port in the Island of Hayti, at the time of the great insurrection in 179– and barely escaped with his life.[2] The horrors he witnessed on that occasion caused him afterwards to be strict but just in his government of Negroes. Subsequently, he was for many years steward over the great Estate of Pierce Butler, which lay near the mouth of the Altamaha River on the Sea Coast of Georgia. He was a very successful manager of that large force of Negroes, & his son Roswell after him, extricating the estate from a load of old debt.[3] The Butlers were absentee proprietors, lived in the City of Philadelphia and probably had other resources to back their style of living, for I understood that before Mr. King's time, the Negro property and plantation in Georgia ran them in debt. Pierce Butler was the lineal descendent of the Dukes of Ormond, attainted long ago and banished from Ireland for their politics.

Pierce Butler, the Son, was the husband of the play actress Fanny Kemble, & thereby is supposed to have come under petticoat government.[4] Occasionally in the winter season Mrs. Fanny Kemble Butler spent a short

*"Roswell in the rough. First view of Mr. Roswell King from near 'Lover's Rock'
(1835)." The first of six pencil sketches of early Roswell life by Henry Merrell.
These sketches were found among the Smith papers, separate from his
manuscripts and bound in a brown wrapper labeled "Uncle Henry's
Sketchbook." Roswell King was the founder of the "colony," and it was named
after him.*

*"Roswell. 1 Mile." Merrell's caption reads, "The straight forwards, main direct
public road takes you right thar."*

"Digging Major Bulloch's gold 'On Sheers.'" James Stephen Bulloch's family, along with the Archibald Smith family, was one of the six founding families of Roswell.

"Mr. King trades a horse for a 40-acre lot of land and gets the worst of the bargain." Roswell King squats on his haunches to the left.

"The first season at Roswell. Boarding out." The feast appears to be in the King household before its move in 1839 to the site of Barrington Hall.

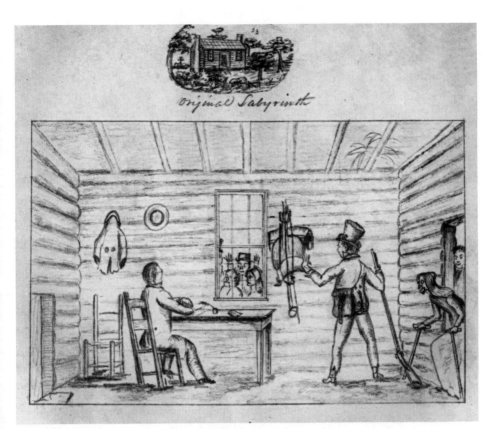

"The first glass window, greatly admired by the natives." Roswell King sits
being admired inside the *"original labyrinth"* (inset above) or *"the castle,"* the
first home of the Kings in Roswell.

time on the Estate, & came to Church alone in her cypress dug-out, rowed by her boat's crew of Negroes, & managing the boat herself. On those occasions she was dressed rather theatrically in red velvet, & carried herself queenly.

I never heard that her husband said anything, or was thought to be of any consequence in her presence.

I never knew much about Old Mr. Roswell King's affairs. He had too many projects to be a very fortunate manager of his own private interests. In forecasting, he was ten years ahead of his contemporaries. The title of a good deal of property was in him. I remember myself, signing a bond for $20,000 to accommodate his son B. King in saving some real estate in the City of Darien. Probably he lost money by the decline in the value of real estate in and about Darien, for the construction of the Central Rail road carried to Savannah the trade that had formerly been floated by the waters of the Altamaha river to the wharves and warehouses of Darien. I think also I remember hearing that he lost money by the failure of the house of R. & W. King in Savannah.

Note: I should have said that it was understood that Mrs. Roswell King, the mother of Barrington and others, was in her lifetime a very superior lady and gave character to her family. I never saw her. She died before my time at Roswell.[5]

The same remarks are due to the memory of my wife's mother.

I have said that I over-worked myself at the Roswell Factory. I did so to the damage of my health & spirits, until I have since had no pleasure in re-visiting the place, & always get away from it as soon as I can. I cannot tell exactly why. I had no need to do so, but I did not give myself enough time to sleep, and constant anxiety about the business preyed upon my mind, until some times a dark cloud would settle upon my spirits, & I would suffer apprehensions of Evil, when at the same time my good sense told me there was nothing to be apprehended.

Literally all my powers, more or less, were thrown into my business, so that I had no wit or relish left for anything else. If I went into society, I had no conversation & no relish for it, but hurried back to my writing desk. On the Sabbath in Church, I either slept from exhaustion, or my mind wandered so that I got no good out of the sermon. I read some, but not in a solid or substantial way, and enjoyed music as I enjoyed food, in a fatigued and dyspeptic way. And I think now if I were to revisit Roswell, such is the power of old associations that I should be oppressed with the same sense of fatigue & indigestion.

When Cousin George Camp first came to Roswell, he brought with him my poor sister Lucretia, his bride.[6] They sailed from N. York for Charleston or Savannah in the New Ship "Catherine": Capt. Berry. It proved to be a stormy time, and they were driven out to sea after coming nearly into port. The passage between the two ports lasted twenty days & was very uncomfortable to them. All this time I was daily and hourly looking anxiously up the road for their arrival at Roswell. It made me sick. I was too proud to talk with anyone much about my sorrow. My heart turned into stone. I was sulky. All the joy I had promised myself was turned into bitter sorrow. So low down did my spirits sink that I had no spring or reaction left, and when they did come at last, I positively cannot say that I had any pleasure, "my heart was dead within me." So that my sister asked me if it was possible I was not glad to see her!!

If I was called upon to give reasons for thus over-working myself in the service of the Roswell Manufacturing Company, I might say briefly, that it was my natural disposition, or I might go further and say that my unlucky position in the business required it, and finally that my responsibilities begat work, & my industry begat promotion, & promotion begat work again until my place became untenable even to myself; & I had, so it seemed to me, no remedy but to throw up all my offices at once and leave. Mr. Parker's efficiency in the Factory left me free while he lived to take upon myself the duties first of store-keeper, then of book-keeper, & then — as Mr. B. King was opening new lands & building for himself, & at the same time was sometimes about winding up his low country affairs — the correspondence, & sometimes the whole duties of the Agent devolved upon me. As I have said before, the office of Assistant Agent was created to cover my case, & I accepted it quite gladly as a promotion, although it brought me no increase of salary.[7] The death of Poor Parker brought the care of the machinery back in my hands; at the same time I had no idea of going back in the grade of promotion, & I undertook to do it all. Mr. King, more thoughtful than I, insisted upon having a book keeper, Mr. Proudfoot, even before the death of Parker.[8] I finally saw that there was no hope of a permanent promotion to the Agency, or even that I could maintain myself in the position of Asst. Agent. There were too many Cadets of the wealthy families coming forward who would be likely to fill the offices & leave me the work, so I thought. Mr. King was not himself a man to surrender his office to any one. I could not go up. I must go down. For three months together, Mr. K. would leave nearly all the business to me, until at last I would of necessity assume responsibilities that belonged to him. Then suddenly he would drop everything else & establish himself in the office, check my work, ask searching questions with the tone & manner of an injured man, & seemed to be bursting with suspicions of something wrong. Then he would attend to all the details of current business until, satisfied in his own mind that all was right, he would subside & go leaving the work to me again.

Had not I honored the man in my heart, I never would have put up with such whims the first time. As it was, we several times came to high words. I have often, without thinking, blamed myself for leaving Roswell, & have oftener been blamed by others; but when I review the whole ground, & remembering that I had honest aspirations after the highest official grade attainable in my profession, I do not see that there was anything for me that I could do but leave the place. What I have before stated about my impracticability in the matter of improved machinery. I am satisfied, as I before stated, that my leaving at the time I did was a good thing for the Roswell Company.

Barrington King, Esq., was very much of a man and gentleman. Every thing about him was firm and steady like his hand-writing. He ruled his white family and his servants absolutely, but with dignity & a pleasant humor.

I have no doubt I had to encounter the roughest side of his character, for at the factory he was acting as agent for others, and with a severe idea of his duty. He used to say we were too much alike in temper, ever to agree entirely. I would be glad to think I ever was as much of a gentleman & as brave a man as he.[9]

Mrs. Barrington King was born a "Nephew," but by blood somehow was also a McIntosh.[10] It was her father who founded the "Nephew Scholarship" of the Theological Seminary at Columbia, So. Car. B. King was a trustee of that Seminary. I have before stated that Marvin Winston married a McIntosh. Mrs. Winston was a niece or cousin of Mrs. King. When I was a boy, Mr. Winston brought his Southern bride to my mother's house in Utica.

She had a brother, Lachlan McIntosh, who, being at the North that same season, came to our house occasionally to visit his sister.[11] But Lack got drunk & had fits, & gave his sister great uneasiness. He was at that time a fine-looking fellow, & the ladies pronounced him a gentleman. But that a gentleman should get drunk & be as fond as he was of the double-barrel gun & a horse served as a wonderment to us people of steady habits.

After I had been at Roswell several years, poor Lack came there to visit & out-stayed his welcome. He was a ruined, broken-down man & had become prematurely old. Still subject to epileptic fits, he was sometimes quite wild and crazy, but generally his derangements assumed the jealous & sulky type.

One day in the store he sat as usual by the stove scolding and watching all that passed, but saying nothing, when suddenly he cleared the counter at a bound, seized a vial of laudanum, struck off the neck with the blade of his knife, as he had often in his time broached a bottle of Champagne wine, & drank off the contents before anyone could get to him. Cous. George was at the writing desk, & seeing at a glance the whole transaction, he ran to the rescue, & jumping upon Lack's head and shoulders, got his head down and shook him well to try to shake the dose out of him; but this novel remedy failing of success, the would-be suicide was carried to the house and laid on the sofa to go to sleep and die. But thanks to the weakness of Tom Barrett's laudanum, the patient could neither go to sleep nor die at that time, but lived until one day he fell into the fire while in one of his fits & was burned to death. But his death did not happen in Roswell.

Some time after Lack's attempt at suicide, Mr. King, at whose house he was a guest, being absent in the low country, Lack got into one of his ways and created a panic among the women & children. That seemed to be his crazy pleasure. Mrs. King sent for me as the one most likely next to her husband, who was absent, to have influence over "Mack," either through respect or fear. Upon going to the house, I found that he had flourished a good deal with his knife, & among other exploits had begun cutting up the furniture. The servants had turned the key on him, & he was thus shut up in a room. Mrs. King required that I should take the crazy man and carry him somewhere, anywhere, so she never should see him again. I did not half like the part assigned to me. I could look for no assistance from the servants; they were scared already. It was hardly a fair fight for me alone to capture an armed man stronger than myself, & do it in a spirit of kindness and forbearance. The fact is, I was a little scared myself. I had heard so much about the poor fellow's savage disposition at such times. But a man does not like to seem to be afraid of anything where women are concerned; so I put a good face on the matter & quietly but firmly unlocked the door and stepped into the room where he was. There he sat on the bed with his long knife open in his hand, just as I expected. I went in with an air as though I had just dropped in to see him, & that was all. "What do you want?" "I want you to go with me." Keeping his eye. "I have a wagon about starting for the head of the Rail-Road at Madison, & you are to go back down the country." I knew well that with a crazy man my best course was to defeat his cunning by going directly to the point. "How much money can I have for my expenses?" "Your expenses on the cars will be paid by the wagoner, & you shall have a draft on our Factor in Augusta for any reasonable amount besides." "Make it —— Hundred Dollars, & I go." "It shall be made as you say, —— Hundred Dollars."

"When?" "I am ready." & so we went, he following me very quietly and apparently afraid I would forget or delay the arrangements for starting. I got him off, & he was very proud of his draft for —— Hundred Dollars. But I had no idea of trusting him with money which he would have spent all on one spree, & then been back again in a few weeks. By mail I wrote the Factor in Augusta not to pay the draft but only Lack's travelling expenses to our Factor in Savannah. It happened that Mr. King himself was in Augusta when McIntosh arrived with his famous draft. How he managed I forget, but we were never troubled again with poor Lack. Some of the casuists thought I did wrong in putting even a crazy man off with a bogus draft. I took care to promise him no money. He had no money due him. I did not think it would have been more conscientious in me to have had a violent struggle with him & sent him off by force, even if I had succeeded in getting rid of him in that way. That transaction never troubled my conscience, yet I have for obvious reasons generally avoided that style of doing things, except as a "war measure," if I may so call it.

At the first, the Roswell people, having brought with them their low country ways, their cooks, & table furniture, enjoyed a round or two of mutual entertainments. In time, however, they fell into hum-drum ways & gave dinner parties only during Christmas times, and at the arrival of visitors whom they wished to distinguish. In the social pleasures of the first settlers I had my full share—quite as much so as I had leisure to enjoy. In truth I had not the leisure. I was in more need of rest & sleep. I remember once I accepted an invitation to dine with Old Mr. Dunwody, & it was to be quite a dinner; but I forgot all about it.[12] It was some time after that before I got another invitation to dine at his house, probably not until I had me a wife to remind me of my engagements.

Mr. Dunwody gave a grand wedding to his daughter, who was married the first time at his farmhouse, before he had built a residence in town. The piazzas were enclosed with sheets or tent cloths, and in them the supper tables were elaborately laid out, and lighted brilliantly. The house— thus converted into a wall-tent & lighted up among the trees, with crowds of admiring Negroes without & guests flitting back and forth within— was an enchanting scene. A few nights afterwards a wedding party was given by Major Bulloch at his farm house.[13] A grand time we had to be sure! Everybody was there, & the ladies as fine as could be; but when the time came to disperse and go home, the appearance of things changed. It was very late. The night was pitchy dark & cloudy. The roads at that time were too stumpy for carriages by night. The horses stood ready-saddled for gentlemen and ladies, each held by a Negro, and a huge blazing fire of light-wood illuminated the whole with a red glare very picturesque and all that. I had already become interested in the young lady who has since become my wife. To her & to her sister I aimed to give special attention, but directly we rode away into the darkness, there was no distinguishing one from another in the cavalcade.[14] On we went, jostling each other in the dark, until by the time we had ridden a mile and had arrived opposite Mr. Dunwody's farm house, it was determined that the ladies should turn in there and remain until morning while the gentlemen rode home as best they could.

Away we went tearing. I could not hold in my horse at all, and the other young fellows were not disposed to be outridden by me. Our pace increased. What could possess the whole party, horses as well as men, to ride at such a rate down hill and up, over stumps and through mud holes! However, after the ride of three miles we all got home safely. Turning my horse over to George, I went into the house, but before I could get my boots off, I heard him call, "Massa, looka here!" I went out. "Jes' look a hea, Massa. You done rode all the way wid de bridle bit hangin loose, so!" Sure enough! In the dark, & in the hurry of saddling so many horses, the servants at the farm had failed to get the bit into the mouth of my horse, & I had ridden him with only the strap across his nose to govern him by; and he was by no means a gentle horse to ride. To the sagacity of the horse under the good providence of God alone, I owed my safety that time, & not to any skill of mine; & when was it ever otherwise?[15]

CHAPTER 33

I have said that, while organizing the business of the Roswell Company, it was not easy to decide what we ought to do with our products, over and above what we disposed of in the way of barter and exchange for supplies. We could have sold millions on credit & had not a cent for collections, after deducting the expense of collections. There was a law of Georgia making it a penal offense for commission agents to sell property & fail to pay over the proceeds to the owner; and, thinking to profit by that law, we declined generally to sell on credit, but placed our goods in the hands of the parties for sale on commission. Those commission agents of ours were not only country merchants, but any old settler who happened to live at a cross road or near an election precinct and had a brick or stone chimney to the house, or the neighborhood title of Colonel, Major, or Esquire.

Like everything else we undertook, this system, once decided on, was followed up with vigor until we had depots of our goods, at our own risk, almost everywhere, extending even into the confines of Alabama and Tennessee. It was a pernicious system, as one can now see, but we could not see it in that light at the time. It absorbed our floating capital, so that we had to borrow dividends from our stock-holders, sometimes from others, in order to get on. If our capital could have been kept in hand, & applied to the improvement of our works, the net results would have been larger & more substantial in the long run. Those agencies, scattered all about, created the necessity of a new office: that of travelling agent. That post was filled by John Dunwody, Jr., & often I had long journeys to take myself, on horseback, running after bad debts, to the neglect of more important matters; for bad debts they were.[1]

The penalty of the law never helped us to our own in a single instance that I remember. It was designed, like most of the laws, to be good for the planters as a class, against others, and was not intended to work both ways; so that no neighborhood or County jury would have given us a verdict, unless it might have been against some obnoxious person whom they wanted to be rid of for some unproven offense against their own interests. It must be something about a Hog or marking the wrong yearling; otherwise, the defendant would come off with flying colors. All the uncurrent money in the country was sure to flow towards our coffers. Did a Bank fail flat, our next collection round would be very unusually successful in that particular kind of notes. Was there any misfortune anywhere—a fire, a flood, a "harricane"—anything that ever befalls, we were in the way of it all.

By means of these collecting tours, I came to know the country and to be better known in return. Seeing so many people both on my rounds and at the Factory, I could not remember them all, but all remembered me.

I met with hearty welcome in the most out-of-the-way places, & from the poorest folk. The hardships of those journeys were considerable, but probably served as a wholesome relaxation for mind and body. Almost everywhere, even in log houses where the whole of the furniture could have been hauled away at one load of an ox-wagon, I could find the Yankee clock, & always dead & would run no more. Being such a wonderful machinery man, in their opinion, I could certainly fix the clocks; & so I could, but I grew tired of that, & after a hard day's ride, was careful not to say clock to anyone. All that ailed their clocks, generally, was that they were out of plumb.

It was painful to hear the prices they had paid for those clocks. I felt sorry for the meanness of Yankee clock peddlers. I heard of one who, finding no place in the little log cabin for the clock, screwed it to a tree in the open air, and having secured his pay, went off and left it there to be ruined by the next fall of rain.

The tin peddlers had likewise left a bad name behind them. Map & book peddlers in the same way; & such books! The Yankee clock was really a good machine at its original cost in the North, which was probably $5.00; but the peddlers made it cost the poor back-woodsman as much money as he could hope to lay by in six months or even a year. After all, the poor man could tell the probable time of day better without a clock; his water tasted to him better in a gourd than when drunk from a tin cup; the map of the United States was all confusion to him; he could take his course through the woods to any place he was ever likely to visit. & as to books! No labor so severe as that of reading them. It almost made me think meanly of myself, being a northern man, to hear how honestly they could curse the Yankees. I never took advantage of their ignorance to wrong any of them, but I knew others that did. One of the Bradleys of Whitesboro in the state of N. York, who had returned from the South a rich man, told me as a smart thing, & a thing to be laughed about, that he, or some other tin-peddler that he had to do with, once stopped overnight with a simple-hearted family & sold them a tin oven, receiving in payment, say Two Hundred Dollars. But soon after leaving in the morning, he looked back & saw a number of neighbors ride to the house on horse-back and go in.

Thinking that certainly, among so many, someone would be sure to detect the fraud & pursue him, he determined to put a bold face upon the matter and go back. Back he went in great apparent haste, with anxiety upon his countenance, & told them he had hurried back to rectify a bad mistake. But seeing directly that the company were as ignorant as he could wish, & had no ill will to him, he told them that he had sold the wrong size by mistake. It was a smaller size that was priced $200.00, & he must have $25.00 more for that one or be allowed to make the exchange; and he got the $25.00 more.

The greatest imposition of all was in shoes, and in short weights and measures. The Boston-made shoes, were really too bad. Short weights and measures, when understood, are compensated by the price, but shoes made on purpose to wear out in a month and make room for the sale of more, rendered leather scarce and high, so that there could be no compensation in the price; beside that, the sacrifice of health & life among poor people & Negroes wearing shoes that burst open and were neither warm nor dry in winter must have been very great, & may be set down as one of the causes of this War. The great Southern dislike towards Yankees has not been a groundless and unreasonable prejudice as many believe, and the events of this war will doubtless aggravate the same into a hatred as enduring as the generation, at least.

Major Dunwody, our travelling agent, was even better known than myself. Our business, riding over the country to collect money, was as well-known as our persons. We often travelled quite alone over lonely roads, and from one gold mine to another where the worst of the population lived; yet neither of us were ever robbed, and if we ever fancied we were in danger, we had reason afterwards to be ashamed of our fears. This general honesty is remarkable among people so poor & generally so vindictive. It was not peculiar to the mountain country. When I lived in Greene County Georgia there was an Old man named Park ("Dicky Park") who had a plantation and mills, & a toll bridge, at a noted crossing of the Oconee River. Everything seemed to cross his bridge, before the rail-road gave him the go-by. He spent nothing, loaned no money, and converted his funds into gold and silver. He was for many years an old bachelor and a feeble old man. It was understood that he kept his hoard of specie in a notable red wooden chest underneath his bed.

There he lived and died at a very advanced age. All sorts of people, white and black were about him, & passed & stayed over night; but he was never murdered, or robbed, or molested in any way, & I never understood that he had any fears on that score. After his death, his executors counted $62,000 in coin out of that chest. One of them (Dr. Curtright) told me so. Had he thus lived anywhere at the North, either in the country or in a crowded city, how long would he have enjoyed his store of wealth, unmolested by professional thieves and cut-throats? Not a month.[2]

I admitted that in my travels I sometimes took the alarm. If a responsible man, entrusted with the funds of others, has the misfortune to be robbed, there is general suspicion hanging over him all his life afterwards. The best thing he can do is to sell all his property and offer to pay the loss; otherwise he will never have any office of honor or trust again. These considerations should cause one always [to] decline being made the bearer of any package of money either with or without remuneration.

Yet I have sometimes had the weakness to feel flattered by having valuable Bank packages placed in my charge. I have learned wisdom & will not now suffer any Bank officer or lawyer ever to leave me alone a minute in company with his open safe, or with valuable papers lying about, lest his own defalcation or carelessness might cause suspicion to rest on me.

But I used to carry about considerable sums, as a part of my duty, for the Roswell Company. A good deal used to be said in those times about the Murrell gang, and although his career had long since drawn to a close, certain confessions, true or false, of his associates had implicated many people here and there in the region of country where we did business. In almost every large neighborhood, some one or more persons were pointed out by the neighbors as "Murrell men"; & as they were generally persons well to do in the world, neighbors made the most of it to worry them until they would sell out their property and move away. Some such transactions came within my knowledge, which caused me to think that the Murrell story was only another way that evil-disposed persons had of ridding their neighborhoods of better men than themselves.[3] But those were conclusions that I afterwards arrived at. One evening, it was before I had learned to doubt the stories I have referred to, I was drawing near a place that had a bad name. It was near a place called Ledaga in Alabama. I happened to be in a buggy that time & getting over the mountain road slowly, night overtook me in a very bad place for wheels. It was the dry bed of the Hurricane Creek, & the road was like going down stairs over the rocks. Before I was quite well through, the night came on very dark.

As I said before, the neighborhood had a bad name, & I was carrying a good deal of money. Directly I heard a man on horse-back coming up the road. I reflected that nothing was easier than for a horseman from the rear, knowing all about me, to pass to the front, or carry word to others to waylay me in this mountain gap. So I quickly hid my money under the seat, & got my pistol ready for action.

The man drew nearer. He had on a drab or other light-colored overcoat. I thought I never saw a man look so big! The darkness was such that I did not suppose a man could recognize his brother. "How do you do, Mr. Merrell," said he. I thought it was all over with me now. He knew me! He must have been expecting me & my money! "Pretty well, I thank you. How far is it to ——," said I. "Abouta mile." "Plain road?" "Yes." & we passed.

So I had been scared for nothing. "Hallo!" said I. "Who are you?" "My name is ——. Seen you at the Factory." "How on earth can you tell one man from another in this dark place?" "Why, I should know your shape & the turn of your head any where in the World. Seen yer once at the Factory." And that is the way with those mountain people. They observe with great sagacity, & what little they know, they know it for a certainty & remember it always.

During the hard times, the Suit at law was a poor remedy for the wealthy creditor, even in the best regulated circuits; but especially in the extreme northwestern corner of the State of Georgia was it worse than useless. Murray County lay in the judicial circuit of Judge Kenan, about whom I knew nothing personally, but have heard stories to his disadvantage.[4] He had not the reputation of a man of courage. Col. Young, who lived at the "Long Swamp," had a story to tell that the Judge (who by the way was very tall & one of the stoutest men in Georgia) stayed overnight at his house under circumstances that made him suspect what was true: that the Judge had come to view his rich lands & go away to enter them. He accordingly watched him. By day the next morning, the Judge had left the house quietly, as he thought, without disturbing the family & bent his steps towards the timbered land. Col. Young quickly dressed himself with his shirt outside his pantaloon and a red handkerchief tied round his head like an Indian &, rifle in hand, followed the Judge's track. Dodging from the shelter of one tree to another, he soon found him, as he expected, looking for the "blazed" trees that marked the lines and corners of Government lands. On the other hand, the judge saw what he supposed to be an Indian dogging his footsteps & began dodging too & running until he was safely back in the house. At breakfast, of course, nothing was said, & soon afterwards Judge Kenan called for his horse & never more troubled Col. Young's land.

There was at that time living at the Cross Plains in Murray Co. a man named Bishop (Col. Bishop), who had established his reputation as a bully by a bloody rencounter in the State House at Milledgeville with another member of Legislature named Riley.[5] On the strength of that one fight, Bishop ruled the politics of Murray County and forbade Judge Kenan to hold courts except at his (Bishop's) pleasure. On one occasion when the Judge made a feeble attempt to open his court, Bishop, with his clan from the mountains & his wife, who was also a fighter, broke open the U.S. Depot of Muskets at Spring Place & made use of the arms. The Judge had not the firmness to proceed, and for a long time there were no courts held in that County. We found that our best way to collect a debt in those parts was to give Bishop 10 percent, & he would bully the pay out of our debtors. The principal motive that Bishop had in interrupting the Courts was to save himself & his followers from impending suits for debt & prosecution for offenses.

But in the meantime, as soon as possible after the Indians were gone, a better style of people came in with their Negro property, from the Carolinas mostly, and settled the rich lands of Murray County. They settled usually in neighborhoods comprised of those who had been neighbors before they moved into that country, and the state of things I have described was not suited either to their interests or feelings. Ere long it became a question whether the balance of power lay with the new settlers, in favor of law and order, or with the mountain people & Bishop as their leader. In order to bring this question to the test of the ballot-box, it was necessary to find someone who had nerve enough to run for the office & fill it efficiently if he should be elected. If Bishop's candidate should be elected, there would be no courts. If his opponent, then there would be courts, and judgments, and executions with such force as might be found necessary. In other words, the county would no longer be tenable to Bishop & his men.

A wealthy gentleman of sickly but refined and genteel appearance named Irwin offered, for the public good, to take the dangerous position. He was modest about it, but it was understood by those who knew him that he was quite equal to the emergency. The great election day came on, big with the destiny of Murray County. The whole strength of the parties on either side was paraded. Bishop strained his influence until it amounted to a tyranny against which his old followers were half-inclined to rebel, if but one man was bold enough to set the example. There was a little tailor working in his shop at the Cross Plains. His name was Cox. A native of Greene County in Georgia, his sympathies were with the better class of people; and on election day at the polls, he declared his intention to vote against Bishop, and that too at his own precinct. Bishop undertook to intimidate him with his customary violence of language and gesture; whereupon the little Tailor gave him a sound thrashing & ran him off the ground ignominiously.[6]

After that, the election of Bishop's opponent was easy; his party was annihilated; he was forced to leave the state, and the future prosperity of Murray County [was] secured.

Years afterwards, Bishop turned up again, in the office of Agent at Chattanooga in Tenn., for the Georgia State road. The appointment surprised everybody who was unacquainted with the way politicians manage. It was thought that perhaps he had become a better man. But no; he was not even cured of bullying, as I had occasion to know. There was some stoppage of Corn at his Depot, where I had several car-loads, of which we stood in passing need. Col. Bishop's polite answer was that if the people troubled him much about it, he would "cut their g——ts out." And he was the official agent of the great Western and Atlantic Rail Road, belonging to the State of Georgia, of which the Hon. Wm. L. Mitchell was then Chief![7]

CHAPTER 34

A chapter of Digressions

(This chap. should have been at p. 52)
[In order to follow Merrell's directions above, I have moved this chapter, running from pp. 463 to 468 in the Owen's volume, to fall between chapters 8 and 9.]

CHAPTER 35

*R*eturn we to the times at Roswell during the years from 1839 to 1845. I will not dwell upon the days of my courtship. "The heart knoweth its own bitterness, & the stranger intermeddleth not with its joy."[1] I had no leisure for courtship except at nights, & by that time I was enough tired to need sleep. I remember one night riding home quite asleep on my horse, and suddenly coming upon a pile of hogs sleeping in the road. With a sudden snoot & grunt, they woke &, scattering, caused my horse to start & wheel so suddenly as to leave me on the ground as near as possible to where the hogs had lain an instant before.

That riding in my sleep was no new thing to me. The intense heat of the sun in Georgia renders one very sleepy sometimes in the day time. I have been overpowered by it & have ridden mile after mile sound asleep. One's security in the saddle is not greatly compromised by sleep. The least start or stumble of the horse brings the proper muscles into action instantly & quite as effectually as if the rider was awake. Of course, one must first know how to ride when he is awake before he ventures to sleep on horse-back.

There are some accidents on horse-back that no rider can guard against, sleeping or waking. One time I was riding from Van West in Paulding County to Marietta, a dismal road at that time, over Blackjack mountain, where the road went over everything, regardless of obstacles. I rode "Buck," a fine horse but "swinnied" a little, so that sometimes, quite unexpectedly, his shoulder would fail him, and down he would come by the head, as suddenly as if he had been shot.[2] I had become accustomed to this, so that I could pick him up with a firm bridle-rein, or failing that, strike on my feet all right. But at the time I speak of, I must have forgot myself. My head was woolgathering, and as I descended a mountain so steep that my saddle seemed like it would slip over the horse's ears, down he came!

This photograph of Merrell, found inside his wife's locket and here considerably enlarged, was probably made around 1850, when Merrell was managing two textile mills in Greene County, Georgia.

Away I went over his head & down the hill on my stomach, with hands outstretched. It was one of those ridges of quartz burned white & broken fine by the action of fire when the woods are burned. My hands and face and clothes were excoriated, & I had to lead my horse awhile in great pain.

I was to be married in July. The lady was in favor of putting it off a few months, but I was of the mind that a project [that] is once decided upon will admit of no delay. Charley Magill, the youngest brother of my intended wife, arrived from the "Low Country" in time to be at the wedding, and it was desirable that we should become acquainted; so thought our mutual friends. It would not be difficult to assign good reasons for that opinion of our mutual friends, but the Doctor is quite competent to write his own memoirs, and I will not tell anecdotes of him until I find that he is not likely to give us his own story. I had one of my collecting tours on hand, & invited Charley to go with me, to which he agreed, & we went together in a buggy.

During this trip we met with adventures enough to make us pretty well acquainted with each other. Enough so to be tolerable brothers-in-law afterwards. One adventure I must tell. Arriving at Cassville in Cass Co., we concluded that we would visit the cave we heard so much about. We found it in the forest about four miles from that village.[3] Taking our horse from the buggy, we secured him to a tree & ascended the face of a hill a few yards to the mouth of the cave. The entrance was spacious and imposing and descended profoundly into the bowels of the earth. We had understood that the underground extent of the cave, so far as it had been explored, was about four miles, and we resolved to see for ourselves at least enough of it [to] talk about. Matches we had and a hatchet, but no light wood for torches was at hand, except what had been dropped by former visitors. We found no part of the cave more impressive than the grand entrance itself, & it would have been as well, perhaps, for us if we had been content with seeing that only. But we lighted our torches of pine & walked away into the darkness of the cave, setting up & making marks of our own to guide us on our return, but not reflecting that, if our torches should fail us, we could not see the marks. We enjoyed the visit very much for a while. The passages very narrow, or so low that we had to go upon our hands and knees, suddenly opening into some large hall of huge stalactites & stalagmites, filled us with huge admiration, & there is no telling how much poetry we spouted between us like two fools, while our torches were fast burning out and no pine at hand to replenish them!

Suddenly we were left in profound darkness, not such darkness as we ever see out of doors in the darkest night, but a "thick darkness."

In this we groped our way we knew not where, nor how far, or for how long a time — but we had the good sense to keep together. At last, as our strength failed, our situation came to be understood between us as one of extreme difficulty, but neither complained or censured the other. We were not yet good friends enough for that. The roof over our heads dripped water on us. The Stalagtites knocked our heads, & the stalagmites tripped our heels when we attempted to walk erect. The floor was ankle-deep with a material like sawdust, & we knew not how filthy it might be when we crawled on all fours. We were hungry & tired, & the air was close through damp & cold.

In truth I began to reflect that my marriage, appointed for the next week, would have to be indefinitely postponed, like the bride in the "Mistletoe Bough."[4] In this situation, we thought at last that we espied a light like a star, shining in the darkness a great way off, & we made the best of our way to it, taking good care not to fall into any holes or chasms of the rock. We found the distance not so great as it appeared, & to our great joy, came to a shaft like a well, up which we could see a long way the open air, and the warm blue sky, & the summer clouds floating by. But how to get out was the question after all. To wait for help was a dim chance, for no one knew we had gone to the cave. The road was unfrequented, & if any one happened to pass & see our horse & buggy standing there, they would pass on, taking it for granted the owners knew what they were about & would return in due time.

There was a dead pine tree standing in the hole, the top of which reached nearly to the open air. Probably the place was what is called a "Lime-sink," & this tree had come away with the ground when it sank. Be that as it may, I undertook to make the ascent and succeeded. Charley followed.

The sensation upon arriving in the open, warm, fresh air was indescribably sweet to me. We soon found our patient horse tied where we had left him & proceeded on our journey "sadder and wiser" young men, I should hope.[5]

In the month of July, 1841, I was married according to agreement, and all in a very business-like way, for I was at my writing desk in good time next day.

There must have been a terrible sameness about my subsequent life at Roswell, for I do not recollect at this moment any incidents worthy of record. My wife charged herself with the care of my health, which had begun to give way, and she regulated my social relations. I have thought that she was not contented at my subordinate position there, but am not able to affirm that. I had already given reasons enough without that to account for my removal from the place, upon my own motion. That event took place early in the year 1845. I owned the "Mars Hill" factory in Clarke Co., Georgia, about seven miles from Athens, about six months nearly, and selling that for twice what I gave for it, became Agent of a new and wealthy company in Greene County, Georgia, and for them proceeded to erect a new Factory at the Long Shoals of the Oconee River about sixteen miles south from Greensboro.[6] That manufacturing village was named for me "Merrell" and will be found on the latest maps of that State.[7] I never liked the location. It was sickly, & that consideration alone ought to condemn any location for a factory town. The water power was of a character not to be controlled without a very great outlay of money. The country round about was too wealthy to furnish the required amount of cheap labor and provision. I demurred at the location & pointed out a better, but they would have the Factory in their own County or not at all. As it turned out, it has seemed to me that I had better [have] closed the negotiation by letting them have it not at all. But I went on with the undertaking in not seriously doubting good results with proper energy & skill in the management. I worked very hard and managed many things well, but some parts of the undertaking were beyond my skill and the means at my disposal. I never did succeed in obtaining good drinking water for so many hands; hence, unusual sickness — even for that place — &, from sickness, a

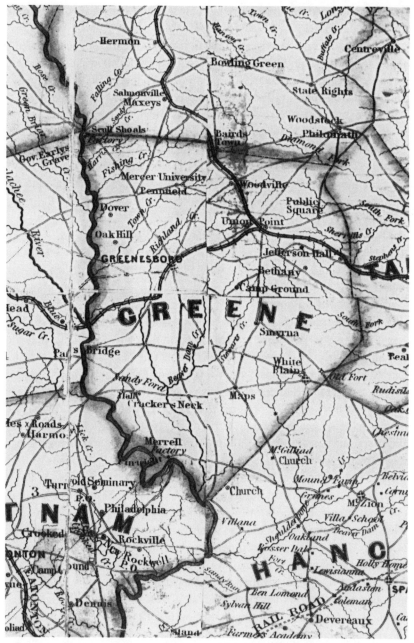

Greene County, Georgia, before the Civil War, with "Merrell" near the southern tip. Detail from James R. Butts, Map of the State of Georgia. Macon, 1859. Hargrett Rare Book and Manuscript Library, University of Georgia.

reduction in the number of hands. I never was able, with the capital at my disposal, to control the river in low water and in high water, so as to give me permanent and reliable water-power. And when I had done building there was not money enough left to purchase first-rate machinery for spinning; so I was fain to content myself and risk my reputation on low-priced machinery of New England manufacture. I have tried them twice & have come to the conclusion that an abolition machine-builder at the North will not furnish a Southern manufacturer with the best machinery. I ought to have known better than to trust them at all.

But in spite of all these disadvantages, such is the virtue of hard work and a determined purpose that, so long as I could give that Factory my personal attention, I made money for my Company. Their books show that in four or five years I made them dividends to the amount of more than $50,000 on a capital which in the same time was increased from $55,000 to $90,000.[8] But the loss of hands by sickness was enormous. Not that so many actually died, but the most thrifty among them became discouraged and moved away to other factories, leaving me only indifferent families and some of bad character who could not easily obtain employment elsewhere. I am speaking now of white hands. No owner of Negroes would be likely to have hired us Negro hands to work at a place with such a reputation for bad morals & bad health.

Under these circumstances, so greatly was I straitened for hands that I went [to] N. York City and brought out at our own expense a drove of Irish immigrants, taking care to have only those who claimed to be Protestants.[9]

It was all in vain. The results were the same, with only this advantage — that those people came to me with a stock of rosy health which carried them through the first year, but the second year (as is generally the case with Northern Constitutions) broke them down to a level with all the rest. The worst of them turned out to be Roman Catholics of the bitterest kind, and would kneel down in the office and curse my Superintendent with a pathos and energy truly wonderful. Some of the women went very far astray, which is, I believe, a thing unusual among Irish girls who have their confessions to make to the Priests.

Even the most promising among them all turned out to be a traitor to me, whenever my interests came to conflict with his. His name was Joshua Neary. He came from Drogheda, was without a father or mother, a little Irish boy in the streets of N. York City, just arrived. I found him at the Intelligence office of the "Immigrant Aid Society." He had a £5 draft in his pocket which I had him keep for his own use, and brought him out with me as a body servant, and he called me "Master" like a Negro, until I told him better. I gave him more wages than others because he was bright and attentive to business. I gave him promotion as I thought he deserved it, until finally he became store keeper and had charge of a great deal of property and the handling of no little money. Somehow the store made no money, as the books of that Company painfully show. Whose fault that was, I can only conjecture. There was a divided responsibility in that store, which is no responsibility at all. Finally I found my boy married to the daughter of a planter of some wealth and, shortly after, a partner in a leading store and Bank agency in the City of Greensboro.[10] Mr. David Howell was the other partner. Neither of them ever had anything but kindness from me; yet I found them both to be my determined foes at the most trying conjuncture of my life.[11] I could hardly believe that of Mr. Howell, though it was told me by others; so one day long afterwards (in the year 1860), meeting him in the Street in the City of N. York, I asked him to walk a little the way I was going. He replied that he *could* do so. I then questioned him categorically as to his relations to me, and I was satisfied by his indirect answers that he had no further use for his old friend and benefactor. So I left him forever. He was a Welshman. I consoled myself by repeating to myself, a distich that was current in my boyhood, & which I had perhaps done well to remember sooner. "Taffy was a Welshman &c." [12]

The state of health, & the want of Society at the Long Shoals Factory caused me to yield to my own wife's wish to live in the town of Greensboro, sixteen miles distant. This move was just as it should be in respect to my family, but the worst thing possible for the Factory. A Cotton Factory, of all things, is the worst to be managed by an absentee. When I located my home in Greensboro, I should have resigned my Agency of the Factory. From that time things gradually ran down on my hands. I saw it year after year growing worse and worse. My anxieties increased to irritability. My frequent rides to and from the works in all kinds of weather impaired my health and spirits. I became indifferent to society, & made no friends. All this time the grinding effects of the Tariff of 1846 began to be felt by the Manufacturers of Georgia, as it had been already felt by those at the North. Profits reached the lowest living point & below. Imported goods did not exactly take the place of ours, but they did take the place of Northern manufactures, driving their looms and spindles into direct competition with us.[13]

And it finally became manifest that we had too many factories in the State of Georgia for the trade of our own Country, & too many for the floating population of factory hands, & that only those Factories which had the most improved machinery in the place of manual labor could hope to succeed—the rest must go under. Here was a change! Five years before, labor was so abundant and so cheap that it was no object to save labor by machinery, but rather a charity not to do so. Five years before, Cotton was so very low that it was not worthwhile to be at the expense of perfect machinery and close management to prevent the wastage of raw material. But now labor and oil and Cotton had all gone up in price several hundred percent & were often not easy to control at any price. I began to regret bitterly that I had set my face against the improvements so far as to go on in the old way instead of keeping up with the times. In the Long Shoals Factory I had actually gone backwards, and adopted new machinery of the style ten years gone by. And I had been fool enough to make a virtue of my conservatism in so doing![14]

Fortunately for the Roswell Manufacturing Company, a son of Mr. Barrington King (James) was then at the North learning the business of Machinist. There he witnessed the rapid outcome of improvements that met the Tariff of '46. He witnessed the discussions of leading mechanics & adopted their new improvements, discarding what was spurious. The result was that the New Factory at Roswell was erected in a style to cope with the hardest times, and upon the success of that, the Old Factory was improved [on] the same model. Thereby securing the present high prosperity of that excellent institution, of which I am always proud.[15]

For myself, I was not yet up to the times. A residence of six months at the North would set me right, but the plodding round of my old business and the growing necessity for hard work and close management blinded me quite.

Money was becoming very [plentiful] in Georgia and sought for investment. The system of Rail Roads could absorb no more capital, & the value of their stocks appreciated greatly. I had myself Georgia Rail Road stock which I had bought at 44 that had gone up to 110. The rate of Interest was reduced by law, and the question was often asked me if I could not invest more money for them in manufacturing. I ought to have said no. But my temperament is sanguine & hopeful, and finally I said yes; and I undertook, in an evil hour, to erect a new Cotton Spinning Factory in the town (City) of Greensboro. It was partly for the profit of the business, & partly to improve the value of property in the town, which was tending to decay.[16]

Greensboro had been for a time the terminus of the Georgia Rail Road & remained so long enough to build up a trade, which died out when the R. Road passed on to Madison and finally to Atlanta. It was to revive this trade and to bring into market certain vacant premises, that it was deter-

Remains of the factory that Henry Merrell built for the Curtright Manufacturing Company. Photo, taken before the inundation of the site in 1979, courtesy of James J. Shive.

mined the new Factory should be located there. Of course the Factory had to be propelled by steam power, but seeing Greensboro was a healthy place, I considered that the advantage of health among my hands more than compensated for the probable cost of steam compared with water power. Moreover, Greensboro was directly on the Rail Road, which was an advantage in the important matter of transportation. I thought I weighed the matter profoundly. I had a doubt about the sure supply of fuel, & stated that doubt to parties concerned, whereupon one of them came forward & set my mind at rest by entering into a written contract for a supply at satisfactory rates. A contract which he afterwards found means to evade, & became my enemy accordingly, as men always do when they have done you wrong. The name of that party was Jesse Champion.[17]

Another tendered the good offices of the Georgia Rail Road for the supply of wood, he being a Director in that Co. But the Georgia Rail Road, which began in good faith, had need of fuel itself &, coming to regard me as a rival in the wood-market, put up the price on me intolerably; and finally, under a new supt., they tore up the switch by which the car loads of wood were run in to the works. Those things baffled me afterwards. In the construction of the Factory buildings I was quite up to the times,

& made the most of rather an indifferent and sidelong place. The bricks furnished me by another of the stock-holders were not well burned, but I had no remedy. I believe the building stands to this day, thanks to a strong cement which I attended to myself; but years afterwards I learned that the chimney, which was an obelisk 80 or 90 feet high, fell down one day. Probably the drainage of the foundation was neglected, and the bricks several feet above the foundations, softened by moisture, became at length unfit to sustain the weight of the superstructure.

But it was not intended by a kind Providence that I should succeed in that undertaking. Again I was straitened in the purchase for machinery. At the moment I should have had the very best and most improved machinery. I was short of funds most unexpectedly, and had to be content with that which was very low-priced, although at the same time I was able to adopt some but not all of the current improvements.

The Curtright Manufacturing Company now looked upon me as a rival manufacturer & no longer their friend. This was unexpected to me, but quite natural, & I ought to have foreseen it. I did not expect it because the leading Stock Holders at Greensboro, were also leading stock holders in the other Company. Mr. Howell, my own protégé, was found to be willing to fill my place, and I was invited to resign.[18] The profits of the Curtright Company were falling off, and they had exacted Dividends from me until their floating capital was exhausted & money had to be borrowed to go on with the business. Still they demanded more Dividends, encroaching upon the Capital Stock. This I objected to, and demanded an investigation. Apprehensive that the result of such an investigation might silence those who now began openly to calumniate me, it was delayed; and considering it was not in their interest but in my own that the investigation I demanded was to take place, they wished me to pay the expense of the same. Several years arrearage of my salary they likewise feared they would be required to pay up if the investigation failed to make out their case of malfeasance in the duties of my post. I exacted from the Curtright Manufacturing Company an investigation, which was conducted by themselves alone, not one person in my interest being on the board. Yet the result was favorable to my administration. They found but one error, or discrepancy, & that was not my own. It was this. Cyrus H. Baldwin, who had for a while been the Store Keeper & after that book-keeper, had carried forward on my Ledger to the credit of the Store which he had recently conducted $4,000 too much, showing a profit to that amount which had never been made. Since Mr. Baldwin stood higher than I did at that time in the estimation of our fellow citizens, & has since become rich, if I mistake not, I had nothing to say as to whether he probably made that mistake with design or inadvertently, but I noticed that Mr. John Cunningham took occasion not very long after to part with him from his store, where it had been expected he would become a partner.[19]

But pending that investigation, which was slow, those same men who had been the opponents of my administration had made up an administration of their own to account for, which showed to a very great disadvantage by the side of mine. They created a board of Directors among themselves to oversee their new Agent, Mr. Howell. They raised $20,000 floating capital upon their Bonds & Mortgages. The Bonds were dated 1st April! When their administration drew to a close, all that $20,000 was gone, no one could tell where, so some said, but I knew very well or guessed it had been sunk in following up awkwardly a losing business. Besides that amount, so much other money had disappeared that, when the $20,000 mortgages came to be foreclosed, their whole property, which cost $120,000, sold for only enough, or as I understood it, not quite enough to pay their debts. During their Directorship, to the best of my recollection, no Dividends at all were made to the Stock holders of the Curtright Co. Their own administration would have set me right before the community, if the investigation referred to had not done so already. And at the same time they were losing money in their wisdom, I was by plodding industry at the Greensboro Factory making a little, but under the most disadvantageous circumstances.

All that discussion preceding the investigation above referred to, and the investigation itself while pending, were a positive injury to me. *First,* in the good opinion of the Greensboro Manufacturing Co., for whom I was still in full powers as President, for some of my stock holders were unfortunately also stock holders in the Curtright Co. *Second.* It cost me the good will of Bankers, upon whom I had to rely for discounts of my bills of exchange against yarns shipped to the north for sale, so that I had to pay higher rates of Discount, and in one year my Interest & Discount Account balanced against Profit & Loss $10,000 upon a business of about $70,000. Any business would require to be very profitable in order to stand that discount. Nevertheless, I made small Dividends. In the year 1854 the net profit was $6,000 or &7,000, but in 1856 [1855], the times hardening down, I lost about as much. I intimated that I had lost the good will of my Greensboro Stock Holders. They had several times oversubscribed to resolutions of their own body, authorizing and instructing me to go on completing their works, and contracting for machinery to fill them up, and they promised and agreed in writing to pay for the same, but in the paying up they fell short about one half my outlay. In order to meet my engagements promptly as Prest. of their Company, instead of letting their business come to a stand while they parleyed, which would have been ruin to them but relief to me, I used my private means and credit to carry it on, and went so far as to buy in with my own property the stock of some who were weak in the knees. This was very well, so long as the business paid a profit & there was a reasonable prospect that delinquent share-holders would pay up, but when the year 1854 [1855] came round and brought with it no profit but a loss, the whole business seemed to me a hopeless case. I had thoroughly lost confidence in my share holders, and in every thing else about me. For the first time in my life, I was discouraged. I looked forward to the loss of my fortune as a positive relief and a boon, which, once resolved upon, I set about it with as much determination as though the transaction was one of great profit instead of a total loss.[20]

I should have said that one cause of loss in business during that last year was the action of a new superintendent on the Georgia Rail Road, greatly increasing the cost and convenience of fuel for our Steam Engines. Also I should have said that I made those purchases of Stock with my own means, not for myself, but for the account of Mr. H. A. Crane of Savannah, who commissioned me to purchase the same for him, but failed to take it off my hands when it turned out that his funds were invested in Sea Island Cotton shipped to Liverpool which was to net him that amount of profit but turned out to be a loss.[21]

I resolved not to carry on a losing business. The businesslike shifts (flying of "Kites" & "Shinning" they are called) customary in such cases, did not accord with my views of integrity, and soon after I became sensible of my situation, I resolved that even if my Stock holders would at the last pay up and go on, I would not be their President nor own stock with them after what had passed between us. The loss to me involved in this determination amounted to quite all I had accumulated by fifteen years of hard work & several successful speculations. It may be set down at some where between thirty and forty Thousand Dollars. I had purchased stock for Mr. Crane to the amt. of, I think, $25,000.

Accordingly in December 1854 [1855?], I called a meeting of the Greensboro Manufacturing Co., and gave them a speech in which I recounted the history of the Company from its commencement to the present time. Announced its certain failure unless they paid up the stock & quit the borrowing of money & discounting of Bills, resigned my office, and surrendered the Works complete, in good order, & all running, to their entire control. They asked a month or six weeks to look into matters, & I retired, leaving it in their hands. In the meantime they passed a flattering set of Resolutions upon my personal character, industry, integrity, &c. of which I have a copy on file.

Their object was to induce me to go on with the business. This I firmly declined, preferring, as I said before, to lose everything but honor rather than serve men in whom I had lost confidence. Whereupon they became my foes, as I had expected, but I was equally indifferent to their friendship or their enmity.[22] I was resolved to have no more to do with stock-jobbing companies. I was resolved not to subside at my time of life into the mere book-keeper for more prosperous men. Had I been sixty years of age, I might have done so gracefully, but not in the prime of life. I would go to a new country. I would begin life over again. A man, neither himself or his friends & enemies, know what he is good for until he is a broken man and has a new start to make. It is not known whether a man is honest and true & brave until after he has failed in business. Any man can be honest when he is prosperous. Any man may exhibit fortitude for others' woes, having none of his own. Any man's energy may be equal to a good business and a high credit. But let him once have to face the loss of all these and his good name besides; let him see that men will believe he has failed full-handed, whether he has done so or not, and we shall presently see whether he has the pluck to begin the world again upon nothing but the mind conscious of rectitude!

So I left them and came to Arkansas to start again in life, upon about $10,000 capital not my own, but furnished by my friends as follows: my Wife $3,000 of her own secured to her by her marriage contract, the principal & Interest of a sum I had never suffered to be involved in my losses; $5,000 loaned to us by her cousin John Joyner Smith Esq., Mr. Duncan his factor, which has since been repaid with Interest; $1,000 by Mr. A. A. Nesbit the cousin of my Wife & an equal amount by Miss Helen Z. Magill my wife's Sister.[23] My mind was made up, & I went. Judge Dawson, my friend & legal advisor, thought I ought to remain a year and live down the "town talk," but I had not a year to spare, & I felt that by a year's delay I might lose my nerve & sink into insignificance, like other men I had seen failing in business.[24] I regretted the necessity I felt for going against advice, but I think I should have died by slow degrees had I remained and done nothing; and to do anything at all in my situation was to entangle myself in other people's affairs.

So I came to Arkansas in the Spring of the year 1855 [1856].[25]

CHAPTER 36

My ten years, the very prime of my life, spent in and about Greens-boro Georgia was not quite altogether a period of labor and toil and thankless responsibility.[1] I had a pleasant home, an undisputed position in society, and some friends. The first of these in point of rank was the late lamented Wm. C. Dawson, U.S. Senator from the State of Georgia. He was my near neighbor, and when he was at home I saw a great deal of him. When at Washington City, he corresponded with me freely. In his society & in that of his excellent family, I have enjoyed some of the most agreeable passages of my life. The life and character of Judge Dawson be-long to the history of times before this war. They were public, & I have no occasion to dwell long upon them in these private memoirs. He was a kind neighbor and a steadfast friend. Had he and such as he lived, this war could not have taken place, but alas! the great peace-makers all died. Judge Dawson once told me that he had arranged in his own mind the materials for a little book that should be a treatise upon the Lord's "Sermon on the Mount." It should be a book for politicians. He owed his usefulness in life, and his elevation also, to his own reputation as a "peace maker." "Blessed are the Peace Makers," said he. He kept his party together when others would have driven them asunder. He performed the same part among his neighbors and his friends. He would drop everything & go over several counties to adjust a family quarrel or a duel. His first marriage into the Wingfield family was in the highest degree happy. By that marriage were born and raised all his children. His second marriage, which shortly pre-ceded his death, was I think a mistake. He died suddenly in the Spring of the year 1855 [1856]. I opened the news-paper which contained the first news we had of his death, in our log house on the frontiers of Arkansas under circumstances of great gloom and despondency.[2]

The Hon. A. H. Stephens, at present Vice President of the Confederacy, I believe I may count among my personal friends of that time, although he did not reside in our village.[3] His home was at Crawfordville in the adjoining County. Mr. Stephens, when I first knew him, was a newly-made member of the U.S. House of Representatives. He bore the appearance of a very sick boy. His weight was about ninety pounds. His complex-ion the color of old parchment, & there was about his visage no index of his mental powers excepting his two eyes of fire. It has been said by ill-natured opponents that the wonder about the man was not so much at his intellect as compared with the intellects of other men, but in the prodigy that such a stripling and such "a natomy" could so sway men and parties by his eloquence. I was at first much inclined to that opinion myself, but after closely observing him through almost the entire period of his rise, I am prepared to say that the foundation of his influence was laid in pure intellect, and his personal disadvantages, so far from being a help to him, were a positive hindrance. Had he enjoyed good health and a fine person, his influence would have been much greater.

Mr. Stephens has been compared to Mr. Randolph.[4] So far as I am able to judge of Mr. Randolph upon what has been published by his friend and biographer, Mr. Stephens is by far the superior man of the two, morally & intellectually. Mr. S. is a humane man. He originates his own politics. I do not think he ever was much influenced by the mere opinions of any other man, or by the views of his party when they cut across his ideas of right. The simple divisions of all questions in his mind are into "Right & Wrong," & the rights he intended to maintain. He is not a deeply read Lawyer, his ideas amounting to no more or less than the right & wrong of a case. He did not cite authorities like other lawyers, except the authority of the Bible, which he read with more clearness than I ever heard from the pulpit. His simple reading was an exegesis by itself. I never knew him to make an attempt at theatrical elocution and effect but once, & then it was rather a failure, being so very far short of his own downright power and pungency of language and look & gesture.

I have several times seen Mr. Stephens come home at the close of a session of Congress, when he had given a vote running counter to his party or to the prejudices of his constituents. It would be the general opinion that he had ruined himself as a politician, & so it would be represented by his opponents. Sometimes the opposition ran so high that his life was said to be in danger—once indeed he was thrown down and stabbed seven times on just such an occasion.[5] But no sooner had Mr. Stephens taken the "stump," and obtained a hearing from the people, than he made it all right with them, and brought them round to his own way of thinking. I do not by any means class Mr. Stephens among the peace makers of those times; he was too much of the debater for that, yet he was not an ultra man.[6] At the final consummation and winding up of all the politics, when the question was shall we fight for our rights in the Union or out of it, he was very decidedly in favor of preserving the Union.

It was in the year 1847 (I think) that the General Assembly of the Presbyterian Church in the United States met at Richmond, Va. I attended that meeting as Delegate from the Hopewell Presbytery in Georgia. I was on the finance committee. During the Session I was a guest at the house

of Horace L. Kent, Esq. On this occasion I renewed some of the acquaintances of my first visit to that city in 1838 and made the acquaintance of
the distinguished men of our Church. Dr. Thornwell presided as Moderator of that Assembly. I afterwards had opy. which I improved to become
better acquainted with that great man. He died last year (1862), and I read
the magnificent Eulogy of the Rev. D. Palmer upon his life & character
last spring at Pine Bluff in Arkansas.[7] When I find myself living to read
and hear of the death of such a man as he, or such as William C. Dawson,
I wonder at the ways of Providence in taking them away and leaving such
as me to read their obituaries!

I am not disposed to dwell upon the events of that Session of the General Assembly, although very interesting to me. One incident, however,
made a peculiar impression on my mind. There was handed in a letter — a
large letter, in size and form equal to a deed of a continent or a treaty of
Peace. It was from the General Assembly of the Free Church of Scotland,
admonishing the Genl. Assembly of the P. Ch. in the U.S. against the so-
called sin and curse of slavery. It was read and referred to the appropriate
committee, who reported back a resolution that we desired no further correspondence with the . . . free church of Scotland. This letter was felt, by
the majority of members, to be an impertinent & self-righteous intermed-
dling of foreigners with our own domestic institutions. I advert to this
incident as serving to illustrate one of the methods adopted by foreigners
to involve this country in the present Civil War on the question of Slavery.

Other ecclesiastical bodies of Christians received such advances with
complacency & were proud to be honored by the correspondence &
personal attentions of great meetings in England & Scotland, at which
Lords — real Lords and Ladies — took a part! And now that we are warring
to please them, brother against brother, we see the same people running
after the same self-seeking foreigners, asking for their sympathy & com-
plaining that they have it not. See the late speeches of Henry Ward Beecher
at Exeter Hall in London as reported in the Cincinnati papers of the
5th Inst.[8]

During my administration of the affairs of the Curtright Manufacturing Company, I had a good deal of trouble with a stock holder in that
Company named Ross. Col. David Ross, whose mills and plantation lay
opposite that Factory on the other side of the river.[9] It appeared that, previous to my appointment as Agent of those works, some promises had been
made (or at least he so understood it) that as an additional inducement
for him to embark in the enterprise, his mills should have a monopoly
of supplying the village with the products of his mills. I could never get

any other evidence than his own understanding in the matter, & as he put higher prices than I thought was right on his products, I ignored the contract, if any such there was, & purchased supplies where I could get them cheapest. I considered it my duty to do so, upon the principle that I was acting in the interest of all the stock-holders & must not show favors to one at the expense of the rest. Col. Ross was a violent man, and some altercation ensued between him and me. He became unfriendly to my administration. Knowing my earnest desire to keep our place clear of lewd women, he [   ] his influence and his practices against me. One of the Irish emigrants becoming his mistress, I took such measures as finally threw her upon his hands for support, and that in a public manner. I had evidence that my life was endangered twice by these circumstances. The first time was by a rifle shot apparently fired at me as I was walking by myself on the river bank below the Factory. I heard the bullet whiz quick & sharp past my head &, instantly after, the crack of the rifle near his mill. At another time, an anonymous letter, which proved to be from one of my former hands who desired to give information without danger to himself. He notified me that I stood in personal danger from the Ross family, and that on a certain evening when I was expected at the Factory, I had been waylaid by them, & had missed being killed by not coming until the next morning. It so happened, in the good providence of God, that on that evening I had accidentally met Col. Ward who asked me to turn aside & stay at his house all night.[10] I did so, and it appears that my life was saved by it. I kept my own counsel about these incidents, but stood upon my guard.

By and by Col. R.'s courses, especially with the woman, brought him into trouble with his own wife and family of young men. He had pursued towards his grown up sons the unwise and doubtful policy of keeping them about him at home, dependent upon him for support instead of portioning them off to start in life for themselves. That, and the liquor, & the women brought him into great trouble with his family. He wanted somebody to advise with. To my surprise he made advances to me. He would have me at his house to stay overnight, and read the Bible, & hold family prayers. He got up a great neighborhood fox hunt for my special entertainment, in which I rode with him, & he brought me through with credit & "in at the death." And a great rabbit-hunt, where they burnt the dry sedge-grass & shot the rabbits as they ran from the smoke and flames. Partridge shooting on the wing with his dogs was another sport that we enjoyed together, until at last he told me that he had never understood me before, & I was considerable of a fine fellow, & we must become better acquainted. He never entered fully upon his family troubles, but seemed anxious to talk with me about them. I did not care to be involved in his affairs, so I discouraged his intended confidences.

A few months (or weeks) afterwards, a messenger to me arrived one morning at Greensboro, 16 miles distant, with a hasty note for me to come, for Col. Ross had been shot dead the night before, on his own grounds. I made haste to go & found him prepared for burial. A murdered man! His death had been instantaneous. One charge from a double-barreled gun had entered his heart, & another his head, at not exceeding ten steps' distance. The gun had been fired by a cool, determined, and expert hand. The paper wads were torn from a newspaper which was taken by no other family in those parts but his, & the piece from which that had been torn was found in a game-bag at the house. The measure of the gun, where it had leaned against the tree behind which the assassin had stood in ambush, corresponded with a small bird gun in the family, known as the "Spoonhandle," because the stock had been broken & marked with the handle of a silver spoon. The track of the murderer was that of a Nr. 6 gentleman's boot. He had waded the mill race, & wet boots of that size were found at the house belonging to one of the sons. Upon these facts, his son John was arrested &, bail being refused, was imprisoned to stand his trial for the murder of his own father.

I did not attend the trial & cannot say what doubts were made by Counsel in favor of the prisoner. He was not convicted. The verdict was of course "Not Guilty," but had it been in Scotland where the law allows such a verdict, I presume the words of the jury would have been "Not Proven." [11]

Considering that Greene County Georgia was a rural district, wealthy and refined as any, there was a great deal of killing going on among the men while I lived there. I am bound to think there was something radically wrong in their education. There were no duels. No one was killed in order to rob, & seldom upon any property question. It appeared to be all for revenge. To kill someone appeared to be the remedy for everything wrong. Not that somebody was killed or even hurt one time in a thousand that it was threatened, but that such & such a man "ought to be killed" was a common form of speech.

The ladies particularly would aggravate a man who had been wrong, by saying, "If I was a man I would kill him," or advice to that effect. I cannot help thinking that this war is the grand and natural result of that habit of feeling & speaking, and I am sure I am correct in the observation that young men who go to the war and return, do so with views a good deal modified and softened down on that very subject.

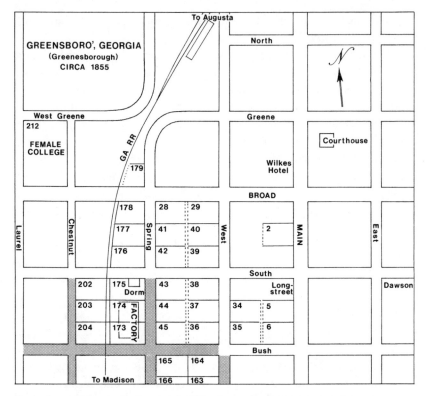

Greensboro, Georgia, as it was in 1855, the year before Merrell left it. He owned the numbered lots at one time or another during his years in Greensboro and may have lived at numbers 34 and 35. The shaded streets may never have been cut through.

Among other public-spirited things that we undertook in order to improve the decaying town of Greensboro and to win for it the rank of "City," we made it the site of a new Presbyterian Female College. Colleges for girls as well as boys were just then the fashion and little as we thought of the name and style, we Presbyterians were unwilling to fall behind other denominations in anything that pertained to education.

I gave, as my subscription, the land upon which the Greensboro Female College stands. I think it consisted of eight town lots within the Corporate limits. I served as a Trustee of the College as long as I resided in the State.[12] My own personal relations to the professors of both sexes were always pleasant, but I have to report unpleasantly upon the general relations of Professors and Trustees to each other, especially when the latter are short of funds. Moreover, a faculty of sharp professors can, by putting their heads together, start questions of college etiquette and discipline too abstruse for the plain common sense of a board of Trustees.

There was in our town of Greensboro a Dr. Martin, who had been raised there and remembered the first spring carriage that ever passed through that village with lamps. It was a chaise, then all the fashion. The population of the village surrounded the vehicle and demanded that the lamps should be lighted, and in that condition they escorted the stranger out of town triumphantly.

The Doctor could tell a good story, but he was slow. His conversation sprouted onto other subjects. You must give him time, and at the end he would give you an anecdote of great point and humor. He told a story on himself that was good in the way he told it. The Doctor was a young buck, & by this time had a chaise of his own. The date was soon after the close of the War of 1812. Taking his evening drive out of town, he happened to stop at Allisons', a mile from the Court House. Alighting, he entered the log house of one small room & one chimney, which was still standing in my time, and still occupied occasionally by the old bachelor Allisons, although their fine new house stood by the side of it. As I was saying, the Doctor walked into the small room. It was evening, & the only light came in, as usual in log houses, through the open door so that the visitor saw at first only the man of the house, with whom he opened a loud conversation upon the merits of the battle of N. Orleans, which was just then the fashionable topic. The Doctor was quite at home on that subject, and animadverted severely upon the plans of General Jackson, who, he thought, should have conducted the battle quite in another way. By this time, he had noticed a stranger sitting on the other side the fire-place, who mildly questioned the accuracy of some of the Doctor's strongest points; whereat he became only the more emphatic in his assertions, and finally bore down rather too hard upon the absent hero. The stranger could stand it no longer, but rising in great wrath, in a threatening voice & with characteristic oath, announced that he was General Jackson himself & ought to know best. The Doctor said that he did not wait to hear any more. The General seemed to him to keep rising taller & taller as he spoke, until he looked to be as tall as the house chimney itself. As to the dandy, he was quickly in his chaise & off towards town in a de-moralized condition. The next day the towns-people gave a public dinner to the General, but it is not to be supposed that the Doctor honored it with his presence.

The Allisons were brothers, both bachelors & rather eccentric. They had been boys together with Jackson, & he had come to pay them a visit. Probably he was up on one of his horse-back journeys on public business with the Indians, & his old friends were not far off his route. I believe the Oconee River seven miles from Greensboro was at that time the boundary line of the Creek nation.[13]

Greensboro in Georgia had been the early home of Judge Longstreet & his comrades, & that country furnished some of the incidents for his "Georgia Scenes & Characters." Upon my land stood an old office which had been occupied by Longstreet when he was a young lawyer in Greensboro, & I was told it had been the scene of many a nightly frolic. When I knew the Judge, he had become a Methodist preacher and since then the President of one college after another, but always his distinction lay in his authorship of the "Scenes & Characters," his humor in reading the same aloud better than any one else, & his skill in playing the flute.[14]

Besides Judge Dawson, the Ga. Senator before referred to, I do not know that any of Longstreet's early companions remained in or about Greensboro, with the single exception of Col. King (Yelverton P. King). A perfect gentleman was he, of the old school, who never pushed his fortune in politics, but was nevertheless chosen, & well-chosen, by Mr. Fillmore when Prest. of the U.S. to represent his Government at Bogata, the capital of New Granada. Col. King was not a man about whom many anecdotes could be told. There was a certain propriety about all he did or said that might not admit of anything striking or unusual in a lifetime. He was the best shot at birds on the wing that I ever knew, yet he never hurried himself, even when he had to kill one with each barrel of his gun. I was told that he was the best of Whist-players. The personal acquaintances he formed in South America amounted in the end to dignified friendships. He was not wealthy and could not afford to maintain much display at the seat of Government in N. Granada. I have been told by an American who about that time resided in the country that his quiet housekeeping was not understood by the citizens or foreigners, and many thought him haughty. A true friend of his, who was at the same time a wag (I think it was Don Patancio Wilson, a Scotchman by birth) determined to draw Col. King & his lady into general Society, sent written invitations to every body (unknown to Col. K.) that he would be happy to receive all his friends at his house that evening. The whole fashion of the City of Bogata made sure to drive up to the door of the American Minister in due time & in full dress. The Col., taken by surprise, but always a gentleman, made the best of it. Refreshments were speedily forthcoming, & the evening passed off finely, & his position in society was attested by abundant invitations to dine & hunt & visit country seats, as usual in such cases, notwithstanding the joke was all over town the next day.[15]

During the time of my residence in Greensboro, the sport of the spirit-rapping and table-turning discussion was in full blast. We tried some of the experiments at my house, in a skeptical way. Certainly tables would move in a remarkable manner, but I thought I could account for it without super-natural agencies, upon the fact that when a number of persons united, strongly wish or will a movement under their hands, their muscles will act with their wills, unconsciously.

CHAPTER 37

*B*efore I take my reader with me to Arkansas, I cannot, perhaps, better illustrate what I have said about the decline of manufacturing in Georgia, than by tacking into these pages some newspaper articles from my pen, which I find preserved among my papers.

[Under the title "Manufacturing in Sober Earnest," four of these articles appeared in the *Milledgeville (Southern) Recorder* on March 30, April 13, April 20, and April 27, 1847. They lament the effects of the tariff law of 1846 and of overproduction in the southern textile industry. Merrell also has glued into his journal four similar articles that he wrote, over the signature "Profit and Loss," for the *New York Journal of Commerce* from August 31 to September 17, 1855. These articles appear below in the Appendix.]

CHAPTER 38

*T*he close of Chapter 35 left our family resolved to leave Georgia against all remonstrance, against all inducements, & at the cost of losing all I had laid by in the course of fifteen years of hard work. I had erected three of the largest factories at that time in the State of Georgia, and I had reconstructed an old one. I had organized the business of those Factories, and trained up efficient hands for the same, as well as for other establishments that were accustomed to run on me for hands and overseers at their pleasure, regardless of the amenities that should prevail among rivals in business.

I have frequently been asked why, if I must go to the west, did I go to

Arkansas? And if to Arkansas, why almost to the confines of the Indian territory? I will give my reasons as they arose in my own mind.

My capital was very small, & I did not feel inclined to go into any more joint stock companies. I had already visited Tennessee & Alabama, & conversed with gentlemen from Mississippi, & was satisfied that there was for me no out come in the Factory business on the East side of the Miss. River. I must go further west. My late experience with steam had determined my mind in favor of Water power as the most steady, the most reliable, & the most economical for Cotton spinning.

West of the Mississippi river I had before me the Western part of Louisiana, an old country, & in no way that I could learn, suited to my views. Also Texas and Arkansas. As it respects water-power, a glance at a good map is sufficient to show that nearly all the water west of the Mississippi River flows in very long, and of course sluggish rivers, running from North West to South East. All water courses running towards the North are short and rapid, but do not drain extent of country enough to insure their permanence. A profile of this Western country would represent slopes of a northern exposure not generally exceeding twenty-five miles from the large streams to the summit of the Watershed, while at the same time, waters from the same ridge, flowing in the opposite direction, that is, southwards, have from 100 to a thousand miles to run before reaching the great affluents of the Mississippi. Through the greater part of all that career, they pass through swamp lands, with no rapids or falls fit to be regarded as waterpower, except within twenty-five to fifty miles of their sources. Among the spurs of the mountains in which they took their first rise: there I might expect to find good water power and a healthy location for my work-people. Where then should I find such a country? The prerequisites of such a location, after I found it, were to be that it should furnish on the one hand a population of poor people who should be glad to find employment in the Factory, or if they had little farms, to make it a near market for their surplus productions; and on the other hand it must [be] near the cotton-growing country.[1] In other words, the place must be in the hill country which divides the mountains of every Southern state from the rich alluvial bottoms where good cotton grows. Such a place would, in a new-settled country where no rail roads were at hand to bring in cheap goods or carry the produce to a better market, give me cheap cotton, cheap labor and supplies, and retail prices for my manufactured goods. In a word, it would be such a place as Roswell in Georgia was in the year 1839, & that was my model. I designed to enact over again the business done at Roswell between the years 1840 & '45, taking care to profit by experience and avoid the mistakes of those times. In so doing, I calculated that in five or six years of persevering industry I should pay back the money I had borrowed with interest and lay by a fortune equal to that I had laid down in Georgia. Was it not at least a manly resolution compared with the alternative of lying on the shelf, a broken man in Georgia?[2]

The Northern half of the State of Arkansas was too far north in point of climate, and politically too near the free States for a permanent location depending on Cotton. Texas was not then settled as far West as it is now. All the Northern ranges of counties in that state, lying near the Red River Cotton lands, were destitute of Water power for reasons before stated. The noble Water powers in the West of that State were too near the Wild Indians and too far from Cotton. The intervening prairies were out of the question, and so my choice was narrowed down to the Southern half of the State of Arkansas.

The Country of the Choctaw Indians would have answered my purpose better than any other that ever rejoiced my eyes. A lovely Country! But not to be thought of, for there is no fee simple to land and no security for much property under Indian rule. As to the South half of the State of Arkansas, I could at that distance, being in Georgia, only arrive at my conclusions by maps, by the public documents of the United States Congress, and by Correspondence.

The Swamp lands maps of Arkansas narrowed me down to the five counties lying West & North of the Ouachita River, and skirting the mountains from Little Rock South West to the Choctaw Nation. Leaving one tier of Counties between me and the Indians, I found that I had but four or five counties left that were at all likely to meet the conditions I had laid down for myself. In order to verify my researches, I purchased a list of Post Offices in all the Counties of the State and wrote to them explaining my views and asking questions. The desire to have a Factory among them prompted many to answer me.

I then turned to the U.S. Census for 1850, and with a pen marked opposite each county the population in 1850 against that of 1840, showing the drift of emigration & the increase of population. To get at the probable healthfulness of each county I compared the no. of Deaths as stated in the Census with the population. For the state of Society I looked to the number of Schools and Churches, & what sort of Churches. And for the probable Capacity of those Counties for trade, I inquired into their productions as laid down in the Census. By these means, when I reached Arkansas in order to "prospect" the Country in person, I had not much ground to pass over, but knew right where to go and look for what I wanted, as well as if I had been living there; for when I reached the State, I found myself to be even better informed than many citizens & quite prepared at all points to be on my guard against the misrepresentations of land speculators.

Arkansas

MERRELL LEFT BEHIND HIM in Utica a developed and stable community. In Roswell he found a developing community. In journeying to Arkansas, he was, in terms of social and economic development, traveling into a wilderness and stepping backward in time. He made these choices consciously and deliberately, for he was searching for an opportunity to use his skills and to make his fortune in the quickest possible way: by monopoly, cheap labor, and barter. "I had the Roswell business to do over again," he says.

Almost one-half of Merrell's autobiography concerns his epic removal to and achievements in Arkansas. Somehow this proportion seems fitting. From his youth in Utica, he seems to have been an explorer, an energetic young man who did not learn in the usual way, act in the customary fashion, or find solace in traditional manners. All through his narrative are accounts of his unwillingness to do things the way others did them, to accept solutions that others offered, to remain in place. It could be argued that a place like Arkansas was the inevitable land of opportunity for a man of Merrell's time and talents. He found in Arkansas what suited his economic, social, and religious tastes: "I had found the missionary ground for a manufacturer."

In January 1856, when the rivers were choked with ice, Henry Merrell, against the advice and conventional wisdom of his best friends in Greensboro, burned his Troy and set out for the West, heartened by his faith in his skills and his unswerving belief that hard work and fortitude could overcome all difficulties and misfortunes. It seems appropriate that the point of departure for his odyssey was Atlanta, which did not even exist when he came to Georgia in 1839.

Merrell chose a five-county area in southwest Arkansas as the location for his new enterprise. Accompanied most of the way by his young nephew William Seagrove Smith, he journeyed by rail, riverboat, and horseback to Washington in Hempstead County and there, with the help of General Grandison D. Royston, selected a site in Pike County then called "Hugh's Mill" on the Little Missouri River three miles north of Murfreesboro.

With characteristic dispatch, he surveyed a five-hundred acre wilderness site, which was then occupied only by a brush dam and its small accompanying stilted mill and log cabin, then returned to the land office in Washington to purchase it. He journeyed back through Antoine and Little Rock to Memphis, where he took leave of his nephew, who had become homesick for Georgia. Yet "Willie" would rejoin his uncle once more in April of 1859 and would work for him, according to the 1860 census, as a clerk in his Arkansas enterprise.

Merrell traveled by river to Cincinnati, where he purchased some machinery, ordered more from Paterson, New Jersey, and started back on a river trip that went all the way to New Orleans, for he had to buy stores there and bring them up the Ouachita River to Camden, not up the Arkansas River to Little Rock. Camden was only 80 miles southeast of his factory site, and Little Rock was more than 110 miles northeast of it. Before returning from Cincinnati, Merrell was joined by his wife's brother, Charles Arthur Magill, who had been living in Chicago since visiting his sister and Merrell in Greensboro. Magill, from now on an associate of Merrell's in his every venture, was to help him set up the Arkansas factory, but his immediate assignment was to return to Georgia to bring his sister and the Merrells' servants out to Arkansas. When they arrived in Camden on a riverboat, Merrell was waiting for them, and the party traveled by wagon to the Pike County mill site in what must have been a sad caravan. Merrell does not hide the discontent of his "family" with both their location and their prospects. Almost two years after her arrival in Arkansas, Mrs. Merrell wrote to Willie Smith: "We lead a very lonely life out here & I see nothing romantic or interesting in life at the West. Your uncle H. is the only one that is satisfied."[1]

Mrs. Merrell, her husband, and her brother had to share a low, spider-infested log cabin with a miller who did not want to make way for her husband. Because she was used to the polite, elegant surroundings of coastal Georgia and Roswell, living conditions in the Arkansas wilderness were particularly trying for Elizabeth Merrell. Henry implies that his "family" remained in a state resembling mutiny for some time, that "my successes over-ruled it generally, but it broke out afresh at every reverse, & every time of sickness," and that it was only under his promise that their stay in the wilderness would be for a limited time that they remained with him at all. Some of his slaves ran away from him. He reflects, "I may truly say that in all that arduous undertaking I was only sustained, at those times when one needs comfort & support at home, by the mind conscious of rectitude."

Noting the similarity between himself and Robinson Crusoe, he began work. His first task was to build his "famous dam" across the Little Missouri, "with little more than the wild woods for resources, and the wild Arabs for my helpers." This dam, the foundation of his fortune, he completed in 1856, and it "gained for me a reputation over the country." He constructed it of local materials and with local labor, framing it with fourteen-by-fourteen-inch oak sills pinned together with iron rods that he had forged on the spot. The part of the dam that remained underwater survives to this day. The sills that Merrell piled into the river bottom and pinned into its banks, with their joining iron rods projecting upward, can be seen clearly when the Little Missouri's waters are low.

Merrell's dam still marks what has been called "the pioneer cotton factory in the state."[2] Dallas T. Herndon, in his *Centennial History of Arkansas*, lists it as the first factory in Arkansas for the production of cotton and woolen goods.[3] In his *High Lights of Arkansas History*, Herndon says that Merrell's was "the first cotton factory established" in Arkansas.[4] Merrell's factory has been termed not only the "state's first Textile Mill," but "the first effort to industrialize Arkansas."[5] Merrell mentions that an earlier textile mill, built at Van Buren, had ceased operations when his began. This would have been the enterprise of John Henry and Alfred Wallace.[6] John B. Ogden, a lawyer and merchant of Van Buren, who was a director of the company, began soliciting funds for a cotton spinning factory in 1848, and the company was granted a charter from the state in 1852.[7] This factory was reported to be in full operation by January 1852.[8] There were similar efforts in Arkadelphia in 1849 and in Benton County in 1854.[9] Merrell mentions that, prior to his operation, one Mark Bean began a small spinning mill in Washington County, which is just south of Benton County in northwest Arkansas, and that Bean's mill ceased operations with his death.

But these ventures do not seem to have been successful ones. Even if the "Royston" factory was not the first attempted, it was certainly the first successful textile mill in Arkansas. Thus, Merrell and his stockholders, his wife, and John Matlock of Camden chartered in 1856 what was appropriately named by the state legislature "The Arkansas Manufacturing Company."[10] The act to incorporate the company praises "the laudable exertions of a portion of the citizens of this State, who are endeavoring to promote the general prosperity and independence of our State, by erecting cotton and wool factories." It names "Henry Merrill" as agent and establishes the company not only for the purpose of manufacturing cotton and woolen goods, but for grinding grains, sawing timber, and "mechandizing in the most advantageous manner."[11]

Merrell advertised for workers in the *Washington Telegraph:*[12]

HANDS WANTED

I will give Thirteen Dollars per month, and customary allowance of food, for able-bodied Negro Hands, to work at the NEW FACTORY, three miles north of Murfreesboro, when crops are laid by. Each hand must bring an axe or mattock. Labor and treatment reasonable. Pay cash. Reference — Ge. Royston. Apply on the spot, or address at Murfreesboro, Pike County, Arkansas.

HENRY MERRELL, Agent

May 14, 1856

The "cash" was clearly to be paid to the Negroes' owners, for he announces in his memoirs his intention to pay workers in kind with goods from his store. According to a letter that Mrs. Merrell wrote on August 18, 1856, there were at that time eighteen people living on the site, plus eight or ten more who left Saturdays at noon and returned Sunday evenings.[13]

The system that Merrell borrowed from Roswell of paying his workers with supplies from his store served him well in establishing his prosperity. He had originally brought from New Orleans "a general assortment of merchandise for a Store I intended to establish on the ground as the nucleus of my Factory town. This was an essential part of my plan." Thus he planned to use a barter system that he had seen work in both New York and Roswell, a system that worked well where specie was scarce and where close relationships existed between the manufacturer and the people.

"Profiting by our experience at Roswell," he says, "I made calculations to pay money only for land and machinery, leaving all materials and labor to be paid for in goods from the Store. By this means, I expected to make as great a profit on our capital while erecting the works as I could expect to make by the works themselves when completed." Not only were profits assured by this system, but a docile labor force as well. "By means of our Store we kept our hands close at their work, & controlled labor that could not have been steadily controlled by wages in money."

By not paying wages, Merrell not only kept his workers close at their work; he kept them close at hand. With money, he says, "our hands would have spent their time, a great part of it, in straggling many miles away to make their purchases. Paying them in supplies, we made a handsome profit to ourselves, & kept the hands under our influence." The company store, then, was at the center of his enterprise. He says that it was "the center around which all our business revolved; and the business, in that frontier location, could not have gone on without the Store any more than a wheel without its hub."

In one other respect Merrell duplicates a pattern established at the beginning of the industrial revolution in America. He is the teacher of all the unskilled labor. He instructed his "wild Arab" hands in everything from sawing wood to installing and operating machinery. His hands would then operate the machines and pass on their knowledge to others. If his workers caused him trouble, he would reduce their credit at his store. If they proved unmanageable or dared to strike, he would replace them and train others. His reader must judge for himself how humanely Henry Merrell used the power and advantages that knowledge and lack of competition gave him.

Work on the dam progressed speedily. Charles Arthur Magill, Merrell's brother-in-law and assistant, who would later be his partner, wrote to William Seagrove Smith in Roswell on August 20, 1856, "The Factory work is tremendous. The dam has to be built across a river which at the present hour you can walk across but which in some winters has been 23 ft. deep, a perfect mountain torrent rising, the people here say, sometimes 8 ft. in an hour." [14]

Mrs. Merrell's trustees, her brother-in-law Archibald Smith and Barrington King, would grant Merrell power of attorney on August 26, 1856, to make quit-claim deeds on the site to the Arkansas Manufacturing Company. They, along with John Matlock and his wife, deeded the property they had purchased to the Arkansas Manufacturing Company in July 1857.[15]

Henry Merrell's factory caught the attention of the Little Rock *True Democrat* on September 9, 1856. The report, entitled "A New and Laudible Enterprise," is interesting both as it relates to Merrell and to the state of the state, and it is therefore quoted in full:

> We were much gratified, a few days since, to observe at the warehouse of Messrs. Merrick & Wassell of the city, a large quantity of machinery in transit to Murfreesboro, Pike county. This machinery is intended for an extensive cotton factory, grist and saw mills, which will, no doubt, be a first rate establishment. Mr. Henry Merrill is the manager for the company, and is a gentleman of fine business capacities.
>
> We say success to every enterprise of this kind. It is a step in the right direction, and of great importance not only to the section where it is located, but to the whole State. We feel sure that this is but the beginning of a new era in Arkansas manufactures. We raise our own cotton, then why not, in the name of common sense, manufacture it? If we desire to be independent of the North, nothing will so effectually conduce to that end as to foster and encourage our own manufacturers and artizans. Such a policy will accomplish more than a hundred resolves by public meetings about southern rights and southern institutions. Interest as well as duty should prompt the South to encourage home manufactures. We would thereby save all the expense of

transporting the raw material to the North or to England, as well as the cost of bringing back the manufactured article. Arkansas ought and we hope she will, in a short time, furnish most of the cotton goods used by her people. We again say success to this and all similar enterprises.[16]

Merrell's factory had between 3,500 and 4,000 spindles, which seem to have been delivered by the Red River and overland by ox-cart from Lanesport to Murfreesboro.[17] According to another article in the *True Democrat*, the factory was equipped by 1857 with enough machinery "to turn out fifty bunches or two hundred and fifty pounds of spun yarn per day." This article, "Factory on the Little Missouri," by one Carolus, reports on a visit to the factory. "Twelve months ago," he says, "the present site was a wilderness of timber, logs and rocks." Now, "we found a little village of handsome frame houses. One large storehouse in erection, blacksmith shop, etc. The foundation of the factory building is (we think) 60 × 60 feet." The writer reported that a gristmill, circular sawmill, and woolen mill were in operation and that "something near a dozen families are living there connected with the working department." Described as "a gentleman of intelligence, high-toned address and enterprising industry," Merrell informed the correspondent that his spinning machinery had arrived on the Red River. "The first thing that attracted our attention," he says, "was the 'stars and stripes,' unfurled and gracefully wafting to the breeze, hoisted high on the liberty pole."[18]

Progress on construction was rapid, and Merrell soon advertised for customers. He placed advertisements in the Little Rock *True Democrat* from late April to mid-June of 1857 and entitled them "How to Prepare the Wool for the New Carding Machines in Pike County":[19]

> Wash it, this is in the interest of the Sheep owner. Send at the rate of one gallon of Lard to each 100 Pounds of Wool, but do not grease the Wool yourselves. Send sheets or blankets sufficient to pack the rolls. Send a paper with your name and instructions on each parcel. The price for Carding is 10 cents a pound, or one quarter toll as you like.
>
> *Burs.*—No extra charge on Wool that contains BURS provided the pay is CASH: but if the pay is to be in toll, one eighth extra toll will be charged for burring. In all cases the Wool must be well washed and dried.
>
> WOOL ROLLS Always on hand for sale.
>
> HENRY MERRILL, Agent
>
> April 14, '57

It would appear that by the middle of 1857, Henry Merrell was so famous in Arkansas that well-known figures such as Augustus Garland could refer to him in correspondence as "the manufacturing man" and expect that their readers would know of whom they spoke.[20] We may account for his spreading fame because of his ambitious work to found a community as well as an enterprise. On August 29, 1857, Charles Arthur Magill made application to the Post Office Department for a post office to be set up at Royston. In the application he stated that ten families lived in the "new manufacturing village," which was "little more than one year old."[21]

In 1857 the Arkansas Manufacturing Company was assessed taxes on 207.72 acres of land worth $621. The tax record shows that the concern had a sawmill, goods, wares, and merchandise worth $4,000 and a total investment of $28,000.[22] Profits were coming in and Merrell's experiment seemed to be working. Then two disasters struck: water and fire.

Merrell wrote Archibald Smith on February 11, 1858, "Recently a freshet, the highest in the memory of white men, crippled us, but not seriously." The works were not damaged, he tells Smith. He goes over in the letter the same events that he covers in his memoirs: the river made a new channel, and following his repairs and his outlay of a thousand dollars, "we shall feel glad it has happened because then we shall have more than double the discharge for surplus water in case of another such rise." With his works standing on rock, Merrell concludes, he will have "the best water power that I ever saw almost." But it took over a year to repair this damage fully. On November 16, 1859, Willie Smith again wrote his father, "The New Dam has been finished, and is a good piece of work; it is about two feet higher than the old part, so as to throw the force of the stream on this side of the River, lest it should work round again."[23]

The Merrells new home had burned in September of 1858 under circumstances that made Merrell suspect arson. He gives a dramatic account of the efforts to salvage clothes, books, and other valuables, especially his harmonium. Undaunted, he sent his wife back to Georgia for a vacation and began rebuilding at once.

Again he wrote to Archibald Smith, this time December 1, 1858, to report,

> Our misfortunes by flood & by fire are not such as to be very discouraging in the face of a brisk trade. We seem to accumulate rapidly enough around in everything that is the same as money to our operations; but of *money* I confess we are often short. We live in a state where the *hard* money theory prevails & has prevailed long enough to work out its legitimate results: no money at all, scarcely hard or soft; but a delightful barter trade in which the trader makes two profits off the producer, at which I am content. Not a bank in this state. Small bills of other states proscribed by law. People take each other's *Notes* of hand to represent debt & credit.[24]

Merrell's profits were again substantial, according to Willie Smith, his clerk from 1859 to 1861. In 1859 Smith wrote his father, Archibald Smith, a letter which included the company's sales figures, labeled "Returns for the year ending Nov. 1st, 1869." They include merchandise, $14,197.19; breadstuffs, $1,546.97; wool rolls, $1009.62; lumber, $669.02; thread, $8,485.11. His figures also include $10,436.36 for thread made on consignment and $900.08 for rolls on consignment.

Willie Smith's letter of November 16, 1859, gives some idea of the routine and schedule of the mill, as well as of some recent improvements:

> The spinning began on the 12th of last Augst. and continued without interruption until the 20th of last June. Since that time there has been very little done. The demand for thread has been considerable, and we have been obliged to run the Cotton machinery a little to keep up.
>
> The Wool Cards have been kept busy thro' the Fall Months. The quantity of Wool in the country seems to increase every year. Toll ¼ of weight or 10' [cents] pr. lb.
>
> The Flour Mill does good business. It is not expensive and brings a good deal of trade to the place. . . .
>
> In the Store we have a large stock of goods, which sell readily. Our business is *cash*. The wages of the Hands are paid principally with goods out of the Store.
>
> Cotton is abundant. We do not pay cash for it yet, but take it in Trade @ 2½' [cents] in the Seed.
>
> We are looking anxiously for Rain now, as it is time that all the works should be running.[25]

According to the "Products of Industry" section of the 1860 census, the Arkansas Manufacturing Company had a total capital invested of $55,000. Although entries are scratched over and overwritten, it appears this amount of capital broke down into $30,000 on cotton spinning, $20,000 on wool carding, and $2,500 each in the gristmill and sawmill. Merrell converted 150 bales of cotton, valued at $6,750, into 60,000 (skeins?) of thread valued at $15,000; 25,000 pounds of wool valued at $7,500 into 20,000 rolls valued at $10,000. When grinding and sawmill operations are added, it appears that his gross annual product was $32,000. If I interpret the scratchovers correctly, it would seem that there were, on average, twenty men and ten women working in the mills and that their total wages for the year were less than $9,000.[26] Merrell tells us that after he sold the factory to Matlock it could spin 550 pounds of cotton yarn per day and produce 700 pounds of wool in a day and a night.

These figures are all the more remarkable in context with the economic condition of the rest of Arkansas. Waddy William Moore, writing in the *Encyclopedia of Southern History*, says, "Arkansas had almost no manufacturing establishments in 1860. The entire capital employed in manufacturing consisted of only .13 percent of the national total." [27]

Merrell says that "the story of all my contrivances in order to get on under these circumstances would make an engineering book by itself, much after the manner of Robinson Crusoe." "Remote from foundries and machine shops, with only bungling self-taught mechanics about me, I was all the time at my wit's-end to get along." Yet he endured and prospered through flood, fire, and local hostility. He would certainly have fulfilled all his dreams of prosperity and plans of retirement had not the Civil War intervened.

When the Civil War broke out, Royston was extremely important to the Confederacy. On May 21, 1862, the *Washington Telegraph* said, "The manufactory for cotton yarns in the neighboring county of Pike is of such immense importance to our people just now, that it might become an object with the enemy to destroy it." [28] Richard W. Griffin has said, "The state was largely dependent upon the products of the Arkansas Manufacturing Company of Royston, and it was feared that the Federal Army, which was destroying industrial establishments in Tennessee, would attempt to burn this factory." [29]

Even though his northern birth made his best efforts on their behalf suspect to the natives of Arkansas, Merrell never wavered in his loyalty to the southern cause after he had made his anguished decision to remain in Arkansas, and he continued to keep his mill running from 1861 to 1863. While he did, he was obligated to allocate one-half of his production at fixed prices to the Department of the Trans-Mississippi. He got into trouble for the prices that he charged his customers. By the middle of 1862 he was charging $2.50 a bundle for thread and was discounting Confederate money. It was widely reported that he would accept $1.50 in specie in lieu of $2.50 in Confederate money.[30]

Merrell writes that before New Orleans fell he always did business on the discount rate that the city's banks gave on Confederate notes: 30 percent for gold. A Camden newspaper, the *Ouachita Herald*, complained that Merrell's goods could be bought only for gold and silver, but the neighboring *Washington Telegraph* defended Merrell, even though it noted: "Many have become incensed with Mr. Merrill, and there has been much talk of taking forcible possession of his factory, and running it for the benefit of the community." The paper added that scarcity had caused farmers to double the price of bacon and shoemakers to double the price of shoes.

It therefore concluded: "Why taboo spun thread? There is a very homely maxim abroad which fits the case. 'Sauce for the goose is sauce for the gander.'"[31]

In May the *Washington Telegraph* had commended Merrell, "the enterprising and industrious manager" of "the manufactory for cotton yarns in the neighboring county of Pike," for "conducting the operations in a manner most advantageous to the whole community and in a spirit of justice to all." It said:

> The prices charged are moderate, being considerably below those charged by similar establishments in Georgia and other parts of the South. This is the only factory here accessible to our citizens. People anxiously flock to purchase this necessary article from a hundred miles distant, and that in such numbers as to render it impossible to supply the demand. Being thus without competition Mr. Merrell deserves high credit for his anxiety to accommodate the wants of the community at moderate rates, when he has it in his power to act the extortioner.[32]

Two weeks after this defense, and following the *Ouachita Herald*'s complaint, the *Washington Telegraph* said: "We . . . still assert that Mr. Merrill is doing good. He serves the public. That is no less true, even although he may enrich himself thereby, as is likely enough. We had better let him alone. Whether he be a bad or good man is between him and his Maker and is no concern of ours. What we want is spun thread."[33]

To provide that need seemed an impossible task. Because he kept his factory going and because he continued to prosper, he was subject to great stresses placed upon him from Pike County, from the state, and from beyond. Merrell brings to life the scene around his factory where people camped for days waiting their turns for goods. They came from as far away as four hundred miles: war widows, mothers, soldiers home on leave, even county delegations. "Every particular tree, or stump, or post seemed to have a horse or a mule tied to it & often without provender, horse and rider both," he says. And they petitioned, cried, begged, railed, and threatened. "Every form of claim, requisition, demand that could be importunately put on paper" was used. "To all such I was obliged to have a civil answer and an explanation." Yet, he maintains, he was not able to meet the needs of one in ten.

Merrell has much to say of the public's hostility toward him, a hostility that took the form of rumors that he was carrying specie out of the country, of public meetings that demanded fixed prices or a public takeover, and of violent stump speeches calling him "a d——d Yankee and a speculator." "Had it not appeared that no one could be found capable of carrying on the machinery but me myself, it would have been taken from me." He also had to confront possible arrest by Confederate authorities, and attacks on the factory by bands ranging from "bogus volunteers in squads" to "banditti." As the possibility grew of attacks by raiders, Merrell and his men worked with weapons near at hand.[34] General Theophilus Holmes had commissioned him a captain in the Partisan Rangers so that he could defend his own mill,[35] but the strain and danger forced him to sell out to his partner, John Matlock of Camden, in February of 1863, and he returned his captain's commission to General Holmes. Merrell says that he sold out owing more to pressure from the people than from the government, yet he also mentions that the future for manufacturing would be bleak with a Confederate victory, for the Montgomery constitution, he said, declared that no encouragement should be given to domestic industry.[36]

Shortly after selling the factory, Merrell accepted Holmes's commission as a major and the task of placing an abatis in the Arkansas River in order to block Federal ships from approaching Little Rock.[37] He finished that task on the river soon after July 4, 1863, and he left for "The Retreat" on the Little Missouri near his old factory, where, in August of 1863, he began to write his autobiography.[38] He had written nineteen chapters, and had almost completed the "New York" section, when he noted on September 15 that Little Rock had fallen on September 10, 1863.

Although Merrell had sold the Royston factory to Matlock, in large measure owing to the complaints and pressures from local citizens, Matlock was to fare no better with them. Merrell says that he raised his prices 300 percent over his own. According to a letter from Mrs. Merrell to William Seagrove Smith, he may have fared even worse than her husband. She says people "from different parts" have told them that "the whole country is in rebellion against Mr. Matlock, & wonder how they ever could have been dissatisfied at the way things were conducted before; so people from different parts tells us."[39] She gives some interesting insights into the way the business was conducted at that time: "No thread can be obtained except for cotton or lard 50 pounds of the former or 30 of the latter for one bunch." The government takes three-quarters of what is made, she adds, and "the guard are paid in thread, & some of the hands, & last week they sold it as high as 25 dollars a bundle."[40]

Following his return to "The Retreat," Merrell was apparently released from further military duty. Owing to the increasing importance and exposed position of the nearby factory, he thought it wise to "get away from that exposed position before it should become too late." Therefore, carefully concealing his plans in order to invite neither hostility nor robbery, Merrell moved his family to Camden. They were settled there by October 1863, and most of his writing in the Owen volume must have been done in Camden. He moved just in time, for a Federal cavalry force was sent to attack the Matlock factory in November, but it was turned back, Merrell says, by a Confederate force that was backed with artillery support.

Once again, Merrell and his family had to start over. He says, "It was like beginning the World anew, our settlement in Camden." But they seemed to make new friends quickly and to become, once again, pillars in their community. Depending upon the interests and tastes of the reader, Merrell's memoirs become, after his removal to Camden, either burdened or enriched with several meticulous accounts of fighting in Arkansas.[41] He describes such battles as Arkansas Post, Prairie Grove, Little Rock, Pine Bluff, Mansfield, Pleasant Hill, and Camden itself, to the capture and re-capture of which he was an eyewitness. He endangered his life by remaining in Camden with his wife, for he could have been executed as a spy. As readers, we should be grateful for his loyalty, for his accounts of the sights and smells of an occupation, together with such vividly rendered moments as the one of his slaves trying to decide whether or not to leave with the Union forces, make for some of his most immediate and most graphic writing.

Most of these accounts of battles, however, seem to be secondhand, although they were based on eyewitness reports, visits to the battlefields, and conversations with Confederate officers. Although he almost never mentions the direct sources for his often highly detailed and dramatic renderings of the fortunes of battle, his friendships with Generals Hindman, Holmes, and Kirby Smith, and the following statements indicate that he had access to firsthand accounts and accurate information: "I was up a good part of the night preparing pocket maps for the officers"; "The Genl. [Kirby Smith] regretted that he had not sent for me before"; "I have said before that the Genl. [Kirby Smith] was personally acquainted with Mrs. Merrell"; "He [Hindman] once told me so"; "I never could discover by conversation with him [Holmes] that . . ."; "to [Holmes's] sharp question, 'What do we do?' I could only answer . . ."; "I had interviews with the Generals [Walker, Frost] having commanded in that region"; "I was assisted at a review at Head Quarters"; "It was then that Col. Parsons told me . . ."; "My views were several times called for"; "I was frequently consulted about the fortifications round the town, about the topography of the Country"; "Since the War I have had the pleasure of telling what I knew about it to General Breckenridge"; "General Marmaduke halted at my gate & asked for the map I had prepared for him." Merrell's credibility in reporting these battles is sustained by his frankness about his own affairs and by such comments as, "I could not say as to the Cavalry, for they were mainly on out-post duty & I could only know so far as I saw."

Some of the Camden property that Merrell and his brother-in-law Charles Arthur Magill had received from John Matlock in exchange for the Royston factory was pressed into service by the Confederacy soon after they arrived in Camden. Magill had become a financial partner in the Royston factory shortly before it was sold to Matlock. For the rest of their lives "Merrell and Magill" would be a major business concern in the Camden area. Merrell preserved among his papers a signed Confederate quartermaster's certificate of 1864 which notes that the Confederate States of America, for the period of September 13 to December 31, paid "Merrell and Magill" $107.00 rent for a brick office building in Camden that was used by the district inspector general, $356.67 for a two-story brick storehouse that was used by the post commissary, and the same amount for a large brick cotton warehouse, used for a military prison and guardhouse. Although Merrell does not mention the event, Magill wrote the Smiths that "our own troops ruined the County far more than the Federals." They tore out "all the doors, windows, counters, & shelves" in one of their buildings. "Complaints to officers were received with laughter," he adds, and "answered by insult." [42]

During the early part of his stay in Camden, it appears that Merrell concerned himself largely with his writing and with the safety of his family. But a man of his talents, energies, and experience was not to be long unnoticed. Following the capture of Camden by General Frederick Steele and its recapture by General Edmund Kirby Smith, Merrell assumed an active role in Confederate military matters. His accounts of his orders from Generals Theophilus Holmes and Edmund Kirby Smith, which are corroborated by documents that he kept among his papers, show that, in some of the long-range planning for the Department of the Trans-Mississippi, Confederate military men relied to an unusual degree upon the recommendations and advice of a man who was basically a civilian, and a Yankee one at that. [43]

Although he wrote of battles, made maps, and designed defenses, Merrell was to be of greatest use to the generals in what he knew best: manufacturing. Writing almost twenty-five years after the event, Judge J. W. Bocage, for whom Merrell shows great respect in his own account of the project, says that early in 1863 the Confederate authorities took charge of the Pike County factory that Merrell had built and which now belonged to Matlock. By the end of the year, it "was hurriedly taken down, thrown promiscuously into wagons and transported over rivers, hills and dales to Mound Prairie, Anderson county, Texas nine miles north of Palestine, to be readjusted and operated by the government, for the benefit of the army of the trans-Mississippi department."[44]

Part of a letter from Mrs. Merrell to her niece Helen Zubly Smith indicates what was in store for her husband in 1864:

> Gen. Holmes has insisted on uncle H. going out to Texas to put up the Fac. I don't know if you know any thing about that as our letters have been lost. In Nov. the Gov. bought it from Mr. Matlock & moved it to Tyler Smith Co. Texas. They were very anxious your uncle should attend to it then but he would not. They employed a Major Busby & sent him out to do it & about 3 weeks ago the news came here that he had not done the first thing about it, he was just a storekeeper at Pine Bluff & knew nothing about Factories. That is about the way Gov. business is carried on this side of the Miss. On hearing this Gen. H. sent for your uncle & urged him very much to undertake it. He hates it very much for he was in hopes never to see the old thing again, but he felt it his duty as it is a matter of so much importance to our army. They are going to send off & get Machinery so as to have quite a large affair of it. He is just now waiting for some papers that have to be drawn out. I cannot bear to have him go, it is 8 days ride from here, & cannot help hoping that Gen. Holmes being called to Richmond may make some change.[45]

Although Merrell tells us in his memoirs that he recommended the idea of a manufacturing village in Texas to furnish "Clothing & Blankets, ordnance, fabrics, shoes, & hats for the army," he was apparently drawn into the project himself against his will and did not go to the Mound Prairie village until much later. Mrs. Merrell writes on July 3 that he has not left yet, that General Kirby Smith "is so taken up with Military matters I think likely he has forgotten all about the Fac. It keeps Mr. Merrell at home." While he waits for orders, "he is studying out all the time something for the good of the cause." He has helped Fagan and Marmaduke, she says, by planning breastworks for them, and "he has been to one of the battlegrounds since & is now improving upon them." She indicates that her husband would prefer to remain at such tasks, "but if Gen. S. thinks it more for the good of the cause that he should go to the Fac. he will go." She says that General Kirby Smith will soon come to Camden and that the matter would be decided then.[46] It was, and Merrell went to Mound Prairie, where, he tells us, "I never worked harder in my life."

According to a receipt for "necessary expenses" that he submitted to the Clothing Bureau, he left Camden for E. Kirby Smith's headquarters at Shreveport on September 12, 1864. His orders from Smith to proceed "to Foreign Parts upon business for this Department" to "purchase and forward . . . certain machinery required by the Clothing Bureau" are dated September 27 in Shreveport. The phrase "foreign parts" refers to England, and the orders specify further that Merrell will be "permitted to return to the Confederacy accompanied by as many foreign mechanics as he may find it expedient to employ by contracts to labor in the Public-Works."

It was necessary for him to go to Texas before leaving for England, for he left Shreveport on October 8 in the company of William W. Bell, his old factory manager who had followed him from Georgia to Royston, bound for Marshall and Mound Prairie, Texas, where he stayed from October 13 to November 15. An interesting document that he kept in his papers is the list of instructions that he gave William Bell, who had remained to be Matlock's superintendent after Merrell had sold out to him. Apparently, all the machinery had not been removed from Arkansas to Texas in 1863, for Merrell gives "Instructions for Mr. Wm. W. Bell's trip to Shreveport and the Pike County Factory Arks., leaving Mound Prairie Anderson County Texas 17 Oct 1864 at noon." After attending to various errands in Camden, Bell is to bring from Pike County to Texas the steam engine, boiler, belting, shafting, bolts, and gearing that remain there.[47]

Having decided to send Merrell to England, Edmund Kirby Smith wrote to Colin J. McRae, the Confederate Financial Agent in England, on October 25, 1864. In this letter, which is printed in the *Official Records* of the Civil War, Kirby Smith tells McRae that his chief of the cotton office has been directed to transfer the sum of $100,000 to McRae's credit with the firm of Fraser, Trenholm & Company of Liverpool, "to be held for the purchase of machinery for the Trans-Mississippi Department, under special instructions from these headquarters." This letter to McRae was to be hand carried by Merrell himself, for the next sentence reads, "You will apply these funds to the payment of such invoices of machinery as may be presented to you, duly authenticated by Mr. Merrill, the bearer of this letter."

Kirby Smith's description of Merrell follows. "This gentleman is a practical manufacturer of long standing and good social position at home. He is familiar with the wants of my department, and I have sent him to England to make all necessary purchases." He asks McRae's help in carrying out his mission. "As he will be a stranger in that country, and may seek advice of you as to the best and cheapest places to make his purchases, I shall esteem it a favor if you will aid him in this as well as in all other respects tending to promote the interest contemplated in his mission." After some details about invoices, Kirby Smith concludes, "Mr. Merrill, please understand, is sent for the purpose only of selecting and purchasing the machinery, payment being made by you or your successor in office. You will also advance him sufficient funds to defray his expenses and the cost of such assistance as he may require."[48]

According to J. W. Bocage, who was in charge of the Mound Prairie project, it was in operation by September of 1863,[49] but Merrell, who is for the most part complimentary of the work of Bocage, was working to bring things together until the time of his departure for England in December of 1864. Bocage's reminiscence in 1887 about Mound Prairie says that there was much disarray when the Merrell-Matlock machinery was originally delivered, "the parts of spinning and drawing frames, cards, railway heads, speeders, lappers, spoolers [sic] and reels were badly mixed, many parts broken and many parts lost." To put everything together, he says, seemed impossible, especially because the blockade was rigid and no one in the South was manufacturing cotton machinery: "The ingenuity of the Confederate artisans was taxed to its utmost."[50]

William H. Etter, the owner and editor of the *Washington Telegraph*, wrote an eyewitness account of the "Busby Cotton factory" to his children on November 16, 1864. "The cotton machinery is in its place in the building—but no Boiler or Engine up yet and no shafting. Nor did I find any hands at work upon the machinery." He saw only a few hands "building the chimney stack" and "some hands working in the shops." Inquiring of someone there "at what time he expected the factory would be in operation," he received the answer of the first of January. He says, "My impression is it will be fully three months before they will be able to commence spinning." The main building "has the appearance of its having been put up with a view of its being a *permanent* institution for the benefit of the country after the war." But the most interesting feature of Mr. Etter's letter is this sentence: "Mr. Merrill who formerly owned the factory in Pike County started yesterday via Houston and Matamoros for England to purchase additional machinery for the factory, and they are framing another building for more machinery."[51]

Merrell left Mound Prairie on November 15, 1864, to inspect the factory run by penitentiary inmates at Huntsville, Texas. He went from there to Anderson, the headquarters of Major General Walker, commissary director, then returned to Huntsville and Anderson, Navasota, and Houston, where he arrived on November 22. On December 1, 1864, Merrell received instructions from Major W. H. Haynes, chief of the Clothing Bureau, to leave on his trip to England to procure machinery for the Mound Prairie factories. This date is corroborated by a letter from Mrs. Merrell to her sister in Roswell, which contains the information that he expected to leave from Houston on December 12. Major Haynes told him, "You will thoroughly inspect work shops and manufactories of army goods in England & France, adapting and purchasing such machinery and appliances as in your judgement are suited to our wants."[52]

Merrell also kept among his papers his copy of an order releasing Private James Lawson from his duties in the Regiment of Volunteers at Mound Prairie, Texas, to accompany him to England as his secretary. They had to leave from Matamoros, Mexico, the closest port that was not blockaded, but there was some delay in getting the final approval to depart. Major Haynes wrote him from Shreveport on Christmas Day, 1864, explaining the necessity of placing himself under the direction of the Confederate agent Mr. C. J. McRae in England: "His opinions, I know from competent sources, have great weight at Richmond & a damper can be thrown on all your efforts by his opposition. In fact I believe he could suspend them altogether." Haynes's convictions about the support that their project would have in Richmond surely must have troubled Merrell as he set out on his journey, for Haynes said, "I am convinced that the Govt. is inimical to becoming its own Manufacturer. I therefore wish to put this business through without exciting the comments of any one, having official relations direct with the Dept. at Richmond."[53]

Merrell also kept among his papers a letter to McRae from P. W. Gray of the Confederate States Treasury Agency in Marshall, Texas, dated December 22, 1864, urging him to make available to Merrell funds to the amount of £20,000 which he had forwarded to Messrs. Fraser, Trenholm and Company. Gray added, "Should these Bills of Exchange not be honored by payment, it will cause Mr. Merrell great embarrassment, which the General desires to guard against, and will call on this agency in such event for the funds at Liverpool." He concludes: "As I have no funds to draw against at this time should you carry out the views of the General, and in default of the collection of the Bills referred to, provide the means of payment, to the extent of Eighty or Ninety thousand dollars, I will as soon as I am able, return to you the amount so advanced."[54]

In the second letter that Major Haynes wrote Merrell on December 25, he told him, "It is the wish of the Genl. that you go forward *at once*." Merrell received this letter, according to his note on it, in Houston on January 12, 1865, and he then began his journey with Lawson to Matamoros, where they took ship for Havana and Southampton. According to his wife, she received a letter from him that was written the day he sailed from Havana, March 8, 1865.[55] Merrell says that he arrived in England on April 1. One week after he had arrived to complete his mission, Lee surrendered.

CHAPTER 39

*I*n the month of January 1855 [1856], I left my family at Roswell in Georgia & started on my expedition to prospect for a new Factory location in some of the five counties in Arkansas, to which my attention had been directed, as set forth in the preceding chapter.[1] My wife's nephew, Wm. Smith of Roswell, late from College and scientifically inclined, accompanied me.[2] We came by rail via Atlanta, Montgomery, & Mobile to N. Orleans, which was at that time the radiating point for all the West. Very cold it happened to be. The Mississippi & Ohio rivers were so frozen over that travelers from the North West bound for N. Orleans were taking this route via Nashville, Chattanooga, and Atlanta. Of those we had a crowd.

Arriving at the city of Mobile, we concluded to begin an economical scale of expenses. I felt poor, & thought I would begin in time to accustom myself to a line of strict economy. So we took our little baggage in our hands and walked to a second class hotel. A thing I had never done before in my life & promise never to do again if I can help it. I doubt if we saved two Dollars by it, and in return had to eat revolting food, and were put to sleep in a cock-loft with nearly a dozen others, in filthy beds, and were kept awake half the night with the slang conversation of our fellow lodgers. Next morning we carried our own baggage with much pain a long way & in much perspiration though out-of-the-way streets to the N. Orleans steamer, cured of the false economy of carrying our own luggage to a cheap Hotel! In N. Orleans I had some letters of introduction to present, which in return procured me letters of introduction to reliable men in Arkansas. I remained [in] N. Orleans only long enough to obtain those letters; then we proceeded in the Memphis Packet "Injomar" to Napoleon, on our way to Little Rock, the Capital of Arkansas. The Arkansas river was we found to be at too low a stage for navigation, & quite frozen over. Napoleon was then, and always, a miserable place to be detained at for an indefinite time, or any time at all, so we proceeded to Helena, near which place I had to look after some land belonging to my friend Duncan of Savannah. At Helena I first made the acquaintance of the Revd. Mr. Welch at that time

William Seagrove (Willie) Smith (1834–65). The oldest son of the Smiths, Willie often accompanied Merrell and worked for him. He did not, however, take to manufacturing, as the Smiths and Merrells hoped he would.

pastor of the Presbyterian Church at that place, and now holding the same relation to the Little Rock Church.[3] From Helena we took passage back to Napoleon on a fine-looking but miserably managed stern-wheel boat, called the "Tennessee Belle," which finally managed to navigate as far as we were going, but probably went to the bottom not long after. On board that boat I became acquainted with Capt. Tilghman, a fine fellow, or at least good company.[4]

All who have read the history of the Mexican War remember Tilghman's [   ]. At the time I speak of, & for several years afterwards, the Capt. was acting as Chief Engineer of several contemplated Rail Roads in Arkansas, but with inferior success because of the same complaints that killed my last manufacturing enterprise in Georgia: & that was want of funds. During this war he has flourished as General Tilghman, very brilliant, but with scarcely more success. He commanded at the loss of Fort McHenry [Henry] & surrendered. My own belief is that he deserved no censure but much praise for his defense, and the manner of his surrender.

Arrived at Napoleon again, we found the Arkansas River still low but rising, & the ice breaking up. After some delay, got under way for Little Rock on board a very different boat, which had no accommodations for passengers. During this delay at Napoleon, we stayed at the public house kept by Gracy—Mike Gracy. Mike was an Irishman, & Napoleon was a

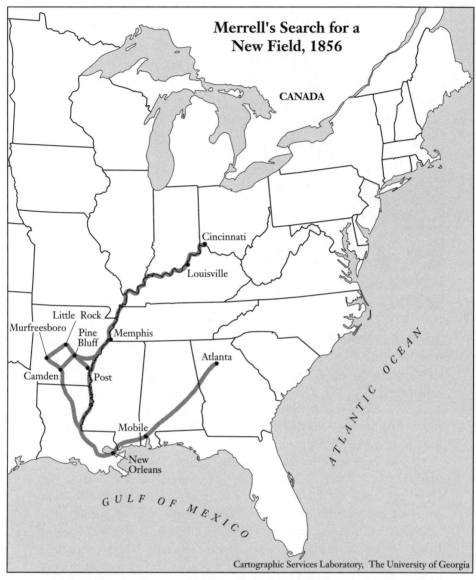

Merrell's Search for a New Field, 1856

CANADA

Cincinnati

Louisville

Little Rock

Murfreesboro

Pine Bluff

Memphis

Camden

Post

Atlanta

Mobile

New Orleans

ATLANTIC OCEAN

GULF OF MEXICO

Cartographic Services Laboratory, The University of Georgia

From Greene County, Georgia, Merrell travels by railroad, steamboat, and horseback to Pike County, Arkansas, searching for the ideal location for a water-powered textile factory. He then goes by steamboat to Cincinnati to purchase machinery and returns through New Orleans to pick up stores for the barter trade that he will carry on.

bad place, not for rows with the fists and shalaley, such as he would have delighted in, but for street fights and nightly assassinations with pistol & bowie-knife. Any day there was somebody killed or wounded, or somebody died that had been so wounded; or at least some one thing or other about a "difficulty." Mike had his own way of getting along without trouble in that Sodom. "I niver," said he, "I niver hears a word that's said, and whinever a man is kilt, I'd not see it if I was looking. I niver has any opinions at all at all, and kinslequently I sees no trouble." In a word, Mike undertook to have no friends or enemies, which he thought the best way "intirely." But, as might have been expected, having no friends, he had no one to stand up for him or to avenge his death, & it was not long before I heard that he too had been killed by somebody.

This state of things at the very threshold of Arkansas was poor encouragement for me, but I considered that the population of a river town on the Mississippi represented not the population of Arkansas, but the floating population of the river people. To a considerable extent, I have found this conclusion to be the correct one. Nevertheless, the influence of those river towns extended some distance back into the country. Thirty miles back I found a family of a wealthy planter who told me that the father had been wounded nine times in neighborhood affairs & finally died in his bed. A Mother, who lived at about the same distance in another direction, told Dr. Magill that she had raised seven sons, of whom six had died by the knife or pistol, & she expected the seventh son to do so likewise. She gloried in it, & said she never wanted any of hers to die in any other way! I have found, in the back country of Arkansas, a reckless disregard of human life, but by no means so bad as the tone of society at and near Napoleon. I suppose the general estimation of human life in Arkansas, or any where else, is the correct one, & quite up to the actual value of the lives in question.

The difficulties of the navigation were such that we landed at Pine Bluff & hired a conveyance to take us as far as Tulip in Dallas Co., which would be within the range of public conveyances carrying me, I thought, where I would like to go. At Tulip I made the acquaintance of several gentlemen whom I came to know more intimately afterwards. Viz. Judge Summerville, Genl. Nat Smith, & Howell Taylor.[5] There Young Smith, my nephew, expressed a desire to visit the Hot Springs of Arkansas and the "Magnet Cove" for scientific purposes. Having no time myself to spare, we parted, & he went to those places by public conveyance, while I purchased a horse, saddle, & bridle, & proceeded on my journey in that manner. I bought the horse because it suited me & not because I needed one so soon. I might have gone further by public conveyance but should have had the horse to buy at last. While we were at Tulip, the gentlemen treated us to a deer-drive, Howell Taylor being the Nimrod. Although a Methodist preacher, & a wealthy planter to boot, he was a mighty hunter, killing as many as forty bears in one season. In this deer-drive I gained the credit of shooting the deer as it ran past my stand. We killed but one, & it was said to go down at the crack of my gun, though some other men fired nearly at the same time, & I was not disposed to claim the shot. One of our party shot another, which lay apparently dying while he re-loaded his gun. In its agony it had left its hair upon the saplings against which it had thrashed itself; but just before he had finished re-loading, it sprang to its feet and ran away very fast. I have since witnessed other instances of the great vitality of the deer under certain circumstances. I once shot a power-ful buck coming at full speed towards me. One buckshot entered between his breast & the shoulder-blade so that his leg hung entirely loose; yet I could see no difference in his running except that he ran faster; and finally, when we got him, he fought the dogs after a knife had been some time in his heart. They will at times run a long way and very swift with both fore-legs broken by a shot. They have been found with old rifle-bullets buried in the heart and healed over.

From Tulip to Camden I rode in company with Judge Summerville who was on his way to attend a meeting of the Directors of the Ouachita & Red River Rail Road. I thought it best to attend also, expecting to see at that meeting persons from all parts who could give me the information I desired, thus saving me much time and expense in travelling, and I was not disappointed. What I thus learned respecting the country served to confirm me in the views I had arrived at before leaving Georgia.

From Camden to Washington in Hempstead County alone on horse-back. There I presented my letter of introduction to General Royston who immediately entered into my views with all his might, and all who know him well understand what I mean by that.[6] The General goes either for or against a thing at once and with all his might. It so happened that while I was talking with Genl. R. in the parlor of Smith's Hotel, Judge White from Pike Co. came in, & Genl. R. said there was "the man of all others that I should see at that stage of the business."[7] We were introduced, & when I had stated my views, he told me that the only place in the whole country was a mill-seat of long standing but still on Government land, situated three or four miles north of Murfreesboro in Pike County. Others were of the same opinion. The place had been forty years known through all the counterfeiting and territorial times as "Hugh's Mill," and had a good reputation.

Col. Blevins and others were of the same opinion about the place.[8] The location precisely answered to my wants, & I went with Judge White to see it. It pleased me. But not to decide by first impressions, I reconsidered the whole matter thus. Within the scope of country to which my search was now reduced, there were only the following water courses large enough for my purpose.

The Sabine, Ouachita, Caddo, Little Missouri and the Cossatot. The two first were too large for me to dam up with my limited means, with any reasonable hope of success. The Cossatot was too near the Indian Country, and a very dangerous river in times of flood. The Caddo was the best stream of all, but the only water-power on it that would answer my purpose, was already occupied by an expensive mill, for which the owners asked a sum equal to my entire capital. Therefore, the Little Missouri River was my only chance, and the old "Hugh's Mill seat" was the only location on that river answering to the conditions I had previously laid down. There were, moreover, some advantages at this location over any other. It was near enough the frontier to command trade from both Texas and the Choctaw nation. It was in the midst of a grain-growing region, and yet near enough to the best cotton lands in the World, *i.e.*, the Red River bottoms. As to a population of poor people for laborers, there were certainly enough of them, and there appeared to be no local causes whatever for sickness. I purchased the right of the occupant (Mr. Dorsey) at a low rate, I thought, and immediately returning to the land office at Washington, entered and paid for the land more than enough for the site of a manufacturing village: say six or seven hundred acres in all.[9] And once more I felt myself to be fairly embarked in business. Others wondered at what I could be at, but to me it was no experiment. I had the Roswell business to do over again, with a more limited capital, to be sure, but with far better advantages, and I went about it with all my heart and in excellent spirits.

My nephew, Smith, was to have rejoined me at Washington, but the water-courses were swollen by rain, & he was water-bound somewhere.[10] The stages did not arrive. I could wait no longer. My time was now precious. I must forthwith go to the North and purchase machinery, & I determined to make my way on the Little Rock road until I found my nephew & then proceed with the journey. We came to-gether at Antoine. I left my horse in good hands, & with some trouble (for it continued to rain), we arrived at Little Rock. There I introduced myself to Roswell Beebe Esq. who was then Prest. of the Cairo & Fulton R. Road.[11] I had been his correspondent years before. It appeared that, out of business, & full of system if not energy, he was anxious to invest largely in a public-spirited &

profitable way. His first thought was in favor of a Cotton Factory. Understanding that Georgia was at the head of Southern Manufacturing, he had obtained an introduction from Senator Borland of Arkansas to Senator Dawson of Georgia.[12] Judge Dawson referred him to me, & that opened the correspondence referred to, which continued a long time, and did not end with the subject of Manufacturing. I turned his attention to Rail Roading as the best thing for Arkansas, and advised him to have nothing to do with Cotton Manufacturing unless he had been raised to the business. It is probable that he embarked in the Cairo & Fulton Road upon ideas suggested during his correspondence with me. My first personal acquaintance with him was upon my arrival as above at Little Rock, and it was my last, for he died not long after, so that his words to me may almost be regarded as his dying words.[13]

He had us to tea at his house, and the next morning came to the Hotel & went to the steam-boat to see us off. I was shocked at the change one night had made in his appearance! On the evening before, at his own house, with his young wife and charming daughter at the piano, he was the picture of robust health. In the morning he looked as though he had the cholera! I knew the cause. Before he called on me that morning, I had seen in the newspaper a scurrilous assault on Mr. Beebe.[14] One of those low, vulgar philippics that carry their refutation on their face & excite sympathy for the victim. Of course, I did not allude to it, but he, assuming that I must have read it, gave me his parting advice, nearly in these words.

"You have now determined to locate a Cotton and Woolen Factory in this State of Arkansas. It is a good thing & a public-spirited thing. Make up your mind before-hand to be insulted & abused. You say you are no part of a politician & expect to flourish only in private life. You will not be suffered to remain in private life. Politics will be thrust upon you. Every thing in Arkansas runs into politics & politics in everything. Even the Church is used for political purposes here, & family social relations are regulated by them. You will find yourself constrained to join in with some one or other of the political coteries; otherwise, you will have no friends at all. And once in, you will find Arkansas politics to be more bitter than death." I felt sorry for him & listened to his views with profound respect, but I regarded them as the sorrows of a disappointed old man. Subsequent experience, however, has satisfied me that he was not far wrong as to the very bilious character of the Arkansas politics.

Arriving at Memphis, my nephew expressed himself satisfied & tired of the trip, & homesick. So we parted, he going home to Roswell in Georgia by Rail Road, & I by the first boat to Cincinnati. The navigation of the

Mississippi River was greatly obstructed by fields of floating ice, so that we were ten days making the trip in a good boat (the "Belle Key") from Memphis to Louisville. Very cold it was and the boat thronged with passengers. I cannot better fill up the time of that journey than by narrating one of the incidents of travel. Of course, there is no end of writing when it comes to that. I will, however, indulge myself in one now and then, taking care that it shall be characteristic of somebody or some thing.[15]

I did not travel any further North than Cincinnati. Some heavy articles of mill wright work I could purchase there, but my fine machinery for carding and spinning I had to obtain from the Eastward. That however was no material disadvantage, for my mind was all made up as to exactly what I wanted. My circumstances did not admit of any more mistakes in the purchase of machinery. I had made up my mind to have carding and spinning machinery of Charles Danforth of Paterson, N. Jersey. I scarcely would have had the machinery of any other builder as a gift. This opinion of his machinery was the result of my own experience. I did get machinery from him for this my last chance of success, & I have had no occasion to regret it.

Charles Danforth was a factory boy once. As far back as my memory carries me, there was always on trial some improvement of his in the machinery for carding and spinning Cotton, but like everything that is genuine and good, he and his improvements encountered the most unaccountable opposition. I never could tell why, but although his great genius made substantial & undoubted improvements in every department of Cotton Carding and spinning, until he had a system of his own, unlike any other, no one, that I know of, was found to adopt his improvements as a whole, except himself. For himself he had him a spinning Factory in his Machine Works at Paterson that was a mint to him when all other spinners were doing badly. He became very wealthy, but never so as to be above his business. It was this success of his own that compelled others to recognize the superiority of his machinery, & I among the rest. But this recognition did not take place until he had become indifferent about Cotton Machinery & turned his genius to the improvement of Rail Road Machinery. However, he made what machinery I wanted & it was a success. Mr. Danforth was a man of large frame. He was a slow-spoken man & not disposed to push himself or his inventions upon any one. He advised me, years before, when I was building the Greensboro Factory to adopt his machinery, but I thought he was talking in his own interest, & I knew best. Had I been governed by his advice, I should have been living in Georgia yet and a prosperous man. But such was not the Will of God. For in starting the Greensboro Factory, I was left to go and purchase machinery from Mr. Leonard of the Matteawan Machine Co., of N. York City. A man that I had long known to be a sharper, whom I had been warned to have nothing to do with, and whose machinery had many a time in my early life given so much trouble that I had resolved to keep myself clear of it. And yet I long afterwards went out and bought it! It shows the power of circumstances to constrain a man out of his own way, and against his judgment. My funds were short, & Mr. Leonard undertook to furnish much more machinery for the same money than other men. I purchased from him & was ruined. So this last time, when I was reduced to one single chance in Arkansas, I determined to get my machinery from the right man at last, & I did so. I purchased from Mr. Danforth, who took special care to give me a good start in my new business.[16]

Dr. Magill, my wife's brother, was then living in Chicago Ill. It had been understood between him & me, by correspondence, that [when] I broke up in Ga. and removed to the West, he was to go with [me]. I do not know his reasons for throwing up his position in Chicago, but I understood that he held himself in readiness to do so, and go with me. From Cincinnati, therefore, I sent him a Telegraph Dispatch, & he immediately came. The Doctor, by the way, has had his ups and downs in the world as well as I. First he studied law at his native place, St. Mary's in Georgia. Admitted to the Bar before he was twenty one years of age, he tried that awhile & did not like it. Then he studied medicine, & spent several years at the different medical Colleges & finally graduated at the N. York University. He was much pleased with the Student life of his new profession, but the practice of Medicine he never could [   ] a way with, & he took a Writer's position under the U.S. Government at Washington City, and at the incoming [of] a new party exchanged for some other like post at Chicago, Ill. From thence he came and joined me at Cincinnati. From that time to the date of this writing he has been connected with me in business.[17]

Having completed my machinery arrangements at the North, and quite recovered the tone of my health, we left together for N. Orleans on the fine new Louisville Packet the "Montgomery." This trip of ten days, we are agreed, was the most agreeable time we remembered ever to have had on board a steamboat.

The large number of passengers were generally agreeable people. The waters of the Miss. were at a height that we could overlook the Country. Every day as we descended the river, changing our latitude by so much further South, so that a gradual but rapid change came over the landscape from hard winter to early spring, & finally, as we descended the "Coast" and neared the City of N. Orleans, the face of the country seemed to us to revel in an opulence of vegetation. It was the first time I had passed by daylight through the "Coast" of Louisiana, so famous for its refinement & the high state of cultivation. We had for fellow passengers a corps of professional musicians, among whom were Paul Julian & the little Patti, who gave us a Concert on board. While I am on the subject of music, let me mention that while in the City that time, I had the pleasure to hear Ole Bull play his violin, with Paul Julian for an auditor. I thought that Julian looked very pale. Ole Bull was a performer of much more genius than Julian, but understood to have less knowledge of the science of music. And it is worthy of remark that the most popular Artists are seldom those who claim to be very scientific in their profession. Of course that is so. Art will go in advance of popular taste.[18]

My business in N. Orleans was to lay in a general assortment of merchandise for a Store I intended to establish on the ground as the nucleus of my Factory town. This was an essential part of my plan. Profiting by our experience at Roswell, I made calculations to pay money only for land and machinery, leaving all materials and labor to be paid for in goods from the Store. By this means, I expected to make as great a profit on our capital while erecting the works as I could expect to make by the works themselves when completed. I knew exactly what I was about in this matter, for we had tried the same thing partially at Roswell nearly twenty years before. By means of our Store we kept our hands close at their work, & controlled labor that could not have been steadily controlled by wages in money.

With the money, our hands would have spent their time, a great part of it, in straggling many miles away to make their purchases. Paying them in supplies, we made a handsome profit to ourselves, & kept the hands under our influence. This Store turned out as I expected, to be the center around which all our business revolved; and the business, in that frontier location, could not have gone on without the Store any more than a wheel without its hub.

CHAPTER 40

*W*hile I was making my purchases in N. Orleans, Dr. Magill went to Georgia in order to fetch my wife and family of servants.[1] Fortunately, we had no children. None were ever born to us. Having completed my purchases, I accompanied my goods on the Steam Boat the "Stacy" to

Camden, in order to be ahead of time and hold a conference with Mr. John Matlock, of whom more hereafter. The season was rather late for Steam Boating on the Ouachita R. and our boat, being a larger one, could proceed no further than Beech Hills, a landing fourteen miles (I think) below Camden. There a small boat undertook to carry passengers and freight forward to Camden. Others of the passengers who had freight on board ordered it transferred to the little boat, but as for myself, I went on board, but declined to interfere with my freight, for it was Insured to Camden on the "Stacy" & nothing said about privilege of transshipment. Although the captain seemed disposed to bully me, I replied that I had nothing to do with it. He had given me a through Bill of Lading to Camden, & I could not hazard my insurance, nor assume his responsibility by assenting to anything. He must do as he thought best under the circumstances without reference to my approval or disapproval. This view of the case caused him to give special attention to the forwarding of my packages, & put me quite at my ease, so that when the little boat, while ascending the river ran upon a snag with such violence as to throw all into confusion, and the mate ran below to report damages; while he was gone I saw many pale & anxious faces, but felt no anxiety at all myself.

Arriving at Camden I saw for the first time Mr. Matlock. He was then doing business in a wooden building now demolished upon his removal into his new brick Store house. Everything about him indicated the thriving merchant. The way I came to know him was as follows. During my first visit to Camden, the inquiries I had to make introduced me pretty generally, but I did not happen to meet with Mr. Matlock. Indeed, he was not a talker & never much on the street. He may have seen me. I was generally asked in Camden if I wanted Capital, & I invariably answered no, because in truth I had seen enough already of capitalists and joint-stock companies, and hoped never to have any more to do with them.

I also knew that an entire stranger asking for Capital to undertake a novel enterprise, would be treated as an adventurer. As for me, all I wanted was correct information concerning the back country trading to Camden. Upon this the gentlemen talked Capital quite freely, & the more freely, as I afterwards learned, in proportion as they had no Capital to spare, but rather the reverse.

But Mr. Matlock was not one of those. He had the money, but was not disposed to talk about it. After I had left, he wrote me a letter, saying that he understood a stranger was in the country seeking a location for a Factory. It was a good idea. Did I lack Capital? If so he had $15,000 or $20,000 at my service if I would take a partner, and he would await my answer. That letter was handed to me at Antoine in the month of February as I went, half-drowned, in the Stage to Little Rock. I had not intended to take a partner on any terms. But there was a straight out Western way in which he tendered to a perfect stranger a risk of so much money, which struck me very favorably, & I reconsidered the matter until I made up my mind to give a conditional assent to his proposition.

I wrote to him that I was on my way to purchase machinery & should be absent until April. I would return via Camden & give him opr. to know me personally. In the mean time I desired him to inquire into my antecedents in Georgia, and if after all that, when we came to see each other, he continued to be of the same mind, we would make a partnership, the practical effect on our business being simply to make it more extensive than I intended. The result was that when we came to see each other in April, after my round-about tour to Cincinnati & N. Orleans, we were mutually pleased, and he being entirely satisfied after the references he had written to in Georgia, we agreed to make up a co-partnership, in which the Trustees of my wife (B. King & A. Smith) should put in $15,000, Mr. John Matlock $15,000, & I should have a salary for my services, & Dr. Magill a salary for his services under me. By the time these arrangements were consummated, Dr. Magill rejoined me, with my wife and her servants, and we all proceeded to our new home among the Mountains of Arkansas; quite a caravan, but, to tell the truth, all but myself quite disheartened at the manifest want of thrift among the settlers and the old tumble-down appearance of the settlements along the road. This was unexpected in a new country, & my family did not understand at first sight what they afterwards learned. The state of Arkansas had not settled at the first intention, or the second. During many years, this Southern portion of the State lay on the confines of Mexico, the Red River being the boundary line; and all that bad population of counterfeiters and horse-thieves which can flourish only on the outermost verge of society were congregated here. The Counterfeits were of Mexican Silver Dollars, and for a blind the counterfeiters sometimes made excavations in the ground, pretending to work silver mines. Those traces of their work have misled many as to the mineral resources of Arkansas.

The Austin Settlements in Texas carried away not only the population I have mentioned but many good families of citizens. Forty such families, as I understand, went from Hempstead County alone at one time.[2]

Then came the War of Texan Independence, drawing for adventurous men; and following that, the final settlement of Texas from the old States, an Exodus in which the Territory & State of Arkansas served only as a thoroughfare for others to pass through on their way beyond. Then came the Mexican War, calling for more men, and after that the settlement of California. Throughout all those mutations of our time, Arkansas has thus played little more than the part of a high-way, raising food one year to supply the transit of emigration for the next year. Moreover, because of the unusual extent of swamp or overflowed lands in Arkansas, the country is generally more sickly than other new countries, the extraordinary richness of those overflowed lands being no inducement to white settlers equivalent to good health. And in this connexion I may as well say what my subsequent experience has proven, that different in that respect from other countries, the Mountainous parts of Arkansas are perhaps more sickly than the low country. Some charge this to the mineral character of the water, but I have not detected more mineral in waters here than elsewhere. I apprehend that the miasma, or whatever it may be, rising from the extensive low country, being of course lighter than good air, floats or is carried away by the winds to the mountains, and there is perhaps condensed until it comes within the range of human lungs. I have observed that in our new home we might look for sickness following the long prevalence of a south wind blowing to us from off the lakes and bayous of the Red River.

However all this may be, I found myself at the very outset of my enterprise in Arkansas, checked simply by discontent and sickness, and finally mutiny in my family, involving all, both black & white — *all* were involved. Not one exception. It was definitively proposed that I should sacrifice what had been already done, & carry them all back to Georgia. They could not see things from my point of view. They could only feel the present inconveniences without one ray of hope that we ever could improve upon our condition. On the other hand, I considered that this was my last stake. That I was not going blindly, but knew exactly what I was about. That our condition in a new settlement was at the worst in the beginning and must improve gradually to any pitch of refinement and good living that we desired. Under these circumstances I dared not yield my point, and in order to make it good against so much and such violent opposition, I assumed a firmness, something amounting to sternness (they called it tyranny), which I did not altogether feel. This state of mutiny never did quite die out in my family so long as I remained at that place. My successes over-ruled it generally, but it broke out afresh at every reverse, & every time of sickness, so that I may truly say that in all that arduous undertaking I was only sustained, at those times when one needs comfort & support at home, by the mind conscious of rectitude, & not always by that, for sometimes I felt that I must be in the wrong where so many were against me. I managed,

however, to effect a compromise by agreeing not to make that our permanent home, but to sell out & return to polite society, as soon as I should
have achieved sufficient success, say in five or six years if possible.

During this state of things I lost several servants by desertion. John, the
husband of Tabby, ran away and contrived to get back to Georgia under
the escort of a gang of gamblers who had been attending (professionally)
on a session of the Arkansas Legislature. He left his own wife with me,
who besides being the best servant and one of the best women I ever knew,
was & still is a most affectionate wife to him, & sends him all the money
she can lay by. He, the rascal, left her & ran away from me to get back
to Georgia where he had a mistress whom he preferred to Tabby. Tabby's
fidelity to that villain, through bad treatment and evil reports, has been
one of the most beautiful passages of human nature I ever have witnessed.
In this instance at least, the institution of slavery has had a tendency to
keep man & wife from separating, & I am satisfied from experience that it
is often so. Perhaps such cases are quite as frequent as the cases of forcible
separation by sale. The other case of desertion from my family was the
case of Pratt (John) whom I had trained up to be a good machinist. He
was always flush of money & dressed finer than I. Having got our Factory
going, I allowed him to return to Georgia on a visit, upon his promise to
return. Once there he coolly wrote me (for he could write) that he had
concluded not to return & had found a master of his own choosing there!
He also had a mistress in Georgia, whom he had dressed finely, having deserted his own wife. His new master sent me in money about half his value,
i.e., just what I had paid for him before I had made him a proficient in his
trade, with which I was fain to be content. But the rascal, no longer under
my restraints, was soon after detected in practices to procure abortion, &
had to be sent somewhere to the West again to save his life, justly forfeited
to the laws. Those Negroes who remained under me have maintained a
good character, and it will evermore be just so. The Slave, as compared
with the free Negro, or the Negro who has his own way, lives the innocent
life & is the happiest man. Both those run-away Negroes of ours were
"stuck-up" Negroes. The first was a Barber by trade, the last, as I have
said, was a machinist. All our other Negroes have been simply "servants,"
which is the position for them, & as such I can truly say they have been
happy, & generally have done all they could to render my family happy,
excepting Helen, who, having been raised a pet and taught to read, has
had a spirit of discontent above her fellow servants, her light complexion
misleading her into the society of lewd white people.[3]

Among all our servants first & last, next to Tabby, I must record the name of Edmund. Though a black Negro, & in the strictest sense of the word a servant, he is a *gentleman*.

From my white family, during all the time of what they would call their "banishment" into Arkansas, I have never actually had a desertion, but those of them who take the trouble to read this will know for themselves how near it came to that several times, and how much nearer it would have come had they not been relieved by occasional journeys to Georgia & to the Northern States.

All this can be reasonably explained. On my part, and from my own point of view, I could see no hardship about the undertaking except the occasional sickness, of which, by the way, I had more than my own share. As to local attachments, I had none, except for my native place in the North. In Georgia I had buried a sister. There I had worked many years, as it were, within an inch of my life & had at last no reward, but much the contrary. No consideration on earth would have induced me to go back there a disappointed man to be a poor relation dependent upon others. Starting a new enterprise was in itself a pleasure to me. If I possessed any genius, it was for that very thing, and beginning life over again in Arkansas was less a hardship to me than it was in 1839 to come from N. York State to the Mountains of Georgia & make my first beginning there. It was by so much a less hardship, as I had now a more substantial experience in my business, & success could not this time be scarcely called a problem. On the other hand my wife (although fond of work, and in point of fact, and "not to put too fine a point upon it," she was and still is the most thoroughgoing housekeeper probably in the world) was at the same time accustomed to polite society, and could see no good in keeping house for any other purpose. Of an old and genteel family herself, she considered that the acquisition of Wealth could add nothing to her respectability, but rather the reverse, for she had been raised to cultivate the intimacy of respectable people in reduced circumstances, rather than that of Wealthy folk who valued themselves upon their wealth alone. Indeed, I rather think she preferred herself to live the dried up economical life of a genteel person in reduced circumstances, a life that would have been torment to me.

I have said that I compromised all this by agreeing not to make a permanent thing of our mountain home in Arkansas, but to return to what she would have called "White Settlements," as soon as practicable after having secured a competency. The sequel will show how I have kept this promise. In the mean time I considered that, as a general average, between my wife's predilections and my own misfortunes, that was doing pretty well, for we had enjoyed a good time in Georgia in her line of things. We had lived very well & seen plenty of company of such as she preferred, & I thought a probation of five or six years not an intolerable thing under the circumstances.

I think I have written enough on this point to set myself right, or wrong as the case may be, in the eyes of those inquiring friends who have so often wondered that I should have carried such a wife as I had to such a place in Arkansas.

And I may now proceed with the Robinson Crusoe details of my Factory engineering in Arkansas, with little more than the wild woods for resources, and the wild Arabs for my helpers.

CHAPTER 41

*O*ur new home Pike County, Arkansas was indeed, in this year of 1855 [1856] a rough place to begin with! By the way, what can be the reason why in every state "Pike County" is the poorest county? So far as my knowledge extends, that is the case, until the fact has become a proverb. Our County of Pike was poor enough & mean enough to make good the saying referred to. Situated in the immediate vicinity of very rich counties, it seemed to have been excluded from their set, and elbowed away into the coves of the mountain and among the gravel ridges, scarcely enough arable land being assigned it to feed the miserable population, who did not look as though they ever could have much appetite to eat what little they had. In the first place it was a sickly county. This was a surprise to me, for in all other States I had found the mountain counties more healthy than other parts. When I found the fact in this case to be the reverse of what I had been led to expect, I hunted up the letter which had been written to me in Georgia by the County Clerk of Pike County Ark., assuring me as to the healthfulness of the location. When I showed it to him & asked how he accounted for that, he coolly replied that he thought it right to offer such inducements, at the expense of a little truth, for men of capital to settle in the county! While I am about it, I may as well add that his view in the case was only too much in accordance with frontier ethics generally, at least on the question of location.

We found the County well-nigh shoeless, hatless, and in rags. Even the rifle of the hunter had often the old flint lock wrapped and tied with a whang of deer skin. Their houses of logs, & very rude logs at that, scarcely higher than a man could stand up in, with stick & mud chimneys not a great deal taller than the man himself. So little before-hand were they, that the failure of a single crop, of which they raised only a patch, reduced them to starvation, which had been actually the case the year before we arrived. Many had lived and died upon wild roots such as they could find in the woods.

Their trade consisted mainly of the Exchange of deer skins and venison hams for a little powder and lead and Tobacco, and a very little "seed-tick Coffee." A few years before, they had been stimulated by the local trade to raise some cotton for market, and upon the strength of it they had been allowed to trade on credit to the probable amount of several years' incoming Crops in advance. As might have been expected, said crops were not forthcoming. In the first place, the people being paid before-hand, and protected against their own debts by the "Homestead Exemption Law," had no motive recognized in their code for paying their creditors; and, in the second place, the uniform sickliness of every fall season of the year prevented the gathering of such crops as were made, until the frost and rains had nearly ruined them for market. For those reasons, in addition to the general good-for-nothing & lazy disposition of the mountain people, we found the raising cotton in Pike County to be nearly extinct, while at the same time, in the adjacent counties where rich lands lay in large bodies and could be cultivated in systematic plantations of Negroes, Cotton of the best kinds was the staple production, and in large quantities. The short-lived credit system above referred to had "worsted" the costume of our new neighbors, for instead of the picturesque buck-skin hunting shirt, leggings, & moccasins, or the comfortable & enduring homespun, we found them as I stated in the rags of "boughten" finery. The Northern brogan with several toes out making tracks in the mud, the silk hat rimless and crownless, and red tags of broad-cloth and calico here and there upon them. Afterwards, when they began to improve in personal appearance, under the influence of our trade which we exchanged with them for supplies and labor, I undertook to keep a museum of old hats, shoes, &c. shed and cast off at our store, so as to illustrate the improvement they were bound to make [under] our hands. Of education, of course there was, among such people, worse than none at all; for if one among many happened to have a glimmering of arithmetic & writing, it only served to make him the greater rascal, and the laws had to be administered with a view to protect the ignorant against the knowing.

The County & Circuit Courthouse & Clerk's office was a log house of one room, juries holding their sittings in the open air among the forest-trees. The original Courthouse, upon which this appeared to be an improvement, had been burned with all the records, by an incendiary as was believed. As to who among them it could be that had done the deed, they could only form an opinion upon Cato's "qui bono," of which quotation, however, they had never heard, often as they acted upon the principle.[1]

As to the state of religion among them, the least said about that is the best. The state of denominational religion was belligerent—decidedly. The Methodist order had had a footing once, as they always do have on the frontier, and were doing good until one day along came a preacher of some other denomination who was great at Controversy. Whereupon, instead of cooperating to do good, the two preachers fell to debating in public upon the tenets of their religion. The people, instead of adhering each party to its own champion right or wrong, went over generally to the one who in their opinion "beat." And in their opinion he was the victor who talked the loudest and longest & bore on the hardest. The successful champion, having thus broken into the existing state of things, & committed the population to his side, went away, leaving nothing behind worth mentioning in the form or substance of religion. Their religion [was] worsted by the controversy much as their costume was worsted by the credit system.

And now when I have added that my new neighbors sat down on their heels to talk, and slept (at least the women did so) in their frocks and bonnets, the same they wore by day. That the greater number had "ague cake" or enlargement of the spleen, ate with a one-tined fork or no fork at all, at tables so high & chairs so low as to bring the plate to the mouth, nearly, and that a still greater number, soured by indigestion, labored in their feeding to masticate hard cornbread or still harder biscuits as black & heavy, nearly, as grape shot. And that in order to arrive at even that pitch of good living, they had to go to mills from ten to fifty miles distant from their homes and often wait a week or more. I say, when I have added these few out of many traits of frontier life in Arkansas, it may well be conceded that I had found the missionary ground for a manufacturer. How I succeeded finally in getting those same people in the way of good preaching, good eating, comfortable clothing, & more industrious habits will hereafter appear; but alas! this wretched war! this wretched war has undone all that, & more good besides.

When we arrived there were persons living in the vicinity who had killed the Buffalo on the spot where the Factory village now stands, and one man in particular still persevered in trapping for beaver in our mill pond. There was one panther occasionally seen or heard in our vicinity, & now and then a Bear. Wild cats were numerous, but the only abundant game was the Deer, which were killed for their skins, the meat being left to the buzzards. But at the best, so precarious is the livelihood obtained by hunting, that the demand for labor and provisions at the building of the factory soon put an end to hunting as a business except for the meat. Fishing was always fine in the spring of the year, & our dam, too high for them to leap, was the head of navigation for those fish that ascend the rivers to deposit their spawn and then return to deeper waters. Such an abundance of fish, fine as they may be, soon cloy the appetite and cease to be a luxury. It may be that, as we grow older, the taste for food meets with a change; it may be that the same food in different parts of the country varies in quality; perhaps it is owing to both causes that we soon tired of the food most abundant in Arkansas: to wit, Fish, Venison, & the beef of wild cattle.

Our new home was in the midst of romantic scenery, and the location appeared to be all that could be desired towards the building of a town; but, as I have said before, the first sight of the premises was not very inviting to my family, who could not foresee with my hopeful eyes the future rows of houses, the grounds neatly trimmed into rows of shade-trees, & the throngs of customers from all parts trading with us. When we first arrived, the grounds were covered with a tangled undergrowth or thicket, strewn with fallen and decayed timber, which bred insects by millions, and tainted the air with a sickening vapor. The night was vocal with the tiresome drone of this world of insects, the hooting of the owl, the mournful song of the whip-poor-will, and occasionally the bark of the wolf or the fox & the scream of the wild cat. The only shelter for our heads was a double cabin log house, which the four winds were free to enter by every chink & cranny. Crowded as we were into this narrow space, we had not undisputed possession. One half the house was claimed by Capt. Snell, the Miller, who stood by his rifle and claimed that he had the mill from my predecessor for the year on "sheers" and could not be ejected. The other half of the miserable house, was a disputed possession between us and the bed-bugs by night and the long-leg-grandfathers by day. Those pestiferous insects were more numerous than I had supposed possible, although I had in my time travelled and slept with "strange bed-fellows" before. Capt. Snell was an old man with a young wife, whereupon his jealousy of Dr. Magill, (without cause, I believe), soon drove him away & gave us the whole house, but not so the insects I have referred to. Nothing short of a conflagration of the whole premises could rid us of them; so I resolved to build us a house, even before I could afford to do so. But before that I had, of necessity, built a store-house of logs to receive our merchandise and offer it for sale. This first log house that I had ever built satisfied me in the building of it that the log house is the most costly of all houses and never is a house at last. I therefore never built another after that kind, but having as yet no saw-mill of our own, purchased the lumber for our new dwelling, when I could ill afford it.

The Mill referred to was a curiosity, yet rude as I shall describe it to have been, it was one of the best in the country. The mill dam was built of alternate layers of logs and pine tops or brush, weighted down with stones. This leaky structure was made watertight by the leaves of forest trees floating down the stream and depositing themselves by suction upon the leaks. Nature being assisted occasionally in the same way by the labors of customers at the mill impatient with their grinding.

The mill itself was built of logs, perched on stilts so as to be out of the reach to an ordinary freshet, but at the same time so inartificially constructed as to tempt destruction in the most reckless manner. Wonderful to tell! such rude works often stand where more expensive erections are swept away by the flood. There is a proverb which says "a fool for luck," but not so, say I. Those rude and ignorant mill-wrights on the frontiers work with no science to be sure, but with an instinct like that of the beaver suited to their circumstances. The brush-dam is in fact an imitation of the beaver's work, and for a mountain torrent and a rock foundation is the very best dam that can be made by men of limited means. It will even stand when more scientific work is washed away.

The Little Missouri river, at the point I had selected, was at times a mountain torrent. The neighbors generally, not to discourage me at the outset, did not give me a full idea of the dangers of my new location in that particular; yet there were some who from a motive of ill will gave me exaggerated ideas of the same. I learned enough by the water-marks on the banks to warn me that my utmost skill as an engineer would be necessary in laying the foundations of my work. The river above me drained a radius of about thirty miles of mountainous country which had no marshes to retain the waters that fell from the clouds; but when they fell, as sometimes they did, in torrents, the freshet came upon us all at once without any reservation, & sometimes like a great wave. A wagoner might be camped by a ford which would scarcely reach the axles of his wagon, & suddenly, before he could well harness his team and get away, the river would be raging around him.

The south winds most prevalent during the dry seasons, carried the clouds towards the mountains north of us, where they condensed and came down in rains with tremendous thunderings and lightnings. I could sit in my back piazza on a sultry evening &, looking out towards the mountains, witness the gathering and breaking of those storms. A few hours afterwards, I would have the same waters to fight as they came thundering over our dam. Fortunately for my location, although our river above us, as I have stated, drained an extent of this mountain country, it did so by means of two affluents running nearly parallel to and emptying into the main river below the factory. Had they discharged their waters into the main stream above the Factory, that place would have been untenable. As it was, although they were dry beds of rivers a great part of the time, whenever the floods came, they relieved us of the drainage over an extent of many miles on either hand, leaving us little more than the headwaters of the Stream to contend against, and that not until twelve to twenty-four hours after the Storm, according to circumstances. The names of those streams are the "Muddy Fork of the Missouri" on the West, & Prairie Creek on the East. I enter into all of these particulars, & shall do so with other particulars because they form a part of my Engineering Experience which may some day be useful to the person who takes the trouble to read what I shall have written.

To begin with, my means in money were scarcely equal to the undertaking of controlling this river by a dam high enough to carry on extensive works. Besides that I had had no previous experience in managing so mad a stream — I had hitherto operated on the comparatively peaceful watercourses in Georgia. Among the conditions upon which I had to proceed were these. *First*, that I must work frontier fashion, without the mechanical means and appliances of civilized countries. *Second*, I must not stop the log mill, poor and slow as it was, until the new works were ready to start. The convenience of the Country for many miles round, & indeed the subsistence of my own hands, imposed this inconvenience upon me. The old brush dam occupied the better site for my work, but I had to build on the best rock foundation I could find lower down the stream.

And now the question arose, and a vital question it was, what style of dam should I build? The Brush Dam of the country could not be made to raise a head of water above four or five feet, & at best was leaky. My business required ten or twelve feet of water and perfect tightness, if possible, so as to be sure and carry on the works at the driest seasons of the year. Wherever I have been, the popular opinion is that a stone dam is the strongest of all dams. This is a fallacy growing out of another fallacy, to wit, that it is the downright weight or specific gravity of a dam [that] holds it down against a great pressure of water. The truth is that the stone dam is the weakest of all dams against the blows of drift-wood and large trees, roots and all, which come riding at great speed on the freshets of all rivers in a new Country. It is not the specific gravity of a mill-dam that holds it down, but it is the pressure of the water itself acting upon the flat angle or inclined plane which a well constructed dam presents to the stream. For these reasons I decided upon the timber-framed dam, notwithstanding a bluff or excellent rock overhung the work. Next, the question arose what kind of a frame dam should it be? There is the plate dam. No, that is liable to the same objection with the stone dam. A large tree dragging over it, roots branches and all, would surely carry away the plate, whereupon the whole dam would soon follow. I decided to build thus. Upper and lower & middle sills of about 14 × 14 white oak timber, scarfed and pinned across the whole river & into the banks. Cross girders the same, dove-tailed and pinned Piers 2 Inches thick. Cross girders at, say, every nine feet. This foundation was let into the rock, not bolted down with iron as some would do, for that is of no use. Along the up stream face of the up stream sill we then piled with two inch planks, dressed on end to a feather edge, and that feather edge driven into a channel or groove chiseled out of the rock. So successfully was this piling done that no part of that work ever had to be rectified that I can remember.

Upon this foundation I erected a rafter dam with no plate, but each rafter standing on its uprights separate and distinct, so that if one should decay or happen (as actually occurred) to be broken down by a drifting tree, it could be removed & another put in its place without interrupting any other timber of the dam. Those rafters were about thirty feet long, each of white oak timber, hooked and pinned to a cross girder of its own, which in its turn was boxed onto the main sills with a gain of about an inch depth. To each sill and rafter were two posts of white oak or post oak. See illustration on the margin.

On the Factory side of the river I had a bluff of rock to build to, but on the opposite side of the river there was a reach of bottom land about 500 feet from the river to the rock bluff. Unfortunately, I had not money enough to warrant me in attempting to excavate and build all the way to that bluff, & I was obliged to content myself with ending the dam on that side with a strong abutment of oak logs and rock. This expedient answered very well the ordinary rises for several years, but the action of the water below the dam formed a huge pot on that side [of] the river, in which the water & drift wood on a freshet went round and round in a circle of a hundred feet radius, eating away the alluvial bank below and beyond the abutment. This I was able to meet as fast as the bank wore away, by a facing of log pen filled with rock, extending the same diagonally as the bank on that side wore away with each successive freshet. Until (I forget what year

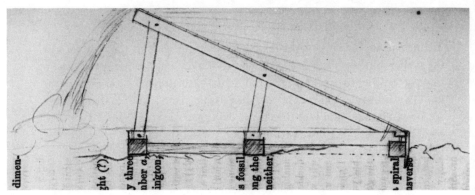

Merrell's sketch of his "famous dam" on the Little Missouri River, Pike County, Arkansas. This dam, which he sketched at the edge of his manuscript, was the foundation of Merrell's new fortunes.

it was) there came a perfect inundation.[2] The water reached knee deep on the second floor of the Factory building and stayed up longer than usual, and when it subsided, behold! the river had made for itself a new channel between the abutment of my dam and the mountain. The works on the Factory side of the river, & the dam itself were uninjured; indeed all the work that we had done was all right; it was only work that we had not done, the soil itself, that had washed away.

I was in N. Orleans at the time & remember well meeting, as we ascended the Ouachita River, that great rise. The steamboat seemed to be climbing up a hill; that was the very observation made by Capt. Kirk of the "Messenger," at the time.

In my absence Mr. Scarboro, the head workman, tried at first to float a raft into the crevasse, intending to lodge it & make it the basis of a brush dam; but the raft got foul and went through. He then felled an oak tree which happened to stand convenient, and swung it round against the abutment just as he wanted it. Upon this he laid alternate courses of old field pines and stones with occasionally a binder of timber, stopping the leaks with sawdust & leaves, until he had a very tough and tolerably tight dam, which answered very well until I had time to continue the dam in permanent style two or three hundred feet further with a new abutment at the new bank. This so widened the river that future rises, nearly or quite equal to the highest, have since gone by without damage. One new and unexpected difficulty arose. The gravel washed out of the gap made by the river had formed a bar across the channel below the factory, backing the water two feet on our water wheels. Through the gravel I made a canal by running a scraper down stream hauled by oxen, who came back by land; but the gravel would again shift into the same plane on the next rise of the river, & I finally had to add enough to the top of our dam to compensate for the loss of power occasioned by back-water. This addition I made on the old dam by means of false rafters, building the new extension to a corresponding height.[3] This famous dam, withstanding the mountain floods against all precedent and in spite of predictions to the contrary, gained for me a reputation over the country and for some time was the distinguishing characteristic by which I was known. Years afterwards, when visiting the Indian Nation I found I was best introduced by the name of "The man who dammed up the Little Missouri river."

That dam, as I have described it, stands to this day. I afterwards made a low dam across the river below the great dam, and upon that built a flouring mill, thus using the same water twice over. I purchased land enough up the river above the Factory to take in another Shoal, and erect still another dam to drive more works, whenever the increase of our business should warrant the same; but the War setting in put all such ideas out of my head.

CHAPTER 42

*T*he conditions of my location in Pike County were such that I could not use to good advantage the best form of water-wheel: *i.e.*, the Breast Wheel or the Overshot. The accumulation of gravel below, & the sudden rise & fall of waters, threw me back upon the use of the re-action iron wheel, and a copy of the same built of wood. The results were entirely satisfactory. I only met with one practical difficulty, and that was in finding an "ink" or step for the lower end of the heavy upright shafts. Those upright shafts were of the heart of yellow pine timber, very heavy; and the lower ends to which the iron water wheel was framed were of course under water. In the woods, hundreds of miles from any adequate machine shops or foundry, I had to make out with such materials as I found at hand & easily replaced in case of accident. The result of my experience is that for the bottom step of the water-wheel shaft to run under water with great super-incumbent weight the best step is a "pine-knot," first turned or dressed down nearly to the size, then bored with many small gimlet holes, & then boiled in tallow until those holes are filled with the tallow. I have had one such ink last seven years, and then it did not give out upon fair usage. Those inks answer perfectly under water, but will not last an hour running dry. They

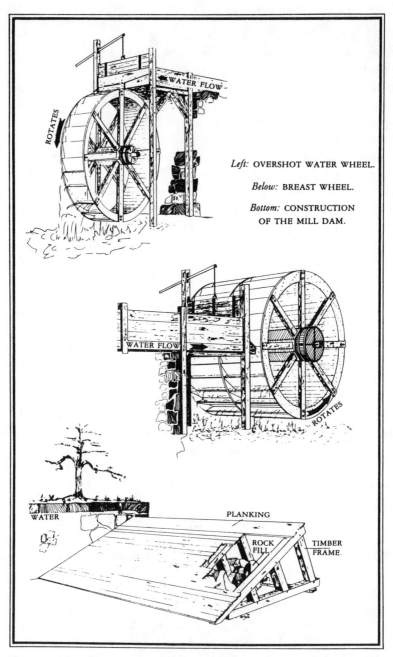

Left: OVERSHOT WATER WHEEL.

Below: BREAST WHEEL.

Bottom: CONSTRUCTION OF THE MILL DAM.

The types of water wheels and dams used in early nineteenth-century textile mills. From Rockdale *by Anthony F. C. Wallace (illustrations by Robert Howard). Copyright © 1972, 1978 by Anthony F. C. Wallace. Reprinted by permission of Alfred A. Knopf, Inc.*

should be as large as an infant's head and larger according to the weight to be carried, & must be so constructed, concave downward, as not to accumulate sand in the saucer of cast iron or composition metal in which the pine-knot fits like a socket-joint.[1] Thus:

I have neither space nor inclination to give a minute account of my essays at engineering and mechanics by means of the back-wood resources at my disposal. Remote from foundries and machine shops, with only bungling self-taught mechanics about me, I was all the time at my wit's-end to get along, but at the same time always confident of being able to meet any emergency likely to arise, & generally by fore-casting already prepared for accidents before they took place. The story of all my contrivances in order to get on under these circumstances would make an engineering book by itself, much after the manner of Robinson Crusoe; but I must put a restraint upon myself, and avoid those mechanical details as much as in me lies.

The mountaineers of Arkansas, just because they were so very poor and rude in their living, possessed a certain rude skill in all the branches of industry necessary for their bare subsistence, nothing more. In their *savoir-vivre* there were many interesting things, very ingenious, & a great many country fallacies. They were especially skillful in the use of the axe, the favorite axe being the Collins Hartford axe of the Kentucky pattern; but at a pinch they could make a tool for themselves.[2] It is almost needless to say that I made a study of their ingenuities & their methods, adapting the same to my manufacturing business, and that I availed myself of the same to the best of my ability. One does not know until he tries how near he can come to getting on without many of those means and appliances which he has been educated to regard as quite necessary.

Success in any enterprise is a good deal dependent not less upon the facility one has in placing men in their right places than in the management & control of the same. I had the good fortune, at the outset, to secure a man for these works who suited me exactly. His name was Scarboro'.[3] I found him in the wood, living in a log house, very poor but cleanly. Riding by on business, I happened to see him with his children about him trying to set up a sun-dial which he had made of lead or pewter. I dismounted and inquired into his circumstances, his own knowledge and the use of tools. The results of my inquiries were sufficiently satisfactory, & I at once secured his services. He remained with me as long as his usefulness continued & was of great advantage. I regard Enos W. Scarboro as a man of original genius in his way, with indications of good blood in his general deportment & style.

I had little difficulty at first in securing the services of the country people in large numbers, with such tools as they possessed; but I experienced great difficulty in getting out of them a good day's work. Several times the stringency of my regulations drove them into mutiny, but their mutinies were as feeble as their characters — I always could manage to maintain any ground I found it necessary to take against them. As to their trifling views of what was due to their employer, I had it in my power to reconcile all that. They would quit work & never return, if upon pretense of sickness, or upon any pretense whatever, they could get in debt to me. My only safeguard against that was to give them no credit, & to believe not a word they told me; & of this I availed myself very effectually. As to their [   ] services, I watched them closely and, where I became satisfied they wronged me, I made it up to myself in the prices of the merchandise they got from me in exchange for their labor. In this delicate adjustment of my interests to their rights & wrongs I think I exercised a sound judgment, and endeavored to wrong no man, yet at the same time I am free to acknowledge that it creates many difficult cases of conscience, when one has to be umpire & has this power in his own interest. It is not, however, so very difficult to be honest under those circumstances as might be supposed. One man dealing with many men who are free to come and go, while his property is located & can get on only by the good will of his neighbors: such a man, if he knows his own interests, will be a just man.

It is even so in the case of a master towards his Negro slaves. The cunning of the Negro, his irresponsibility, & the superior means of annoyance on the part of the many against the few, has, according to my experience, rendered the masters, especially on large plantations, at least just in their dealings with their own people — and I more than doubt whether emancipation itself will ever bring about in the long run any relations between the white man and the black so natural, & at the same time so satisfactory to the Negro, as the relation of master and servant has generally been.

In due time, I managed to have some thousands of pieces of timber hewed in the woods and hauled to the place where I wanted them. The work done out of my sight among the timber subjected me to the greatest impositions because the workmen were so much out of my sight. To diminish that risk, I divided them into gangs consisting of one hewer &,

under him, as many cutters and scorers as he could keep employed. I knew how much timber so many men in each gang ought to cut and hew, & from each hewer I required nightly reports; but in spite of these precautions, when the timber came to be framed, I should say that not exceeding two-thirds the lumber reported was anywhere to be found. This was about as I expected, & I tell it only to illustrate one characteristic of the people. Nearly all other work I could have done on the ground under my own Eye, but even under my personal attention, I found there was compelled to be a great discount on the labor of the Arkansawyers, all of which, as I said before, I endeavored to reconcile in the pay. Poor work, poor pay!

My new home had been selected with a special view to health. There was apparently no local cause whatever for sickness. I had made, as I thought, sufficient inquiry among those who ought to know, and I had concluded that I had certainly a healthy location. But in spite of all my precautions, it turned out very shortly that I had a very sickly place indeed. This I did not discover until too late to abandon the enterprise. On the 4th of July 1855 [1856], we were all still in good health, and celebrated the occasion by erecting a flag staff and throwing out the old flag to the breeze with a salute. Forthwith we were waited upon by gentlemen from the town of Murfreesboro inquiring if we were "Know Nothings."[4] It appeared that the American flag was best known to them as the symbol of the Know Nothing party in politics, and that to be a member of that party was little short of a crime. We gave the parties satisfactory answers, & kept the flag flying until it wore itself out flapping in the wind.[5]

It was not long after the 4th July that I had my first "chill & fever." I did not know what it was then; but, once begun, I think I knew all about the Arkansaw chills before I got through. I took my first chill by wading barefoot in the river to feel for myself the foundation for our dam. I treated it for a cold with caster oil, which reduced me like an attack of Cholera. I never was so completely prostrated in my life. I expected speedy death & gave directions what to do when I was gone, and that was to abandon the place and return to Georgia. But it was not the will of God that I should die then, or that we should abandon the enterprise. The doctor we sent for happened to be the right one. He laughed me out of my apprehensions, & soon had me going again. Poor Tom Conway! With all his faults he was a great fever-doctor, and a good friend. Afterwards he fell a victim to his own professional labors, and in his death was a great loss to his county. From him Dr. Magill learned the right methods adapted to the diseases of the country, so that between Dr. Conway and Dr. Magill we lacked in all our sufferings nothing in the matter of professional aid.[6] All of us were finally sufferers by the diseases of the country. My wife least of all, & for some time myself most of all; but in the course of two years we all seemed to become partly acclimated, but Dr. Magill grew more and more liable to bilious attacks. The servants all got the better of their chills, but Tabby the Cook suffered most because of her exposure to extra heat over the stove. As for myself, I was more than two years specially subject to the chills & fever; sometimes as I was told, looking like a dead man, but never conscious of any abatement of mental energy so far as my business was concerned. Thanks to the medical treatment, none of us acquired the "ague cake" or were injured by the use of calomel, although we swallowed that drug, as I thought, to excess. I found the shower bath of cold water to be an excellent prevention against chills, and the occasional use of cod-liver oil but little less beneficial. I do not remember that I ever had a chill when I was in the habitual use of either of the above remedies, but a chill and fever, once taken, could not be broken without recurring to the calomel and quinine.

Besides the chills past counting, I went though one attack of typhoid fever with a relapse of the same, and the Diphtheria once. The last named was a very bad disease. It was called in that country the "Black tongue." Many cattle perished by it, and nearly all the deer in the forest. One-hundred of our neighbors perished, & more, for when we had counted to that number we stopped counting. Such a country for sickness I never saw! When it was not one mortal disease it was some other; or, when there was no prevailing complaint, one man would die by the bite of some insect, or by a whiskey sore on his leg, so bad was the blood that crept slowly in their veins. Calomel! Calomel! is the specific against all those ills. Calomel by the spoon-full! & I judge by our own exemption from the loathsome consequences of disease so common in Arkansas that we escaped by the judicious use of Calomel, while others rebelled against the same. And if Dr. Conway died & Dr. Magill came out of it worse than the rest of us, was it not because, like all doctors, they were slow to take their own prescriptions?

This unexpected sickliness, worse upon others in poor circumstances than in my own family, proved to be a great drawback against my expected successes. All the year round, and every year, I had to keep about me quite double the number of hands that would have been necessary for the same works in a healthy region. Since all those work people had to derive their support from their labor, and their labor generally did not exceed half time, my expenses were double what they should have been, to say nothing of the inconveniences attending such a state of things. Besides this sickness & worthlessness of hands, and the difficulty I found inducing the country people to resume the cultivation of Cotton, I do not remember anything else concerning our new business that was different from what I expected & had fully calculated upon. Yes, there was one other thing. I did not find the public generally gratified at my success or indeed at the success of anyone. I was by this time old enough not to [be] discouraged by any of these considerations, but I did think that I was entitled to good will in a country where the people themselves, without risk or capital on their own part, were to be more benefited by my labors than I could be. When the first great floods came to test the strength of my mill-wright work, crowds came to see it washed away, with remarks discouraging and looks unfriendly. It was enough triumph for me that they had to go away disappointed. Finally several annoyances were put into practice against the discipline & the good name & the general prosperity of the place, some of which may come up in the progress of my narrative.

They served to cure me of any lingering spark of public spirit in my business relations that may have survived my experience of public life in Georgia. I have been told that this same envious temper of mind towards any one who is by his own efforts more successful than the rest is a trait, if not a peculiarity, of all Western & frontier society, where all have come in order to better their condition, & only a few succeed; the rest are "down upon them." It is unreasonable, but it is no less true. And now I began to learn the truth of what Mr. Beebe told me about Arkansas politics. I found them "sweet to the mouth" but bitter afterward. I tried to keep out of them, but like Mike Gracy found that neutrality left me no friends on either side. I tried to be moderate, with little better success. It was not manly to withhold my influence or the influence I might have at those crises which, according to each candidate, pended in his election. Did I say ten words either way, they were directly wrested from their original mean-ing, so that by the time they were reported back to me I would have to deny them as any words of mine. Did I say nothing, my silence was worse misunderstood than my words. I tried to make friends among those who were not likely to want any office, but if their own names were not before the *people*, they would be sure some day to put up a friend, whereupon they would effervesce, make the cause their own, and friendship, good will— even the slightest acquaintance amounting to a strict recognition must all make way for the rancor of politics. Personal slights & coldness between families were the unavoidable followings of an election canvass, let the office in question be ever so mean. Family connexions, denominations in the church, secret societies, all must bend to the one condition of party or personal advancement. I never was so disgusted with anything else in my life as I have been with free suffrage and its concomitants. It was this that has caused me at all times to regard "self-government" as a failure, and perhaps all governments as an evil continually among which we have to choose the least. But since this war, I have learned to see that any government at all worthy the name is better than the anarchy to which man will drift away when left without restraints. So that instead of Government being the evil, human nature is the evil, & government the antidote.

CHAPTER 43

I must again pledge myself not to run into the details of my Factory business lest I seem to mount a hobby. It must suffice for me to say that by three or four years of persistent effort, through "evil report and through good report," often well-nigh defeated & again lifted up with great success, but in the main, having very much more success than failure, I succeeded in building up the manufacturing village which we called "Royston," and making it the centre of a trade more extensive than I ever contemplated in the original design. And that in order to achieve success, I had to make many a shift & contrivance in machinery which for originality might have been thought to merit a patent-right. For iron, I had to substitute wood; for bricks, stones such as I could procure. Parts of machinery broken or worn out and easy to replace at a nominal cost in the old states, I had to cast or forge, file, & chip out of unsuitable materials and at heavy cost. Oil, leather &c. we made when we could not buy. Mechanics & work-people we had to unlearn much they already knew, & teach them what we knew ourselves, & there keep them at work, until, swelled up in their own opinion by what we ourselves had taught them, they took the notion that we could not get on without them, put on airs, & struck for unreasonable wages, leaving us to begin over again and teach new hands. All this and much more we had to wade through, not occasionally but all the time, making it requisite and necessary for me, in order to get on with my works, to have a smattering, at least, of all the arts and mysteries involved in every stage of the business, & to know more about the machinery than the man that made it. It was like a perpetual game of chess, upon which my last chance of success in life was staked. Many a sleepless night it cost me. Many a time I have worked when I ought to have been sick in bed. I remember once in particular, short-handed & hard-run with business, with the typhoid fever upon me, having a pallet made by the side of the machinery & transacting business on my back. I got well, perhaps in spite of such exposure, perhaps because of it, & because of the necessity that was laid upon me not to give up for sickness.

First, a store building & a house to live in, next a saw mill, then a grist mill, and flouring mill of three runs of burr stones. After that wool Carding machinery capable of carding into rolls 700 to 800 Pounds of Wool in twenty-four hours, and finally the Cotton-spinning factory, with dwellings, gardens, outhouses, & wells for the operatives; a black-smith shop and a shop for wood workmen. Also ware houses for cotton, wool and supplies; and stables for the stock. Quite a village upon our own lands and surrounded by our own lands, all under our own municipal regulations, & depending upon us for a livelihood. The place was a success long before the war. Its relations to the war times will be another part of my story. I have said before, that success in Arkansas is a matter of spite & envy. I can truly say that whatever success I achieved before this war was without the aid & in spite of the people, who refused to see that they themselves were more benefited than I by my own labors and risks. I found them living in log houses, & I made them sawed lumber at ⅘ the price I had to pay when I first came among them, besides hauling it a very long way. I found them eating biscuits as heavy nearly as lead & blue with smut & other dirt. Such flour they could obtain only by going many miles to mill and getting back about half the weight they carried. I gave them full weight of excellent flour, with a prompt dispatch of business in place of the loss of time in milling to which they had been accustomed. I found the women carding & spinning by hand the Wool & Cotton for the clothing for their families, a life of labor from one year's end to the other almost. I erected wool carding machinery of capacity large enough for all their wants, and as to Cotton yarns, or "Spun Thread" as they called it, I made it "a drug." I found them paying 40 cents a pound for Cotton yarns with Cotton at 6 cents a pound, & before the war I furnished them a better article & honest weight at 25 cents a pound with Cotton at 10C. Did I get any thanks for all this? O No! I knew better than to expect any such thing. I received in return cursings and bitterness. The merchants especially, held me up to public distrust. "What is one man's gain is another man's loss!" I was making myself rich at the expense of others! I ought to be put down &c. &c. Those merchants, some of them, actually brought Cotton yarns from N. Orleans and sold them at less than cost in order to put me down; &, with the same praise-worthy intent, the people would buy of them rather than me. I had finally to ship Cotton yarns to N. Orleans for a market, &

I remember well one time rolling a large shipment of that kind on board a Steam boat at Camden, and while I was rolling on, someone else was rolling off an importation of the same to be thrown upon my own market. And yet after all that, when this War began, public meetings were held to take away my property and otherwise interfere with my rights, upon the ground that it was by the special patronage and good will of the people that I had been able to erect the works! I may here anticipate my story so much as to say that I never suffered myself to be put down by any of these things.

When we first came to Pike County, the Laws were not vindicated in all their majesty, & I may as well add that in the matter of jury trials, the courts were feeble and often unjust. Any offense about a hog or a horse or even a bee-tree was sure to meet with severe punishment, either by the Courts or otherwise; but for the taking of human life, or violent assaults upon the same, there was but indifferent redress. One reason assigned for that was that one man had once been hanged in the County, unjustly as it afterwards appeared, and that event had engendered a public aversion to capital punishments. This could not be the true reason, because there was no such public aversion to neighborhood law even unto death, and indeed there was no call to furnish reasons in one county more than another why killing could not be judicially punished with death.

Under this state of things, the temptation was great for even a peaceable man to carry deadly weapons; and almost everyone did so. I was myself averse, from principle, to that practice because I considered that the fact of having arms always by one was pretty sure in the long run to lead to the wearer's injuring someone or being injured himself, perhaps killed, and so "dying as the fool dieth" in a street fight or a duel. I have always felt that the greatest misfortune that can befall any man, next to being killed himself, is to kill a fellow man, unless it be in actual warfare. I have generally got on very well without wearing, as others did, the pistol and Bowie knife, and that too without backing down for any body. The fact of being known to carry no weapons is itself a safeguard against the chief ground of all stabbing and shooting, & that is the fear every bully feels of being shot or stabbed himself. In my experience, ten men are killed by bullies through fear, where one is killed through courage or revenge. Bullies are cowards generally. This war has brought out that fact, even if it was not understood before. The bully carries deadly weapons concealed about his person because it is his fore-gone determination to kill someone who he is afraid intends to kill him. His antagonist arms himself with the same amiable idea. Both are inwardly resolved to take the sly advantage; they never expect to fight on equal terms. They avoid each other while they would have it understood that they are both anxious for the encounter. Accidentally they meet, & the quickest kills first through fear—the other runs if he is not hit. That is about the history of all street fights, so far as my knowledge extends. I was never in one, although I have been in situations very favorable for it, had I carried arms; but being understood to wear no arms, until this war, no one had any excuse to shoot me for fear I might shoot him.

Soon after I began in Pike County, I went through a scene, the account of which must serve to illustrate the general state of society. Politics was King. At least that was the case in our County town, Murfreesboro, which after all its turbulence was scarcely so much of a town, in extent and appearance, as the Negro quarters of a middling planter. Election times in Murfreesboro were like a "tempest in a tea-pot." Whatever was not politics, was nothing there. The man who took no interest in politics was nobody. The Church, the grog shops, the blacksmith shop, & stores all drifted into politics; & sometimes the preacher, sometimes the bar-tender were the candidates.

I have said that I went there resolved to shun politics, but it could not be understood by that community, nor was it believed, that a person who might have so much influence in the country could be content to mind his own business and hanker for no office. I gained no credit by forbearance, but rather suspicions of a deeper design, and it was not for the interest of some of those who controlled the county that I should flourish unmolested. I do not assert that such were the views of the many, but of the few who by intimidation or finesse held the power.

There was a bully, named John Owens with a rowdy mother and sister and father and brother, all of the street-fighting order, who had once carried on a Store of merchandise, but by my time had come down to keeping a tavern and a doggery.[1] They had influence sufficient left, when backed by the pistol and the knife, to control enough votes to gain a Clerkship or a seat in the Legislature—almost, not quite. The vote of our factory village (which soon became more important than the County town), if cast in their favour, would carry them into office; if against them, there would be ruin. My perfect indifference therefore to either side became a sin against their influence. As it was, they just had votes enough at one election to encourage them to run for some office at the next but never with success. If this does not explain the antagonism of John Owens the bully & his set against me, I cannot account for it, except upon the ground that his hand was against every man, & he rejoiced in being a terror to the

County. Not long before my arrival, a wealthy settler in the County from Georgia named —— had been run off with his Negroes, partly by threats against his life, because he had entered and paid for lands upon which squatters claimed a right but would not pay for & cultivate themselves or allow others to do so. But I had entered no lands without satisfying the squatter.

Let the reasons be as they may, John Owens sought a quarrel with me. On my own place we were too many of us together for him to dare much, & I had no business in Murfreesboro; so it was no easy matter to get a quarrel on me with the advantage on his side, and that was the only way he quarreled. I could hear of many things he said, but did not think them worthy my attention.

I had a stout Negro named John, a first-rate mechanic of my own raising.[2] John had a wife in Murfreesboro and spent his Sundays there. John played the banjo & made himself generally entertaining; and he indulged in fine clothes—finer and more of them than I or any one else in the County could parade. I never heard (except from Owens) that my boy John was otherwise than respectful to the gentlemen & ladies of Murfreesboro; at the Factory he was a favourite. A good way to draw me into a personal rencounter was to abuse my Negroes. A Negro has nothing he can do in self defense against a white man but to run, & one of the conditions of respectable ownership is that the Master must protect his own Negroes, even to the loss of his own life; otherwise, his neighbors & even his Negroes themselves will regard him as a man unfit to be a Master.

John Owens fastened his quarrel upon my Negro man John. The Negro was dressed too fine, he said, & so he tore his clothes from off his back. The Negro insulted him, he said, & so he beat him on the head with his own banjo. The Negro ran when he told him to stop, & for that he went about to kill him. Cornered & with a knife at his throat, I thought the forbearance of the Negro very remarkable and praiseworthy, for he went no further than the most strict self-defense required, although he was possessed of strength sufficient to have killed a man with one blow of his fist. I have known him to lift 500 lb. weight in a keg, with only a hold of his fingers on the chine. No one who knew John suspected him of being afraid of anybody, but I had often warned him, if he expected my protection, to keep within the law as prescribed for Negroes, & be humble in his deportment towards white people of all classes. He could read & write, & the temptations to sort with low white people were great, but if he could not preserve his relations as a Negro in company with whites, he must keep away from them. I am thus minute in all this, because it illustrates a state of society about which there is a great difference of opinion.

My duty as a Master came in when my servant was set upon by a white man. First satisfying myself that the Negro's version was not only correct but could be sustained by white testimony, I mounted my horse & rode to town, pondering by the way what course should I pursue. I carried no arms. I saw as yet no occasion to depart in this instance from my usual practice in this respect. I regarded the affair as a crisis for my enterprise. If I allowed myself to be intimidated, this was only a beginning of a line of outrages that would finally drive me from the county. If I should have to appeal to arms, that would inaugurate a line of retaliations in which the Owens' would have all the advantage of assassins against an honest man. I may be excused for saying that, as I rode to town, I prayed God to guide me in every thought, word, & action, & to carry me safely through.

I resolved to use no arms even if they were handed me by friends, unless at the last extremity. To use but few words and those to the point, & if attacked to ride down my antagonists & in that way I felt confident of being able to run them from the public square without firing a shot; for I had an extraordinary horse. It was "Stuart," a large sorrel with a small head & ears, powerful in the hams & the worst eye that ever was in a horse of mine. A fine horse to look at with his white mane & tail, but of no earthly use except under the saddle. He would have destroyed a carriage directly. I used to ride him over anything I liked, & no ordinary fence could keep him in or out unless he liked. I have seen him stand and jump over a nine-rail fence without so much as clinking a foot. With this horse under me, a double girth to the saddle, and a strong spur on my heel, I rode into town feeling myself to be a match for several bullies. In case of a fight, my plan was to ride round them at speed while they fired & ride them down when they ceased firing or attempted to change positions. I expected to be hurt, but did not believe they could make a center shot at a man in motion, & as to their knives, it must be between them & the horse about that. I had high boots above my pantaloons. If I could once scatter their crowd, I doubted not I could run them to cover & expose them to ridicule, which would serve my purpose better than killing. But the main idea was to do what I had to do, & say what I had to say, without giving Owens what he wanted, a ground to begin the assault with the plea of justification for threatening acts or words spoken.

The town was full of people, for it was some court day. It was soon known that I was in town collecting evidence to make out a case against Owens for assault upon my Negro with intent to kill. In a few minutes, as I expected, he waited upon me much excited with liquor and a crowd at his back. He demanded to know what I was going to do about it. I replied, quietly, that I was about to appeal to the laws of my country for protection to my property, & if I failed in that appeal, I intended to protect it myself by all the means at my disposal, & I believed I had the means of doing so very effectually. The manner of my addressing him was unexpected, & while he was pondering a reply, I passed him & his crowd, or through them, stiffly to where my horse was standing hitched close by. Leading my horse in a manner to wheel him between me and him in case of a shot, & then to mount instantly, I returned to renew the interview.

By this time Owens was "rampaging." I was a coward that would not fight! On the other hand my advice was that he would know more about that when he had got through with me. I appealed to the laws did I? I should find out that I was not in Georgia now. I should have Arkansas law, & Pike County law at that! And so it went on, few words & to the point on my side, & great excitement on his. Two things I quickly observed. *First* that I had friends in the crowd. *Second* that my antagonist was scared at my composure & apparent determination to do something that he was not prepared for. He fidgeted a good deal & watched every motion of my hands & feet with great uneasiness, his tongue going all the time. He maneuvered to keep a crowd in his background so I could not fire without the risk of killing others. This act of cowardice and his high words, increasing in heroism as he increased in loudness, satisfied me of what I had suspected all along: that he possessed no real courage. So I ventured to irritate him & stir up his raw places, with dry humor, until his father-in-law, Henry Brewer, a respectable man, fearful of the consequences, came to me and asked as a favor that I would withdraw in his company.[3] I did so slowly & indifferently. Owens, pretending to regard my withdrawal as a backing down, ran to his horse and double-barrel gun for a pursuit. Seeing him mount & ride towards me, I wheeled & rode at him to meet half way on the square. His horse, a mere pony & low in flesh, would in another moment have been rolling on the ground & he under him; but he wheeled & left the town by the road I had to go. Thinking if he got out of my sight that he would ambush me, I dashed on and over-hauled him in the woods. Riding up on his left side so as to give me free use of my right hand against his left, taking care not to range up with the muzzle of his gun, which lay across his saddle in front. I addressed him quietly as though resuming the conversation where it left off. He appeared greatly relieved, for had I been armed with a pistol as he supposed, I had a "dead thing on him." Quite as quietly as I spoke, he turned the muzzle of his gun away, & laid it across his saddle with the breech towards me. This was the pipe of peace. There was no mistaking that signal. I then entered fully into an explanation of my position in the county. Although disposed for peace, & much interested in the preservation of order, I had too much at stake to be timid now. I was resolved to carry out my plans and hold my position in the county at all hazards, & it was in vain for any man if he was as big as a mountain to put himself in my way.

Averse to shedding blood, & especially my own blood, I had nevertheless made up my mind to as much of it as would secure my position in the country & protect the property entrusted to me. I should first appeal to the Law, & that failing should see what virtue there may be in the strong arm. As to killing, two could play at that game. If he began it on me, I had some friends who would give themselves no rest until the last of his race had paid the debt, &c, &c. He professed to see it all from my point of view, & promised if I would drop it so, I should never have anything more to complain of at his hands. I said, with that understanding I would drop the business where it was, but what about the insulting language he had used to me before a crowd on the public square; did he expect me to take a verbal apology with no witnesses for a public insult? He answered no, he would make his apologies on the same spot and before as many men.

I never had any more trouble with John Owens after that, although others tried to stir it up again. But his prestige in the County was gone. Every successive Grand Jury had some bill against him. After paying a fine or two, he finally left the County, & not long afterwards we learned that he had died.

This one narrative must stand for all I have to say about the bullies in Pike County. They flourished always, but generally they let us alone after that, until this war broke up the very foundations of society—such as they were.

CHAPTER 44

I labored hard to forward the erection of our new house, so much needed for the comfort of my disheartened family. We could not afford to wait the starting of our own saw-mill, but hauled the lumber a long way & hewed the square timber & even the rafters. I commenced framing the house with my own hands, but my chills quite disabled me for working in the hot sun. Finally it was completed, a costly house it was for us; but, owing to the above circumstances, not such an one as I desired. We were not permitted to enjoy it long. Wife had put forth her house-keeping energies, which were mighty, and made our new home very comfortable, and for Arkansas quite luxurious. Her resources in the way of bedding & bed linens, tables and table linens, furniture, crockery, knives, forks, & spoons, & stores put away for sickness, were always prodigious. On this occasion she had surpassed herself. Even the flower-garden was in a forward condition, & gravel walks. In a word, we were living finely & had really nothing to complain of except the chills; when one bright moon-light night in the month of September 1848 [1858], I was roused from my slumbers after midnight by a doleful cry, & from Edmund our old carriage-driver, who slept in the loft over the kitchen. At a glance I saw flames bursting and roaring above & around the kitchen; a hopeless case, for the building was entirely of rich pine lumber, with no walls of plaster to check the progress of the flames. All our servants excepting one were sleeping there, & it is well known how soundly Negroes sleep. The kitchen was connected with the house by a gallery. Could I have help in time, I might possibly remove that, but the help was not at hand & the flames were fierce. All this I saw & felt at a glance, & wife says the words with which I woke her were "Betsey, we are ruined!"

Without stopping to dress myself except in a pair of pantaloons, I ran to the kitchen to save the servants; they were up and were saving their little property. I seized the axe & commenced cutting down the posts of the gallery. I did not call the Negroes from saving their own property to assist me in what I felt to be a labor in vain. Neighbors came in. The heat drove us from that work, & I had only to decide what first to save, for there was not time to save much. It did not seem to me ten minutes of time elapsed after the first discovery of the fire before our house was enveloped in flames. I first got Mrs. Merrell out of the house, much against her will, & seated her among the women spectators at a safe distance. Dr. Magill took one half the house & I the other, directing the laborers & working ourselves. His department comprehended the bed room and clothing, mine the parlor & finery. He saved a great deal more than I expected, but omitted some things I think I should have saved: for instance my wife's watch & jewelry were lost. On my own side of the house I had to decide between the useful & the ornamental. When it was all over, I could think of many things I had rather saved, but did not. And even now that five years and more have elapsed, occasionally I think of things that I miss very much &, inquiring for them, find that they were destroyed in the fire. The first thing I laid hands on was my melodeon. It was hot to my hands. The varnish was blistered, but I got it out of a window on the safe side [of] the house. Next my books. I had about 500 volumes & saved less than half that number, though I think I saved the best,—at least the largest. In the midst of this hot work, my attention was suddenly directed another way by a cry from my Negro man John. "Master, just look at Missus!" I looked & there she was back in her bed room, in her night clothes, with the flames on both sides of her & overhead! She was searching for some clothing, which she would be likely never to need if she remained longer where she was. I think she was not rightly conscious of what she was about, but she retorts by saying that it was me & not she that was excited. Let that be as it may, I ran to her through fire that singed me &, laying hold of her, brought her away in my arms, or began to do so, but right in the door my feet became entangled in her night clothes & down we both came on the floor to-gether. I called to John, who was as strong as a mule, to save his mistress, & he did so, handing her through a window to the women outside. Her head was bleeding from a wound. Finally, the danger of the roof falling in upon us became so great that I went round and with difficulty called off the men from their work of trying to save property. At that instant I thought of a certain red chest in which were all my private papers. Was it saved? said I to Dr. Magill, for it was in his side of the house. "No. Where is it?" "There," said I—"In the bathing room." And a hot place it was in! "Rest easy; [I] will save it," said the doctor. The doctor has no caution. Never took a precaution in his life; but I saw at a glance that by shutting a door, the flames could be kept out long enough to cover his movement. I shut to the door against the flame & then fell to gathering my clothing which was hanging on pins & nails round the room &, while so employed, I saw the doctor, not as I expected with several laborers but alone, take up that big chest and pass it out of the window! At any other time he would not have attempted to lift more than one end of the same chest! Such is the strength a nervous man can lay out under excitement. The Doctor says, however, that he was not at all excited! I think he was.

It seemed to us all that the whole conflagration did not occupy many minutes; but, to judge by the quantity of things saved, it might have been an hour before we were forced to desist from our efforts. We estimated our loss at $4,000; but, as our business was prosperous, we did not greatly feel it, except the inconvenience of living again in a log house. Not that we had formerly occupied. By this time the increase of our business had caused us to build a new store for merchandise; &, when we were burned out, we immediately moved our effects into the old store, which was a comfortable log house with one window only.

Under these circumstances, it did not require much persuasion to induce my wife to take her best servant Tabby and visit her kin in Georgia, while I was to go on and build a new house, ready to be furnished on her return. She went and returned under the escort of her nephew Wm. Smith in the April following. It was during her absence at that time that I suffered the attack of Diptheria, before alluded to, which brought me to the gates of death.

I believe that my house was set on fire by an enemy. I had several such who were bad enough to do the deed; but one circumstance fastened it, in my mind, upon a man who had no cause to be my foe, but much the contrary. At first I had no suspicions of foul play. The carelessness of Negroes in the kitchen is always reason enough for anything that happens, but my wife's plate was missing. She had it all together in a box & in the store room which adjoined the kitchen. Under it was a hollow in the ground. The melted silver could go nowhere else. There we looked and dug for the precious lump, but never found it. It was not stolen after the fire. It was doubtless, we think, taken first, & the fire applied to conceal the robbery. Finally our suspicions fixed upon a man named D'Orsey, but we had no redress.

Our new house was, of course, much more of an affair than the first, but the years of my promised stay at that place had so far expired that I had not the heart to build a residence equal to our improved circumstances. I built a comfortable house, & this time placed the kitchen far enough away; but our noble shade of forest trees was ruined by the fire — we had to set out young trees and wait for their growth. I never had quite patience enough to wait for trees to grow. Never planted an orchard of young trees in my life. Wife had had it done, & not I. Once, in my wisdom & impatience, I bought an orchard of full-grown fruit trees, & with great labor transferred them to my home. Of course I failed in getting fruit [at] all. I might have known it, but I never had as good sense in planting matters as I suppose I have had about other things.

There was a fellow named Charley Ray. A genuine Arkansawyer. Born and raised that way, he knew nothing else. He grew up under my eye from a bad boy to be a bad man. I could not get rid of him. Raised to gorge himself when the hunt was fortunate, and famish when the precarious supply was exhausted, he soon formed the habit of resorting to our place for a more regular subsistence. The only terms upon which any one could get a living out of us was to work for it, but work was precisely what Charley Ray had no idea of doing. Nevertheless, he managed to worry along & make believe work, or at least to keep up such relations with the families round about that he could eat like the anaconda occasionally & then lie torpid for a while.[1]

I describe him because he was the type of a class to be found no where else in such perfection as in Arkansas. Large framed but not firmly knit, he was capable of a great outlay of strength for a while, but failed in endurance. He could pack home on his back a large deer that he had killed five miles away in the wood, but he could not work half a day without sleeping more or less on a log. His countenance—I came near forgetting his countenance. No one could put him out of countenance. He had such an one as a bungling hand could any time fashion out of duty, dough, or putty; but the greatest artist must have failed in the impudent expression. Charley Ray was barely tolerated about the village because there was no getting rid of him, but especially because most persons, myself among the rest, deprecated his sly revenge. Low cunning & revenge were not only written but stamped on his countenance. Some desperately mean things were laid to his charge, such as shooting his enemy's mules and oxen in the "range" out of revenge, but so sly was he that nothing could ever be proven against him, and so fearless that he went about unconcerned among men who were more than half-inclined to kill him at sight, and yet he was a coward face to face with a determined man. A strange compound was he altogether! I can say this for the Arkansas folk grudgingly. They die and leave their country with less regret than any other race I have seen.

I have in my possession the skin of a bear killed in a fair single-hand fight by that same Ray. The holes in the skin & the testimony of those who heard the outcry, witness to the desperate character of the fight. It was a she-bear; &, true to his instincts, Ray had stolen her Cub. His dog was whipped & ran to him for protection. It was summer and the she-bear was low in flesh. The two brutes fought desperately, the man & the bear; & the man conquered as much as anything through fear, as many a man has fought & conquered before and since.

I worried along with this fellow Ray year after year. Sometimes I would be compelled to discharge him & run him off, but it always ended in my giving him work again to get rid of him, for he would hang on, and dog my foot steps, & lounge on my desk looking at me all day with hungry eyes. Well, things went on so until one day he took into his wise head the idea of robbing Edmund's fish lines. Edmund, our old carriage driver, was the fisherman of the family, & kept his hooks set out along the river. Ray could think of nothing better he could do than fish up all Edmund's lines & put the hooks & sinkers into his dirty pocket. As I have said before, one's Negroes must be protected, even if he thinks best not to be too particular about his own rights. To be sure, I had only the Negro's testimony, but that was as good in my eyes as anything Ray could say. I took pains to make sure by other testimony that he had done the deed, and then I deducted the value of the stolen things from his pay, handing the proceeds over to Edmund. I did so fully expecting his secret revenge either upon me or my Negro. It came that night.

It was a bright moon-lit night. The wool-cards were running. Before retiring for the night, as was my custom, I walked down from my house to the factory to inspect the works and give the night watchman his charge. Returning, I had scarcely walked five steps from the Factory door when, bam! went a pistol so near to me that I felt the concussion of the air like a shock, but I was not hit by the bullet, neither did I hear the rush of a bullet through the air. Probably a leaden ball does not produce that sound until a later period of its flight. The distance in this case was about twenty steps. Instantly I wheeled and there stood Charley Ray at the above distance confronting me! He was nervously cramming his pistol, which had a long rifle barrel, into the pocket in the tail of his coat. It appeared to me that the lining or pocket had torn so that he had difficulty in finding the place. I had no weapon. I did not think of that, but made a charge upon the first impulse of rage, but could not get at him. The pile of logs in front of the sawmill blocked the way; &, before I could get over it, he vanished down the bank & into the dark under the mill, whither I did not feel like following him. At the explosion of the pistol, a man came out of the Factory who was unknown to me, but he was a respectable customer whose wool was in the Cards at the time. He seemed to take my view of the case, and after talking with him a few minutes, I went home, disguised myself & loaded my double-barreled gun with buck shot, came back to the factory waiting for my turn to shoot, but I saw no more of Ray that night.

I suppose he laid himself down some where, anywhere, & slept the sleep of innocence. I concluded that now I was at last rid of Charley Ray for ever; he would certainly leave the country, but no, the next day he was on hand as usual, denied the essential facts, & seemed to have no more concern about the consequences than an idiot. I could prove nothing. The man who came out at the firing was not in time to be a witness; so I had nothing I could do about it but distinctly to give Charley Ray to understand that I would kill him as I would a wolf or a rattle snake at the very next motion he made with so much as a finger to harm me or mine. This understanding seemed to reconcile his mind amazingly, for after that I think he seemed to enjoy following me round, & feasting his eyes by looking at me. The reader might infer that the fellow was a fool, but he was no such thing; he had a shrewd low cunning & took many striking views of things. It may be thought that I should have gone before a magistrate & taken the oath that I was in bodily fear, & then have him imprisoned for lack of security to keep the peace. But one does not like to acknowledge himself afraid of any one, and the particular course above alluded to would be the worst possible position for me to take among a frontier population, who do not much respect any defense a man can set up except the strong arm and stiff upper lip.

What finally became of Charley Ray, I do not know. When this war broke out, the volunteers, before leaving home, took the idea that it would not be for their interest to go from home, leaving such rascals behind to plunder & eat out their families in their absence. In our country [were] several such, and among the rest Charley Ray, whom the volunteers gave their choice to go along with them as soldiers or stay behind hanging by their necks to the trees. Of course they concluded to go, but to make them fight was another question. They would straggle, shirk their share of the camp duty, steal from their comrades, & cheat them at cards; & in a battle were suspected of shooting at their own officers. Finally Charley Ray disappeared. Some said he had deserted to the Federal side, & some hinted that his comrades had left him somewhere in a situation not to shoot or steal again on either side; but for my part, I expect to see him again some day following me round, & looking at me with his hungry, longing, admiring eyes.

CHAPTER 45

I have said that I came to Arkansas strongly averse to doing business for any more stock companies, but the unexpected magnitude of my undertaking compared with my means rendered it fortunate that Mr. Matlock desired to become a partner; & the conditions of his co-partnership were necessarily such as to make a Charter from the State very desirable. So I found myself once more, as we men often do, going once more into a line of things I intended to avoid. "The best laid schemes of men and mice oft gang aglee."[1] So I found myself asking a favor of the Legislature. It was amusing to see the new-born zeal of some members in the cause of manufacturing. They greatly magnified the coming event of a live factory in Arkansas. (There was already a dead one at Van Buren).[2] I must by all means be exempt from taxation & have the privilege of exemption from liability for my debts.

To both of these I objected firmly & much to the surprise of my new friend, but I did so understandingly and out of my past experience. In the first place, favors received at the hands of politicians are too dear at any price; they lay you under an obligation that you will never hear the last of. Favors from Legislatures are like an Indian's gifts: they can be taken back, & they are sure to bring extraordinary taxation in the end. Moreover, I had no idea of belonging to a privileged class in this country; and, as to being the responsible agent for any company of men, however virtuous, who were by law exempted from liability for the debts of the concern, I had no intention of ever holding that relation to such men or to the public. I had witnessed, in Georgia, how good men would shuffle their responsibilities in case of accidents or misfortunes in the business. So I wrote a letter to our member who had the matter in hand, setting forth my views, which caused us to have a simple charter to sue & be sued, hold property &c, under the name and style of the Arkansas Manufg. Co., with no franchises more than any other partnership of good citizens. Under this Charter we worked and prospered & had no competition. Had we obtained a privileged charter, others would have asked for the same. Manufacturers would have left other states to come to Arkansas in order to enjoy those privileges. We should have had great competition, & no doubt several "bogus" concerns, bringing us all into disrepute. As it was we had no serious competition, & we enjoyed undisputed credit to the end.

Mr. Matlock, our partner in this business, was a Georgian by birth & raising. Successful as a merchant, he possessed a great deal more than customary nerve for any undertaking he made up his mind to. He either would, or he would not do a thing, certainly; and it required a very great deal of convincing to turn him against his will. He made an excellent partner, for he was a silent partner, living at Camden, eighty miles distant & seldom visited the works. I was generally able to comply with his wishes, & it was to him that we finally sold out our share of the business and property, but that did not take place until February in the year 1863, after a partnership of nearly eight years.[3] That transaction calls for a more extended account in its chronological order.

When I first came to Arkansas, I brought a letter of introduction to Genl. Royston of Washington in this State. I am not in the habit of using or giving letters of introduction freely. I could give some curious reasons, but have not space. However, I had occasion to use that one, and some other things occurred to improve the acquaintance into a friendship so cordial that I named our village after him and called it "Royston." This good will continued & was, I believe, mutual until the evil times which attended the beginning of this war. I could [not] keep up with his politics; and since he is a strong hater, as well as a strong friend, I am not surprised that he is now cold to me. I have regretted the probable loss of his good will, but it is impossible in time of Civil War to shun all the points of collision between man and man. Indeed to be able to do so would be no credit to any man. Since Genl. Royston has been to Congress, I have not seen much of him.[4]

It was my original plan to have no more business in Arkansas than Dr. Magill & myself could attend to, Dr. Magill at the merchandise, & I at the machinery; but the accession of Capital upon the reception of Mr. Matlock as partner caused me to withdraw a good deal from the immediate management of the machinery, after it was once set going, and place myself at the head of affairs generally out of doors & in the Office. This made it necessary that I should have an experienced Superintendent in the Factory. Such a man could only be found in Georgia or in the old states. I sent for one. He came, sent by my friends. His name was Tippins — Cicero Tippins. He had been a factory boy under me at Roswell nearly twenty years before, but I had lost sight of him.[5] He did not answer my purpose at all. He had habits and ways that he never learned from me. He drank spirits to the neglect of business, and coming to the wilds of Arkansas, he thought it necessary to carry about with him a Colt repeater, loaded and ready to shoot somebody or other. I soon got rid of him and attended to the business myself until one day, unexpectedly (for I had not yet made up my mind to send after another Superintendent), arrived Mr. Wm. Bell, my last Superintendent in Georgia.[6] He came with his family & household goods, & said he had come all the way from Georgia upon his own desire to work for me. He had no terms to make about wages or anything else, only a house for his family & work for himself. Nothing could have been better timed or more satisfactory to me. Mr. Bell was the very man, of all others that I wanted, & I immediately gave him the post of Superintendent. That position he continued to hold so long as I continued in the business, discharging his duties with singular fidelity. When we retired, I made him a present of $5,000 in money as a token of my good will, and he went on managing for Mr. Matlock as well as he did for me. His savings in the long run have been considerable. I presume he has property enough about him, if he can save it, to be in independent circumstances the rest of his life.

Before Mr. Bell came to me, another of my old hands had followed me from Georgia unasked, John Garrison. He had grown up under me from a very little boy, and he had been a good boy. All he knew of books he had acquired in my Sabbath Schools. I know of no motive that could have induced him to follow me so far, unasked, except personal attachment. He was too young to expect any office, yet he came all the way alone; the low waters in the Ouachita River at that time stopping the Steam-boat at Ouachita City, he was put on shore and had to proceed on foot. Garrison likewise remained with me, & went over with the good will of the business to Mr. Matlock.[7] Instances of personal attachment to me have been few in my lifetime, except among my work people; and those I take pleasure in recording. I never thought I was a very lovable man, but I do think I have enjoyed a good deal the confidence of those under my command. I tried to be a just man to them, and that is the reason.

Dr. Magill, my wife's brother, remained with us & left with us after we sold the property. He all along preferred to draw a salary, rather than become part owner of the business. An interest in the business was several times offered to him and declined until a late day, but toward the last he took $5,000 of the stock, which was 1/11 of the whole capital stock invested, exclusive stock in trade and undivided profits on hand. Which returned him in the selling out & profits nearly $12,000 in real estate besides about $3,000 in money on hand, besides the support of his family. The $3,000 may be said to represent the proceeds of his salary during the period of his ownership. Dr. Magill did the greater part of the medical practice on the place after the death of Dr. Conway.[8] Had he taken out a license to practice medicine, and taken pay for his medical services, he might have done so; & he now intimates that he would have done better in that way. He always had that privilege, but he preferred to receive a salary by the year, which, as that disposed of his time for the year without reservation on his part of the privilege of practicing medicine besides, left no opening for him in that direction. Indeed such a reservation as that never would have been admitted by the Company on the part of a salaried officer. He was employed by the year. He might have declined to practice medicine on our place, and he often did in particular cases; it was his right, & other Doctors were sent for; but if he gave out medicine from the store, as he generally did with advice how to take it, it was in the Company's time; & if there were any expense about it, it was at the expense of the Company. Under these circumstances I deny that the Doctor would have done well to practice for pay. No other Doctor in those parts realized half so much by his practice as Dr. Magill did from his salary, to say nothing of the riding by night & day in a sickly country, which other doctors had to do, & from which Dr. Magill was exempted. I do not think Dr. Magill was satisfied. His declining for so long to have interest in the business indicated that he intended to keep himself free to go when he liked; but if he was overworked, it was his own fault, for he could have had any assistance in his department that he would ask for and often declined assistance when it was tendered. If the Doctor has failed to come out of the business with as much money & property as he would like, it is not because of his practicing or not practicing medicine, but it is because he failed to invest and take his share of the risks in our partnership at an earlier stage of the business. Had he done so, his results would have been more to his satisfaction. It is not those who prefer to work for salaries that prosper with a business if it does prosper, or are ruined if it fails. The Profit or loss is for those who invest their capital and take the risks, & they earn what they get. Dr. Magill married & brought his wife to live at our place in the spring of 1860.[9]

My wife is a great Presbyterian & enjoys herself well under no other order in the Church. So am I a Presbyterian, and have been an elder in a Presbyterian Church, & so was my father before me, but I have learned to enjoy one form of worship about as well as another, provided it is hearty. I have learned that it is in vain to pass upon a community a style of worship unsuited to their position, their education, or their habits. For the frontier, undoubtedly the Methodist circuit-rider is the most useful man, & I have worshipped with the Methodists in the woods with great satisfaction. For the good of my work-people under such circumstances, I would encourage the Methodist preachers to come, leaving highly educated preachers to instruct congregations that could appreciate them; but, in deference to my wife's views, I endeavored at the outset of our new place to establish the Presbyterian doctrines and forms of worship. The attempt was, as might have been expected, a failure. The preacher sent to us was a young man newly married & brought his wife with him. His name was Orr from Georgia, educated for a minister at the Columbia Seminary in South Carolina. A man of learning, I believe, & a good teacher, but the laziest man I ever knew. The seat of his black pantaloons was glazed & polished to a remarkable brightness by sheer dint of sitting at the fire warming his shins. A good man, I believe, & happy, but good and happy after the manner of a clam or oyster. His preaching was as dull as his temperament. Such a man could have no influence in a village like ours, which was like a beehive for industry. He soon discovered that fact himself and left without any violence to his feelings or ours. He was afterwards more successful as a schoolteacher. I afterwards learned that his powers as a preacher had been rated very low before he left the Theological School, & no censure fell upon us for not being able to appreciate him.[10] His salary, which was considerable, and would have satisfied five or six Methodist preachers, we paid with some assistance from an old friend Jos. C. Stiles D.D. formerly of Georgia, but then of N. York City and acting as Secretary of the Southern

Aid Society.[11] Our Church membership we had already put in, by letters from the Greensboro church of Georgia, to the Washington Church in Hempstead Co. Arkansas.[12]

Soon after the departure of Mr. Orr, we made arrangements with the Methodist Conference (Ouachita Conference) to furnish us a Circuit preacher, to preach on our place two Sundays in each month, for $100.00 pr. anm., which we paid, besides entertaining the preachers & their horses while on the place. On the alternate sabbaths I read a sermon with the forms of worship as practiced in the Presbyterian Church. This practice of keeping up the public worship of the place by public reading, singing and prayer, dated from the beginning, long before Mr. Orr's arrival, and continued to the end, with this addition: that after the coming of Mrs. Magill, who is an Episcopalian, we had morning worship according to their ritual—besides the evening service, as above stated—according to our own views. A Sabbath School was always kept up, & its success, which was considerable, was due to the efforts of Mrs. Merrell. A bible class also was conducted by Mrs. Magill. It must be that in the course of the eight years of our residence at that place, a great deal of good must have been done by the means above described.[13] Wife thinks that the constant changing of our factory population, who came and went like Arabs, was a hindrance. I apprehend not. By that means a great many people, first and last, heard the words of eternal life, and that was about all the knowledge that would do them any good in their circumstances. As to "the three R's," as they have been called, viz. "reading, riting & rithmatic," the amount they could have acquired under the most favorable circumstances would have only served to make them greater rascals, by so much as they would have the advantage in their dealings with others more ignorant than they. It is worthy of observation that very ignorant people cultivate a natural cunning or sagacity which stands them in very good stead of education. It answers their purposes even better. An educated man is often, by reason of his education, unable to cope with them in a transaction. In point of memory, close observation, & shrewdness, the back-woodsman has nothing to gain by book-learning. I have seen cases where I thought a few month's schooling made them stupid.

Our saw mill had a circular saw. Whenever it was running, I felt anxiety lest some one should get hurt, & took a great many precautions to prevent accidents. A circular saw-mill, or any very swift-running saw mill is a dangerous place for careless hands. I always felt an oppressive responsibility concerning the safety of my work-people while on duty, and it is owing to the precautions, probably, that I have had few accidents in all my career as engineer and manufacturer. I was able to contrive sufficient guards upon all cotton & woolen machinery and flouring mills; but the circular saw there, it was ready to devour all that came within reach of its fangs! It made me nervous to think what might happen, & was sure to happen some day. A piece of water-mellon rind or a sliver any day might trip the passer by & off would come a head or an arm! I have seen circular saws that I considered safe comparatively, but this one was not; it was dangerous, & I had no help for it, the way it was constructed.

One day there came along a stranger, who had an anxious hungry look but otherwise seemed to be above the general run of laboring white men. The sawyer afterwards said that before he came to me for employment he sat for hours watching the running of the saw & seemed to be fascinated by it. He applied for work, & I immediately put him at carrying off lumber from the saw. In the course of half an hour I saw him borne up the hill, faint and bleeding. He had fallen upon the saw, & though it had been instantly stopped by the sawyer, there had been momentum left to wound him dreadfully on the arm. Instantly I made a tourniquet with my pocket handkerchief, a gravel stone, and a stick; & before that was completed, Dr. Magill had arrived, & doubtless the application was under his direction. Finally, we thought him in a good way to recover, but he continually tore off all bandages & rebelled against his own recovery. A surgeon was sent for, with the same result; he seemed determined to die, and he did die. He had something he wanted to tell me, but never told it. Others said he told them that he had murdered a man in Mississippi & did not wish to live.

The sawyer said he did not fall upon the saw by accident, but threw himself upon it. Our people would not allow his dead body to be buried in the grave yard, & he was interred in the woods away by himself. Some months afterwards, perhaps a year after, a stranger came, apparently with no other business but to learn certainly that the man was dead. Said he was his brother. Did not want to visit his grave, but only wished to know the particulars of his death, and then went away. With that same saw mill we had another accident, but not so fatal. Looking upon the business as extra-hazardous, I never put Negroes to work upon it when I could possibly avoid it. If white people chose to attend to it for extra pay, it was at their own risk. Whenever I had Negroes about the saw mill, I laid down a mark on the floor, beyond which they were not to pass, even to obey the orders of the sawyer. Nevertheless, one day Alfred, a Negro boy, must needs disobey orders, & stumbling over something, he fell & would have fallen across the saw at full speed had not the sawyer met him with a straight out blow in the breast or shoulder which sent him spinning, but not until the saw had nearly destroyed two fingers on one hand. Amputation of the two fingers followed and very nearly the lock-jaw. I came at last to have a thorough dislike to the saw mill & did not carry it on for the purpose of making money, but only to meet the bare necessities of the place & neighborhood.

CHAPTER 46

*T*he events of our stay at Royston in Pike County are so recent that I could fill what remains of this volume, and more besides, with incidents characteristic of the people and the times, but I must pass on to the events that have transpired since the beginning of this "dreadful war."

Our stay at that place was by no means monotonous. On the contrary, it was a very stirring life to those of us whose business kept us stirring about and in daily contact with all sorts of men. Wife says she found it dull in the house, but it was certainly not so for any want of company— we had quite too much of that. During the eight [seven] years, wife made two visits to her kin in Georgia and one to our friends in the Northern States, and one or two visits to her friends the missionaries in the Choctaw Nation, besides visits to and from friends she had made in the neighboring counties of Hempstead and Clark.

Dr. Magill did all the travelling to the North that was done for the purchase of goods, & sometimes he traded to N. Orleans, and it was upon one of those trips that he married & brought home his wife. She was a daughter of a Dr. Bacon of the town of Princeton in Ill.

As for myself, I had frequent journeys to make, always upon the business of the Company, until the year 1860, when wife and I made a journey through the Northern States and further, mainly for our own recreation & pleasure.[1] Several times I journeyed as far as N. Orleans on business, and on one of those occasions took wife with me. Indeed we made two visits to N. Orleans at that time; for while we were about it, we made rather a complimentary trip from N. Orleans up to Camden and back to N. Orleans, on the splendid new packet the "Lizzy Simmons." The same was afterwards altered into a gun-boat & called the "Ponchartrain," which escaping, with several others, from the Naval defeat above Memphis in the winter of 1862,[2] fled into the waters of the Arkansas River; and after putting off her guns, which were mounted at the "Post of Arkansas," lay at

Little Rock until the fall of that place in Sep. 1863, where she was burned, together with eight or nine steam-boats by the retreating Confederate army. The "Lizzy Simmons" was in her time the finest packet ever in these waters. But I am digressing.

When wife returned from her first visit to Georgia, after the burning of our house, she brought back as escort her nephew Wm. Smith. That young gentleman remained with us until the summer of the year 1860, and made the Northern tour in our company. I was near forgetting two visits we had from wife's cousin Jack Magill, whose adventures would by themselves make a book. During his first visit, they made up a party comprising Jack, Dr. Magill, my wife, & Edmund to drive, & spent a month or more at the Hot Springs of Arkansas.[3]

When wife returned from her short visit to her Georgia kin in the fall of the year 1860, she was accompanied by her Sister Helen, & her nephew Archd. Smith, both much loved by us all.[4] They returned to Georgia in the Spring of the next year, 1861, by the way of N. Orleans, & afterwards wrote us that they passed through Montgomery, the Capital of Alabama, on the day Mr. Davis was inaugurated as Prest. of the Confederate States.[5] During that winter while Sister Helen and "Archy" were with us, I took Archy with me on a business tour into Texas, and back through the Choctaw Nation, visiting several of the Missionary stations. We had some adventures well worth relating, but I have not space to tell them. Now I think of it, the whole journey was an adventure which, well told, would make an interesting story for boys. Archy was an interesting boy, and sick on the road, threatening Typhoid fever. We persevered in getting nearer home, so he might be nearer his Aunty & Dr. Magill in case of the worst. Day after day he kept up his courage to travel on, laying his head in my lap, & suffering much & suffering patiently. Indians were kind, Missionaries more than kind. The rain fell in torrents. We forded mountain streams that were past fording and ran every risk to get nearer home before he should have to be put to bed. The result was that, with the blessing of God, he got through safely; & before we reached my home, again he was well! I have since been told that constant travelling, a little every day, & change of scene is a good treatment in case of typhoid fever; that emigrants who keep moving in wagons recover, while those who stop in houses along the road are very likely to die.

I should have said that I have mentioned all these journeys and visitations in order to show that our Eight [seven] Years residence in Pike Co. Arkansas was by no means such a steady and perpetual banishment as might be supposed. We had in the main pretty good times, and a great deal better than, for our sins, we deserved. The real hardships of our situation were, first, that we were all growing older every year; we had all reached the downhill side of life, & there is little satisfaction in that. We had sickness as I have before stated, but I observed that those among us who suffered least by sickness were the most discontented, and we had not as good nor as constant preaching as we desired, which led me to observe that it was poor religion that could not flourish in our own hearts, and among ourselves in the family, without constant talking to by the preachers. While I would not undervalue preaching as a means to grace, it may be, at the same time, a test of true religion to live a while without that aid to a religious life & yet preserve a religious temper of mind.

Accustomed as my mind has been for many years to forecasting in my arduous business of manufacturing, I had, (although no part of a politician) made up my opinion that somehow there would grow out of the next presidential election a war between the Southern and the Northern States of the Federal Union. I had no clear idea that there would be a "secession" of one part from the other, but I thought it would be a war inside the Old Union upon questions [of] rights and wrongs under the Old Constitution. I thought that, inasmuch as the Old Constitution guaranteed the institutions of Slavery in the States where it then existed, the South would hold on to that Constitution &, if necessary, fight for its provisions; so that if any section of the country became so far disgusted in the quarrel as to slough off & hoist a new flag, it would necessarily be those Northern states, wherein it was the foregone determination of the majority of people to allow no more slave states at the West, & no more rendition of fugitives, whatever might be the compromises of the Constitution. In such a War, I had little doubt of the ultimate success of Southern principles. The events which have already transpired in this present War of Southern Secession show clearly that had the South retained the *prestige* of the Old Constitution and the old flag, & the existing treaties with foreign powers, thereby forcing the Northern States into the position chosen for themselves by their radical leaders, of determined violators of the Old Constitution, who, in the words credited to Mr. Lincoln, "could see no warrant for the institution of Slavery in that Constitution." I say the events of this unhappy war show that there could have been no reasonable doubt of the success of a war under the Constitution, & for the Constitution, not against it.

But even such a just war as that, short as it must have been, met with no approval before hand in my feelings or my intellect; for, though I was no politician, I thought I saw a better way than even that. I wish to be understood as here expressing no opinion one way or other about this war as it is. I regretted it bitterly at the beginning. So bitterly that I could not eat or sleep; it made me sick. The modifications in these views that have arisen in the progress of the War, I cannot here stop to record.

What I started to say was that immediately upon the nomination of Mr. Lincoln, I concluded that Wife and I had better be sure and visit the North during the ensuing summer; otherwise, we might not be able to do so for several years to come, & perhaps never. I longed to see my mother again, and my brother & his twin boys, and Uncle John & Uncle Harry, God bless them! I longed to see once more the old house where I was born, and the street where I had played plays, & the well, & the grave-yard, & the Deerfield hills![6] And the more I thought, the more I pined to go. So we went.

Leaving our Arkansas home late in June of the year 1860, we passed through Camden & reached the Mississippi River at Gaines' Landing on the 4th July. Our party consisted of Wife & myself, with our nephew Wm. Smith of Roswell in Ga. Baggage of course we had, since there was a lady in the party, but not so much baggage going as returning. Down to the time of our taking passage on board the splendid packet "Atlantic" at Gaines' Landing, our journey gave us little more pleasure than fell to the lot of Strain's expedition over the Isthmus of Darien.[7]

We were packed thirteen in a nine-passenger stage. One passenger was deranged & several sick. The sun pelted us hotter than I ever felt it before or since, & the mosquitoes bit as they never bit me before. No wonder the captain of the splendid Louisville packet refused us State Rooms at first sight & reconsidered the matter when we had taken our bath and gone through the barber's hands. Once through this ordeal of escaping the wilds of Arkansas, all the rest of our summer tour proved to be as pleasant as the starting had been disagreeable.

I must not dwell upon it, although the journeyings of that summer & fall furnish me now, in some respects, the most agreeable reminiscences of my life.

We made a stop at Cairo and at St. Louis. From thence we ascended the Mississippi River on a fine packet, "Gray Eagle," to St. Paul in Minnesota, stopping long enough at Galena to visit the lead mines and Smelting Works. From St. Paul we travelled by Stage to the Falls of St. Anthony, where we enjoyed the brook trout & cleanliness of the "Winthrop house." We visited the sweet little water-fall of "Minnehaha" & from thence rode across the prairie to Ft. Snelling. Back in St. Paul, we descended the Mississippi, taking a second look at the enchanting scenery of that region, enjoying the finest of all summer climates, viewing the track of the late

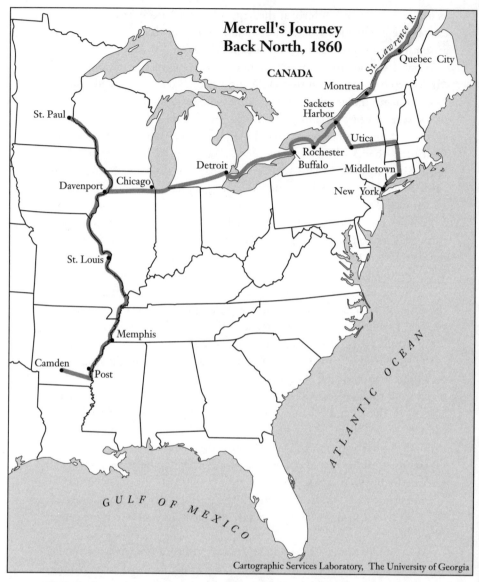

Merrell's Journey Back North, 1860

CANADA

St. Lawrence R.

Quebec City

Montreal

Sackets Harbor

St. Paul

Utica

Rochester

Detroit

Buffalo

Middletown

Davenport

Chicago

New York

St. Louis

Memphis

Camden

Post

ATLANTIC OCEAN

GULF OF MEXICO

Cartographic Services Laboratory, The University of Georgia

Fearing the outbreak of war, Merrell travels with his wife and Willie Smith through the Midwest and North. He visits his mother, family, and friends in Utica before returning to Arkansas, the trials of war, and service for the Confederacy.

tornado, and dining on board in too much luxury for our own good, until it came to be time for us to leave our elegant quarters on board the steamer in order to take the cars for Chicago. From Davenport to Chicago by rail across prairies boundless, and everywhere, as far as the eye could reach, waving grain, yellow-golden for the harvest. Not the reap-hook or the scythe, but the reaping machine drawn or pushed by horses, & surmounted by the inevitable native American guiding this chariot of peace and plenty over the serried ranks of grain. It had been a long time since I had visited the North before. In my dreams even, I had not enjoyed such visions of prosperity and plenty as the reality that swept by us on either hand, like a panorama of some painter's ideal! Such were the prairies of Illinois in the harvesting of 1860. I felt proud of my country. My heart swelled with delight at viewing the prosperity of others, such prosperity as never before gladdened my eyes. I verily thought that a people so prospered had no occasion to envy any Southern planter the tedious labor, all the year round, and the careful picking, by little hands full at a time, of the uncertain Cotton Crop.

In the City of Chicago our little party was entertained in a princely manner, for we had kin and acquaintances residing there—both Wife & myself found friends. And this is as good a place as any to record a fact worthy to be recorded. During that memorable summer and fall of 1860, immediately preceding the election of Mr. Lincoln, all tourists, so far as my own experience or observation went, all tourists from the South were treated with marked attention, and deprecatingly so. In our own case we felt that we were received with distinction. I could tell anecdotes illustrating the point. Even in Chicago, even in N. England, as soon as our unknown names were recorded & it appeared that we were from the South, all difficulties about accommodations vanished. We had the best of everything. Even the servants, black & white, seemed to anticipate our wishes, & the doors of public institutions were thrown open to us, & we were welcomed without reserve into polite Society as ordinary tourists never were before. I met several parties of Southern people travelling with their own Negro servants (slaves). We travelled in their company & thought them rash in thus tempting the Abolitionists, but we never saw or heard of any Negroes kidnapped or enticed away when travelling with their owners. All this to my mind indicated a deprecating apprehension of the consequences likely to grow out of Mr. Lincoln's election; but, at the same time, I could detect no wavering in the foregone conclusion or determination that he must be elected. By the election of Mr. Lincoln, I mean not that event in particular. I mean the domination of the Republican party, of which he was the representative man.

Under these circumstances common politeness restrained us from bringing forward the all-absorbing question for discussion in conversation. I myself seldom or never alluded to it, except in company with my own kin, & then more to get at their views than to present my own. Yet in spite of this general forbearance, I gathered many items: quite enough to satisfy my own mind that the movement towards a civil war would not come from the North, and that the materials composing the great Republican party at the North were thrown together so hastily and so incongruously, & withal were so badly cemented together by conflicting interests among themselves, that the edifice could not stand, unless, as it has actually turned out, it should be propped up by the bayonets, and cemented by the blood of a civil war.

For instance, I was assured by a leading man in the City of Chicago, who was present at the deliberation of the "Wigwam," which resulted in the nomination of Mr. Lincoln to be the Republican Candidate at the next election for the Presidency. He told me that the Republican Party was not strong enough by itself to elect Mr. Lincoln. Hence, overtures had been made to the old Whig party at the North and accepted on these conditions: that in return for the election of Mr. Lincoln, the Republican party did promise and agree to restore the American System as it flourished before the time of Prest. Jackson.[8] The truth of this statement is proven by subsequent events. As soon as the withdrawal of Southern members had left a Republican majority to do as they pleased in that Congress, they did not wait for Mr. Lincoln's inauguration, but proceeded at once to pass the "Morrill Tariff Bill" & put the onus of signing it upon poor old Mr. Buchanan.[9] As to a National Bank, the war has perhaps made that a necessity. But the directness with which the country has been flooded with a National currency indicates the pre-existence of financial doctrines made ready for that line of things. No other plan was tried. I was much impressed by the knowledge beforehand of this coalition & the terms of this coalition between the Republican & the old Whig parties at the North, and its bearings upon the Southern question.

I knew that the old Whig party at the North—wealthy, influential, & highly respectable—rankled over its old defeats. Nearly a generation had passed away since their time, & some of their doctrines on political economy had been laid away among the fossils of an older period. I knew those respectable and wealthy old gentlemen could not help but regard the interests of the Southern planter as antagonistic to their own, since the doctrine of a Protective Tariff was obnoxious to the planting interests; and blaming the South for their own overthrow in the struggles of the past thirty years, they must naturally affiliate with that party which held out the promise not only of a resurrection of their doctrines, but revenge upon the institution of Slavery, which had been the cause of all their defeats. But at the same time I knew that the political economy of the North Western States must be inevitably antagonistic to the Whig doctrine of Protection. The North Western people were even more an agricultural and less a manufacturing people than they of the South. Like the Southern planters, they desired the freest possible trade in order that they might sell on the best terms their own productions and buy as low as possible what they needed for consumption. At the same time there was a growing dislike at the West towards Eastern influences. Eastern Companies controlled at the West almost every rail-road, steamboat, mill, & Hotel. Eastern Capital, in the form of Mortgages at usurious interest, lowered like a black cloud over all their affairs. Laws had already been passed taxing enormously non-resident owners of property at the West; and one could hear any day curses deep against "Eastern Capital." In a word, the whole North-West was at that time in a repudiating state of mind against "Eastern Capital." It needed only a spark of fire to all that tow, in order to set the whole in a blaze. The flint & steel that were to ignite the mass was the coalition between the Whig and Republican parties, under promise of a protective tariff. "When your Enemy is making a mistake, give him time." The passage of the Morrill Tariff would inevitably have reacted in the North West to the destruction of the Republican party. All that lacked was time for public discussion. But alas! the time was not granted. Events crowded one another. Sumter was bombarded. The war spirit swept everything before it; and the Noble West, which has furnished the troops for well-nigh every Federal victory of this War, was lost to the South!

Our journey in the Summer season of 1860 was extended from Chicago to Detroit, thence through Canada to the Falls of Niagara. Through Rochester to Lake Ontario and to Sackets Harbor & Cape Vincent at the foot of that Lake where my dear Mother and brother Samuel resided. I will not speak of the inward satisfaction attending such a visit. We fished among the Thousand Islands in the St. Lawrence River. We descended the "rapids" of that noble stream. Spent a day at Montreal, one or two at Quebec, & from thence made pleasure excursions to the falls of Montmorency, also to the Saguenay River two hundred miles further, which was quite as near the North Pole as I cared to go. Returning southward, we travelled via Utica, my native place, to New England, where my Wife and I both found worn tombs of our remote ancestors near together. At Middletown in Ct. are the graves of the Magills, & seven miles distant in the town of Durham are the Camps.

Of course we made a stop in N. York City, but in all our journey we fell in with none of the excitements of the season. We did not go out of our way to see the Prince of Wales, or the Japanese, or the "Great Eastern."[10] The Manifest tendency of Northern folk to Frenchify themselves with picnics, hotel life, mass meetings, and great excitements did not make a favorable impression upon me. We traveled quietly, & I am free to confess that I was myself so much of the "Old Fogy" as to return, after all our journeyings, with pleasure, to a quiet life at home.

But I came home with great thoughts of heart about the condition of the Country—my whole country. All the Northern man there was in me had been warmed up by the genial influences of my visit. The views I have spread on the preceding page were uppermost in my mind. I believed the Country might be saved by a little forbearance—a little waiting for events—on the part of Southern politicians. Wherever I had access to them in Georgia, in Arkansas, in Texas, I endeavored to impress my views upon them, but failed to gain anything more than a respectful hearing. The reply generally was, "The course you lay down does not lead to secession. We want nothing short of immediate, entire, perpetual separation from the North. We have put the question to the North in every form but that, & they deny us our equal rights in the Union. We will have them out of the Union." "But," I replied, "you cannot expect to do such great violence to the Country as secession would be without bringing on a War, and that a Civil War. In such a War the fortunes of either party would be, to say the least, uncertain. Perhaps the very existence of the Institution of slavery would be staked upon the doubtful event of such a war." To this were several answers. Some believed there would be no cause of War. Others longed for the War, & still others counted upon the alleged cowardice of Northern folk!! Against all these forms of opinion I made little or no head. Such was the public excitement that I have no idea the question was fairly discussed. In the Presidential Election I voted for Bell & Everett.[11] Lincoln was elected. States held Conventions. One after another seceded. The Confederate Congress met at Montgomery. An attempt was made to relieve Fort Sumter. Sumter was bombarded & surrendered—from that time both sections of the Old Union seemed to let go all holds. The fire had been set to the tow. The flame of Civil War became unquenchable. The first battle of Manassas put reconciliation out of reach. In the meantime Arkansas held a Convention like the rest but did not "secede."[12] The majority were for waiting at least until after the Frankfort convention, which was to be in May. I myself had a hand in the resolutions instructing the delegate from Pike County to vote for delay until after that convention.[13] Those resolutions we copied almost word for word from a printed set of resolutions sent to me by Genl. Royston, whose name was at the bottom as chairman of the meeting that passed them, yet I lived to be censured by Genl. Royston, after he became a secessionist, for the Pike County resolutions! The fact is the times had already become dangerous among ourselves. It was more than most responsible men dared to do, to own themselves Union Men. Here and there men began to be marked for confiscation, for banishment, & even for death for opinion's sake.

The turning point with Arkansas was Mr. Lincoln's call for 70,000 men of whom this State was to furnish her quota; whereupon the feeling became pretty general that if it had come to that, and they must fight, they would not fight among themselves neighbor against neighbor, county against county, kindred & friends in Arkansas against kindred and friends in Georgia, and the State seceded.[14] Pike County was already committed against the *doctrine* of secession, so our delegate was instructed to vote for a "Declaration of Independence," on which, in the convention, insisting rather too pertinaciously, it was intimated to him over night by somebody that he would have to be hung if he did not vote the straight ticket; whereupon he caved in and voted with the rest. His name was Kelley, Sam Kelley, a Baptist preacher.[15] Afterwards in telling me about it, he said it "hurt his feelings!" I should think it would.

Pending this storm, it was for me to take my own latitude and longitude accurately, lest I should make a shipwreck of everything: honor, life, property, domestic happiness, all that man holds dear in this life, and my immortal soul besides.

There was I a Northern man by tradition, by descent, by birth and education. In point of enterprise, ingenuity, & perseverance, I was perhaps regarded as the type of the Northern Man. Yet I had lived the greater part of my life at the South. Had married into a Southern family, all of whom I esteemed too highly, (to say nothing of my own wife), to take any course that might seem dishonorable to them. All the property I had was in the South, for part of which I was in debt & had no right to retire & leave those debts unpaid. We were identified by ownership with the institution of slavery, and I myself was thoroughly convinced upon the careful study of the Bible on that question, that the institution is not in itself wrong in the eye of God; that the relations of Master and slave rightly sustained, were as innocent as any other relation, & I had endeavored always to make it so in my own case by doing my duty as a Christian Master. Therefore, after the Secession of the sovereign state of Arkansas had become a fact accomplished, and the decree was published that all those who could not acquiesce in the new condition of things must depart within so many days, and leave their property to be confiscated to the Confederate government, I did not depart—I remained. Of course I did! I remained with my wife and family and having done so, Common law, the law of God, my own Ethics, & my own honor constrained me not only to submit, but to do my whole duty under "the powers that be." This position is impregnable and cannot be successfully assaulted from either the North or the South—for a Christian man to stand in his lot and do his duty under the "powers that be." No counter theory of alleged "rebellion" can move one from that. If any one should be disposed to deny that the Confederate Government is a Government *de facto*, I would like him to test it by placing himself under it once, & then trying to set his face against it! I think he would find it to be a very strong Government indeed.

The issue of War-Bonds and the raising of State troops was set on foot. Volunteers were plenty. There was no Conscription or drafting of the Militia necessary, and if it had been, I was myself getting past the age to be subject to military duty. No call was made on me, at that time, to take up arms, only to carry on the factory with all my might for the clothing of soldiers and their families at home.

This duty was exacted from me by every means that could be brought to bear & by some means that ought not to have been employed. I am speaking now of the people, not of the Government. The people were unreasonable with me. I never was an unwilling worker. I would have been a fool if I had been, for working was becoming very profitable, & I was joyfully & rapidly paying my debts. The people could not endure the thought that a Northern raised man should be making money out of their necessities. The demand was so great for our products that it appeared as though I could get any prices I chose to ask; and that, said the stump speakers, was too much power to be vested in one man, and should be taken away from him. Public meetings were held, violent speeches were made, Resolutions passed, Committees appointed to wait upon me, and the measure was greatly discussed whether it was not expedient to take the Factory from me and carry it on for their own benefit—they the people! Had it not appeared that no one could be found capable of carrying on the machinery but me myself, it would have been taken from me. My hands & overseers were tampered with, but refused to turn against me. Specific prices were fixed by public meeting, and served on me by committees, with threats;

& beyond those prices I must not go. I always met such deputations with politeness, but told them the property was our own, not theirs. We had paid for it & built it up without public aid, & without even popular good will. We would cheerfully acquiesce in any public law that would bear on all alike, but never would we succumb to popular violence. The tendency of their line of things was to anarchy, and it was for their interests in the long run as well as ours that I should stand up firmly for my rights.

It was true I was a very fortunate man to be in possession of Works that were a source of profit at a time when the planter, the lawyer, the Storekeeper & the politician had a losing business; but all that gave them no right to take that business from me, any more than it gave me or any set of men a right to what they had.

The wheel of Fortune had simply turned, & I was up while they were for the present under. Once I was down myself—lost all I had, lost it precisely by selling my manufactures to the people for less than they cost to make them; but at that emergency I never heard of any public meetings with resolutions and committees to reimburse my losses, and now that the hour of my prosperity had come, I would hear to no public meetings or committees to take from me the fruits of my labors. As to the prices of my products, I could fix none, neither should they. The law of supply and demand would govern all that. The man who bid the highest should be the fortunate purchaser. The right of the highest bidder was as good for the buyer as for the seller, &c. &c. As it respected the threats to come in a body and subject me to personal violence, compelling me to spin for a mob, or hanging me for a "d——d Yankee" as was frequently talked of, they would know more about that when they got through. I was disposed to peaceable measures—but at the same time I was no Quaker, and killing was a game that two could play at, and as to being forced into measures by a mob, I did not remember having ever done anything under compulsion in my life. This was the substance of my arguments. It was rather a "bluff game," for I had not exceeding twelve or thirteen men that I could rely upon in a fight, yet it was a defense that answered all purposes for the time.

I felt sure of my ground for several reasons. *First* because I knew from past experience that a logical position well put and calmly but firmly maintained has great influence with an excited populace. *Second* I knew the leaders generally to be men who could not cast the first stone at me for a speculator, which I was not, only a producer; while they, many of them, had put off all their old mules, and wagons and harness onto the State troops at factitious prices, and then run over the country forcing the payment of their Specie debts with the depreciating paper currency. A thing I would not do. *Thirdly* I knew & they knew that in hanging me, they would "kill the goose that laid the golden egg." The factory could not get on without me.

It must be borne in mind that I am now describing my relations to the *people*, not to the Government. That is a separate story. This pressure from the people continued with greater or less intensity until, at the end of about two years, worn out in body & mind, over-worked night & day, disgusted, I sold out to Mr. Matlock who, being a southern born man, could have what prices he chose and it would be all right. I sold out partly because I felt that being a man of Northern birth, that circumstance disqualified me to do as well for my own partner as he might, or thought he might do, for himself, and partly because I had read in the Montgomery Constitution that clause which says "there shall be no encouragement to domestic industry." Whereupon I determined, as probably the Southern Manufacturers did generally, to make what we could with our factories while the War lasted; & then, since our business was constitutionally tabooed, have no more to do with manufacturing industry. If so be that planting was to be the privileged order in the Confederacy, our remedy lay in becoming planters ourselves, whenever the War should end. Here I may be allowed to remark that from my point of view, the clause above referred to is a blemish on the Confederate Constitution, which carried out in spirit during this war, has like a fracture in a pane of glass spread and ramified in directions unexpected. The encouragement of mechanics and manufactures, at least during the progress of the war, would, I think, have been the better policy for the Confederate Government. I have known mechanics, accustomed to more consideration and better wages than ordinary laborers, unwilling even to own that they were mechanics, to be put on detailed duty at 40 cents a day. I have known several superior workmen to abscond and find their way as best they could to the Federal lines, and I suppose such cases to have been frequent.

Had encouragement been given to mechanics, & certain conditional exemptions, then no man's son would have been above learning a useful trade, and the blockade would have enriched the South by raising up a class of Southern mechanics and manufacturers that would have rendered the Southern people practically independent, whether the Confederate Government had been a success or not.

But I was saying that we sold out to Mr. Matlock. He advanced the prices of his manufactures as high as 300 per cent upon the prices I had received; yet he was less annoyed by the people than I. I being a Northern raised man & he a Southern. One news-paper did indeed express the

opinion that they had "swopped the d——l for a witch," which I understood was intended to be complimentary to me — but never was able to see
it in that light. Dr. Magill went [out] of the concern with me. Mr. Bell
remained under writings with me, for the consideration of $5,000 — which
I paid him out of private funds in advance, to remain and carry on the
business for Mr. Matlock with good will, one year. By this time Mr. Bell
was competent to carry on the machinery, which I had brought to great
perfection. Of this any spinner will judge when I say that with 400 of Danforth's cap spindles, he spun 550 pounds of Cotton yarn per day, which is
9 or 10 skeins to the spindle and with two double wool cards 700 Pounds
Wool in a day and night, well done, & no discount for stoppages to clean
machinery.[16] Our work of all kinds was extremely well done and faithfully.

The pressure from the people, to which I have referred, came in other
ways besides the public meetings, committees, and mobs. It did not always
turn upon the question of prices, but the contest was who should have the
"truck" at any price. Planters whose Negroes were in rags, asking nothing for themselves, but a little for their poor servants. War-widows, and
mothers anxious for their sons in the War, often in the rain and sleet, fifty
[or] a hundred miles from home, alone and in parties, poorly clad themselves, & draggled in the wet & mud; crying, railing, begging for only a
little, or even a promise of a little if they would come again. Their absent
ones were to them heroes — they must and would have something for them
to wear. Such as this was quite another affair from the mobs and committees. My heart was wrung. It well nigh made me down sick. Of course I
could relieve many. I could furnish materials for about 400 suits of clothes
daily; but that was not enough to meet the wants of one in ten that came
or sent to me. The woods round about our village was an encampment of
people anxiously waiting [for] their turn. Every particular tree, or stump,
or post seemed to have a horse or a mule tied to it & often without provender, horse and rider both. They came from Louisiana and from Texas as
far away as the Comanchee Country. From the Chocktaw, Chickasaw and
Cherokee Nations of Indians, and of all the complexions the blessed sun
ever shone upon. Soldiers came who were at home on leave & would not
return to the army without clothing. Texan soldiers came far out of the
way to get the materials for clothing as they went homewards three or four
hundred miles on furlough or on duty. Sometimes they tried to see what
virtue there might be in bullying. Long subscriptions came, and petitions,
signed by counties and attested by the County seals. Threatening letters.
In a word every form of claim, requisition, demand that could be importunately put on paper, not forgetting letters of introduction from people

who never before cared a straw for me, in favor of people that I cared the same for in return. They came in fine carriages and they came on foot, & in every other way that man has invented for getting over the ground, except the locomotive.

To all such I was obliged to have a civil answer and an explanation. It was reasonably expected that at the end of a long and anxious journey, forlorn women with their tears, and savage men with their oaths should at least have a hearing, and a polite reception. I endeavored to maintain the deportment of a gentleman, though at times sorely tried, and always overworked in mind & body, & especially in the tongue. Consequently among all the throng I had any day many friends, and whenever confederated clans of neighbors came, or men already on the ground labored to collect a crowd to lay violent hands on me, or to take by force what they wanted to the exclusion of others, they soon found so many on the spot who had more confidence in me than they had in each other, that I never had any serious fears as to the result of a collision with the male populace. I never, except upon one occasion, that I now remember, thought it worth while to wear arms because of them. Of the female populace I own that I generally stood in a wholesome fear, all the time. With the real military authority, I never had any trouble any longer than was necessary to come to an understanding, for this reason on my part: that my creed was to submit to authority—and on their part the fact that constituted authority is bound to be *just*. This necessity is more binding on a despotism than upon a popular government. If Hindman was an usurper, as some allege, so much more was it necessary that he should make his government a just government; otherwise, (such is the power there is in a passive resistance on the part of the people), he must fail.[17] Sure of the correctness of this view, I always met promptly the requisitions laid upon me, and whenever I felt myself aggrieved, laid the same, with my reasons annexed, before the Commander in Chief, & not before any subordinate officer, and never failed to get redress. First there were the Arkansas State troops to be clothed, of whom the Governor (Rector) was Commander in Chief. The battle of Oak Hills was fought and won, turning back the first invasion of Arkansas.[18] The discovery that their Antagonists in that battle were mostly Dutchmen and other foreigners sent to over-run their country greatly exasperated the public mind in Arkansas and facilitated the raising of more volunteers, and the subsequent transfer of the State troops to the Confederate service. The battle of Elkhorn, which was a drawn battle, and by no means discreditable to the troops engaged on either side, however it may have damaged the reputation of commanders, had a like result in checking

& turning back the second invasion of Arkansas, & from the Federal point of view, may be said to have checked a contemplated invasion of Missouri by the Confederacy.[19]

The extraordinary secret and most successful march of the army under Genls. Van Dorn and Price from the North West to White river & thence by transport to reinforce the army at Corinth, immediately succeeded the battle of Elkhorn.[20] That army carried out of the State the elite of the young men, those who had volunteered at the first intention. On their backs they carried away all the substantial dry-goods, hats, & shoes (or nearly all) in the State of Arkansas; also the arms and ammunition, and many a last blanket or counterpane, by the women themselves stripped from their beds and presented to the soldiers. Only one iron field-piece remained behind, & that had been condemned. The State was defenseless, and at the mercy of the invader. The public Archives were removed from the Seat of Government, & the Governor, if I remember rightly, retired with them. What the Federal General could have been thinking about that he did not take advantage of that inter-regnum to march in & possess the land, I have wondered. The fair inference is that Gel. Curtis had suffered too severely in the battle of Elkhorn to be able to follow up advantages.[21]

During the interval between Elkhorn and the coming of General Hindman to take command of the Trans-Mississippi Department, we began to taste the bitterness of Anarchy, more particularly in the Mountain counties where the authority of law never had been fully recognized. There were regulating committees in the place of Judge and juries. In respectable neighborhoods such tribunals would generally act in the right, but even there it was not the law-abiding portion of the population who composed those committees. But in neighborhoods not so respectable, a regulating committee was very likely to punish a better citizen & a better man than themselves. There were also clubs or gangs or squads of men roaming over the country with a captain quarter master commissary &c. so called, and a muster-roll or a bogus paper so called, who under pretense of being volunteers, searched people's houses and took away what they wanted, quartered on neighborhoods until they had eaten them out, would take a poor man's house from him when plowing in the field, and if a man was denounced by one of their number who happened to have his own revenge or other private ends to serve, they would capture him or shoot him if he fled, & give him an exparte trial and hang him if they felt like it—ruin him anyway. Against such I found it necessary to arm myself and my men. Nothing but a firm front kept them off me. Those rascals so ready to shed others' blood, had no idea of shedding their own. They gave me several visitations in force, once with hands reeking with the blood of a man they had that morning shot. When I look back upon those scenes, I cannot account for the influence I had over those men, more influence than their leaders, to restrain their violence, except by giving the praise to God in his good providence, to whom I had committed myself in prayers.

I knew better than to ask those bad men for mercy—a confession of weakness would have ruined me. My position towards them was peculiarly trying. My own true men said (some of them) just give us the order & we will see how many we can kill, & I myself would have engaged them any day or night with a heart light and happy compared with what I felt could I have made sure that I was fighting with banditti. But here were men organized who claimed to be Confederate Soldiers, embodying among themselves all the virtue there was left in the Country, & Self-licensed to plunder because they were going to war. I believe they had, the bulk of them, no intention of going to the war. From what I knew of them, I believed they would desert if they were ever compelled to go into the service. And so it afterwards turned out. Some disbanded when it came to actual service. Others deserted & came home confederating again into bands, robbing & murdering on the credit of Federals and Union men.

I believed I knew them as well then as I do now; but if I should kill any of them in self defense, could I make others see it from my point of view? Me, a man of Northern raising, to kill a Confederate Soldier! I had better submit to almost any wrong. I say it was a trying position. Somehow, under God, I worried along until the coming of Genl. Hindman as Comr. in Chief of the Trans Miss. Department. That event took place in May or June of the year 1862.

Genl. Hindman, with a clearness that was surprising, took in at a glance the condition of the country, which was fast drifting into helpless anarchy. He seemed to think, and rightly too, that civil law, having played itself out, was not competent to restore order. Immediately he commenced issuing military orders, which under his vigorous government had all the force of Imperial decrees. Having no precedents & no experience in any analogous cases, he seemed to treat the matter empirically, but with unflinching nerve. Orders appeared in the Little Rock papers in rapid succession—reconsidered, canceled, & other orders [appeared] in their stead a few days after. Offices were created & men put in them who were taken down immediately it appeared they did not work well. A kind of nervous energy was infused into every department of Government within his reach, and it presently appeared that there was no dark corner of Arkansas where a bad man could hide himself so that Genl. Hindman would not, from his office in Little Rock, put forth his hand and have him up to Head Quarters for trial.

Bad as it seems that there should ever be so much power in one man, it was in Genl. Hindman's case a very great improvement upon the state of things before his coming, and quiet citizens in our part of the country breathed freely once more. Hindman was sometimes very rough to me, and cut sharp across what appeared to be my rights & for my immediate interests, but as he was the Government for the time being, it was my duty to obey & to do so cheerfully—moreover, I was glad to have any Government, however despotic, in place of the Anarchy through which we had passed.

CHAPTER 47

*D*irectly Genl. Hindman began to have an army about him. The country was ransacked for arms, and many an old flint-lock rifle wound with whangs of deer skin appeared on parade. Saw-mill saws and scythes were beaten into cutlasses, and bayonets for double-barreled guns. Those wandering squads of pretended volunteers were peremptorily ordered to report for duty. Head Quarters at Little Rock were nearly 150 miles from our part of the country. It seemed a long way for one man's power to reach into the coves of those mountains. Some went forward at the General's call. Others were always going but never went. Still others hid themselves among the hills; but behind them came the volunteers from Texas. Great regiments 1200 strong of mounted men, as healthy and as wild as the horses under them, hurrying to the front exhausted the provisions and the forage. No money in the Department and no power to issue any. Quartermasters & commissaries gave us bogus receipts (single receipts) for supplies, which could not be recognized at Head Quarters, and it was not for the private interests of the Commissaries to have them paid. Who cared! Genl. Hindman, I believe, did care and labored to do justice, if for no other reason because it was for the interest of his Administration that he should be just. No crops next year if the produce of this year is seized without pay. Somehow—all hows, in an incredibly short time an army was on foot in Arkansas amounting to nearly or quite 50,000 men, and three more Federal invasions of Arkansas were checked and turned backward, more by sticking close to the invading armies and annoying them than by any victories.[1] The forces on foot were not of a quality to secure great victories against disciplined troops; but the results, under the circumstances, were all the same.

But I am running ahead of my own story. It left me harassed by the people on the one hand & on the other hand worse annoyed by bogus volunteers in squads, in point of fact little better than banditti. One day in the month of June 1842 [1862] came in the Little Rock news-paper an Order by Genl. Hindman (No. 27, I think it was). It ran thus, or words to this effect. "All good citizens are called upon to defend themselves against robbers and marauders, and if overpowered in so doing call on me for aid. No good soldier will plunder. All who trespass on the property, or assault the persons of private citizens, are robbers and marauders." I put that paper in my pocket. This was just what I had been wanting to see. This was calling things by their right names. Here at last was law for me to defend myself under.[2]

It so happened that I had just then for several days had warning that a company was organizing to come and take from the "D — d Yankee" what they wanted. And by the way, the Capt. of the company they belonged to was one of the first afterwards to go over to the Federals, & is now a Capt. in that army; and doubtless has under him in the Federal army the same men nearly that he had at the time I refer to. With Hindman's order in my pocket, I loaded with my own hands every gun on the place, arranged signals, & prepared my men for a movement that would have been a dead thing on any number short of a hundred resolute men.

Everything in readiness, we went on with our business as though nothing was on our minds. My writing-desk was so posted as to secure me against a rush on either flank or the rear, & within my reach were a sharp artillery cutlass, a navy six-shooter, and two double-barreled guns loaded with buck shot.

Dr. Magill was equally as well posted at his desk, covered by the iron safe; and the back door stood ajar ready for a rush of my men upon call. The crowd came, quite full of confidence. We were all very busy with our writing & had not much time to waste in talking. What did they want? They declared their intentions plainly enough to warrant me in acting, had I desired to shed blood, but that was not my wish. I took from my pocket Genl. Hindman's order against robbers and marauders, and read it aloud. "There," said I, "is something to go by. I am expected to defend myself and my property. I am prepared to do so. Let any one who feels disposed to plunder now begin as soon as he likes." They backed down. The idea of *any* constituted authority coming in where they expected to have their own way must have made more impression upon them than any threat of mine, for they could see nothing of my plan. The scene made a deep impression on me as illustrating the moral power of a Government — any Government, when it acts in the right against a wrong.

It is impossible for me to give any more than a few sketches character-istic of the times. I find myself again outrunning my story. Long before Genl. Hindman's time, it had become necessary that our works should run by night as well as day, and that the speeds should be increased beyond the capacity of our water-power. A steam engine must be purchased. No one could get up the right thing but myself, & I was too sick to under-take the journey. Just out of the typhoid fever, I could scarcely keep up with business at home; nevertheless, I must go. First, I went to the Red River about 80 miles and back to look at the machinery of a wrecked steam boat, but the boiler & pipes had been carried away to Texas & made into a whiskey still. I came home and started for N. Orleans. It was in December and January before N. Orleans fell. With a pallet made in a wagon so I could lie down, I was hauled to Camden, feeling miserably. There was no water for steamboat navigation on the Ouachita, & I had to go by stage to Gaines' Landing on the Mississippi — in all, about 175 miles on wheels. There was no other passenger in the stage, and I made a bed of corn-shucks (could get no fodder) & lay on the bottom of the Stage. The stems of the shucks hurt me badly on the rough road. It was Xmas time and very cold. I had with me a large amount of specie, besides Bank Notes. I had to visit both Memphis & N. Orleans. Memphis first. Could not get much that I wanted there. In N. Orleans not much better. Concluded we must try & build the Steam Engine in Arkansas, at the Camden furnace. Purchased what I could in N. Orleans toward it, and laying out the balance of our spare funds, a considerable sum, in such merchandise as was most needed by the destitute people in Arkansas, started for home; but alas for me! there was yet no navigation on the Ouachita. Had to come home by rail from Vicksburg to Monroe in Louisiana, & from thence home on wheels. Fortunately I had purchased in N. Orleans a new carriage for my wife, & had a comfortable shelter from the rain and cold. Hired horses from one Livery Stable to another. I was very sick in N. Orleans & quite miserable generally; but somehow the idea of dying at that time never got hold of me. Others shook their heads & looked wise, but I was hopeful. Had a dreadful cough & diarrhea. Poor Me! I tell all this by way of contrast to my reception when I returned to Arkansas. I had undertaken the trip, sick as I was, & taken with me all the hard money and Bank Notes I could raise to get a Steam Engine in order to meet the public necessities. I laid out that money, which I could never hope to replace except in the paper currency, in merchandise much needed by the country. No other merchant in Arkansas had the faith and the public spirit to do that at such a time. Yet on my return home, I was met by a hue and cry that I was a public enemy. I had carried specie out of the country! Some said that I had taken away a barrel full. Rival merchants said they knew I could not have found those goods in the Confederacy, and that I was Yankee enough myself to have carried all that hard money to the North—been trading with the enemy. At any rate the goods ought to be taken from me and confiscated to the public use! Other stories grew out of these, and arriving at my home, I found public action in my affairs suspended only until my return. During my absence my relations with the people had been complicated in other ways besides, so that I had a very rough time. The steam Engine, a very good one we got up in Arkansas, by a little here and there, at considerable cost. The merchandise I took care not to receive until the people were in a better humor to do me justice, but even then subjected to a quasi-military search warrant and several seizures. No wonder then I was glad at the coming of Genl. Hindman, who was a "terror to evil-doers." Under him we enjoyed security against all but himself, & he was not unreasonable.

Genl. Hindman's administration was down upon speculators. I was no "speculator." I was an "operator." The precise difference being that a speculator is one who, producing nothing and adding nothing by his labor or capital to the value of anything, buys up or holds back from the market, waiting for or forcing an advance in prices. The Operator is one who produces by his labor or capital what he sells, or purchases a raw material and increases its value by his manufacturing skill and capital, and then puts it upon the market, taking what it will bring from day to day without holding on for speculative prices. This last was I, nothing more or less. But my fellow citizens could not see it in that light. A deputation of them went up to Little Rock and entered complaints against me at Head Quarters. I have no idea they told Genl. Hindman how they had badgered me and failed with their public meetings, and committees and mobs; only that I was a d——d Yankee and a speculator. The gentlemen who rode all that way, 150 miles to Head Quarters and back, were one a noted Jew trader, and another who had not long before lost a lucrative office under the old U.S. Government because of his notorious mal-practices in that office! Directly there came a little Colonel with a buggy and driving two little black mules, their tails shaved very close, but the Col. himself was very hairy about the head & smoked a very dirty pipe. He said he had authority to arrest me and carry me to Little Rock to answer for my offenses! He had tried to bring over a squad of soldiers from Murfreesboro to aid him in the arrest, but the officer in command, learning that he had no written warrant, told him he was a fool & should have no force from him. The officer in question, being friendly, advised me of his action in the matter. I myself took the same view and told the Colonel politely that I had no time to leave my business to go to Head Quarters and answer to fool charges. It was not for the public interest that I should stop the Factory and go with him. He smoked and studied over it a while; & then he said he thought so too, & getting once more into his buggy, went away with his little mules. I immediately wrote to Head Quarters that I was hurt—wounded in my feelings, thought the threatened arrest a breach of faith &c., & the next I heard of my Colonel was that he was relieved from his command, for it appeared that the whole affair was an extra-official undertaking of his own.

The fact was, my relations to the Government were better defined than the Col. knew anything about. The Factory had become a military necessity. To arrest me, & so suspend the operations of the Works, would have been a public loss, even had the charges against me been true, which they were not. The Government had therefore sent me a letter, letting me know the charges against me, desiring my answer in writing "before proceeding to ulterior measures." Those were the words of the letter. Of course I immediately sat down and put my reply in writing. All the charges I could truthfully answer with a flat denial excepting one, and my denial was accepted by the Government as satisfactory & conclusive. The charge that I could not deny was one upon which Government laid the greatest stress; and it was, that in my transactions I was putting Confederate Notes at a discount compared with gold and silver. It was true that, having as before stated, spent all our gold & silver in N. Orleans for merchandise which the bogus military had been taking away from me, I was trying to get some of the specie back by the very method charged against me. My reply was that the difference in value between specie & the paper currency was a thing beyond Government control. It was a real difference in value. In all flush times of paper currency it had been so & would again be so. I don't remember the words, but such were the ideas I intended to convey without offense to the Government.[3]

The difference therefore in Value between specie & paper money was not of my creating. N. Orleans, before its fall, was as loyal a city to the Confederacy as any. Yet the N. Orleans papers quoted Confederate notes at 30% discount for gold. I had always done business upon the N. Orleans quotations, & was doing so still. Yet if my so doing was offensive to Government, I must of course stop it.

The document cost me some labor. Having answered the charges against me, I proceeded to put in my charges against my accusers, generally. Not to put too fine a point upon it, I did not, I am afraid, give them a very good character. In point of fact, I denounced them bitterly.

Mr. Matlock, our partner, carried the document to Head Quarters in person. So far as he could judge by appearances, it was regarded as not only satisfactory but rather amusing. The immediate results were that exemptions were sent me for my hands from military duty, our Cotton from burning, & our tools and implements from seizure for military purposes. I thought it my duty, while I had the ear of the Government, to put forward some views tending to mitigate the hardships of the war, which had arrived at a pitch well-nigh intolerable; for it will be remembered that the year 1862 was the famine year in Arkansas, and the question of clothing for the women and children, to say nothing of the Army, was being fast reduced to first principles: *i.e.*, no clothing at all. Subsequently my views were several times called for, & I had the pleasure to see that they prevailed with Government. The people were no longer forced to supply their own husbands, sons, & brothers in the Army, either here or those East of the Miss. River. The Clothing Bureau was organized, which undertook to clothe the Army, leaving the poor people to clothe themselves. The Quartermaster department undertook to take the place of merchants, & import goods from beyond the Mississippi River by running the blockade for the benefit of the people, exchanging the same for their labor, & for the little surplus of provisions that some had concealed, & would not bring forth from their hiding places except to exchange for clothing.

West of the Mississippi river within the Confederate lines there was but little machinery for carding and spinning. The fine Cotton Factory at Baton Rouge which had supplied West Louisiana had been burned at the fall of that place.[4] There were in Texas several machines for carding Wool into Rolls, but there was only one spinning & weaving Factory, & that not a large one. It was at Huntsville, Texas, belonged to the State, & was worked by penitentiary hands. In Arkansas there was a Factory at Van Buren in a low condition at the best.[5] In private hands it was producing about half what it ought to do. Pressed by the Government and carried on by a Colonel, matters grew worse and worse; it finally took fire and was destroyed, but not until it had been restored to its owners in mutual disgust. There was some spinning machinery at Norristown on the Arkansas River understood to be of good quality, but I never heard of its producing any yarns.

There had been before the war a very small spinning concern at Cane Hill in Washington Co. belonging to Mark Bean. He died & I heard of no more spinning done there.[6] Besides those I have mentioned, I know of no others in the Department, except our own, which I have sufficiently described already. In anticipation of the War, I had in the fall of 1860 laid in at least three years supply of "findings" necessary to keep our works in order. Our machinery was in high condition, and under the pressure of the times, I ventured to increase our speeds & increase our production to 150 percent upon what we had thought to be very fair spinning at the start. In order to do this, we had to be up at night a good deal, not only to run the works but for repairs, and we increased our force so as not to stop running even for meals; but I never ran the machinery or did repairs upon the Sabbath day or night. It seemed to be expected of me that I would, but I never did.

Government wanted all I could produce for the Army. The people wanted it all for the women and children, who were willing to work or do anything to get clothing; but the hand cards were worn out by constant use and borrowing from house to house; & the women could no longer spin for themselves. I laid the case before Government; they believed my statement, and we settled upon a compromise that I should spin one half for Government & one half for the people. Pending this controversy, people became very bitter against the Government, and against me, assuming, as they always did, that I was finessing for my own interest. Nothing could be further from the truth. Government might well have taken that view of the case, but not the people. It was not for my interest to work for Government at all. Government fixed its own prices. The people by this time had given up the question of price, & would cheerfully have paid me twice what the Government paid. I might have been $50,000, at least, better off had Government let me alone.

Whatever may possibly be the future events of the war, it seems to me that the fall & winter of 1862–63 must stand for the darkest time, that is from the humane point of view. The crops had failed because of drouth. Famine and sickness followed. Great scarcity of medicines for the sick, & few substitutes yet discovered, as they afterwards were. The people and the army shivering in the remains of thin clothing from the stores. The public economy was in a transition state, from a state of dependence upon imported things to a state of self-reliance upon home productions; and a miserable transition state it was! Shoes which, although they were still worn as Shoes, left the prints of bare toes in the mud; and it was alleged that the soldiers left tracks of blood where they had marched over the frozen ground. Multitudes were entirely barefooted in the heart of winter. Shocking bad hats, if any hats at all. Clothing which for want of change and blankets had been worn and slept in until they rotted off the person & fell into rags; and, withal, a craving for food that was seldom satisfied.

The first natural resort as a remedy for this destitution would have been the skins and meat of wild beasts and game, but the ammunition and guns had been bought up or pressed into the army, and the wild deer walked into town and out again unmolested.

Right here is, I think, where Genl. Hindman made a mistake, but it was a mistake that he found ready-made in the organic law of the Confederacy. He assumed that private interests were of necessity the antagonist of the interests of Government, and in many cases of bargain and trade, no doubt, he found it so; but it ought not to have followed that private enterprise was not the best reliance of a Government in want of everything — much less that private enterprise should be put at a discount and discouraged or seized for Government uses.

I think that, seeing he had more troops than he could either feed or clothe, he had better, not for a day, have put any check or restraint upon the class vulgarly called "speculators" and so denounced in his orders, *provided they were producers of actual value.* A liberal and judicious detailing of young men to learn trades and of old men to carry them on with no check whatever upon prices but the inexorable "law of supply and demand," all this subject to Government inspection as to quality & quantity, would have resulted in a rivalry and competition which must have brought down prices permanently & filled the country with supplies. Genl. Hindman did in certain cases, not generally, encourage private enterprise; but at the same time he published a tariff of such prices as amounted to a prohibition, or amended the same so frequently and made such seizures as to destroy all confidence & take away "that hope of reward which sweetens labor." Genl. Hindman learned better wisdom as he went along, and I believe was not above learning by experience. When he left Arkansas, he was a sadder and a wiser man than when he came. He began with the idea that Military discipline is omnipotent and good for all the ills of a body politic. He found that it was not strong enough even to control his army, to say nothing about developing the resources of the country under his command. Could he personally have been present everywhere, or infused his spirit, vigor, and industry — together with some sparks of his clear intellect — into his subordinates, he might possibly have succeeded; but he was singularly unfortunate in the selection of his officials. I do not refer to those immediately about his person, for he was such a worker himself that I suppose it did not matter a great deal who was about his office. I do refer to the agents he sent into the country. In many instances, if not all, they out-

Hindmaned Genl. Hindman himself. They were men just able to take in
& understand his violent measures, without a spark of his good sense and
forbearance. The consequence was that the discouragements outweighed
the few encouragements, and very few persons had any heart to risk capital
in any enterprise. The hides of beef-cattle killed for the army lay in heaps
& in a state of de-composition, when they ought to have been immediately
in the tanner's hands, or carefully dried for shipment to the rear. Wool
abounded on the prairies of Texas, but was bought up by speculators and
shipped to Georgia. Cotton, of course, was everywhere, but it remained
in the condition of raw material for want simply of hand-cards, which any
enterprising merchant would have found means to procure at his private
risk, could he have been sure that he would not be denounced as a "speculator" and the whole taken from him, or put into a tariff of prices so low
as to deprive him of his profits & fair reward for his trouble & risks.

Moreover, the country was ransacked by men detailed to procure clothing for their Companies whose homes were West, but their fighting east of
the Mississippi River. That was especially unreasonable since there were at
least a hundred factories there to one here. At the same time, large quantities of Salt Peter were purchased and carried away to the East, while the
powder mill here was standing for want of it.

General Hindman had all this, and a great deal more besides, to contend
against. His administrative and organizing ability must have been great
indeed to accomplish so much as he did in the short time that his councils
prevailed. My own impression, as a disinterested looker-on, is that if the
line of things he commenced had been carried out, in spite of all its errors,
it would have created a military power very formidable indeed on this side
[of] the Mississippi. He would in time have corrected his own mistakes. I
look upon his removal and the abandoning of his policy as a mistake on
the part of Mr. Davis, and above all things the disingenuous ignoring of
his credentials by Mr. Randolph, the Secretary of War.[7] Now that a year
and more has elapsed since he was superseded, I see that others are adopting this view. The Confederate Congress itself [has] now at last, when it
is perhaps too late, established the independent provisional government,
the issue of Treasury notes, & other powers needful for the isolated position of things in the Trans-Mississippi Department. I am not so capable
of judging in military matters, but I am told that the same observations
might be applied with equal justice to his plans of military organization.
One thing is certain: before the force of his decrees had died out, the
Army was clothed, with the exception of rather a short supply of shoes and
blankets, and the fabrics of which the clothing was made, although motley

in appearance, was twice as durable as the store-goods with which they had started out. I understood that desertions and plundering were pretty effectually checked, and, in the short space of sixty days, three invading armies turned back.[8] Inasmuch as these great events transpired without any general engagement, or any Confederate victory to boast of, I will try and explain the Fabian tactics by which so much was accomplished with an army so hastily collected & so poorly armed and drilled. No part of a military man myself, I can only tell how it seemed to a looker-on.

After the battle of Elkhorn, the Federal army under the command of Genl. Curtis fell back to Springfield in Missouri, while the Confederate army under Genl. Van Dorn and Price also fell back & made a forced march across the country to reinforce the army at Corinth in or near the N. Eastern corner of the State of Mississippi. Genl. Curtis, abandoning his first intention of entering the valley of the Arkansas River at Van Buren, in the month of May, 1862, put his army again in motion and descended the valley of White River in a south easterly direction towards Batesville in Arkansas, and from thence by the way of Searcy to Little Rock. At that conjuncture there were no Confederate troops in Arkansas ready [except] for a very few men at Little Rock under Genl. Roane, armed with pikes and one condemned field piece of iron, and a part of Col. W. H. Parsons' 12th Texas Dragoons awaiting near the mouth of the Arkansas River the arrival of transports to carry them to Memphis.[9] About 200 with their Col. had gone on; about 1000 remained. The whole regiment was about 1200 strong.

Gov. Rector & Senator Johnson used their influence with Genl. Beauregard & obtained an order for the return of Col. Parsons & his men to Arkansas.[10] Succeeding in this, Col. Parsons, at the head of his own Regt., crossed the country from Red Fork, near Napoleon, and confronted the enemy at or near the town of Searcy, and a collision took place called the battle of Searcy.[11] The Federal force retired, leaving 203 men dead in the cane. The Federal commanders, Genl. Carr & Genl. Osterhaus, holding after the battle a position on the North bank of the Little Red river, and Col. Parsons with his 1200 dragoons playing a "bluff game" in front, looking anxiously for reinforcements. Hd.Quarters near the Des Arc Bayou. Col. Taylor's Regt. of Texas Cavalry arrived. I forget whether it arrived before of after this battle of Searcy. I got these particulars from Col. Parsons himself.[12]

Col. Fitzhugh's Regt. of Texas Cavalry arrived shortly after, and Col. Parsons found himself at the head of a Brigade.[13] His plan of operations was to stick close to the Federal Army, consuming or retiring the subsistence

Places and Battles in Merrell's Account of 1862-1864

Pea Ridge

Prairie Grove

Batesville

White River

ARKANSAS

River

Cache

Fort Smith

Arkansas

Searcy Landing

Cotton Plant

Memphis

River

Bayou

Devall's Bluff

Hot Springs

Little Rock

St. Charles

Helena

Merrell's cotton mill

Jenkins' Ferry

Pine Bluff

Men

Murfreesboro

Arkadelphia

Arkansas Post

Merrell's abatis

River

Little

Marks' Mill

Washington

Missouri R.

Camden

Saline R.

Poison Spring

Ouachita R.

Red

LOUISIANA

Ouachita

Mississippi

Marshall

Shreveport

Vicksburg

Mansfield

River

TEXAS

Pleasant Hill

Cartographic Services Laboratory, The University of Georgia

Important Arkansas cities and battle sites, as mentioned by Merrell, including the abatis that he placed in the Arkansas River between Napoleon and Arkansas Post in 1863. Crossed swords mark the locations of important Civil War engagements that Merrell mentions.

in front, with a small force detached to threaten their communications by the rear. Certainly the Federal commanders did not understand the art of war as well as they do now! Col. Parsons assures me that the prowess of men & officers in actual combat, on the part of the Federal army, was admirable, and always has been wherever he has met them; but they were easy to outwit on the field. I apprehend that want of experience made all the difference. The Southern officer had all his life been accustomed to the fox hunt, the deer drive, and hunting stock. Even lawyers and merchants in the South were accustomed to the Sports of the woods and fields, & the common men even more so. Hence a natural aptitude for the topography of roads, short cuts, and positions. I am no believer in the alleged inferiority of either the Northern man or the Southern man in point of pluck. I have heard good soldiers say that if no other good comes of this war, it will leave among the soldiers at large a mutual respect for each other's prowess in arms. Let that be as it will. I have always felt it to be in bad taste, if not bad policy, to belittle an enemy because, if they are not a brave enemy, there is little merit in beating them; and, on the other hand, very great disgrace if you are beaten by them.

But I am leaving Genl. Curtis' invading army a long way in the rear! The Confederate Col. commanding had now a Brigade of Three Regiments of Texas Cavalry: viz., Parsons', Taylor's, and Fitzhugh's, with three or four companies of Arkansas mounted men, in all less than 4000 men, against 6000 Federals under the immediate command of Generals Osterhaus and Carr. The battle of Cold-Wells was fought, & the Federal army fell back to Batesville. That was about the 10th June 1862.[14] The Confederate forces accumulating rapidly by reinforcements from the rear, Genl. Rust arrives and takes command, but by losing time in what was called the Parchd. Corn Expedition on the head waters of White River, failed to prevent the juncture of the Federal column under Genl. Steele from Ironton in Missouri, which increased the Federal force to 20 or 25,000 men under command of General Steele.[15] So large a force could not subsist in the country through which it had to pass in order to reach Little Rock; accordingly, General Steele's plan of the Campaign was to descend by the East bank of the White River and the Cache, keeping those watercourses between him and danger, until he reached Devall's Bluff, the head of the Rail Road to Little Rock, while at the same time a fleet of Gun Boats and transports under Col. Fitch should ascend the White River, and he relied upon this junction at Devall's Bluff not only for provisions but for an adequate supply of ammunition.[16] Such combinations by land and water seldom turn out well, according to my reading of history. Genl. Rust's army was thrown across White River into a position where defeat would have been ruin. The battle of Cotton Plant was fought. It was by no means a Confederate victory, but it had all the effects of a victory by putting an end to Genl. Steele's advance in that direction. Owing to the nature of the country, he could form no idea of the Confederate force in front of him. Short of supplies and ammunition, & hearing nothing from the fleet, he changed his course and took possession of Helena. The fact was that his Gun boats had been checked and turned back with considerable loss by Lt. Dunnington's battery at St. Charles, near the mouth of White River.[17] In that engagement the gun-boat "Mound City" had a steam pipe or boiler hit by a shot, and nearly all on board were scalded by the Escape of steam.

The battle of Cotton Plant, as described to me by Col. Parsons, was about on this wise. It was 7th July 1862, at about 10 o'clock A.M. that the head of the Confederate column came upon the Enemy who were in line of battle. I understand that the collision was rather unexpected. There was an under-growth of rank cane. Col. Parsons' Brigade was in advance, consisting of 5 Regiments: Parsons, Fitzhugh, Taylor, Sweet, & Darnell's Texas Cavalry.[18] Genl. Rust was riding with them. He gave orders for them to keep the Federals in check while he would ride to the rear and bring up the Infantry and Artillery. Col. Parsons made one spirited charge, designed by its audacity to make the impression that he was well-supported, which he was not. Having made that impression, he maneuvered in presence of his enemy in such a manner as to improve upon that mistake. This caused General Steele to feel his way very cautiously, and the battle went on in this manner about five hours, Col. Parsons expecting to hear from the Infantry and Artillery on the flank and rear of the Federal lines. Finally, after five hours of this suspense, finding that the Federal right and left wings were closing in around him, he withdrew by columns of companies in perfect silence, leaving about 70 of his men dead on the field. In the absence of orders, he did not retire until he was nearly surrounded. Four miles in the rear he found the Infantry quite safe, and General Rust lying on a blanket by the side of a gun. The General rose as though he had seen a ghost. Col. Parsons saluting says, "General, I bring you back the Cavalry under my command, all safe and sound, deducting the casualties of this day." To which the General replies, "Colonel, you have covered yourself & your men with glory. I had given you up for lost." It afterwards appeared that the Commanding General had already sent a dispatch to Head Quarters reporting the loss of five Regiments of those Cavalry. But, says the colonel, it never appeared in his dispatches that he had gained any credit that day.[19]

The Federal loss that day must have been considerable. A young man of Darnell's regiment who was desperately wounded & left on the field told me that the Federal surgeons sent to the house where he was lying for the sheets to tear up for bandages, & he heard them say they had about 250 rotten bandages, but they were all used & more required. That young man's wound singularly illustrated how much man can endure sometimes. He was sitting on his horse when a minnie ball hit him in the breast and came out behind his back. He felt that he must be mortally wounded. Alighting, he asked a comrade to take care of his horse and walked into a house not far off and lay down to die. Some ladies who lived in that house dressed his wound, and he recovered perfect and robust health, although the Federal surgeons examined him & pronounced it all of no use.

I know another young man (Simms) wounded at Oak Hills in like manner by a grape or spherical case shot, which, entering his breast & escaping behind, tore away several ribs from his spine; yet he recovered.

Turning from the Battle of Cotton Plant, the Federal Army under Genl. Steele marched to Helena on the Mississippi River, which was not defended. There they entrenched and established a base for future operations in Arkansas.

The battle of L'Anguille took place on the 3rd August 1862 between Col. Parsons' command and the 1st Wisconsin Cavalry, which was moving down Croley's ridge towards Helena, aided by several hundred Negroes whom they had collected in the country through which they passed. Col. Parsons says the battle was a desperate struggle, the Negroes and all fighting with such desperation as to render the giving or taking of quarter quite out of the question so long as it lasted. About 400 of the Negroes were brought to Little Rock as prisoners. I understand that the Regiment (1st Wisconsin) was destroyed, or nearly so, and all they had was captured.[20] The captured Negroes were, I understand, returned to their owners, & those not claimed put on duty as grooms, cooks, etc. in the Regiment that captured them.

Several unsuccessful advances were subsequently made from Helena upon Little Rock, one by General Hovey late in August 1862, but with too small a force, say 5,000 men. Another, which was a false start, by Genl. Steele with about 25,000 men early in November of the same year.[21]

In the North Western part of the State of Arkansas, the successive advances and retreats of either army—the Confederate & Federal—had by this time exhausted that rich country; and neither army being able to subsist so far from its base, that portion of the State enjoyed as much rest from the war as was compatible with the scalping propensities of the Pin Indians, who were near neighbors, and the Jay Hawking ways of the whites.[22] I have never visited that section of the State, but have been told that it is ruined. The same, I understand, may be said of the country lying round about Helena for many miles. I will not undertake to record any of the thousand (more or less) atrocities that I have heard of. Such things in the telling are very repugnant to my taste; and even if true, all of them are no more than what might be expected in a state of civil war, when the worst passions of the lowest and meanest men are turned loose.

In the Autumn of the year 1862, Major General Holmes superseded Genl. Hindman in command of the Trans Miss. District, the latter taking command of the army in the North Western part of the state, which at that time was understood to amount to about 25,000 men.[23] In front of him was the Federal army under Genl. Blunt, advancing by the old route from Springfield, Missouri, to invade the valley of the Arkansas; and it may be that at the same time Genl. Hindman was advancing to invade Missouri.[24] If so, his advance was impracticable; for, as I said before, it was the famine year. His army could only subsist, as it were, from day to day; and, at the same time, a large proportion of the Soldiers were without shoes or blankets in the dead of Winter. In this condition, Genl. Hindman made a forced march to meet General Blunt. The Battle of Prairie Grove was fought [in] Dec. 1862.[25] It was not a general engagement. On the part of the Confederate army, only one brigade (Fagan's) of infantry was engaged, and the artillery.[26] The Federal General burned his wagon train and fell back, leaving Genl. Hindman in possession of the field. A Federal flag of truce obtained for permission to bury the dead. The Confederate army fell back after the battle to its old base of supplies on the Arkansas River, & the Federal army retired also to Fayetteville. Both sides claimed a victory on the ground that the battle had checked the further advance of either army.

The battle of Prairie Grove was soon followed by the fall of the Post of Arkansas, indicating that the attack on that Post and the forward movement of Genl. Blunt were a combined operation, drawing the Confederate force away to the N. West corner of the State at the time it would be the most needed near the mouth of the Arkansas River.[27]

I am aware that this view is contrary to the statements which appeared in the Northern papers at the time, to the effect that the Federal General McClernand made the attack upon the Arkansas Post without orders.[28]

I have walked over the battle-ground at the "Post" since the battle, & conversed with officers who were engaged. By these means, I am able to give a correct account of the battle from the Confederate point of view, which I will reserve for another chapter.[29]

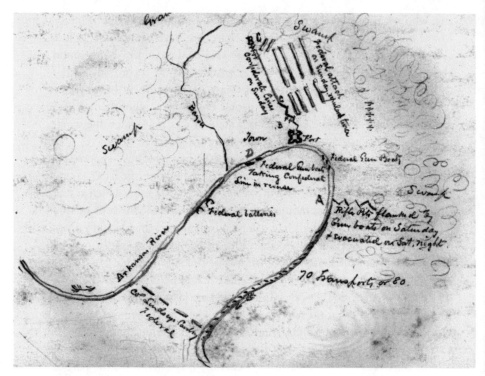

Merrell's sketch of Arkansas Post, which he made to illustrate his comments on its capture by Union forces.

CHAPTER 48

*T*he Federal General had correct information about the situation at the Post of Arkansas and arranged his attack correctly according to the knowledge he had; but he fell into an error nevertheless.[1] The Federal spy, a young, intelligent, and very attractive woman pretending to be in search of her husband, was known to the Confederate officers and received a good deal of attention from them. She was not molested but sent back to Helena under a Flag of Truce, escorted by Col. Carter, a Texas Col. of Cavalry. Once safely there, she made no secret that she had brought away plans of the Works. At the time of her visit the line of rifle-pits extending from the Fort to the Swamp was not completed, and just there was where the Federal General made a mistake that was fatal to many of his men. He marched boldly to turn the Fort and was twice repulsed with very great loss by the infantry in the trenches. Had he relied less upon his previous information, but more upon actual reconnaissance, he would have made no attempt to carry the line of rifle-pits until the gun-boats had silenced the Fort and, running by it, had taken up their position in reverse of the Confederate lines, and not even then until the gun-boats had shelled the rifle-pits effectually.

The attack began on Saturday upon the part of the Federals who landed and attacked the first line of rifle-pits at **A** in the plan. This line, which was a very good dry-weather position, had, since the winter rains had made the river navigable, become untenable because the Federal gun-boats could pass and take it in reverse. This was what took place, and on Saturday, after a brisk firing on both sides, the Confederate guns were retired from that position, repaired over night, & placed in position at B.B. In the meantime the gunboats moved up and engaged the Fort until some time after dark, when they retired, one of them in a crippled position. The next day being Sunday, the combined attack was made by land and water. The Cavalry taking position on the Grand Prairie to cut off a Confederate retreat & intercept reinforcements from the Garrison at St. Charles. The infantry in heavy masses to turn the Confederate lines at **C.C.**, and the Gun-boats to engage the Fort. The attack of the Gun-boats was successful. Com. Porter commanded in person.[2] He laid his gun-boats along-side the Fort at 60 or 70 yards distance and fired in at the port holes of the case-mates, which had no shutters! Of course the guns in the case-mates were soon dismounted. The cheeks of the embrasures were so constructed, funnel-like, as to guide the Federal shells in, even if they had been going wrong! One shell entering a case-mate exploded in that close place & killed one-third of all the Confederates killed that day. I have since examined the dismounted guns. Their trunnions were knocked off. They were split by shot striking them in the muzzle, pock-marked with grape and spherical case shot, and one had a fragment of a shell fused in the chamber, where I saw it by turning the light of the sun in with a piece of looking glass. A 9-inch Dalgreen gun that was mounted on the Fort en Barbette burst itself, & so the Fort was silenced on the river side, but not so on the land side, where two bastions mounted with field pieces commanded the field of battle & destroyed a great many men.[3]

The Fort silenced, several of the gun-boats passed it and took the position at D, having the Confederate line of battle in reverse.

In the meantime the Infantry and field Artillery of the Federals had been repulsed twice from the rifle-pits with great loss. The third time, the attack of the Federal infantry was made with greater caution & most imposing effect, while at the same time the gun-boats opened on the Confederate rear. The overwhelming character of this last attack was more in appearance than in fact. The Federal infantry, twice repulsed already, must have lost confidence, and the gun-boats were too low under the bluff bank of the river to throw any projectiles at point blank. They could only use shells, & those by the parabola, at which they were liable to overshoot the rifle-pits, and did actually overshoot, killing more of their own men than of their enemies. Genl. Churchill, commanding the Confederate force, expected to defeat this grand attack as he had done others, & so prolonged the battle until night, withdrawing his entire army in good order before the next day.[4] In this he was disappointed by the giving away of a Texas regiment of dismounted cavalry under the command of Col. Wilkes, who with his own hands raised a white flag; and the word being passed up and down the line that a surrender was about to take place, about 2000 men, who were resolved not to be taken prisoners, broke & made their way to escape, & did escape before the commanding General could restore order. The surrender now became necessary.[5] But when orders came to strike the flag at the fort, Col. Dunnington, although wounded, ran it up again & refused to surrender without orders in writing, & then only to the Navy.[6] Finally he surrendered to the Navy. The main body of the army surrendered to the land forces. The former, I have understood, were well-treated. The latter report, since they have been exchanged, that their treatment as prisoners of war was very bad indeed, so that 700 or more of them died in a captivity of only a few months. Genl. Churchill says he saw one officer freeze to death, & they all suffered intensely from cold and abusive language which they had not power to resist.

Col. Wilkes was, I am told, afterwards tried by court martial for that surrender & condemned to death; but I never heard that he was executed. Reinforcements were on the road to relieve Genl. Churchill at the Post, but it was as well they did not arrive. They could have done nothing in presence of so large a force. The Federal army was 47,000 strong besides gun-boats. They were returning from an attempt on Vicksburg, which had been a failure, & had taken the Post of Arkansas on their way home.

It is alleged that they had no less than 10,000 men killed, wounded, and deserted at the taking of this post. I have made an estimate upon the interments of dead in the trenches and in graves and find their loss must have been at least 6,000 & probably 8,000 men killed, wounded, & paroled deserters or prisoners.[7] Since the Federal army retired after burning the town & destroying the Military Stores and wagon-trains, leaving the Post to be re-occupied by the Confederates, I am at a loss to know what good end they gained by the victory. Had they proceeded to occupy the lower valley of the Arkansas, or even to visit that portion of the river with their gun-boats, they would have compelled the Confederate army in Arkansas to fall back upon Red River for subsistence; but they did no such thing.

The Post of Arkansas was never again occupied in the Confederate interest, except occasionally as an outpost. The cannon that had been disabled and thrown into the Well in the Fort by the Federals were afterwards recovered and mounted for the defense of Little Rock; and so late as June in 1863, Government mules, arms, and other property were collected in that vicinity by officers detailed for that purpose.

While all these events of the Campaign of 1862 were going on, there was a growing discontent in the Confederate army of Arkansas. The old Revolutionary army at Valley Forge could scarcely have suffered so much, for it was in winter quarters; but here was no rest; marching and countermarching through mire and sleet and frozen ground; without shoes, or blankets enough, & very few tents. With no salt, no flour, not enough of corn meal by half, and beef that had journeyed several hundred miles on foot with nothing at all to eat but the buds of trees and underbrush along the road. Great sickness followed this low fare, exposure, and hard duty; and hearing of the destitution of their families at home, men became dejected, ferocious, & finally deserted, singly and in squads. The punishment of death for desertion was not inflicted in many cases because of these extenuating circumstances; but there were some deserters who richly deserved all that military authority or society could inflict. The worst men in the camps, they came home to plunder and murder in the absence of those who had been conscripted and were gone to the war. It was remarkable to see how many of those were the same men who had robbed and murdered in the year before under the pretense of excessive zeal for the Confederate cause!

We could hear of such gangs in almost every mountain county, and in some of the river bottoms where concealment was easy. In our county (Pike), the first organized party that made head established itself in the "Greasy Cove," a mountain pass at the source of the Little Missouri River. There they forted their position, & sent out boasts that they could not be dislodged. Their leader was a Capt. Greer who had been elected Capt. of a Company in the Confederate service, but failing to pass the examination was reduced to the ranks; whereupon he deserted after writing passes for a number of soldiers who also deserted and met him in the mountains, forming the nucleus of the band above referred to. Of course they had to plunder in order to subsist, but it was not long before they proceeded to an attempt at murder, which roused the citizens, who organized a company under the Command of Capt. Morgan, who stormed their entrenchments and broke them up, killing some in the battle & hanging their leaders. This band of marauders had several times threatened me with a visitation, and I armed my people to resist their attack whenever they thought fit to make it; but none of us joined in the expedition against them, for these reasons. *First*, we were employed day & night carrying on the Factory, and our duty was there. *Second*, I would never take part in the hanging of any man, however much he might deserve it, without a fair trial, & that by law. The immediate occasion of the destruction of that band of deserters was their robbery of old Mr. Henderson, leaving him for dead. Mr. Henderson was a citizen of Hot Springs County. He was on his way to the Salt Works in Sevier Co. with a wagon and team of mules and a Negro driver, himself on horse-back, and money around him in a belt. Camped for the night, he was roused by four horsemen, & asked them where they were going. They said they were on their way to kill a neighbor (naming him) four miles beyond, and rode on. In a few minutes they returned & told Mr. Henderson that they had changed their minds & were come back to kill him and take what he had. So they tied him to a tree, and drinking farewell to him in his own whiskey, one of them shot him with a rifle, and they left him for dead after taking his Negro and wagon with the horse and mules & all the money they could find. Henderson was not killed but recovered after a very long time; he was able, however, to identify the men who did the deed, & none of them except the Capt. were hung without being first confronted with him.

Capt. Morgan was afterwards shot & killed by some one in ambush by the road side. Judge Flowers also, sometimes called Capt. Flowers, whose home was in the adjoining county to ours, was shot in the back and killed as he journeyed from Head Quarters towards home. That event took place in Hot Springs Co. Capt. Flowers and his Company had been conspicuous as "regulators," and had hung at least one man and shot another, which causes me here to make the reflection that "the way of the transgressors is hard." I think I have before made the remark that the Bullies have not proved to [be] brave soldiers in this war; I now add that those who have taken the lead in "regulating" the country by acts of violence have turned out so far to be unhappy & unfortunate men. They come to no good afterwards.

There was a man hung in Pike County in these times by an enraged populace, but those who did it were not citizens of our county; they were from Hempstead County. I did what I could to prevent it. The name of the victim was Lester, a one-armed man. He had come into the county from Texas with a very bad name. It seems he had killed a man in Texas after the same man had shot off his arm. I never heard of his committing any crime in Arkansas except that of returning to his neighborhood after having been once banished by a regulating committee. A gin had been burned, but it was by daylight, & although there was no evidence, he was suspected, and suspicion was enough in that reign of Terror; he had to be hung. I have no doubt Lester was a bad man, it may be he was a dangerous man—he certainly had that appearance; but he was not bad enough or dangerous enough to be put to death without law.[8]

He had been as threatening towards me as he had been to anybody & probably more so; but I never thought he deserved hanging for that. Worse men were at large.

This event took place during court-week; a fair trial might have been had. I was Foreman of a Jury. Just as we were coming out of the jury-room with a verdict, I heard the cry, "They've got old Lester!" The Court room was quickly deserted. Sheriff, Jury, Lawyers, witnesses, audience, all ran to the Court-House square, leaving the Judge and myself with one or two others. Looking from the window, we saw them dragging their victim across the square. When he struggled or made an out-cry, a double bar-reled gun was put to his head. I said, "Let us go and rescue that man & give him a fair trial," but the Judge said it was in vain to interfere with an excited populace. And a friend standing by intimated that I, of all others, had better not interfere. I said no more. The best terms that could be obtained of the regulators was a promise that they would not hang the man in Pike County, a promise which they violated. Jeff Cottingham, who was Captain in that business, died soon after. He fell dead of a heart disease while drilling his men.

Matters now became so complicated that I forted the Factory at our own expense & prepared an armory. Several military men who looked at my preparations expressed their opinion that we could hold it with thir-teen resolute men against 200 or even 300 assailants without artillery. Our position on the outskirts of the population, in the spurs of the mountains, with a wilderness extending many miles to the North and West, exposed us to the attacks of confederated deserters, who could come upon us without passing any house for fifteen or twenty miles. Our circumstances invited such attacks. We were reported to have on hand fabulous amounts of money. We had always more or less of Stores accumulated for the supply of our hands. We had guns and ammunition and horses and mules, all things much desired by such gentry. Moreover, we were not popular with the people, and to rob us would have been regarded by many as a good joke rather than a crime. For me personally as a "d——d Yankee" and a "speculator," I might look for nothing less than hanging to be my portion if they got hold of me.

This brings my narrative down to the month of January 1863. I have said that by this time I was nearly sick and run down by the combined labors and anxieties of my business. Dr. Magill, my bro-in-law, was of the same mind, and we began seriously to talk of selling out and retiring from the business. Government itself was likely to be the only purchaser, and that at its own price, assuming the Confederate notes to be equal to Gold and silver and at par. The business was very profitable, & our part-ner, Mr. Matlock rather than sell, preferred to buy us out & go on with the business himself. He had never lived at the place. His home was at Camden. He had no idea of the toil & care he was taking to himself, only my word for that. He knew very well what I had gone through, but he, a Southern-born man, could get on better. He was not deceived as to the danger. The very night we were making out the Deeds of Sale, and Bal-ance Sheet and Inventory, we had for several days and nights before [been] expecting an attack. The ladies and their valuables had been several nights in succession forted. We wrote with our arms at hand & a guard sleeping by us on the floor. That very night our pickets were twice driven in, the last time in considerable force. Upon looking over those documents, I am surprised to see so few mistakes. I think the mind acts with more clearness at a time of pressing danger, & the nerves too seem to be hardened down. Mr. Matlock is a man almost insensible to danger. I never saw a man more so. He lacks the caution necessary for a well-balanced character. He, upon his own proposition, purchased our share in the Factory & other works of the Company, at its full value, in the face of all the dangers that en-vironed it. Such men for luck. He carried on the works, leaving all the mechanical part to Mr. Bell, my old manager, and at the end of eight or nine months sold out to the Confederate Government; but not until he had been literally run off the premises by a raid of Federal Cavalry who came on purpose to destroy it, but were turned back by a timely advance of a Confederate force with artillery to defend the place. That took place in November, 1863.

The Confederate Government took the machinery out of the Works, and hauled it in one large train of wagons to Texas.[9]

So ended my manufacturing career! ?

Of all the Factories I had built up—four in Georgia—my first at Roswell, Ga. and my last at Royston, Arkansas, have been the most successful. That at Mars Hill in Clarke Co., Georgia, had been destroyed by fire, but not until I had sold out of it. That which I left in good condition at Greensboro in Ga. would have made great fortunes for that Company if they had held onto it; but they quarreled, & rashly sold the machinery out of it before the War. The Curtright Co. Factory fell into the hands of Henry Atwood Esq. of Darien Ga., a planter who had befriended me & loaned me money in my time of need. He was father-in-law to my cousin George H. Camp.[10] In closing up my business I had endeavored to secure him by turning over to him certain Bonds of the Curtright Co. which I had received for money loaned to the Directors of that Company, after I ceased to be Agent. Those Bonds Mr. Atwood foreclosed (they were Mortgage Bonds) and became himself the purchaser of all that property, but afterwards took a partner, Mr. Rochambeau. The price he paid, I understand, was $40,000 for what had cost that Co. about $140,000. He afterwards wrote to me in Arkansas that he greatly feared that by my means he had undertaken more than he could carry out. However he removed his Negroes from the Seaboard, put some at work in the Factory and others on a plantation which he purchased near at hand.

I have not heard from him since the War, but of course it found his business in the best possible train. His Negroes already removed to the interior & well employed. His factory a public necessity and extremely profitable. I hope some day to have a letter from him saying that by means of me he has saved what he had, & become one of the wealthiest men in the Confederacy.

Note — 1873. I have since heard from a relative of Mr. Atwood that he died before the close of the war, but not until he had verified the above Expectation, & expressed himself in so many words as quite content with the results. This announcement was very gratifying to me, as may well be supposed.

Here my narrative was interrupted by military duty which took my time until the close of the War. This book was then laid away & finally lost as we thought, but this day Nov. 5, 1873 it is recovered.

Let this be considered then Vol. I. The remainder I will endeavor to write in a separate book.

CHAPTER II

*T*he last public event of the War in Arkansas recorded in Vol. I was, I think, the fall of the "Post of Arkansas."[1] Genl. Churchill, who commanded the Confederate army on that occasion, has told me since that, but for the flag of truce carried out of our lines without orders by a certain demoralized Col. of a Texas regiment, he could certainly have held his position & effected a good retreat that night. Said Col., subsequently tried for that business, succeeded in raising so much doubt as to who it was that put up that flag, as to secure his own acquittal.[2]

I myself went over the ground some months after the battle, & am able to say that I have never seen elsewhere signs of so hard a struggle as that must have been while it continued. "Gaines' Mill" & "The Crater" in Virginia presented no such spectacle after the fight. My estimate was that the Federal army buried about 1,000 men.[3] We know the Confederate killed to be about 120.[4] The debris of battle & the marks of shot along the whole line, especially among the trees, surpassed my expectations; & as to the Fort, it was evidently untenable under the fire of so many gun-boats.

At nearly the same time all this was going on near the mouth of the Arkansas River, another active campaign was progressing near the Western frontier, three or four hundred miles distant towards the sources of that river. Simultaneously with the advance of McClernand's great armament upon the Post of Arkansas, another army under Genl. Blunt marched down from Kansas & Missouri upon "Van Buren" & "Fort Smith": towns which mark the limit of White settlements in that quarter. This diversion was very destructive to Lieut. Genl. Holmes, who had but one ill-fed & ill-clothed army to go against these two, either of superior force & in opposite directions.

Against the army of Genl. Blunt he sent General Hindman. How many men he had I never knew. Hindman's strategy always was to make the enemy, and his own people also, believe if possible that he commanded an overwhelming force. My own impression is that, deducting the sick & otherwise disabled by cold & destitution of whom there was a vast number, he could not have set out with more than about 10,000 men.

It was in the month of December. The weather & the roads well-nigh intolerable. By the time he encountered the enemy, he must have had but a poor front to show. However, he fought the Battle of "Prairie Grove," and it really did turn out that the Enemy burned some of his wagon trains, if not all, & fell back upon reinforcements, allowing Hindman to claim a victory. But at the same time Genl. Hindman & his army fell back also, as he explained it, for want of rations, their advance having outmarched their wagons & teams, which were by this time jaded sorely.

My own judgment at the time was that the "Prairie Grove" campaign added less than nothing to the reputation of either General. As to the troops, they suffered unreasonably by cold & exposure, hunger, & inadequate clothing; & it [was] almost like creating a new army to make one out of what was left of Hindman's men after that expedition. Indeed multitudes never did come straight back, but deserted & went across the Country to their homes in Texas, not to appear again as soldiers until afterwards & in some other command. Genl. Hindman did not consider himself a General fit to manage a campaign. He once told me so. He could carry a Brigade into action gallantly & bring it out all right, but he was no master of strategy in war. His organizing & administrative powers were very great.

This advance of Blunt in the North west was adroitly timed by the Federals time enough in advance of McClernand's arrival in the mouth of Arkansas River, so that the greater part of Genl. Holmes' available force was westwards, beyond recall, leaving him but few troops with which to relieve Genl. Churchill at the Post; & those only arrived in time to learn of the surrender. The roads were extremely bad everywhere at that particular season, the water-courses up, & the cold intense. Thousands of men were placed *hors de combat* without ever seeing the enemy. Four months afterwards I assisted at a review at Head Quarters, & we could scarcely parade 9,000 men. I scarcely think the Federals could have suffered much from hardships in Arkansas that winter. They were better clad & better shod. Their transportation was doubtless excellent, & as to Genl. McClernand's 40,000 men, they came & went on transports very comfortably, I should say, indeed. That they did not then & there march to Little Rock & take possession of the State is one of the things I never could understand.

One circumstance regarding the army of Genl. McClernand, which gradually came to our knowledge, partly accounts for the inactivity of Federal operations at that conjuncture. The morale for Genl. McClernand's army was not sound. Great as that army was, & well-equipped, it was easily discouraged. It had been turned back from before Vicksburg after prolonged & exhausting efforts, & large numbers of the men had no more stomach for the war. After the battle of Arkansas Post, although victorious, the men of Genl. McClernand came in to our outposts & surrendered in great numbers, taking their paroles in due from & starting across the country for their homes in the North, free, as they supposed, until it came their turn to be exchanged. I myself knew of one outpost where not less than 300 Federal soldiers were after the battle thus taken in & paroled after the battle by the handful of men who had marched to the relief of the Post but failed to arrive in time. I have heard the opinion expressed that probably as many Federal soldiers surrendered after the battle as were captured of our soldiers at the battle.[5]

However, the U.S. Government soon put an end to this voluntary surrender of their men by refusing to recognize the Paroles, an arbitrary & unwarlike proceeding which was finally most disastrous & demoralizing in the interests of prisoners & their treatment. It vitiated all the remainder of the war in that respect, for our people were positively not in a condition to feed & clothe well their own armies, much less prisoners of war for whom there was no parole or exchange. But in the case of Genl. McClernand's army, fatigued with six or seven months' vain efforts against Vicksburg, I suppose that self-preservation prompted the U.S. Government to do something effectual, right or wrong, to keep its armies from straggling.

Note. Turning back to the closing chapters of Vol. I, I find that I did then & there, while the events were fresh in my memory, record the Battle at the Post & its results more fully & doubtless with more accuracy than I can now after ten years lapse of time.

CHAPTER III

*T*he disasters of December & January left us in a poor way to hold the Trans-Mississippi Department. We had become much exhausted in resources. 29,000 stands of arms intended for this Department were shut up at Vicksburg, & as I said before, we had in Arkansas not exceeding 9,000 or perhaps 10,000 Infantry & Artillery. I could not say as to the Cavalry, for they were mainly on out-post duty, & I could only know certainly so far as I saw. More men were forthcoming, but the arms they brought were not fit to encounter the regulation arms & fixed ammunition of the Northern armies.

Lieut. Genl. Holmes was still in command of the Department, notwithstanding his application to be relieved. His duties & responsibilities were too great for any one man.

His authority comprehended all that was still Confederate in Louisiana, Arkansas, Texas, & the Indian nations westward. If Northern armies had gained & held a considerable foot-hold in Louisiana & Arkansas & in the nation, so much the worse for Genl. Holmes & his government. He was ably seconded by the Civil Governors of the several states. Gov. Flanagin in Ark.[1] I scarcely remember who held the same position in Louisiana, unless it was Gov. Allen.[2] As to the Governor of Texas, we never heard him mentioned; indeed it did not matter much about the Civil power in those times.[3] The Confederate power was dominant & almost everything was military or nothing.

Genl. Holmes was a good man, as a soldier brave & experienced; but as an organizer not equal to Hindman, partly because he was decrepit & had not the work in him, partly because he had not, like Genl. Hindman, enough of the "mustang" in him to deal with Wild Western men.

Genl. Holmes was pre-eminently a *just* man. He came to us a hale, hearty man of large stature. Before we had reached the middle of the year '63, he had perished away until his legs were quite loose in his cavalry boots, & his temper irascible, sometimes almost past endurance. In point of fact, he had come to be called "Grandmother" by the army.

This was probably due to his habit of scolding officers when they came to Head Quarters on business, and it was so far subversive of discipline, but I never could see that it weakened his power to command when in the presence of the enemy. I never could discover by conversation with him that he had any plans at all; yet that may have been because of his reticence. All his instructions to me were a seeming *carte blanche*, leaving with him all credit for success & all the blame of failure to myself. This, from what I have seen, I take to be one of the little arts of Military men, which finally becomes a life-long habit — & there is some sense in it.

It was in June, 1863, that I was called for to report at Head Quarters to take a "position of great Responsibility."[4] That was about the language of the letter placed in my hands. I did not like it, but had it to do nevertheless. I needed rest. My physical & mental powers had been overtaxed almost to exhaustion during the period of a year or more that the Factory had been, as it were, in a state of siege, & I had sold out of it, mainly for the sake of rest. But I could not well decline to report when desired to do so, especially considering the complimentary tone of the letter. My Commission as Captain I had already resigned & handed back in person to Genl. Holmes in person, on the ground that the purpose for which it had been sent me was accomplished.[5] But unhappily for my love of quiet & rest, I had somehow gained under my commission a reputation for holding a difficult post against odds; & Col. Alexander of the Ordnance Office had specially reported, upon inspection, favorably as to my Engineering skill.[6]

So I procured me a respectable outfit, & in due time appeared in presence of the irascible old General. I never could tell whether he personally liked me or thoroughly disliked me; nor did I care much. I expected to do my duty if possible. I found the Genl. quite out of humor with his Engineer Capt. Mackey, who was at that time absent on a visit to his family in Texas. Capt. Mackey was not a good man, but I always thought him an efficient Engineer.[7] At least he had two assistants who did a great deal of work & did it well. I wish I could remember their names.[8] As to Capt.

Mackey, he was of the temperament of a mercenary soldier, most thoroughly. His violence & profanity were very repulsive to Genl. Holmes, who was a religious man, & further than that, I surmised that his unscrupulous ways of taking for the public service, or burning the property of citizens, must have made situations distasteful to the General.

At any rate, it soon appeared that what he wanted of me was to do his Engineering. The office of Chief Engineer was vacant & its functions were for the present vested in Major Burton, who was at the same time Chief Quarter-Master.[9] By the way, Maj. Burton was from first to last one of the very best executive & administrative men in the Army. In all his military career I never saw or heard anything about him to the contrary. He was especially good-tempered & courteous under circumstances often the most trying. Sick or well, he was always the same.

It was no child's play to hold positions like his—Chief of Clothing Bureau, Chief Quartermaster &c. with such meager supplies, & to satisfy Colonels & Generals clamoring for more, their commands often absolutely destitute.

I had no idea of becoming an office man & to settle down into a thing of requisitions & printed forms. From the Factory into an official position of that sort would have been from the "Frying pan into the fire." If I soldiered at all, I wanted it to be in the open air, & so we soon came to an understanding.

The general situation at the front was this. The Federal military power was established at Helena on the North East, & at Van Buren & Fort Smith towards the North West. The Mississippi River, as far down as nearly to Vicksburg, was patrolled by their gun-boats, of which they possessed some of light draft & swift speed, whose rendezvous was in the "Cut-off" at the mouths of the White & Arkansas Rivers.

This military occupation held the country in subjection within the range of their guns, but no further. The Confederate Head Quarters were, as I said before, at Little Rock. A post was maintained at Pine Bluff, near which a Fort was in a forward state of construction, at a place so much out of the way as to suggest the inference that it had been built more to interest the men & keep them employed than for any use against the enemy.[10] The main chance was to hold Little Rock.

The Northern army, once there, would of course establish a Politico-Military Government; & so Arkansas would to all intents and purposes be lost to the Confederacy. In order to hold the seat of Government at all, we must have rations for the men. The army was patient. The Soldiers would go in rags. They would march, if necessary, shoeless & hatless; &

as to pay, that was of no kind of consequence since Confederate money would by this time buy almost nothing. A quart of whiskey would bring Seventy-Five to One Hundred Dollars in Confederate Money. The soldiers could stand all this, but they could not do without something to eat for themselves & their horses.

The Cavalry, generally on outpost duty, & well up with the Enemy, could & would take [care] of themselves. Anywhere that they could no longer stay for want of supplies had not much to fear from the enemy. But the Infantry & Artillery at Hd. Quarters depended solely on two sources of supply. All the meat came from Texas. After being driven several hundred miles, & the last hundred miles without any thing at all to eat except buds in winter time, it was very poor beef. It shocks me even now to recall to me how poor & sickly it was.

I was saying the meat, such as it was, all came from the rear—from Texas. That line of supply was not likely to be interrupted by the enemy; but one other only article of food, viz. Indian Corn, all came from the lower Arkansas River, between Pine Bluff & the mouth of that river. It was hauled from the Plantations to the River Bank & housed in rail pens, from which it was loaded into our steam boats by means of a chute.

This being the situation, it is manifest that whenever the enemy should get it through his hair so as to understand it, he had only to come in with his Gunboats up the Arkansas, with a sufficient force to land occasionally & set fire to corn cribs, & the evacuation of Little Rock on our part without a chance to fight for it would become a necessity for want of food; & falling back, our next base of supply would have to be on or near the Red River of Texas & Louisiana. I say this was the situation in Arkansas when I reached Hd. Quarters in May, 1863.[11]

To the General's sharp question, "What must we do?" I could only answer that "I would study about it & we would see what could be done." I went to Pine Bluff & examined the Fort, but could not see how that could answer, for it was situated at the wrong end of the river. By the time the enemy's gun boats could come under the fire of that Fort, our Land of Egypt would be already lost to us & the supplies destroyed.

I concluded that we must establish a post, & obstruct the navigation of the river at some point below & as near as possible to its mouth, & so reported to the General. He gave me a *carte blanche*, & I lost no time in going about what I had to do, & indeed there was no time to lose. The Enemy were again pounding away at Vicksburg. This time under Genl. Grant, they had a better prospect of success. Whether they were to bear another defeat or a success, we knew not; but we knew that in either case they would be sure, [when] it was over, to give us a visitation in force. As the bad boy said at school, "Well, if I cannot whip you, I can kiss your sister." So they turned against us to make reputation or at least a "Report" as they returned from their failures elsewhere.

Now there were two lines of Military approach from the Eastward to Little Rock open to the enemy: one, as I have stated, was from Napoleon up the fertile valley of the Arkansas R. as far as Pine Bluff. Halting there — probably without any hard fighting, for "The Fort" was situated four miles above Pine Bluff on the river — halting there, the evacuation of Little Rock sooner or later would have become a necessity to us through want of food & breadstuffs. Moreover, from that point their cavalry would have been in position to intersect the military road in the rear of Little Rock, & so cut off also our supplies of meat.

The other line of approach was that which they had before attempted in vain. That is by ascending the White River to Devall's Bluff & from thence following the line of Rail Road to Little Rock. This last is the road we wanted them to come because it threatened none of our communications. It was over a country bad for an army in Autumn, which is here the droughty season of the year.

We could make the road of little immediate use to them by destroying bridges & rails; the simple crossing of the "Grand Prairie," where no water is at that season, would greatly discourage an army, & we could fight them on the line of the "Bayou Meto," ground of our own choosing where we had the timber & the water on them.

Before recommending this plan of the campaign at Hd. Quarters, I had interviews with the Generals having command in that region: General Walker was genial & communicative, but he was on the eve of removing to Texas.[12] Genl. Frost succeeded him, but I found him to say that he was not going to put himself to inconvenience about fighting the enemy at all.[13] Col. Wm. H. Parsons, commanding the 12th Regt. of Texas Cavalry, was hearty & enthusiastic as he always was; for he loved soldiering, & had no poor opinion of the grandeur of commanding men. In order to confirm ourselves in our views, we spent a night with Judge Scull near Pine Bluff & had a full expression of his views. He had been educated at West Point, was room-mate there with Jeff Davis, & had good ideas respecting military campaigning.[14]

To get the enemy where we wanted them — they out on the prairie & we in the timber along the Bayou: there was the plan we decided upon; & so I reported to Head Quarters, but not a scrap of the pen did I get to confirm our views, or commit the Genl. to our plan. However, I afterwards learned that our plan of the campaign was adopted, & it was understood that I must proceed with my part of the programme, & Col. Parsons was ordered to cover my operations with the force at his disposal.

CHAPTER IV

*B*ehold me then, Chief Engineer for want of a better, with the rank of "Major," uncertain of the sympathy of Head Quarters & liable any day to be superseded any day by somebody—anybody sent at random from the Court at Richmond Va.—of my own head pushing my operations close to the enemy near the Mouth of Arkansas River. I was fortunate in having the good will of Col. Parsons, commanding in those parts. His regiment of Cavalry formed a thin shelter behind which I might project. He had about 700 to 800 Cavalry, very enterprising & well in hand. He himself was on the alert both night & day. The rendezvous of the enemy was about ten miles from us as the crow flies. Parsons' horse was always within reach of his hand in case of alarm; & his saddle, bridle, & holsters, if not mounted, were ever close at hand & in condition for instant departure. His outposts were distributed in the form of a "T," the stem along the Arkansas River & the cross up & down the Mississippi or White Rivers. I always understood there was another regiment of Cavalry under Col. Dobbin keeping watch & ward over the Federal posts from the mouth of White River up to Helena, & that he did not suffer them to forage or journey far into the Country with impunity; but it so happened that I never saw him or any of his command to know them.[1]

I had subject to my orders two steam boats—one good one named the "Julia Roane," the capt. of which was a contrary man, & the "Sunny South," a poor little thing, with an obliging little man for capt. Owing greatly to this difference in the temperament of officers (& in their loyalty perhaps), the inferior boat was finally the most useful to me.

The only writing I had from the General, was an order which I will endeavor to find & insert it here.[2] Its purport was, to the best of my recollection, that I was to obstruct the Arkansas River somewhere near its mouth, by means of an *abatis* that should stop the advance of Gunboats in that quarter and, to that end, the meager resources of the department were placed at my disposal.

Notwithstanding the sandy, treacherous character of the bottom & banks of Arkansas River in those parts, I had little doubt I could construct an abatis of heavy timber or trees across the river that would stand the action of the water; but I was sure that I could place nothing but what the Enemy could saw out with their machinery, unless we had heavy artillery enough in position to drive them from their work. There were only two heavy guns at the Arsenal at Little Rock. They were the wreck of two out of the three used at the Post of Arkansas. They appeared to have been damaged in the action. They were pock-marked with grape & shrapnel, deeply indented. One had the remains of a shell which seemed to have been fired into the muzzle & embedded firmly in the chamber. Both were split the whole length of the chase nearly, & one trunnion at least was knocked off.[3]

The fire of those gunboats carrying probably 40 heavy guns, at 70 to 80 yards distance, had eventually been too much for those three. The wonder is that Dunnington made any fight at all 'gainst such odds. These two fragmentary guns were of 9-Inch Caliber. They had been cast at the Tredegar works in Richmond, & the worksup pronounced the metal to be of the very best.[4] The enemy had left them to us after casting them into the well of the Fort. Col. Parsons had recovered them by digging an inclined plane, & sent them to Head Quarters for what they were worth. The machinists at the arsenal had cut them off midway of the chase & mounted a wrought iron trunnion on one.[5]

I could not bring myself to risk my reputation on the performance of such pieces against the perfect artillery of the Enemy. So I was fain to be content with an old 12 Pounder of Cast Iron, which Genl. Price had brought away from Missouri. It was very heavy in proportion & probably had been cast by some enterprising foundry man, upon his own ideas, & early in the war. It was mounted for Field operations & had fixed ammunition, so that I might at least hope to get off with my gun & so avoid the disgrace of a capture. I took that gun, but never ventured to fire it at any thing, & I never let it fall into the hands of the Enemy. I had heard of Genl. Price making a good fight loading his guns with log-chains, paving stones, & bits of old iron; & I suppose this must have been one of the guns he did that with. It was rough enough, to be sure.

With these appliances all I could hope to do was to make the Enemy believe, by making a great parade of small means, that I was obstructing the river in such a way as to forbid them coming that way, at least without great loss & delay, while at the same time the White River was left free for them to go the way we wanted them to come. Their spies were numerous, more numerous, I had reason to think, than was consistent with the fierce Southern sentiments paraded by some Citizens. Negroes were going &

coming by night through the lines, & there were several well-known spies, as it turned out, of whom it was concluded that the best use they could have been put to was not to hang them, but to coach them up with such information only as we desired the enemy to have. No one so easy to deceive as a sharp, conceited, self-conscious Spy, unless it may be the parties who employ him & give him credence.

As for myself, nothing in all the war so demoralized me as the deceit & low cunning I learned to practice towards the Enemy. Nothing I so much regret. To be sure, I had started in life upon the Ethics of Paley, but let a man reason as he will, suppression of the truth, & deceitful strategies, even in war, are degrading to a man in his own self esteem.[6] To make a clean breast of it, once for all, I think I lied to the enemy on several occasions during the War, & I have not thought so well of myself for it ever since.

However, in the bogus obstruction of the Arkansas River, I had only to make my parade of great works, & every mouth was ready to magnify their importance. Planters made arrangements to move off, with their Negroes & household stuff, in anticipation of heavy warlike operations; & Steamboatmen especially were annoyed, for there were several fine boats lying above my obstructions who had to be watched all the time lest they should get up steam & run off to the enemy. Spies, as I said before, were coming & going, & our own scouts themselves, frequently visiting families within the enemies' lines. All I had to do or say was to be very much in earnest about my work, & very courteous & conversable when strangers appeared at my quarters.

My proceedings at the outset were the best possible calculated to fill the country with exaggerated rumors concerning the magnitude of our works. Having selected my location, which was at "Smith's Cut-off," & established my quarters at a heavily timbered spot on the immediate bank of the river, I sent my Quarter Master (Curry) over the adjacent country to summon the planters to send me without fail on a certain day, each in proportion to his force, so many able-bodied Negroes, each to come with a good axe & rations sufficient.[7] From some we made requisition of Ox teams & heavy timber wheels & with drivers for the same.

I got what I wanted amid a storm of protests & objections, which I had reason to believe would have taken the definite form of resistance, but for the presence of Cavalry ready & willing to enforce my orders. All the time of the War, so far as my experience went, a wealthy planter owning many Negroes was the hardest man in the country for a soldier to get anything out of; &, as to the soldiers, since the war had by this time taken definite form as a planter's war, which going against us would leave no rich planters, nor any Negroes they could own, they (the soldiers) were quite ready enough to exact what was necessary. So my requisitions for laborers, tools, & supplies, backed by a sufficient Cavalry force, were of themselves sufficient advertisement; & the Enemy were not slow to hear of it, as I said before.

The work I did was done in very good faith. I did intend to obstruct the river the best I could. My reputation as an Engineer was at stake, & my duty as an officer. My "navy yard," as we called it, did look like business to be sure. The Cotton-wood tree was the only timber, & that was in abundance. Tall, straight, & easy to work, it was well-suited to my purpose. I wanted to construct a dense abatis across the river of those trees, the largest ends resting on the bottom & the tops pointing downstream. My first idea was that the tree roots & all, with the soil adhering to the roots, might be lodged where I wanted them & that they would stay there as we see snags without number at many points on that same river. With that idea I rigged a Capstan & other machinery on the forward deck of the "Julia Roane" with other appliances, but soon found that plan would not succeed. I might lodge a tree now & then, & perhaps it would stay, perhaps it would not. If successful, the expense would be enormous, employing a steam-boat at $500.00 per day to deposit one or two trees or less per diem. I had been raised, as a manufacturer & mechanical engineer, to do things economically or to drop them at once. So I discharged that steam-boat & tried other plans, retaining only the steam-boat "Sunny South," which, being small & cheap, I could employ to advantage.[8]

My next project was to frame the trees, after trimming off the tops, into rafts of four to six trees to the panel, not lying close alongside each other like the timber in a commercial raft, but each tree about six feet apart from the rest. These we secured by cross girders & strongly pinned, so as to float to the spot & be anchored there. The next thing to be done was to sink the upstream end to the river bottom & make it stay there.

Driving piles was out of the question. That had been tried at the unlucky Post of Arkansas, but the first good rise in the river wiggled them loose at the bottom, so that they shot themselves up in the air & floated away.

The sandy bottom of the river was so shifting & treacherous that whatever I did must be so adapted as to be subject to & aided by natural causes, or it would not stand at all.

And that I hold to be the essence of good Engineering. Not to resist & overcome the powers of nature, but to court & win those powers until they reinforce & strengthen the work. Of all the tight places for an engineer I ever saw, the bed of the Arkansas River is the last place to undertake

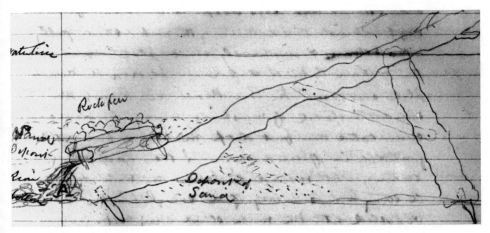

Merrell's sketch of the abatis that he placed in the Arkansas River in 1863 to impede the Union capture of Little Rock.

anything in spite of the caving banks, the shifting sands, & the immense volume of waters in times of freshet. So I must coax the river & see what she could do for me. Of course the current floated my rafts to the spot where I wanted them.

I had provided each tree with, say, two strong oak pins like the flukes of an anchor to hold on at the bottom by one end while the other should remain above the surface. Then, in order to sink that end of the raft, I had loaded each with a log-pen, pinned & divided into compartments, which compartments I filled with rocks of heavy iron ore (bog iron) which the "Sunny South" brought down from the rocky bluffs high up the river.

It was slow getting these rocks, & we kept the little boat quite busy. We had on the spot a barge, one hawser, & one anchor, by means of which we kept ourselves afloat above our work, & did not have to put hands into the water much.

By this time we were well into the month of June. It was not wholesome to be much in the water, & the glare of the sun upon the water was almost intolerable. The following sketch will serve to illustrate the present stage of the work.[9]

The leg & brace were hinged by a joint & let down after arrival of the raft on the spot.

All went on smoothly until I planted my first section of timber-raft. Niggers & all applauded the job. It looked formidable, to be sure. A plenty of such in the channel of the river would delay the enemy's boats some time, no doubt; &, if they could be deterred from reconnoitering in force, we might really bar their passage this way! But, alas, the deceitful river. Next morning it was found that the current had washed a deep hole under the log-pen of my raft. That end had settled down until my timbers were well-nigh perpendicular in the air, with a fair prospect that another twenty four hours would undermine the whole structure & float it away.

Robinson Crusoe was never more at his wits' end than I was for an hour or two that morning. But "there is always a way."

I thought certainly the same current & the same shifting sand which now washed my work away, might be constrained to cover up my work & hold it there. It was my only chance. So I built the next raft with a tail like the tail of a bird. Young Cotton wood bushes made the quills & feather. The same, laid side by side & several tiers deep at the bottom of the raft behind & held there by the rock, sank gently & instantly shut flat upon the bottom like a valve. It was a complete success. In less than an hour, the sand, instead of washing away, had accumulated three feet deep, making a bar at the foundation of our work. I then had the steam-boat "round to" below the work, & with a strong hawser try if a single timber could be pulled out. The work stood every test.

For illustration of this tail, or saving clause in my structure, see *A* in the sketch.

By this time the work was reduced to a method which might be carried on by the master of Construction (Mr. Westerman) & the Quartermaster to keep him in laborers & supplies. And it was high time, for I was sick of fever. Lying in my tent my mind wandered, & I talked nonsense by the hour. That is a very unhealthy region, & I had undergone unusual exposure with some anxiety.[10]

CHAPTER 5

*F*ortunately, the enemy had not hitherto advanced upon us, but he soon now became more active.[1] The war was lively near at hand. Genl. Grant's operations against Vicksburg were progressing daily. We could hear the reports of heavy guns frequently. The Mississippi river was active with gun-boats & transports almost every day; but as yet I had remained quite unmolested. The first alarm came while I was lying sick.

There was a large side-wheel steamboat lying about seven miles up the river from my barricade. The Capt., I had good reason to know, was not friendly to the obstruction of the river. He had an extra supply of ropes

& tackle which I needed badly. The same belonged to the Confederate Service, & his boat had been employed early in the war at Columbus laying the boom across the Mississippi R. He had them concealed in a State Room. I did not feel like respecting his rights, if he had any in the matter; so I sent by some Cavalry for what I wanted. The things could not be found. I got one anchor & nothing else. The remainder, we were led to infer, had been put in one of his yawls & pushed up the waters of Bayou Meto, where it was impossible for us to go at present. That circumstance, together [with] the fact that our first Federal Spy had disappeared in his company, both in a buggy, on the road to the Enemy. By this time I had encountered so many of about that style in those parts that I restrained my indignation. Capt. Miller, for that was the skipper's name, had a daughter, full grown & quite a belle with the officers.[2] I never saw her, but could hear. Never heard any harm of the girl. I suppose she loved admiration neither more or less than others of the sex at her age. She lived on board the "Bracelet" with her father, & made her home quite a popular resort for respectable officers. One day cards of invitation went round for all the officers of Col. Parsons' Command, with the Col. himself to come on a night specified & have a Ball on board the "Bracelet." I myself received no invitation. That night, for the first time, the Enemy advanced on us.

I lay sick & in a dreamy state. I had all the time my plans laid to evacuate at a few minutes' warning & escaping by a neighborhood road to leave the Enemy nothing they could capture. In the night there was a storm of wind & rain. It blew down my tent flat & made the situation dangerous by limbs torn off trees & falling heavily. After the storm all was still again when I heard a courier on horse-back tearing up the road at full speed. The Enemy had crossed the river at Red Fork.[3] They were cavalry. Before the courier was well out of hearing again on his reckless ride to find the Colonel, my own plan was arranged mentally thus. "Red Fork seven miles — courier at his gait has been half an hour coming — Enemy cavalry — in the dark, cautionary. Head of column have to wait for rear. 'Twill take them two hours to get here — deduct courier's time net say one hour & a half I have to spare — & a half — & aff. No hurry. Half an hour all I want. Believe I will sleep half hour — 'affour — only half — & then I will be up & off time enough ahead — ahead — a-head"; & so I went off sound asleep, prostrated & enfeebled in mind by my fever.

Of course I did not wake again until broad day-light. The Col. & I looked each other in the eye but never exchanged views about the treachery of the "Bracelet's" Captain & his daughter. Neither of us felt inclined to report our share in the night's work at head quarters. Enough for us that the Enemy found his road obstructed more than expected & so went back the way they came. Col. Parsons was quite too old a soldier to leave the road open in his rear while he was dancing with the girls, nor is it likely he was altogether deceived as to the fidelity of his host that night. On the contrary he had left on duty his very best officer for such a duty, Major Farrar, who was quite equal to the emergency & gave the enemy no success in their raid that he could boast of.[4]

Of course the arrival of the Courier broke up the ball on board the "Bracelet." As usual the Col. had his saddle & bridle in a corner within reach; lady's society & a fine supper had no longer any charms; in a very short time the invited guests were all in the saddle again, leaving the ladies & the non-combatants [to] make the most of what was left. The officers afterwards told me they had a rough dance at the best. The rain poured, & the wind drove it in at every opening. The roof of the boat leaked until the dancers were wet to the skin, & the water on the floor draggled the ladies' dresses wet & muddy to their knees. So the Captain's Ball on board the "Bracelet" was a failure, & I, the uninvited, had the best of it & lost no sleep. I never heard any more about the popularity of Capt. Miller & his daughter among the officers of the 12th Texas Cavalry.

The plot now thickened fast. The fighting was growing heavier daily at & about Vicksburg, & it soon became evident that the Confederate authorities on that side the Mississippi were growing nervous about the result. Orders came for Genl. Frost's Brigade to advance from Pine Bluff to the banks of the Miss. R. below Napoleon, in order to operate against the Transports which daily, under escort of the gun-boats, went down with troops & supplies for Genl. Grant. Amongst them they made a great deal of noise with their cannon, but I never learned the extent of damage done. I did not think the Missourians much liked that sort of warfare.

There were also indications of another aggressive movement, from Head Quarters at Little Rock towards Helena. This was so wild a scheme considering the sickly season of the year & the small force we had fit to move, that it could not have originated with Genl. Holmes; the orders must have come from as far off as Richmond, Va., & it afterwards turned out that was the fact.[5]

First a Steam boat was sent down to me, a large fine one. I now forget her name—but her Capt. was a Van Buren man of the Northern persuasion. He brought written orders for me to let him through my barricade, which I did, after satisfying all on board that I was really putting formidable obstructions across the River. The Captain's orders were to proceed up the White river & report at and above Clarendon, to assist in Transportation of men & stores. As might have been expected, after a few hours the Pilot returned alone & on foot. His name was, I think, Fraser. He was of Van Buren, Ark. He reported that they got safely through the cut-off, no Federal squadron in sight; but, at the point of turning northward in the White R. the Capt, Engineer, & others entered the Pilot House with pistols in hand, & demanded peremptorily if he would put the boat about & "Steer for the United States." He said "No." Then they made him jump into a yawl which they had stolen on their way down & were about to land him then & there in the Cane brake, but he persuaded them to give him the oars & let him row himself to a place of safety, which he did, landing at Red Fork & proceeding inland on foot. I gave Fraser a letter to Head Quarters which resulted in his promotion.[6]

Another Steam boat passed us with similar orders. She was named the "Kaskaskia" & had side wheels. The officers of that Boat proved to be true men, & went through all right. I suppose the Federals must have withdrawn their guard boats from the Cut-off in order to escort Transports to and from Vicksburg; otherwise no boat of ours could have got into White River from the Arkansas.

As to the run-away boat, she did not go far. We afterwards learned that she was seized & put in Calaboose at Memphis for debts contracted before the war. So I reckon the Capt. of that boat had better done as he agreed to do.

These symptoms of a general forward movement from Head Quarters were not slow in developing evil results, as might have been expected at that season of the year. On the 4th July heavy firing could be heard in the direction of Helena, & shortly after the whole army came back, what there was left of it, in a sad plight. It turned out that untimely & peremptory orders had come from Richmond, Va., for Lt. Genl. Holmes to advance in force & capture the strong fortifications at Helena as a diversion in favor of our troops in & about Vicksburg! A far-fetched & ill-timed diversion! For the assault on Helena did not & could not take place until the very day Vicksburg surrendered. In order to reach Helena at all, the water courses being up & a great extent of over-flow lands quite under water — in order to get at Helena at all, Lt. Genl. Holmes had to make Northing many miles towards the head-waters of the streams. The weather was hot & sweltering, the men & artillery often up to the middle deep in mud & water. Daily more and more sick & stragglers fell behind on the road.

The Enemy had timely warning of their coming & were all snug & well-prepared. The Genl. behaved gallantly. The troops, what was left of them, were game, & for a few hours they gave the Federals all they could do.

One fort was captured by assault; another was pretty well silenced, but the whole thing was a hopeless case from the beginning. If the entire fortifications had been captured & the entire force of the enemy to boot, the place could not have been held; for there lay the gun-boats in the river, ready to enfilade everything.

Little Rock was lost at the Battle of Helena. The order came from Richmond, Va. Those unlucky orders from Richmond were the bane of the whole Trans-Mississippi war. It was too far away for even the best strategist to send orders for execution, where time & distances to be traversed constituted so large an element in the probability of success. And the best of advice did not always prevail in Richmond. Did an inefficient officer, in bad repute with the army here & shelved by Head Quarters, yet enjoying personal acquaintance & some influence as a politician, did he above all belong to the old original Secession order of men, he could go to Richmond & become an oracle there — a perfect "Mar-plot"[7] — until some day, without an accident, he would come back to the department promoted in rank over the heads of those who remained at their posts.

Did a Chief Quartermaster or Commissary turn out to be absolutely inefficient & obstructive in the hour of danger, no summary measures on the part of the General would rid us of him in time. The whole matter had to be referred to Richmond, Va., the delinquent action in securing friends & representatives of his own at Richmond, while the Commander in Chief, too busy & too high-minded for intrigue, would, after six months delay, wake up & find himself badly misrepresented & misunderstood by the Authorities. It was so continually. The "Dead beats" of the army, who should have been put in the ranks, still retained their stars on the Coat Collar, & repaired to Richmond.

The true policy of the war, I think, should have been to give no audience to such men; & as to the movement of troops, let this department hold its own. Thinly settled, distances great, people divided in their opinions about the War, it should have been understood from first to last that the Trans-Miss. Department had all it could do to take care of itself. And it might have been so but for the pig-headed politicians in Congress assembled at Richmond, who very early began to parade their law-knowledge against the manifest necessities of the times. "There is danger all the time," said they, "of a military usurpation & a separate Confederacy west of the Mississippi."

So the troops were perpetually ordered away from us to reinforce the Eastern people, leaving us little or nothing in exchange but promises which were never fulfilled, to re-inforce us in our time of need.

Alas! The curses of our land have been the Politicians. So I think of them, not personally & individually, but in the direful results of their wranglings. They embroiled us in this dreadful war. They disturbed & mismanaged the war when it was upon us, & subsequently by their continuous ignorance, malice, & corruption, cumulative all the while, they have the peace more intolerable & more destructive than the war itself. Had the Trans-Mississippi Department of the unlucky Confederacy been left to stand on its own bottom. Had a first-class Commander, say Genl. Kirby Smith been placed in command from the first, & no troops taken from him nor any sent to him; had politicians been disqualified for any but subordinate positions in the army, & put under ball & chain whenever they practiced their arts of popularity in Camp; I doubt not the Confederacy would have held its own this side the Mississippi River & at least as far north as the Missouri. In that position it would have given our Northern friends a frontier to defend so extensive as to have kept quite busy one-third, if not half, of all those splendid regiments that were left free to operate against Atlanta, Vicksburg, & Port Hudson.

If the Eastern States of the Confederacy were not strong enough in themselves to cope with the Middle & Eastern states of the North, they ought to have thought of that in time & let secession alone. As it was, however, we find our men of the Southwest in every active campaign from first to last of the war. They were at Bull Run. They were at Bowling Green & Ft. Donaldson. They were in force at the battles of Shiloh, Murfreesboro, Chickamauga. They saved Bragg's army after Missionary Ridge. They held Dug Gap against all that Genl. Sherman could do. They were at Resaca, Hope Church, & Atlanta. They helped mightily to defend Vicksburg & Port Hudson. In Virginia, too, in and about Richmond we find such as Grigg's Texas Brigade serving as the very forlorn hope of the Army.

Any good soldier who will examine the ground at Gaines' Mill, where that Brigade charged down a slope without shelter into a ditch or gully ten feet deep, hoisting each other out on the other side, under the fire of infantry & artillery in three tiers crowning the opposite heights, how they pushed on & on, capturing all that artillery, with Genl. in command. How without breathing time, they received an advance of Cavalry of the Regular army & sent it the way it came. How the "Irish Brigade" came on & on with colors flying & music blowing & then & there lost their reputation forever. I say a good judge of war will not fail to rank our men of the Southwest equal, when disciplined, to any troops in the world. I went over that ground with a young gentleman from Boston whose father had brought him to re-new the scenes of his labors in the war. The young man could point out the positions but said he was confused & never could tell how the thing was done! Sorry I am to say of our Western men, that undisciplined, they were sometimes quite as troublesome to their friends as to their enemies.

Where was I? O! The miserable business at Helena. In the multitude of fresh orders came one sending Col. Parsons & his regiment away to re-inforce somebody about Milliken's Bend in Louisiana. I seemed to myself to be forgotten. No orders, no officer or command sent to cover my works or defend them, so far as I could know officially. I removed the pub-lic property under my charge to a place of safety & reported for further orders.

The Lt. General was sick of a nervous fever. No one could see him or send him a letter. Genl. Price was in temporary command, & he did not believe in Engineers. Never looked at a Topographical map, he said, & as to works, when he wanted any he could always take them from the Enemy! After advising with my friends about Head Quarters, I got an informal leave to go home & recuperate my health until Genl. Holmes should resume command, if he ever did. My home was then still in Pike County. I did not get home any too soon for the welfare of my family.

Vicksburg & Port Hudson fallen, as we expected, the Northern army advanced in force upon Little Rock. They came just as we wanted them, across the Grand Prairie, & as we predicted, they had by their own official report 4,000 of their troops placed *hors de combat* by the difficulties of that Country before they were in sight of Little Rock.

But thanks to the Helena Expedition, our army was in no condition to fight such a force as that, & our fighting General was sick. As for Genl. Price, he was great on a retreat. This rear-guard fighting was, they say, magnificent, & he was personally as brave as Julius Caesar, but for defen-sive or active offensive operations, he had no genius. Moreover, the troops were discouraged. The Evacuation of Little Rock was made necessary by a flank movement of the Enemy, who forded the Arkansas River on a sand bar a few miles below the City.[8] They might have been fought to advantage on the Fourche Bayou, but that battle would have left the city under fire of Federal batteries advanced to the river bank opposite, & in case of defeat no retreat would have been practicable. So that in spite of the disgust & abuse of citizens, I suppose the Genl. did well to get out & away from there in a hurry as he did. There was no fight to speak of in our discouraged army just at that time.

At or about the same time, an advance in force on [the] part of the Fed-erals took place from Fort Smith. It came in the direction of the Caddo

Gap, thirty miles above where I was residing with my family. Once established there, they could raid the whole flat country below for a while, with impunity perhaps. But Col. Cloud commanding the "Feds," though a good fighter, did not seem to have any strategic plan. He was met at the "Back Bone" mountain by our Genl. Cabell, who was also an exceptionally good soldier, but his men would not stand.[9] About twenty-five of the Enemy were killed & wounded by an ambuscade at the head of the Column, & in the delay occasioned by that interruption, our men took up the retreat.[10] I never heard that any of them were hurt, or that they stood fire at all. The fugitives I saw seemed to think the war was at an end. As for themselves, they said the ammunition furnished them would not penetrate the skull of an ox at ten steps. They had tried it. They would not fight at such a disadvantage. Upon inquiry, I found that to be even so. The powder had been made at Arkadelphia in this state & was, as they said, of no account. However, if our men retreated, so did the Feds. At least we heard no more of them for that time.

As for myself, I concluded it was time for me to get away from that exposed position before it should become too late.

To move with our entire household, bag & baggage, leaving nothing behind to fall into the hands of the enemy, was no [little] achievement. Nevertheless we made the trip. The household consisted of Wife & myself—no children—Dr. Magill, my wife's brother & his wife with also no children. Servants Edmund, Tabby, Munroe, & Niddy. The two first very aged. Munroe, a sprightly young Negro man, & the other one the grandchild of Old Tabby.[11] We had accumulated for ourselves besides the customary bedding, plate, & household furniture, enough Bacon, flour, Coffee, sugar, tea, &c. &c., enough to do us probably as long as the war could reasonably go on. We had a Carriage & horses & one wagon. We had some Specie, but not near so much as we had the name of, & it was this last consideration that made our removal specially dangerous.

CHAPTER VI

We fortunately had a place to go to. Otherwise we should have fallen upon the hard lot of that very large class of Southern people, known as "Refugees." We could go to Camden, which was still within our own lines & not likely for some time to come to be a point of consequence to the Enemy, enough so to provoke any considerable raid or invasion. In our trade with Mr. Matlock, we had taken in exchange for the Factory several dwelling houses in Camden & other property as much as we could well take care of under the circumstances.[1]

Indeed that property began to need our personal attention. Abandoned or neglected property in those times was but little respected & poorly protected by the military.

With the unlucky reputation we had for owning "Hard money" in a large amount, the direct road from Pike County to Camden would have been for us a very unsafe road to travel. We therefore established a Depot about 30 miles southward, & off the direct road to any place. That place we approached from the rear through a swampy Creek bottom. To it we forwarded our things—a load at a time in such a manner as to excite no remark, until we had nothing left but ourselves to carry, & that final movement of ourselves was effected rapidly & with as much secrecy as was practicable. How much of all this was done in the night, I am now unable to say, but probably all arrivals & departures were nocturnal. I may as well here say that this safe harbor for our effects was on the plantation & in the house of Rev. Dr. Williamson, our beloved pastor. The old gentleman carried it out in a spirit of fun as well as of hospitality. Never a whimper from him that peradventure we might be bringing him & his household into trouble. I am happy to say he never did incur any loss or damage by it.[2]

Our precautions in this respect were none too great. The country was swarming with stragglers from the Army, & especially in all that region lying between the Prairie D'Ane & the Little Missouri Rivers, were squads of deserters, & men who had always resisted the Conscription, & there were some citizens too, who never intended I should get out of that country safe & sound with money in hand. But I out-generaled them all that time. The transfer of our stuff from Dr. Williamson's to Camden was made in like manner by sections, but in this I was aided by Confederate Government wagons by the Good Will of Capt. Taylor, then Quarter Master at Washington, who was one of the few in that region who by personal knowledge knew of my past services to the Government.[3]

Here it occurs to me to tell of one little incident which took place previously in my dealings with Capt. Taylor. As Quarter Master one of his duties was to collect Wool in the Country, & sometimes to fetch it from Texas, to make clothing & blankets for the Army. The spinning & weaving was done "On shares" by the women all over the country, but the Carding had to be done at our Factory. For that we got Confederate Money.

In order to wash & dry such large amounts of Wool fast enough, we had a "Dry House." The Dry house took fire one night & burned to the ground with all its contents—the same being mostly Confederate Government Wool & that to a large amount. To the best of my recollection, I should say about 5,000 pounds of Govt. Wool. Well, it was bad enough to lose the dry house, & our own share of the lost Wool; but what to do about the Government Wool? If we officially reported its destruction, it would not be for the interest of Government to believe a word we said. We knew all the time they wanted only a pretext to take Factory & all away from us; so we concluded to say nothing about it officially, but make up the loss out of our own pockets. It was this fact, among other things, that subsequently won Capt. Taylor's good will in the matter of transportation. And I may as well add that from that time to this, mutual good will has prevailed between Capt. T. & ourselves. He was an exception of a just Quarter Master in the War, & he has been a prosperous man since. Which is saying a good deal for any man in these times.

It was like beginning the World again, our settlement in Camden! Few knew us, except by our partnership with Mr. Matlock, & our ownership of his property in & about Camden. None knew of my half-military, half-civil status in Pike Co., & they knew less of my Engineering rank at Head Quarters, & as we wanted now most of all rest & quiet, it was not likely any of us would "Blow our own horn." I might at any time be ordered away on duty again. We had fences & outhouses to repair, Gardens to make, Corn & other supplies to purchase & haul, & not a few things to hide away for future subsistence.

The army under Maj. Genl. Price, *i.e.*, what was left of that army, had made a temporary halt at Arkadelphia, but finally fell back for Winter-Quarters to Camp Bragg, situated about ten miles westward from Camden.[4] Genl. P. must have been conscious of great numerical inferiority; otherwise, he would not have retired from a position of such strategic importance. At that point he was, so long as he liked it, able to keep the Enemy under the necessity of protecting both Little Rock & Pine Bluff. At the same time, by holding the "Caddo Gap," he could hold in check the Enemy raiding from Fort Smith & Van Buren. In other words, every one of his men under this arrangement might keep three of the Enemy employed, which is all that could have been expected of this Department under the circumstances. I don't know if Maj. Genl. Price ever had any plan other than to fall back, inflicting all the time all the injury he could on the enemy by desultory warfare.

As the season advanced, rain & cold prevailing, the Quarters at Camp Bragg failed to give satisfaction. Men & officers were sick in great numbers, & no little discontent prevailed, especially as the winter clothing for the men was not forthcoming. I will here add that here was another painful thing about the Confederate Military service. Often no pay, bad as that pay was in "Confederate Money." Very often no shoes, nor hats, nor clothing in the dead of winter, their bare feet on the frozen ground; &, especially after a retreat, no blankets. As to over-coats, they were rarely to be seen, even among officers. So 'far as the Clothing Bureau was concerned, the winter clothing reached the soldier in the field after the winter was half spent, & again the summer clothing when that season was likewise well spent. "Want of Transportation" was the prevailing excuse, but from what I subsequently discovered in the Department of the Clothing Bureau, want of method, if not of zeal as well, was at the bottom of it. A foolish idea that French & British intervention would any day end the war interposed from the first to prevent any timely and adequate provision for anything to be made long in advance. We had very few men who even realized the magnitude of the undertaking we had in hand.

Well, the army was pining & dwindling away at Camp Bragg. I think it was upon my suggestion that Head Quarters were removed to Camden. It took place in a brief conversation with Maj. Gallagher, the Judge Advocate, who by this time had quite recovered from the effects of a grape-shot which he got in his mouth at the battle of Helena.[5] A bad accident for a Lawyer, but [he] finally found the use of his tongue again, & is to this day quite able to hold his own in any Court. Well, Gallagher went round & found the sense of the people quite favorable & the vacant houses numerous enough. Soon Head Quarters came, & we began to have a gay time. Every decent housekeeper felt bound to make things agreeable. There was dancing. There was whist. There were serenades by brass bands & by string bands & glee singers. There were parties, recitations, &c. &c., & to offset the same, there were the serious drawbacks of depredations & tricks by some very bad soldiers. In point of fact, the destitution in the army did seem to justify almost any depredation the soldiers could perpetrate.

The rank & file of the Soldiers attended public worship well & were more than respectful. Many were added to the Church in Camden, & not a few who had not long to live, for they were slain in [the] spring campaign following.

My old General (Holmes) was by this time again in command, but he suffered me to remain quietly at home. I was in frequent communication with him, not so much direct as through Judge Watkins, of whom more hereafter.[6] I was frequently consulted about the fortifications round the town, about the topography of the Country. I had some maps to make, & took no small part in the consultations held in the N.W. Room of my house. Once only was an expedition to Dardanelle tendered me which I accepted, but the Genl. said he thought it would cost more than it would come to, & so it was dropped, & I was glad of it.[7] It was to fetch away from within the Enemy's lines the Machinery of a Factory. The garrison afterwards turned out to consist of 300 men, & unless the Genl. had given me more men than was probable, our success would have been no ways sure. Indeed I don't know but the Enemy were in force this side of there to have prevented our advance at all. The plan was not mine. It was the owner of the Factory himself who suggested it. The distance would have been more than 300 miles there & back, through a very rough & sometimes unfriendly country.

I do not remember any important enterprises undertaken during that winter except the attack on Pine Bluff made by Genl. Marmaduke, another in a small way upon the Federal stockade at the mouth of Arkansas River on the Cut-off Island: both unsuccessful. The latter was under command of Col. Lawther.[8] But all the while there seemed to be work enough for the mounted men of either side to gather in the live-stock (especially pork) still left running at large in the woods & cane bottoms between our lines. The sudden & unexpected presence of regular military forces of one army or the other was quite necessary to keep in check the devilments of squads of men styled "Jay Hawkers," "Bummers," "Graybacks," &c., who, whatever their name or whatever their claims to loyalty for one side or the other, were nothing more or less than Banditti of a very cruel & unscrupulous sort.[9]

One of the wonderments since the War is the facility with which those consummate villains have absorbed—dissolved themselves—subsided (or whatever one may call it) into Society again—especially how readily they have become "trooly lile," ready for any iron-clad oath, & adapted to fill any office under the Government. But more of that when we come to it in course.

As to the Attack on Pine Bluff, [it] was I think ordered by Lt. Genl. Holmes. I was not consulted about it, but I had asserted that in falling back from Little Rock, the army should have fallen back upon Pine Bluff. The elbow of the Arkansas River bending Westward & coming to an angle at that point rendered it possible for us to hold a line from there through Arkadelphia to the Caddo Gap, & from Pine Bluff we could every day threaten their line of supplies by the Rail Road to Devall's Bluff & the White River. I say I was not consulted, & I am glad of it. The Expedition turned out badly. Genl. Marmaduke had men enough to ensure success. His secrecy at setting out & in concentrating his men promised a surprise,

& a surprise it was to the Enemy. Everything went right! All pickets & outlying squads were already captured, & had the Genl. moved right on, entering the town at mid-might, the entire garrison would doubtless have been bagged without a fight. Indeed, as it seemed good fortune would have it, an escaped prisoner (escaped in woman's clothes) just then met them & assured the Genl. that he could lead him in the night to the quarters of every commissioned officer; but the Genl. replied that they would have the town anyway in the morning, & the men & horses must have rest. So they camped there that night, & the next morning, while bells were ringing for church (the day was Sunday), Genl. Marmaduke was before Pine Bluff in force; but it was too late. The Federal Commandant of that Post was no less a person than Col. Clayton, since General Clayton, Governor of Arkansas, & later on United States Senator from Arkansas.[10] All this he has made out of his successful defense of Pine Bluff. So, in that light alone, this fiasco of Marmaduke's has been a costly affair to our state. The fact is that your old-time West Pointer is hard to persuade out of his routine. A night attack, especially, is disagreeable to a lion of order & method. He summoned the town to surrender, when he could have gone in without permission. Genl. Clayton demanded time to consider & used that time, while the ardor of Marmaduke's men was cooling off, to barricade the public square with cotton bales, & converting the brick court house itself into a citadel. Time up, of course he declined to surrender, & made good his position at the end of a stubborn fight. We may suppose that probably Marmaduke had orders from Genl. Holmes to manage about as he did in order to avoid damage to the town, which was inhabited by the wives & friends of many men who were in our ranks.

Col. Lawther's attempt on the Stockade at the Cut-off I knew nothing about until it was over. Lawther was a fine officer who gave all his time & attention to his duties as a soldier. He probably made this expedition on his own hook. Expecting to effect a surprise, but finding the enemy quite ready, he had the good sense to come away & let them alone; for that position, in reach of gun-boats if captured, was untenable by us, & of no strategic value whatever.

During this time the Feds from Little Rock made one Cavalry raid as far as Arkadelphia. Their Commander was a Col. Caldwell. He found no garrison to defend. Came at dead of night. It does not appear that he allowed his men to plunder. Appeared to keep them well in hand, but there were men enough at hand in Federal overcoats who sacked the town pretty thoroughly. He scarcely could have been ignorant of that.[11] One notable thing done by his soldiers illustrates the spirit of the war. The contents of the Drug Store were methodically taken out into the street & destroyed!

CHAPTER VII

*O*n the whole, the winter of 1863–64 was rather a quiet time, for war times, in Arkansas. The fun & amusement we had was enjoyed with greater relish because of the dangers impending.

Lt. Genl. Holmes had now command of only the Department of Arkansas — *i.e.*, what was left of it to us. As far back as the winter of '63, full Genl. Kirby Smith had been ordered from Richmond, Va., to relieve Genl. Holmes of the command over the entire Trans-Miss. Department.[1] No degradation or disgrace to Genl. Holmes, for he had desired it & so petitioned. Genl. Smith established his Head Quarters at Shreveport in Louisiana, where he could be more central to his entire command. From that time forward, movements in Arkansas became of secondary importance. We, of course, would have preferred to have the head of the Army here, at what was to us the front; but by this time there were other fronts to be guarded. The naval power of the U.S. Government in the Gulf of Mexico facilitated the unexpected landing & supply of troops anywhere. Accordingly, we find a Federal Garrison at & near the mouth of the Rio Grande. Another very considerable force at & below Galveston, & an attempt at the Sabine Pass. At the same time, the aggressive operations of the Federal forces, both land & naval, radiating from New Orleans were of themselves a study & a campaign, especially during the winter while the weather was tolerable to Northern folk & the water courses navigable.

It had become the Camp talk in Arkansas that we were neglected by Genl. Smith, but that was unjust to him. We had no news-papers to inculcate general information, & it was only at long intervals through men at home on furlough, or by letters passing between friends quartered far apart, whose own means of information were little better than Camp talk at last, that we had any way of knowing what was going on even in our own Department. Now & then the Scouts brought in files of Northern newspapers, which never encouraged us much; indeed, we could but infer from the imperfect & partial accounts they gave of events within our own knowledge that the news was, outside of Official Documents, wholly unworthy of credence. Indeed, their Official reports of their own Exploits often excited the derision of our soldiers who knew better.

Very soon after his first arrival in the winter or spring of 1863, Genl. Kirby Smith's staff visited all our front, as high up as Little Rock, reviewed the troops, & examined the situation. That time he came in the Steam Boat "B.L. Hodge" around down Red River & up the Ouachita River to Camden, himself & staff with their horses on board. From Camden they proceeded on horse back. It was then I first saw him. He was in the prime of life, cheerful & laughing, his hair dark curling & in profusion all over his head. Alas, in one year more he was bald & gray as a rat. Verily! the Trans-Mississippi Department, under conflicting orders from Richmond, Va., was a hard place for a Commander in Chief. No changes that I ever heard resulted from this first visitation of Genl. Smith. From a word he let fall, I concluded he did not think the line of Arkansas River very defensible under the circumstances; & I have no idea he was disappointed when he afterwards heard of the evacuation of Little Rock. Indeed, by this time the worn-out condition of wagons & teams made a perpetual puzzle how to keep up supplies at the front &, at the same time, to maintain that overland commerce with Mexico which was every day becoming more of a necessity, as the Federal navy in the Gulf became more active against the Blockade runners.

The next visit we had from Genl. Smith was at & about Christmas time, 1863. I know he took Christmas dinner at my house, Mrs. Merrell & he having been born & raised neighborly in & about St. Mary's & St. Augustine in Florida.[2] The families were acquainted. At that time the Genl. exhibited great vigor & activity in his ambulance drawn at speed with four fine mules attached, his dinner of hard corn bread & baked sweet potatoes on the seat before him, he flew from place to place, a surprise to us all his coming & his going.[3] He examined the country as high up as Arkadelphia at least, &, without an escort, he must have incurred no small risk of falling into bad hands.

I forget the relative dates. But if this flying visit on the part of Genl. Smith was before Marmaduke's attempt on Pine Bluff, I should conclude that he himself gave the order, & that by it he meant a general advance of our lines.[4]

What confirms me in this is the fact that we could hear of Genl. Magruder as far north as Monticello. Whenever Genl. Magruder was heard of, it meant business, & my own impression now, as I write & think more about it, is that the Genl. intended seriously to give the Enemy all they could do to hold their rear lines of communication without advancing on us.[5] Indeed, the Genl. said in my presence, & in reply to a remark of my own, that as good a thing as he wanted was to keep a very large force of the Enemy employed watching him, thus diverting them from the continual pressure in Virginia & in Tennessee. Under this view of the case, Marmaduke's failure at Pine Bluff may be regarded as a disaster in Arkansas. As it turned out, vigorous measures were now become necessary in order to be ready for what the Enemy might see fit to do in the Spring.

No more advancing on our part could be thought of. The ranks must positively be filled up by the return of men from their furloughs (or without furloughs) at home. A publication of amnesty for past offenses was generally satisfactory to them. The convalescents from hospitals might be expected generally for duty in February, for our first spring weather comes in February, & a few pleasant days will bring out smiling many men from the hospitals. So severe had been the Exposure of the winter that of one Cavalry regiment alone (Col. Parsons' 12th Texas, in which I was always treated like a comrade) there were at one time 700 men on the sick list.

Here let me break the monotony of this narrative by an anecdote in point. One day I heard that my old guardians, the 12th Texas, had arrived. I at once rode out of town to see them again, & have some of the officers at my house & introduce them to society. I found them encamped in the river bottom near the Lone Pine Ferry. One of those long, cold, soaking rains was falling. The roads & camping ground were muddy & disagreeable in the highest degree. They had but one tent, scarcely enough to shelter a dozen men. The men were squatting or standing over fires that gave out little but smoke, & their poor horses, head down, draggled in mud & wet & cold with eyes shut, seemed to be dreaming of the warm sun & green waving prairies of their native Texas! I thought the men looked discouraged & as much disposed to go home as their mustangs themselves. No sports were going on, not even card-playing. Approaching the Colonel's fire, I found the state of things little better. All thinking of home, I doubt not; the tears in their eyes were however occasioned, not by thoughts of home & wife & child, but by the smoke of a fire that would not burn.

It was then that Col. Parsons told me he had 700 men sick. I did not think he had 250 men with him. My visit cheered the officers, & they soon had better quarters, but to my anecdote.

Said I, "Colonel, this scene reminds me of a picture I have seen on Bank Notes of South Carolina. Marion in the swamp inviting the British officers to dine with him on roast Sweet Potatoes." "By —— boys," said the Col. "Do you hear that? Major Merrell says we remind him of Marion dining on sweet potatoes! As sure as a gun is iron, if we could get sweet potatoes to eat we would think we were in hog heaven!" & Sure enough, the poor fellows were tired enough of blue-beef & hard corn bread & nothing else. Such rations were [the] next thing to starvation, & I have often thought that the hard fare in prison, so much complained of by prisoners of war, was probably the same rations our own soldiers had to be content with in the field. However, of prison matters I know little from personal observation. What I do know, I may perhaps put in a separate Chapter to itself.

It soon came to be understood in our Army that an active campaign was close at hand. The rumor was current among the disaffected that a large Federal army would take possession of this whole country "as soon as grass springs." From this one idea of Campaigning on grass, we could draw a pretty good idea of what was in the mind of the Federal Commander. Multitudes of Cavalry & wagons & teams. Plenty of leisure to come along slowly & hobble out his cattle to feed with impunity! We thought he would be likely to know more about that when he got through! We stood greatly in need of some wagons & teams ourselves. Even if we should, under pressure of superior force, be compelled to fall back, it was more than likely we would manage to replenish our stock at their expense.

Soldiers improve in character, & in our Army they daily swelled in numbers, at the near approach of active operations. No more languor, no more discontent. Drill no longer seemed fatiguing. Discipline hardened down. Horses improved in appearance & were better groomed, & ere the Enemy developed his plans, we had again a well-conditioned but motley army in Arkansas of, say, 8,000 mounted men, about 4,000, perhaps 5,000, Infantry. Of Artillery there was not much, & among the rank & file what was had was not highly valued. It was thought to be too much trouble to haul about, make & repair roads & bridges, & wait for Artillery to come up in this rough country, where the oprty. to use it to advantage was so rare. But after all, it turned out that there were several things an army cannot do without artillery.

The mounted men, with the exception of Parsons' 12th Texas, were not Cavalry in any sense, except that they moved on horse-back. Some had pistols, & some even holsters; but their regulation arm was the Enfield rifle & bayonet, the same as infantry. In action the mounted men were expected to dismount, leaving one man to hold four horses; the remainder went into line of battle. In this two-fold capacity they became, sometimes, very formidable troops but, after all, not so entirely reliable as good Infantry.

One thing in particular was noteworthy: that by this time our entire army was well-supplied with the very best of arms & ammunition; but of ammunition we had not always by any means enough. It soon appeared that by some oversight (probably by the unlucky Captain of some Blockade runner) we had at the greatest emergency but ten rounds of percussion Caps in the department.

CHAPTER VIII

In April the Enemies' lines were hermetically sealed against us. A flag of truce sent by Genl. Holmes, probably to see what was going on, was not permitted to approach near to Little Rock. Evidently, they were in a high state of preparation for some mischief.

At last they came out in martial array, to be sure. Our scouts reported a thousand wagons & no end of men & artillery. Indeed, there was some exaggeration. Our army was soon in the field. It appeared that the Genl. had no idea of waiting to be attacked. Every regiment that moved at all moved towards the Enemy, whom they began to feel at about fifty miles from Camden on the Little Rock road to Washington. The first collision was at or near Spoonville, this side of Arkadelphia. The first to fall upon the Enemy was Genl. Jo Shelby with his Missourians. At that time I think he was only Col. Shelby.[1] It seems he annoyed the Enemy's rear very much, & an entire regiment of Federal Infantry lay down to receive him, behind their knapsacks, which they arranged in a long line to shelter their heads. Col. Jo routed them out of that & captured the knapsacks & blankets with twenty-two prisoners. I saw the prisoners myself. The knapsacks & blankets came in good time for Shelby's men. Those I saw in charge of the prisoners complained that they might do much more, but they were already short of ammunition.

This was the opening act of the great Campaign of May 1864 in Arkansas & Louisiana. I will be more circumstantial in telling it than I otherwise might, because I think the merits of this campaign are not generally understood. Since the War I have had the pleasure of telling what I knew about it to Genl. Breckenridge, who was Confederate Secretary of War towards the close; & he said it was a new view of the matter to him, for at Richmond they could never get the right of Trans-Mississippi affairs.[2]

I said that Shelby's affair near Spoonville was the first act of this campaign. I may be in error there. There was an official report from a Scout named Jacobs, who came into camp with about sixty mules captured from the Feds. It seems he had fallen upon a train when out of sight & hearing of its escort & that he was so energetic about it that he cut loose the mules from their wagons, stampeding them away. His narrative & that of his men, of the flight & hot pursuit made quite an impression at the time. My memory does not serve me as to the exact time of that exploit. Nevertheless, the name of Capt. Jacobs deserves to be preserved. He was from Missouri. His services as a scout were highly appreciated at the time.

Some of the citizens remembered him kindly. But his successful eluding or resistance [to] that hot pursuit of sixty miles, encumbered with a drove of contrary mules, struck my fancy at the time.

Let me gather up some facts before I proceed with the campaign. At least one is worthy of record; indeed, it ought never to be forgotten by the people of Arkansas, and some day he should have a monument at Little Rock. Young Dodd. Before the war a student of St. John's College at the Rock, he either remained after the Federal occupation, or he went, or he was sent — I know not which.

At a conjuncture when correct information was very important, he was captured trying to escape, & upon his person were found plans & memoranda going to show that he had been furnished with correct information by intelligent parties within the Federal lines. He was, of course, condemned to be hung as a spy, but in consideration of his extreme youth, his pardon was promised provided he would tell who furnished that information or knew beforehand of his design. This was pressed upon him, & no doubt several, both men & women, in Little Rock trembled for their lives, expecting no less than that the love of life in one so young would overcome his fidelity. But no! the young man died & made no developments. He was hanged in front of the College where he had passed his happy student days.[3]

Dodd was a native of Saline Co., Ark., & his father's house was standing, the last time I passed, near the town of Benton. The fact that, after a lapse of ten years nearly, no public or private testimonial to his memory exists, & no one is yet found so hardy as to attempt it, shows what? Shows that our people do not understand that this was a Hero? No. They understand that; but it shows that they understand it would be displeasing to the Conqueror, & so they do it not. This is too abject. It is not honorable, even in the eyes of our Enemies. I do not believe such a monument would be insulted by any Northern man.

To return to my narrative. We left it where our troops from all quarters were passed on as fast as they arrived, onto the front to feel of the enemy wherever they could find him. No one here had any idea of the plan of the campaign. Maj. Gen. Price was in command. Lt. Genl. Holmes had, at his own request, been ordered to Richmond Va.

His farewell address to Fagan's Brigade, his favorite troops, was made from the iron balcony in front of the Court House in Camden. To me it was affecting. The old gentleman, much emaciated, trembled like a paralytic, which perhaps he was to some extent.

The good will extended to him at his departure could but have been to him satisfactory. He was a good & a brave man, worn out with cares more than he could endure.[4]

I said I have no idea there was as yet any plan of Campaign. The night before our troops broke camp at Camden, I was present at a free conversation upon that subject, which took place in a room of my house. I was up a good part of the night preparing pocket maps for the officers. The ground I took was this. That we had reliable information concerning the transportation of Genl. Steele. We knew the country he traversed to be exhausted. That army could not subsist, both men & teams, at the rate they were coming on, longer than to reach the Little Missouri River. If their wagons contained more rations for men & less for horses, then so much the worse for the horses. The spring season was unusually late & cold that year, & they would be disappointed about grass. They could stop & feed their horses on the Cane in [the Little] Missouri bottoms, but eventually their objective point would be the Prairie D'Ane.[5] There they would expect to find grass. Genl. Fagan replied, "I thought of that & sent an officer out to see if there is any grass on the Prairie, & he reports that there is none to speak of."

"That is so, no doubt," I replied, "but the enemy do not know that. They have set out on this campaign upon information furnished by disaffected citizens who could not know before-hand that this spring season would be so backward. Genl. Steele will go for the Prairie, you may be sure, & if you fight him, you should do so at his crossing of Little Missouri, or in the river bottom & among the points of ridges before he gets into the open Prairie where he can display his entire force." It turned out my reasoning was correct. Genl. Fagan & Genl. Marmaduke did find the enemy in force, & fight them as best they could at & near the crossings of Little Missouri.

The morning after this consultation, Genl. Marmaduke halted at my gate & asked for the map I had prepared for him. His command were marching past at the time. I noticed then a look of daring & command in his hard face that I had never seen before. He had hitherto seemed dejected, & I had concluded he was unhappy & remorseful at the fatal result of his duel with Genl. Polk [Walker].[6] But this morning all that had vanished from his face & manner, & he was all over the resolute commander, inspiriting his men by every look & every movement of his wiry frame.

I may as well here add that it was understood in the Army that Genl. Marmaduke was cornered into that unhappy duel with Genl. Polk, & Polk [Walker] with him, by subordinate officers who persisted in making a situation from which neither could decently back out, at least not as opinions then went in the army. That duel took place about the time of the evacuation of Little Rock.

And now I have made such a mess of this Chapter that I must throw it away & try again. As Mr. Alex' Stephens said in an anecdote I once heard him tell to illustrate some change in his political views: "In one of the back counties of Georgia, at an early day, a boy & his father undertook to butcher an ox, but for want of practice did it badly. Finished & hung up, the lad walked back, & with arms akimbo viewed the work artistically. Said he, 'Dad!' 'What is it, Sonny?' 'Well,' says the boy. 'We've sure enough made a mummuck of this one; let's kill another & try again.'" So I will try a new chapter.

CHAPTER IX

*W*e left Genl. Steele's finely-appointed army marching southward from Little Rock, harassed more or less by our light troops on his flanks & rear.[1] At or near Spoonville the Federal army was heavily reinforced by its junction with Genl. Blunt's army from Ft. Smith & Van Buren.[2] It had come through the mountains by the way of Caddo Gap.

At the very head of that army, in advance some distance ahead of the advanced guard, rode one of the extraordinary [men] of the war. He was a long, lank, sallow, hook-nosed, tow-headed man, whose name I have forgotten if I ever knew it, but he was a very noted scout, & cruel as a wild beast. We could hear of him, always alone, coming & going unexpectedly, a terror to lone women, especially if they wore little articles of jewelry. He finally met his fate in the front yard of Mr. Samuel's (or Solomon's) house near Poison Springs & was buried in that yard with nine or ten bullet holes in him. And there he lies yet, unless his remains have been reverently exhumed at the public expense & transferred to a National Cemetery. The immediate occasion of his death was this. On the morning of the Poison Springs battle, he presented himself alone, as usual, at Mr. Solomon's & demanded a cooked breakfast, which having eaten, he eased himself according to nature in the middle of the floor, & used the clean coverlet of the best bed as paper is used on such occasions.[3] But, unlucky for him, as he stepped from the front door into the yard, a squad [of] Choctaw Indians halted at the gate, & so he happened onto the bad accident as before stated. Alas! I am digressing again!

Reinforced by Blunt's army, Genl. Steele advanced, still keeping [to] the Old Military road. Reaching Antoine, he detached a command to follow the Wolf-Creek road westward, after supplies doubtless, for they had friends in Pike County anxiously awaiting their arrival; but their advance was disputed by Genl. Cabell's command on Wolf Creek to such an extent at least that they gave up the expedition, leaving their wounded on the ground.

It is noteworthy that this Command of Cabell's was the same that broke ranks without engaging the enemy at the "Back Bone" affair. The sequel shows that our whole army was thus inspirited by offensive operations against a superior force, as much as it had been dispirited by the retreats of the previous year.

The genius of our troops was always better suited to active & offensive operations.

From Antoine Genl. Steele's army deflected from the Military road Eastward & made tracks straight for Prairie D'Ane. But this was not until after some delay to feed their stock on young cane in the Missouri bottoms. A slow business for a large Army, to be sure! and a situation that must have subjected their outlying men to daily & nightly losses, in situations not very heroic for either side. Here Genl. Steele made a bon-fire of the trunks & carpet-bags of his officers. This was for want of transportation. I do not remember that he began burning his wagons until later on.

At the small prairie near Okolona, I understood there was a combat, but it must have been a slight affair.[4] Our army by this time had mainly retired to the south side of the Little Missouri. The Federals foraged with impunity as far down that river on the North side as twenty miles, at least, below Okolona but were no doubt closely watched & reported.

It was now manifest that Genl. Steele aimed to get possession of Prairie D'Ane, but where would he cross the river & when? He would be sure to cross at some point where he had the bluff on his own side [of] the river, so as to command the river bottom with his superior artillery. It was a time of suspense & watchfulness. If resisted at all in force, it must be at or soon after his crossing the river. In point of fact, as will be hereafter seen, we had not the available force fit to offer the splendid army of Steele anything like a fair battle. The Fabian warfare was the only chance for us.

Genl. Steele threw his army across Little Missouri River at a place anciently known as the "Nacatoch Ford." It seems that in Indian times there was a noted trail to the Spanish settlements on Red River, & this was the crossing. That crossing was so long out of date that I never heard of it before — at least I had not put it in my topographical maps.[5] However, no time was lost by that. Marmaduke was near enough at hand to fall upon the head of their column as soon as it was well out from under shelter of their cannon on the opposite bluff. This fight in the edge of L. Missouri bottom could scarcely be called a battle, but it was a hard-fought combat.

Marmaduke had his men well-placed in the timber on the south side of an open field or deserted plantation. His main body on the right of the road & his artillery on the left. Awaiting the arrival of the head of the Federal column until it was well exposed in the open field, he opened fire with effect. The first Regt. was an Illinois Regiment of Veterans, which of course stood its ground at first, but finally gave way & retreated at double quick before a bayonet charge from Marmaduke. The next Federal Regiment in course was from Iowa, also veterans, which instead of coming into line in front, lay down & out of sight about a hundred yards from Marmaduke's left obliquely. Whether he was conscious of their presence or not, I don't know; but when he made his charge, they fired into his left flank with severe effect. Had the Iowa Regiment, after that well-directed fire, sprung to its feet & charged bayonets, Marmaduke would have lost his Artillery, which was at that moment ill-supported on his left. But it does not seem that the Federal Colonel had sense enough for that. So they all fell back to re-form, & as the advantage of surprise was lost & Marmaduke could not expect to do any more good then, he fell back among the pine ridges. He lost 28 men killed & wounded in that fight, probably only two killed outright. At least that was all the graves I could find a month afterwards.

It was in that Affair that Marmaduke had another duel, but this time with a foe, & not with a brother officer. In the heat of the action, someone called his attention that a Federal officer was firing at him in particular with a six-shooter. I can imagine how Marmaduke hardened into welts & ridges! He calmly took the carbine that he carried attached to his saddle, & with deliberate aim, fired at his antagonist. The cotton was seen to fly out of the cap of the Federal officer, but he did not seem to be otherwise hurt. Except in his feelings. He did not shoot any more at Marmaduke in particular. I afterwards learned that it was Genl. Rice of the U.S. Cavalry. He was subsequently wounded in the foot at the battle of Jenkins' Ferry on the Saline & died of his wound. Said to have been an excellent officer.[6]

Our people had entrenched themselves by timber works, among the points of ridges commanding the Nacadoche trail, near Mrs. Carnahan's house, but it was optional with the Enemy to come that way or head Eastward.[7] Inasmuch as it was not for their interest to come the way we wanted them, they made a flank movement Eastward suddenly & in heavy force,

& so they reached the Prairie D'Ane to find little or no grass, after all, for their Cattle.

There, at the head of the Prairie, they halted & took their own time. Evidently they were waiting for some thing, & so they were. Our people entrenched again diagonally across the Washington road & so awaited their pleasure. The Federal General had evidently some ulterior object in view, superior to fighting & killing man for man of our army & his own. What that strategy might be was a puzzle to the rank & file, but it was perfectly understood at Head Quarters, for by this time the original plan of the Campaign was fairly developed.

While all this was going on in South Arkansas, a much larger Federal Army under General Banks was advancing up the valley of the Red River, its objective point apparently being Shreveport, the Head Quarters of the Commander in Chief.[8] It was accompanied by a fleet of Transports & Gun-boats ascending the river at the same time. I say their "apparent" destination was Shreveport. Their real intention was to give Shreveport the go-by, for it was well-fortified & provisioned, & march directly for Marshall in Texas, thus compelling the evacuation of Shreveport without a siege.[9] That would have been equivalent to the evacuation of all Louisiana on the part of the Confederacy, & the Federal army established at Marshall would have set up and probably maintained a politico-military Government there which would have set free the latent discontent in Texas. It would thus have cut off the source of supply for our Army in Arkansas, compelling in like manner the Evacuation of all Arkansas, thus shutting in (for all the remainder of the War) shutting in the Confederate power to that part of Texas only which lies, say, beyond the Trinity River. It was a magnificent scheme on their part, & they came with military power sufficient to have accomplished it, if the battle was always to be "with the Strong." I have heard Northern people themselves characterize Banks' Red River Expedition as a "Cotton-stealing trip." In so doing they underrate its importance. No doubt he had plenty of Cotton thieves with their wagons in his wagon-train, but the main object of the campaign was practically to close the war in the Trans-Mississippi Department.

Genl. Kirby [Smith] had means of information positive & correct in advance. Moreover, our men captured one Courier passing from Banks to Steele whose dispatches confirmed the above theory of the Campaign. Genl. Steele was ordered to cross Red River at Dooley's Ferry & proceed at once to report with his army to Banks at Marshall, Texas.

It does not appear that Steele's fine army was expected to perform any heroic things in Arkansas. The main thing was to co-operate with Banks in Texas, leaving Arkansas behind him to be evacuated for want of supplies from Texas.[10]

Genl. Kirby Smith's counter-plan of the Campaign was framed upon the above theory. He ordered the Infantry & Artillery from Arkansas all to march & reinforce him at Shreveport. Leaving Genl. Price too weak to offer Genl. Steele a pitched battle, he was not expected to do any more than hinder him a while by Fabian operations from foraging & destroying far off his direct route. Genl. Steele was to have the road left open for him to cross Red River at Dooley's Ferry, not at once or prematurely, but in due time after Genl. Smith & Genl. Banks had fought a pitched battle. For that battle Genl. Kirby [Smith] had the time & the place fixed. His reinforcements were hurrying up from Arkansas & from Texas. He might calculate to meet Genl. Banks' army of 30,000 men with about 22,000 Confederates on ground of his own choosing, which he had already viewed in person.[11] That ground was the line of a creek about two days' march for the Federal army North westward from where the battle of Mansfield took place. Having defeated Genl. Banks, as he expected to do under the circumstances, his further plan was to leave Genl. Dick Taylor with his mounted men to follow up the Enemy's retreat, while he Genl. Smith, with his remaining troops, should march, not into Arkansas to reinforce Genl. Price, but up the West bank of Red River only 80 or 90 miles to the line of the Sulphur Fork of Red River, & there to bar the way against Genl. Steele's advance into Texas.[12] While at the same time Genl. Price should pound away in his favorite style at the rear of Steele's army.

Genl. Steele's situation without supplies, in the wretched country inside the forks of Red River at that season of the year, it is easy to [see] would have involved the surrender of his entire Army. Genl. Smith needed not to fight him any battle at all, but only check the Enemy & await his surrender.

We now understand Steele's protracted halt on Prairie D'Ane. The battles of Mansfield & Pleasant Hill in Louisiana were going on.[13] By some means, Genl. Steele knew quickly enough, or at least suspected, that Banks was not completing his part of the programme, & he was too wary a General to be caught west of Red River without the support of Banks' Army. He laid his plans thenceforward independent of Banks. One Sunday morning he got up a most gorgeous parade. His men were drawn up in one long line clean across the Prairie five miles long, his left in the timber & his right in the timber: — it was very imposing. The sun of Arkansas never before shone on such a spectacle.

Of course, neither army had been quite idle all this time on & around the prairie. The Confederate position was almost or indeed quite within range of the Federal guns. The dense underbrush was most favorable to secret movements & ambuscades. The men in [the] picket line of one army could nightly hear the opposing pickets hawk & spit. On our side, movements were directed not by word of command or by bugle, but by cow-bells, which, as there were cattle feeding, would not certainly betray the presence of human beings. Under these circumstances it was impossible but that collisions must take place—sharp shooting, & personal exploits, & some acts of revenge—without any effect whatever on the general result. Our men asserted that in falling back & again advancing, they found comrades, whom they left wounded, with their throats cut, & that it was done by the Negroes, of whom there were two regiments from Kansas in Steele's army. That savagery produced its legitimate fruits later on.

CHAPTER X

While Genl. Steele is sunning his fine army that Sunday morning on Prairie d'Ane, turn we to contemporary events on the line of Red River in Louisiana.

Genl. Banks on his advance had captured Fort De Russy, which, being a water-battery only, could not well be defended against considerable land forces. Genl. Dick Taylor, son of the late Genl. Taylor, President of the U.S., was in command of the Confederate forces, about 8,000 strong, which fell back slowly before the Federal advance. Taylor had more than enough mounted men & could keep his antagonist from foraging or plundering much off his direct line of march. His orders from Genl. Kirby Smith were to fall back doggedly enough, annoying the Enemy all he could, but by no means to suffer himself drawn into a general engagement until the Commander in Chief could reinforce him & take command in person.

What ulterior views Genl. Taylor had is not for me to say, but it is manifest those instructions galled him, & he finally resolved to disregard them & have a battle of his own. His ground was well-chosen, & so was the exact time. His army behaved gallantly, & he won the victory at Mansfield. But it was an ill-timed victory. It was premature, & it vitiated the whole remainder of the campaign. The whole affair well-illustrates the wide difference there is between popular heroism & the conscientious discharge of a soldier's duty. Next day, at the battle of Pleasant Hill, General Taylor, though partially reinforced, was not so fortunate. At first driving in the center of the Enemy's line & capturing a multitude, his right, instead of engaging the Enemy's left, telescoped itself upon his own center, creating confusion which ended in a tumultuous retreat, which would have ended in a disaster had the Enemy's whole line advanced; but, night approaching & Genl. Kirby Smith & staff appearing on the field, the battle ended; & to the surprise of all, the Federal army of two army corps was gone like a flock of pigeons at full retreat the way they came! It was a shameful affair on their part. Then General Banks, expecting to walk over the track, we were told, was completely disconcerted at the violence of the Confederate attacks & the apparent multitude that came against him. "Not less than 70,000 men!" he was reported to have said. He had only 8,000 against his 30,000 at Mansfield, & not exceeding 12,000 men at Pleasant Hill; but it is true those men were in earnest.[1]

Genl. Kirby Smith suffered himself to lose no time after "Pleasant Hill" in marching to the support of Genl. Price. Indeed, there was no time to lose. He had a Telegraph wire from Camden to Shreveport, by means of which hourly intelligence passed between both armies on our parts. The enemy had no means of communication that we knew of, except the espionage which is comparatively easy in times of Civil War, where both sides speak the same language & both sides also have with them disaffected & mercenary men. Genl. Steele, halting at the head of Prairie d'Ane, learned enough of Banks' disaster in Louisiana to stop his advance in that direction. On our part, Gen. Kirby Smith hastened to the support of Genl. Price. Banks in full retreat, he left Genl. Dick Taylor with his command to watch the Enemy & escort him out of "the country," but not in force strong enough to strike any very heavy blows.

This was the occasion of a serious misunderstanding between Genl. Taylor & Genl. Kirby Smith: all the talking, so far as I could learn, being on the part of Taylor.

It appeared that Genl. Taylor wanted nothing less than that the entire army should follow Banks back, if possible, to New Orleans. It would be surprising, the way military men go, if General Dick had [not] some aspirations to be himself Commander in Chief of the Department. Certainly very hard Camp talk was started by some means against Genl. Smith, who, without ostentation, was trying to do his duty by the whole of his people, & refused to abandon Arkansas for the exclusive advantage of Louisiana. I heard a courier say that he left Genl. Taylor on a "Big bust," which was the army slang for very drunk.

However, Genl. Smith stood to his own plans, & I presume never made any official report of Taylor's contrariness. The Enemy, out of humor, went burning & destroying back down Red River & Taylor after him, getting what satisfaction he could in the way of pursuit. We heard no more of his successes. By the time Banks reached Alexandria on his way backward, Red River had fallen too low to float his gun-boats & transports over the falls. Then & there was Taylor's opportunity; but we heard of no fire boats or rafts. The Enemy were left at leisure to tear down buildings in Alexandria &, with the material, throw a wing-dam into the river, forming a Chute through [which] the whole flotilla escaped.[2] While all this was going on in Louisiana, Genl. Kirby Smith, at the head of his remaining troops, marched into Arkansas to confront Genl. Steele. Had the battle of Mansfield never taken place, Genl. Smith expected to have marched only about ninety miles up the West Bank of Red River through a country as yet abounding in supplies. This would have given him the "Short lines" on Steele. As it turned out, Smith had to counter-march by the "Long line" all the way to Camden, through a country pretty well exhausted by the war. Genl. Churchill afterwards told me that his Division, consisting of Infantry & Artillery, had to march in this Campaign 575 miles.[3]

We left the Federal Genl. Steele on a fine Sunday morning with his army on parade five miles long, all the way across Prairie d'Ane. This ostentatious display meant business. Yet it does not seem that Genl. Price so understood it until too late. It meant nothing less than retreat. At about sundown, Steele began to pound away with all his artillery. For more imposing effect, he let it off by the section in salvos. This continued until nine or ten o'clock at night. All that night all his army decamped & marched, not back the way they came, for that road was exhausted of supplies, but he took an Eastward course. At the crossing of Terre Rouge bottom, one mile wide, he encountered that night a serious obstacle to his retreat. All night, until just before day, his army worked repairing the causeway & the bridges, so that just before morning his entire army & trains complete was in motion on the road to Camden with Price behind him, instead of before him as he would have been could he have anticipated this adroit movement on the part of Steele. Price lost some time in a rear-guard fight at & about the Village of Moscow. The mounted men under Marmaduke hastened by the lower Washington road which heads the principal water courses, & by that means contrived to confront Steele again about at the Poison Springs.

There he made a brief stand with his artillery, but it does not appear that Steele's army halted at all. Marmaduke had barely time, after firing a few rounds, to get away with his guns. The Enemy spread out like a fan & came upon him in force & with great spirit.

Camden had been pretty well fortified. Could Genl. Price have thrown any considerable force with artillery that second night into the works round this town, Genl. Steele's flank movement would have been checked, & another change of direction towards Tate's Ferry would have been his course. In that case, Steele's situation would have been critical, provided Genl Smith arrived in time.[4] It would have been disagreeable in any case. But Genl. Price's command now consisted mainly or entirely of mounted men, the most unsuitable for garrison duty, & I have no idea Genl. Price at all liked being sent in to the defense of Earth works. He greatly preferred to fight in the foxhunting way & in the open country.

As for myself, I was still in Camden with my family. Genl. Holmes' departure left me in no position. My relation to the army had been purely a personal relation to him & his staff. I therefore remained at home, watching events & giving what comfort I could to neighbors, mostly lone women, while listening to the heavy firing as it approached nearer to the town. There was another little stand made by some of Marmaduke's command at the forks of the road near Lee's house, & there ought to have been a decided stand at the "Hurricane" if there was not. Lee's house was burned by the enemy.[5] Although the Telegraph operator had fled with his instruments, & later on a detachment of Lawther's men had come into town for the purpose of securing the pontoon bridge, my own theory still was that the works would be manned in time, & that Steele would arrive too late to carry the works by first assault.

The sound of nearer & nearer approach of our Artillery was calculated to confirm me in my views, & had Steele delayed until morning, that might have been the result. But he made a forced march of it & came in that same evening.

Too rapidly indeed for me to weigh the pros & cons to know what best to do. My wife is too deaf to negotiate or temporize. She had servants that could not be relied upon. To leave her alone with no white person in the house in the midst of an excited Soldiery & under fire of cannon & musketry: I could not bring myself to do it. To remain as a citizen forfeited my life as a spy whenever the Federal Commander chose to take my case in hand. I stayed. I could not leave. I think that, under all the circumstances, I should have stayed if I had known I would be arrested. It turned out that Genl. Steele, while in occupation of Camden, had quite as much as he could attend to, taking care of himself without hunting down Confederates.

Lawther's detail of men had barely time to cut loose the pontoons & float down stream on board of them before our videttes were in the outskirts of town with the head of the Federal army in full view on the hill at Dr. Whitfield's place. Those pontoons with anchors & hawsers complete did good service at or near Newport fourteen miles below, in passing portions of them back & forth, thus maintaining the campaign on both sides of Ouachita River. It was the facility of crossing & recrossing the river that made both the subsequent battles of "Marks' Mill" & Poison Springs possible. The Feds. also maintained a bridge of India Rubber pontoons at Camden while they stayed.

At the summit of Whitfield's hill the head of their column halted, while the rear deployed into line to the right & left of the Washington road. Their left seemed to rest upon the grave-yard road. They were not long about it, & then they advanced in line, but with a heavy column on Washington Avenue. They evidently expected resistance. Their firing heavy, especially in the direction of the grave yard. But there was no force in Camden to resist them. A few men of Lawther's, under an officer whom I knew well by sight but forget his name, sat in their saddles at the corner in front of Judge Elliott's residence, & the officer was so intent with his field-glass that he stayed too late.[6]

Their presence I thought would draw a shell or two from the enemy, & I persuaded a group of ladies all to scatter to their homes. I thought they behaved very well. I particularly remember Mrs. McElrath, Miss Molly Malone & I think also Mrs. Judge Elliott. Mrs. Graham came away with me and to her house. As for me, I had my wife & servants to provide for.[7]

I said Lawther's videttes stayed too long. At the instant they started at full speed up the road to Ageeville, a column of the enemy suddenly deployed & charged up the ravine back of Judge Elliott's house, towards the Southerland fort. Seeing Lawther's men crossing their track, they fired, & one Confed. fell from his saddle wounded. Him the ladies afterwards took special pains to look after in the hospital. In a few minutes it was all over, & before dark Genl. Steele's army were making themselves quite at home in Camden.[8] They went about it as old soldiers will do, turning everything in reach to good account. I thought they spread out too much. Probably they did that to create the impression of imposing force. Upon entering Camden, they had about 14,500 men of all arms.[9] Their Infantry was excellent, & their Artillery too, but their Cavalry I thought poor. Of course they were well-clothed & battle-armed. All Federal troops were, but the Cavalry men appeared to be a hard lot of men & their horses were jaded & emaciated for want of food.[10] As to the clothing of Federal soldiers generally, it was of course more uniform in appearance, but the shoddy material of which it was made soon went to rags. After a few weeks of

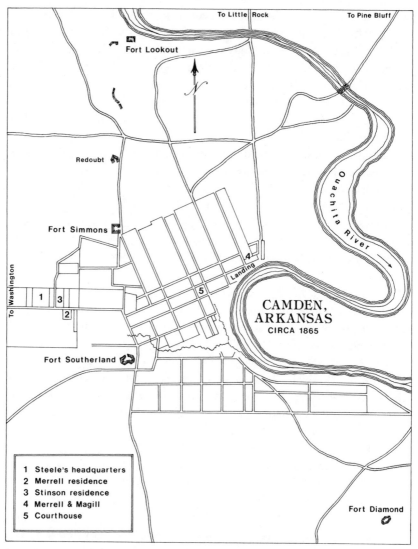

To Little Rock

To Pine Bluff

Fort Lookout

N

Redoubt

Ouachita River

Fort Simmons

To Washington

4

Landing

5

1 3

2

CAMDEN,
ARKANSAS
CIRCA 1865

Fort Southerland

1 Steele's headquarters
2 Merrell residence
3 Stinson residence
4 Merrell & Magill
5 Courthouse

Fort Diamond

Map of Camden, Arkansas, around 1865, showing the location of Merrell's house and business, together with the location of Union headquarters during the town's occupation in 1864. Based on a map drawn by Union Lt. Fred Sommer, National Archives, Record Group 77, Drawer 123, Sheet 5-1.

active operations in this rough country the Confederate Gray, of domestic make, presented a less shabby appearance than the Federal Blue made by contracts. Dust & dirt at the same time more discolored the dark blue. The truth is that neither officers or soldiers of either side looked much like going into ladies' society shortly after several weeks of hard fighting.

CHAPTER XI

*T*he close of the last Chapter left Genl. Steele & his army in peaceable possession of our own fortified town, Camden. So far, his change of direction had been an apparent success. It had certainly been executed with military skill, & the result doubtless read like a great Capture in his Dispatches & Northern newspapers. But the fact was Camden had captured him, & he was in great straits. All the Cotton in town had been burned by Genl. Price's orders in advance of Steele's arrival. So his empty wagons found nothing valuable of a public nature to carry away. As to Forage there was scarcely one night's feed in the town, & he was at the last of his rations. All the family supplies in town would probably not have fed his army a day, if so much as one meal.

I could hear remarks frequently but asked no questions. The troops were on short rations. The thickets around the town, they said, were swarming with rebels, & I soon felt assured that Genl. Kirby Smith was outside at the head of the Army, for things were becoming lively. One expedition at night sent outside the town to secure & bring in a Corn-mill, barely made the trip & reported the danger great. Next, an expedition consisting of about 200 wagons & a Brigade of Infantry, some Cavalry & 4 guns of artillery was sent westward about 15 miles but never got back.

They went out safely enough, & were suffered to forage, but on their return, reaching the place called Poison Springs, they were attacked fiercely & irresistibly by Gano's Brigade, composed in part of Choctaw Indians.[1] The shock of their charge, its suddenness & perhaps its surprise, telescoped the whole Federal force. A regiment of Kansas Negroes was driven back among the tangled mule teams, & the only methodical fighting was done by a Veteran Iowa Regiment of Infantry which covered the retreat by making a fresh stand at the summit of every ridge over four miles of country, fighting all the way.[2] The four pieces of artillery & all the wagons & teams with their plunder fell into Confederate hands. Not many prisoners were taken. The Indians behaved badly about that. The efforts of

Confederate officers to save wounded prisoners from the hatchet & scalping knife were at the risk of their own lives & did not always succeed. As to the Negro regiment I doubt if many survived. White soldiers, no less than Indians, had become exasperated by the Negro outrages on Prairie d'Ane, & I understand that little quarter was given. Indeed I have heard our own people call it the "Poison Spring Massacre."[3] That kind of warfare, however, does not prosper. Our own soldiers afterwards suffered in return at the Saline when the war cry of the Negroes was "Poison Springs." As to the Indians, I had the pleasure to stand by & see Genl. Smith send them back to their own country, & that on the eve of another battle. He had no idea of tarnishing his reputation with their deeds. How they came to be here I never learned. Their Treaty was to defend their own frontiers only.

Just at dark that day I stood lounging at my front gate & saw the fugitives march into town. They came in from the North & must have made a great circuit in their retreat. A more leg-weary & forlorn body of men I never saw. A crowd of soldiers from the Camps followed them up with eager questions. I heard an officer remark, "I apprehend this will encourage the rebels. They must have watched our expedition & counted every man as they went out." All of which I thought more than likely. Next morning I witnessed the parade of Iowa men encamped in Judge Greene's field opposite ours.

As near as I could judge by the vacant spaces, about half were missing. One wounded officer was at Mr. Stinson's house, & one came to my house wounded in the knee.[4] He brought a present of Coffee to my wife & questioned me in a way that put me on my guard, for I could see that he was sent. That man kept me under his watchful care until the very instant of evacuation. I am quite sure I made no *faux pas* in my conversations with him, & I am equally sure he gave me a deal of valuable information.

The biggest fool in the world is a spy, who thinks he is tolling you on, when all the time you are pumping him.[5] However, my friend Capt. B. was a very clever fellow & good company for such times, & I hope he recovered the use of his leg, which is not likely since he was hit in the knee.

From this time on it was easy to see that the Federal army, both officers & men, were sadder & wiser men. They drew in their lines, & their personal deportment when conversing with any of us was actually humble. At least it was a great improvement upon the rollicking way they had when they first came. I suppose the fact was they were hungry & disgusted at coming so far & staying so long without any victories. I thought I could see that the possibility of defeat was beginning to dawn on their minds. As for Genl. Steele, he had something instant to do if he was to hold this fortified place as a military fort, & so parade some results of his campaign by extending the Federal occupation to the line of Ouachita River. Ere long he might expect a flotilla of Gunboats & transports with abundant supplies, but in the meantime they were starving, & he must forage or evacuate.

He accordingly fitted out a more promising Expedition, consisting of one Veteran Brigade of Infantry, ten pieces of Artillery, & 500 or 600 wagons. These were to hasten to Pine Bluff, 75 miles Eastward, & return with provisions. I understood they were to meet halfway & exchange trains for one already coming. [It was] at this conjuncture that the pontoons saved by Lawther's men came into play. Genl. Smith threw Fagan's & Marmaduke's commands of mounted men across the Ouachita, in hot pursuit. They overtook the Federal train & escort near "Marks' Mill," about 30 miles Eastward from Camden.[6]

The battle which ensued was extremely well-contested by the Federals. It so happened that no Brigadier, nor any full Colonel, was in Command. The Federal Commander was a Lieut. Colonel named Dodge or Drake. He was a fat man & was captured with the rest; had a bullet in one or both thighs.[7] He proved to be a very game man & did not at all lose his head. In point of fact, he was overpowered. Our people, for once, had more men than was needful on the ground.

For several hours the Federal line remained firm against the best efforts of Cabell's Brigade. The Federal firing was especially fine. Cabell could stand it no great while longer, when a heavy force, by a preconcerted flank movement, came just in time upon the Federal rear. Finding himself between two fires, the Federal Commander faced his line of battle to the right, moved out in a column of twos, leaving both Confederate lines firing into each other. It was in the timber, & some minutes elapsed before the mistake was found out. In the meantime, the Feds., with admirable discipline, were hastily forming a new line to enfilade; but Jo Shelby was too quick for them. They were captured rallying by twenties, & before they could quite establish a new line. I never heard that any of that Command got away. The fruits of the Victory were all that wagon-train, ten pieces of Artillery, & 1320 Prisoners of War, besides a multitude of Negro servants who had followed their camp, & no little plunder of household stuff which they, or the Negro servants, had carried off.[8]

Those prisoners had to spend one night in the Ware House belonging to us, which had been seized long before by the Confederate authorities & used, first for storing salt & sugar which had been run by steam boats from Louisiana soon after the fall of New Orleans, & afterwards as a Military prison.[9] There were many unhappy men confined in that Ware House first & last, but not many so crest-fallen as the long line of prisoners captured at the Marks' Mill battle. As they marched back prisoners through the streets they had so recently walked as conquerors, they looked to me as though they would fight again with pleasure. Indeed, some were loud in threats of what they would do yet! They remained in Camden one night only & next day were forwarded to the prison-camp at or near Tyler in Texas.

The news of this disaster was brought to Genl. Steele by a wagoner of his trains who had cut loose from his team a mule, & so escaped capture. Directly preparations for evacuation commenced. The town was closely watched by chain pickets. My friend the wounded Captain, I could feel, was keeping his eye on me. It would have been impossible, I think, for any citizen to have got out alive to carry information to Genl. Smith. Blankets & surplus clothing were carefully burned. Camp kettles & other utensils were destroyed, also wagons, & the harness was thrown into Ouachita River, from whence our people afterwards fished it out for immediate use. It was plain to be seen that Genl. Steele was thoroughly in earnest about getting away, yet the quiet & discipline of his entire army was admirable, I thought. Indeed I think the rank & file were as anxious as he could have been to get away without any more fighting.

Even before this, the gravity of the situation had been materially heightened by an event which I ought to have narrated in its place. One afternoon at about three or four o'clock, most unexpectedly the noise of artillery in full play apparently close to the south side of the town, startled us all, citizens as well as soldiers. Matters became lively in an instant. Amidst the roar of cannon & the sound of bursting [shells], officers went dashing about with orders, & very soon indeed the entire Federal army was in position for a battle.[10]

I thought Genl. Steele's arrangements very sound considering the short time he had to consider. His first line of Battle extended so far as I could see from the Southerland fort, through Leak's lane & Green's lot to the fort at Simmons' house. As to his second line, all I could see of it was the muzzles of his artillery just looking over the summit of the hill at Mrs. Darnell's house. In advance, along the ridge extending from Southerland fort to Ageeville, a regiment of a thousand more or less of Negro men were marching in the direction of the firing, & I observed that they marched & counter-marched as though the faint courage of the Negroes made it necessary they should be kept in motion. Suddenly the firing ceased, & the sun went down, & night came on very cold indeed, cold for any season of the year in this climate, too cold by half for an army to be lying out under arms, without fires & awaiting an attack. But no attack came.

I afterwards learned from Genl. Boggs, Chf. of Staff to Genl. Smith, that the occasion of that firing was this. The pickets reported all too quiet in Camden. They feared Genl. Steele was evacuating or had nearly done so, Genl. Kirby Smith thought nothing more likely. He advanced his forces to be in readiness for pursuit, & still in advance of the army he sent his Artillery or at least a part of it to open fire towards the town, & then as suddenly to cease fire & listen. They did so as I have stated, but directly hearing the long roll all over the Federal Camps, the Genl. was satisfied that his advance was premature, & so he ordered his men back to Camps, for he had no idea of fighting Genl. Steele in our own entrenchments & so exposing the town to entire destruction. The effect of all this upon the Feds was very salutary. They drew in their lines again & kept very close. Much to the relief of towns-people, mostly women-kind who were at their homes unprotected. This occurred before Genl. Steele sent away that ill-fated expedition which ended at Marks' Mill.[11]

Genl. Steele's uncomfortable stay in Camden was from the 11th April to the 22nd of same month—say eleven days in all.[12] His first Head-Quarters were at Mrs. Graham's house in the suburbs. That too much exposed, he removed to the house of Jas. Brooks Esq. opposite the Methodist Church. Genl. Salomon first encamped in Dr. Magill's front yard. Next he retired to Judge Elliott's front yard & home, & later on I lost sight of him.[13] The whereabouts of the other Brigadiers I never knew. Their Ammunition was stored in Jim Brooks' fire-proof store. Their hospital in the Court House. Their Commissary, what there was of it, in our store & ware-houses. Jim Brooks was all this time under arrest in the Confederate Camp. What for, I never knew, but supposed he probably cursed a little about the Cotton Burning.

CHAPTER XII

*T*he close of the last Chapter left Genl. Steele & what was left of his Army & equipment in full retreat, back towards Little Rock. Any thing but a victorious army, although he had until within a few days managed to make it seem so.

To sum up the results of the joint Campaign of Banks & Steele, with their splendid out-fit, down to the departure of Steele from Camden, the advantages accruing to the Confederate army were greater than could have been expected. More prisoners taken than we were able to feed as we would like. A very large amount of ammunition, much needed at the time. Nearly two thousand wagons & teams, which just then were of prime necessity in the Department. How many cannon captured in Louisiana I never heard, but I saw myself one fine Battery called Nims' Battery that had been captured at Mansfield, & in Arkansas Steele lost at Poison Springs four pieces & at Marks' Mill ten pieces; after that he lost no guns but captured two from us at the Jenkins' Ferry fight on the Saline.[1] And the essential fact [was] that two invading armies, together outnumbering our force two to one, had been sent back the way they came, & so roughly handled that they never afterwards repeated the attempt. Yet I never saw a Confederate officer that I remember, from Genl. Kirby Smith down, who seemed to feel elated. There seemed to be a general feeling of humility at so much & such unexpected success.

The Federal army completed the evacuation of Camden at about one o'clock in the night, carrying away their rubber pontoons, which afterwards saved them at the crossing of the Saline River. The night of their departure was one of great watchfulness & anxiety in Camden. Especially among the ladies was [it] understood that, in general, the worst of a Federal army would remain & do deeds after the main body had gone on that the General would never hear of. Burning the town, as some expected, would not have accorded with the secrecy of the evacuation. Genl. Steele, who was no doubt a humane man as soldiers go, neither permitted the burning of the town or plundering in his rear. At any rate, it was not done to any noteworthy extent. The fact is the Confederates were too close behind them to favor bummers or stragglers.

Several pretty bad robberies were committed during the occupation, some almost laughable to relate; & the disabled officers took a fancy to ride away in the ladies' fine carriages, causing great resentment.

I think the ladies never will get over their resentment at the accidents of the war.

Most especially did the Feds labor to entice Negro men to join their Negro regiments. My body servant "Munroe," who had been very faithful to me close up to the enemy before, now told me that he could not stand the pressure any longer—he must go. He told me they said they would hang him if he did not stand up in a line with some others & take an oath to be a soldier.[2]

The women servants, who the Federal officers said were an encumbrance & must not go, were crazy to go & wanted to stay, & the evening of evacuation was a scene of wild cries & confusion. A Negro woman, formerly a servant of ours, whose mother & child still remained with us as house-servants, gave us a deal of trouble about it. Neither the grandmother or the child could have survived the fatigue & terrors of a retreat. The Feds had not transportation enough left to carry away their own sick & wounded. Yet that woman persevered. She made interest in a Negro regiment & brought a squad of Negro soldiers armed to take our servants any way. The scene was harrowing. The servants did not want to go & filled the air with outcries.

I interposed a long-winded argument to the colored patriots & they listened respectfully enough, until suddenly the drums beat for "Roll Call," & my audience vanished in obedience to discipline. That was the last of them, & the house servants stayed at home.

I said that the Federal rear crossed the river at about one o'clock in the night. The Confederate advance was in the town by or before sun-rise the next day. One of our citizens carried them information as soon as it was possible to leave the town. I am sure I felt that fine morning as though a weight was lifted off my spirits & my conscience too. As to the town, it literally stank with the bad smells of the departed Feds. A prolonged stay would certainly have bred fatal sickness among both soldiers & citizens. Soldiering reads finely, when well told, in Poetry & in History; but, in point of fact, an army shut up in a beleaguered town, or the same staying long in one camp is—nasty!

Upon Genl. Smith's arrival, he made his Head Quarters in the Law Office at the Corner of Dr. Ward's office, now Geo. Wright's. A foot-bridge & a ferry boat were immediately thrown across the Ouachita at Neill's Ferry, & from that moment began a hot pursuit. Genl. Kirby Smith sent Genl. Gano up the West bank of the Ouachita to Tate's Bluff, expecting to cross them there by means of some pontoons we had left there, but nothing was found remaining of these except the coals & ashes where they had been burned.[3] That column failed to get across ahead or on the flanks of Genl. Steele, as was expected. Another expectation was that Genl. Fagan, victorious at Marks' Mill, would get wind of Steele's retreat & proceed at once to annoy & retard his movements; but Fagan, with his mounted men, had already crossed Steele's route ahead of him & does not appear to have known it until afterwards.[4] From Fagan's habitual longing to "march into Little Rock" in the absence of the garrison, I judge that was what he was bent upon. Anyway, at the time of the Jenkins' Ferry battle, he & his fine command were thirty miles away.

I doubt myself, from what I saw of the discipline & temper of Steele's remaining troops, whether any force Fagan had could have halted the head of Steele's column an hour. It was one of those orderly & determined retreats that 'twere better let well enough alone.[5] The Enemy were leaving the Country as fast as ever they could, & that was all we wanted of them. But the Army failed to see it in that light. Any order to desist from the pursuit would have been misunderstood to the injury of discipline. So Genl. Kirby Smith pressed on to the front. His army, small as it was—still much inferior in numbers to the Enemy, was scattered all along the road forty miles long. The slow method of crossing the Ouachita & the jaded, ill-shod condition of the men made it so. Nevertheless, on they pressed in hot pursuit, until the head of the Column overtook the rear of the Federal army at Jenkins' Ferry, the crossing of the Saline River, & immediately went into action.

All that Genl. Steele had to do was to make a rear-guard fight, while his remaining trains & the main body of his troops passed the river by his Rubber Pontoons. Nothing could have been more timely for him, & if he had searched the whole world, he could not have found a better position for his purpose. Because of heavy rains in the Mountains, the Saline River was rising fast. If the rise had been a few hours later, our army would have forded as well as his. A few hours later, & his army could not have passed at all, for the Saline well up is near two miles wide, including the bottoms. The river was just at that stage that Steele's army covering the bridge formed on the ridge of dry land next the river, while the approach to him across the intervening bottom was under water in that uncertain fashion that one minute our soldiers would be wading to their knees, & the next to their armpits. On those conditions the battle had to be fought, if fought at all.

Marmaduke began the fight.[6] The troops, as they hurried up & formed, were sent in & came out again defeated. The drizzling rain fell, & the smoke of the battle settled down upon the field so that little could be seen. Our men said afterwards they had this poor advantage: that although obliged to load & fire with their arms elevated in the air, they could see underneath the smoke then as high as the knees of their Enemy, while they could not see our men at all, except by the blaze of our guns. Fighting in this manner, the lines approached at one time within about forty yards. There were the Missourians under Genl. Clark.[7] As he was about to make a bayonet charge, his attention was called to the fact that they were under an enfilading fire very hot; so he & his men got out of that place as fast as they could. Genl. Kirby Smith, arriving, could make nothing of the situation, only that the Federal firing was, as he said, the heaviest roll of musketry he had ever heard in all his experience. He could only send in pieces of Brigades as they arrived, to be beaten back like the last. One Lieut. of Artillery made a dash with a section of guns to get into position on a dry knoll within range, but his horses were shot down directly, & a struggle for the possession of the guns followed, which ended in the Enemy sending out Negroes who crawled & waded, as best they could under fire; &, attaching a prolonge to each gun, & they were in time hauled into the Enemy's lines.[8] So we lost two cannon, which, we afterwards saw by a Little Rock paper, were paraded in that City as trophies, saying nothing of the 14 Guns they had themselves lost.

Genl. Kirby Smith next tried a flank movement against the Enemy's left. This was commanded by Genl. Walker, in considerable force; but the Federal position was impregnable.[9] A bayou intervened, & the Enemy had no lack of men to hold it. Cannot say that Genl. Walker was beaten off, but that the Enemy held his own until he had completed his crossing of the river & destroyed his pontoons by cutting large holes in the Rubber Boats. Genl. Smith regretted this battle, but it was one of the things he could not prevent. Fortunately, it was not very bloody. Our loss was but a little over a Hundred men killed, but a great many were wounded, especially about the head & arms. The Enemy left on the field 113 Dead.[10] As we afterwards learned that their Genl. Rice had died of a wound in the foot, we inferred that our fire had perhaps done as much damage among their legs as theirs did among that part of our men which was exposed above the water. This disagreeable & muddy fight closed the Campaign. There were many recriminations as to what *might* have been done, but opinion in the Camps settled down into a feeling of content at the general results. The army, by the help of arms & transportation captured from the Enemy, soon presented a better front than at any time before during the war.

Genl. Kirby Smith, in his checked flannel shirt, and as much soiled from head to foot as though he had been driving a wagon instead of leading an army, returned to Camden.[11]

The Genl. had a rule that neither he nor any of his staff should sleep under any roof during a campaign, but all were glad by this time to have some rest. His staff pitched their tents in Stinson's shady front yard opposite my house.[12] His personal train & couriers occupied my pasture lot west of the house; & he made my house his home. I have said before that the Genl. was personally acquainted with Mrs. Merrell, their families having been raised near enough in Florida to know each other. He had dined with us on Christmas day, & another little incident had occurred to renew the acquaintance.

At dinner on Christmas day the Genl. had been pleased to praise some home-made wine of the Muscadine, or scupernong Grape. Upon his entry into town in pursuit of Genl. Steele, Mrs. Merrell made up a basket of

Cake & Wine & sent it upon her best plate to the General's Quarters, with a note. The General must have been very busy writing orders, for the basket & plate came back all right & a note in pencil, which being deciphered read nearly as follows: "Major Genl. Price will immediately detail sufficient force of Cavalry to patrol the town & preserve order to-night." Signed. Kirby Smith, Genl. I inferred of course that by mistake the Genl.'s thanks for Cake & Wine had gone to Genl. Price & in the mean time the town was becoming turbulent, with Indians & all in high glee. Of course, I sent the order to Genl. Price, & for fun also wrote the Genl. a letter of thanks for the rank of Major General bestowed upon my wife, assuring him that it was a judicious appointment, for that I had served under her command myself several years & had found her to be a strict disciplinarian &c.

The story got out in the County, & in Shreveport La. I afterwards heard it narrated with this improvement: that Mrs. Merrell had replied, "She had no Cavalry in her command, but only considerable force of Light Infantry." Which was impossible, though very good, for we had no children & never had.

I was afterwards told by Judge Watkins, who was one of the three judges of the Military Court for this Department, that he had suggested to Genl. Smith to provide me an early appointment.[13] So when the Genl. left my house, he left word for my wife to tell me to write him & say what sort of position I wanted. I also met him in his ambulance, & he asked me to get in & ride a way, which I did, & he said the same & more to me. I told him I wanted an independent position in which I could report to him alone, but I had tried it before, & the interposition of Brigadiers & Colonels, in Engineering matters was a positive obstruction. He assented to that, & the next chapter will narrate what came of it.

In closing the narrative of this Campaign, it is proper I should add that a strategist may differ with me as to the theory of Banks' & Steele's campaign, on the ground that the Federal Army could not have passed on to Marshall & there maintained themselves with Kirby Smith at Shreveport & Price in Arkansas hovering on their rear. The answer to this is that neither could those Confederate armies have obtained supplies with Banks & Steele occupying Texas. The Federal army went expecting to find the sheep-growing counties glad to receive them. They had advice of a wheat crop growing, & they brought in their wagons Scythe Cradles for their soldiers to go in & harvest those crops, & their money would have purchased beef & mutton more than enough.

CHAPTER XIII

*I*t was not easy to provide me such a position as I required. In the line, it would have been subversive of discipline. I knew that, & was not surprised at having to wait several months before anything turned up. Neither did I care, for I was quite content to be at home with my wife.

In the mean time the army was improving in all respects. The probability of any more Federal invasions in this direction became less & less. To keep so fine an army idle did not pay. So Genl. Price got permission to carry 12,000 or 13,000 men, including his Missourians, northward into Missouri.[1] That this was Genl. Kirby Smith's own plan, I do not think. I judge from a remark he made when they started: "That is the last of that army." It was always Genl. Price's favorite idea to "go into Missouri," & he had (like other subordinate officers) more ways of pursuing his views at Richmond, probably, than the Commander in Chief himself. To march into Missouri in the summer of 1864 & so make a lively diversion of Federal troops, as far as possible from Grant & Sherman, was not a bad idea, supposing Major Genl. Price had the genius for aggressive warfare — which was not the case. But to send back into the neighborhood of their own homes a whole military Division of Missouri troops who had been absent from their homes several years was not very wise or prudent. For brave as those men were, they were but men after all. The result was about what might have been expected. Genl. Price marched up, & he marched back again. He fought about forty combats, but scarcely any that could be called a battle. He went with a good army of about 12,000 men, & he came back at the head of a rabble of about 20,000 men.[2]

He carried away from us every wagon, team, & ambulance he could lay hands on. I never heard of any coming back; & he left a large Federal force probably double or triple his number entirely free to go & reinforce Genl. Sherman in Georgia. Had he been content to place himself between the Federal garrison in Little Rock & their supplies, at the same time threatening an invasion of Missouri, he might have kept a very large Federal force amused watching him, & counter-marching in cold weather without the satisfaction of a battle. This was a kind of strategy well-suited to the genius of Genl. Price, but I think he was tolled on by advisors from that part of Missouri lying North of Missouri River promising a cordial reception & heavy reinforcements. But North Missouri lay beyond a broad & hostile country. The statement of Gov. Reynolds of Missouri, who accompanied the expedition, was that Genl. Price in that march greatly consulted his own pomp & popularity. Every day he would turn his army end for end, causing the rear of yesterday to "march past" him & his staff to be the front of this day's advance. Also that he would lie, apparently asleep, on his blanket in an attitude of touching innocence for his soldiers, & especially the new recruits, to admire & applaud. There was Genl. Price's weakness. He was one of the finest-looking men I ever saw. Not handsome or symmetrical, but portly, large, & when he pleased, an air of majestic bonhomme that was inimitable. No politico-military ever lived who was half as good as Genl. Price looked. He had one quality which with soldiers saves any man from ridicule. He was as brave as Julius Caesar. He would forget in the heat of a battle that it was necessary for him to overlook the whole & provide for contingency. He would so far forget himself as to go & stay in the hottest part of the fight, doing personal acts of valor like a paladin of olden times.

Finally came an order from Genl. Smith for me to report at Head Quarters in Shreveport, La., & an ambulance with four mules with a driver in Artillery uniform. According to regulations, no one under the rank of Major General could have four horses or mules to his ambulance. I had already learned in the army self-assertion was a necessity. A certain amount of display was necessary to command respect, at least where one's position was not already well determined. So I took all the state that was offered me, although Genl. Price & his officers were grabbing all the rolling stock for themselves to carry away into Missouri. In order to get off at all with my cortege, I had to leave rather between two days, & stop one night off the public road. It was fortunate I was so persevering, for that ambulance & team was, I reckon, all that was saved to the Confederacy out of all that army's equipage.[3]

Arriving at Shreveport, the problem for me to solve was this, & fortunately for me it was more in my line of engineering than obstructing rivers or throwing up Earth-works.[4]

The fall of Vicksburg & Port Hudson closed the line of Mississippi River, & practically shut out or in the Trans-Mississippi Department of the Confederacy to its own resources.

Blockade running on the Texas coast, which had been for a time a sufficient source of supply for imported things, was daily becoming more uncertain as the Federal blockade became more intense.

Importing through Mexico was costly in the extreme, for Maximilian's Government exacted a Transit duty, & the hauling across the plains from the Rio Grande to Shreveport was at terrific expense. Even this poor reliance was subject any day to interruption from the Federal land forces at Boca Chica, who maneuvered daily almost within sight of Confederate Cotton & merchandise.

It was clear that ere long we should be shut in to our own resources. There was no time to lose. The Genl. regretted he had not sent for me before, but red tape was in the way. Would I mature a comprehensive plan for the future, & put it in a written form upon which the Commander in Chief could predicate his future action? I said yes, certainly. I shut myself in a room with pen, ink & paper, & you may be sure I tried hard to get off a good thing with me at the head. No one in the Department fit to carry it on but me. My plan was:

To establish, in the heart of Texas, so far inland that by the time the Feds got there, we would necessarily be past wanting supplies, a manufacturing town belonging to the Department & carried on by mechanics & disabled men of the army. Also for Factory operatives the families of War-widows.

That this manufacturing town should be projected on a scale so extensive as not only to furnish Clothing & Blankets, ordnance, fabrics, shoes, & hats for the army but a surplus to be bartered with the Country for Commissary stores when Confederate money would no longer purchase supplies. And that this thing should be commenced at once & carried out with all the energy of military discipline.

The Genl. was pleased with my recommendation, & gave me as far as he could, subject to military forms, a *carte blanche*, to carry out my schemes. He told me to collect at our centre all the manufacturing machinery in the Department, & getting that well under way, to then lose no time but proceed to Europe & purchase whatever else was wanting, running the same in sections through the blockade before it should be too late. As to reporting to him, he had a great deal to think about; he would like things to progress smoothly without annoyance to him; but I must report directly to him in case I was obstructed by the ignorance or contrariness of officers of whatever rank. So I took congee of Genl. Kirby Smith & have never seen him since, though what I did passed under his Eye often enough.[5]

While these preliminaries were going on at Shreveport Head Quarters, I came near, in what I thought my clear line of duty, cutting across the *Esprit de Corps* of the Army.

One evening returning to my quarters, I found my landlady in tears. Two young officers, she said, had called to see if they could borrow my ambulance. They were principal & second on the one side & had a duel to fight the next morning, & it was to be a duel with six-shooter pistols *à la outrance*, & they wanted an ambulance to haul away what was to be left of them, more or less. And one of them she knew intimately, & he was a good young man, & she was sure he would be killed because it was the good young man that always got the worst of it, & what on earth was to be done about it. Could not I interfere? &c. I thought of it, & I came to think at last it was my duty as an officer to stop it if possible; otherwise, I should always feel myself blood-guilty. So after supper I walked round to Genl. Kirby Smith's private Quarters. He was out visiting with his lady. Upon reflection, I concluded to tell my business to the medical Director, Dr. Yandrell.[6] He asked me to put it in writing. I knew that, in military parlance, that meant for me to make myself responsible. I had no objections to being held responsible for a good deed. So I wrote, not in any official form or official language fit for to be filed in the General's office, only a pencil note on a page torn from my memorandum book, something like this:

> Genl. I think it my duty to advise you of a duel between two officers (naming them), the same appointed for to-morrow morning early.
>
> The parties seem to me very young men to be shooting pistols at all, & yet my information is that the contemplated affair is to be very desperate: six shooters at twenty steps, & firing to continue until one or the other is down. I am sure you will desire to prevent the meeting, if possible.
>
> Signed

I left my note & went home to bed with the mind conscious of rectitude, & thinking of course there would be no duel. What was my chagrin then when at breakfast next morning some army gossip came into the piazza &, leaning his elbows on the window sill, said, "Heard of the duel this morning?" "No. What about it?" "Well, not much. Only young so and so had a fight, all regular, & second round one fell, pretty badly hurt, I hear." Of course my landlady was greatly beshocked, & I went out to learn the particulars. Upon rct. of my note, Genl. Smith had immediately notified the Commandant of the Post to arrest the parties. He detailed a young Lieut. to effect the arrest. He was green. The first of the young duelists asked to see his written orders, & having none, told him he must go & get his orders in writing; & while the Lieut. was gone on his fool's errand, the young scapegrace went & hid under a bridge until time should come at daylight for his duel. He also sent word to his antagonist, who took equal pains to hide himself until morning. I learned it was of no use trying to prevent a duel when the parties are in earnest; moreover, I soon learned that I had "put my foot in it." The young officers wanted to know what I had to do interfering in their private affairs, & one of them had got sight of my unlucky note, which was not thought to abound in that reverence which was due from the man of mature years towards the rising generation! From what I could hear, my friends had something to do to prevent some of them insulting me. It ended, however, in a dinner party to which hostile parties were invited, some good stories told, & good feeling restored.

My good landlady told me all about the occasion of this duel. It seems there was, as there generally is, a lady in the case. This time a young one. She was a Miss. Sibley, daughter of Genl. Sibley of Arizona fame.[7] Young, petite, a belle, & specially a fine singer, she lacerated the very heart strings of the very young officers about Head Quarters.

Conspicuous among whom was a really fine young man named Waymouth, or some such name [Weightman]. The father had been a Missouri General [Colonel] & was killed in the battle of Oak Hills.[8] Young Waymouth [Weightman] was in the Adjutant General's office, & a great favorite in the army. His age about nineteen years.

Finally, he addressed Miss Sibley, & she accepted him, but stipulated that the engagement should be kept a great secret until she divulged it! The young lady went on, as captivating as ever, & the next thing young B— (I really quite forget his name), midshipman on a gun-boat, also addressed her in form. She said no, & he asked if she would tell him had she any prior engagement? She said, "Yes." If it was not too much, he would ask her to tell him who was the happy man? Not at all. It was Lieut. Waymouth [Weightman]! Here was a row! It seems the midshipman was intimate friend to Waymouth [Weightman]. Had told him he intended to address the lady & asked his good word with the lady & her family. To all this young W. could make no objections, for his tongue was tied; yet he felt he was in a false position. On the other hand, the fiery midshipman felt himself outraged, so that nothing but a duel would satisfy his honor. And seeing he was near-sighted & wore spectacles, the shooting must be within his range. Just as might have been expected from young men shooting at each other, one of them was hurt directly. He got a bullet behind in that part of him where both of them ought to have been kicked.

I understood that Miss Sibley was not so popular in the army from that time, & that ere long she left & went somewhere.

I never had any good luck interfering with other officers in the army. Once I interposed on behalf of a private under my command who reported to me that a Capt. of another Command had used violent & profane language, seized him by the throat, & held a pistol at his head; & all that about something that did not concern military affairs at all. After a big muss, I learned that my private had deceived me as to the facts in the case.

Another time, at my quarters near the mouth of Arkansas River, when

Frost's Brigade was there, one moon-light evening was introduced a Count or Baron something, who was teaching the officers the use of the Sword & Bayonet. Said he was a Pole, I think, & of a military school in Russia. Certainly he was skillful & active with his weapons.

Some officer suggested that the titled fencing master should show Major Merrill his sword exercise. Major M. admired, but being something bilious at the time, asked what sword exercise he called that? It looked to me like monkey shines. I suppose I inwardly resented the foreigner's title, in which I lacked faith. He took offense, & said perhaps Major Merrell knew more about the use of the sword than he did. Would I step out & try him? I saw the officers looked upon it as a challenge which I could not decently decline, especially as I was the local representative of Head Quarters & must not show the white feather. So at it we went with sabres. I soon found that in the moonlight, against an active & skillful young man, & he dancing & capering round me with the light in his favor, I had a slim chance; and, after sufficient swordplay, I dropped my point, saying I set up no claim to superior swordsmanship. I thought I could probably defend myself sufficiently well by daylight, but moon light was too uncertain, & so it passed off for the present in good humor.

But after breakfast next morning, for this was in the front Piazza of a Mrs. Smith's house, as I was conversing with the lady of the house over her table, a messenger came in to say I was wanted.[9] I went out, & there was my impossible "Baron" & all the officers congregated to see a fight. The foreign rascal said it was now good daylight, & we must finish what we had begun the night before.

I saw it was a trap. There was really no escape, so I said, "Very well." "How will you have it: bayonet or sword?" said he. "All one to me," said I. "I shall use the sabre." So, borrowing one from Col. Musser, I took my place as coolly as I could & waited his attack.[10] It was a poor place for a fight. The floor was covered with oil cloth, for it was in the wide hall of the house, but that oil cloth was worse for him than for me, he jumped about so much. He, however, had the light of the open front door at his back, which was to my disadvantage. I resolved I would have no trial of scientific skill with him, for in that he had all the advantage. I intended to, & I did, parry his first lunge instantly, had my sword through him to the hilt. Not that I shed his blood at all, but it was through him as the actors do on the stage. I intended upon that to insist that the officers should decide that my antagonist was dead, to all intents and purposes, & had no more he could do. He on his part, however, intended to draw blood, at least, & perhaps to kill. Paying no attention to my sword, which was through him, he shorted his sword, grasping it with his left hand half way, & sprang at my throat. I dodged my head & neck instinctively & received his point in my neck, left side, underneath the cravat. Whereupon I assumed lofty indignation, threw my sword upon the sofa in disdain. "Here is blood plenty, I hope, gentlemen. I call upon you to witness that I had my sword clean through him. He had no business going on after he was hit. At any rate, I feel no call to do so myself. I have more important business entrusted to me than this; & so good morning, Mr. Count." The fellow seemed scared at my lofty deportment, & I learned afterwards that he very shortly ran into the Enemy's lines. A spy, no doubt, all the while.

I do not think I ever did learn to keep a guard upon my tongue as I ought, if I was to keep out of scrapes in the army.

CHAPTER XIV

By the time I had gotten through at Head Quarters, & upon reaching the place designated beforehand for the future Military Manufacturing town, very considerable progress had been made. Machinery had been collected by purchase & by impressment from all quarters too near the Enemy for safety. Our old factory in Pike County was there. Six steam engines in all were on the ground & a mass of building material lying about, besides several buildings already in a forward stage of erection.[1]

The resident Quarter Master was Major Busby, then of Pine Bluff—but now a leading man in Memphis, Tenn.[2] I never quite understood Major Busby. I think he was probably shy of me as a man from Hd. Quarters; but I incline to think he was an efficient officer, & quite able to maintain his own position. The Master of Construction on the ground was another well-chosen man, Judge Bocage, also from Pine Bluff. I could not fail to understand Judge Bocage. The position exactly suited him. He was really a fine mechanical Engineer without much science. No one understood better the resources of the backwoods & streams.[3] He had one standing grievance. There was no "steam whistle" among all the engines. He was nothing without a steam whistle! Requisitions were kept going, & I do not know but couriers were sent all over the Department until the Judge had got possession of a Steam Whistle, & then he was content. A terrible man to "blow his own horn" was Judge B. He was really the only boastful man I ever knew that was really as good as his word. I could quite understand Judge Bocage & put him to the best possible uses. I think, however, that

he also was shy of me, but I went along about my own business, surveying, measuring, & making drafts & specifications, which were submitted
by courier to Genl. Smith at Hd. Qr., who ordered them copied into the
Ordnance Department & the original sent back for working plans.[4]

I never worked harder in my life. I had to draft in a way to work up
rather incongruous material already on the ground, providing beforehand
for every bolt & pin, at the same time in red ink on the same plan, that
which had yet to be made or purchased. I felt it to be a great responsibility
to answer for drafts & plans made to work up unsuitable materials, without
being present myself to point out the particulars. I learned afterwards that
no mistakes occurred. By January all the available machinery was well at
work, producing supplies for the army at a rate surpassing expectations.[5]

In the mean time I was well on my way to Europe. Leaving Mound
Prairie about 1st December, 1864.[6] I halted to inspect the machinery of
the Texas Penitentiary at Huntsville. Found the same in excellent working
order, & the goods turned off were as perfect as could be made of the
materials. The Convicts in that prison were in the main a bad lot, demoralized by the prison itself. They had secret means of communication among
themselves, as prisoners will have, & what do you think was their Esprit de
Corps? Why, of course, it was "Loyalty to the U.S. Govt.!" They seemed
to think that was a virtue that would some day bring its reward. Should
not be surprised if it did not turn out just so. I have lived to see many great
rascals, whose crimes merited the Penitentiary, flourish & triumph over
better men by dint of loyalty to a party, which has come to be all one with
fidelity to the Laws of the Country, or at least a substitute for the same.

Getting on under Military orders, I found, as usual, to be quite a different thing from going by my own head as I did at Mound Prairie. Arrived at
Houston Texas, that thing took place which I had tried to guard against in
my understanding with Genl. Kirby Smith. Subordinate Officers countermanded me. By this means I was detained in Houston about a month.[7]
At last I was allowed to proceed just to Matamoros in Texas [Mexico], &
from thence by way of Havana & the Island of St. Thomas, first tread-
ing on the shores of Old England at Southampton, about the 1st of April
1865, & proceeded without delay to report myself to Genl. McRae, the
Confederate financial agent there.[8]

The narrative of my adventures down to the time of leaving Havana is
best told in my letters to my wife, which I will endeavor to preserve by
securing them in this or the other volume.[9]

Some of those letters must have been lost or miscarried, for I find in
them no account of my journey from Houston to Matamoros & the mouth
of Rio Grande.

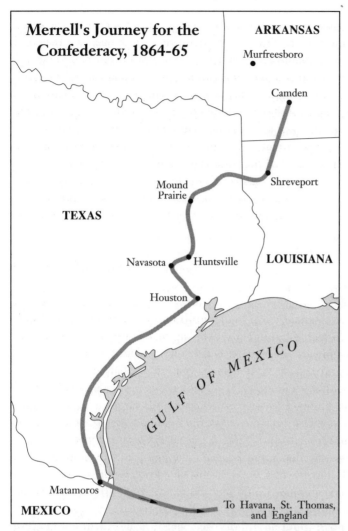

Merrell's Journey for the Confederacy, 1864-65

ARKANSAS

Murfreesboro

Camden

Mound Prairie

Shreveport

TEXAS

Navasota   Huntsville   LOUISIANA

Houston

GULF OF MEXICO

Matamoros

MEXICO

To Havana, St. Thomas, and England

Ordered by the commanding general of the Trans-Mississippi Department to travel to England to purchase needed machinery, Merrell leaves from Shreveport and, after stopping at manufacturing centers in Texas, travels into Mexico, embarking from Matamoros on his way to England via Havana, San Juan, and St. Thomas.

I was not alone on my journey. A secretary or adjutant had been provided to do my writing. His name was James Lawson. Age about twenty years. Son of a Widow Lady of Little Rock.[10] We started from Houston in company with quite a party all going the same road. Genl. Polignac (Prince Polignac) on some mission first in Mexico & then in France.[11] Lt. Col. Miltenberger of the Staff of Gov. Allen, the Gov. of Louisiana, & they were finally joined in Matamoros by Major C. J. [——] [T. C. Moncure], but whether he was attached to Polignac or Col. Miltenberger I never knew. I understood afterwards in London that the upshot of Genl. Polignac's mission was to advise the Governments disposed to favor the Confederacy that we could not hold out much longer without foreign recognition & the opening of some ports by which we could get supplies. The supply of Lead was especially running low. The Trans. Miss. Department was hauling it from Mexico across the plains, the cost being at Houston 25c pr. lb. paid in Gold. It came in shapes in bulk like to a turtle. I may as well say here that the scarcity of lead in the Confederacy was all along a great drawback. Southern people were not a mining people any more than they had been a manufacturing people — nor as much. Early in the war the few veins of lead that were known in Tennessee & Missouri fell into the hands of the Enemy.

When I was in Havana, Maj. Holm told me confidentially that for want of lead the war must now shortly end. The fall of Fort Fisher left no place where he could land it with any reasonable chance of success.[12] He said I had my orders & must go to Europe, but the war would necessarily end soon after I got there, which proved to be true. I reached England 1st April, & before the end of that month came the news of Genl. Lee's surrender.[13]

In crossing the plains, under circumstances of no little danger, travelers become pretty well acquainted, & I for one learned to dislike Prince Polignac very much. He was a mere "scold" in point of temper & seemed to think his convenience must be consulted always. This we were all disposed to do in deference to his rank in the Confederate Army, but we did not like his way of exacting it. He was not a pure-minded man. Of course, his bravery was undoubted, & he was otherwise a good soldier; but I made up my own mind that if the Bourbon family were generally like him, the French did well to be rid of them. Intense littleness, I should say was theirs, & no princely grandness of character, unless it might be possibly at an emergency of great danger, when every brave man appears well.

Until within ten miles of Matamoros, we had the weather warm & were wearing our linen coats; but, as we entered the Chaparral not far from the place where Genl. Taylor fought the battle of Resaca de la Palma, beginning the Mexican War, a "Norther" blew up, which continued more than twenty days.[14] All our clothing came into requisition & some more besides that we purchased in Matamoros. I never felt cold so intensely before or since that I remember, not because it was so very cold as the thermometer goes, but the piercing wind, & the fact that our Hotel at least had no adequate preparation for cold. There was one fire place in the dining room, but it was small & was built not on the floor with a hearth, but several feet from the floor like a Dutch oven. The fuel was excellent, what there was of it. It consisted of the roots of "Muskeet," I think they called it, dug up in the Chaparral & hauled in by miserable Mexican Indians.

The City was lively & expensive in the highest degree. An usurper had just been expelled; his name was Cortinas.[15] Although the supreme power was at that time in Maximilian the Emperor, it did seem that in remote places of Mexico any reckless fellow with a feather in his hat & a rusty sword might get up a "Pronunciamento," driving out the authorities by shooting at anything, especially at the Cathedral, & taking possession, levy a contribution on all reputed to have money, & holding possession until the next fellow of the same sort came along to expel him, in like manner levying another contribution. Miserable Country! Miserable people! Their favorite pastime seemed to be that of shooting at each other. The Cathedral & the buildings in & about the Grand Plaza were pockmarked by musket & cannon balls, & blood on the pavement was a thing one would not stop to enquire about. It so happened that when we were there, Majia (pronounced Mehea, as Mexico is pronounced Meheco), Majia was holding Matamoros in the interests of the Europeans. He was a full-blood Indian, fond of gorgeous trappings for himself & horse, & very gracious in returning salutations as he rode the streets. He looked elegantly, but his Indian soldiery, besprinkled with Negroes, were rough enough.[16] I understood their pay & rations were of the smallest, & their conduct just as it happened. Their officers used the Cow-hide freely, as I can bear witness.

At the Boca del Rio, which is the seaport of Matamoros & lies thirty miles Eastward, we found better regulations. They were about changing the Mexican garrison for one of French soldiers, or at least of French officers. Such a miserable hole as the "Boca" was! Built in the mud. Crowded with people of all nations, the Norther blowing cold, houses mere shanties, water brackish. I doubt if many drank water at all in that town, & the streets belly deep to a mule, a perfect "lob-lolly." No harbor, the vessels in port, about Eighty in number including men of war, lay not inside the bar but several miles out & at anchor. Their cargoes had to land through a surf that was at that time too dangerous. For want of facilities to ship safely through such a surf, Cotton had accumulated in very large quantities, & shippers were distressed. We put up at the only decent house, called Hotel Faranti, & had adventures daily. From the Cupola of the Hotel, where a good spy glass was kept, we could see the in-comings & outgoings of the Federal garrison at Boca Chica daily. The gale had driven out to sea about thirty of the eighty vessels in the offing. One French Brig or ship was driven ashore on the American side [of] the river, & a squad was detailed from the Federal garrison to look after her. Nearly loaded with Cotton, she would have been a prize sure enough, but she broke up, & her Cotton came our way, propelled by the gale from the north. So the Feds had the mortification of looking on while the Mexicans landed the wet Bales.

All that need be told of my adventures from the time I left the Coast of Mexico until I left Havana & embarked for Europe will be found in the letters above referred to.

At that time there was (& still is, I presume) an excellent line of British mail steamers, of about 1,000 tons burthen each, plying from all important points in the Gulf of Mexico & the Caribbean Sea, to a Central station at "St. Thomas," meeting there a line of very large seagoing steamers which ply regularly between that port & Southampton England. These last steam packets are probably the largest & best in the world. About 5,000 Tons American Measurement, & under man-of-war regulations. The population, the social intercourse, church service, the music & the dancing on board seeming more like a well-regulated town than like a ship at sea. Our ship was named the "Atrata," after a river of that name in the Isthmus. But I should have said that in transit from Havana & St. Thomas we coasted so near the Island of Haiti as to examine the shores as clearly as I ever want to see them. Desolate mountains with little habitation for man, I should say, was the Geography of Haiti, & that more so every year. We ran in to exchange the mails at the port of St. John's in the Island of Puerto Rico. The most delightful place to look at from the water that I had yet seen. Passengers did not land. Left in an hour or so. Delightful that cruising among the West Indies Islands. Found St. Thomas just as it is described, a very hot, earthquaky fern-hole. Harbor fine. Nature lovely but very mountainous, & population of Negroes very degraded. Santa Anna, who had so long flourished at the head of Mexican Affairs, was at that time resident at St. Thomas. His house was conspicuous about half way up the mountain side overlooking the town. I was told that he was living in sin at a very fast rate, & apparently had not long to live, for he was well in years.[17]

We stayed only a few hours in St. Thomas. That time was spent in transshipping ourselves & luggage from the small steamer to the large one, in looking about us, & in conversing with the impudent natives along-side. Great Depot of Coal. Danish fortification, not much force, probably old-fashioned guns, for a Confederate blockade runner had recently run out safely under fire of the fort. She was named the "Banshee," had the Confederate flag flying, which at the solicitation of U.S. Consul occasioned the firing. Possibly the Danish gunners did not try very hard.

We were twelve or thirteen days running from St. Thomas to Southampton. Did not see the Azores Islands. Probably we passed in the night.

Did not slow the engine to speak ships as we passed. Wrote what they had to say on a black board, saluted flags & passed on. Passengers contented & jolly, but finally the Capt. announced that after dinner that day we would sight the Scilly Island light, & from that time preparations for going ashore began. Sure enough after dinner, from the Ship's forward deck, after dinner with a good field-glass, there was the light twinkling at the water's edge, but many miles away.

Next morning the sea was lively all around us. Coasting vessels & sea-going craft plying in & out. Mackerel fishermen in Smacks by the thousand. I understood there were 4,000 smacks in that trade. The rocky shores of Cornwall or Devonshire on our left, & something new to call for our attention every hour. At last we passed the "Needles" & the Isle of Wight, up the beautiful "Southampton Water," & by Noon or soon after found ourselves inside a granite dock with gates to shut us in afloat when the tide should leave us. As we went in, we passed a German steamer going out, black swarming with emigrants, mostly men, with a brass band of music, bound to reinforce the Federal power in its war against the South. I felt then, all over me, that it was a hopeless case. The Confederacy could not win against all Europe, Africa, & America combined. But just then we had other things to distract our thoughts. Parting with so many traveling acquaintances, not sad at all but very lively. An Express train was waiting, & a short run carried us to London. All of us Confederates put up at the British Hotel in Trafalgar Square. Our party consisted of Col. Pascal Smith, agent for Texas and his lady. One Mr. Granger & his young wife. He was a merchant from Brownsville or Corpus Christi, & myself & Secretary. Col. Smith's wife & Mr. Granger were both invalids, & I subsequently learned that Mrs. Smith & Granger [were] both dying. Col. Smith married the widow & now lives & prospers in Texas.

For my part I had to go to work. The first thing was to purchase for Lawson & myself an outfit of good clothing, & at the same time to report to Genl. McRae & hand in my dispatches. My reception was cordial. I was expected. As to personal appearance, we were a sight. Lawson being a younger man & quite handsome, could manage to look well in anything, but for myself, I was a sight. A soft, drab slouched hat, in which I had slept often, the same discolored by salt-water, perspiration & smoke. Thanks to my wife, good under clothes, clean but frayed out. Gray regulation pantaloons, worn through at the seat & elsewhere, & a coat that was no longer a coat at all!

However, I had no time to lose. I was under military orders again. We must commence seeing London while our new clothing was making, & it was in vain to put on a new Hat or any other over article new without the rest. It was better taste for us to go as we were. Lawson was worried very much. He would have preferred to lie in bed & make no showing until we could appear in style. But I did not feel that it was anybody's business but our own. We cared for nobody in London, & a little in the spirit of contrariness, I did "the Parliament House," Westminster Abbey, St. James Park, & the Palaces first. People stopped & turned & looked after us, & then went on, puzzled in their minds. Very few, I suppose, were able to "Locate" us from our outward appearance.

At last our outfit was all done & sent in to our quarters, & we put these things on all at once: 2 span new from head to foot! The old things we sold to the Jew Old Clo. man. It did one good to see the smile with which the waiters & landlady at the Hotel greeted our first appearance in good clothing. Indeed it must have been almost disreputable to the house, where members of Parliament did resort, to have such demi-savages as we appeared, in the dining room.

I made it a point to myself to dress as much like a member of Parliament as I knew how, & in point of behavior to look as much like a lord.

In point of fact, I have sometimes had reason to think that a modest, well-disposed Southern man, who has been accustomed life long to be of the dominant race & to expect obedience, & most especially if he has had military command—reason to think that such an one in a quiet way might pass anywhere in Europe for a lord, provided he would not say too much. Let that be as it will, Lawson & I got on very well, & enjoyed quite as much consideration as we were entitled to.

Postscript

If the missing letters to his wife that Merrell placed in his memoir included descriptions of negotiations with McRae or with any English manufacturers, their loss is greatly to be regretted. It is possible, however, that they contained accounts only of his travels from Matamoros to Havana. As he says, the letters that concern his journey from Houston to Matamoros miscarried at the time or were lost before he began his memoir. Furthermore, he may not have had much to say about any negotiations or diplomacy, for he landed in England April 1, 1865, and Lee surrendered one week later, on April 9.

The Department of the Trans-Mississippi was the last to yield. On June 2, 1865, General Edmund Kirby Smith, who had sent Merrell to England, accepted in Galveston, Texas, the terms of a convention approved by his agents in New Orleans on May 26. What happened to Merrell between April 1 and Kirby Smith's surrender? Indeed, what happened between Merrell's arrival in England and his return to the United States?

Colin J. McRae, the agent for the Confederate States Treasury Department in England, wrote to Kirby Smith on April 1 that Major Merrell had arrived, had sent him a note and letters, and would call on him on Monday the 3rd. McRae acknowledges receiving, through Merrell, Kirby Smith's letter of October 25, 1864, containing instructions about how to handle Merrell's purchases. He also acknowledges the receipt of a draft for $100,000 to be applied to the purchases. On May 1 McRae wrote Kirby Smith that Merrell "has just returned from a tour amongst the foundries and machine shops of the manufacturing districts of this country and is now ready to commence his purchases." Merrell had obviously been busy in the month of April and planned to complete his mission shortly. McRae continues, "He will probably be able to get off *all* the machinery required by him in about two months." [1]

When Merrell curtailed his mission, he did not return to the United States immediately. He may have been afraid of being arrested as a foreign agent and uncertain how agents such as himself were included in the terms of surrender. He kept in his papers a map of England that he purchased there, and arrows and dates that he penciled on this map show that he crossed the English Channel from Newhaven to Dieppe in June of 1865, and that he recrossed from Calais to Dover in August. He also kept a map of Paris in which he wrote the date "3 July 1865." Private Lawson accompanied him on this trip.[2]

Mrs. Merrell had not heard from her husband as late as July 1865. She wrote to her sister, "I have not even heard of his arrival in Europe. His last letter I received was written the day he sailed from Havana the 8th of March."[3] The only other document that provides information about Merrell's movements after the collapse of the Confederacy is the petition for pardon that he applied for on October 26 and filed in Washington, D.C., on November 2, 1865.

In support of his application, Merrell submitted affidavits from Little Rock dated September 30, 1865; from Utica dated October 9; and from New York City dated October 16. He petitioned for pardon before a notary public in Washington, D.C., on October 26. The affidavit written in Little Rock on September 30, which is signed by a United States attorney named Jennings and which refers to Merrell as an "industrious and valuable citizen," notes that "he has just returned" from Europe. When this document is coupled with a passing reference in his wife's letter to her sister Helen in 1866 ("He went in March & came back in Sept."), we may safely assume that he left England for the United States in early September of 1865, almost five months after Lee's surrender.[4]

A stipulation of Andrew Johnson's Amnesty Proclamation of May 29, 1865, may have caused Merrell to worry and delay, for he was technically excluded by exception 7 for "all persons who have been or are absentees from the United States for the purpose of aiding the rebellion." In his application Merrell maintained that he was not a foreign agent but a military officer under orders and that he should be included in the surrender terms that Kirby Smith signed.[5]

Another interesting question raised by Merrell's mission to England concerns the money that Kirby Smith had deposited with C. J. McRae to pay for Merrell's purchases. Merrell said in his application for pardon that "want of funds or credit, & subsequently the closing disasters of the war prevented him, so that he made no purchases or contracts at all under his Instructions." Merrell's cousin Walter B. Camp, speaking before a group of Utica citizens celebrating the city's semicentennial, told the interesting story that Merrell, while in England, "deposited the funds, half to the order of Kirby Smith and the other to the U.S., and with honorable mention by Mr. Seward, returned to allegiance."[6] The matter of these funds troubled Kirby Smith himself in his exile. On his way to the Yucatán, he wrote the former Confederate Secretary of War John C. Breckenridge from Havana on August 1, 1865, enclosing a letter that he had received there from McRae, saying that "the funds referred to are not under my control. In any disposition made of them, I would request that Mr. Merrill be paid his expenses back to his home in La. and that the account of Alexander Ross & Co. of London against the Confederacy for £1944.17 ? be adjusted."[7] Merrell kept a document from the United States Treasury Department, dated December 10, 1866, attesting to the receipt from him on November 23 of four hundred dollars.[8] It is tempting to believe that he kept this receipt to prove that he had deposited with the U.S. Treasury any funds that he had left from his trip to England on behalf of the Confederacy.

It should be noted that Merrell says "he tried to be a Union man" in the beginning of the war, "but the time arrived when it became necessary for him to declare himself a rebel or sacrifice home, property & strong personal attachments." He adds further that he was in debt "& felt that it would be infamous in him to desert his condition." Although asking for pardon, Merrell had the courage to add: "Under pressure of these considerations he decided to stand in his lot: and having done so, acknowledges that even previous to his enrollment as a conscript, he did what he was called upon to do with fidelity to the so called Confederacy." His application was supported by letters from two very influential New York politicians: Thurlow Weed, William H. Seward's friend and ally and Lincoln's special envoy to England during the Civil War; and Roscoe Conkling, the radical Republican who would press in the United States Senate for a severe Reconstruction policy in the South.[9]

When Henry Merrell returned to Camden, Arkansas, he found that his property had not been confiscated, perhaps because it had been transferred to his wife's name. As far as finances were concerned, he came out of the war well enough to be able to make a tour of Europe in 1866 with his wife and her Smith sisters-in-law, Elizabeth Ann ("Lizzie") Smith and Helen Zubly Smith. On his way to Europe, the group visited Merrell's mother and his brother, Samuel, in New York, and there was an awkward moment when the Smith girls, still mourning the death of their brother Willie, failed to follow their father's instructions to avoid meeting Merrell's cousin Walter Bicker Camp, who had been energetic in raising Union troops from New York.[10]

Merrell's path had crossed that of Edmund Kirby Smith in Louisville, Kentucky, in January of 1866. Apologizing that he would not be able to see him in person, Merrell wrote an affectionate letter from his hotel to

Henry Merrell in 1878.

Merrell's wife, Elizabeth Pye Magill Merrell (1815–90).

financial malfeasance had been proven against Kirby Smith for dealing in cotton in the Trans-Mississippi Department. "When I finally got back from Europe," he says," I found the report current that I had been your *private* financial Agent to dispose some Cotton which it was alleged you had sent to England for your own account!" Merrell tells Kirby Smith that he had been summoned in Camden to appear before the committee of a Federal treasury agent "upon the question of my expedition to Europe" and that after answering their questions he "determined to draw their fire on the Cotton question." They replied that they had investigated the cotton dealings of all Confederate officers of the Trans-Mississippi Department and only a Major Broadwell was implicated in any cotton frauds.[11]

Merrell was for the rest of his life a resident of Camden, Arkansas and was active in its business and church affairs. Although Charles Arthur Magill had gone into a partnership as a druggist as early as January of 1866, a letter from him to his niece Helen Zubly Smith shows that he lost money in this business and was going to "hold myself at liberty" to join

Merrell's brother-in-law and business partner, Charles Arthur Magill (1817–84), in 1878.

his old commander, assuring him that, to his knowledge, no charges of Henry Merrell, "if he should conclude to do anything in the Manufacturing or Mercantile business."[12] Merrell soon became associated with his brother-in-law in a series of enterprises involving merchandising, timber, and even banking, inasmuch as they acted not only as cotton factors but as creditors.[13]

The firm of Merrell and Magill placed advertisements in the *Camden Daily Bulletin* for furnishing plantation supplies and for buying and selling cotton. They also handled general merchandise, for they claim that "Merrell & Magill under the hill can fill your bill."[14] "Under the hill" refers to the location of their business at the foot of Washington Street at the bottom of a long hill that drops from the city of Camden down to the Ouachita River and the wharves. The diaries of Robert F. Kellam of Camden show that on at least one occasion "Bully Ferguson" was "buying cotton for Merrill and Magill—buying more than any other. We have several foreign buyers in our town. Some buying for foreign a/c. So terms are lively on cotton."[15]

In the same issue of the *Camden Daily Bulletin* mentioned earlier is an editorial entitled "A Manufactory in Camden." "The subject has already become one of earnest discussion," it reads. "We hope our townsmen will not let their interest in this important subject die out, but that they may astonish the world by actually going to work to add this much needed improvement to our city and surrounding country." The paper counsels against discouragement and negativism in regard to the important move. "How few enterprises of the kind we are here speaking of, have ever ended in failures when once gone into, especially when engaged with earnestness and zeal, and conducted with practical good sense?"[16]

It is not difficult to guess who one of the moving spirits behind this project was, for Merrell had returned to manufacturing by 1869. According to a letter Mrs. Merrell wrote to Archibald Smith, this factory started up in July 1869, and it was appropriately William Bell who helped Merrell install the steam engine that drove it: "You ask about the Factory in Camden. Uncle H. writes that he started the Engine & it works beautifully. Mr. Bell was moving down when he last wrote & they would start up as soon as he came."[17] This factory was apparently in an old brick building near the wharf at Camden, where wool was carded from 1869 to 1886.[18]

Merrell was clearly a leading businessman of Camden by 1868, for he introduced a resolution that was unanimously passed in a meeting of the merchants and business men of Camden on November 17. We can see Merrell's thought and style in the motion: "That as it respects the present government of the State of Arkansas, although it exists under the circumstances, against our suffrages, and (as we think) against our interests; yet, it is a *de facto* government, and as such, (so long as it acts within the legitimate scope of its own Constitution.) it is infinitely better than anarchy, and we counsel obedience to all its laws until repealed by authority."[19]

The *Camden Beacon* complimented Merrell on August 14, 1875: "Maj. Merrell sent us a package of flour last week ground at the city mills, from fine wheat, which we pronounce equal to Plants best."[20] The Sifford Scrapbooks include pictures of Major and Mrs. Merrell with the clipping.

Always active in Presbyterian church affairs wherever he lived, for the rest of his life Henry Merrell remained a pillar of the Camden Presbyterian Church, which he joined in October of 1867, becoming a ruling elder a month later.[21] The church frequently appointed him delegate to Presbytery meetings, and he was the only elder selected to represent the Southern Presbyterian church in the "Pan-Presbyterian Council" of Edinburgh in 1877. He kept a small travel diary about this trip, and he wrote a series of articles under the by-line "Back-County Elder at the Council" for the *South-Western Presbyterian* of New Orleans.[22]

Certainly the energy that he threw into the building of Royston and into the Confederate cause was directed in his later life both to Merrell and Magill and to the Presbyterian church. According to the obituary of Merrell written by the Reverend Eugene Daniel, a minister whom the Merrells had brought to Camden in 1871 and who was at the time the minister of the First Presbyterian Church in Memphis, Merrell was president of the area Bible Society and, as "Back-Country Elder," the author of a series of learned articles entitled "Retrenchment and Reform" in the *South-Western Presbyterian*.[23] Interestingly, the complements to these articles were those written by his brother-in-law Archibald Smith for the *Southern Presbyterian* of Columbia, South Carolina, as well as the *South-Western Presbyterian*, under the pen-name "Low Country Elder."

In an obituary that she published in the *South-Western Presbyterian*, Mrs. Merrell noted that her husband was a trustee of Southwestern University at Clarksville, Tennessee, and also of Batesville College (now Arkansas College), both Presbyterian institutions. She adds: "Being a true Presbyterian, he was also a true believer in a Republican form of government, for the writer has often heard him remark that the principles of our representative Republican government were derived from Presbyterianism, and that they are the only true safeguards of civil and religious liberty. He espoused the cause of the South in the late war, because he believed she was contending for these very principles, and he believed that since the war these principles were maintained in their purity only in the Southern Presbyterian Church."[24]

About the time he stopped writing his memoirs, Henry Merrell began writing a long, thinly veiled autobiographical novel, *The Refugees*, which he published in numbers in the *South-Western Presbyterian* from December 27, 1877, to April 15, 1880. Although the work is fiction, it may be read on one level as a continuation or amplification of these memoirs, for recognizable people, such as the Smiths, appear with different names, and if the reader is steeped enough in Merrell's family, friends, and adventures, the book may be read as a roman à clef. In the last part of his life Merrell visited the Smiths at Roswell at least four more times: in 1869, 1870, 1877, 1881. On the 1877 visit his nephew Archie twice took him to see the mills of the Roswell Manufacturing Company.[25]

At Merrell's invitation, his nephew John Merrell (1854–1933), son of his brother, Samuel (1822–1900), came to Camden about 1870 to work for Merrell and Magill. The young John Merrell would settle in Camden, join the Presbyterian Church there in 1872, and marry in 1875. It would appear from a draft of Merrell's will that he wanted John Merrell to inherit a large portion of his business and property following his wife's death, but after his own death Mrs. Merrell, her brother Charles Arthur Magill, and John Merrell agreed to settlements that left most of Merrell's property in her control. John Merrell moved to Prescott, Arkansas, following his uncle's death, then moved to Springfield, Massachusetts, about 1886.[26]

In later life Henry Merrell apparently became deeply interested in church order and church history. The minister of his own church said of him: "There is not a minister in the Church who could more intelligently tell of all the vicissitudes of Zion in all her past experience — her triumphs, her reverses, the various persecutions, the heresies, the Councils, the names of the Popes, the controversies, the Reformation — with all these things his mind was completely familiar."[27] Mrs. Merrell said, "He was well acquainted with ecclesiastical law, and made the constitution of his own Church a special study. He had read perhaps everything that had ever been published on the subject of Church order. . . . He was perfectly familiar with the whole history of the ecclesiastical controversies."[28]

His intellect and memory seemed to have impressed all who knew Henry Merrell. "In him the faculty of memory was even wonderfully developed," said his minister, Eugene Daniel. "With a natural taste for historical research, his mind grasped names and dates and facts with a firm hold, and retained them with a precision and fidelity that were simply marvelous. His wife remarked on his "extensive reading and acquaintance with the best authors" and "his marvelously retentive memory that was a magazine of knowledge, always full, always fresh, and always at his command — these things eminently qualified him for the social circle, and made him an interesting and instructive companion."[29]

Other people who knew him described him as a "gentleman of philanthropic views and notions — rather a reformer, I thought, but of a generous heart and disposition." Yet another observer commented, "Mr. Merrill was a man of fine intellect and held positions of peculiar honor and trust during the Confederacy." The editor of the *South-Western Presbyterian*, Henry M. Smith, commented, "He was no common man. Large-hearted, generous, clear in his convictions, and thoroughly loyal to principle, he was loved, respected and trusted wherever he was known."[30]

Merrell's health was not good during the last ten years of his life. His wife wrote to her sister Mrs. Smith in February of 1873 that her husband has been very ill recently and that they were planning a trip to New Orleans for his recovery. She says, "I do not mean you must not refer to his sickness when you write, but to its being a perhaps fatal sickness. He says it is so cruel to distress friends in that way. He will not let either his mother or brother know what is the matter with him." She concludes that

Camden, Arkansas, at the turn of the century. The camera is pointed west down Washington Street toward Merrell's residence. His business establishments were to the rear of the camera, in the wharf area at the foot of Washington Street. Photograph courtesy of Larry Morrison and the photo collection of Southern Arkansas University Tech, Camden, Arkansas.

he has been so sick recently that they could not have gone to New Orleans even if there had been a boat available. Her references in this letter to his coughing, to his debilitation, and even to the possibility of their going to Cuba for his recuperation make one suspect that Merrell had contracted either tuberculosis, which had killed his father, or "brown lung" disease from his years of manufacturing.[31] It was during this illness in 1873 that Merrell began his memoirs over again, thinking that he was on his death bed and believing that his earlier effort had been lost.

Merrell was well enough in 1877 to go to Edinburgh to the Pan Presbyterian Council, but as he got on board his ship to depart, he had a hemorrhage. In a small travel diary that he kept of the trip, he noted on June 21 "the first hemorrhage I have had in several years."[32] Yet he seemed to participate energetically in the affairs of the council and returned from it with the project of publishing his novel, *The Refugees*, which began running that December.

His death must have been sudden. Elizabeth Magill Merrell had left

Camden to travel to Georgia to help nurse her sister Helen, who had fallen and broken her hip. She was in Roswell at the Smith House when she received word from Camden that her husband had died on January 19, 1883.[33]

The minutes of the Camden Presbyterian Church note that he was characteristically active until the last. He reported his attendance as delegate to "the last meetings of Presbytery and Synod" on January 12. At its next meeting of January 29, following Merrell's death on January 19, the session officially mourned its loss of "a most efficient & faithful member who was thoroughly acquainted with ecclesiastical law & who ever manifested great interest in ecclesiastical matters & whose sound judgment & wise counsel will be sorely missed." In the loss of this "faithful and zealous" member, they stated on behalf of the church, "one of its pillars has been removed & this loss seems to be irreparable."[34]

The only copy of Henry Merrell's will that survives contains a paragraph that begins with directions that his body be interred as his wife thinks fit. But the paragraph concludes with a request that tells us something about the man, his life, his relocations, and his loyalties. He asked to be transplanted once more. He said, "I would, however, if perfectly convenient, prefer in due time to lie by the side of my sister Lucretia at Roswell, Ga., & near my first workmen Mr. Parker & Mr. Smith, who were very true to me at a trying time in my life, & I want their monument which was erected on the spot, to be kept in repair, & my name with theirs."[35]

This request was not carried out, and Merrell's grave was made in the Confederate Cemetery in Camden. Mrs. Elizabeth Magill Merrell prepared an inscription for her husband's stone which reads: "God calls his chosen home. For so he giveth his beloved sleep." The business firm of Merrell and Magill effectively ceased operating within a year of Merrell's death, and his partner Charles Arthur Magill himself passed away in Niles, Michigan, in 1884. Elizabeth Merrell remained in Arkansas until she was put to rest beside her husband in June 1890.

Freshly arrived from New York in steamy Savannah, Georgia, in May 1839, Henry Merrell stayed in a hotel room that had recently been occupied by two young ladies. He later noted the irony of the fact that one of these women later became his wife. She had come there from Florida. Here, he noted, were two people who would marry, one from near Canada, the other from the deepest South. Together, these transplanted Americans helped to settle the southwest frontier, and there they remained.

As for the central enterprise and most extraordinary accomplishment in a long life of enterprise and accomplishment, Merrell's Royston factory in the Pike County wilderness continued to operate after its builder's death. Following the Civil War, the machinery had been returned to Pike County from Mound Prairie, Texas, and Merrell's old partner, John Matlock, operated it so profitably that, in 1875, he built a large new mill on the site and a two-story mansion for himself facing the Little Missouri River. The population of Royston had reached two hundred by 1875, "with homes built close to the mill." [36]

About 1880, however, John Matlock began to have financial problems. He "became involved in litigation and the factory was sold in 1885 to satisfy an execution against him." [37] Legend has it, says *The Early History of Pike County*, that in 1886 John Matlock "went across the river and buried what money he had, then came back to his house and took poison. Others say that he died by shooting himself." [38] The *Nashville News* of June 12, 1886, records that Matlock "committed suicide last Monday by taking an overdose of morphine." [39] By 1890, a single tenant occupied Matlock's fine mansion, and all of the other houses at Royston were "falling rapidly into ruin and decay." [40]

The *Southern Standard*, of Arkadelphia, Arkansas, had reported in March of 1888 that negotiations were then underway to move the Merrell-Matlock factory to Arkadelphia. A joint stock company had been formed there, it seems, which had "purchased the Pike county mills, known as the Royston cotton factory, whose entire property consists of one of the most magnificent and by far the most capable and desirable water powers for manufacturing purposes anywhere to be found in southwestern Arkansas." The paper records that the cotton mill machinery "is now being taken to pieces to be shipped under a contract with the lowest bidder for removing it to this place by June 1st." [41]

Perhaps most of the machinery had been removed by late May. If much was remaining, it was to be lost, together with almost everything that Merrell had built. The *Nashville News* of June 2, 1888, records the destruction of the Royston factory on May 27. Two days of torrential rains had brought the Little Missouri to "the biggest rise for years past." "Some of the oldest citizens" maintained that "the river was higher than it has been since 1848; others say since 1874," but all admitted "that it is by far the most destructive of any previous one." The community lost fencing, stock, and houses, and most of Merrell's enterprise was carried away by the rampaging waters. [42]

Thereafter, Royston was abandoned. But the fourteen-inch oak sills and their iron connecting rods that Merrell laid as the foundation for his re-

Henry and Elizabeth Merrell, probably taken during the 1870s.

markable venture can still be seen on the river bottom, marking to this day the wilderness location that he chose in order to repair his ruined fortunes over one hundred and thirty-five years ago.

This site is, finally, the most fitting memorial for a Victorian missionary of industry who cut himself off from his native North to come to the South with an idea and a hope, which, if adopted by more southerners, may have led the region down a different road from the one it took. But for himself, though he never mentioned it, Henry Merrell would have readily accepted for his own the motto of the New England state of Connecticut from which his own ancestors had moved to New York: *Qui transtulit sustinet* — "He who transplants, sustains."

Appendix

[Merrell pasted into his text at chapter 37 two series of newspaper articles on manufacturing that he wrote in 1847 and 1855 while he was in Greene County, Georgia.
These articles are reprinted as they appeared in the *Milledgeville (Southern) Recorder*
and the *New York Journal of Commerce*. The dates, numbers, and pages of these
articles are listed in the Bibliography under Merrell's name. The Milledgeville
series did not extend beyond four articles.]

CHAPTER 37

Before I take my reader with me to Arkansas, I cannot, perhaps, better illustrate
what I have said about the decline of manufacturing in Georgia, than by tacking
into these pages some news-paper articles from my pen, which I find preserved
among my papers.

1847 Milledgeville *Recorder*, Ga.

Communicated.

MANUFACTURING IN SOBER EARNEST.

No. I.

Messrs. Editors: — The business of manufacturing at the South, whether we consider it as a new way for employing capital, or as accessory to local interests and the
general good — as a means of livelihood with individuals, or for the improvement
of classes — view it in any way, if divested of its present novelty, and the "pomp
and circumstance" of chartered companies, becomes at last like any other business:
a question of profit and loss, of success or failure; and like any other business, it
must make or lose agreeable to the times, and *very much* according as it is well and
skillfully followed.

Considering that we are now engaged with the question of success — more so
than at any former stage of our business — it becomes an object of deep solicitude with all concerned, to know the difficulties we have to encounter, and their
remedies, as far as there may be remedies for the same. We are often asked now-a-
days (as often as anyway by very good factory stockholders themselves) "Well! how
comes on the spinning and weaving these times? How does the price of cotton
serve you? Cut down the profits a button hole — eh!?" Of course, we put a good
face upon the matter; but to tell the truth, not only cotton, but the price of every
other article that we consume, is higher than we can afford until we are paid better
prices for the goods we make.

And why do not our prices go up in proportion to the expense of manufacturing? What is the reason that our business does not participate in the general prosperity? Is there anything about the manufacturing interest that is antagonistic to the general good, so that one must be depressed to promote the other? Not at all! Then some adverse influences must be at work, and it becomes a matter of self-preservation to find them out and oppose them in every proper way.

Several new cotton factories have very recently gone into successful operation in our State. These are for the present mostly engaged in spinning "Thread" for the Southern market and they are, in connection with those before at the same business, making *too much thread.* — This is the reason why we cannot now get former remunerating prices. But it does not follow, because we are over doing a single branch of our business, that we have reached the ultimatum of Southern manufacturing — on the contrary, we think it but just begun. This is only one instance among many, where we are gaining that wisdom through experience which is essential to success. There is now much more of the one article, thread, made in the State and Georgia, than is consumed within the same limits. For several years past, the consumption of thread in this region has undoubtedly diminished, so that although the spinning by hands is much less than formerly, our increase of manufacturing has outstripped the demand for Factory thread.

The causes operating to lessen the demand for thread are consequent upon the increasing prosperity of the State; therefore there is no prospect of a change and no desire that there should be one. But no doubt, as the country improves, the people in better circumstance and education different, the ladies will get altogether above weaving at home, and the gentlemen above wearing their homespun if they make it — or what is more reasonable still, they will all have learned the truth that it is neither "polite or wise" to keep the gentler sex at home in bondage to the loom and distaff, while the Factories stand ready to furnish better goods ready woven, at a less price, and glad to take produce in return. Such has been the invariable result in other sections of our country where manufacturing and the mechanic have the time and opportunity for development. The "good old way" of doing things by hand has been gradually superseded, domestic affairs simplified, and the necessaries of life, as well as many of its luxuries, brought within the means of all because cheaper and more easily paid for than before.

The same causes are now in operation here, and we are glad to see it. The new facilities for transportation to all the up-country have made near markets for small planters, where their produce (not only cotton, but grain and almost any of the products of the soil) is easily convertible into money, or what is still better, into the necessaries of life; while the same process of transportation has so much reduced the cost of those supplies, that the purchasers are made comparatively rich, and can very well afford for the future to live without that hard economy which condemns the females of a family to profitless drudgery at the loom.

The gradual failure in the demand for thread indicates therefore a good state of things in the country, but it is "death to us" unless we can find a remedy. As we observed in the commencement, we consider the business of manufacturing yet in its infancy at the South. There is room for its almost unlimited increase; but the period of infancy is one of peculiar helplessness, and the greatest care will be necessary if we would bring it to ultimate success.   M.

GREENSBORO', 23rd March, 1847.

[To be continued.]

For the Recorder.

MANUFACTURING IN SOBER EARNEST.

No. II.

We have seen, that owing to recent increase of operations, together with a certain falling off in the demand for *thread*, the young and vigorous manufactures of our state, in the midst of superior advantages—just starting in life with anticipations of a prosperous career, suddenly feel the heavy hand of competition—not from abroad, but with ourselves! Paradoxical as it may seem, in infancy we have become old. We are now suffering from over production and the other evils of high competition, not less than the old established manufactories of the Northern States.

The legitimate remedy for over production is to make less, or find a new market for the article. The *preventive*, which in our case would undoubtedly have been the safer course, is to scatter—to diversify our employments, and not limit ourselves to the one or two branches of this business, with which we have been hitherto almost exclusively occupied. And it is a matter of surprise that all this did not occur to our minds a year ago, while we were planning the increase of our business, and before the mischief was done. But so it is ever with human foresight. The Vicar of Wakefield's picture was too large for any room in his house, and Robinson Crusoe's boat too far from the water to be of service when completed.

For several years past, the manufacture of thread in our State has exceeded the demand for consumption within the same limits. None has been brought from the North; on the contrary, during every summer season, it has been found necessary to ship more or less to the North in order to prevent it accumulating here, a dead weight upon our market for the ensuing seasons. What room then was there for additional factories to turn off more of the same kind of goods? Nevertheless the business has recently very much increased, and the consequence is such as might have been expected. At present this is most burdensome to small concerns, and others long established. Factories with large capital and more improved machinery will always possess advantages; but it is a melancholy state of prosperity—quite necessary in the present case, that the moderate success of a few must be disastrous to all the rest.

Every man in Georgia knows from experience the compound lever power with which a small surplus in any article will depress the business of the producer. The consequence in our case has been to depress the manufacturing business at a crisis of its destiny—at a time when its future greatness would seem to depend upon present success. Cotton, our raw material, has unexpectedly advanced in price, and with it almost every item of cost in its manufacture. We see indications of renewed prosperity in every other department of business — but our own does not respond. We struggle for prices corresponding to the advance in cost, but with only partial success. We turn another way and endeavor to economize in the details of business, but competition here also bars the hope of amendment, and we are obliged to see that some change must be effected in the physical constitution of our Factory system.

It is not necessary that manufacturers should be the natural enemies of each other, as they now certainly feel or suspect themselves to be. There is room enough here for all now concerned; also for as many as will be likely to embark in the business for years to come; but there must be some system observed by which they will not all be crowded into one branch of the business, while others equally promising remain untried.

The error is now that we have persisted too long in the one idea of spinning thread; rapidly increasing the quantity, while the demand in our own proper market gives signs of decrease almost as great. This proposition cannot, at the present time, be too distinctly understood. The remedy is in our own hands. We are not at all helpless in the matter — as it will be our object in another number of this series to show; but it is in the meantime exceedingly desirable that those who are about commencing to manufacture in our State, or who contemplate an increase of business already begun, should understand this matter well enough to take up some one amongst the numerous branches of this business which will not clash with those already engaged.   M.

GREENSBORO', April 5th, 1847.

[To be continued.]

For the Recorder.
Manufacturing in Sober Earnest.
No. III.

Next to the evil of over production in our one leading article, the greatest difficulty with manufacturers at present grows out of our relations toward each other — if, indeed, we may be said to have any relations towards each other where each one acts for himself without regard for the general welfare or even to his own future good.

The reserve and distrust that characterize our intercourse with each other, although naturally enough engendered by a state of competition, are very far from the right spirit for mutual aid and comfort. The great success of Factories at Lowell, and in every other manufacturing town, is owing mainly, if not altogether, to the *advantages of competition* rightly understood and kept under good control. Picture to yourself the comforts of manufacturing in a city or county wholly devoted to the business. Forty factories all prosperous and neighbourly, reciprocating favors, rendering prompt assistance in times of accident or danger, and seldom governed by any worse feeling than a right spirit of emulation. You have facilities for the construction, the repairs, and the supply of our works, with superior economy and skill in every department. You have daily intercourse with men superior to yourself in science, skill and capacity, with whom you consult about your difficulties or debate the merits of an improvement. You enjoy uniform practice in the wages and discipline of hands, in the purchase of material and the disposal of goods; and you have it well understood by all parties, and their hearty co-operation is necessary to the general good. This looks like the Eutopian dream of a manufacturer; but it is not — it is the real life of numerous manufacturing towns and counties in our own country as well as abroad — nor is it difficult to imagine how the same good understanding might pervade the limited manufactures of a whole State like ours with equal benefit to all concerned.

During the past year or two, and especially since we have been made sensible of interfering with each other, it has come to be generally admitted that something of a community must be made of the manufacturing interest here, in order to have any further advancement, or even to hold that which we have already achieved. Several praiseworthy efforts have been made towards this object, but with indifferent success — so much so, that it is clear that the measures taken were not of a kind suited to the end in view.

It is said that matters of this kind will regulate themselves, and so they do in time. They cannot be controlled by arbitrary enactments, yet nothing of the kind ever "regulated itself" without either physical or moral agencies of some sort; therefore we must study our interests and aid nature by the active use of remedies. In the present case, it seems the best thing to be recommended, that we notice the ways and profit by the experience of those at the North — our countrymen — who are many years our seniors in the business, and have been successful to a degree proverbial the world over. At the same time, we should discriminate rightly, and adapt their maxims to the circumstances in which we are placed; for it is worthy of special notice, that there are some matters peculiar to southern manufacturing, which it requires a southern experience to understand.

The tone of our business was impaired at the outset by a certain smallness, or rather a want of dignity in making arrangements. This was perhaps unavoidable in a small beginning; but it served to establish some very bad precedents, and we should see to it, that practices which crept into our affairs in early times, before the Indians left, are not suffered to hang about us, to our manifest injury and reproach, long after the circumstances which brought them into use have died away with the past.

For instance What propriety is there in selling your thread and osnaburgs at first hands on time? Especially goods which devour such immense proportions of the raw material! — Your Factory costs a sweet sum of money to begin with. Cotton is a cash article, and every item of your expense is equal to cash. Are not fabrics thus made, as it were, of gold dust, entitled to as much respect in our market as corn and bacon? It is dreadful to be under the necessity of superadding to the proper capital of every manufacturing company a large surplus of the purposes of general credit. — If credit must be extended to the consumer and to the country merchant, that is a business to itself; it belongs to another set of men, and a very precarious business it is — without better facilities for knowing whom to trust than most manufacturers can command. Right here our profits are very much cut down, and the permanency of the manufacturing interests really endangered. Few manufacturers, making their own sales on time, with the present inducements to favor customers, will realize enough, over and above the cash value of their goods, to cover all risks and the interest; much less will they be able to divide upon a large floating capital the profits which stock-holders expect from their investment.

Our products are as precious to us as cotton is to the planter, and we can no better afford to wait for the money, because we have daily use for it. The present awkward and unmerchantlike arrangements by which our excellent goods are put out for retail on commission, or hawked about and peddled in wagons, and each manufacturer compelled to act as broker, commission-merchant, jobber and peddler, now and then leaving his business to ride over the country drumming new customers and dunning for his money — this bad arrangement, with which no one is satisfied yet all persist in, is one of the relics of barbarism that have been entailed upon us, innocently enough, by our fathers in the business, but which is certainly "more honored in the breach than in the observance."   M.

GREENSBORO, 15th April, 1847.

[To be continued.]

For the Recorder.
MANUFACTURING IN SOBER EARNEST.
No. IV

From being accustomed to witness the great anxiety of manufacturers to sell, customers have come to regard it as a favor if they take our goods on any terms.

We have seen the Factory travelling-agent turned away from the merchant's door like a mendicant, or a strange man with a subscription paper.

The merchant had perhaps been deceived by some other travelling agent, or by the manufacturer himself, and was very justly incensed; or it may be that he had become principled against goods which are peddled through the country, or set down at every cross road, to the manifest injury of the regular trade. In this manner, no doubt, very innocent persons have been made to feel quite guilty for offering to sell — not a forged acceptance or a counterfeit note — but an honest bale of factory goods, that are, as far as they go, if rightly considered, an honor and a blessing to the State.

During short periods of scarcity, there has been better demand; but generally speaking, such is the estimation in which our manufacturers have been held, especially the article of thread. This is no fault of the country merchant, for it is not his business to appreciate our goods. Our business and the products of our machinery will be honored by others precisely according to our own dignity and self-respect. Let us then accustom ourselves to look upon goods of our own manufacture as inferior to nothing else in importance, and no matter whether they are in brisk demand, or accumulating for want of purchasers, hold them to be as good property as the cotton on hand, or money in the pocket.

Is it not wonderful that men can calculate to gain anything by underselling below the fair value of their goods? The poorest salesman in the world can come down, and gain a temporary advantage by relinquishing a portion of his profits; but it is a shallow artifice, soon found out, and when others have come down also, he is utterly helpless to gain what he had lost.

Every manufacturer who reads this, will say at once that it is the very thing he has been trying all along to get at, but that someone in particular, or all the rest together, are pulling the other way. He has several times promised to abide by certain prices, and perhaps went to a convention; but directly finding that he was to be only a "cat's paw" for others, he did like the rest, and sold at any price he could get. And in this he is really sincere, although he may have been himself the first to knock under.

It seems to the writer, that all arbitrary arrangements for the regulation of prices and terms are contrary to the spirit of trade, and in our own case sure to fail through want of confidence between parties. They are especially injurious when accounted through a public meeting, or in such a manner as to provoke ridicule or excite suspicion of monopoly. It was once rumored in the country that a certain sea-port town had established a "chamber of commerce" to regulate business. What sort of a tribunal it might be no one pretended to understand, and it was doubtless a very inoffensive thing, having no improper designs whatever; yet it was so misunderstood or misrepresented by rivals, that had it been the Inquisition itself it could not more effectually have turned away the current of trade from that city.

If, then, combinations are powerless and even injurious, and there is no hope of independent action, are not manufacturers utterly powerless in their own behalf? We think not, but will hardly undertake to recommend where there is certainty of doing no good. If certain leading *principles* relating to our affairs could be stated to the satisfaction of all parties, buyers as well as sellers understood to be mutually advantageous, and kept fixed and unchangeable before their minds, the success of our business could be reduced to a demonstration. No doubt of it. — The general prevalence of one right idea is worth more in such a case than an army with banners. But perhaps as good a way as any will be to wait patiently for the legitimate results of the present state of things, and afterwards all start fair again. At the present rate confusion will soon be "worse confounded." During the coming summer, several factories in Georgia will stop altogether or in part, because either too old, too small, or too slow to be profitable: or for the reason that they have too much money "coming to them;" and it will not be surprising if a few, when compelled to value property agreeably to the times, and allow the wear and tear of machinery, should discover that they are broke — and have been so for some time, but they did not know it.

As we remarked before, no doubt new or extensive works with improved machinery will have very good success, especially if they make it a cash business. But we trust that no new beginners will have the hardihood to embark in the manufacture of Thread. Let the present surplus of the article be shipped off to distant markets, until looms can be procured to weave it into coarse fabrics, for which there seems to be an increasing demand; and if new factories about to be erected will take up the finer branches of the business, we venture to promise that in a very short time the manufacturing interests of our State will rally and present a new and formidable front which shall not only suppress disaffection in our own ranks, but repel competition from abroad, like the invasion of a foreign enemy.   M.

GREENSBORO', 21 April, 1847.

[To be continued.]

(For the New York Journal of Commerce.)

COTTON MANUFACTURING IN GEORGIA.

No. 1.

The past two or three years have been a critical period to this important interest. — What may be said of Georgia in this respect, is doubtless more or less true of all the Southern states where cotton manufacturing exists.

It is self evident that the manufacture of cotton, at least into the coarser and more simple fabrics is the legitimate business for any surplus capital that the cotton plants may possess, provided the same can be made profitable. Undoubtedly the "up country" of Georgia is well adapted, in every essential particular, to this business: and in one important respect, to wit, in a mild and equable climate, it has greatly the advantage of any Northern or Eastern State. It has therefore seemed to many wise and public-spirited men at the South, that there must be the same fitness in spinning cotton in Georgia where it grows, that there is in grinding wheat in our own "Genessee County"; in either case, saving the transportation by nearing the fields which produce the raw material. They have thought it as poor economy to send cotton to the North to be spun and brought back at their expense, in the shape of goods, as it would be for the Genessee farmer to send his wheat to the South to be ground, and sent back for consumption in the shape of flour. With some qualifications, this was undoubtedly the correct view for them to take; and it was this sensible idea of Georgia, and has nourished it until at length the very large amount of capital at stake renders its ill success a matter of serious consideration.

At this time, there are about fifty factories in the State of Georgia. Some of them small, illy constructed, and worse managed: — others of the very best machinery and construction and as large as factories ever ought to be. As before stated, the past two or three years have been very hard upon these factories, so at this time a number of them are stopped, others partially so, under circumstances of discouragement so great as to render it very uncertain whether they will ever resume operations without a radical change of ownership and management.

It is a pity that it should be so, — for, apart from the interests of those who have invested there with the hope of honest gain, the stoppage of these works will be a public loss. Just such a loss as will be more deeply felt and appreciated by the public after it shall have transpired, than it would be possible for any public to understand in anticipation. These factories have been doing a good work in the South, leaving much good yet undone which they might do if they had prosperity. They have, in common with the Railroads, diverted a proportion of capital from the business of planting, thereby helping to limit the production of cotton to something like the wants of the world,—otherwise the crop of the Southern States might have reached 4,000,000 bales per annum, selling at 5 cents per pound, instead of 3,000,000 bales at 10¢ per pound. They have increased the consumption of cotton by bringing into favor styles of cotton goods, such as osnaburgs, bags and cordage, in the place of linen and hemp. They have forced into active employment, and into something like discipline, a very unruly and unproductive class of white population, who, when idle, are, to say the least, no friends of the planter. There are now no paupers, to speak of, in any county of Georgia where a cotton factory exists. By employing the children of such, factories preserve their parents from want. It may be estimated that during the late scarcity of food which has run through two years, the factories in Georgia have saved the state from a poor tax which would otherwise have exceeded all other taxes put together.

Within the writer's memory, which goes back fifteen years, the factories of Georgia have by competition among themselves, not only improved the clothing of the negro, but they have reduced its cost quite to one-half the old rates. When we add to all this, the fact that those factories provide each a local market for numerous items of surplus provisions, (in the aggregate a large sum), which would otherwise bear no value, we may be justified in declaring that they have proven themselves to be (in the sense of political economy) perhaps the most productive of all the productive interests at the South.

All these considerations are of importance in the economy of any State:—therefore it is to be regretted on behalf of the commonwealth, as well as of individuals, that so important and useful an interest should be so depressed. Indeed it ought not to be so. There is no necessity that it should be so.

PROFIT AND LOSS

[To be Continued.]

For the Journal of Commerce.
COTTON MANUFACTURING IN GEORGIA.
No. 2

It is to be regretted that the Southern manufacturer, who has a peculiarly arduous and responsible calling, should enjoy so little permanent success. Nevertheless, it is all natural and regular, and precisely in accordance with the history of manufacturing elsewhere. It is the old story, as familiar to the New England man as to the Georgians; which may be told something on this wise.

In the course of events, a certain neighborhood, or a village, or a county, as the case may be, becomes ripe for a fresh enterprise. What shall it be? The Railroad is finished and paid for; and having arrived at that age when repairs and material decay begin to absorb the profits, stock is below par, and no more of that is to be undertaken. A Cotton Factory is the next thing to a railroad in the succession of Southern ideas, and very properly so. The Factory is decided upon; about half money enough paid in. The worst possible location is selected, in order to favor the predominating interest, and mistakes or whims prevail throughout the construction, frittering away all advantages. In spite of all this, however, some money is made at first, and so long as everything is in good repairs, — yet not half so much as ought to have been made, considering the advantages of a Southern location.

The Factory proves to be a great curiosity, and a plaything for its stockholders. They cannot keep away from it. They purchase books on the subject, and read them. They bring troops of friends, unto whom they explain the mechanical operations, not perhaps in the most lucid manner, yet with sufficient unction. They insist upon calling the workpeople "operatives." So precious to them is the property, for a season, that if they insure it against fire, they wish the Insurance Company itself insured against failure, — while at the same time they feel it to be an outrage upon the dignity of stockholdership, should they be required not to smoke their cigars in the lint-room.

Shortly comes Dividend No. 1. Great excitement. That dividend is looked upon as better money than other money. Dividend No. 2 follows; the great inflation. Our village becomes an epitome of Wall Street. The stock goes above all prices. Other factories are projected upon the strength of this one. The manager, a clever Northern man, gets his head turned, buys a horse, and rides at a gallop; becomes a great man and is talked of for the office of Sheriff. Of course, Dividend No. 3 is not forthcoming. Thereupon ends forever the overweening popularity of the Cotton Factory, and henceforward it suffers by neglect and disgust, just by so much the more as it was at first over-rated.

The manager is disgraced. His functions devolve upon a board of directors, very good men in their way, but no manufacturers, nor the sons of manufacturers. Disastrous consequences ensue, because this is peculiarly a business which, perhaps more than any other, requires experienced and steady management in order to succeed.

The unfortunate factory finally passes, at a reduced cost, into other hands, who succeed with it either better or worse, according as they profit by the experience of their predecessors.

The preceding observations relate to a class of small establishments, which take their rise during the early history of manufacturing in every State. It is not intended, however, to make the impression that all such are invariably unsuccessful. On the contrary, there are to be found among that class, many instances of unostentatious, plodding industry, attended with permanent success. Indeed, it may here be remarked, that perhaps the most meritorious of all manufacturers, whether of cotton or of any other raw material, and the most successful according to the amount of capital invested is a small, neat, and well managed establishment, owned by one man or one family, who are not above their business, and have the skill within themselves, from father to son, to carry it on like a plantation — always. The most conspicuous manufacturers in Great Britain and France, have grown up from this very class, by natural increase, and have founded families surpassing worth and influence. The most notable instance is that of the late Sir Robert Peel, whose father dug with his own hard hands, the ditch that conveyed water to his factory.

We now pass on to the "secondary formation" in the Natural History of Manufacturing.

Large Factories succeed the little ones, in the hope of over-shadowing them or swallowing them up; upon the rule that, "if a little is good, a great deal must be better." But it is to be observed, that Factories, like Hotels, sometimes many get to be too large: — so very large, indeed, as to exceed the capacity of the man to manage, and of the location to support. Now it is undoubtedly true that in very favorable locations, where skillful labor, water power, and the source of supply, are already fixed and established, the large companies with extensive works do have the advantage. Yet it does not always follow, even in large manufacturing towns, that the greatest establishments return the greatest profits in proportion to the capital invested. Management is everything there, as it is elsewhere.

Large companies, with large cotton factories, have succeeded in effecting a permanent "stand," even in some of the Southern States. There are several such in South Carolina and Georgia. Their successes are due mainly to the indomitable perseverance of some one or two men, who have served as salt and ballast in such Company, through evil report and through good report. When you meet these men, you may distinguish them from the rest by the deep lines of responsibility and care, and the premature "gray hairs here and there upon them." It is to such men, (seldom appreciated until they are gone), that those prosperous companies owe that success which is now confirmed, we trust, past ordinary contingency. So long as they go on, demonstrating by their results what may be done by good management, there is no ultimate danger to the cause of Southern manufacturing. But should they also pine away, then indeed the shadow will go back many degrees upon the sunny dial-plate of Southern prosperity; for we hold that no State can be independently wealthy, and prepared for war as well as peace, which is altogether dependent upon other States, for the consumption of its products, and the furnishing its supplies.

The writer does not name those institutions referred to as prosperous at the South, because it is not the object of this article to puff any, or to damage any; but to do some good, by discussing the real causes of the successes and the failures. There have been, we are sorry to say, some instances of bad management on large capital and big factories, so notorious and conspicuous as to bring others besides themselves into disrepute, casting a dark shadow of discouragement over many who might otherwise have achieved success.

The writer met, only the other day, an old man, a stranger, whose experience, as he narrated it in touching and simple style, illustrates sufficiently the whole thing.

The old gentleman said that, by dint of hard work and saving in the retail line for many years, the prime of his life, he had at last attained the darling object of his toils—rest. Having converted all his property into cash, he knew exactly what he was worth, and now he had nothing to do but to invest it judiciously for income, and spend the remainder of his days, free from care, in the society of his only child, a daughter. This was several years ago. He determined to do nothing rashly, but to take plenty of time in making his investments. He consulted the richest and most knowing men, and worked himself up to be, as he fancied, one of the shrewdest and most cautious of men. By no means would he "put all his eggs into one basket."

The result was, that he invested as follows, viz:

1st. Ten thousand dollars in a Railroad Company, because its stock was above par, and that was a good sign. His railroad soon after required all its profits, years in advance, to lay down new iron and cross-ties.

2nd. Ten thousand dollars in a famous Marine Insurance Co. for that also was above par;—but directly the storms on the ocean converted the "floating capital" of that Company into a "sinking fund."

His 3d and last investment was made with extreme caution. He was recommended to put it into a Cotton Factory already permanently established; but, improving upon that advice, he put it into a new one, of large capital and huge dimensions, that was to swallow up all the small ones,—which, in truth, it has done in a measure, like Pharaoh's lean kine, without any benefit to itself. These works were as yet but partly under way, all new and beautiful to look at. Money was plenty, as it always is when capital is first paid in; and not even the bookkeeper himself could exactly distinguish between what was profit and what was capital stock. The President informed him confidentially, (what he no doubt believed to be true), that they were afraid to make as large dividends as they could, for fear of inflation. Our aged friend invested his other $10,000 in this Company, and it proved to be the worst operation of the three. It turned out that the location was sickly, the water-power only half enough to drive all the works when completed, the legitimate supply of hands inadequate, provisions entirely too high for poor people to live by, and the morals of the place such as to be wholly incompatible with prosperity. Money was sunk, not made. The consequence has been, divided councils in the Board, stormy meetings of the stockholders, no dividends, of course; until now, he does not believe that any one can be found, who would be willing to take the whole concern as a gift, and be obliged to carry it on in its present unfortunate location.

We turned from the old man, and went away in sorrow; for under all his disappointments, he expressed no feelings of acrimony or revenge.

PROFIT AND LOSS

[To be Continued.]

For the Journal of Commerce.
COTTON MANUFACTURING IN GEORGIA.
No. 3.

We stated at the outset that the present unhappy depression of the manufacturing interest at the South, is all perfectly natural, and regular, and in accordance with the history of manufacturing elsewhere. The remedy has been Time — Experience — Industry — which having conquered like difficulties elsewhere, will not fail us here.

That same progression which enables the plants now to raise five bales of good cotton, with the means that produced one poor bale of cotton forty years ago, will make a good manufacturer of his son by and by.

As to the failure: — the giving up of the idea of a Southern manufacturing system: that is not be thought of. The advantages of the Southern manufacturer are manifestly too great to be relinquished because of one or more failures. Had he the hard Northern winters to contend against, locking him up from commerce four months of the year; an agrarian white population, half foreigners, to subdue; provisions to bring from the Western States, timber from Georgia, and cotton from the far off Mississippi, like the manufacturer of Massachusetts, he might have reason to despond: but since he has nothing but his own blunders to rectify, and nature is still favorable to him, let him be encouraged to try again. The causes of his ill success hitherto might be summed up in one phrase: — viz. "Amateur manufacturing" by gentlemen who know nothing about the business; but it may be profitable to specify more particularly.

So long as the factories were few in Georgia, and no more goods were produced than could be sold at home, money enough was made under any sort of management. Before the construction of Railroads, provisions and labor and cotton were very low in remote sections of the Southern States, and goods, on the other hand, were very high indeed. The original factories, therefore, were constructed without much regard to those improvements in machinery which economize labor and raw materials. Railroads, however, wrought a speedy change in these respects. By fetching the plantation nearer to the sea-board, the value of cotton increased; substituting broad-cloth for copperas colored homespuns in the back woods of Georgia, they brought the Southern manufacturer, in his feebleness, into direct competition with the most powerful competitors now in the world, viz., the Northern manufacturer, with none of that protection from government which the Northern manufacturer enjoyed under like circumstances, in his infant struggle against foreign competition.

Under these circumstances, ten years ago and for several years following, the manufacturers in Georgia found themselves under the necessity of increasing their capital and adopting the best improvements in machinery, in order to meet the exigencies of the times. In doing so they increased likewise the production of their particular styles of goods beyond the home consumption. Shipping a large surplus of these goods to the Northern markets, brought them still more into direct competition with the Northern manufacturers, — under this very great disadvantage in a large market, that the Southern goods, though made of the better material, and as the saying is, "upon honor," were much less sightly, and less skillfully made. Unsatisfactory sales were the result.

In the meantime, the manufacturers, instead of following any system, or cooperating in any way for the common good, fatally mistook each other for enemies, and ran against each other, beating down the prices of goods, (already too low) and tampering with each other's work people until they became worthless, and a good day's work could not be had for a good day's wages. So far as this want of charity towards each other may have contributed to their common misfortunes, no doubt they deserve bad luck: but those other evils, imperfect goods and bad salesmanship, were precisely the kind of evils to be corrected by experience. The manufacturers (at least those among them who will ever learn anything by experience), have well nigh mastered these defects; when the late scarcity of provisions supervened to test once more to the very utmost their powers of endurance. For, whatever the price of food, the manufacturer must foot the bill; unless he would have his hands go upon the county or parish, as they do in England.

Under this last and most helpless pressure, several of the factories in Georgia have become silent, perhaps forever. Others have gone on, content to make little or nothing, rather than disorganize; and a few have made money, but not so much as they could wish.

This is the present condition of manufacturing in Georgia. Where it will end, remains to be seen. The indications are, that the worst is over. The incoming crops are very promising, and provisions will be low enough soon. The stoppage of so many factories must reduce the production of goods within bounds; and it is to be hoped that manufacturers will learn from the past, among other things, that it is for their advantage to co-operate for each other's benefit. We shall see.

As might be expected, the temporary ill success of manufacturing in Georgia has disappointed and embittered many, who can see no more good in it. They would feel the want of it directly, should their wishes be fulfilled in its extermination. But any such result as that, is past the power of such men to accomplish. There is by this time too much capital concerned, there are too many local advantages involved, for this important interest to suffer elision, without violence to the commonwealth. The business of cotton manufacturing in Georgia is not obliged to be carried on to ultimate prosperity; into whose hands it may pass before that time, is another question.

There ought to have been rendered in its proper place, another reason for discouragement, and we will also add, discontent also, among these manufacturers. They had never asked protection, and therefore did not look for proscription at the hands of their State government. They asked only to be let alone. Struggling against foreign and Northern competition combined, with none of that protection from Government which the English and the Northern manufacturer each enjoyed from their respective governments under like circumstances, they felt that they had need of all the chances for success. It was with dismay therefore, they learned, after it was sumptuary law, limiting their hours of work: — and in a peculiar manner too, "from sun rise to sun set," — which renders the law intolerable. For the winter, when the cotton is at the door, is the harvest time to the Southern manufacturer. At that season of the year, daylight is very short. Again, in winter the hands are best able to work long hours: in summer they are debilitated. It is very much as though the miller should be required by law to stop his mill when the grain comes in, and run it more than he likes when there is no grain to be had.

Many thousands of dollars were sunk last winter by the manufacturers of Georgia in an honest endeavor to keep that law. But seeing ruin staring them in the face, and their hands about to be thrown upon the public for support, the greater part concluded to break through the law, at any risk, resuming customary operations. Those who continued to observe it, made losses from which they will not recover. The law was ill-timed, even if it was right. It was to the manufacturer like the last feather which broke the camel's back. But what is most provoking about it, is the fact that there was not public demand for such a law; only some local demagoguing such as was not supposed to have any influence in Georgia. It is not surprising that such enactments should prevail in sections of the country where lawmakers are made and unmade by the votes of foreigners, fresh reeking from the great European struggle of labor against capital—the poor against the rich: but Georgia has not that radical and agrarian element in its population—the negroes keep it away. But even if it were not so,—if the foreigners were creeping into our very kneading-troughs, there would be no occasion for statutory laws, in this free country, to protect labor against capital. Free labor is here every way competent to protect itself; and every day tends to tyranny. There is far more need for laws to protect the small capital of our country against the aggressions of labor:—but alas! Capital can't vote, but labor can vote, with a confusion of tongues. However, as before stated, it is not so in Georgia, and never will be. It is therefore deeply to be regretted that the State, whose province it is to cherish those great conservative interests which pay the taxes and support the State, should so inopportunely have used its power contrarywise.

These articles, already longer than was intended, must close. Should they meet the eye of any Southern man who is interested in the manufacturing business, the object of the writer has been gained, if his remarks throw any new light upon the subject in a manner to revive drooping spirits, and contribute to better success in the future.

PROFIT AND LOSS

For the Journal of Commerce.
COTTON MANUFACTURING IN GEORGIA.
No. 4.

The preceding articles under this head, written in too much haste, have missed at least one important consideration, which the writer thinks it best to bring forward at the risk of over-writing his subject. For this he asks the reader's indulgence.

The effects of recent "*Hard Times*" upon the manufacturing interest of Georgia.

The former No.'s of this series limited the discussion to matters concerning Southern manufactures as distinct from cotton manufacturing elsewhere; and irrespective of those considerations which bear upon all alike,—at the South and at the North equally. The impression intended to be made was distinctly this; that as compared with manufacturers in their early struggle for a footing elsewhere, at the North, and we may add in Europe also, the Southern manufacturer, so far, has at least shown himself to be a match for other pioneers, and considering that he has achieved so much, not only without that aid or protection from government which Northern and British manufactures early enjoyed, — but in spite of laws that discriminate against him, there must be some genuine advantages about his Southern location.

It might be inferred from the preceding remarks that Southern manufacturers alone have suffered depression during the recent hard times — but that is not so. The truth is the late intolerably high prices of provisions and money have depressed the business everywhere, and it is not believed that the Southern manufacturing interest has suffered more than others except for lack of an adequate floating capital. For it must be borne in mind that "hard times" are the best of times to those who are not in debt, and have ready money to take all the advantages.

Few of the Southern factories have any floating capital. Many are in debt even for part of their capital stock never paid in, but borrowed. Those that have sufficient capital find little fault with the times. But those who have usurious interest and discounts to pay, and are constrained to make disadvantageous sales of their goods in order to raise the wind — whether at the North or at the South — cannot make much headway against hard times, — if they could, they have a better business than any other trade whatever, under like circumstances.

Aside from this very important difference in the item of trading capital, and consequently of salesmanship, there is not so much difference as may be supposed between the present condition of Cotton manufacturing at the North and at the South.

As it respects *public opinion* in Georgia concerning Southern manufacturing, much could be written: — we will barely touch upon it. We have observed that too much capital is already concerned, and too many local considerations, to admit of their loss to the commonwealth, whatever may be the necessary changes of individual ownership and management, and of location. — What has been done must be made good. Time, industry, economy, will harden it all down at last into a reasonably paying business; but any propositions to build more factories for many years to come, would now be received, everywhere in Georgia, with derision. That is well enough; but there are some respects in which public opinion upon manufacturing, not only at the South but over the United States, generally is unreasonable: because founded not upon experience, but upon the reading of English books, reprinted in this country.

Ex parte books they are, written for the patronage of the aristocracy, who live by the value of *land*, against the manufacturer, who patronizes only scientific books and has the misfortune to stand, in those *parts*, in self defense, (as he can never stand in America), the declared and powerful antagonist to the landed interest.

Money would hire the same authors to write for either side. Some of those fictions bear the same relation to the manufacturing interests of Great Britain that the book called "Uncle Tom's Cabin" has to the "Southern institution" of our own country, — reasoning from the abuse of the thing against the use of it. Such books, for the mere interest of the story, reprinted in our own country, where no corresponding state of things exists, have contributed too much towards the formation of a morbid public opinion here; and that they have also influenced the legislation of the States upon this question, there can be no doubt, because we often see them quoted as good authority in the speeches of our members. Any quantity of such discourse may be heard next winter at Washington city, in the coming discussion of the new tariff. The gentlemen would do well to strengthen their minds by reading something on the other side: — say for instance Macaulay's strictures upon Southey. A little of that kind of substantial reading in place of the novels, might improve materially their statesmanship, if not their rhetoric.

It was not the writer's intention, at the outset, to touch upon any of the political bearings of the question, but since he has done so, will close by calling the attention of Southern manufacturers, and of all Southern men, to a deadly blow, from some quarter, aimed at the vitals of the Southern manufacturing interests, in the contemplated new tariff. Cotton *yarn* is the staple of the Southern manufacturer. In the list of articles to be admitted free of duty, as recommended in Secretary Guthrie's report, near the bottom in alphabetical order is found the little word "yarn." Cotton yarns to be admitted free of duty, but woven goods, the staple of the Northern manufacturer, to bear 20 per cent duty as before! The circumstance is very suggestive, and needs no comment. There is reason to believe that the little word was afterwards erased in the committee room, but if it was not — if it should re-appear in the free list of the revised tariff at the next session of Congress — we recommend Southern manufacturers to look out for themselves.

PROFIT AND LOSS

Notes

Abbreviations frequently used in these notes are *DAB* (*Dictionary of American Biography*, ed. Allen Johnson and Dumas Malone. 20 vols. New York: Charles Scribner's Sons, 1928–36) and *O.R.* (U.S. War Department, *The War of the Rebellion: A Compilation of the Official Records of the Union and Confederate Armies*. 70 vols. in 128. Washington, D.C.: Government Printing Office, 1880–1901. All references are to series 1 unless otherwise noted).

Introduction

1. The memoirs, letters, and papers of Henry Merrell and his wife are a part of the Smith Papers, which are currently being catalogued by Arthur Norvell Skinner and the staff of the Georgia Department of Archives and History in Atlanta. Any box and folder numbers cited for these papers will reflect their disposition as of July 1990. If no box or folder number is cited, the reference is to a still-uncatalogued part of the Smith Papers. The letter referred to here is in box 100, folder 5.

2. Shryock, "Industrial Revolution," 119.

3. Clarke County, "Deed Book S," 139, 148–49, 265–66.

4. Smith Papers, box 100, folder 10.

5. Letters of Anne Magill Smith to Archie Smith, April 17, 1867, and Archie Smith to Gulielma Riley Smith, June 16, 1890, Smith Papers, box 7, folder 4; box 62, folder 2.

6. Arthur W. Smith, "Books Collected, Classified, & Boxed," Smith Papers.

New York

1. Ryan, *Cradle of the Middle Class*, 8.

2. Bagg, *Memorial History of Utica*, 128–30.

3. Durant, *History of Oneida County*, 296; Bagg, *Memorial History of Utica*, 236, 387; Wager, *Our County and Its People*, 202.

4. Ryan, *Cradle of the Middle Class*, 17.

5. Prude, *Coming of Industrial Order*, 261, 13.

6. Clark, *History of Manufactures* 1:536–37.

7. Wallace, *Rockdale*, 5.

8. Prude, *Coming of Industrial Order*, 125, 116.

9. Johnson, *Shopkeeper's Millennium*, 6.

10. Ibid., 22, 27. On the genesis and role of the factory "agent," a term that Merrell uses for himself in Georgia, see Prude, *Coming of Industrial Order*, 78–81. The fact that Merrell records his experiences both as the agent of other men and as his own man increases the value of his account of early American manufacturing.

11. Sernett, *Abolition's Axe*, xv; Cross, *Burned-over District*, 82.

12. Dunbar, *History of Travel in America* 1:312.

13. Preston and Ellis, "Ethnic Dimension," 59.

14. The evangelist Charles Grandison Finney (1792–1875) coined the term "Burned-over District" to describe the area between Lake Ontario and the Adirondacks. He believed that the early Methodist circuit riders had "burned out" the area, leaving behind souls that were hardened. Later usage of Finney's term "suggests that the burning-over process fertilized luxuriant growths rather than merely destroying old ones." To almost everyone the term meant "the place where enthusiasts flourished" and was synonymous with upper New York or, more specifically, New York west of the Catskills and Adirondacks (Cross, *Burned-over District*, 3–4). Of all the moral and cultural reforms that originated in the evangelical fervor of this district, "the most dynamic and divisive" was abolitionism (McPherson, *Battle Cry of Freedom*, 8).

15. Ryan, *Cradle of the Middle Class*, 15.

16. Manzelmann, "Revivalism and Reform," 53.

17. Cross, *Burned-over District*, 3–6.

18. Johnson, *Shopkeeper's Millennium*, 14, 47, 45.

19. Harrington, *Utica Directory, 1829*, 34–35, 136.

20. Manzelmann, "Revivalism and Reform," 57.

21. Daniel, "The Late Major Henry Merrell," p. 1, col. 1.

22. Tucker, *Samuel Slater*, 15, 27.

23. Ryan, *Cradle of the Middle Class*, 47.

24. Cyclone: Bagg, *Memorial History of Utica*, 219; riots: "Mob members belonged by and large to a commercial and professional class in Utica which feared that abolitionists intended to sow the seeds of communal disorder and social revolution" (Sernett, *Abolition's Axe*, 43); the bank was robbed of $110,000 (Bagg, *Memorial History of Utica*, 228); fire: Durant, *History of Oneida County*, 296, and Bagg, *Memorial History of Utica*, 230.

Autobiography. Ch. I

1. John Henry Hobart (1775–1830) was bishop of the diocese of New York from 1816 to 1830 while, during the same years, holding the office of rector of Trinity Church in New York City. In 1806 he founded the Protestant Episcopal Theological Society, which later became the General Theological Seminary. He was the

founder of the Protestant Episcopal Tract Society in 1810 and of the Protestant Episcopal Press in 1817.

2. Monroe (1758–1831) was president from 1817 to 1825, but Daniel D. Tompkins was not the governor of New York during those years. On the contrary, Tompkins was Monroe's vice-president for the entire term of his presidency. Tompkins was elected governor of New York in 1807, 1810, 1813, and 1816. He was instrumental in supporting the legislation to abolish slavery in the state, which passed in 1817 and became effective in 1827.

3. Old Fort Schuyler was built in 1758 on the site of what was to become Utica. At the time of these events, this fort had been abandoned, and Herkimer was approaching the "new" Fort Schuyler that had originally been named Fort Stanwix and would remain known as Fort Stanwix. This site later became the town of Rome. See Ellis, "Military Developments," 37. Old Fort Schuyler was never called Fort Stanwix; therefore, Utica does not stand on the site of Fort Stanwix. These name changes probably account for Merrell's confusing the two places.

4. Merrell is summarizing events of July and August 1777, when Nicholas Herkimer (b. ca. 1715) called out the New York Militia to defend against Indian and Tory attacks. Attempting to relieve St. Leger's siege of Fort Stanwix (known temporarily as Fort Schuyler), Herkimer was himself attacked on August 6 near the modern town of Oriskany. The battle in the woods there was drawn. While it was raging, a sortie from the besieged garrison, led by Colonel Willett, attacked a Tory camp on the west bank of the Mohawk River. Herkimer died soon afterward of wounds that he received at Oriskany, but his strategy repelled St. Leger and helped lead to the failure of Burgoyne's overall strategy of severing New England from the rest of the colonies (Ellis, "Military Developments," 39–44).

5. Merrell is, of course, referring here to Natty Bumppo (or Hawkeye), the wilderness scout and hero of the Leatherstocking Tales by the American novelist James Fenimore Cooper (1789–1851).

My Autobiography Begun in August A.D. 1863

CHAPTER 1

1. The name of Merrell's grandmother seems to have been spelled Damaris. She was baptized January 1, 1757. There were New Hartfords in both Connecticut and New York.

2. Merrell's beloved uncle John Camp was still living when Merrell wrote this page. He died July 21, 1867.

3. Harry Camp died October 9, 1875.

4. Brackets indicate that Merrell left such dates blank. Bildad Merrell died September 28, 1851.

5. Ira Merrell died April 17, 1849.

6. Isaac Merrell died May 7, 1860.

7. Nancy Camp died June 13, 1850, and her twin brother Horace, March 8, 1817.

8. George Camp, the father of Merrell's cousin and brother-in-law George Hull Camp, died December 23, 1850.

9. Although she was still living when Merrell wrote about her, his aunt Zelinda died within the year, on November 10, 1863.

10. The ditto mark after the birthdate indicates that Eunice Camp has died, but Merrell gives no date. It was March 11, 1793.

11. Merrell's mother lived until December 12, 1880.

12. John Merrell, of Hartford (1635–July 18, 1712), had ten children. Merrell's ancestor is John's son Isaac (March 11, 1682–1742). He was the father of Eliakim (baptized August 8, 1714), who was the father of Henry Merrell's grandfather Bildad (baptized January 28, 1749/50–November 11, 1815).

13. Nathaniel Merrell was born in England, probably about 1610. He came to Newbury, Massachusetts, in 1635. His sons Nathaniel, Abraham, and Abel stayed there, while John (1635–1712) went to Hartford.

14. John Camp, Sr., was born in 1639 or 1640 and died March 14, 1710.

15. Lieutenant John Camp died February 12, 1795.

16. It would seem that Merrell is referring here to Lieutenant John Camp's father, John Camp (February 13, 1675–February 4, 1747).

17. Elnathen Camp was born January 24, 1734.

18. Here Merrell seems to be noting two sons of Nathaniel Merrell (b. ca. 1610): Daniel, who stayed in Newbury, Massachusetts, and John, Merrell's great-great-great-grandfather, who went to Hartford, Connecticut.

19. According to Merrell family records furnished by Chester Talcott Park, the Merrell name was probably originally du Merle.

20. The Mix family was of West Hartford, Connecticut. Merrell's grandmother Damaris (baptized January 30, 1757) was the fourth child of Isaac Mix of that town.

21. Henry Merrell's grandfather's mother was Eunice Talcott (1736–1804), the daughter of Hezekiah Talcott (1686–1764).

22. Samuel A. Talcott (1789–1836) was a prominent lawyer in Utica. He served in Congress, on the state court of appeals, and the state supreme court.

CHAPTER 2.
"Before I Was Born"

1. "Cow-boys" were bands of loyalist guerrillas that operated in New York during the American Revolution.

2. Ezra Stiles (1727–95) had been involved in many religious and secular activities before being elected president of Yale in 1777, a post he did not accept until the next year.

3. Talcott Camp (1762–1832) assisted his father, Elnathan Camp (b. 1734), in the Commissary Department of the revolutionary army (DAR, "Revolutionary

Soldiers' Graves" 2:234). His grandson Walter B. Camp tells an interesting story of his efforts to get a message to a distant outpost concerning supplies needed to feed Washington's troops. With the words "For Washington says so," he impressed a fine horse from an unwilling owner, who had been on his way to church, and secured the needed supplies in time. Walter Camp also maintains that, before coming to Utica, Talcott Camp helped to lay out the city of Cincinnati (Oneida Historical Society, *Semi-Centennial History of the City of Utica*, 19). While he was a merchant in Glastonbury, Connecticut, Talcott Camp happened to see, in New York City in 1796, a barrel of silver coins brought in by a businessman from Whitesboro. He was thus stimulated to visit Utica, where he came to settle and open a dry-goods store the next year. He was "prominent among those who made honorable the beginnings of Utica," and after serving as village treasurer and trustee, he was elected the first village president, or "mayor," of Utica. (Bagg, *Memorial History of Utica*, 40–41, 50, 102; Cookinham, *History of Oneida County* 1:524). He was also a trustee of the United Society of Whitestown and Old Forts and later of the Presbyterian Society of Utica (Bagg, *Memorial History of Utica*, 397; Jones, *Annals and Recollections of Oneida County*, 569). He served as trustee of the Utica Academy when its charter was granted in 1814 (Wager, *Our County and Its People*, 346). But he was primarily remembered by his city as "an upright and esteemed magistrate" (Bagg, *Memorial History of Utica*, 41) and by his grandson Henry Merrell as a warm, affectionate old man sitting by the fireside in his mother's house. Talcott Camp boarded with his daughter Harriet Camp Merrell in the last part of his life (Harrington, *Utica Directory, 1828*, 9; *1829*, 48). He died of cholera in 1832 (Durant, *History of Oneida County*, 295).

4. Talcott Camp married Nancy Hale on March 21, 1785.

5. Merrell's parentheses. British Major John André (1750–80) was hanged as a spy after being caught by American militiamen with papers on his person detailing his negotiations with Benedict Arnold for the surrender of the fort at West Point, N.Y.

6. One of Merrell's occasional references to the Bible: "Drink no longer water, but use a little wine for thy stomach's sake and thine often infirmities" (1 Tim. 5:23).

7. The quotation is from Samuel Johnson's poem "The Vanity of Human Wishes" (1749), line 220.

8. "For, when we were come into Macedonia, our flesh had no rest, but we were troubled on every side; without were fightings, within were fears" (2 Cor. 7:5).

9. Today New Hartford is no longer a village, but Henry Merrell would be pleased to find that the members of the New Hartford Presbyterian Church worship in the same sanctuary that his forefathers built almost two hundred years ago.

10. For Merrell's confusion concerning the two forts around which the towns of Rome and Utica sprang up, see note 3 to chapter 1. Utica's growth was rapid. Harrington's *Utica Directory, 1829* shows a growth from 2,972 inhabitants in 1820

to 4,017 by 1823; 5,040 by 1825; 7,466 by 1828; and 8,010 by 1829 (p. 136). By 1825 Oneida County was the second most populous county in the state, second only to New York County (Larkin, "Three Centuries of Transportation," 33).

11. Talcott Camp was elected the village's first president, or "mayor," in 1809, and he held the office for five successive years (Bagg, *Memorial History of Utica*, 41).

12. James Carnahan (1775–1859) was pastor of the United Churches of Whitesboro and Utica from 1806 to 1812, when he resigned because of poor health. But in 1823 he was elected president of the College of New Jersey (now Princeton), virtually preserving the institution through a difficult period of its existence (*DAB* 3:498).

13. The street is still named First Street today.

14. Harry Camp (1787–1875) was Merrell's other favorite Camp uncle. In 1882, a few months before his death, he affectionately told the story of the "whittling club" at their store for the Oneida Historical Society, *Semi-Centennial History of the City of Utica*, 95–102.

15. "Fret not thyself because of evil-doers, neither be thou envious against the workers of iniquity" (Ps. 37:1).

CHAPTER 3.
"About the Time when I was born"

1. Andrew Merrell (1792–1826) was the seventh child of Bildad Merrell, Sr., and Damaris Mix. He came to Utica from New Hartford, New York, and is listed as a bookbinder in the first *Utica Directory* (Williams, *Utica Directory for the Year 1817*, 10) in 1817, the same year that he began a new bookstore at the sign of the Bible, Number 40, Genesee Street, one door west of the post office (Bagg, *Memorial History of Utica*, 139). To this bookstore was soon added a publishing house and a circulating library, which offered history, biography, and select English novels to the Utica public (*Catalogue of Books*). His partner in these ventures was Charles Hastings. Together Merrell and Hastings published religious works — *The Missionary Arithmetic*, for example, by William R. Weeks, one of Henry Merrell's teachers. In 1824 the firm began publishing Thomas Hastings's *Western Recorder* (Bagg, *Memorial History of Utica*, 139), one of the early religious periodicals produced by the Second Great Awakening in the Burned-over District. Merrell's father is a good representative of Utica's publishing and book trade, "which would lead upstate New York for a decade or more" (Cross, *Burned-over District*, 64). Andrew Merrell died January 25, 1826, "after an illness of several months, which he maintained with Christian character and resignation" (*Utica Sentinel and Gazette*, January 30, 1826, p. 3, col. 4). It seems that he was a victim of tuberculosis, the disease that may eventually have claimed his son.

2. The partners of the earliest stage of his father's firm seem to have been Talcott Camp, Ira Merrell (1779–1849), and George Camp (1790–1850), who moved to Sackets Harbor, New York, upon the dissolution of the firm in 1817. George Camp's son George Hull Camp (1816–1907) married Henry Merrell's sister Lucre-

tia (1818–45) and followed Merrell to Georgia to help him with the company store of the Roswell Manufacturing Company.

3. After becoming the organ of evangelists such as Charles Grandison Finney for six or seven years, the *Western Recorder* ceased publishing in 1834 (Cross, *Burned-over District*, 106–7).

4. The Reverend Henry Dwight (b. 1783) was installed as pastor of the Utica Presbyterian Church as soon as the United Society of Whitestown and Utica was dissolved in 1813. When he was discharged in October 1817 because his voice had failed (Jones, *Annals and Recollections of Oneida County*, 568; Bagg, *Memorial History of Utica*, 398–99), he went to Geneva, New York, and opened a bank there. As Merrell maintains, he remained active in church affairs, serving on the boards of trustees of Hamilton College and Auburn Theological Seminary, as well as the Presbyterian American Home Missionary Society (Fowler, *Historical Sketch of Presbyterianism*, 521–33).

5. The lines are from "On the Receipt of My Mother's Picture Out of Norfolk" (lines 108–11), by the English poet William Cowper (1731–1800).

CHAPTER 4.
Early Religious Training

1. Although he died young, Merrell's father seems to have impressed Utica with his "excellent business and personal qualities," and an obituary notice, rare in his day, maintained that "few men, in the ordinary walks of life, have been more distinguished for piety. His zeal . . . never tired: he was instant in season and out of season, doing the work of his Master. The friendly admonitions and Christian counsels which dropped from his lips will not soon be forgotten. He was amiable in disposition, frank and kind in his manners—a peacemaker—probably without an enemy" (Bagg, *Pioneers of Utica*, 408).

2. After becoming a doctor, Gerrit P. Judd (1803–73) was converted in 1826 and decided to become a missionary. He was appointed physician to the Sandwich Islands Mission of the American Board of Commissioners for Foreign Missions and served there for fourteen years. He mastered the language and customs of the Hawaiians and sided with them in 1843, when they were threatened with being overwhelmed by foreigners. He served the native king, developing a policy that would integrate natives with foreigners without allowing the native population to be overwhelmed, and virtually running the affairs of state. After 1853 he returned to missionary and agricultural work (*DAB* 10: 229–30).

3. Rockwell (1808–31) became apprenticed to Merrell's father after his family moved to New York from Connecticut when he was about fourteen. Interest in his poetry was soon more than local. At age eighteen, Rockwell went to Boston, where he worked as an editor of the *Statesman*. He became editor of the *Providence Patriot* in 1829 and is known for such poems as "Lost at Sea," "The Drunkard," and "To the Ice-Mountain," which Merrell calls the "Iceberg."

4. Alfred North (1807?–69) boarded for a time with Merrell's mother (Harring-

ton, *Utica Directory, 1829*, 89). Although he was learning the printing trade, which he practiced from 1832 to 1834, North studied Hebrew, Latin, and Greek privately. He was a mission printer in Singapore from 1834 to 1843 and in Madura from 1843 to 1847. Returning to the United States, North was graduated from Auburn Theological Seminary in 1850. Ordained in 1851, he served several churches in New York before moving successively to Kansas (1866), Missouri (1867), and Wisconsin (1868) (*General Biographical Catalogue of Auburn Theological Seminary*, 108).

5. Pliny Fisk (1792–1825) and Levi Parsons were sent to Jerusalem by the American Missions Board in 1819, but they selected Beirut as the location for their mission station (Bliss, *Concise History of Missions*, 128).

6. Sylvester Larned (b. 1796) was a popular preacher in New York after being licensed to preach there in 1817 (Nevin, *Encyclopedia of the Presbyterian Church*, 416–17).

7. Harrison Gray Otis Dwight (1803–62) spent thirty years as a missionary to Turkey and wrote frequently on Christian missions in the East. Having crossed the Atlantic six times in the course of his work, he died in a freak accident in Vermont when his rail car was blown off the tracks (Fowler, *Historical Sketch of Presbyterianism*, 513–17). The Reverend Dennis Marvin Winston (1801–40), whom Merrell calls "Mervin Winston," appears several times in Merrell's memoirs. Born in Utica, Winston was graduated from Hamilton College in 1825, served as an agent of the American Bible Society in North Carolina from 1827 to 1828, was graduated from Andover (Massachusetts) Theological Seminary in 1828, was ordained in Greensboro, Georgia, in 1829, and resided in Darien and Bryan, Georgia, before removing to Kentucky with his friend Joseph C. Stiles (*General Catalogue of the Theological Seminary, Andover*, 103). He served two churches in Kentucky, Bethel and Upper Benson (near Frankfort), before his early death. Merrell's father was apparently very close to the Winston family and helped them. When Merrell visited Marvin Winston in Kentucky in 1838, the Reverends Winston and Stiles suggested that he look to Roswell, Georgia, as a field for his endeavors.

8. Thomas Hastings (1784–1872) was the brother of Charles Hastings, the business partner of Merrell's father in Merrell and Hastings. The firm published Thomas Hastings's *Western Recorder*. Thomas Hastings directed choirs, taught music, and wrote several books on religious music, but he is most famous for the music to Augustus Toplady's "Rock of Ages." Moses M. Bagg discusses him at great length in his *Memorial History of Utica*, 137–39.

9. Mary Merrell (1811–98) was the oldest daughter of Merrell's uncle Bildad (1777–1851) and Lana (or "Lany") Palmer (1781–1859); Eden Platt was her third husband. Zelinda Merrell (1786–1863) was the sixth child of Merrell's paternal grandparents; she married Hezekiah Hulburt in 1809.

CHAPTER 5.
Boyhood

1. Merrell's uncle Bildad (1777–1851) had a livery stable in Hotel Street, Utica. During the War of 1812 he was called upon to organize an express mail system for

the army between Sackets Harbor and Plattsburg. In partnership with his brother Andrew, Merrell's father, Bildad Merrell ran an excursion boat on the Erie Canal, naming it the *Montezuma*, after the town west of Syracuse that was one hundred miles from Utica. He later engaged in staging lines north and south of Utica (Bagg, *Pioneers of Utica*, 254; and Larkin, "Three Centuries of Transportation," 33).

2. Lewis Merrell (b. 1799) was the only child of Merrell's grandfather Bildad's second marriage to Hannah Lewis (1764–1836).

3. Henry Merrell's cousin Horace (1817–38) was the fourth child of his uncle Ira Merrell (1779–1849) and his aunt Nancy Camp (1788–1850).

4. The bill to abolish slavery in New York was passed in 1817, but it did not take effect until 1827. This particular slave must have belonged to James S. Kip, a resident of Utica as early as 1794, who owned four hundred valuable acres, was a "conspicuous member of society" and frequent sheriff, and was the first president of a local Utica bank (Bagg, *Memorial History of Utica*, 31–33).

5. The Van Rennselaers of Utica were prominent export merchants and "scions of the colonial New York aristocracy" (Ryan, *Cradle of the Middle Class*, 82).

6. Nehemiah Brown was a Utica butcher, grocer, and tallow chandler.

7. David Prentice was appointed principal of the Utica Academy in 1825. He left in December 1836 to go to Geneva, New York, as a professor in a college there (Bagg, *Memorial History of Utica*, 454).

8. "Gum" Hunt's aggressive father (d. 1837) was the first real banker in Utica, having been sent by the Manhattan Bank to open a branch there in 1809 (Bagg, *Pioneers of Utica*, 273, 315; Bagg, *Memorial History of Utica*, 571–72). Another one of his sons, Ward Hunt (1810–86), became mayor of Utica, helped to organize the Republican party in New York, and was appointed by President Grant to the U.S. Supreme Court.

CHAPTER 6.
Several Celebrations and Some Excitement

1. The "emancipation day" of all slaves in New York was July 4, 1827. Freedom was extended to all blacks not already freed by the gradual emancipation act of 1799.

2. The 1799 bill passed in the New York Assembly freed all children born after July 4 of that year, girls at age twenty-five and boys at age twenty-eight. This provision allowed for them to work long enough to compensate their masters for their loss (McManus, *Black Bondage in the North*, 177).

3. Merrell glues into his book at this point a cartoon that he cut from an issue of *Harper's Weekly*, dated February 2, 1861. The cartoon depicts a black man, dressed finely and smoking a cigar, walking on a dock amid great shipping. Seeing him pass, one of two loafing white boys says to his companion, "Hello BILL! there goes the CRISIS!"

4. Ground was first broken for the Erie Canal in Rome on July 4, 1817. The first boat on the sixteen-mile section between Rome and Utica passed through on October 23, 1819.

5. This boat, belonging to Merrell's uncle Bildad, was named after the town that was west of Syracuse and one hundred miles from Utica. The *Montezuma*, together with the *Chief Engineer*, made up an excursion from Utica to Seneca River in April 1820 (Durant, *History of Oneida County*, 181–82).

6. The grand opening of the Erie Canal was October 26, 1825. Henry Merrell was almost nine years old.

7. Probably the son of Merrell's grandfather's brother George.

CHAPTER 7.

"Before the Indian was hung," and after that event

1. Merrell is seconded by several historians of Utica in pointing out the importance of this singular event. Moses M. Bagg tells us that Tuhi was a Brotherton Indian who killed his brother while intoxicated. He describes the hanging and notes that "the spectators were careless and unfeeling, and there was much laughing and swearing under the gallows, but not much drunkenness except among the Indians, of whom a number got intoxicated." He concludes, "The execution formed a memorable day in the calendars of the men of that generation, an epoch not easily forgotten, and people dated events as happening before or after the Indian was hung" (Bagg, *Memorial History of Utica*, 136–37). Durant notes "hilarity, profanity, and drunkenness" at the scene and comments on the "usual farce of religious services performed by two Baptist clergymen." He also calls it "an event long remembered by the people of Oneida County" (Durant, *History of Oneida County*, 289). Utica's modern historian, Judge John J. Walsh, quotes an interview with John Tuhi in which Tuhi states that he became angry with his brother for dunning him about a debt of three cents. Walsh also notes that military force was required to get the execution procession through the crowd and that over five thousand people were counted thronging the roads to the execution. The troop of cavalry was commanded by Captain Camp (Walsh, "Trials and Tribulations," 19–22, 25–26). Merrell seems to offer an original view of the importance of this execution in noting that it involved white men passing judgment on Indians for crimes not committed against whites.

2. Morris Smith Miller (1779–1824), after being village president and a member of Congress, was the first judge of the Oneida County Court of Common Pleas, appointed in 1810. He held the job until his death. Moses M. Bagg refers to the "pleasant home and ground" of Judge Miller (Bagg, *Memorial History of Utica*, 130), which he had begun to lay out in 1820 but which were not finished at his death (Walsh, "From Frontier Outpost to Modern City," 97–98).

3. Hull and Theodore Pomeroy (1785–1860) were both doctors. Amos G. Hull was "one of the earliest and best remembered surgeons of this county" (Wager, *Our County and Its People*, 252) and is noted for "Dr. Hull's Utero Abdominal Supporter" (*Utica Whig*, March 5, 1839, p. 1, col. 2), "almost the sole truss employed in the vicinity" (Bagg, *Memorial History of Utica*, 109). He was the first president of the Oneida County Medical Society, elected in 1806. Pomeroy, who bought

out Hull's practice and drugstore when he moved to New York City in 1821, was medical adviser to "some of the best families of Utica" and was among "the liberal, the useful, and the trusted" citizens of the town (Bagg, *Memorial History of Utica*, 145–46). Contemporary readers who look closely may find an advertisement for Pomeroy's wares reproduced on the surfaces of tables in Wendy's restaurants.

CHAPTER 8.
Go back and try it again

1. Merrell's account of his education at various schools in and about Utica gives his modern reader one of the most interesting contrasts between childhood then and now. Utica seems to have been a very progressive town in its attitude toward education, for in a town of just over eight thousand inhabitants in 1829, there were no fewer than thirty-three schools (Harrington, *Utica Directory, 1829*, 34–35, 136). After attending the variety of small private schools that he mentions, Merrell enrolled at the Utica Academy in Chancellor Square, chartered in 1814. Later, about 1828, he was sent outside Utica to Paris Hill, to a school kept by the Reverend Dr. William R. Weeks. Then, still later, he was sent to the famous Oneida Institute in Whitesboro, chartered in 1829.

2. Anson J. Upson (1823–1902) held the chair of Logic, Rhetoric, and Elocution at Hamilton College from 1849 to 1870 (New Century Club, *Outline History of Utica*, 92). He was vice-chancellor of the University of the State of New York from 1890 until his death (*Appleton's Cyclopedia* 6:214).

3. Eliasaph Dorchester (1780–1864) first appeared in Utica at age twenty-eight in 1808 as teacher in a grammar school held in the Welsh Church on Hotel Street. He apparently combined his teaching with being a bank clerk and journalist. He was an assistant on the *Columbian Gazette* from 1815 to 1816 and in 1817 founded the *Oneida* (later *Utica*) *Observer*. He took this paper to Rome, New York, from 1821 to 1823, then returned to Utica as a teacher. Soon he was off lecturing on geology but returned once again to teach and to work at a printing press, which he kept in his house on Lansing Street (Bagg, *Pioneers of Utica*, 266–67; Bagg, *Memorial History of Utica*, 105, 478). Beginning in 1828, he was principal of the Utica Public School (Wager, *Our County and Its People*, 348; Harrington, *Utica Directory, 1833*, 38). He was principal of the "Lancaster School" in 1832 (Walsh, *Vignettes of Old Utica*, 107).

4. Nathan Williams (1773–1835) had been a lawyer, a librarian, a village president, a bank president, a district attorney, a New York state assemblyman, and a U.S. congressman before becoming a circuit court judge in 1823. He was appointed clerk of the New York State Supreme Court the year before he died.

5. Thomas E. Clark (1788–1857) was a learned attorney who began practice in 1811. For James Beardsley, Merrell may mean Samuel Beardsley (1790–1860), a four-term congressman, state attorney general, and chief justice of the New York State Supreme Court. For Hiram Dennis, he may mean Hiram Denio (1799–1871), a law partner of Ward Hunt, who was a circuit judge and a judge on the court

of appeals from 1853 to 1866. Joshua Austin Spencer (1790–1857) became a U.S. attorney, a state senator, and a mayor of Utica. According to Daniel E. Wager, he was "among the foremost men who have shed luster upon the bar of this State" (Wager, *Our County and Its People*, 239–40). William H. Maynard was Spencer's law partner. Erastus Clark (1763/68?–1825), by "common report" pulled the "heathen name" of Utica out of a hat at Bagg's Tavern in 1798 (Bagg, *Memorial History of Utica*, 48–49). He later was a village trustee and president, was twice elected to the New York Assembly, and "his name was proverbial for originality and decision of character" (Jones, *Annals and Recollections of Oneida County*, 510). William Curtis Noyes (1805–64) fulfilled the promise that Merrell observed. He became district attorney of Oneida County before he was thirty; accumulated a large library, which he later donated to Hamilton College; became well known for eloquent legal briefs and defenses; pushed the causes of temperance, black emancipation, and union; and helped to codify the laws of New York (*DAB* 13:592).

6. John E. Hinman was often elected sheriff of the county during the 1820s. In 1850 "Colonel" Hinman was elected mayor of Utica and was reelected for three successive terms (Bagg, *Memorial History of Utica*, 110).

7. Bagg's Tavern, begun by the grandfather of the Utica historian Moses M. Bagg in 1795, is perhaps the most famous early landmark of Utica. It was on the corner of Main and John streets, near the river, the railroad, and the house where Henry Merrell was born. In 1812 Moses Bagg, Jr., took over the tavern and built a larger hotel (Bagg, *Memorial History of Utica*, 35).

8. On Dwight and Winston, see note 7 in chapter 4.

9. The Dana boys were the sons of James Dana, a substantial city merchant who dealt in hardware, harness, and saddlery. George S. Dana became a bank director, and James Dwight Dana (1813–95) became a famous geologist, mineralogist, and zoologist. He went to Yale to study under Benjamin Silliman (1779–1864), the university's first professor of chemistry and natural history. He assisted Silliman until 1838, when he acted as mineralogist and geologist on the expedition to the South Seas led by Captain Charles Wilkes (1798–1877), which lasted until 1842. James Dana married Silliman's daughter in 1844 and took over his father-in-law's position at Yale when Silliman resigned it in 1849. His celebrity rests on hundreds of articles, books, and manuals on geology and mineralogy.

10. Colonel Comfort Butler was discharged from the army in 1813 and, with one William Jones, operated a saddlery shop in Utica from 1813 to 1816. In 1828, in cooperation with a Linnaeus Peale of Philadelphia, he opened a museum. For two years it was known as Peale's Museum; later, when Butler assumed the management, it was called the Western Museum and, still later, the Utica Museum. Butler soon became blind, but he continued to show his "moral and instructive" exhibition of stuffed birds and animals, wax figures, Indian relics, etc., enriched from time to time by the services of giants, magicians, ventriloquists, albinos, fire-eaters, and jugglers (Waldron, "A Hundred Years of Amusement in Utica," 6–7). Colonel Butler's museum was located on the east side of Genesee Street (173–75),

just south of the Erie Canal, and was, according to Bagg, "the chief place of resort of its time" (Bagg, *Pioneers of Utica*, 355).

11. William A. Barber had the title of David Prentice's "assistant" at the Utica Academy (Harrington, *Utica Directory, 1829*, 13).

12. David Prentice was principal of the Utica Academy from 1825 until 1836, when he left to become professor of languages at the college in Geneva, New York (Bagg, *Memorial History of Utica*, 454).

13. Charles Stuart (1763–1865) was surely one of the most extraordinary people the young Henry Merrell knew. He was born in Jamaica, served as a captain in the British East India Company, then migrated to Canada, where he had received a land grant. Deeply religious, he began to teach school and to distribute, at his own expense, bibles and tracts. After he became principal of the Utica Academy in 1822, he met and began his long support of and relationship with Theodore Weld. Both were converted by Charles Grandison Finney and began their lifelong commitments to the cause of abolition. Stuart supported Weld at the Oneida Institute and returned to England in 1828 to carry on, again at his own expense, the campaign against slavery in the British West Indies. His lectures and pamphlets on the subject were one of the leading causes in turning British public opinion. In 1834 he returned to the United States to lecture against slavery and also did pioneering work in the temperance movement before retiring to his Canadian property about 1842 (*DAB* 18:162). He was principal of the Utica Academy from 1822 to April 1824. Alexander Dwyer succeeded him, and David Prentice replaced Dwyer in January 1825 (Bagg, *Memorial History of Utica*, 453–54).

CHAPTER 34.

A chapter of Digressions

1. Running from p. 463 to p. 468 in the Owen's volume, this chapter is placed here in order to abide by Merrell's directions at the beginning of the next chapter.

2. According to a tradition discussed by John J. Walsh, Eliphalet Remington of nearby Ilion, New York, had Morgan James do the original rifling for the barrel of his famous Remington rifle. When James went into business with George H. Ferris about 1850, the firm of James and Ferris became one of the leading gun shops in America (Walsh, *Vignettes of Old Utica*, 237–38).

3. Bagg places Rogers's gunsmith shop at 118 Genesee Street in 1832 (Bagg, *Memorial History of Utica*, 208).

4. Seymour (1810–86) was governor of New York from 1852 to 1854 and from 1862 to 1864 and ran against U. S. Grant for president of the United States in 1868. In 1832 Seymour was felt to be a "newcomer to Utica," but he had been elected mayor by 1842. He had attended a military school in Middletown, Connecticut, after two years at Hobart College (Bagg, *Memorial History of Utica*, 210 and part ii, 3–4).

5. The "Maine liquor law" was the Maine Law bill of 1854, which favored prohibition. Seymour was elected governor again in 1862.

6. James Henry Hackett (1800–71) was the first American actor to appear in England (Kane, *Famous First Facts*, 753). He had come to Utica in 1819 to open a grocery store and had been very popular for his exhibitions of wit and mimicry (Clarke, *Utica for a Century and a Half*, 35). He returned to New York City in 1825, having accumulated eighteen thousand dollars in Utica (Bagg, *Memorial History of Utica*, 145), but he tried his wife's profession of acting after he lost all his money speculating. It would appear that his most famous roles were Shakespeare's Falstaff and native American characters such as Rip Van Winkle.

CHAPTER 9.
In which it turns out that this "Autobiography is . . . nothing more than . . . Memoirs"

1. Lorenzo Dow (1777–1834) was a famous traveling evangelist who, in 1802, preached at Western and at Paris Hill in Oneida County. In a single three-hour sermon at Paris Hill he is said to have converted one hundred people. He therefore earned a great reputation in the county and returned to preach there four times between 1802 and 1817 (Cross, *Burned-over District*, 10).

2. This imaginative German was Joseph Masseth (d. 1832). An early map shows that the creek west of Utica on which he lived was called Nagal Kill, Dutch for "Nail Creek." About 1813 he established there a "dog nail factory," so called because he used two dogs to operate his bellows, and a description of this factory appeared in many newspapers in the United States. The name of the creek, however, is older than the factory (Jones, *Annals and Recollections of Oneida County*, 493; Walsh, *Vignettes of Old Utica*, 50).

3. Merrell mentioned earlier, in chapter 5, the braggart butcher Nehemiah Brown. James C. Delong (b. 1790) is listed in Harrington's *Utica Directory, 1829* as a "morocco manufacturer" (56). As ardent in his religion as he was in his desire to abolish slavery, Delong made his home a station on the Underground Railroad (Walsh, *Vignettes of Old Utica*, 118).

4. Matthew Codd, whom Merrell remembers as "Cobb," was the "proprietor of the Utica brewery" (Bagg, *Memorial History of Utica*, 173) and the husband of Mrs. Bradstreet.

5. The vivid community memory of the notorious Martha Bradstreet (b. 1780) is preserved by several historians of Utica, who devote pages to chronicling her complex claims (Bagg, *Memorial History of Utica*, 65–67; Bagg, *Pioneers of Utica*, 123–26; Jones, *Annals and Recollections of Oneida County*, 529–37; Walsh, *Vignettes of Old Utica*, 4–5). She was the daughter of Major Samuel Bradstreet, a stepson of General Bradstreet. General Bradstreet had been one of the joint owners of a large portion of the land on which the town had been built. Her portion of that inheritance she believed came to her in a double devise, for she had been named heir of both her father, a half-brother of General Bradstreet's unmarried daughter Martha, and her aunt, a half-sister of that same Martha. She was the wife of Matthew Codd, an Irishman who ran a brewery in Utica. But she had trouble with Codd and often fled next door to Talcott Camp, Merrell's grandfather, for protec-

tion. Bagg says, "More than once did she flee into Squire Camp's for protection, and there carry on an altercation with her husband, as he stood on the stoop of his own dwelling." When she divorced him, the state legislature allowed her to use her own name, under which she continued to terrorize the citizens (Bagg, *Pioneers of Utica*, 123–26). Writing in 1851, Pomroy Jones says, "although she has sometimes obtained *verdicts*, yet those verdicts have never enabled her to gain *possession* of city property after having been reviewed by higher tribunals" (Jones, *Annals and Recollections of Oneida County*, 529).

6. Benjamin Walker (1753–1818) served as von Steuben's aide at Valley Forge and superintended all his correspondence. By the end of the war he was also acting as Washington's aide. He came to Utica in 1797 and "soon became the village's outstanding citizen," devoting a large part of his income to charity (Clarke, *Utica for a Century and a Half*, 29; Bagg, *Memorial History of Utica*, 42–43).

7. The publishers and bookdealers Seward and Williams (Asahel Seward and William Williams) operated from 1808 to 1824 in their shop at 60 Genesee Street. Asahel Seward (b. 1781) came from Connecticut to Utica and in 1803, with Merrell's uncle Ira, printed the *Utica Patriot*, later the *Patriot and Patrol*, in which he retained an interest until 1824. William Williams (1787–1850) bought the *Patriot and Patrol* in 1821, renamed it the *Sentinel*, and ran it for four years (Bagg, *Pioneers of Utica*, 164–65; Bagg, *Memorial History of Utica*, 75–77, 477). Williams is important for beginning the *Utica Directory* in 1817, a publication that was later taken over by Elisha Harrington, and, with Harrington's successors, A. P. Yates and William Richards, ran until 1843. Merrell's friend Alexander Seward became an editor and was joint proprietor of the *Oneida Whig* from 1843 to 1853 (Bagg, *Memorial History of Utica*, 479).

8. According to Moses M. Bagg, the dam was erected in 1823 for a gristmill after the Erie Canal replaced the Mohawk River for navigation. The dam, built by William Alverson for proprietors Parker and Seymour, flooded property upstream to depths of four feet. The suit brought against them by angry property owners was unsuccessful, but they dropped their defense against a second suit and gave up the unpopular enterprise. These events took place about 1829. The flour mill below the dam eventually burned, and the dam was broken up and never rebuilt (Bagg, *Memorial History of Utica*, 159–60, 219; Durant, *History of Oneida County*, 292).

9. This may be Thomas S. Mitchell, a farmer and constable who lived in Utica and owned or rented meadowlands below the town (Bagg, *Pioneers of Utica*, 514).

10. Alexander Robinson (1812–87) is listed in Harrington's 1832 *Utica Directory* as boarding at T. S. Mitchell's (88). If Merrell's account of his being Mitchell's apprentice and of running away from him is accurate, then Robinson did indeed go far. According to a fascinating account by Judge John J. Walsh in his *Vignettes of Old Utica* (240–42), Alexander Robinson's brother John Robinson (b. 1807) had a famous equestrian troupe that became the John Robinson Circus, a circus that was one of the largest in the United States and that lasted until 1929, when its property was bought by John Ringling. Alexander performed with his brother John's circus

at first but formed his own company in 1860. After the Civil War his company became Robinson and Deery's Metropolitan Circus, which lasted through tragedy and triumph until 1879.

11. Merrell refers to *The Life of P. T. Barnum, Written by Himself* (1855). Barnum's revised version of 1869 is more pompous than his original.

12. Merrell is escorting his brother, Samuel Lewis Merrell (1822–1900), who became a Presbyterian minister and remained in New York for the rest of his life. The Potter boys were the sons of Merrell's mother's sister Eunice (1795–1851) and W. F. Potter (d. 1850). Jason Parker (1763–1828) was one of Utica's most famous citizens. Arriving in the area in 1793, he farmed until his health made it necessary to find other employment. He became a postrider on the route between Whitestown and Canajoharie in 1794 and in the following year began running a stage from Old Fort Schuyler (later Utica) to Albany. This stage line grew into one of the largest transportation systems in the state (Jones, *Annals and Recollections of Oneida County*, 505–6; Bagg, *Pioneers of Utica*, 288–90; Bagg, *Memorial History of Utica*, 34–35; Walsh, *Vignettes of Old Utica*, 13–16). He employed both Theodore Faxton (1794–1881) and John Butterfield (1801–69). The former would create the first telegraph company in the state, and the latter would create the Pony Express, the Overland Mail Company, the Butterfield trail to the West, and the American Express Company. See Walsh, *Vignettes of Old Utica*, 164–72, 193–95, 228–32.

13. A spencer was a short, double-breasted jacket or overcoat that was named after the English politician George John, second earl of Spencer (d. 1834).

14. Faxton (1794–1881) drove on Jason Parker's stages from 1813 to 1817, but he became, with Silas D. Childs, Parker's partner in 1822. His business ventures included stages, packets, steamboats, railroads, and banks. In 1845 he and John Butterfield formed the company that laid down the first telegraph line between New York and Buffalo. He was county sheriff in 1842 and city mayor in 1864, and his civic interests were great. Faxton built a public hall, a home for elderly ladies, a school for the children of factory operatives, and a hospital. The Genesee Nursing Home and Faxton's Children's Hospital serve the area to this day. See the accounts of his life in Bagg, *Memorial History of Utica*, 9–11, 625; Durant, *History of Oneida County*, 292, 349; and Walsh, *Vignettes of Old Utica*, 164–66, 282–84.

15. Lafayette's visit to Utica took place on July 9, 1825. Theodore Faxton drove his coach and six (Clarke, *Utica for a Century and a Half*, 32).

16. Trenton Falls, fourteen miles north of Utica, was a tourist attraction more accessible to early nineteenth-century travelers than Niagara. Through the century it "rivalled Niagara as a mecca for thousands of tourists from America and Europe" (Dorow, "Trenton Falls," 194). Joseph Bonaparte (1768–1844) visited the United States in 1830. The first railroad to Utica, the Utica and Schenectady, did not open until 1836, although the line from Albany to Schenectady (the Mohawk and Hudson) ran its first trip on August 9, 1831, missing Joseph Bonaparte's company by a few months.

17. Eliza Mesier Suydam, the seventeen-year-old daughter of Joseph S. Suydam of New York City, drowned at Trenton Falls on July 21, 1827. She and her cousin

were walking in advance of the party, and she fell from a projecting point below the falls (Jones, *Annals and Recollections of Oneida County*, 458).

18. This drowning took place on July 15, 1836. Herman Thorne, "a celebrated *millionaire* of New York, then recently returned from Paris," lost his eight-year-old daughter Zerlina, who fell from the same point as Miss Suydam. A servant, who had taken the child from her father, fell with her, but he was pulled out (Jones, *Annals and Recollections of Oneida County*, 459).

CHAPTER 10.
Sunday Reading

1. Revivals were common to the "Burned-over District" of upstate New York. Mary P. Ryan speaks of a "cycle of religious revivals" that swept through the area from 1813 to 1838 (Ryan, *Cradle of the Middle Class*, 16), and Whitney Cross dates several peaks of religious excitement in the area (1799–1800, 1807–8, 1815, 1825–29), noting that the Presbyterians of Utica had many converts during the revivals of 1815, 1819, and 1821. These revivals led up to the "peak of fervor" reached in 1826 under Charles Grandison Finney (1792–1875) (Cross, *Burned-over District*, 9, 11, 13).

Because Henry Merrell was born in 1816 and left the state in 1839, we may accept his descriptions of the spiritual awakenings of the time as a firsthand account and note the importance of the revivals on the formation of his character. Michael Barkun counts 1,343 revivals in the state between 1825 and 1835, with most of them between 1829 and 1832 (Barkun, *Crucible of the Millennium*, 23). Merrell's father may have been watching for a new revival, because he had been caught up in one about 1813. Mary P. Ryan mentions members of the Camp and Merrell families and their friends who were added to the church rolls in 1814 and 1819. They include Bildad Merrell, Jr., Horace Camp, Nancy Camp Merrell, Charles Hastings, and Asahel Seward (Ryan, *Cradle of the Middle Class*, 82).

2. Jedediah Burchard (1790–1864) began preaching in 1825, following his failure in business. He studied under George Washington Gale, as did Charles Grandison Finney, and these two may have been the most popular preachers in the district (Cross, *Burned-over District*, 188). Burchard organized a church in Utica in 1828 and stayed there for a time, but he was mostly employed in protracted meetings such as those he held in 1833–34 in Auburn, Homer, Ithaca, Buffalo, and other places. Wherever he went, "there was large attendance, high excitement, many professed conversions" (Fowler, *Historical Sketch of Presbyterianism*, 278–81; Hotchkin, *History of the Purchase and Settlement of Western New York*, 169–70).

3. "For they have sown the wind, and they shall reap the whirlwind" (Hosea 8:7).

CHAPTER 11.
In which the story makes an effort to progress

1. William R. Weeks (1783–1848), a graduate of Princeton and Andover Theological Seminary, was pastor in New York churches from 1812 to 1832, when he

left to go to New Jersey. Weeks was pastor of the Paris Religious Society from 1820 to 1831 (DAR, III [Records of the Paris Religious Society], 28). When a new church had been erected there in 1818, Weeks moved the old structure and had it fitted out as a residence and school building (Durant, *History of Oneida County*, 500; Rogers, *History of the Town of Paris*, 55). It was to this school that the young Henry Merrell was sent, probably in 1828. As Merrell will maintain, Weeks took authorship seriously. One of his books, published by Merrell's father's firm, was *The Missionary Arithmetic*, which taught mathematics based on missionary or religious topics (Bagg, *Memorial History of Utica*, 139). One of Weeks's pamphlets attracted the ire of Charles Grandison Finney, the revivalist. In his capacity as leader of the Oneida Association of Presbyterian ministers, Weeks issued a pamphlet against Finney's revivals in 1827 (Finney, *Memoirs*, 144, 178–79, 195; Ryan, *Cradle of the Middle Class*, 78). Weeks and the Oneida Presbytery may have disliked Finney's techniques, " 'but God was with him,' and their hands were tied" (Cross, *Burned-over District*, 162).

2. A Hopkinsian was a follower of Samuel Hopkins (1721–1803), a Connecticut theologian who was a pupil and friend of Jonathan Edwards, but Hopkins offered more optimism about human possibilities than did older Calvinists. Hopkins had a "profound influence on New England theology" by carrying "the principles of the New Divinity to their logical conclusions." So acceptable was his school of thought that it was called Hopkinsianism, and it "quickened the spiritual life of New England" (*DAB* 9:217–18).

3. Giles Mix (b. 1761) may have been the youngest brother of Merrell's grandmother Damaris Mix.

4. Moses M. Bagg lists William Backus as owning a dry-goods store at the corner of Liberty and Genesee streets in 1832 (Bagg, *Memorial History of Utica*, 208).

5. Talcott Camp died September 5, 1832. Charles Camp (b. 1796) did not die until 1834.

6. Before the Civil War, Merrell's compatriot William H. Seward (1801–72) was an antislavery Whig and Republican. After terms as governor of and U.S. senator from New York and after losing the Republican nomination for president to Lincoln in 1860, he was Lincoln's secretary of state during the war. He remained in that office until 1869 and is known for "Seward's Folly": the purchase of Alaska from Russia. In a speech of March 1850, Seward outraged southerners by saying that there was a "higher law" than the Constitution, a law that did not sanction slavery (McPherson, *Battle Cry of Freedom*, 39, 72–73, 216–17). To Merrell and to many southerners of his time, Seward is important for coining the phrase "irrepressible conflict" in 1858 to describe the growing differences between the North and the South. See the note at the beginning of the next chapter.

CHAPTER 12.
In which the story makes no effort to progress

1. Mr. Ward seems to have been Major Frederick Ward (d. 1832?). Seward wrote in his *Autobiography* that he came to Putnam County, Georgia, in 1819, after

running away from Union College in Schenectady, New York, over a dispute with his father about finances. He had landed in Savannah and had sought out friends in Hancock County. These friends told him that he might find work at the new Union Academy in Putnam County. He was hired as principal and lived with Major Ward until a letter from his father called him back to New York, where he returned to graduate from Union College in 1820. See pages 38–46 ("Six Months in Georgia") in Seward's *Autobiography* and page 219 in Rice and Williams, *History of Greene County, Georgia.*

2. In March 1846 William Freeman murdered a Mr. Van Nest, a farmer of Auburn, New York, along with several members of his family. He was in danger of being lynched, and Seward took upon himself the unpopular task of defending him. Finding that Freeman had been wrongfully arrested earlier and that he had been beaten senseless in prison, Seward unsuccessfully pled insanity as Freeman's defense (Seward, *Autobiography,* 785–88, 809–22).

3. Dawson (1798–1856) became Merrell's friend and legal adviser in Greene County, Georgia, when Merrell built and operated mills there between 1845 and 1855.

4. This may be the Rowan H. Ward (b. 1815?), who lived in Greene County, Georgia, when Merrell lived there, but it is unclear whether Rowan's father is Frederick because Frederick Ward's will mentions his wife, Eliner, and a Mary Ward, who died in 1856, names Rowan H. Ward as her son (Putnam County, Georgia, "Record of Wills," 230, 279–80). Both Rowan H. Ward and Cullen Reed, mentioned later, are listed as living in Greene County, Georgia, in the 1850 census. Rowan H. Ward was a state representative when Merrell corresponded with him in 1847 concerning the charter and water rights for the Curtright Manufacturing Company in Greene County, Georgia. An almost illegible tissue-paper, ink-blot volume of Merrell's correspondence as the agent of the Curtright company is filed in box 102 of the Smith Papers. I have labeled this volume "Letterbook," and it will be cited as such below. For Merrell's correspondence with Ward, see pp. 76, 134, 137, 164, 191, 198, 217, 220, and 247 of the Letterbook.

CHAPTER 13.
The Oneida Institute, a School of Fanatics

1. George Washington Gale (1789–1861) became pastor of a church in Adams, Jefferson County, New York, after graduating from Princeton Theological Seminary. Here he converted Charles Grandison Finney (1792–1875), who became a major figure in the revivals of the 1820s and 1830s. When he resigned this pastorate in 1824 because of his health, Gale moved to a small farm at Western, Oneida County, New York, where he took in several young male students who paid for their theological instruction by working a few hours each day on the farm. He later applied this method to the Oneida Institute at Whitesboro, which he founded in 1827 on the heels of the 1825 revivals in Utica. The Oneida Presbytery gave two thousand dollars in 1827 to support the school, and it opened in the second week of May with 27 students, its announced purpose being "to educate those

who intend to preach the gospel." There were two teachers for these students: Gale and Peletiah Rowson (Cross, *Burned-over District*, 234; and Harrington, *Utica Directory, 1829*, 14–15). The students worked twenty-one hours a week to defray their costs. In 1830, 500 students were turned away for lack of space (Sernett, *Abolition's Axe*, 35), and by 1833 there were 120 students and three teachers. Beriah Green (1795–1874) was inaugurated president in August of that year (Harrington, *Utica Directory, 1833*, 42–43; Rohman, *Here's Whitesboro*, 39). Gale left New York in 1835 to found Knox College and Galesburg in Knox County, Illinois. After he left, the school became, under Beriah Green and Theodore Weld (1803–95), more and more dedicated to the cause of abolition. Green's outright abolitionism caused the Oneida Institute to collapse, and it was sold to the Free Will Baptists for a seminary in 1844 (Cross, *Burned-over District*, 234).

2. The effect, or lack of effect, on Henry Merrell of "America's first truly interracial 'college'" (Sernett, *Abolition's Axe*, xii) creates one of the most absorbing questions raised by his memoirs.

3. Merrell is recording some of the ferment that attended these debates in Utica. For example, during some 1834 debates with the American Colonization Society, Beriah Green was hanged in effigy (Sernett, *Abolition's Axe*, 39–40).

4. Most items in Merrell's list of "anti's" are comprehensible, but "Graham bread" gives us pause. Apparently Merrell is ridiculing Sylvester Graham (1794–1851), who, in addition to advocating the causes of temperance, vegetarianism, and cold showers, developed and advocated unsifted, coarsely ground whole-wheat (graham) flour. Such a person with such a regimen must have appeared to Merrell as yet another fanatic of his time.

5. Although Green, another native son of Connecticut, was elected president of the Oneida Institute in 1833, he actually took over from Gale as president of the institute in 1834, when the school had 134 students. It does not seem that Henry Merrell could have been one of them. If, as he says, he spent the seven years before 1838 learning textile manufacturing at the Oneida Factory, then he must have left the institute by 1830 or 1831 after staying there only one or two years. In an article that he wrote for the *South-Western Presbyterian* in 1875 entitled "The Last of the Great Abolitionists," Merrell said that "about the year 1830" he had been in "a college at the North" whose president "foamed at the mouth and shook his fists on the slavery question" (*South-Western Presbyterian*, December 23, 1875, p. 2, cols. 3–4). Merrell seems to be describing Green, but it does not seem that it would have been Green in 1830. If Merrell were still at the Oneida Institute in 1833, then it is likely that his mother, hearing of Green's abolitionist fervor at Western Reserve College in 1832–33, would have withdrawn him before Green arrived. In any event, Green quickly alienated the Oneida Presbytery that had supported Gale, and the school "soon lost its predominantly 'Presbygational' identity" (Sernett, *Abolition's Axe*, 21–30, 38). Green even denounced the Oneida Presbytery as guilty of slaveholding, and "a wide gulf of alienation opened between the Oneida Institute and its original patrons" (Wager, *Our County and Its People*,

274). The Presbyterian Education Society struck the Oneida Institute from its list of approved schools in 1834 (Sernett, *Abolition's Axe*, 41).

It is therefore uncertain that Merrell knew Green personally. But it is likely that he often heard at the institute "the son of thunder" (and of Connecticut) Theodore Dwight Weld. After Weld and Charles Stuart had been converted by Charles Grandison Finney in 1826, Stuart sent Weld to the first class of the Oneida Institute in 1827 to prepare for the ministry (*DAB* 18:162). Weld remained there through 1833 to teach. Although Weld helped to recruit Green and may have lectured with him, he did not teach under Green, for he left in 1833 to attend a seminary in Ohio. Weld's abolitionist lectures made him, by the spring and summer of 1836, "the most mobbed man in the United States" (Cross, *Burned-over District*, 222). His *American Slavery as It Is* (1839) used advertisements in southern newspapers to condemn the institution of slavery with slaveholders' own statements. Often reprinted, the book was influential in that it was a source used by Harriet Beecher Stowe for *Uncle Tom's Cabin* (McPherson, *Battle Cry of Freedom*, 38).

6. Green was president of the Oneida Institute until 1843, shortly before financial difficulties caused it to close, but he remained as a pastor in Whitesboro until his death in 1874.

7. This Phineas Camp may have been the son of Merrell's great-great-grandfather, Lieutenant John Camp of Durham, Connecticut.

8. Phineas Camp (1788–1868) published the following title in Utica in 1859: *Poems of the Mohawk Valley, and on Scenes in Palestine, Together with an Essay on the Origin of Poetry, with Miscellaneous Poems and Sketches.*

9. The terms *ultraism* and *ultraist* refer to a radical lifestyle prompted by the atmosphere of religious conversion in the Burned-over District. Whitney Cross describes ultraism as "a combination of activities, personalities, and attitudes creating a condition of society which could foster experimental doctrines" (Cross, *Burned-over District*, 173).

10. Jared E. Warner began his drug business in Utica in 1812 (Wager, *Our County and Its People*, 302). His partnership with Sylvanus Harvey (d. 1843) lasted from 1817 until 1829 (Bagg, *Pioneers of Utica*, 447; Walsh, *Vignettes of Old Utica*, 99). Although Jared Warner retired from his historic drugstore in Bagg's Square in 1867 (Walsh, *Vignettes of Old Utica*, 275), his name continued on the drugstore as late as 1892, when Bagg noted that the present generation of Utica could still visit the shop (Bagg, *Memorial History of Utica*, 139).

11. Angelina Emily Grimké (1805–79) was one of two wealthy and aristocratic sisters from Charleston, South Carolina, who broke from their heritage to become famous advocates of abolition and women's rights. Her *Appeal to the Women of the South* (1836) urged her fellow southern women to speak out and act against slavery. She became a famous lecturer and married Weld in 1848.

12. Merrell's brother, Samuel Lewis (1822–1900), was the father of John Merrell (1854–1933), who came to Camden, Arkansas, in 1870 to work for Henry Merrell. Samuel named John's twin brother Henry (1854–74).

13. Lucretia Hale Merrell Camp (1818–45); Harriet Merrell (1825–47). Lucretia died when she and Henry Merrell were in Roswell, Georgia. She is buried in the Presbyterian Church cemetery there. Harriet died when Henry was in Greensboro, Georgia.

14. When he was the overworked "Assistant Agent" of the Roswell Manufacturing Company, Merrell asked his cousin George (1816–1907) to come south to run the company store. In chapter 32 Merrell writes of his anxious waiting for the arrival of his sister and cousin in 1842. Lucretia died in childbirth three years later (chapter 29).

CHAPTER 14.
I go to work and work goes against me

1. Charles Camp (b. 1796) was the eighth child of Merrell's grandfather Talcott Camp. Charles died two years after his father, in 1834.

2. William Walcott, Merrell's "master for seven years," was the second son of Benjamin Stuart Walcott, Sr. (1755–1824), "the only bona fide industrialist in the region before 1845" (Ryan, *Cradle of the Middle Class*, 9). The older son, Benjamin S. Walcott, Jr. (1786–1862), was the father of Merrell's friend "Little William," William Dexter Walcott (1813–90); Elizabeth Walcott, with whom Merrell was in "puppy love" for a time; and Charles Doolittle Walcott (1818–52).

3. Textile manufacturing in Oneida County began in Whitestown some three miles west of Utica on sites along the Sauquoit Creek where it completed its rapid fall into the Mohawk River. There in 1809 a small group of former New Englanders led by Seth Capron and Benjamin S. Walcott, Sr., built a small factory that spun yarn for local inhabitants. They formally organized themselves in 1810 under the name Oneida Manufacturing Society. This was "the first cotton manufactory established in the western part of the state" (Harrington, *Utica Directory, 1828*, 87). In 1825 Benjamin S. Walcott, Jr., who built and superintended the factory, joined the British investor Benjamin Marshall in an agreement that would become the basis for the New York Mills, and a second factory named the New York Mills was completed in 1827 (Berkhofer, "Industrial History of Oneida County," 19–20, 45, 47). The original factory of the Oneida Manufacturing Society burned on March 13, 1828 (Harrington, *Utica Directory, 1828*, 87). New construction was begun on this site almost immediately, and the Oneida Factory, where Henry Merrell was to learn his trade, was built during the year 1828 (Jareckie, "Architectural Survey of New York Mills," 24).

4. Merrell is referring to the Tariff of Abominations (1828). Tariffs had a great deal to do with the rise and fall of Merrell's textile ventures. The following brief survey should provide a background for his enterprises until the Civil War: The first tariff act of 1789 was urged by Alexander Hamilton in order to protect the country's infant industries. Henry Clay pushed through a temporary tariff in 1816 to protect manufacturers in order to build up a home market for agricultural products. In 1824 Congress excluded various foreign goods that competed with

American products, but the famous Tariff of Abominations (1828) placed pro-
hibitive duties on cotton and woolen goods, particularly. Southerners protested,
fearing that the British would retaliate against their cotton imports. Opposition
to the Tariff of Abominations led to a general lowering of tariffs until 1842, when
another high tariff bill was passed as the result of the depression of 1837–42. Upon
the return of prosperity in 1846, tariffs were lowered until the protectionist Morrill
Tariff of 1861.

5. John Camp (1786–1867) was largely engaged in general merchandising in
Utica, but Merrell applied to him for insuring the Roswell Manufacturing Company in 1840.

CHAPTER 15.
Bad Boys!
1. Another allusion that shows this manufacturer's familiarity with the popular
poetry of the day. "Oft in the stilly night" is the first line and title of a poem
written in 1816 by the Irish poet Thomas Moore (1779–1852).

2. Barrington King (1798–1866) was the son of the founder of Roswell, Georgia, Roswell King (1765–1844). After Merrell applied to him in 1838, Merrell went
to Roswell to help Barrington King build the Roswell Manufacturing Company
and to become his "Assistant Agent" at the factory.

CHAPTER 16.
A Friendship
1. Samuel Irenaeus Prime (1812–85) was a well-known Presbyterian clergyman,
author, and editor in New York. He edited the *New York Observer*, a Presbyterian
weekly which included articles of education, literature, and politics. His "Irenaeus"
letters in the periodical were popular and later published separately. Prime also
wrote the "Editor's Drawer" column in *Harper's Magazine* from 1853. Merrell
met him in 1877 when both were on the same committee at the Pan-Presbyterian
Council in Edinburgh.

2. The Croton Distributing Reservoir was located at Fifth Avenue and Forty-
Second Street, now the location of the New York Public Library, opened in 1911.

3. James Lenox (1800–80) inherited the wealth of his father, a New York City
merchant and investor in real estate, and devoted his life to book collecting, philan-
thropy, and writing history. His collections finally reposed in the Lenox Library,
which was incorporated in 1870. He gave land in New York City to Presbyterian
institutions and gave away millions of dollars to other charities.

4. Wells married Jessie Henderson in 1849. They had two sons and three daughters.

5. Wells was pastor of the Third Street Presbyterian Church of Williamsburg
(now a part of Brooklyn) from 1850 to 1903. John Dunlap Wells (1815–1903) was
born in Whitesboro and became a clerk at the Oneida Factory at the age of fifteen.

He experienced a religious conversion when he was seventeen and left the Oneida Factory at age eighteen to study at an academy in Cambridge, New York, and to study at the Mount Pleasant Academy, Sing Sing, under the Reverend N. S. Prime. He was graduated from Union College, Schenectady, and took charge of an academy in Huntsville, Alabama, before entering Princeton Theological Seminary in 1840. His health caused him to interrupt his theological studies, but he was graduated from Princeton in 1844. He first served at the private chapel of James Lenox in New Hamburg, New York, then at the Lenox Chapel at Madison Avenue and Twenty-Ninth Street in New York City from 1844 to 1847. Wells was principal of the First Presbyterian Church parish school from 1847 to 1849, but in 1850 he was installed as pastor of the Third Street Church of Williamsburg (Brooklyn), a position that he held for fifty-four years until his death in 1903 at the age of eighty-eight. He received an honorary doctorate of divinity from Union College in 1864 (*Necrological Report*, 265–66).

CHAPTER 17.
Novercalis, and the "Faculty"

1. *Novercalis* is Latin for "stepmother," or for something that has the character of a stepmother. In this case Merrell seems to be referring to the Oneida Factory as his stepmother and college, and to his friends and supervisors as the faculty of that college. The Oneida Factory that Merrell sketches was built in 1828 to replace the original mill of the Oneida Manufacturing Society, which had been built in 1809. This beautiful Federal-style structure with an octagonal cupola centered on its roof ridge was designed to stand at the head of a street (Mill Place) that was lined on both sides with houses for workers. Apparently these houses were constructed at the same time as the factory itself. The factory, known as the "Oneida Factory" while Merrell worked there, was later known as the Lower Mills of New York Mills after the Oneida Manufacturing Society sold out to New York Mills in 1851 (Jareckie, "Architectural Survey of New York Mills," 5, 8, 25).

In 1833, while Merrell was working at the Oneida Factory, it employed 175 people, contained 4,500 spindles and 126 power looms, and manufactured over one million yards of thread. It was one of sixteen factories in Oneida County by that date, but it produced more than any factory except New York Mills (Harrington, *Utica Directory, 1833*, 85).

A new building was erected behind the Oneida Factory in 1854, and a decision to replace it was made in 1879. This new "Lower Mill" was completed in 1880 (Jareckie, "Architectural Survey of New York Mills," 37–38). The building, at this date owned by Utica Cutlery, still stands on the site that Merrell affectionately sketched in 1835, still flanked by some of the original workers' houses.

His affection for his real "school" extended to its owners, the Walcotts, especially to the brothers William and Benjamin, Jr., who were able to create in New York Mills "a quiet, orderly village that was much in the image of the old New England community, an epoch away from dense and busy Utica" (Ryan, *Cradle of the Middle Class*, 114). That which was transplanted sustained.

2. Ezra Wood came to Utica from Rhode Island to establish in 1812 a weaving shop of six looms. There were no power looms in the United States at that time, and weaving was still done by hand. The first practical power loom in America was built in Massachusetts by Francis Cabot Lowell in 1813. Such looms were apparently in operation in Oneida County by 1818 (Clark, *History of Manufactures* 1:541). After the Walcotts acquired the technology, Ezra Wood was asked to take charge of running their power looms. He also began and was active in the Sabbath school of the Whitestown Presbyterian Church (Durant, *History of Oneida County*, 623, 617). Merrell probably calls him "Deacon" in reference to his church activities.

3. See the references to William Ballantine (or Balentine) in chapter 29.

4. Amos Wetmore was an original investor in the Oneida Manufacturing Society (Berkhofer, "Industrial History of Oneida County," 21).

CHAPTER 18.
The "Walcotts"

1. Samuel Slater (1768–1835) founded the cotton textile industry of the United States by establishing the first successful cotton mill in Pawtucket, Rhode Island, in 1793. See Tucker, *Samuel Slater*.

2. Benjamin Stuart Walcott, Sr. (1755–1824) established the Oneida Manufacturing Society in Whitesboro, New York, and built its first factory in 1809. When this factory burned in 1828, the Oneida Factory that Merrell worked in was constructed on the spot in the same year. Walcott built the Whitestown (Burstone) Factory in 1812 and, with Benjamin Marshall, the New York Mills in 1825 (Harrington, *Utica Directory, 1828*, 86–87).

3. Near the end of this chapter in his manuscript, Merrell glues to a page an engraving of Benjamin Walcott, Jr., and photographs of "Little William" Walcott and his wife. But Little William is the son of Benjamin Walcott, Jr., and is not the William Walcott ("my master") of whom he speaks here. Merrell's "master" was Benjamin's brother and Little William's uncle.

4. At this point, and beneath the picture of David Dale Owen that is printed on p. 206 of his volume, Merrell writes: "*Note*. The above D. Owen, when engaged in the State Geological Survey of Arkansas, encamped a while near my house. I formed a pleasant acquaintance with him; but his countenance at the time did not resemble this picture. He gave me an honorable notice in his book on Arkansas 2 Vol. and I think my nephew Wm. Smith gave him much information in the Mineralogy and Geology of the Vicinity which he might as well have acknowledged while he was about it."

5. The business connections of Benjamin Walcott, Jr. (1786–1862), and Benjamin Marshall (1782–1858) seem to have dated from 1825. Marshall had come to New York in 1803 and had become a famous cloth importer. Later he sold cotton to England and went to Georgia to get better prices by buying his cotton directly. In 1823 he made a fortune by investing in a packet line (Berkhofer, "Industrial History of Oneida County," 45). Marshall moved from importing to manufactur-

ing following the enactment of the 1824 tariff (*DAB* 12:305). New York Mills, the Federal-style factory erected under the partnership of Marshall and Walcott, was built in 1825 (Harrington, *Utica Directory, 1828*, 86), although Merrell maintains in his next paragraph that the capstone of the building read "1824."

6. The Oneida Manufacturing Society sold out to New York Mills in 1851 (Durant, *History of Oneida County*, 623).

7. Benjamin S. Walcott, Jr., was about sixty-four years old in 1850, ten years before Merrell's visit. He retired and sold his interest in New York Mills to Samuel Campbell and to his son William Dexter Walcott in 1856 (Jareckie, "Architectural Survey of New York Mills," 35). William Dexter Walcott (1813–90) would have been thirty-seven years old at the time Merrell says his father turned over the business to him, but it seems that he was actually closer to forty-three when the transfer took place. "Little William" Walcott, who is closer to Merrell's own age, should not be confused with his uncle William Walcott, whom Merrell calls "my master."

8. The visits of Benjamin S. Walcott, Jr., and William Walcott may be dated certainly by means of Merrell's Letterbook. The former visited Merrell in Greensboro during the last week of October 1847, and the latter came a little over a week later. Both the tone and the content of a letter to his stockholders concerning William's visit are worthy of note. The letter is dated November 12, 1847: "I had a pleasant family visit last week from W. Walcott, former partner of Benj. Marshall of N.Y. Mr. W. is owner of the N. York Mills in my native county & is in some sort my 'old master.' Mr. W. is travelling for health. He has been for forty-odd years a manufacturer & has seen vicissitudes in his business. I can remember when his place was in the woods & he worth about $5,000. Now he is worth more than half a million, I presume, and his income not less than $100,000 per. anm. He has 2,000 well-conditioned people dependent on him for a livelihood. Well, I took Mr. Walcott to see our works. He appeared to be pleased with our business & encouraged me very much. He says that manufacturers, especially at the South, have more before them (of success) than there has been in the past" (Smith Papers, Letterbook, box 102, pp. 117, 137).

9. Charles Doolittle Walcott (1818–52).

10. The son was named W. Stuart Walcott.

11. D. Marvin Winston (1801–40). See note 7, chapter 4.

CHAPTER 19.
Whitesboro Village & round about

1. The village of Whitesboro, about three miles west of Utica, was settled in 1784 and should not be confused with the town of Whitestown, of which it is a part. On some early maps, the settlement is called Whitehall Landing.

2. Lewis F. Berry, a bookkeeper and village trustee who kept a tavern that was the center of activity in Whitesboro, died in 1869. The Berrys had four sons and seven daughters. Of the Berrys' four sons, Merrell mentions Morris (1799–1881)

and Lewis T. (b. 1809). Of their seven daughters, he seems to have been closest to Elizabeth (1806?–56), Frances Miriam (1814–52), and Katherine (1817?–65) (Wager, "Whitesboro's Golden Age," 131, and Sperry, *Families of Old Whitesborough*, 21–24).

3. Apparently Elizabeth Berry's husband spelled his name Barbour (Wager, "Whitesboro's Golden Age," 131).

4. Frances Miriam Berry married the Reverend B. W. Whitcher in 1847. She died January 4, 1852. She contributed to such periodicals as *Neal's Saturday Gazette* (poems and "Bedott's Table Talk"); *Godey's Lady's Book* ("Aunt Maguire" and "Letters from Timberville"), and the *Philadelphia Saturday Gazette*. Her "Widow Bedott Papers" were not published in book form until 1855, with a new edition in 1864 (Allibone, *Critical Dictionary*, 2682).

5. Katherine Berry, the youngest of the Berry daughters, wrote for newspapers and magazines. She married Colonel H. P. Potter in 1855 and died in 1865 (Wager, "Whitesboro's Golden Age," 132).

6. "M.L.W." (probably Martha L. Ward Whitcher, who married Frances Miriam Berry Whitcher's husband after Frances's death and edited her sketches in 1867) gives an interesting picture to complement Merrell's memory of the Maeonian Circle in her book entitled *A Few Stray Leaves in the History of Whitesboro* (1884). She refers to "a society of persons of literary ability, who formed a reading circle. The members met at each other's houses, and their productions were read in the form of a newspaper. The objects of the society seem to have been mirth and enjoyment quite as much as literary improvement. The paper was called the *Momus*, in honor of the God of Mirth. Some of the society thinking it too much devoted to the harmless comedy of life, it was changed to a little more grave character, and became the *Maeonian*. . . . They were written in fine old fashioned round hand, on paper about twice the size of ordinary foolscap. These papers at last became a part of the stock in trade of an itinerant tin merchant. A few numbers were rescued from the wagon by a young gentleman who was attracted by their fine penmanship, but the larger part went to the oblivion of paper rags" (42).

7. The issue of "The Cotton Bug" that Merrell inserted at this point is filed in the Smith Papers, box 100, folder 1.

8. "Cousining" is a New England dialect term that means visiting relatives, especially distant ones.

CHAPTER 20.
An Episode

1. Little Rock was occupied by the Union general Frederick Steele (1819–68) on September 10, 1863.

2. Merrell sold his interest in the Pike County mills and village at Royston to his partner John Matlock (1817?–86). Matlock had been born in Georgia, had become a successful businessman in Camden, Arkansas, and had been Merrell's partner since 1856.

3. The forces of the Confederate general William Lewis Cabell (1827–1911) and the Union general James Gillpatrick Blunt (1826–81) fought at Devil's Backbone, or Backbone Mountain, Arkansas, about sixteen miles southeast of Fort Smith, on September 1, 1863, the same day that Fort Smith was occupied by Federal forces. This skirmishing occurred only thirty miles from where Merrell was writing and convinced him that he should move to a safer location, for Royston would be a logical Union target. General Sterling Price (1809–67) had taken command of the District of Arkansas upon the illness of General Theophilus Holmes following the futile attack that Holmes had led on Helena July 4.

4. Steele's troops laid a strategically placed pontoon bridge across the Arkansas River that Price could not cover with his artillery. (*O.R.*, vol. 22, pt. 1, pp. 476–77, 515, 522, 524. All references to *O.R.* are to series 1 unless otherwise noted).

5. Albert Rust (1818–70) had emigrated to Arkansas in 1837 and had settled in El Dorado in Union County, which is too far to the south to be the specific "place" to which Merrell is referring. Rust had served under Lee and Stonewall Jackson in western Virginia, and he was now back in the Trans-Mississippi, but not near his home. During this time he was serving in Louisiana. As for Price's location at this time, he was ordered to fall back on the Ouachita River on September 12 and moved into Arkadelphia on the fourteenth; he was there when Holmes reassumed command of the District of Arkansas on September 25 (*O.R.*, vol. 22, pt. 1, p. 522; pt. 2, pp. 1014–15, 1027).

6. The first Confederate Conscription Act, with its exemptions, was enacted by the First Confederate Congress on April 16, 1862. See the first Confederate conscription act (*Confederate Statutes at Large*, 1st Cong., 1st sess., chap. 74). Exemptions were enlarged in the second conscription act, passed on October 11, 1862. In the last part of the paragraph, Merrell seems to be referring to the law passed on February 17, 1863, which provided for slaves to work in the army as teamsters or cooks, upon fortifications, or in workshops, hospitals, etc. (Richardson, *Compilation of the Messages and Papers of the Confederacy* 1:493).

7. Charles Arthur Magill (1817–84), Merrell's brother-in-law, had come to Arkansas to work for him in 1856.

8. Southern resistance to the 1828 Tariff of Abominations had resulted in the Nullification Crisis of 1832. A South Carolina state convention passed an Ordinance of Nullification that declared the 1828 tariff and a recently passed 1832 tariff null and void in the state. It further prohibited the federal government from collecting duties in the state after February 1, 1833, unless the tariff was lowered 12 percent by that date. This crisis led to maneuverings by President Jackson and Henry Clay that culminated in the Compromise Tariff of 1833, which provided for the gradual reduction of the tariff to 20 percent in 1842.

9. The Tontine Coffee House (1792) on the northwest corner of Wall and Water streets in New York City housed the stock exchange and principal insurance offices of the city. Important tradesmen and merchants met daily to transact business in this fine neoclassical building (Kouwenhoven, *Columbia Historical Portrait of New York City*, 107).

10. The battle of Navarino was an important naval engagement in the Greek war of independence against Turkey. It had taken place in the harbor of Navarino in southwestern Greece in October 1827 and was fought between a combined British, French, and Russian fleet and an Egyptian-Turkish fleet.

11. Although he confuses two rail trips, Merrell's paragraph provides a fascinating glimpse of early rail travel. On his earlier trip, perhaps in 1832 or 1833, he could have traveled on the first steam railway in New York, the Mohawk and Hudson, which had its first run between Albany and Schenectady on August 9, 1831. Both the Saratoga and Schenectady and the New York and Harlem began running in 1832, but there was no other railroad in New Jersey at the time other than the Camden and Amboy, and neither it nor the New York and Harlem ran to Paterson. Merrell could not have traveled from Utica to Albany by rail until after August 2, 1836, when the Utica and Schenectady began running trips. Both the Mohawk and Hudson and the Utica and Schenectady were parts of a series of successive independent rail links through the middle of New York that would eventually end in Buffalo and make up the New York Central Railroad, which was not chartered until 1853 (Dunbar, *History of Travel in America* 3:801, 974–75, 4:1384–85; Bagg, *Memorial History of Utica*, 384).

12. It is natural that Merrell was drawn to Virginia, for it was the first state in the South to charter enterprises for manufacturing cotton. Two charters were issued in 1803: one to the Petersburg Manufacturing Society and the other to the Halifax County Manufacturing Society (cited in Bateman and Weiss, *Deplorable Scarcity*, 8). Two large mills operated on the Appomattox River at Petersburg following subscriptions for their erection about 1827, and there were a large number of mills operating in Richmond as early as 1840 (Hall, "Utilization of Southern Water Powers," 582, 585). In the decade before 1840 a group of mills had been constructed in Richmond and Petersburg, "which were receiving-points for cotton from the Carolina uplands." More than half the spindles in Virginia were at Petersburg (Clark, *History of Manufactures* 1:551). A factory near Charlottesville, possibly the Shadwell factory mentioned below, was described in the thirties by an English traveler as comparable with the better mills in Lancashire and Yorkshire (Clark, "Manufactures during the Ante-Bellum and War Periods," 329).

13. Messrs. John Timberlake (d. 1862) and his son Edward J. had begun a carding factory in Shadwell, Virginia, in 1835 (Rawlings, *Albemarle of Other Days*, 127; Woods, *History of Albemarle County*, 330–31). Edward J. must be Merrell's "Ned" Timberlake.

14. There is a Valentine Peyton (1801–40), the son of Craven Peyton (d. 1837) of "Mont Eagle" in Albermarle County, Virginia. Craven Peyton sold eleven hundred acres of Albemarle County to Thomas Jefferson in 1811 and married Jefferson's niece Jane Jefferson Lewis, the daughter of Charles Lilburn Lewis and Jefferson's sister Lucy Jefferson. Their children were Margaret, Valentine, Lucy, Mary, and Charles (Woods, *History of Albemarle County*, 295). If this Valentine Peyton is not Henry Merrell's "Volney," then Volney Peyton continues to escape detection, unless he be the Volney H. Peyton who served under General N. B. Forrest, lived in

Memphis, and "went west" after the Civil War (Hayden, *Virginia Genealogies*, 556, 527–28).

15. Another literary allusion, this time to Oliver Goldsmith's sentimental novel *The Vicar of Wakefield* (1766). Little Moses Primrose, the vicar's son, is a naive child who is described in the first chapter as one who has received "a sort of miscellaneous education at home" and who shares the family character of being "equally generous, credulous, simple, and inoffensive."

16. Thomas Jefferson's elder daughter, Martha ("Patsy"), had married David M. Randolph, who had sacrificed all his property instead of paying his debts and had gone to England. Mrs. Randolph then set up a boardinghouse in Richmond (Malone, *Jefferson the President*, 528).

17. Merrell knew Dr. Francis Bowman (1795–1875) as the pastor of the Greensboro, Georgia, Presbyterian Church, which he served from 1837 to 1856. Bowman had previously served as pastor of the Presbyterian Church of Charlottesville, Virginia, from 1824 to 1836 (Scott, *Ministerial Directory*, 93).

CHAPTER 21

1. Thomas Jonathan ("Stonewall") Jackson (1824–63) became a professor of both artillery and natural philosophy at the Virginia Military Institute in Lexington, Virginia, in 1851. Jackson died in May 1863, and Merrell wrote this account only a few months thereafter.

2. The Saguenay River empties into the St. Lawrence River about 120 miles northeast of Quebec city. Merrell visited the area on a trip that he made to the North in 1860.

3. Merrell mentioned Winston earlier in chapters 4 and 18. But his purpose in visiting the Lexington area was surely not entirely to renew old ties. Cotton manufacturing had begun in Kentucky before 1820, at which time the state had more spindles than Maine, Vermont, or any other state in the West or South. "Enough Alabama and Tennessee cotton came to market down the tributaries of the Ohio to encourage its manufacture in Kentucky" (Clark, *History of Manufactures* 1:542).

CHAPTER 22. – *1838*

1. See note 7 of chapter 4 on Merrell's friend Dennis Marvin Winston. Merrell also mentions Winston in chapters 18 and 21.

2. The McIntosh clan, in the person of its chief, John Moore McIntosh, came to Georgia with its founder, General James Edward Oglethorpe. General Lachlan McIntosh was an American Revolutionary War hero and is particularly associated with the battle for Savannah, Georgia.

3. The Reverend Dr. Joseph Clay Stiles (1795–1875) appears twice in Merrell's memoirs. Here, as a minister who had been sent to Kentucky in 1835 on a nine years' assignment, he is the companion of his friend Marvin Winston. Later, in the Arkansas section of Merrell's memoirs, he will appear as the man who organized the Southern Aid Society in 1853 (Nevin, *Encyclopedia of the Presbyterian Church*, 863). See note 11 to chapter 45. Stiles was called by a Yale elocution professor "the

first pulpit orator in America" (Myers, *Children of Pride*, 1690). In 1835 Stiles and Marvin Winston had moved to Versailles, Kentucky, from Georgia in an attempt to free their slaves. These two men provided Merrell with his link to Roswell, Georgia, for they had family connections with "the colony," as it was called. Stiles had married Caroline Clifford Nephew (1810–79) from Darien, Georgia, of the same family as Barrington King's wife (Myers, *Children of Pride*, 1690). Later Winston's daughter Susan lived with Barrington King's family, according to the 1860 census. Winston had married a Miss McIntosh.

4. The Cherokee were evicted from Georgia in December 1831. A land lottery was held for settlers in October 1832, and settlers were arriving in a steady stream by early 1833 (Temple, *First Hundred Years*, 32–33, 37).

5. The colony of Roswell, Georgia, consisted of the families of the following six founders from the Georgia coast: Roswell King (1765–1844) and his daughter Elizabeth Hand; Roswell King's son Barrington King (1798–1866); James Stephens Bulloch (1793–1849); John Dunwody (1786–1858); Archibald Smith (1801–86); and the Reverend Nathaniel Alpheus Pratt (1796–1879). The colony was named for Roswell King.

6. Frederick Seymour Winston (1806–75), after attending the Utica Academy and becoming a clerk in a New York City dry-goods store at the age of fifteen, owned one of the largest stores in the city, the F. S. Winston Company, and directed the Mutual Life Insurance Company. When Merrell was managing the Curtright Manufacturing Company in 1847 in Greene County, Georgia, he made drafts on Winston's company in his business. Winston also helped Merrell to arrange transportation from New York to Greensboro for a group of Irish immigrants who were to work at Curtright. Further, Merrell helped with the education of F. S. Winston's nephew Frederick, the son of his brother Marvin, who died in 1840. Frederick arrived in Greensboro on or near November 27, 1847, and the letter that he wrote to F. S. Winston should be quoted both for the light that it sheds on the following paragraphs and for what it shows about Merrell and the education of a manufacturer of the time: "Frederick is with me. If his plan of learning the mfg. business under me meets the approbation of those concerned, I will with pleasure give him the same chance that was given me when I was a boy. I take it to be not only a duty to bring up young men to the business but in this case a pleasure. If Frederick learns with me, he must off coat & go into the factory shoulder to shoulder with ordinary hands in each department until he is capable of keeping up his end with the best. Mr. Gordon's son, about Frederick's age, has just commenced in the same way" (Smith Papers, Letterbook, box 102, pp. 41–42, 154, 186).

CHAPTER 23.
(1838)

1. Horace Merrell (1817–38) was the fourth child of Henry Merrell's uncle Ira (1779–1849) and his aunt Nancy Camp Merrell (1788–1850).

2. Henry Merrell's paternal grandmother was named Damaris Mix.

CHAPTER 24

1. Merrell's beloved uncle John Camp (1786–1867), after years of bachelorhood and at the age of almost fifty-nine years, married Abigail Doolittle, a widow, in 1845. They had one daughter, Harriet.

2. Harry Camp (1787–1875), the partner of his brother John in the business on Genesse Street in Utica died a bachelor.

3. Bagg lists these and other Utica businessmen and their locations in his *Memorial History of Utica*, 573.

Georgia

1. Sherwood, *Gazetteer of the State of Georgia* (1837), 86–87; Shryock, "Industrial Revolution," 111.

2. Mitchell, *Rise of the Cotton Mills*, 21; Merrell, Smith Papers, Letterbook, box 102, pp. 132–33; Clark, "Manufactures during the Ante-Bellum and War Periods," 325–26; *DeBow's Review* 5 (1848): 189.

3. Shryock, "Industrial Revolution," 124–26.

4. Boney, "Part Three: 1820–1865," 170.

5. Griffin, "Textile Industry," 1228. But Victor S. Clark maintains that in 1860 the number of spindles in the South was 290,000, compared with 5,236,000 in the country; and "they did not equal by over 100,000 the number running in the single city of Lowell [Massachusetts]" (Clark, *History of Manufactures* 1:558). James M. McPherson notes that by 1860 southerners had a smaller portion of their capital invested in manufacturing than they had had in 1850 (McPherson, *Battle Cry of Freedom*, 99). Two different perspectives on the extensiveness of the South's industrial output are offered by Fred Bateman and Thomas Weiss. On the one hand, southerners were far behind the rest of the nation in both 1850 and 1860 in industrial output per capita. With 36 percent of the nation's population in 1850 and 33 percent in 1860, the South "never accounted for more than eleven percent of the nation's industrial output." On the other hand, in 1860 the South was the fifth most developed "nation" in the world in terms of cotton manufacturing (Bateman and Weiss, *Deplorable Scarcity*, 18–20). It was "backward only relative to the industrial Northeast and to some European economies" (25).

6. Clark, "Manufactures during the Ante-Bellum and War Periods," 313; Clark, *History of Manufactures* 1:553.

7. Bateman and Weiss, *Deplorable Scarcity*, 158, 162. Bateman and Weiss reach this conclusion only after carefully studying, then discounting, other reasons that have been offered for the failure of the South to live up to its industrial potential: the presumed deficiency of aggregate southern income, the supposed inequality of wealth and income distributions, the apparent deficiencies in product market and aggregate level of demand, the apparent lack of incentive for investment, the possibility that slavery created economic incentives to invest in agriculture rather than

industry or that it deterred immigration of white laborers, the South's choice of specializing in staple exports, the charge that planters purposely erected legal and social barriers to block industry from developing, and the hypothesis that white southerners were incompetent in or indifferent to business (26–37, 41, 46, 85, 91, 157, 159–60). They offer specific reasons why the planter class turned away from industrial development: they were "exceptionally averse" to taking financial risks; they were "not knowledgeable about the benefits of diversification"; they did not acknowledge "accumulating evidence on the greater possibility of manufacturing"; and they "attached unagreeably high social costs to industrial diversification" (161).

8. Temple, *First Hundred Years*, 32–33, 37.

9. Myers, *Children of Pride*, 1584.

10. Temple, *First Hundred Years*, 111.

11. Myers, *Children of Pride*, 1579.

12. Roswell Historic Preservation Commission, *Bulloch Hall* (pamphlet), n.p., n.d.

13. Coleman, *Roswell Manufacturing Company*, 3.

14. *Acts of the General Assembly of the State of Georgia, 1839*, 116–17.

15. Smith Papers, box 100, folder 9.

16. Roswell Manufacturing Company, Minutes, 1–11, quotation on 10–11. The originals of these minutes are in the possession of DeKalb College in Decatur, Georgia.

17. U.S. Post Office Department, *Record of Appointment of Postmasters*, roll 23, 17:35.

18. White, *Statistics of Georgia*, 291; Greene County, Georgia, "Deed Book PP," 327.

19. Smith Papers, Letterbook, box 102, pp. 279, 164, 182, 200.

20. *Milledgeville (Southern) Recorder*, July 7, 1846, p. 3, col. 2; *Savannah Daily Republican*, November 25, 1846, p. 2, col. 4.

21. *DeBow's Review* 6 (1848): 293.

22. *DeBow's Review* 12 (1852): 359–60.

23. "Manufacturing in Sober Earnest," *Milledgeville (Southern) Recorder* March 30, April 13, 20, 27, 1847; *New York Journal of Commerce*, August 31, September 6, 8, 17, 1855), p. 3, col. 3; p. 1, col. 1; p. 3, cols. 4–5; p. 3, col. 3. The articles are reprinted in the Appendix.

CHAPTER 25

1. Merrell was a great admirer of Thomas Rogers (1792–1856), the great mechanic of Rogers, Ketchum, and Grosvenor of Paterson, New Jersey. He regretted not buying Rogers's machinery for his enterprises in Greene County, Georgia, and to this fact he attributed his failure there. So great was Rogers's reputation in 1839 that the first textile mill at the Roswell Manufacturing Company was erected according to his drawings. Rogers had started as a carpenter's apprentice and had progressed to blacksmithing when he settled in Paterson at the age of twenty. After serving in the War of 1812, he returned to Paterson to build wooden looms. He

earned enough money at this work and at pattern making to enable him, in 1819, to purchase the rights to manufacture an imported power loom. With John Clark he formed the firm of Clark and Rogers to manufacture the new loom. Rogers used the capital that he acquired from this venture to build a plant for manufacturing textile machinery, and in 1832 he organized the Rogers, Ketchum, and Grosvenor Machine Works, which soon began making railroad locomotives and other railroad machinery, in addition to textile machinery (*DAB* 16:112–13).

2. The steam packet *Home*, one of the first "coastwise" steamers after the *Savannah* and the *Robert Fulton*, was lost during a northeast gale on November 9, 1837, going ashore near Cape Hatteras with a loss of about 100 lives. When the *Pulaski* was twelve hours out of Charleston on June 14, 1838, one of her boilers exploded. The ship broke into two pieces and sank within an hour with a loss of about 110 people. Commenting on these disasters, John H. Morrison confirms Merrell's opinion about their effect on coastal steam travel: "After the accidents to the 'Home' and the 'Pulaski' the public confidence in this class of vessels seems to have been shaken, so much so that on most of the routes they no longer proved paying investments." This condition lasted until 1846, when vessels more appropriately called "steamships" began to be constructed (Morrison, *History of Steam Navigation*, 437–42). The *Great Western* of Isambard Kingdom Brunel (1806–59) had been launched in Bristol, England, in 1837. The ship had proved that oceangoing steamships could cross the Atlantic successfully without refueling.

3. Peter Wiltberger, formerly a sea captain, came from his native Pennsylvania to keep the City Hotel, and later the Pulaski House, in Savannah (Myers, *Children of Pride*, 1734). Mrs. Hardee may be the Isabella Hardee (b. 1806?) who kept a small hotel in the 1850 census of Chatham County, Georgia. Her relative William Joseph Hardee (1815–73) was the author of *Hardee's Tactics*, a book adopted by the army. He became a Confederate major general and commanded a corps at the battle of Shiloh in 1862. He organized the original Arkansas (Hardee's) Brigade and by 1864 was in command of the military departments of South Carolina, Georgia, and Florida. He was in charge of the unsuccessful defense of Savannah against General Sherman.

4. Merrell traveled the first railroad in Georgia. The Georgia Railroad (chartered in 1833) began at Augusta, directly across the Savannah River from Hamburg, South Carolina, the western end of the first railroad in America, the Charleston and Hamburg, which had begun running in January 1831 (Dunbar, *History of Travel in America* 3:962, 1085). Construction of the Georgia Railroad had begun in 1834 and had reached Greenesborough (later Greenesboro' or Greensboro) the very month that Merrell arrived there, in May 1839 (Sherwood, *Gazetteer of Georgia*, 4th ed., 150). Merrell does not note here that he later spent ten years in Greensboro nor that the passage of the Georgia Railroad onward to Madison and Athens in 1841 decreased the importance of the town, a fact which led to his being asked to build a steam-powered factory to recoup the town's fortunes.

CHAPTER 26

1. Barrington King (1798–1866), son of the colony founder Roswell King (1765–1844), the "agent" of the Roswell Manufacturing Company. Henry Merrell was given the official title of Assistant Agent for the company in 1844 (Roswell Manufacturing Company, Minutes, April 3, 1844, p. 9).

2. The colony of Roswell, Georgia, is known to have been founded by six planter families brought by Roswell King from the Georgia coast. Roswell King had managed Pierce Butler's Hampton Point plantation on nearby St. Simons Island. The families that he brought with him to Roswell had lived in such nearby counties as McIntosh and Liberty. In this paragraph Merrell mentions most of them. After Roswell King, who lived with his daughter Elizabeth Hand, they are: Barrington King, James Stephens Bulloch, John Dunwody, Archibald Smith, and the Reverend Nathaniel Alpheus Pratt. Although these families first lived in such primitive conditions as Barrington King's Labyrinth, they were soon building the fine Greek Revival homes that are today the pride of the city. While Roswell King lived with his daughter Elizabeth Hand in Primrose Cottage, Barrington King built Barrington Hall, Bulloch built Bulloch Hall, Dunwody built Mimosa Hall, Archibald Smith built the Smith House, and the Pratts built Great Oaks.

3. The area of northwest Georgia had been cleared of the last Cherokee Indians in 1838, when the United States Army rounded them up for the infamous Trail of Tears. According to a census taken by the state, however, there were over fifteen hundred white people living in Cobb County as early as 1833 (reprinted in *Northwest Georgia Historical and Genealogical Quarterly* 12, no. 4 (1980): 30–31), for the state had held a land lottery in 1832. Although the Cherokees protested the lottery and were still pressing their claims before the U.S. Supreme Court, these people were here about the time that Roswell King was traveling through the area to Dahlonega, the site of the gold rush in 1829 that had increased pressure to remove the Cherokees. King had been sent to manage a branch of the bank of Darien and was living in Dahlonega in 1833 to protect his interests (Coulter, *Auraria*, 10). He must have liked what he saw coming through Roswell, however; he and his son set up a gristmill in what was called Lebanon, a community about a mile to the northeast of what would become Roswell. "The Colony" had arrived by 1838. The rapid fall of Vickery (or Cedar) Creek into the Chattahoochee River nearby must have soon suggested a textile mill. Construction began in 1839 and was well advanced by the time Merrell arrived.

4. "The depression of 1839–43 was one of the severest in American history. Prices fell by as much as one-half in some places; real estate values and stocks declined even more drastically" (Bruner et al., *American Portrait*, 252).

5. Thomas Rogers, the inventor and locomotive builder whom Merrell mentioned in the preceding chapter.

6. The details that Merrell has just given, especially the fact that hewn blocks of granite were used to shore up the factory's first foundation, have helped to docu-

ment the location of the original factory of the Roswell Manufacturing Company for the recent archaeological work on the site sponsored by the Roswell Historical Society. See Wood, *Archaeological Survey.*

7. Merrell spoke of Backus before, in chapters 11 and 24.

8. Captain Allison Nelson (b. 1822) was the son of John B. Nelson, the founder of Nelson's Ferry across the Chattahoochee River near Atlanta. In 1855 Allison Nelson became the first mayor of Atlanta to be born in what is now Fulton County, but he resigned the same year because his city council had reduced the amount of two small fines he had imposed. He moved to Texas, served in its legislature, and became a brigadier general in the Confederate army. He died of sickness in September 1862 (Garrett, *Atlanta and Its Environs* 1:51, 230, 389–90). Farrish Carter (1780–1861), for whom Cartersville, Georgia, is named, was a wealthy planter and speculator in land. As an entrepreneur, Farrish Carter owned many early mills and factories in Georgia and "played an important role in the growth of the state's prewar economy" (Coleman and Gurr, *Dictionary of Georgia Biography* 1:176–77).

9. Henry Rootes Jackson (1820–98) served as a judge on the Georgia Supreme Court and as U.S. minister to Austria. He resigned his judicial offices to command a division of the Georgia militia in the Civil War and helped in the defense of Atlanta. After the war he became director of the Central of Georgia Railroad, was U.S. minister to Mexico, and earned a reputation for such poems as "The Red Old Hills of Georgia."

10. Perhaps Captain Charles James Magill, the son of Merrell's wife's uncle William (b. 1792), but "Jack" Magill has to date refused to be pinned down definitely. Comparative references and dates in Georgia Civil War military records and Smith family letters show that he is the John W. Magill who enrolled as a Confederate private in Captain Wheaton's Company of Georgia Artillery in 1861 and who became a first lieutenant in Captain Daniell's battery of light artillery in 1863–64 (drawer 254, rolls 65 and 51 of microfilm records of Georgia Civil War soldiers, Georgia Department of Archives and History, Atlanta.)

CHAPTER 27

1. Merrell seems to be counting the death of his cousin Horace Merrell (d. 1838) as his first "heavy bereavement." See chapter 23. Henry Merrell was only nine years old when his father died.

2. Archibald Smith's house was not finished at the time of these fisticuffs. It was not completed until 1845, well after Merrell's marriage to Smith's sister-in-law Elizabeth Pye Magill in 1841. At the time of Merrell's first visit to the family, the Smiths were living in a farmhouse north of Roswell.

3. "Charley" is Merrell's brother-in-law, Charles Arthur Magill (1817–84).

CHAPTER 28.
(1839 or 1840)

1. Merrell seems to have produced six thousand dollars worth of manufactured goods at the factory as early as 1840. According to the *Schedules of Mines, Agriculture, Commerce, and Manufacturing in Georgia* (Cobb County) in 1840, the factory had 480 spindles, employed twenty-eight people, and had a capital invested of $45,000 (U.S. Bureau of the Census, *Sixth Census of the United States: 1840*, microfilm, Georgia, roll 1, vol. 16). This may be a good time to note that the Roswell area was in Cobb County until 1932, when it became a part of Fulton County.

2. The word in manuscript is virtually illegible, but it appears to be "Teel." If it is, the word is a variant of "til" (sesame), and "Teel oil" is obtained from sesame seeds (*Oxford English Dictionary*, s.v. "til").

3. Archibald Smith probably furnished much of the cotton for the Roswell Manufacturing Company. He had thirty-three slaves in 1840; he kept a large cotton warehouse; and he seems to have been one of the northernmost cotton planters in Georgia. His notebooks concerning the weather, his times of planting, fertilizers used, etc., are now kept in the Georgia Department of Archives and History in Atlanta.

4. The north Georgia gold rush of 1829 had indeed caused much excitement. It brought white people, such as Roswell King, rushing into Cherokee Indian territory. It is said that the expression "There's gold in them thar hills" was coined about this gold rush. A U.S. mint was built in Dahlonega (the Cherokee word for *gold*), and Dahlonega gold covers the dome of the Georgia state capitol today.

5. The Georgia state legislature granted three railroad charters in 1833. The Georgia Railroad Company was to build a line from Augusta that was to end in Athens. Construction began in 1834, had reached Athens in 1841, and had gone on to what would become Atlanta by 1845. The Central of Georgia Railroad Company was to go from Savannah to Macon. Construction began in 1836 and was complete through Macon by 1843. The third charter issued in 1833 was given to the Monroe Railroad Company, which was to run a line between Macon and Forsyth. It had laid its track between the two towns by 1838, but it went bankrupt soon thereafter. All of these lines would eventually connect to Atlanta, which was first a village named White Hall. It was renamed Terminus when it was selected as the point at which the new state railroad, the Western and Atlantic (chartered in December 1836), was to end its line from Chattanooga, Tennessee. Merrell discusses the many false starts and delays in finishing this route (Sherwood, *Gazetteer of Georgia*, 4th ed., 149–51; Boney, "Part Three: 1820–65," 157–59). In 1843 Terminus was renamed Marthasville, after the daughter of a state governor, then finally Atlanta in 1847; but as late as 1850, its population was only a little more than 2,500, and it did not reach 10,000 until 1860 (Knight, *Standard History of Georgia* 3:1782–83).

6. Colonel Stephen H. Long (1784–1864) had been hired in May 1837 to locate the route of the Western and Atlantic from the Chattahoochee River to the Tennessee line (Johnson, *Georgia as Colony and State*, 408–9). The line of the railroad

today is basically as Long designed it. Long was the first chief engineer of the railroad until 1840. Charles Fenton Mercer Garnett was the chief engineer of the Western and Atlantic from 1842 to 1847. Garnett was succeeded in this office by William L. Mitchell, whom Merrell mentions in chapter 33. (See note 7 to that chapter and Johnston, *Western and Atlantic Railroad*, 19–21, 28–29.) The two Garnetts whom Merrell mentions were two different people. Robert Selden Garnett (b. 1819), the first general officer killed in the Civil War, was a career West Pointer who fell at Corrick's Ford, Virginia, on July 13, 1861.

7. The Central Bank of Georgia had been created in 1828 in order to furnish agricultural loans for which the private commercial banks did not adequately provide. It issued its own bank notes and generally was successful until the legislature began to dip into its capital to pay off deficits and to finance the Western and Atlantic Railroad. During the expanding economy of the 1830s, five railroad banks were chartered, among them the three major railroads already mentioned. All these and other commercial banks were hurt by the panic of 1837 and the depression that followed it. By 1842 the legislature ended the Central Bank's power to issue bank notes and to grant new loans, thus beginning a liquidation process for the state bank which lasted more than a decade (Boney, "Part Three: 1820–1865," 153–54).

8. Governor George Walker Crawford (1798–1872) was, as a hard-money Whig, concerned with liquidating the Central Bank of Georgia during his term of office, which ran from 1843 to 1847. He later served as Zachary Taylor's secretary of war and was president of the Georgia secession convention in 1861.

9. F. S. Winston was mentioned in chapter 22. He is the brother of the Reverend Marvin Winston, who, when Merrell was visiting him in Kentucky, suggested that he write Barrington King in Roswell. Frederick Seymour Winston (1806–75) was, like Merrell, educated at the Utica Academy and became a clerk in a New York City dry-goods store at age fifteen. He later built up the F. S. Winston Company, one of the largest in the city, and became a director of other companies, state boards, and religious societies.

10. According to the 1840 census of manufactures mentioned earlier in note 1 of this chapter, the Roswell Manufacturing Company was capitalized at that time at forty-five thousand dollars. The charter itself mentions no specific amount of capital to be raised before operations could begin (*Acts of the General Assembly of the State of Georgia, 1839*, 116–17). The profits were so satisfactory, in fact, that Merrell himself, at a meeting of the stockholders on October 16, 1844, made the motion, subsequently passed, that a dividend of 22 percent be declared on the last twelve months' profits, that $87.30 be added to the value of each share, and that an 8 percent distribution be made (Roswell Manufacturing Company, Minutes, 10).

CHAPTER 29.

(1840 to 1841)

1. In the frontier economy of Georgia, the Roswell Manufacturing Company could operate without banks, paper money, or even specie by following the fashion

that Merrell learned at the Oneida Factory in Whitesboro, New York, a fashion that was common among the earliest textile mills in America. The factory could pay for raw materials and local purchases in thread or cloth, and workers could be paid in credits at the company store, as were persons outside the company who provided services to it. Merrell would follow this pattern in establishing other factories, except that in Arkansas he would emphasize collecting specie.

Merrell, who is referred to as "one of the shrewdest northern manufacturers," is quoted in an article in *DeBow's Review* in 1848 as saying that he could count on profits of 12 percent and that factories could increase their profits by having stores supply workers and resell articles received in barter (6:293).

2. There is a Jane Green listed as a head of household in the 1840 census of the 845th Militia District (Roswell) of Georgia. From the age and sex of the people in her household (only one girl is under fifteen), it is possible that Jane Green was a widow who ran a small boardinghouse. If Jane Green is Merrell's "Mrs. Green," then he would have been one of the two males between the ages of twenty and thirty listed in the census as resident in her household. The 1840 census was the last to list only the heads of households by name. Of the 136 or 137 heads of households in the 845th Militia District (there is one possible duplication), only 7 appear to be women, and Jane Green is the only Green in the district.

3. There is no Tom Fee in the 1840 or 1850 census of the Roswell district, but there is a Samuel Fee listed in 1840. A miller named Oswell B. Langley, age forty-eight, is listed in the 1850 census.

4. In the 1840 census, a Simon Fraser is listed in the 845th Militia District (Roswell), and the 1850 census lists a Simon Frasier, age fifty, from Scotland. He is still in the area in 1860 at age fifty-nine, and his name is again spelled Fraser. In her exhaustive study of Cobb County, Sarah Temple says that Simon Fraser was the bookkeeper for the Roswell Manufacturing Company until his death, that he had lived in Liberty County for some years before coming to Roswell, and that he had come to the new town at Roswell King's request (Temple, *First Hundred Years*, 115).

5. This David Howell certainly plays an important part in Henry Merrell's story, but details about him are sketchy. If we assume that Merrell brought him from Utica to keep the Roswell Manufacturing Company's store in 1839 or 1840, then he may be the "D. Howell' who witnessed Merrell's marriage settlement on July 7, 1841 (Smith Papers, box 100, folder 2). But Merrell invited his cousin and brother-in-law George Hull Camp to keep the company store in 1842. We may therefore assume that Howell had returned to Utica by that date. Merrell says that he saw Howell again in Utica and invited him to keep the store at his Long Shoals Factory in Greene County. This meeting in Utica could not have taken place before 1845 and perhaps took place in 1847, for David Howell was back in Georgia by August 23, 1847, when he replaced Merrell as the postmaster of Merrell, Georgia, the new manufacturing village that Merrell completed in Greene County (U.S. Post Office Department, *Record of Appointment of Postmasters*, roll 23, 17:35).

Furthermore, the 1850 census of Greene County, Georgia, records David Howell, age thirty-five and born in Wales, as being a clerk married to one Hannah, a native of Pennsylvania. David Howell later succeeded Merrell as the manager of the Curtright Manufacturing Company and, as we shall see in chapter 35, earned Henry Merrell's everlasting anger.

6. Croton oil is a viscid, acrid fatty oil obtained from the seed of the *croton tiglium,* a small Asiatic tree. The oil can act as a purgative, and in the South farmers have protected their watermelon patches by cutting plugs from selected melons, pouring in Croton oil, reinserting the plugs, and waiting for thieves to steal and eat. Here Merrell's cousin is applying the oil, also a vesicant and pustulant, to relieve congestion in his chest.

7. This issue of the "Cotton Bug" is not reprinted in this volume. All of these *jeux d'espirit* are on file among the Smith Papers, box 100, folder 1, Georgia Department of Archives and History, Atlanta.

8. In Elizabeth Merrell's hand is a note pinned into the manuscript, marked to be placed before the paragraph that begins "The case was this." It reads: "This I think is a mistake. It was in regard to money for C. [her brother, Charles Arthur Magill] while studying medicine at the North. The other matter: Mr. K. had money of mine in his hands & brought some of it back, not buying a ladle which I sent for because he thought it unnecessary. I don't remember that there was any hard feeling or any thing said about that. The other story was this way. Mr. K. was going to Sav. You were owing C. for Bank stock you had sold & begged Mr. K. to send on money to him from Sav. C., in great distress for money to pay his board, which had been due some time, wrote to me about it. You were at Mars Hill. I wrote to you, & you answered that Mr. K. had money of yours, & you could not understand why he had not sent it. I told your sister of it, & she was staying at Mr. King's at the time & spoke of it. He was vexed & spoke to brother about it, & brother spoke to you. That was the first coolness I ever knew about."

9. Cicero Tippens will surface again in Arkansas, in chapter 45 of Merrell's memoirs.

10. Henry S. Atwood (1800?–1864) was a resident of Darien, Georgia, and a stockholder in the Roswell Manufacturing Company, although he never lived in Roswell. In 1855 he purchased most of Merrell's Greene County property from him, and in 1856 he bought the Curtright Manufacturing Company that Merrell had built there. George Hull Camp met Atwood's daughter Jane in Roswell when she and her sister Ruth spent several summers there as the guests of Mrs. Hand, Roswell King's daughter. Ruth married Dr. William Elliott Dunwody, a son of John Dunwody and Jane Bulloch (Temple, *First Hundred Years,* 114).

11. Merrell gave his name as Eric Parker in chapter 27.

12. See chapter 17.

13. A William Balentine, a weaver, age thirty-eight and born in Scotland, appears in the census of Greene County, Georgia, in 1850.

14. Merrell first used the term *ultra* in chapter 13 in his discussion of the effects

of such people as Beriah Green on the religion and politics of New York. See note 9 to that chapter.

15. Charles Barrington King (1823–80) was the oldest son of Barrington King. He graduated from Princeton Theological Seminary in 1848 and served several Presbyterian churches in Georgia: Marietta, Sparta, Columbus, Augusta, and Savannah.

16. The new factory, managed for their father by Thomas Edward King and James Roswell King, was the Ivy (or Laurel) Woolen Mill, built near the end of Vickery Creek in 1846, after Merrell had left Roswell (Coleman, *Roswell Manufacturing Company*, 3). Thomas Edward King was killed at the battle of Chickamauga in 1863.

17. But like his brother Tom, young Barrington Simerall King fell in the Civil War, at Averysboro, North Carolina, in 1865.

18. The Reverend Nathaniel Alpheus Pratt (1796–1879), like many of the settlers of Roswell, had a Connecticut background. He was born in Saybrook, Connecticut, graduated from Princeton Theological Seminary, and came south to serve the Darien Presbyterian Church from 1826 to 1840. He married Roswell King's daughter Catharine Barrington King and moved to Roswell to serve as the first minister of its Presbyterian church.

19. Merrell's interest in this subject comes, of course, from the Connecticut background of his grandparents and of his wife's family as well. Not only was the Reverend Dr. Pratt a native of Connecticut, but Roswell King himself had been born in Windsor, Connecticut. John Dunwody (1818–1903) was born in Hartford. The homes of most of these Roswell settlers may have been built by a Connecticut architect, and the square in Roswell is certainly on the pattern of New England towns. Its Presbyterian church (organized in 1839) is built in the style of a New England meetinghouse. Allenbrook, a house built about 1846 that may have served as a residence or office for the manager of the Ivy (Laurel) Woolen Mill of the Roswell Manufacturing Company, is built in the New England salt-box style, as are many houses in the mill village. The style of the Smith House itself was similar to a salt-box dwelling. Barrington Hall had a captain's walk.

20. Of the children of John Dunwody (1786–1858) and Jane Bulloch (1788–1856), Henry Merrell would have been most familiar with young John Dunwody (1818–1903), who worked with him making collections for the Roswell Manufacturing Company. Born in Hartford, Connecticut, John later served in the Georgia militia and in the Mexican War. He was a government surveyor in Kansas, a colonel of Georgia infantry, and the disbursing agent for the Niter and Mining Bureau of the Confederate States. In this post he often carried dispatches and large sums of money from Richmond to the west. His brother Charles Archibald Alexander Dunwody (1828–1905) worked at manufacturing in Roswell until the Civil War, in which he was severely wounded. His brother Henry Macon Dunwody (b. 1826) was killed at Gettysburg in 1863, and James Bulloch Dunwody (1816–1902) was a clergyman. William Elliott Dunwody (1823–91) was a well-known doctor in

Cobb County (Myers, *Children of Pride*, 1510–11; Northen, *Men of Mark in Georgia* 6:345–47; Temple, *First Hundred Years*, 114).

CHAPTER 30.
1842 to 1845

1. William Gregg (1800–77) was from Columbia, not Charleston. He made a fortune in the jewelry business there before turning his attention to his Graniteville factory near Edgefield, the first cotton mill in the South. His essays, "Domestic Industry—Manufactures at the South" and "Southern Patronage to Southern Imports and Domestic Industry," urging the South to build its future on manufacturing rather than on growing cotton, appeared in the influential *DeBow's Review* 8 (1850): 134–46, and 29 (1860): 77–83, 226–32, 494–500, 623–31, 771–78. He planned an ideal factory community at Graniteville. "In public-mindedness, in breadth of view, in qualities of imagination, in sanity of judgment that did not sacrifice understanding of his misguided contemporaries, in power of analysis of the confronting situation, William Gregg stood head and shoulders above other Southerners of his time" (Mitchell, *Rise of the Cotton Mills*, 37). For a good, brief description of Gregg's Graniteville, see Clark, "Manufactures during the Ante-Bellum and War Periods," 324–25; and Clark, *History of Manufactures* 1:557.

2. The first successful textile mill in Georgia was apparently built in 1826 by Gregg's uncle and guardian, Jacob Gregg, on the banks of the Little River at Whatley's gristmill, halfway between Madison and Monticello (Griffin, "Origins of the Industrial Revolution," 356). Victor S. Clark says that a mill was in operation in Georgia "soon after 1810" (Clark, *History of Manufactures* 1:556), but M. R. Hall refers to an unsuccessful factory established on the Little River in Morgan County in 1810. Hall maintains, on the contrary, that the first successful cotton mill in Georgia was built in 1828 near Athens on the Oconee River (Hall, "Utilization of Southern Water Powers," 582–83). Lucian Lamar Knight maintains that the oldest recorded cotton mill in Georgia was chartered in 1810 in Wilkes County, near Washington, and that the next was the Georgia Factory near Athens that was mentioned above, which was incorporated in 1828 (Knight, *Standard History of Georgia* 3:1783–84).

3. This is perhaps Johnson Garwood, one of three men from whom Merrell purchased the Mars Hill Factory on Barber Creek in Clarke County (now Oconee County), Georgia, in December 1844 (Clarke County, Georgia, "Deed Book S," 139, 148). After Merrell left the employ of the Roswell Manufacturing Company, Johnson Garwood became a stockholder in that company (Roswell Manufacturing Company, Minutes, October 7, 1845, p. 12).

4. A contemporary source lists thirteen cotton factories in Georgia in 1837 (Sherwood, *Gazetteer of Georgia*, 3d ed., 86–87). A modern source maintains that there were "about fifteen" factories in the state in 1837, small affairs "near the fall line on rivers or in such towns as Athens, Augusta, and Columbus" (Shryock,

"Industrial Revolution," 111). The 1840 census yields a total of nineteen (Griffin, "Origins of the Industrial Revolution," 362).

5. Elsewhere, Merrell himself listed by name thirty-one factories in Georgia in 1847 (Smith Papers, Letterbook, box 102, pp. 132–33). *DeBow's Review* in 1848 quotes a Mr. Nisbit, chairman of the Committee on Manufactures in the State of Georgia, who says that "we know of thirty-two cotton factories in our State, in operation, or in progress of construction." The same periodical lists thirty-four in 1849 and thirty-six in 1850 (5:189; 7:454–55; 9:557). J. G. Johnson says there were thirty-five factories in Georgia in 1850, when Georgia led the South in number of factories and in value of manufactured products (Johnson, "Notes on Manufacturing in Ante-Bellum Georgia," 224). Merrell himself maintains in print that there were fifty factories in Georgia in 1855 (*New York Journal of Commerce*, August 31, 1855, p. 3, col. 3).

6. The Tariff of 1846 reduced the rates of duty and charged all articles not free of duty with ad valorem rates.

7. Merrell seems to be referring to the completion of the rail links from the area that would soon connect Atlanta to the ocean. The Georgia Railroad, which gave the area connections to Charleston through Augusta, had reached what was to be Atlanta by 1845; the Central of Georgia route, which, through the Macon and Western Railroad connected Atlanta to the sea at Savannah, had reached the area by 1846 (Boney, "Part Three: 1820–1865," 158–59). The links from Merrell's area to the north would not be long in coming. The Western and Atlantic reached from Atlanta to Marietta (near Roswell) by 1845, to Cartersville by 1846, to Dalton by 1847, and finally to Chattanooga by 1850 (Temple, *First Hundred Years*, 103).

8. According to the *Savannah Daily Republican* of November 25, 1846, this prize was awarded to the Curtwright (often spelled Curtright) Manufacturing Company for the "best specimen of cotton yarn" at the "recent Fair of the American Institute in New-York." This specimen was "not a fancy one prepared for the occasion, but taken merely from a lot offered for sale in the New-York market" (p. 2, col. 4). This award came after Merrell had won the award for the "best and finest in the Fair" at the 1846 National Fair in Washington "City." In this case the prize was for "a very beautiful specimen of Cotton Twist" (*Milledgeville [Southern] Recorder* July 7, 1846, p. 3, col. 2).

9. Merrell bought this mill from James Allen, Isaac Vincent, and Johnson Garwood in December 1844 for $4,150 (Clarke County, Georgia, "Deed Book S," 139, 148). He sold it to the Curtright Manufacturing Company on May 31, 1845, for $16,000 (Clarke County, Georgia, "Deed Book S," 265). This fourfold profit makes Merrell's claim of doubling his investment seem modest, but he could be referring to its book value and not to his profit (Clarke County, Georgia, "Receivers Book," 1845, 5–6; "Tax Book" 1846, 5–6). The "extensive works" in "the adjoining county" is the Curtright Manufacturing Company plant, which Merrell built in 1845 in Greene County, Georgia, at Long Shoals on the Oconee River.

CHAPTER 31

1. Elizabeth Pye Magill Merrell (1815–90) should be included among the first settlers of Roswell, for she had come there to live with her sisters Helen and Anne, the latter of whom was the wife of Archibald Smith. All three sisters were among the founders of the Roswell Presbyterian Church in 1839 (Charter of the Roswell Presbyterian Church, History Room, Roswell Presbyterian Church).

2. David Zubly married Elizabeth Pye, one of three wards who came to his father, John Joachim Zubly (1724–81), through his second marriage to Anne Pye in 1767. Merrell's wife is therefore named for her grandmother. The father of Merrell's friend and brother-in-law Archibald Smith (1801–86) was also named Archibald Smith (1758–1830). His second marriage, in 1796, was to Helen Zubly, the sister of Merrell's wife's mother, Elizabeth Ann Zubly.

3. Elizabeth Pye Magill Merrell's father was Charles A. Magill (1782–1854). His first child was Anne Margaret Magill (1807–87), who became the wife of Archibald Smith (1801–86) and the mother of Elizabeth Anne Smith (1831–1915); William Seagrove Smith (1834–65), who accompanied Merrell on his first trip to Arkansas and later worked for him there; Helen Zubly Smith (1841–96); and Archibald Smith (1844–1923). The second child of Charles A. Magill was Seagrove William Magill (1810–84), whom Merrell does not mention. The third child was Helen Zubly Magill (1812–87), who lived with her sister and brother-in-law in Roswell. The fourth child was Merrell's wife, Elizabeth Pye Magill (1815–90); and the last child was Merrell's business partner in Arkansas, Charles Arthur Magill (1817–84).

4. Zubly (1724–81) came to Georgia in 1745. He was elected to the Second Continental Congress in 1775 but took such a strong stand against separating from England that he believed he was not useful, and he returned to Georgia. During the Revolutionary War he was jailed for a time, then was banished from Georgia until Loyalists took lower Georgia. After the war, he never regained his former influence.

5. The six illustrations of life in early Roswell that follow this chapter (plates 11–16) were not included in Merrell's memoir, but they are included here to complement his picture of the community. These illustrations were done in a 7½-by-9½-inch sketchbook ("New Improved Sketchbook") that was found wrapped in bound paper among the Smith Papers. On the front and rear of the wrapper is written in pencil "Uncle Henry's Sketch Book of Early Roswell" (Smith Papers, box 106).

CHAPTER 32.

Intended to be rather Anecdotical

1. King died in 1844.

2. The date of the insurrection was 1794.

3. According to Malcolm Bell, Jr., in *Major Butler's Legacy*, Roswell King was anything but a just manager of slaves. His goal of making Pierce Butler a rich man was "pursued with relentless determination that warped his sense of decency in

his relations with the hundreds of black slaves he controlled. His departure from the Butler estate was not friendly. . . . Second generation Butlers believed him dishonest and self-serving" (531).

4. Pierce Butler (1810–67) and Frances Anne Kemble (1809–93). "After a stormy life together and apart, the Butlers were divorced in 1849, their marriage rent by the infidelities of Pierce Butler and by his wife's outspoken disapproval of the family's ownership of slaves" (Bell, *Major Butler's Legacy*, 489).

5. Catherine Barrington King (1776–1839). She was the daughter of Jessiah and Sarah Williams Barrington of San Sevilla Bluff on the Altamaha River. In her family background were governors of Connecticut, General James Edward Oglethorpe (the founder of Georgia), Oliver Cromwell, and the Tudors (Bell, *Major Butler's Legacy*, 531).

6. Merrell's cousin George Hull Camp (1816–1907) boarded with Merrell's mother, Harriet Camp Merrell (1799–1880), while he was working in Utica for his uncles John and Harry Camp in their dry-goods store (Yates, *Utica Directory, 1839–40*, 45, 72). He would have become well acquainted with Merrell's younger sister Lucretia (1818–45) while living there. They were married in 1842 and moved to Georgia the same year.

7. On the motion of John Dunwody, Henry Merrell was given the title of Assistant Agent of the Roswell Manufacturing Company on April 3, 1844. At the same time, he was allowed to purchase a share of capital stock for $750. His office was confirmed on October 16, 1844 (Roswell Manufacturing Company, Minutes, pp. 9–10).

8. Hugh W. Proudfoot (b. 1795?) was long the bookkeeper for the Roswell Manufacturing Company.

9. Merrell strikes at the end of this sentence the phrase "with all his faults."

10. Catherine Margaret Nephew King (1804–87).

11. Lachlan McIntosh has the same name as his Revolutionary War ancestor who was colonel of the First Georgia Battalion and, with Count Pulaski, the leader of the advance guard at the battle of Savannah (Johnson, *Georgia as Colony and State*, 135–36).

12. "Old Mr. Dunwody" was John Dunwody (1786–1858), one of the six founders of Roswell.

13. "Major Bulloch" was James Stephens Bulloch (1793–1849), another of the founders of "the Colony." His sister Jane (1788–1856) was Dunwody's wife. Merrell's account is of the social life of Roswell before the Dunwodys built Dunwody (now Mimosa) Hall and the Bullochs built Bulloch Hall next to each other near the city square.

14. Both Elizabeth Pye Magill (1815–90) and her sister Helen Zubly Magill (1812–87) were living in Roswell with the Smiths, for Mrs. Archibald Smith was their sister, Anne Margaret Magill Smith (1807–87).

15. Merrell appended to this chapter his long account, apparently written much later, of surviving a hurricane in a sailboat near Beaufort, South Carolina, where he

had gone to visit Archibald Smith's half-brother, John Joyner Smith, and some of his wife's cousins, the Barnwells. This is the first editorial excision from Merrell's manuscripts.

CHAPTER 33

1. See note 20 of chapter 29 on John Dunwody.

2. Merrell's story about "Dicky" Park is corroborated by Arthur Franklin Raper in his survey of the history of Greene County, Georgia, except that Raper puts the money in the chest at one hundred thousand dollars in gold and silver (Raper, *Tenants of the Almighty*, 39).

3. Merrell's reference to a "Murrell gang" is probably to a legendary network of bandits who were supposed to have operated across eight states of the Old Southwest in the 1820s and 1830s. A horse thief, counterfeiter, and slave stealer named John A. Murrell (1806–44) was said to have been their leader. The historical John Murrell was inflated to mythic proportions in 1835 with the publication of what purported to be his life story, written by his captor, Virgil A. Stewart. Although Murrell was never convicted of any crime stronger than disturbing the peace, Stewart portrayed him as the mastermind of a vast conspiracy to incite an insurrection of slaves. This accusation spread fear and paranoia throughout the antebellum South. See James L. Penick's *The Great Western Land Pirate: John A. Murrell in Legend and History* (Columbia: University of Missouri Press, 1981) and *DAB* 13:369–70.

4. According to Charles H. Shriner (*History of Murray County*, 28), a Judge Kennan was a superior court judge from 1836 to 1839. "Several old citizens have informed me that the lawless element defied the courts for some time," he says, and Judge Kennan (which he also spells Kenan), was the first judge "who succeeded in holding court and enforcing respect for the law" (15). It may be that the name that Merrell spells variously "Kenion" and "Kenyon" and that Shriner spells "Kennan" and "Kenan" is actually Augustus Holmes Kenan (1805–65), a famous early criminal lawyer and politician in Georgia who, after vigorously opposing secession, helped to frame the constitution of the Confederate States and loyally supported the Jefferson Davis administration. See Coleman and Gurr, *Dictionary of Georgia Biography* 6:571; Myers, *Children of Pride*, 1578; and Register, *Kenan Family*, 98–99.

5. This may be Colonel William N. Bishop, commander of a militia unit called the "Georgia Guard" and clerk of the Murray County superior court, who was the county's first state representative. His brother, Captain Absalom B. Bishop, knocked down Spencer Riley in Milledgeville and tried to shoot him, but his pistol misfired. The careers of these brothers show that Murray County politics of the 1830s could often arrive at the point where "opposing forces would fight regular battles in a small way with sticks and stones" (Shriner, *History of Murray County*, 13–16). The Bishops' careers are detailed in Murray County History Committee, *Murray County Heritage*, 11, 40–46, 50, 52–54.

6. This brave tailor may be Frederick Cox, who is listed among several county merchants in Murray History Committee, *Murray County Heritage*, 51.

7. William Letcher Mitchell (1805–82), whose father had come to Athens, Georgia, from Virginia in 1803, was a tutor, law professor, secretary-treasurer, and then a trustee of the University of Georgia. In 1848 he was appointed chief engineer of the Western and Atlantic Railroad, and later he was a member of the state legislature (Knight, *Georgia's Bi-Centennial Memoirs* 2:157; Myers, *Children of Pride*, 1626; Johnston, *Western and Atlantic Railroad*, 29). In 1848 Merrell wrote to him about the relationship between the railroad and his business (Smith Papers, Letterbook, box 102, p. 293).

CHAPTER 35

1. "The heart knoweth his own bitterness, and a stranger doth not intermeddle with his joy" (Prov. 14:10).

2. A "swinnied" horse has atrophied shoulder muscles or, more broadly, any muscular atrophy.

3. According to the U.S. Corps of Engineers near Cassville, Georgia, this would be Salt Peter's Cave in Bartow County, about four miles from Cassville. It has been purchased by the National Spelunkers Society and is currently closed to the public.

4. The title of a poem by Thomas Haynes Bayly (1797–1839) about a bride who, "in sportive jest" during Christmas festivities, hides from her bridegroom in an old oak chest which has a lid that springs shut on her. Her lover and the festive company search for her in vain, and her moldering skeleton is found in the chest years later.

5. The Wedding Guest in "The Rime of the Ancient Mariner" by Samuel Taylor Coleridge (1772–1834) awoke "a sadder and a wiser man" the morning after he heard the Mariner's tale.

6. See note 9 to chapter 30 concerning Merrell's purchase of the Mars Hill in December 1844 for $4,150 (Clarke County, Georgia, "Deed Book S," 139, 148) and sale of it to the Curtright Manufacturing Company on May 31, 1845, for $16,000 (Clarke County, Georgia, "Deed Book S," 265). On January 9, 1845, the *Savannah Daily Republican* announced that "an effort is making to form a company for the establishment of a cotton factory at the falls of the Oconee" (p. 2, col. 3). The land at Long Shoals in Greene County was sold by John Curtright to the Curtright Manufacturing Company on June 10, 1845 (Greene County, Georgia, "Deed Book OO," 252–53). Merrell was one of the nine owners of the company. Construction began soon thereafter, and the factory was in operation "within nine months after the first spade was put into the ground" (*Savannah Daily Republican*, April 20, 1849, p. 2, col. 3). Merrell always spells *Curtright* without a *w*. This spelling is used in Greene County deeds. *Curtwright* often appears elsewhere.

7. Although the factory site was first registered with the Post Office Depart-

ment on May 26, 1846, as Long Shoals Factory, with Merrell as the postmaster, its name was officially changed to Merrell on December 28, 1846, with Merrell still as postmaster. David Howell replaced Merrell as postmaster on August 23, 1847, but the post office kept Merrell's name until February 18, 1854, when it was changed to Curtright. The post office at the site was discontinued June 26, 1866 (U.S. Post Office Department, *Record of Appointment of Postmasters*, roll 23, 17:35, 26:83). The following maps of Georgia have "Merrell," "Merrell Factory," or "Merrill's Factory" on them: *Bonner's Map of the State of Georgia* (Milledgeville: William G. Bonner, 1847, 1848, and Savannah: W. T. Williams, 1849), appearing also as a "Pocket Map" in White's *Historical Collections of Georgia* (New York: Pudney and Russell, 1855); *Georgia*, by J. H. Colton (New York: Johnson and Browning, 1855, and J. H. Colton and Co., 1856, 1860); *Map of the State of Georgia, Compiled by James R. Butts, Late Surveyor General*, (Macon, 1859, 1870); *An Accurate Map of Greene County, Made in Accordance With An Act of the General Assembly of the State of Georgia*, by Amanda Barnett (Milledgeville, 1867); *Map of the State of Georgia Compiled Under the Direction of the General Assembly*, by A. G. Butts (Macon, 1882, 1889).

Before its inundation in 1979 by the waters of Lake Oconee, the Curtwright ("Merrell") site was thoroughly surveyed in 1974–1975 and 1978 by a team of archaeologists from the University of Georgia's Department of Anthropology. The site consisted of the factory building — a substantial building on granite foundations with the first floor walls eight inches thick — and more than forty other buildings and structures that dated from construction in 1845 to the cessation of operations about 1870. Merrell was proud of the construction. He noted in the Letterbook that he kept in Greensboro, "In everything relating to the Long Shoals Factory, I have aimed at permanence. I have been at extra expense to make it so. The works are substantial" (Smith Papers, Letterbook, box 102, p. 279).

By 1850 the mill employed sixty-five to seventy-five men, and the population of the mill village itself was as high as five hundred. See Fish and Hally, "Wallace Reservoir Archaeological Project," 1–18; Chester DePratter, "The 1974–1975 Archaeological Survey in the Wallace Reservoir, Greene, Hancock, Morgan and Putnam Counties, Georgia," 317, 320; and Rice, "Towns, Villages, and Post Offices." See also Albert F. Bartovics and R. Bruce Council, "A Preliminary Site Report for Archaeological Salvage Undertaken at 9Ge37 (The Curtwright Factory Site)," University of Georgia, Laboratory of Archaeology, Athens, 1978.

There is an incorrect legend in Greene County that Merrell caused his mill to be spared from destruction by Federal troops in 1864 because he "convinced them that it was his mill and that he was their kind of 'folks.' " But Merrell was in Arkansas at the time (Rice, "Why Sherman's Army Showed Mercy)."

8. George A. White's *Statistics of Georgia* (1849) says that the capital of the company was one hundred thousand dollars (291). The company charter, dated May 8, 1851, allowed it to increase its capital to five hundred thousand dollars (Greene County, Georgia, "Deed Book PP," 327). This factory was the largest in Greene

County before the Civil War (Griffin, "Textile Industry in Greene County," 83), with either four thousand or five thousand spindles and looms (White, *Historical Collections of Georgia*, 479; *Savannah Daily Republican*, April 20, 1849, p. 2, col. 3).

9. The potato famine of 1845–50 forced thousands of poor Irish peasants off their land and across the Atlantic to America. Merrell's interest in hiring only Protestants seems a fond hope, but he apparently went to a great deal of trouble to bring such workers from New York City to Greensboro. His correspondence with F. S. Winston, who helped arrange their transportation, was mentioned earlier. They "came up last week in the passenger train 2d class," says Merrell in a letter of November 26, 1847 (Smith Papers, Letterbook, box 102, p. 182). Merrell wrote Colonel Rowan H. Ward at the House of Representatives in Milledgeville on November 20, 1847, concerning their arrival. The letter is interesting not only for what it says about labor and labor problems in Georgia, but for the ironic tone that Merrell takes:

> I have this week rcd. and installed 19, making in all 20, emigrants of the starving poor who are now made happy with food & clothing at our works. They came to hand in good health & spirits. I never employed a lovelier set of hands. The moral effect upon our fractious & insubordinate is capital. If those people had dropped from the clouds, they would not have produced more dismay. But in a more serious way, I would apprise you that I consider the experiment entirely successful. Factories can at this time be built & manned with decent, humble, Protestant people who can be procured at less expense & will work for more reasonable wages than the corresponding class of native Georgians.
>
> You are aware that it has been a serious question whether white hands could be procured to man [   ] Factories. Also that the hands already employed are restless & exacting because the demand for operatives exceeds the supply. The interesting circumstance is this. The first question asked by these people is, "Can they have a patch of land to cultivate?" They set infinite value upon an acre of poor land & I doubt not [   ]. Those whom I have will all be fully employed as mechanics & will have no time to till the land. (Smith Papers, Letterbook, box 102, pp. 164–65)

10. Joshua Neary married Tranquilla C. Parrot on September 11, 1852 (Greene County, Georgia, "Marriage Licenses, White, 1852–1862," 34).

11. In the 1850 census of Greene County, Georgia, Joshua Neary, David Howell, and David Howell's wife, Hannah, are listed as living with a schoolteacher named Griffin. Neary's age is given as twenty, Howell's as thirty-five, and Hannah's as thirty. It is unclear when Merrell asked Howell to come to Greene County. He had been the "first regular Store Keeper" for the Roswell Manufacturing Company (see chapter 29, note 5) and may have returned to Utica in 1842, when Merrell's cousin George Hull Camp assumed that post. David Howell is back in Georgia by 1847, for he replaces Merrell as the postmaster at Merrell on August 23, 1847 (U.S. Post Office Department, *Record of Appointment of Postmasters*, roll 23, 17:35).

In a letter to the Post Office Department on October 9, 1847, Merrell stated that

Howell was then his clerk. During the next month, he referred to Howell as his superintendent in charge of "hiring and discharging hands." Further, Merrell said that Howell fulfilled his task "very much to my satisfaction." Merrell also wrote Henry Atwood in 1847 that, of all his subordinates at Long Shoals, Howell was his "especially" picked superintendent, and he referred to him as "a townsman of my own & a young man of my own make," one who was competent to carry on the works. Howell "buys & barters for cotton at the Factory, hires, discharges, manages, & settles with the hands. Keeps up the store & the store books." "In a word," Merrell said, "every thing at the factory is under him" (Smith Papers, Letterbook, box 102, leaf between pp. 27 and 28, 149, 280).

Although Howell is listed as a clerk in the 1850 census, by November 30, 1850, he is a stockholder in the Curtright Manufacturing Company (Putnam County, Georgia, "Deed Book R," 235). He has replaced Merrell as the agent of the company by June 23, 1852 (Greene County, Georgia, "Deed Book PP," 426). It is interesting that Merrell's antagonists Joshua Neary and David Howell were living next door to each other in 1860, when Neary was twenty-eight and Howell was forty-one (U.S. Bureau of the Census, *Eighth Census of the United States: 1860. Population.* Microfilm. Georgia [Greene County], roll 125, 7:488).

12. Englishmen are sometimes fond of calling Welshmen "Taffy." The old anonymous English rhyme begins:

Taffy was a Welshman, Taffy was a thief,
Taffy came to my house and stole a round of beef;

The poem continues, in an American version:

I went to Taffy's house, Taffy wasn't in,
I jumped upon his Sunday hat, and poked it with a pin.
Taffy was a Welshman, Taffy was a sham,
Taffy came to my house and stole a leg of lamb;
I went to Taffy's house, Taffy was away,
I stuffed his socks with sawdust and filled his shoes with clay.
Taffy was a Welshman, Taffy was a cheat,
Taffy came to my house and stole a piece of meat;
I went to Taffy's house, Taffy was not there,
I hung his coat and trousers to roast before a fire.
                    (Williams, *Silver Treasury of Light Verse*, 27)

13. Pinned to the manuscript page at the beginning of this paragraph is a slip of paper, the front side of which is written in Elizabeth Magill Merrell's hand, the back side of which is written in Henry Merrell's own. Mrs. Merrell's side reads: "This I think is a little mistake in memory. We moved into Greensboro and took rooms at Willis' Hotel in Octr. '55 [1845] (the same year we moved to Greene Co.) because we could not have a fire place room at Dr. Curtright's. In Decr.'56 [1846] I suppose on account of the Fac. place having proved so sickly you thought best to purchase a House, & go to housekeeping in Town." Although the moves may

have taken place in this order, Mrs. Merrell's dates are off by ten years and have been corrected. Yet her husband writes on the back of her note: "1873, November. I dare say wife's memory in this matter better than my own. This narrative was written twenty years after the event, & now ten years more have passed since the writing. I am content now to believe I was to blame in the matter. Indeed I think I recollect that I was. I pray God to forgive me! Drawing near to the close of my life, I cannot afford to leave any sin unrepented of, or anything that might peradventure have been a sin. I pray for forgiveness for the sake of Jesus Christ our Lord." Merrell's memory is playing him false as he writes his note of apology, for he wrote his account almost eighteen years, not twenty years, after leaving Greensboro in January 1856.

The Willis Hotel, formerly the Grimes Hotel, had entertained Andrew Jackson in 1820 and had become known as the Willis Hotel when bought by Louden Willis (Rice and Williams, *History of Greene County*, 162).

14. Merrell's conservative attitude toward technical innovation was shared by many manufacturers of the period. According to Thomas R. Navin, for example, the Whitin Machine Works of Massachusetts "was obliged to point out to customers that they could not expect to buy the same frames in 1869 that they had bought in 1850." This fact indicates that "changes in design over a period of two decades were neither looked for by customers nor considered especially desirable" (Navin, *Whitin Machine Works*, 110).

15. Merrell is apparently referring to the building of a second cotton mill at the Roswell Manufacturing Company, which seems to have been completed in 1854 (Roswell Manufacturing Company, Minutes, 44). A wool factory had been completed there in 1846.

16. If the Letterbook reflects accurately Merrell's state of mind, then he was more convinced at the time (1847–48) that the concern would flourish than he is now in retrospect. He wrote Henry Atwood on December 28, 1847: "I am now frequently solicited by persons wishing to invest in a new factory. Against building any more at the Long Shoals, I am for the present determined [   ]. The new factory I have to build will make fine goods, whether driven by steam or water power. By fine goods [I] mean the ordinary sheetings & shirtings such as are [   ] course goods at the North. I am desirous of building such a Factory. I was brought up to make such goods. The money seems to be held in readiness now for such an Enterprise. The time appears to be propitious" (Smith Papers, Letterbook, box 102, p. 279).

On March 15, 1848, Henry Merrell bought the land on which the Greensboro Manufacturing Company was to stand, and he sold the "Greenesborough Manufacturing Company" this land on July 26, 1849 (Greene County, Georgia, "Deed Book PP," 78, 183). We may assume that construction began in 1849.

17. Jesse W. Champion (1807–59) was an original stockholder in the Greensboro Manufacturing Company (Greene County, Georgia, "Deed Book PP," 183).

18. Merrell's resignation from the agency of the Curtright Manufacturing Com-

pany must have come between May 8, 1851, when he signed as agent the charter of the Curtright Manufacturing Company that was entered in the Greene County "Deed Book PP," 327, and June 23, 1852, when David Howell signed a document as company agent (Greene County, Georgia, "Deed Book PP," 426).

19. Merrell dealt with both men other than as storekeepers. Baldwin was a stockholder in the Curtright Manufacturing Company, and Cunningham (1794?–1874) was a stockholder in both the Curtright and the Greensboro manufacturing companies (Putnam County, Georgia, "Deed Book R," 235; Greene County, Georgia, "Deed Book PP," 183).

20. If an article by the local historian T. B. Rice in the most important Greene County newspaper in 1938 is any indication of community memory, then it would seem that local people blamed Merrell for the failure of the Greensboro Manufacturing Company, just as a false legend persists that he turned Yankee troops away from Curtright. In reference to the Greensboro Manufacturing Company, Rice reports that " 'They say' one Merrill wrecked it" (Rice, "Why Sherman's Army Showed Mercy").

21. In his papers, Henry Merrell preserved a group of letters that passed between him and Herman A. Crane (1810?–79), a Savannah merchant originally from Connecticut. Crane wrote Merrell on May 12, 1853, that he had been "thinking of our project of joining you in spinning cotton." He asks Merrell for "the fullest possible particulars about the original cost of the Factory," its stock, and its present condition. He continues, "If I do anything, I must first understand the condition of affairs and then go in in earnest. I am no manufacturer but can do something in some of the departments" (Smith Papers, box 101, folder 4).

22. On January 8, 1856, the subscribers to the Greensboro Manufacturing Company, Henry Merrell among them, posted a ten-thousand-dollar bond to agree to the arbitration of Francis H. Cone, Augustus Reese, and Thomas R. R. Cobb in the dissolution of the company (Greene County, Georgia, "Deed Book QQ," 338–39). The arbitrators made their award on the same day, deciding, among other things, that the stockholders who had recently received dividends should repay them before other stockholders were called upon to repay the company's debts, and declaring that the property should be sold to pay the debts. Their most interesting decision relates to Merrell: "We have not considered and do not decide or award any thing as to the liability of the President and Agent Henry Merrell to the Company for his acts in the management of the same" (Greene County, Georgia, "Deed Book QQ," 339–40).

23. Compare these to the similar figures that he gives in chapter 40.

24. On William C. Dawson, see note 2, chapter 36.

25. A full explanation for editorially altering the dates in this chapter is made in note 1, chapter 39.

CHAPTER 36

1. Editorially excised from this chapter are ten paragraphs that deal in a random fashion with a music teacher at the Greensboro Female College, a young man from

New York who worked briefly for Merrell, an abandoned mill, a drunken minister, and a bad carriage horse. This is my second editorial excision from Merrell's manuscripts (see note 15 to chapter 32).

2. After attending law school in Connecticut, William Crosby Dawson (1798–1856) of Greensboro served as a member and clerk of the Georgia House of Representatives and was chosen by the legislature to compile the laws of the state. Following two terms in the Georgia Senate, he became a member of the U.S. House of Representatives. After a term as a superior court judge, he was a U.S. senator from Georgia from 1849 to 1855. Perhaps his most significant achievement was the leading role he played with his friend Henry Clay in the Compromise of 1850.

In 1820 Dawson married Henrietta, the daughter of Dr. Thomas Wingfield; in 1850 he married Eliza M. Williams, a widow from Memphis, Tennessee (Knight, *Georgia's Bi-Centennial Memoirs* 2:221).

Dawson died on May 5, 1866. Merrell has been off one year in his dates for some pages now. See explanatory note at the beginning of chapter 39.

3. An opponent of slavery and supporter of the cause of union until the last possible moment, Alexander Hamilton Stephens (1812–83) is most famous as the vice president of the Confederacy and for being denied entrance to the U.S. Senate following his election to that body in 1866. Before and after the Civil War he served in the U.S. House of Representatives and was elected governor of Georgia in 1882.

4. George Wythe Randolph (1815–67), lawyer, Confederate general, and secretary of war of the Confederacy from March to November 1862.

5. In 1848 Judge Francis H. Cone stabbed Alexander Stephens in the lobby of the Thompson Hotel in Atlanta. Although they had met earlier and seemed friendly to each other, Cone and Stephens were political rivals. Cone was the founder of the Know-Nothing party in Georgia, and he objected to the position that Stephens had taken on the Clayton bill, an extension of the Oregon compromise on slavery, thinking that Stephens had betrayed the South. Their quarrel came to violence when Stephens hit Cone with his cane. Cone then drew a knife. Stephens stopped the downward blow with his hand, which was badly slashed. Cone was later arrested and charged with assault. See Schott, *Alexander H. Stephens,* 91–93.

6. Merrell has used the term *ultra* before, in chapters 13 and 29. See note 9 to chapter 13.

7. The General Assembly of the Presbyterian Church did meet in Richmond in 1847, and James Henley Thornwell (1812–62) was elected its moderator. He was said to have been the youngest man ever to hold the office (Myers, *Children of Pride,* 1702). Thornwell was pastor of several churches in South Carolina; a professor and president of South Carolina College and a professor at the Presbyterian Theological Seminary in Columbia, South Carolina; the founder of the *Southern Presbyterian Review*; and a leading organizer in the move to separate the southern from the northern Presbyterian church.

8. Henry Ward Beecher (1813–87), famous liberal New England minister and orator, had been most outspoken in his opposition to slavery. Exeter Hall in London was the scene of many evangelical sermons, speeches, and revivals during the Victorian period, and Beecher addressed a large gathering there in 1863. His speech was a long defense of the North's reasons for prosecuting war against the South. In it Beecher maintained that any British sympathy for the South would be sympathy with an attempt to build up a slave empire. This speech is summarized in Thomas W. Knox's *Life and Work of Henry Ward Beecher*, 199–205.

9. Ross lived on the Putnam County side of the Oconee River and had a gristmill opposite the Curtright Manufacturing Company. In 1845 he was one of the original stockholders and purchasers of the Greene County land on which the factory was built (Greene County, Georgia, "Deed Book OO," 252–53). He must have had a violent temper, for Merrell mentions in a letter of November 11, 1847, that, while drunk, Ross had stabbed "old Mr. Bell" at the Curtright factory. Fortunately, the wound was shallow (Smith Papers, Letterbook, box 102, p. 128). In 1850, after his death, Ross's heirs sold his Putnam property to the Curtright Company (Putnam County, Georgia, "Deed Book R," 235).

10. Colonel John Ward had a beautiful home near the Curtright factory (E. H. Armor of Greensboro, Georgia. I am indebted to Mr. Armor for showing me many of the sites in Greene County that Merrell mentions).

11. After John R. Ross was acquitted, he and James A. Ross sold his father's land to the Curtright Manufacturing Company (Putnam County, Georgia, "Deed Book R," 235).

12. Merrell did not give his land (six lots) to the Female College outright. On May 21, 1851, he sold to the college for five hundred dollars the land that he had bought on April 22, 1850, for three hundred (Greene County, Georgia, "Deed Book PP," 237, 329). Among other original trustees for the "Female Seminary" was Merrell's friend Senator William C. Dawson, but in 1860 we find the name of David Howell listed among the trustees (Rice and Williams, *History of Greene County*, 216). The college opened under the auspices of the Presbyterian Synod of Georgia on January 2, 1852 (White, *Historical Collections of Georgia*, 477). Its motto was: "That our Daughters may be as corner-stones, polished after the similitude of a Palace" (Raper, *Tenants of the Almighty*, 37). Greene County tradition has assumed that one of the teachers at the Female College was Louisa May Alcott (Raper, "Greene's Goin' Great," *Greensboro (Ga.) Herald-Journal*, February 20, 1942, p. 6, col. 2). Rice and Williams list her among the faculty in 1854 but maintain that there is no documentary evidence to prove that she taught there. The college closed in 1864, attempted to reopen in 1872, and burned in 1874 (Rice and Williams, *History of Greene County*, 216, 218).

13. Dr. Martin may have been Robert E. Martin (1798–1859). The story of Andrew Jackson's visit in 1820 is discussed by Thaddeus B. Rice in the *Greensboro (Ga.) Herald-Journal*, June 23 and 30, 1939, p. 6, cols. 1–2 and p. 6, cols. 1–3, and October 3, 1941, p. 7, cols. 2–3. See also Rice and Williams, *History of Greene County*, 162.

14. Merrell purchased land in Greensboro on February 16, 1847, from Augustus Baldwin Longstreet (1790–1870) (Greene County, Georgia, "Deed Book OO," 396). Longstreet is the author of the well-known *Georgia Scenes,* published first in newspapers from 1827 to 1830 and in book form in 1835. He had settled in his wife's hometown of Greensboro after completing law school in Connecticut. While living in Greensboro, Longstreet served as a state legislator and superior court judge, but he left in 1827 to found a newspaper in Augusta, Georgia. After becoming a Methodist minister in 1838, he was president of Emory College in Atlanta from 1839 to 1848, of Centenary College in Louisiana in 1849, of the University of Mississippi from 1849 to 1856, and of the University of South Carolina in 1857.

15. Yelverton P. King (b. 1795?) was custodian of a gold mine in Greene County and became a distinguished lawyer, legislator, and judge. In an attempt to control trespassing upon the gold mines in northern Georgia, Governor George R. Gilmer appointed King in 1830 as the superintendent "of the public lands in the occupancy of the Cherokees" (Gilmer, *First Settlers of Upper Georgia,* 278–79). Because he had had some correspondence with him, King was on Greensboro's welcoming committee for Andrew Jackson's visit in 1820, and he was mayor of the town from 1856 to 1863 (Rice and Williams, *History of Greene County,* 142, 314, 332, 341, 352).

CHAPTER 38

1. The plantation system was developing in southern Arkansas at this time, changing the nature of the existing small-farm system, and cotton production would quintuple in the state between 1850 and 1860 (Moore, "Arkansas," 61; Bonner, "Cotton," 61).

2. Merrell records some of the information that he sought about his locations on his own map of Arkansas ("A New Map of Arkansas," in *A Universal Atlas* [Philadelphia: S. Augustus Mitchell, 1847], 25). His choice seems to have been shrewd. The area, well watered by the run-off from the Ouachita Mountains and close to Indian Territory set aside by the Choctaw Treaty of 1825, was ideal for beginning a manufacturing business along the lines he envisioned. There is some irony and interest in the fact that the Ouachita Mountains are a distant extension of the same Appalachian Mountain system that watered the Roswell Manufacturing Company in Cobb County, Georgia, and that, when Merrell arrived in Cobb County in 1839, the area had just been cleared of Indians, Cherokee Indians who had been sent on the Trail of Tears to the same Indian Territory that borders the area of Arkansas to which Merrell will now remove.

Arkansas

1. Elizabeth Merrell to William Seagrove Smith, September 29, 1858, Smith Papers, box 100, folder 8.

2. This phrase was used in 1887 by the *Pine Bluff* (Arkansas) *Daily Commercial* in a notice that the factory had been sold. The paper added that the factory had been "of infinite value to the people throughout the southern part of the state" (July 13, 1887, p. 2, col. 1). Joseph W. Bocage repeated the phrase in writing his own account of the factory and its importance. See "The Merrell Factory," *Pine Bluff Daily Commercial*, July 16, 1887, p. 2, col. 3.

3. Herndon, *Centennial History of Arkansas*, 463.

4. Herndon, *High Lights of Arkansas History*, 89.

5. Dickinson, "State's First Textile Mill," 2B.

6. Griffin, "Pro-Industrial Sentiment," 134.

7. Lewis, "Economic Conditions in Ante-Bellum Arkansas," 261.

8. Griffin, "Pro-Industrial Sentiment," 136–37.

9. Lewis, "Economic Conditions in Ante-Bellum Arkansas," 261.

10. Matlock (1817?–86) seems to have nursed the charter through the legislature. When Merrell met him in April 1856, he was a successful merchant in Camden, Arkansas, who dealt in general merchandise, groceries, iron, and farming implements (advertisements in *Ouachita Herald*, October 2, 1856, p. 4, col. 3; March 5, 1857, p. 4, col. 3). Merrell did not like politics and worried about the process of getting a charter. He insisted they be given no monopoly or favors, for he feared that possible competitors would insist on the same.

11. *Acts of the General Assembly of Arkansas* (1856), pp. 123–24.

12. *Washington Telegraph*, May 28, 1856, p. 3, col. 5.

13. Smith Papers, box 5, folder 1.

14. Ibid.

15. "Burnt Records of Pike County," pp. 99–100. Of their original agreement, Merrell says in the text, "we agreed to make up a co-partnership, in which the Trustees of my wife (B. King & A. Smith) should put in $15,000, Mr. John Matlock $15,000, & I should have a salary for my services, & Dr. Magill a salary for his services under me." Although these figures differ from those that he mentions at the end of chapter 35, we may assume that the earlier amounts were used for land purchases that were eventually given over to the company. Of his original purchases, Merrell says, "I purchased the right of the occupant (Mr. Dorsey) at a low rate, I thought, and immediately returning to the land office at Washington, entered and paid for the land more than enough for the site of a manufacturing village: say six or seven hundred acres in all."

Purchases by Merrell recorded in the "State of Arkansas Tract Book" (124–25) seem eventually to have totaled more than six hundred acres, but he did not make all these purchases at once. Land Management Records of the National Archives indicate that his first purchase (certificate 10237) was of a little over ninety acres and was made in the name of his wife's trustees, Barrington King and Archibald Smith, on February 23, 1856. A later purchase (certificate 10306) was made on April 24, 1856, and was also made out to Elizabeth Merrell's trustees. These two purchases totaled 207.62 acres at a cost of $259.53, or $1.25 an acre.

16. *True Democrat*, September 9, 1856, p. 2, col. 2.

17. Bocage, "The Merrell Factory," p. 2, col. 3; Dickinson, "State's First Textile Mill," 2B.

18. *True Democrat*, May 19, 1857, p. 2, col. 8.

19. The ad first ran on April 28, 1857, and kept running for seven consecutive weekly issues until June 16, 1857, although its content was altered slightly in the May 12 issue (p. 3, col. 8) to the form quoted and continued running in that form.

20. Nolan, "Four Unpublished Letters from Augustus Garland," 80. Augustus Hill Garland (1832–99) came to Washington, Arkansas, from his native Kentucky and practiced law. A Confederate congressman and senator, he was later elected to the U.S. Senate (1877–85) and became Grover Cleveland's attorney general (1885–89).

21. U.S. Post Office Department, *Geographical Site Location Reports*. It appears that the Royston Post Office was begun on September 24, 1857; discontinued July 9, 1860; reestablished November 30, 1866; and finally discontinued October 22, 1884 (U.S. Post Office Department, *Record of Appointment of Postmasters* microfilm, roll 8, vols. 14, 25B, 40, and 56).

22. Pike County, Arkansas, *Tax Records, 1834–1875*, roll 10.

23. Smith Papers, box 100, folder 9, and box 4, folder 1.

24. Ibid., box 100, folder 9.

25. Ibid., box 4, folder 1.

26. U.S. Bureau of the Census, *Eighth Census of the United States: 1860. Schedule 5. Products of Industry*, microfilm, Pike County, Ark., Thompson Township, roll 8, p. 1.

27. Moore, "Arkansas," 66.

28. "Important Manufactory," p. 2, col. 1.

29. Griffin, "Pro-Industrial Sentiment," 137–38.

30. *Washington Telegraph*, June 4, 1862, p. 2, col. 3.

31. Ibid.

32. Ibid., May 21, 1862, p. 2, col. 1.

33. Ibid., June 4, 1862, p. 2, col. 3.

34. Merrell's problems were, to a great degree, part of the larger problem of lawlessness in Arkansas during the middle years of the Civil War. He is joined by a modern historian in dramatically rendering the extent of those problems. Speaking of Arkansas in 1863, Robert Selph Henry says: "Conditions there were deplorable, really appalling, as Secretary Seddon wrote to General Smith in March. Civil government had largely disappeared, and military rule was not strong. Bushwhacking, burning, pillage, assassination, violence of all sorts were common" (*Story of the Confederacy*, 232).

35. Elizabeth Merrell to William Seagrove Smith, May 10, 1863, Smith Papers, box 5.

36. Here Merrell may have been thinking of paragraph 1, section 8, of the Constitution of the Confederate States of America, which reads, "nor shall any duties or

taxes on importations from foreign nations be laid to promote or foster any branch of industry" (*Journal of the Congress of the Confederate States of America* 1:913).

37. Mrs. Merrell tells us that her husband rather dictated the terms of this project. She writes Willie Smith on May 10, 1863: "He told Gen. H. he must insist on not being interfered with in any way; & he gave him full authority to have it exactly his own way" (Smith Papers, box 5).

38. Because the paper shortage was so acute, Merrell began his memoirs in the endpapers and margins of David Dale Owen's *Report of a Geological Survey of Wisconsin, Iowa, and Minnesota* (Philadelphia, 1852). Paper was so scarce when Hindman took over the Trans-Mississippi Department that he had to seize the public documents in the state library to tear up and use for cartridge paper (Belser, "Military Operations in Missouri and Arkansas, 1861–65," 376). The closest newspaper to Merrell was the *Washington Telegraph*. It announced on March 19, 1862, that it would reduce the size of its paper to half a sheet, adding, "the paper mill at Nashville is in the hands of the enemy, the blockade still exists. . . . The fact stares us in the face that when our present stock is out, we can get no more" (March 19, 1862, p. 2, col. 1). On May 28 the same paper announced that although they still had some stock of printing paper, "the stock of writing paper in our town is entirely exhausted. There is not a sheet for sale" (May 28, 1862, p. 2, col. 2).

39. It would seem that Henry Merrell came out distinctly better for his sale of Royston than did his partner, John Matlock. For the Camden property that was to be the basis of Merrell's prosperity for the rest of his life, John Matlock received a factory that, within months, Confederate authorities took from him and for which they never paid him. Matlock described himself in his application for pardon on September 9, 1865: "He is a heavy loser, pecuniarily, by the rebellion, much of his property having been impressed and seized by agents of the rebel government, and for which he was never paid" ("Case Files of Applications from Former Confederates," group 1, roll 14, pp. 0088–0089).

40. Elizabeth Merrell to William Seagrove Smith, May 10, 1863, Smith Papers, box 5.

41. Readers may note that even secondhand accounts of Civil War battles in Arkansas may be important additions to the history of a state which witnessed more battles and engagements than all but three Confederate states (Moore, "Arkansas," 67).

42. Certificates: Smith Papers, box 100, folder 10; Charles Arthur Magill to Smith family, August 30, 1865, Smith Papers, box 60, folder 10.

43. Throughout the course of the war, and indeed until her death in 1880 at the age of eighty, Merrell's mother lived in Sackets Harbor, New York, with her nephew Walter Bicker Camp, the brother of George H. Camp, who had been Merrell's successor at the Roswell Manufacturing Company. Although Merrell mentions seeing his mother in 1860, he never mentions her or his northern relatives while he is writing about the Civil War. He does seem to have communicated with them, however. According to a letter to Willie Smith that Mrs. Merrell wrote

in Camden on March 15, 1864, "we have this moment had the pleasure of receiving a letter from dear Mother via Flag of Truce from L. Rock. Friends all well. She is still with Walter. Says they live happily as they did when we were there, & are both growing fleshy. I don't wonder. Plenty of good living & nothing to do" (Smith Papers, box 5, folder 3).

44. *Pine Bluff Daily Commercial,* July 16, 1887, p. 2, col. 3.

45. Elizabeth Merrell to Helen Zubly Smith, March 15, 1864, Smith Papers, box 100, folder 8.

46. Elizabeth Merrell to Anne Magill Smith, July 3, 1864, Smith Papers, box 100, folder 8.

47. Merrell's orders from General Kirby Smith, the list of "Necessary Expenses," and these instructions are in the Smith Papers, box 100, folder 6.

48. *O.R.,* vol. 41, pt. 4, pp. 1012–13.

49. *Pine Bluff Daily Commercial,* July 16, 1887, p. 2, col. 3.

50. Ibid.

51. William H. Etter to his children, November 16, 1864 (Private collection of William H. Etter III, Washington, Arkansas).

52. Elizabeth Merrell to Anne Magill Smith, November 9, 1864, and Haynes's instructions (dated December 1, 1864), Smith Papers, box 100, folders 8 and 6.

53. Smith Papers, box 100, folder 6.

54. Smith Papers, box 100, folder 6.

55. Haynes's letter, Smith Papers, box 100, folder 6; letter of Elizabeth Merrell to Anne Margaret Magill Smith, July 8, 1865, Smith Papers, box 100, folder 8.

CHAPTER 39

1. Merrell often repeats the date 1855 as the year that he left Georgia for Arkansas. See the end of chapter 35 and note 25 to that chapter. Several compelling facts demand that the date of his departure for Arkansas be changed from January 1855 to January 1856. First, we must consider that he wrote his wife from Savannah, Georgia, a letter, now preserved in the Smith Papers, that is dated January 12, 1855 (box 100, folder 9). It is a commonplace letter that mentions people whom he has seen about town, and it gives no indication that he is preparing to be in Arkansas by the end of the month. Second, we must confront the fact that there are deeds of sale of his property in Greensboro that are dated October 17 and November 24, 1855 (Greene County, Georgia, "Deed Book QQ," 319–21). We must add the fact that the final breakup and arbitration of the Greensboro Manufacturing Company did not occur until January 8, 1856 (Greene County, Georgia, "Deed Book QQ," 338–40).

Third, in a long, somewhat tedious section that will be editorially excised from the text of his memoir, Merrell mentions meeting a Catholic bishop, Martin J. Spalding (1810–64), on the train to Arkansas and on the riverboat from Memphis to Louisville. Spalding was traveling to a council that was held in New Orleans in 1856 (O'Connell, *Catholicity in the Carolinas and Georgia,* 186).

Fourth, the weather conditions that Merrell describes could have occurred only in 1856, not 1855. Merrell says that in 1855 the weather was harsh, the rivers were frozen, and water transportation was at a standstill. But on January 5, 1855, there were recent heavy rains in the Little Rock area, and a boat was headed up the Arkansas River toward the town. The temperatures ranged between a low of 38 and a high of 68 degrees Fahrenheit for the week of December 28 to January 3 (*Arkansas State Gazette and Democrat*, January 5, 1855, p. 2, col. 1). Temperatures remained moderate during the week of January 4 to January 10, ranging between 32 and 48 degrees. "The River is at last at a fine boating stage and we hope the season for navigation has fairly set in. There are ten or twelve feet of water in the channel and the river is rising" (*Arkansas State Gazette and Democrat*, January 12, 1855, p. 2, col. 1). No fall of the river or interruption in river traffic is mentioned in the January 19, January 26, or February 2, 1855, issues of the *Arkansas State Gazette and Democrat*. Temperatures remain at successive highs of 70, 66, and 55 degrees for those weeks. No excessive rain is mentioned for the months of January and February.

On the other hand, the conditions of 1856 conform exactly to those that Merrell mentions. In late December, the river is falling and it has snowed (*Arkansas State Gazette and Democrat*, December 28, 1855, p. 2, col. 1). The river has been "frozen over, for several days" on January 5, 1856, and all of the area icehouses have been filled (*Arkansas State Gazette and Democrat*, January 5, 1856, p. 2, col. 1). On January 12, the river is "still at low water mark, and frozen over opposite this place. There has been a continuation of cold, freezing weather for three weeks, which is a longer spell than 'the oldest inhabitant' ever saw" (*Arkansas State Gazette and Democrat*, January 12, 1856, p. 2, col. 1). The river is still too low for navigation between January 19 (p. 2, col. 1) and January 26 (p. 2, col. 1). A "cold, sleety rain" begins on January 24 and continues to fall so that by February 2 the river has risen by ten feet (p. 2, col. 1) and the weather continues bad through most of February.

Almost all doubt is removed by the dates on the documents in the National Archives that Merrell used to make his original purchases of federal lands in Pike County. The earliest, certificate no. 10237, is dated February 23, 1856. The second, no. 10306, is dated April 24, 1856.

Another proof that Merrell moved to Arkansas in 1856 is the scurrilous attack upon Roswell Beebe that Merrell mentions in his text. This attack appeared in the *Arkansas State Gazette and Democrat* on March 1, 1856, p. 2, cols. 5–6. Finally, we have the evidence that his wife and his minister provide in the obituaries that they wrote about him. Elizabeth Merrell says that "in 1856 he removed to Arkansas"; the Reverend Eugene Daniel says, "he went to Arkansas in 1856" (*South-Western Presbyterian*, March 15, p. 1, col. 1, and February 22, 1883, p. 1, col. 1).

2. William "Willie" Smith (1834–65) is perhaps the most tragic figure to appear in Merrell's narrative. The oldest son of Archibald and Anne Magill Smith, he stood to be their heir. It is clear that the Smiths and the Merrells were agreed that the young man should consider manufacturing as his career, for he lived with

the Merrells for a time in Greensboro, accompanied Merrell on his 1856 trip to Arkansas, and worked as his clerk in Arkansas from 1859 to 1861. It would seem, however, that Willie Smith did not have the temperament to be the hard-driving builder and manager that his uncle was. He kept elaborate notes of the flora and fauna that he saw in Arkansas, and family letters indicate that he had a sensitive, artistic temperament. Merrell may have cast him as the son that he never had and may have been disappointed that Willie did not take to manufacturing. In any event, Willie Smith served in the signal section of the Eighteenth Georgia Battery during the Civil War and, to the dismay and anguish of all who knew and loved this gentle, affectionate young man, died of dysentery in Raleigh, North Carolina, in July 1865, months after Lee had surrendered.

3. Thomas Rice Welch (1825–86) was the pastor of the Presbyterian Church in Helena from 1851 to 1859 and of the First Presbyterian Church in Little Rock from 1860 to 1885. He was moderator of the General Assembly in 1872 and U.S. consul to Hamilton, Ontario, from 1885 to 1886 (Scott, *Ministerial Directory*, 759).

4. Lloyd Tilghman (1816–63) was graduated from West Point in 1836 but soon resigned from the army to become a civil engineer, working on railroads and canals. He returned to the army during the Mexican War, then served as an engineer on railroads in Panama and in the South until 1859. He joined the Confederate army in 1861, became a brigadier general in 1862, and was taken prisoner after his surrender of Fort Henry in February of that year. Exchanged in July 1862, he was killed near Vicksburg on May 16, 1863.

5. In the 1860 census, the most likely indentifiable residents of Dallas County who seem to be of the property and status of Merrell's gentlemen are W. L. Somerville, age forty-nine, a wealthy farmer who had been born in Virginia; Nat G. Smith, age fifty-eight, a somewhat less wealthy farmer who came from North Carolina; and Howell F. Taylor, from Tennessee and extremely wealthy for his age of thirty-one (U.S. Bureau of the Census, *Eighth Census of the United States. Population*, microfilm, Desha County, Ark., roll 31, 3:993, 980, 978).

6. Grandison D. Royston (1809–89) was a lawyer, prosecuting attorney, and politician who had been born in Tennessee but came to Hempstead County, Arkansas, in 1832 or 1833. He was a member of Arkansas's first constitutional convention in 1836, served in both houses of the state legislature, and became a Confederate legislator and judge. He owned ten thousand acres and a large number of slaves (Goodspeed, *Biographical and Historical Memoirs of Southern Arkansas*, 382).

7. The hotel kept by Hezekiah W. ("Ki") Smith was for many years the chief hotel in Washington, Arkansas, a town that later served as the Confederate capital of the state (Medearis, *Sam Williams*, 287, 312). Judge Isaac White was sheriff of Pike County from 1835 to 1840 and Pike County judge from 1850 to 1852 (Goodspeed, *Biographical and Historical Memoirs of Southern Arkansas*, 307; Pike County Heritage Club, *Early History of Pike County*, 20).

8. Hugh A. Blevins, a lawyer and speculator, was a partner of Grandison Royston in some of his business ventures, but Allen W. Blevins, a prosecuting attorney for

the sixth judicial district of Arkansas from 1840 to 1861, also served with Royston. It is uncertain which Blevins Merrell is writing about. See Medearis, *Sam Williams*, 52; Goodspeed, *Biographical and Historical Memoirs of Southern Arkansas*, 382.

9. Although purchases of the Arkansas Manufacturing Company eventually totaled more than six hundred acres, Henry Merrell did not make them all at once in 1856 ("State of Arkansas Tract Book," 124–25). National Archives land records indicate that his first purchase (certificate no. 10237) was of a little over ninety acres and was made in the name of his wife's trustees, Barrington King and Archibald Smith, on February 23, 1856. A later purchase (certificate no. 10306) was made on April 24, 1856, and was also made out to Elizabeth Merrell's trustees. These two purchases totaled 207.62 acres at a total cost of $259.53, or $1.25 an acre.

10. The *Arkansas State Gazette and Democrat* shows that "a cold, sleety rain" began to fall on the night of Thursday, January 24, 1856, and was still falling Saturday morning when the paper went to press. By February 2 the river had risen by ten feet (January 26 and February 2, 1856; p. 2, col. 1 and p. 2, col. 1), and the weather continued mostly bad through February 23.

11. Beebe (1795–1856) helped to lay out Little Rock in 1839 and became an active alderman and mayor. He organized the Cairo and Fulton Railroad and became its first president in 1853. See Goodspeed, *Biographical and Historical Memoirs of Southern Arkansas*, 350; Clark, *Arkansas Pioneers*, 352–53.

12. Solon Borland (1808–64) was a U.S. senator from Arkansas from 1848 to 1853. He had previously served in the Mexican War and returned to Central America as U.S. minister to Nicaragua and Central America in 1853 and 1854. He later became a Confederate brigadier general.

13. Beebe died in New York on September 27, 1856. He had gone there on railroad business. Once again we have evidence that Merrell first came to Arkansas in 1856, not in 1855 as he maintains.

14. This "scurrilous assault" in a newspaper provides more evidence that Merrell came to Arkansas in 1856, not 1855, and gives us a rare specific date for his movements in the state that year. The attack on Beebe, entitled "Gov. Conway's Cat's Paw — Sitting No. 2," appeared in the *Arkansas State Gazette and Democrat* on March 1, 1856, and it is indeed scurrilous. Referring to an earlier "sitting" during the summer of 1855, the writer states that "it was our duty to let the public know the manner of man who was trying to poison their minds against the state, and citizens of Arkansas." Beebe's career had then been "characterized as 'a tomb-stone, with the single word — *Failure*, as a black lettered inscription, upon its top and upon its four sides.'" Now, in this second "sitting," the writer launches an attack on Beebe's failure to establish a promised foundry. Further, the writer maintains that Mr. Beebe, "without brains, and without education, has undertaken to be a literary man," writing as a cat's paw for Governor Elias Nelson Conway (1812–92), plagiarizing in the process, and trying to keep the state of Tennessee from helping in constructing the railroad from Memphis to Little Rock (p. 2, cols. 5–6).

The paper's motive for this attack may have been political. Beebe was nominated by the Democratic party for internal improvements commissioner of Pulaski County in 1856, but he lost to a Know-Nothing candidate named Giles. See the *True Democrat*, June 24, 1856, p. 2, col. 1; August 12, 1856, p. 2, col. 3.

15. Merrell indulges himself in thirteen paragraphs that describe his meetings, his theological arguments, and his subsequent visit with Bishop Martin J. Spalding (1810–64) of the diocese of Louisville. Illegible names mar these tedious and digressive paragraphs, but the last part of one paragraph must stand as an example of Merrell's character and religious views. The bishop has asked him to attend a mass: "I must acknowledge that I found myself quite carried away with the occasion. So that when it came to the wail and the cry, in the minor key of music, and the ringing of bells, and the swinging of censers, and the prostrating of the multitude upon the Elevation of the Host, I had not quite the hardihood to sit bolt upright and stare, as I had intended to do, but I compromised between that and kneeling down, by slightly leaning my head on the front of the pew, saying over and over to myself these words in rapid succession. 'I don't believe a word of it. I don't believe a word of it,' etc."

16. Charles Danforth (1797–1876) can be linked to Thomas Rogers (1792–1856), whom Merrell mentions in chapters 25 and 26. In 1820 Rogers organized the machine works company of Godwin, Rogers and Clark in Paterson, New Jersey. Danforth, who had begun as a factory worker in New York and had patented the cap spinner for spinning frames in 1828, became a machinist for Godwin, Rogers and Clark and eventually took Rogers's place in the firm, which became Danforth, Cooke and Company in 1854. When this firm expanded to build railroad locomotives in 1865, it was incorporated as the Danforth Locomotive and Machine Company. Merrell refers to his "Danforth's cap spindles" in chapter 46.

William B. Leonard of the Matteawan Machine Shop in Fishkill, New York, was also an inventor. In 1833 he had patented the "railway drawing head," which was "an important step forward in the integration of yarn-spinning processes" because it provided "a more or less automatic flow from the carding to the drawing process" (Gibb, *Saco-Lowell Shops*, 78, 745 n. 32). The Matteawan Machine Shop was at the time one of seven great centers of innovation in textile machinery (Wallace, *Rockdale*, 188). This shop was famous in the New York area for importing and improving the latest English industrial technology, and between 1825 and 1845 only the Lowell Works in Massachusetts matched the Matteawan Machine Shop in selling "a large variety of machinery over a wide geographic area." Matteawan had a branch office in New York City and, unlike other similar shops, advertised in scientific periodicals. But it may be that other customers had the same experience as Merrell with this company, for by the 1870s Matteawan "appears to have lost its early position in the industry for reasons unknown" (Gibb, *Saco-Lowell Shops*, 169, 90, 753 n. 15, 761 n. 42).

17. And Magill remained connected with Merrell in business for almost twenty years longer, until Merrell's death in 1883.

18. Adelina Patti (1843–1919) was an Italian soprano who had been brought

to America by her parents. She began singing concerts in New York at the age of eight. As "the Little Florinda," she made her operatic debut there in 1859 in Donizetti's *Lucia di Lammermoor*. Ole Bornemann Bull (1810–80) was a Norwegian violinist and composer who considered himself self-taught. After observing Paganini in Paris, Bull toured Europe and the United States, gaining a reputation as a violin virtuoso. He founded the Norwegian National Theatre and hired Henrik Ibsen as playwright and stage manager. According to John Tasker Howard's *Our Tradition in Music*, these two musicians toured together with a concert party that went all the way to California (200).

CHAPTER 40

1. Merrell himself did not own any slaves at this time. They belonged to his wife through her trustees Barrington King and Arthur Smith (U.S. Bureau of the Census, *Eighth Census of the United States: 1860. Slave Schedules*, microfilm, Arkansas, roll 54, 173). The Merrells preserved several papers concerning the servants (Smith Papers, box 100, folder 4; copies of these particular papers are at the Arkansas History Commission and the Southwest Arkansas Regional Archives). These receipts and letters indicate that the Merrells' servants in Arkansas were Edmund, born about 1800; John Marion, "the Barber," born about 1802; John's wife, Tabby Marion, born about 1807; their daughter, Helen or Ellen, born about 1842; John Pratt, "the Blacksmith," born about 1830; and Munroe, the body servant whom Merrell bought from John Matlock on February 12, 1863. Edmund seems to have been bought for Mrs. Merrell by her trustees in 1850. The Marions were bought from Oliver H. Lee of Richmond County, Georgia, on February 6, 1847. John Pratt was purchased from Mrs. Catherine B. Pratt of Roswell, Georgia, on May 10, 1854, for two shares of stock in the Roswell Manufacturing Company. At the end of chapter V below, Merrell mentions Niddy, the grandchild of Tabby, as another servant in his household.

2. Stephen F. Austin (1793–1836), who had settled briefly in Hempstead County, Arkansas, in 1819, later used the county's strategic position on the Red River as a base from which to colonize the 200,000-acre grant that his father Moses (1761–1821) had originally wrung from Spanish authorities in what was to become Texas. One of the settlements was named after Washington in Hempstead County, and it was in Washington-on-the-Brazos that Texas independence was declared on March 2, 1836. See Mary Medearis, *Washington, Arkansas: History on the Southwest Trail*, 1–8, 15–20.

3. In April 1864 Helen ran away with the Federal troops who were leaving Camden (Elizabeth Merrell to Anne Magill Smith, July 3, 1864, Smith Papers, box 100, folder 8). If the Merrells had the six servants mentioned in note 1 above, the only ones that could have been happy would be Tabby, Edmund, and Munroe; but Munroe was not purchased until the month that Merrell sold the Royston mill to Matlock.

CHAPTER 41

1. In writing *qui bono*, Merrell may mean *cui bono?*, a question that Cicero, not Cato, attributed to a Roman judge (*Pro Milone* 12.32). It means literally "to whom for a benefit?" It may also be translated "to whose profit?" or "who stands to gain?" Or it is possible that Merrell may mean *pro bono publico* (for the public good), a phrase that is often heard today in reference to lawyers who give up their fees to plead on behalf of the public or to represent the indigent.

2. Merrell wrote Archibald Smith on February 11, 1858: "Recently a freshet, the highest in the memory of white men, crippled us, but not seriously" (Smith Papers, box 100, folder 9).

3. Willie Smith, who was serving as Merrell's clerk at the time, wrote his father on November 16, 1859: "The New Dam has been finished, and is a good piece of work; it is about two feet higher than the old part" (Smith Papers, box 4, folder 1).

CHAPTER 42

1. Merrell's phrasing "the Breast Wheel or the Overshot" could lead the reader to the conclusion that "breast" is a synonym for "overshot," but the terms, in fact, apply to the two major and different types of wooden waterwheels used in early mills. Both types are turned by the weight of the water that accumulates in troughs built into the outside rim of the wheel. In an overshot wheel the water is brought over the top of the wheel to fall onto its front; but in a breast wheel, the water is brought to the rear and middle of the wheel to fall there and cause the wheel to rotate in the opposite direction from that of the overshot wheel. See Wallace, *Rockdale*, 125–27.

According to the *Oxford English Dictionary*, an ink was originally an iron cross that was set into the bottom of the upper millstone and held the stone to the spindle that turned it. Later usage joined the word *ink* with the term *step* that Merrell uses; both terms referred to the socket in which the end of any rotating spindle rotated. Merrell's sketch indicates that his ink performs the function of a bearing on which the shaft can both rest and rotate.

2. The Collins Hartford ax was mass-produced by the Collins Company of Hartford, Connecticut. American ingenuity was constantly improving upon the European ax by balancing the weight of the cutting edge and the blunt back edge of the ax head and by extending and curving the ax handle to give its user more precise control (Hawke, *Nuts and Bolts of the Past*, 147, 13–14).

3. Enos W. Scarbrough, as his name was spelled in the 1860 census, was born in Tennessee about 1822.

4. A Know Nothing was a member of an American political party that flourished in the 1850s. Members of the party were hostile to what they thought was the excessive political influence of recent immigrants and of Roman Catholics.

5. An article in the May 1857 *True Democrat* includes the fact that Merrell still had his flag flying almost a year later (May 19, 1857, p. 2, col. 8).

6. Thomas J. Conway (1819–59) first came to Hempstead County, Arkansas, from his native Tennessee. He moved to Pike County in 1846 and practiced medicine there until his death in February 1859. He also served two terms (1848–50 and 1854–56) as county coroner (Pike County Heritage Club, *Early History of Pike County*, 20). According to Goodspeed, *Biographical and Historical Memoirs of Southern Arkansas*, Dr. Conway was "the leading physician of his time, and had almost all the practice in the county" (322).

CHAPTER 43

1. John S. Owens's father, Edwin Owens, had come to Murfreesboro from North Carolina and had built the town's first hotel. After selling the hotel, he opened a store and had an extensive trade by 1850. John Owens was prominent in the affairs of the county, for he was barely twenty-one when he was elected to a two-year term as county clerk (1852–54). He died in the spring of 1861 in Texas, after being elected lieutenant colonel of the Confederate regiment that he had helped to raise (Goodspeed, *Biographical and Historical Memoirs of Southern Arkansas*, 312, 334–35; Pike County Heritage Club, *Early History of Pike County*, 20, 26, 71).

2. This is John Pratt (b. 1830?), who had been purchased by Elizabeth Merrell's trustees on May 10, 1854, from Mrs. Catherine B. Pratt of Roswell, Georgia. John Pratt ran away from Merrell in February 1860.

3. The maiden name of John Owens's wife was Rosanna Brewer (Goodspeed, *Biographical and Historical Memoirs of Southern Arkansas*, 334). Henry Brewer was one of the earliest settlers of Pike County. He was one of the commissioners to select Murfreesboro as the county seat in 1833 and was one of three commissioners to plan the town in 1836. He was also county coroner from 1836 to 1840 (Pike County Heritage Club, *Early History of Pike County*, 17–20, 69).

CHAPTER 44

1. There is no Charley Ray listed in either the 1850 or the 1860 census of Pike County, Arkansas. There is a William Ray, however, listed in both as living in the Royston area of Thompson Township, near the mill. His age is given as twenty-five in 1850 and thirty-four in 1860. He had a wife and one child in 1850 and a wife and four children in 1860. William Ray's wife, Emiline, is living alone with one son in the 1870 census of the county, a fact that indicates that her husband's fate in the Civil War may have been the fate of Charley Ray, and that Charley and William are the same person (Partain and Cooley, *1870 Federal Census. Pike County, Arkansas*, 84).

CHAPTER 45

1. "The best laid schemes o' mice an' men gang aft a-gley" (Robert Burns, "To a Mouse").

2. This mill would have been the enterprise of John Henry and Alfred Wallace.

John B. Ogden, a lawyer and merchant of Van Buren, who was a director of the company, began soliciting funds for a cotton-spinning factory in 1848, and the company was granted a charter from the state in 1852. This factory was reported to be in full operation by January 1852 (Griffin, "Pro-Industrial Sentiment," 134, 136–37; Lewis, "Economic Conditions in Ante-Bellum Arkansas," 261).

3. Once again, Merrell is off one year in his dates because he is thinking that he came to Arkansas in 1855. He came in January 1856, and the partnership between him and Matlock lasted from April 1856 to February 1863, not quite seven years.

4. Grandison D. Royston (1809–89) was a member of the Confederate Congress from 1861 to 1863 (Hempstead, *Pictorial History of Arkansas*, 869).

5. In March 1845, Cicero Tippins brought Merrell in Athens, Georgia, the news of his sister Lucretia's death in Roswell. See chapter 29, where Merrell spells his name "Tippens."

6. William W. Bell (b. 1818?) later helped John Matlock to run the Royston factory and traveled to Camden to help Merrell and Magill begin their woolen factory.

7. John W. Garrison's story does seem to have had a happy ending. When Merrell sold the factory to Matlock in 1863, Garrison was only about twenty-one years old. According to the 1870 census, he was then twenty-eight, was still working for Matlock, was married to an Arkansas woman six years younger than he, and was the father of two daughters and a son by her.

8. Conway died in February 1859. Dr. Magill, therefore, would have tended to Royston's medical needs for exactly four years.

9. Aurelia Isabella Bacon Magill (1830–1907) does not play much of a role in Merrell's memoirs, but she became very close to her Magill in-laws in Roswell and to the second and third generation of Smiths. Because she lived longer than her husband (d. 1884), than Merrell (d. 1883), or than Merrell's wife (d. 1890), her correspondence with the residents of the Smith House continued well into the twentieth century, and she continued to visit them until late in her life. There is, for example, an affectionate letter that Arthur W. Smith, the last of the Smiths, wrote in 1907 when he was twenty-six to "My dear Aunt Bell" from Paris, where he was studying architecture. She willed to Arthur Smith, who had been given her husband's middle name, all the remaining Arkansas real estate that her husband had willed to her. In fact, there is a slim chance that the Merrell memoirs came to Roswell through her, if either Merrell or Mrs. Merrell gave them to her husband. Although she is buried in Oregon, there is a marker to "Belle" Magill, as the family called her, in the Smith plot of the Roswell Presbyterian Church cemetery.

10. Samuel Orr (1823–82) graduated from Columbia Seminary in South Carolina in 1854. He seems to have arrived in Royston in 1857. After he left Royston, he became a teacher at Centre Point in Hempstead County, Arkansas, from 1858 to 1860, then at Pleasant Grove Academy in Dallas County from 1863 to 1869. He was a chaplain during the Civil War and served as a pastor in Dobyville, Arkansas, from 1869 to his death (Scott, *Ministerial Directory*, 545).

11. Joseph Clay Stiles (1795–1875; D.D., Transylvania University, 1846, and LL.D., University of Georgia, 1860) appeared earlier in Merrell's memoirs. We saw him during the epic horseback journey of 1838 that Merrell recalls in chapter 22. In 1835 Stiles and Marvin Winston had moved to Versailles, Kentucky, from Georgia in an attempt to free their slaves. These two men provided Merrell with his link to Roswell, Georgia, for they had family connections with the colony. Stiles had married Caroline Clifford Nephew (1810–79) from Darien, Georgia, of the same family as Barrington King's wife. Later Winston's daughter Susan would live with Barrington King's family, according to the 1860 census. Winston had married a Miss McIntosh.

After Merrell saw them in 1838, both Stiles and Winston became involved in an intense struggle between the "New School" and the "Old School" Presbyterians in Kentucky. At one point Stiles was deposed from the ministry because he and his followers, Winston among them, refused compromise along Old School lines. This break led to the establishing of a new synod in 1841. Winston died in 1840. Stiles moved to Richmond in 1846 and to pastorates in New York City and Connecticut before returning to Richmond. He became a general agent for the American Bible Society in the South in 1850. In this chapter Merrell is discussing Stiles's role as general agent of the Southern Aid Society from 1853 to 1859. In this office Stiles raised and distributed money to various southern churches and to home missions. During the Civil War he was appointed evangelist by the Synod of Virginia and served in the command of Stonewall Jackson (Thompson, *Presbyterianism in the South* 1:221, 407–8, 416–17; Gillett, *History of the Presbyterian Church* 2:538–41; Scott, *Ministerial Directory*, 686; Nevin, *Encyclopedia of the Presbyterian Church*, 863; *General Catalogue of the Theological Seminary, Andover*, 103; Myers, *Children of Pride*, 1690).

12. Henry and Elizabeth Merrell joined the Washington Presbyterian Church on July 19, 1857 ("Records of the Washington Presbyterian Church," vol. 1, Minutes of the Session, 1857, p. 21).

13. Once again, Merrell is off by one year in his estimate of the time that he spent in Pike County. He arrived in February 1856, sold the factory in February 1863, and was living in Camden (Ouachita County) in October 1863.

CHAPTER 46

1. Willie Smith accompanied them on this trip.

2. Merrell may be referring here to the surrender of Island No. 10 on April 7, 1862.

3. The fire, his wife's visit to Roswell, and her return to Royston with Willie Smith all took place in 1859. "Jack" Magill may be Captain Charles J. Magill of Chicago, the son of William Magill (b. 1792), who was the brother of Charles Magill (1782–1854), the father of Merrell's wife and of Dr. Magill.

4. Helen Zubly Magill (1812–87) was the sister of Merrell's wife Elizabeth and of Archibald Smith's wife Anne. She lived in Roswell with the Smiths. Archibald ("Archie") Smith (1844–1923) was the son of Archibald Smith, Sr. (1801–86).

5. Davis was inaugurated on February 18, 1861.

6. Merrell's mother, Harriet Camp Merrell (1799–1880), was staying with her nephew Walter Bicker Camp (1822–1916) in Sackets Harbor, New York. Merrell's brother, Samuel Lewis Merrell (1822–1900), became the father of twin boys named Henry and John in 1854. It will be remembered that Merrell's favorite uncles, John Camp (1786–1867) and Harry Camp (1787–1875), kept a store on Genesee Street in Utica where his beloved "whittling club" would meet. The town of Deerfield is northeast of Utica on a high plateau above the Mohawk River.

7. Lieutenant Isaac G. Strain (1821–57) of the U.S. Navy led an expedition in 1853 to find a possible route for what would become the Panama Canal. He had earlier explored in Brazil, and he later investigated laying a cable between the United States and Great Britain.

8. The Whig senator Henry Clay (1777–1852) authored the so-called American System of Tariffs in 1816 to protect the country's infant industrial system and to ensure a home market for U.S. agricultural and industrial products. Protective tariffs were extended in 1824 and in 1828, when the famous Tariff of Abominations led to the Nullification Crisis and a gradual decline of tariffs until the Civil War.

9. The Morrill tariff bill was first enacted in March 1860 as a reaction to the Panic of 1857.

10. Edward, the Prince of Wales, had left England on July 12, 1863, to tour Canada and the United States. He arrived in New York City on October 11 and departed on October 15 (*New York Times*, July 10, October 12, and October 16, 1863, p. 2, col. 2; p. 1, col. 1; p. 1, col. 5). "The First Japanese Embassy to any foreign nation" arrived in New York City on June 16 and departed on July 1, 1860 (*New York Times*, June 18 and July 2, 1860, p. 1, col. 1; p. 5, col. 1). Isambard Kingdom Brunel's mammoth ship, the *Great Eastern*, arrived in the harbor of New York City on June 28, 1860. The ship was opened to the public on July 3, and over 140,000 people went through it. A two-day sail followed at the end of July, and the ship departed August 16 (*New York Times*, June 29 and August 17, 1863, p. 1, col. 1; p. 4, col. 1; Beaver, *Big Ship*, 64–68).

11. John Bell and Edward Everett were the presidential and vice-presidential nominees of the Constitutional Union party, which opposed both the Republican ticket of Abraham Lincoln and Hannibal Hamlin and the Democractic ticket of Stephen A. Douglas and Herschel V. Johnson. Southern Democrats ran a ticket of John C. Breckinridge and Joseph Lane. Unionists of Merrell's sentiments in Arkansas formed Bell-Everett clubs to coordinate their campaign efforts, but the final state vote was Breckinridge, 27,732; Bell, 20,094; and Douglas, 5,227. The Republican party had no ticket in the state (Scroggs, "Arkansas in the Secession Crisis," 188–90).

12. Unionists at the first Arkansas convention, March 4–21, 1861, kept the state in the Union for the time being.

13. Merrell's name appears among those who drafted the Pike County resolution. See the article entitled "Mass Meeting in Pike County." Mass meetings were held during December of 1860 in various counties across Arkansas (Scroggs,

"Arkansas in the Secession Crisis," 194). The meeting in Pike County had been held on December 29, 1860.

14. Lincoln issued a call on April 15, 1861, for 75,000 men. The quota for Arkansas, 780 men, was refused by Governor Henry M. Rector on April 22.

The Arkansas convention met on May 6, 1861. They soon voted 65–5 in favor of an ordinance of secession. Upon a call for a unanimous vote, only Isaac Murphy refused his assent. The convention approved the Constitution of the Confederate States of America on May 10 by a vote of 63–8.

15. Samuel Kelley was a Campbellite minister who had previously been a representative of Pike County to the General Assembly of 1852–53 (Medearis, *Sam Williams*, 289; Pike County Heritage Club, *Early History of Pike County*, 19). Of the five votes against secession, his was the only one not to come from Unionist northwest Arkansas. In explaining his changed vote, he said that he supported the right to revolution but not the doctrine of secession (Woods, *Rebellion and Realignment*, 159–60).

16. In chapter 39 Merrell mentioned his preference for the carding and spinning machinery of Charles Danforth (1797–1876), who patented the cap spinner in 1828 and went on to own machine shops and locomotive works in Paterson, New Jersey. This cap spinner eliminated the clumsier flyer arms of the "throstle" spinner and, according to George Sweet Gibb, "surpassed the common throstle both in economy and in quality" for certain counts of yarn (Gibb, *Saco-Lowell Shops*, 77). In the cap frame the yarn could be guided onto the bobbin by the fixed edge of the cap, "around which it was dragged by the rotation of the bobbin" (Wallace, *Rockdale*, 197). This action made the tension uniform, gave the yarn greater evenness, and "enabled the bobbin to be rotated so rapidly as to increase the product 40 percent," even as it required less power to operate than the Awkright throstle (Clark, *History of Manufactures* 1:426).

17. Thomas Carmichael Hindman (1828–68), "at the earnest solicitation of the people of Arkansas," was placed in command of the new Department of the Trans-Mississippi on May 27, 1864 (*O.R.* 13:28). Previously Hindman had come from Mississippi to Arkansas and had served in the U.S. Congress before joining the Confederate army. After serving in Tennessee, he commanded the center at the battle of Shiloh. When he assumed command of the Department of the Trans-Mississippi, virtual anarchy prevailed. Courts were not held; law enforcement was almost nonexistent; and Governor Rector, who had fled, had only recently returned. Food was in short supply; Confederate money was refused everywhere; and extortionists operated freely. What Hindman accomplished in this situation has been termed almost miraculous (Belser, "Military Operations in Missouri and Arkansas," 371–73). In only seventy days Hindman doubled the number of Arkansas regiments and tripled the number of Missouri regiments (*O.R.* 13:42). He opened lead mines and built factories for smelting iron and for making small arms and percussion caps. He "adopted measures" for manufacturing shoes, harnesses, gun carriages, caissons, powder, shot, and shell (*O.R.* 13:32). "He crushed deser-

tion, established military posts, seized arms, ammunition and supplies, destroyed a large quantity of cotton to prevent it from falling into Federal hands . . . and impressed money from banks" (*National Cyclopedia of American Biography* 22:130). In the field, his troops drove General Curtis back across the White River, thereby saving Little Rock from capture. But his autocratic methods finally resulted in his removal as commander of the department, and he returned to a distinguished battlefield career. Although Hindman earned "more personal opprobrium from his fellow citizens than from any of the Yankees who came as conquerors," he probably deserves "primary credit" for the fact that Arkansas avoided total subjection during the last two years of the war (Ashmore, *Arkansas*, p. 83).

18. The battle of Oak Hills (or Wilson's Creek) was fought near Springfield in southwestern Missouri on August 10, 1861.

19. The battle of Pea Ridge (or Elkhorn Tavern) was fought just south of the Missouri line near Bentonville, Arkansas, on March 7–8, 1862. See the crisp description of this important battle in McPherson's *Battle Cry of Freedom*, 404–05.

20. Although he went to help repel Grant's invasion of Tennessee, Major General Earl Van Dorn (1820–63) promised that he and his troops would return to the Trans-Mississippi area. Killed by a jealous husband in Tennessee in May 1863, Van Dorn never returned. Major General Sterling Price (1809–67), governor of Missouri from 1853 to 1857 and one of the most prominent figures in the Trans-Mississippi Civil War, did return to positions of high command in the area and led a monumental effort in 1864 to recover Missouri for the Confederacy. Yet many of the troops that Van Dorn and Price led across the Mississippi in 1862 never crossed back.

21. Samuel Ryan Curtis (1805–66), appointed major general for his victory at Pea Ridge, continued to command the Department of Missouri until Lincoln relieved him in May 1863. He went on to command the departments of Kansas and of the Northwest.

CHAPTER 47

1. It is not clear what Merrell means by the checking of three Federal invasions of Arkansas. His meaning is even less clear in the light of his statement later in this chapter that three invasions were checked within the space of sixty days. The problem of understanding his meaning is complicated by the fact that the names and dates of some of the battles that he mentions in this chapter seem uncertain. Merrell emphasizes four battles in this chapter that may qualify for his three checks in sixty days, but sixty days does not elapse between them. It appears that his three checks would be Searcy, or Whitney's Lane, fought on May 19, 1862, not on May 27 as Merrell maintains; Cold Wells, which Merrell says was fought on June 10; and Cotton Plant, or Hill's Plantation on the Cache River, fought on July 7. But only forty-nine days elapse between the first and last of these battles, or forty-one if Merrell's incorrect date for Searcy is used.

Complicating the matter is the fact that Cold Wells is a term not in general use for any battle on June 10, although there was a skirmish on the White River that day. If one looks at the major engagements, eliminates Cold Wells, and assumes that the August 3 engagement at L'Anguille Ferry, or Hugh's Ferry, should be included in Merrell's three checks in sixty days, then seventy-six days elapse between Searcy and L'Anguille Ferry, or sixty-eight, if one uses Merrell's incorrect date for Searcy.

Merrell's friend Colonel William H. Parsons of the Twelfth Texas Cavalry played a leading role in the battles of Cotton Plant and L'Anguille Ferry. See Long and Long, *Civil War Day by Day*, 205–47; *O.R.* 13:2–4, 37, 69–79, 103, 141–51, 202–5.

2. The general order to which Merrell refers is clearly number 5, dated June 2, 1862. It appeared in the *True Democrat* on June 5 and in the *Arkansas State Gazette* on June 7, 1862. Because there is a misprint in the Gazette's version and because Merrell seems more likely to have subscribed to the *True Democrat*, the version in the *True Democrat* (June 5, 1862, p. 2, col. 6) is quoted here:

General Orders No. 5
Headquarters Trans-Mississippi District
Little Rock, Ark., June 2d, 1862

I. Private property within this District must not, in any case whatever, be taken or "impressed" by any person, whether officer, soldier or citizen, without special authority, in writing, from these Head Quarters, and such authority must, in every instance, be exhibited and read to the owner or his agent before the property is taken, unless he shall purposely absent himself, to avoid the same.

II. All Confederate officers and soldiers are hereby instructed, and all State officers and loyal citizens are hereby authorized and requested, to resist and prevent the taking or "impressment" of private property, except in strict accordance with paragraph number one, of this order. If the persons attempting to prevent such outrages are overpowered, they must report the facts, at once, to these Head Quarters, where the proper steps will be taken to punish the wrongdoer. The men who take or "impress" private property, without an authority, are robbers and marauders, and will be put to death without hesitation.

By order of Maj. Gen. Hindman,
R. C. Newton,
A. A. General

3. When a Camden newspaper, the *Ouachita Herald*, complained that Merrell's goods could be bought only for gold and silver, the neighboring *Washington Telegraph* defended Merrell, even though it noted: "Many have become incensed with Mr. Merrill, and there has been much talk of taking forcible possession of his factory, and running it for the benefit of the community." The paper added that scarcity had caused farmers to double the price of bacon and shoemakers to double the price of shoes. It therefore concluded: "Why taboo spun thread? There is a very homely maxim abroad which fits the case. 'Sauce for the goose is sauce for the gander.'" Yet the paper did take Merrell to task for taking $1.50 in specie in lieu of

$2.50 in Confederate money. "No man should directly or indirectly discount the money of the Confederacy, who does not intend sometime to leave it." Still, the paper added, "he is no more reprehensible than the banker who buys Confederate notes at a discount" (*Washington Telegraph*, June 4, 1862, p. 2, col. 3). In May the *Telegraph* had commended Merrell, "the enterprising and industrious manager" of "the manufactory for cotton yarns in the neighboring county of Pike," for "conducting the operations in a manner most advantageous to the whole community and in a spirit of justice to all." It said: "The prices charged are moderate, being considerably below those charged by similar establishments in Georgia and other parts of the South. This is the only factory here accessible to our citizens. People anxiously flock to purchase this necessary article from a hundred miles distant, and that in such numbers as to render it impossible to supply the demand. Being thus without competition Mr. Merrell deserves high credit for his anxiety to accommodate the wants of the community at moderate rates, when he has it in his power to act the extortioner" (*Washington Telegraph*, May 21, 1862, p. 2, col. 1).

4. Baton Rouge had been occupied by Federal troops in late July 1862. They held it against a Confederate attack on August 5 but evacuated it sixteen days later.

5. This would have been the enterprise of John Henry and Alfred Wallace (Griffin, "Pro-Industrial Sentiment," 134). John B. Ogden, a lawyer and merchant of Van Buren, who was a director of the company, began soliciting funds for a cotton-spinning factory in 1848, and the company was granted a charter from the state in 1852 (Lewis, "Economic Conditions in Ante-Bellum Arkansas," 261). This factory was reported to be in full operation by January 1852 (Griffin, "Pro-Industrial Sentiment," 136–37).

6. Mark Bean (d. 1862) was one of Arkansas's first immigrants. He came from Tennessee in 1820; at first he manufactured salt, and later he served as a member from Crawford County on the Territorial Council of the upper house of the General Assembly. He moved to Washington County in 1834, first to Rhea Mills and then to Cane Hill, where he lived until his death. He was a Whig leader in Washington County and was elected to the state senate in 1842 (Goodspeed, *Biographical and Historical Memoirs of Northwestern Arkansas*, 144, 171–72, 913–14). Washington County is just south of Benton County in the northwest corner of Arkansas.

7. George Wythe Randolph (1818–67) was Davis's secretary of war from March to November 1862 and had much to do with organizing the Trans-Mississippi Department. But he and Davis had their hands full of objections to Hindman's tactics, which ranged from declaring martial law to shooting deserters and taking into his new regiments men with legitimate leave from the eastern theater. Hindman was at odds with Governor Rector over conscripting and using troops from the state, and planters were furious about having their cotton burned and with being threatened with conscription themselves. Hindman had angered Albert Pike, who commanded in Indian Territory, by taking troops from him. Therefore, Governor Rector, the Arkansas congressional delegation, the planters, Albert Pike, and others put pressure on Davis to relieve Hindman. To appease them, Davis replaced Hind-

man with Theophilus Hunter Holmes (1804–80) in July 1862. See *O.R.* 13:28–44, 831–32, 850–51, 855–56, 874, 877; Belser, "Military Operations in Missouri and Arkansas," 373–83; Buel and Johnson, *Battles and Leaders* 3:444–45.

8. See note 1 to this chapter.

9. John Seldon Roane (1817–67) had been governor of Arkansas from 1849 to 1852. Although originally opposed to secession, he accepted an appointment as a Confederate brigadier general and in May 1862 was placed in command of all troops in the state until Hindman's arrival at the end of the month.

William H. Parsons (1826–1907), often called "Texas" Parsons to distinguish him from General Mosby M. Parsons of Missouri, appears frequently in Merrell's account of the Civil War in Arkansas, for Parsons's Twelfth Texas Cavalry Regiment protected him when he was working to block the Arkansas River in 1863 and appeared in Camden in 1864 after Merrell had moved there. Parsons's regiment was organized in August 1861 and was one of the last Confederate units to yield, breaking up on May 20, 1865 (Crute, *Units of the Confederate States Army*, 331; Kerby, *Kirby Smith's Confederacy*, 422).

"Parsons's Texas Brigade" was, in Parsons's own words, "the sleepless right arm" of the Trans-Mississippi army. It was a command that "participated in forty-eight (48) distinct engagements, mostly independent and unsupported," and in these engagements it was repulsed only twice. From 1862 to 1865 the brigade took part in campaigns in Missouri, Arkansas, and Louisiana and was frequently stretched across outposts covering a front of one hundred miles. Writing for a reunion of his men in 1878, Parsons demonstrated particular pride in the brigade's part in the actions that Merrell describes. "Few successful movements," he wrote, "can be recorded of graver and more decisive significance than those which may be traced directly to your first campaign in Arkansas in 1862" (Parsons' Texas Cavalry Brigade Association, *Brief and Condensed History of Parsons' Texas Cavalry Brigade*, 16–18, 23; most of the letter to his men is reprinted in the *Confederate Veteran* 33 [January 1925]: 17–20).

One of his officers, Lieutenant George W. Ingram, wrote from Arkansas that "Col. P. is the most popular man in the State with the citizens" (Ingram, *Civil War Letters of George and Martha F. Ingram*, 23). Although he was personally popular with the citizens and with his men, and although the regiment earned the distinction of being the only Texas cavalry regiment that was not dismounted in 1862, Parsons was never promoted to brigadier general, perhaps because of General Theophilus Holmes (Bailey, *Between the Enemy and Texas*, 80–81, 161–62). It would seem that Parsons was one of Merrell's major sources for what was happening on the battlefields.

10. Henry Massey Rector (1816–99) governed the state through 1862. Robert Ward Johnson (1814–79) was a U.S. senator from 1853 to 1861 and a Confederate senator from 1862 until the end of the war. Pierre Gustave Toutant Beauregard (1818–93) had commanded Confederate troops at the battle of Shiloh in April 1862.

11. The battle took place on May 19, 1862. Parsons himself did not take part in this engagement, being en route from Memphis to Little Rock. The attack was led by Maj. Emory W. Rogers (Bailey, *Between the Enemy and Texas*, 53. See *O.R.* 13:69–79).

12. The Federal commanders were Eugene Asa Carr (1830–1910), who became a famous Indian fighter after the war, and Peter J. Osterhaus (1823–1917), who finally accepted the surrender of the Department of the Trans-Mississippi on May 26, 1865. Colonel Taylor seems to be James R. Taylor, commander of the Seventeenth Texas Cavalry.

13. William Fitzhugh commanded the Sixteenth Texas Cavalry.

14. There was a skirmish on the White River on June 10, 1862, but it has not been generally known as the battle of Cold Wells. See *O.R.* 13:103, 1087; *O.R.* vol. 17, pt. 2, p. 1018; and U.S. Naval War Records Office, *Official Records of the Union and Confederate Navies* 23:159.

15. Albert Rust (1818–70) had come to Arkansas from Virginia about 1837. He practiced law in El Dorado and served in the Arkansas House and U.S. House of Representatives before becoming a Confederate colonel, then brigadier general. Frederick Steele (1819–68) later commanded the Federal Department of Arkansas, captured Little Rock, and directed the Camden Expedition.

16. Colonel Graham N. Fitch commanded the Forty-sixth Indiana Regiment in a combined attack on the Confederate batteries at St. Charles (U.S. Naval War Records Office, *Official Records of the Union and Confederate Navies* 23:172–74).

17. Lieutenant John W. Dunnington will be mentioned several times in Merrell's accounts of naval engagements in Arkansas. Hindman sent him to obstruct the White River at St. Charles, thirty-five miles west southwest of Helena, in June 1862 (*O.R.* 13:34–36). He helped Lieutenant Joseph Fry engage a flotilla of Federal gunboats there on June 17, 1862 (*O.R.* 13:836–37 and 929–32; U.S. Naval War Records Office, *Official Records of the Union and Confederate Navies* 23:165–68, 172–74, 199–204; Buel and Johnson, *Battles and Leaders* 3:551–53). Dunnington would later command the river defenses of Arkansas (*O.R.* 13:884), would be conspicuous at the battle for Arkansas Post (*O.R.*, vol. 17, pt. 1, p. 791), and would command the Confederate gunboat *Ponchartrain* (*O.R.*, vol. 22, pt. 2, p. 899).

At this point in his manuscript Merrell, who is looking over his 1863 volume in 1873, scratches the following note: "Dec. 1873. News comes of the execution of a Capt. Fry at St. Jago de Cuba by the Spaniards. Fry, say the [   ] was the Com. at St. Charles Battery. But at the time of that Battle I heard no one named as Commander but Lieut. Dunnington." Here Merrell is in error. Fry was in overall command at St. Charles (*O.R.* 13:35), and he was the same Captain Joseph Fry who led the Virginius expedition to relieve the Cubans and was killed by the Spaniards at Santiago in 1873 (Harrell, "Confederate Military History of Arkansas," 109).

18. The commanders and their regiments were all from Texas: William H. Parsons, Twelfth Regiment; William Fitzhugh, Sixteenth; George H. Sweet, Fifteenth;

James R. Taylor, Seventeenth; Nicholas H. Darnell, Eighteenth. See Roberts, "Confederate Military History of Texas," 62; and Crute, *Units of the Confederate States Army*, 333–34.

19. The battle at Cotton Plant, or Hill's Plantation on the Cache River thirty miles northeast of Devall's Bluff, took place on July 7, 1862 (*O.R.* 13:37, 103). Parsons's regiment was heavily engaged in it, according to a letter of Henry G. Orr of the regiment to his parents. The battle was joined between forces commanded by the Union general Samuel Ryan Curtis (1805–66) and the Confederate general Albert Rust. Although no report of this affair has ever appeared, says Orr, "General Rust has reported it a great victory (Anderson, *Campaigning with Parsons' Texas Cavalry*, 54–58). Hindman said that Rust retreated across the river after fighting for thirty minutes and complained that "no report of this affair was ever received, though often called for" (*O.R.* 13:37, 141–51).

Reports of the battle are confusing. Apparently because Rust failed to determine Union strength, Parsons rode into an ambush and was forced to retreat (Bailey, *Between the Enemy and Texas*, 67–68). "Our brigade," reported Bryan Marsh, one of Parsons's men, "had a fight with Curtis Command on the Seventh and got jenteely whipped" (Marsh, "The Confederate Letters of Bryan Marsh," 14). Another of his men, John W. Truss, wrote, "Our regiment stood the shock of the battle and consequent was cut to pieces pretty badly" (Ray, "Civil War Letters from Parsons' Texas Brigade," 214).

We may trust Merrell's report of what Rust said to Parsons following the battle, for according to a report printed in *The Tri-Weekly Telegraph* of Houston, Texas, on August 6, 1862, "the Colonel received the warmest thanks of General Rust, who told him that he had covered himself, his regiment, and his State all over with glory" (J.T.S., "Campaign in Arkansas. Battle of Cotton Plant," p. 1, col. 3).

20. The battle at Hughes Ferry on the L'Anguille River near Marianna was basically as Merrell describes it, although the Union commander, Major Henry Eggleston, said that their casualties fell short of twenty-five killed, forty wounded, and forty taken prisoner (*O.R.* 13:204–5). Parsons and his men surprised the Union camp at dawn on August 2, 1862, scattering them and capturing almost a half million dollars worth of arms and equipment. See Bailey, *Between the Enemy and Texas*, 75–79, and *O.R.* 13:37–38, 202–5.

21. In the first part of this paragraph Merrell refers to the expedition from Helena to Clarendon of Brigadier General Alvin P. Hovey (1821–91), which took place August 4–17, 1862. Hovey was following orders to "make a demonstration in the direction of Little Rock" (*O.R.* 13:206–7). Merrell's description of Steele's advance on Little Rock as a "false start" seems quite accurate, for General Frederick Steele (1819–68) had been ordered to march on the city in late October of 1862 (*O.R.* 13:760), but offered resistance to his superiors in doing so (*O.R.* 13:752), going over the head of his commander, Samuel Ryan Curtis, to complain directly to Lincoln's general-in-chief, Henry Wager Halleck (1815–72), who countermanded Curtis's order for such an attack (*O.R.* 13:782, 790, 793–94, 812–13). Steele was

moving toward Batesville in early November (*O.R.* 13:781, 787, 913), but the attack was indeed a "false start" and was never completed.

22. The Pin (i.e., full-blooded) Cherokee Indians were known as such because of the crossed pins they wore on their coats to symbolize their allegiance to traditional tribal laws and customs (see Josephy, *Civil War on the Frontier*, 142). "Jay Hawking" is from *jayhawk*, a fictitious predatory bird. As the term applies to the Civil War, jayhawkers were antislavery guerrilla bands that operated on the border of Kansas and Missouri before and during the war.

23. Theophilus Hunter Holmes (1804–80) took command of the Trans-Mississippi Department on July 7, 1862, while he was still at Vicksburg. He arrived in Little Rock on August 18 and ordered Hindman to remain in command of the army in Arkansas (*O.R.* 13:876). Holmes had fought in Indian Territory, in the Florida wars, and in the Mexican War. He was in charge of general recruiting for the U.S. Army before he resigned to become a Confederate brigadier general. He had served in Virginia and North Carolina before being promoted to lieutenant general and serving at Vicksburg. His assignment to the command of the Trans-Mississippi probably came from his friendship with Jefferson Davis, who was his classmate at West Point and with whom he had served in Mexico. "Old Granny Holmes," as his soldiers called him, was a timid, hesitant, and ineffective commander of the department, and he was asking to be relieved by October 20, 1862 (*O.R.* 13:898–99). Even Davis complained that Holmes concentrated too much on Little Rock, leaving the rest of the department to fend for itself (Boggs, *Military Reminiscences*, 55). To use a phrase current at the time, those who had complained about Hindman found that in Holmes they had "swapped the Devil for a witch." See Belser, "Military Operations in Missouri and Arkansas," 426, 495–96, 586. In *Never Call Retreat*, Bruce Catton characterizes Holmes as "the sort of general who sees his difficulties clearly but is quite unable to do anything about them" (8).

24. James Gillpatrick Blunt (1826–81) commanded the Army of the Frontier at the battle of Prairie Grove, December 6–8, 1862. He was a physician who had been an ardent Kansas abolitionist and friend of John Brown. He fought throughout the war in Arkansas, Kansas, and Missouri, and played a major role in turning back Sterling Price's Missouri campaign of 1864.

25. The battle was on December 7, 1862.

26. James Fleming Fagan (1828–93), a Mexican War veteran and resident of Saline County, Arkansas, had been promoted to brigadier general after the battle of Shiloh. He remained in Arkansas through most of the war, and Fagan's Cavalry Division played a major role in the repulse of Steele's Camden expedition. He accompanied Price on his Missouri campaign.

27. Arkansas Post surrendered on January 11, 1863.

28. John Alexander McClernand (1812–90) was one of Lincoln's "political generals" of whom Grant had a low opinion. Grant called the Arkansas Post expedition a "wild goose chase" until he learned that Sherman had planned it (Faust, *Historical Times Illustrated Encyclopedia*, 457). When McClernand's army returned to Vicks-

burg from Arkansas Post, Grant took command of it and placed McClernand in a subordinate position. See *O.R.*, vol. 17, pt. 2, pp. 555, 564–67; and U.S. Naval Records Office, *Official Records of the Union and Confederate Navies* 23:605–6.

29. Here Merrell sketches a "Rough plan of the battle ground & vicinity at the Post of Arkansas." Merrell "reconnoitered the Battle Field at the Post" on May 5, 1863. This date can be pinned down because while working to block the Arkansas River from May to July 1863, and later while living through the Federal occupation of Camden in April and May 1864, Merrell recorded some key dates and events in a small notebook which has "Receipts" printed on its spine. But he does not seem to have consulted this book in writing his memoirs, for there are several discrepancies in dates and events, and it seems that what will hereafter be referred to as the Receipts book is more accurate in such instances. Perhaps he had forgotten about or had misplaced this book, but he or his wife must have found and preserved it later, and it is now on file as box 103 of the Smith Papers. A copy of this notebook has been placed with the Arkansas History Commission, and a copy of its Camden portion is on file at the Southwest Arkansas Regional Archives, Washington, Arkansas.

Just above his drawing of the battleground, Merrell places the following notes: "Federal Force: 47,000 men & 4 or 5 Gun Boats. Confederate Force: 5,500 men, of whom 3,500 were taken prisoners. Federal Loss: 1,800–1,000 men at least killed and buried on the ground, 6000–4000 wounded, 1,400–1,000 deserted & more parolled. Confederate Loss: 100–90 men killed, 3,500 prisoners."

CHAPTER 48

1. The general was John Alexander McClernand.

2. David Dixon Porter (1813–91) was the commander of the Mississippi Squadron. He later cooperated with Grant in the assault on Vicksburg, and, after being promoted to rear admiral, was placed in charge of the Mississippi River as far as New Orleans. Porter cooperated with General Nathaniel Prentiss Banks in the Red River Campaign of 1864 and at the end of the war commanded the North Atlantic Blockading Squadron. He was the superintendent of the U.S. Naval Academy from 1865 to 1869.

3. A gun mounted "en Barbette" was mounted so as to fire over a parapet rather than through an embrasure.

4. Thomas James Churchill (1824–1905) had settled in Little Rock after serving in the Mexican War. He was promoted to brigadier general for his part in the victory at Wilson's Creek (Oak Hills) in 1861. He served at Pea Ridge and in Kentucky before returning to command at Arkansas Post, which he was forced to surrender, he maintained, by the cowardice of Colonel F. C. Wilkes of the Twenty-fourth Texas Dismounted Cavalry (see next note). After being exchanged, he commanded "Churchill's Division" during the Camden Expedition.

5. Several white flags were seen among the Twenty-fourth Regiment of Texas Dismounted Cavalry, commanded by Colonel Francis Catlett Wilkes. This regi-

ment was part of the First Brigade commanded by Col. Robert R. Garland. Brigadier General Thomas James Churchill was in command of the area designated the Lower Arkansas and White Rivers. According to Garland's report, there were a "number of white flags displayed in Wilkes' regiment," and Garland bitterly resented Churchill's claim that he had assented to the surrender. The Confederate secretary of war James Alexander Seddon recommended a court of inquiry into the conduct of Garland, Wilkes, and even Churchill, but no inquiry was ever held, as the witnesses were either scattered or dead (*O.R.* vol. 17, pt. 1, pp. 782, 783, 785–86, 789–90).

6. Lieutenant John W. Dunnington. See note 17 in the preceding chapter.

7. The casualties at Arkansas Post for the "Army of the Mississippi," McClernand's term for the Thirteenth and Fifteenth corps, were 134 killed, 898 wounded, and 29 captured or missing, for a total number of 1,061 casualties (*O.R.*, vol. 17, pt. 1, pp. 716–19). Merrell's estimate of 47,000 Federal troops is also too high. Thomas L. Livermore gives their number of effectives at 28,944 (*Numbers and Losses in the Civil War*, 98).

8. A. M. Lester, having been warned to leave the county, refused to do so; he was taken in force in Murfreesboro by a posse of men calling themselves "Independent Soldiers" and was hanged on the bank of the Little Missouri River (Elbert Davis, "Early Crimes," in Pike County Heritage Club, *Early History of Pike County*, 44).

9. In early 1863 factories that produced clothes, blankets, shoes, and harness were so few and so inferior in the Confederate Trans-Mississippi Department that the Merrell-Matlock factory at Royston was given special attention. In his book *Kirby Smith's Confederacy* Robert Lee Kerby says that in early 1863, "in the rebel fragment of Arkansas, only John Matlock's cotton and woolen mill at Murfreesboro was important enough to rate its own military guards" (64). On December 8, 1863, Lieutenant Colonel Owen A. Bassett of the Second Kansas Cavalry reported that as of December 2 a Confederate major named Wood "was encamped with about 300 men near a cotton factory, 2 miles northwest from Murfreesborough, guarding the factory, and preparing to take out the machinery" (*O.R.*, vol. 22, pt. 1, p. 77). I am indebted to Sam Dickinson for pointing out this passage to me.

10. Henry S. Atwood (1800?–64) was one of the stockholders of the Roswell Manufacturing Company, although he never attended their meetings. His daughter Ruth Ann married Dr. William Elliott Dunwody, a son of John Dunwody and Jane Bulloch. Another of his daughters, Jane, met Merrell's widowed cousin George H. Camp on one of her visits to Roswell (Temple, *First Hundred Years*, 114). She later became George Camp's second wife. Before Henry Merrell left for Arkansas, Henry Atwood bought from him most of his Greensboro property (Greene County, Georgia, "Deed Book QQ," 319–21). On June 15, 1856, Atwood bought the Curtright Manufacturing Company for $40,000 (Greene County, Georgia, "Deed Book QQ," 474); he and Jacob Rokenbaugh reincorporated the Curtright concern as the Oconee Manufacturing Company in 1857 (*Acts of the General Assembly of the State of Georgia, 1857*, 213–14).

CHAPTER II

1. This chapter begins the 1873 volume of Merrell's memoirs. The reader will recall that Merrell asked that the 1863 volume be inserted between chapters I and II of the 1873 volume.

2. See note 5 of chapter 48 above.

3. Merrell considerably alters his estimate of the preceding chapter. See note 7 thereof.

4. One source says that the Confederate loss was 60 killed, 75 or 80 wounded, and 4,791 prisoners (Snead, "Conquest of Arkansas," 453). Thomas Livermore places Confederate losses at 28 killed, 81 wounded, and 4,791 prisoners (*Numbers and Losses in the Civil War*, 98).

5. Official reports place the number of Federal soldiers captured or missing at Arkansas Post at twenty-nine (*O.R.*, vol. 17, pt. 1, pp. 716–19).

CHAPTER III

1. Harris Flanagin (1817–74) was governor of Arkansas from 1862 to 1865, succeeding Henry M. Rector (1816–99) at that post.

2. Thomas O. Moore held that post from 1860 to 1864. Henry W. Allen succeeded him from 1864 to 1865.

3. Through most of the Civil War the Confederate governors of Texas were Francis R. Lubbock (1861–63) and Pendleton Murrah (1863–65).

4. Merrell was called much earlier than June. He kept documents relating to this military mission that show he had presented to Holmes on April 27, 1863, a request for equipment that he signed "Major in Charge of the Works" (Smith Papers, box 100, folder 5, with copies at the Arkansas History Commission, Little Rock, and the Southwest Arkansas Regional Archives, Washington, Ark.). In his Receipts book diary, mentioned earlier, he recorded the fact that he began his work on the river on May 15, 1863. He abandoned it on July 4, 1863 (Smith Papers, Receipts book, box 103).

5. Although Merrell never mentions receiving this commission in the Partisan Rangers to defend his mill at Royston, his wife speaks of it in a letter to Willie Smith on May 10, 1863. "Capt. Preston, who is stationed at the Fac. with his Partisan Rangers (the company uncle H. commanded. He resigned & Preston, who was 1st Lieutenant was elected) takes his meals with me" (Smith Papers).

6. Although no Colonel Alexander is listed on Holmes's staff in 1863, it is possible that this is no less a figure than Edward Porter Alexander (1835–1910), who served as ordnance officer to Robert E. Lee and who was promoted to general after becoming Longstreet's chief of artillery. Alexander served under Lee until November of 1862 and later, beginning in March 1863. It seems possible that he could have visited the Trans-Mississippi in the interim (Crute, *Confederate Staff Officers*, 2, 13, 114, 123).

7. Captain Thomas J. Mackey served as engineer officer on the staff of General Albert Pike. Later, as a major, he was the chief engineer on the staff of General Sterling Price (Crute, *Confederate Staff Officers*, 152, 158).

8. These two officers may have been Captains R. H. Fitzhugh and A. M. Williams, both of whom were serving on the staff of General Holmes as early as September 14, 1862 (*O.R.* 13:885). Under General Hindman's orders in June 1862, Captain Williams had attempted to block the White River at St. Charles (*O.R.* 13:34). On one list of Confederate staff officers, Captain A. M. Williams is listed as an engineer officer on Holmes's staff, appointed June 21, 1862. Merrell himself is listed as Major Henry Merring, Engineer Officer, appointed 1863 (Crute, *Confederate Staff Officers*, 89–90). He is listed as "Merrill, Henry, Maj. Engr. Corps; staff of Maj. Gen. T. H. Holmes, 1863" in Carroll, *List of Staff Officers of the Confederate States Army*, 113.

9. Major John B. Burton was the chief quartermaster of the District of Arkansas. He seems to have accomplished such valuable feats of supply as bringing arms across the Mississippi after Vicksburg had fallen. See *O.R.*, vol. 22, pt. 2, p. 1078; vol. 41, pt. 4, p. 1007; and Nichols, *Confederate Quartermaster in the Trans-Mississippi*, 28–29.

10. This was Fort Pleasant, which was located near what is now Pine Bluff Arsenal. Its ruins have long since fallen into the Arkansas River.

11. Merrell earlier warned the reader about his memory for names and dates. See his "Preface" to his 1863 (Owen's) volume. Any failing in this direction is now magnified by the fact that he is ten years older than he was before chapter II above. Earlier in this chapter he said that he reported to Trans-Mississippi headquarters in Little Rock in June. Now he says that he reached there in May, but he was actually there at the end of April. See note 4 of this chapter.

12. John George Walker (1822–93) was one of the most competent generals in the Trans-Mississippi Department. A Mexican War veteran, he commanded the Eighth Confederate Texas Cavalry before serving in North Carolina and Virginia. He was promoted to major general because of his performance at Antietam, then returned to the West to command a division of Texas infantry that became known as Walker's Texas Division. This division played a major role in the Red River Campaign and Camden Expedition of 1864. See Blessington, *Campaigns of Walker's Texas Division*.

13. As commander of the state militia at St. Louis and as Governor Claiborne Jackson's military adviser, Daniel Marsh Frost (1823–1900) played a daring role in the early attempts to commit Missouri to the Confederate cause. He led a division at Prairie Grove and took over Price's division in August and September of 1863, but he was mostly in charge of "Frost's Brigade," which Merrell mentions later in his memoirs. See *O.R.*, vol. 22, pt. 1, pp. 543–44, and pt. 2, pp. 808, 969, 1027.

14. A good guess for "Judge Scull" would be James Scull, listed as a forty-six-year-old and wealthy planter in the 1860 census of Jefferson County, Arkansas. (U.S. Bureau of the Census, *Eighth Census of the United States: 1860. Population*. Microfilm. Arkansas, Jefferson County, roll 44, 4:830).

CHAPTER IV

1. Colonel Archibald S. Dobbin is mentioned, sometimes not favorably, in *O.R.*, vol. 22, pt. 1, pp. 435–36, 523–35, and pt. 2, pp. 309, 316, 674, 869, and 1042–43.

2. No document was inserted at this point. Merrell kept requisitions, lists, and receipts from this mission, even packing lists for the *Julia Roane*. One two-page memorandum of April 27, 1863, notes that Holmes was "present" when it was made, and it appears that Holmes scrawled his signature and added directions to his chief quartermaster, Major John B. Burton, to fill Merrell's requests. There is even a letter from Major Burton dated May 1, 1863, and addressed to "Maj. Henry Merrell, Ch. Engineer, In Charge of River Defenses" that reads, "I wish to see you before you leave or at your earliest convenience." But no actual copy of an order from Holmes has been found among his papers in the Smith House (Smith Papers, box 100, folder 5; copies at the Arkansas History Commission, Little Rock, and the Southwest Arkansas Regional Archives, Washington, Ark.).

3. The trunnions of a cannon are the pins on opposite sides that allow the cannon to drop into a mount and to move up and down vertically in it.

4. The Tredegar Iron Works in Richmond, chartered in 1837 by Joseph Reid Anderson, forged nearly half of the domestically produced cannon for the Confederacy. It was the South's only antebellum rolling mill capable of producing railroad rails and cannon. Some historians maintain that without the Tredegar works, "the South's participation in the war would have been curtailed substantially" (Bateman and Weiss, *Deplorable Scarcity*, 12). The Tredegar Iron Works has been called "the Confederacy's most valuable manufacturer" (Faust, *Historical Times Illustrated Encyclopedia of the Civil War*, p. 762). Although the word is almost illegible in his manuscript, Merrell seems to have written *worksup* that "pronounced the metal to be of the very best" in the cannon he is describing. A search of unabridged dictionaries and several metallurgical dictionaries and handbooks did not yield the term *worksup*. Merrell's penmanship at this point seems more careless than usual; hence, it is possible that in his haste he is creating a neologism that is rooted in his familiarity with his father's printing trade. A "workup" in printing is an unintended mark made on the page by a piece of metal that rises in the chase, the frame of the letterpress. Because the cannon that Merrell is describing has been damaged, it is possible that some metal has "worked up" in the manner of pieces of metal in a printing chase, and that it is these *worksup* that "pronounced the metal to be of the very best."

5. The chase is that part of the cannon from the trunnions forward to the mouth or to the point where the muzzle may begin to swell leading up to the mouth.

6. The Anglican priest and Utilitarian philosopher William Paley (1743–1805) argued, in such books as *A View of the Evidence of Christianity* (1794) and *Natural Theology* (1802), for a natural theology and morality that posited God's existence from the evidence of his creation.

7. The "cut-off" was a small, navigable body of water that connected the Arkansas River to the White River before both emptied into the Mississippi. Because

Merrell is not very specific, and because the rivers have shifted and the old cutoff is no more, the location of Merrell's abatis seems impossible to determine. It was certainly between Arkansas Post and Napoleon, where the Arkansas entered the Mississippi, but its location in relation to the cutoff is uncertain. The site of Merrell's abatis was "Smith's Landing" near "Smith's cut-off" and apparently opposite the plantation owned by Mrs. Emily Smith (1806–96), widow of Colonel J. M. Smith of Desha County, Arkansas. Her plantation, which obviously lent its name to the nearby cutoff linking the Arkansas and White rivers, was on the south bank of the Arkansas, downstream of Arkansas Post. In the diary that he kept while constructing his abatis, Merrell refers several times to Mrs. Smith and her plantation. He says that he arrived at Smith's cutoff and "selected quarters" on May 15, 1863. On May 19 he notes that Colonel William H. Parsons's Twelfth Texas Cavalry Regiment could not fully cover "my work at Smith's cut-off." He notes that he stayed with Mrs. Smith, who apparently offered travelers room and board (see chapter XIII below), on May 21 and even that he sent his wash to her on May 23. But Mrs. Smith objected to Merrell's work so near her, and on June 23 Merrell mentions "a very unpleasant interview with Mrs. Smith concerning the location of the work at her plantation," and added, "I am given to understand that the blockading of the river is decdly. unpopular with the entire populace below Pine Bluff." His impressing slaves from nearby plantations certainly contributed to the unpopularity of his project. Merrell listed these slaves and their overseers in his diary, "about 50 in all say 51 Hands besides overseers" (June 1, 1863). When some of his blacks fell sick on June 3, 1863, he thought that their sickness resulted from a conspiracy of their masters (Smith Papers, Receipts book, box 103).

I am indebted to Russell Baker, deputy director of the Arkansas History Commission, and to Sam Dickinson, chairman of the Arkansas Civil War Centennial Commission, for tracking down information about Mrs. Smith, her plantation, and "Smith's Landing," which appears on a map of the Mississippi made in 1874 by Major Charles R. Suter of the Corps of Engineers.

8. Merrell's diary, the Receipts book mentioned above, records that he discharged the *Julia Roane* on May 21, 1863 (Smith Papers, box 103).

9. Unlike his previous sketch of the dam at Royston, which was placed in the margin and vertical to his written text, Merrell placed this sketch between his written lines and parallel to them.

10. According to his diary entries in the Receipts book on May 7 and May 13, 1863, Merrell's head carpenter was C. D. Westerman and his quartermaster was one E. Curry. Writing this account in 1873, more than ten years after the facts that he records in his diary, Merrell neglects to mention what occupies a good amount of space in the diary: the constant hunger and privation that he and his men suffered while they were working to block the river. Here are some sample entries in the Receipts book: "Thurs., May 28: Provisions gave out today again for the 3rd time. Overseers discontented. Hands made sick by irregular food. Cannot stand this any longer. Ordered Q.M. to get a wagon & train & rely only upon our-

selves in future for meal"; following the notation "out of meal for dinner again" on Monday, June 1, Merrell says that Parsons has a line of pickets thirty miles long to supply, that his quartermaster can receive only through Parsons's command and has no commissary powers himself, and that these faulty arrangements have "already caused our hands several times to go without dinner"; "Tues., June 2: No meal for the hands' dinner"; "Wed., June 3: 14 hands sick (Negro Hands). No Whites (overseers), although the whites drink the same water & eat the same food. Diarrhea the complaint. Have reason to think a great deal of this sickness a false pretense, instigated by their masters"; noting on Monday, June 22, that he is down to fifteen hands, Merrell enters: "Have reason to believe the withdrawal of Negroes a conspiracy against the work" (Smith Papers, box 103).

CHAPTER 5

1. Merrell does not use a roman numeral for the number of this chapter.

2. In the diary in the Receipts book, Merrell says that on June 23, 1863, he asked Captain Miller of the *Bracelet* for ropes, tackle, and chains but that Miller told him he had sent them away and that "he had it so arranged that he himself could not tell where it is" (Smith Papers, box 103).

3. In chapter 47 Merrell told us that Red Fork was near Napoleon. This settlement still exists today, about fifteen miles upstream from where Napoleon used to be, but is no longer directly on the river.

4. Major Lochlin Johnson Farrar of Parsons's Twelfth Texas Cavalry (Henderson, *Texas in the Confederacy*, 128; Crute, *Units of the Confederate States Army*, 331; and Bailey, *Between the Enemy and Texas*, 10–11, 210, 217). In the diary in the Receipts book, Merrell refers to the ball on board the *Bracelet*, to his fever, to the gale, and to the Federal advance as all occurring during the night of June 9 and the early morning hours of June 10, 1863. A puzzling entry on Thursday, June 11, follows, which could challenge his account here of exchanging glances with Colonel Parsons on the morning of the 10th: "On the night of the 9th Col. Parsons received a dispatch to meet Lt. Genl. Holmes at Pine Bluff & started at 12 o'clock in the night" (Smith Papers, box 103).

5. The idea was Holmes's, although the idea may have been planted by Jefferson Davis, who wrote George W. Randolph, his secretary of war, while Holmes commanded the Trans-Mississippi Department: "It was rather hoped that he [Holmes] would be able to retake Helena, which would greatly contribute to the security of the country below, both in and out of Arkansas" (*O.R.* 13:914–15). When Holmes was planning his attack on Helena, he was in command of the District of Arkansas but no longer in command of the Trans-Mississippi. Edmund Kirby Smith (1824–93) had assumed command on March 7, 1863 (*O.R.*, vol. 22, pt. 2, p. 798). Kirby Smith's chief-of-staff was Brig. Gen. William Robertson Boggs (1829–1911), and Boggs's *Military Reminiscences* show clearly that the attack on Helena was Holmes's idea and that he carried it out with little enthusiasm from Kirby Smith. Boggs says on page 69 that Holmes "was arranging for an attack on Helena, as a diversion

in favor of Vicksburg" but that this strategy "diverted the principal purpose for which General Smith had been sent to the department" (i.e., saving Vicksburg). The *Official Records* also make clear that Holmes developed on his own the plan to attack Helena and that he was not ordered to do so by Richmond, as Merrell contends. On May 9, 1863, Smith writes Holmes from his headquarters in Shreveport, "You must act according to your own judgment. At this distance I can give no positive orders. Attack the enemy, should an opportunity offer for doing so with hope of success. You can expect no assistance from this quarter (*O.R.*, vol. 22, pt. 2, p. 835). On June 13 Holmes tells General Sterling Price that "if there are 4,000 or 5,000 men in Helena, fortified as they are, to take it would cost too much," but two days later he tells Price that the garrison is weaker than he had suspected (*O.R.*, vol. 22, pt. 2, pp. 866, 868). Kirby Smith's adjutant, S. S. Anderson, wrote Holmes on the same day, "It is impossible for Lieutenant-General Smith, at this distance, and without any knowledge of the strength of the force at Helena (which is continually varying), to give any orders in the case. It is, therefore, submitted to Lieutenant-General Holmes to act as the circumstances may justify." Two days later Holmes begged Kirby Smith, "I believe we can take Helena. Please let me attack it." Kirby Smith replied the next day, "Most certainly do it" (*O.R.*, vol. 22, pt. 1, p. 407).

6. The following relevant entry for June 5, 1863, appears in the diary in Merrell's Receipts book: "Early this morning both the 'Kaskaskia' & the 'Lady Walton' got safely into White River, but the latter, under the command of Capt. Pennington, turned eastward and went over to the Federals. The Pilot, Wm. Forbes of Van Buren & his brother-in-law, refused to go & were set adrift in a skiff which Capt. Pennington had borrowed" (Smith Papers, box 103).

7. In Mrs. Susannah Centlivre's (1667?–1723) *The Busybody* (1709), the title character is Mrs. Marplot, whose well-intentioned officiousness frustrates the designs of the story's lovers.

8. That day the Arkansas River was fordable at twelve different places within twelve miles of Little Rock, but to enter the city Steele's troops required a pontoon bridge so strategically placed that Price's fire on it was ineffective. See *O.R.*, vol. 22, pt. 1, pp. 476–77, 515 (map), 522, 524–25.

9. The report of the battle at "Devil's Backbone" given by Colonel William F. Cloud, commander of the Second Kansas Cavalry, appears in *O.R.*, vol. 22, pt. 1, pp. 602–4. The battle took place on September 1, 1863.

William Lewis Cabell (1827–1916) was a highly praised organizer and leader who, following service under Van Dorn, had returned to Arkansas as cavalry commander of northwest Arkansas. Yet in September of 1863, his troops were primarily conscripts and unreliable partisans and guerrillas. Desertions forced him to abandon Fort Smith. Cabell's Arkansas Brigade was later to play key roles in the battles of Marks' Mills and Poison Springs, and it went with Price on his Missouri campaign. During this campaign, Cabell was captured in Kansas.

10. Federal casualties were two killed and nine wounded (*O.R.*, vol. 22, pt. 1, p. 602).

11. According to records that Merrell kept (Smith Papers, box 100, folder 4; copy with Arkansas History Commission, Little Rock, and Southwest Arkansas Regional Archives, Washington, Ark.), Edmund would have been about sixty-three years old at this time, and Tabby would have been about fifty-six. Tabby's husband, John Marion, had already run away, as had John Pratt. Merrell had just bought Munroe from John Matlock in February. Niddy was the daughter of John and Tabby Marion's daughter Helen, or Ellen, who would have been about twenty-one in 1863. Although not with the Merrells at this time, Helen appears in chapter XII below (pp. 372–73) to beg that her mother and her daughter leave Camden with her and the departing Federal troops. Helen and her youngest child seem to have run away from William Bell of Royston, to whom the Merrells had sold them (Elizabeth Merrell to Anne Magill Smith, July 3, 1864, Smith Papers, box 100, folder 8). See note 1 to chapter 40 above. Tabby later used Brown as her last name.

CHAPTER VI

1. At this time Camden, Arkansas, in Ouachita (sometimes spelled Washita) County was second in population and importance in the state. It was, according to a Union soldier who took part in its 1864 occupation, "an enterprising town, doing a heavy business. It had many fine houses and beautiful gardens" (White, "Blue-coat's Account of the Camden Expedition," 86). The Ouachita River was navigable to Camden, giving it access to New Orleans. The Confederates placed nine forts around it. See Britton, *Civil War on the Border* 2:276. In 1860 there were 52 mercantile houses, 16 law firms, 5 manufacturers, 11 doctors, 4 churches, 3 schools, 3 hotels, and 3 newspapers in Camden. Its population was about 2,000 (Griffin, "A Social History of Camden, Arkansas," 6). It remained a trading center after the Civil War, and Merrell remained a citizen of the town for the rest of his life. Camden was a river town until the arrival of the Iron Mountain Railway in 1874 and the Cotton Belt Railroad in 1881 (Goodspeed, *Biographical and Historical Memoirs of Southern Arkansas*, 645–46, and see J. E. Gaughan, "Historic Camden"). Today there is almost no evidence of the bustling waterfront area that surrounded the offices and warehouses of Merrell and Magill "under the hill."

2. The Reverend Dr. Samuel Williamson (1795–1882) was a native of York, South Carolina, who had come to Washington, Arkansas, from Davidson, North Carolina, where he had been a professor and president of Davidson College until 1854. He visited Arkansas in the fall of 1855 and moved to Hempstead County, near Washington, in January of 1857. Pastor of the Washington Presbyterian Church from October of 1857 to September of 1876, Dr. Williamson continued to live on his nearby farm until his death in 1882 at the age of eighty-seven (Goodspeed, *Biographical and Historical Memoirs of Southern Arkansas*, 449; Scott, *Ministerial Directory of the Presbyterian Church*, 777; "Records of the Washington Presbyterian Church," 23, 127).

3. Captain Taylor has been difficult to trace. A Captain E. W. Taylor served in Houston, Texas, on the staff of W. H. Haynes, chief of General Kirby Smith's

Clothing Bureau, in June of 1864 (*O.R.*, vol. 34, pt. 4, pp. 657, 659). There was also a Captain E. Taylor, chief quartermaster, serving on Longstreet's staff in December of 1863 (Crute, *Confederate Staff Officers*, 124).

4. During the first week of December 1863 the headquarters of the Confederate District of Arkansas under Holmes was at Camp Bragg, about eighteen miles west of Camden in Nevada County, but it had moved into Camden by December 12. Because Kirby Smith was in the area, the headquarters of the Department of the Trans-Mississippi was also in Camden by December 23 (*O.R.*, vol. 22, pt. 2, pp. 1086, 1094, 1110).

5. Major George A. Gallagher served in succession as the assistant adjutant general for Theophilus Holmes, Sterling Price, and Edmund Kirby Smith (Crute, *Confederate Staff Officers*, 89, 158, 176).

6. Theophilus Holmes had fallen ill after the failed attack on Helena on July 4, 1863, and Sterling Price had replaced him as commander of the District of Arkansas on July 24. Holmes reassumed command of the district on September 25 (*O.R.*, vol. 22, pt. 1, p. 5; pt. 2, pp. 942, 1027). Later, after Holmes had left Arkansas, Judge George C. Watkins suggested to General Kirby Smith that he use Merrell's talents in Trans-Mississippi affairs. See chapter XII below. Watkins was a former justice of the state supreme court, one of a three-judge military court for the District of Arkansas, and influential enough in Arkansas to write letters offering advice to the governor and to Kirby Smith and to expect answers from them. See *O.R.*, vol. 22, pt. 2, pp. 945–47, 1064; Crute, *Confederate Staff Officers*, 90.

7. Dardanelle, Arkansas, had been the scene of a skirmish in September 1863, following the battle of Backbone (or "Devil's Backbone"). Other skirmishes took place there in May and August 1864. As its name might suggest, Dardanelle is a small port on the Arkansas River, halfway between Fort Smith and Little Rock.

8. Merrell later discusses the bungled raid on Pine Bluff by Brigadier General John Sappington Marmaduke (1833–87), at the time the Confederate cavalry commander for Missouri and Arkansas. Marmaduke had fought at Shiloh, Prairie Grove, and Helena; his cavalry had tried to slow Steele's approach to Little Rock. Following the fall of Little Rock, he fought a duel with General Lucius M. Walker (1829–63), which resulted in Walker's death and which Merrell mentions later. In 1864 Marmaduke harassed Steele during the Camden campaign and went with Price back into his native Missouri, where he would be the governor from 1885 to 1887. Colonel Robert R. Lawther commanded the Tenth Missouri Cavalry Regiment of "Greene's Brigade" of Marmaduke's Cavalry Division.

9. The jayhawk was a mythical predatory bird; a bummer was a looter in the Civil War; and a grayback was one who was supposed to be a Confederate soldier.

10. Powell Clayton (1833–1914) was the commander of the Fifth Kansas Cavalry Regiment at Pine Bluff. He became governor of Arkansas when it was finally readmitted to the Union in 1868 and was the Republican boss of the state, frequently charged with fraud and corruption. He was McKinley's and Roosevelt's ambassador to Mexico from 1897 to 1905.

11. This man is probably Colonel Henry C. Caldwell of the Third Iowa Cavalry Regiment, and the action described would have taken place on October 29, 1863. See *O.R.*, vol. 22, pt. 1, pp. 728–29.

CHAPTER VII

1. General Edmund Kirby Smith (1824–93) had come from commanding the District of East Tennessee to assume the command of the Department of the Trans-Mississippi on March 7, 1863. Holmes had then been assigned to command the District of Arkansas on March 18 (*O.R.*, vol. 22, pt. 2, pp. 798, 803). Merrell must have had great affection for Holmes, for he treats him very gently. But Merrell also recognizes the heroic qualities of Kirby Smith, whose character and accomplishments under impossible circumstances certainly merit the book-length treatments that he has received. Cut off from Richmond soon after he arrived and cut off from the rest of the world by the Federal naval blockade, he reorganized the Confederacy west of the Mississippi. According to Merton Coulter, he "controlled this region almost as completely as Davis ran the Confederacy east of the Mississippi" (*Confederate States of America*, 358). He stopped further Federal military gains; he won major victories in Louisiana and Arkansas in 1864; he virtually governed the three states of Louisiana, Arkansas, and Texas while not overly offending their civilian governors; he showed remarkable initiative in controlling the cotton and economy of the area in order to supply the people and to feed, clothe, and arm his soldiers; and he made imaginative use of such people as Henry Merrell. So completely did he dominate the scene that the Confederacy west of the Mississippi was known as "Kirby Smithdom."

Florence Elizabeth Holladay concludes a lengthy study, "The Powers of the Commander of the Confederate Trans-Mississippi Department, 1863–1865," by observing that "it was in a large measure due to the ability, patriotism, and untiring zeal of the commanding general in the use of these extraordinary powers that the Trans-Mississippi Department did not break down of its own weight long before the surrender of the Confederate armies east of the river" (359). Kirby Smith, as he is generally known because of his habit of signing his name as if he had two surnames, was president of the University of Nashville and taught mathematics at the University of the South (Sewanee) after the war. See Kerby, *Kirby Smith's Confederacy* and Howard, *General Edmund Kirby Smith, C.S.A.*

2. Kirby Smith was born in St. Augustine on May 16, 1824. He was therefore almost nine years younger than his hostess, born on November 19, 1815.

3. Kirby Smith's letters to his wife show that he arrived in Camden on December 14, 1863, that he stayed at a Major Elliott's house while traveling about the area, and that he was in Camden on Christmas day of 1863. He went to church Christmas morning and left in the evening to visit the camp of General Price. Unfortunately, he does not mention his pleasant dinner with the Merrells (Kirby Smith to his wife, December 15, 17, 19, and 25, 1863, Kirby Smith Papers).

4. Marmaduke attacked Pine Bluff on October 25, 1863.

5. John Bankhead Magruder (1810–71) had commanded the District of Texas, New Mexico, and Arizona since 1862 and had earned great praise for recapturing Galveston. In late 1864 he replaced Sterling Price as the commander of the District of Arkansas, and after the war he served as a major general under Emperor Maximilian in Mexico.

CHAPTER VIII

1. Joseph Orville Shelby (1830–97) was not promoted to brigadier general until 1864, to rank from December 1863. He had been one of the wealthiest and most influential citizens of prewar Missouri, leading proslavery raids in Missouri and Kansas in the 1850s. He had a high reputation as a dashing Confederate cavalry commander, and his "Iron Brigade of the West" was compared to J. E. B. Stuart's cavalry in the East. Like Magruder, Shelby served Maximilian in Mexico after the war. On April 1, 1864, the advance of Shelby's brigade, consisting of two cavalry regiments commanded by Lieutenant Colonel W. H. Fayth, attacked the Union rear nine miles from Spoonville at the crossing of Terre Noir Creek (*O.R.*, vol. 34, pt. 1, pp. 780, 821). The brigade skirmished continuously with Steele's columns on April 2, 1864, as Steele made his way toward Washington. Spoonville, twelve miles from Arkadelphia, was nine miles from a fork where the main road from Little Rock to Washington branched with a lesser road. The Confederates lay in wait on the main road, and Steele took the lesser-used fork and secured the Missouri River crossing at Elkins' Ferry (*O.R.*, vol. 34, pt. 1, pp. 732, 780, 822).

2. John Cabell Breckenridge (1821–75) of Kentucky, who had been vice-president of the United States under James Buchanan, was not appointed Davis's secretary of war until February 1865, just before the end. It is small wonder that he knew little of the West, for he occupied himself primarily with evacuating Richmond, fleeing to North Carolina, and negotiating surrender in that area. Merrell's date for the Camden Expedition should be March and April, not May, of 1864.

3. "Young Dodd" was David Owen Dodd (1846–64), who had returned to Arkansas to look after some cattle that his family had left behind when they fled to Texas. As he passed through Camden on his way to Little Rock, General Fagan, who knew him, gave him a pass, jokingly on the condition that he bring back the numbers, location, and campaign plans of Steele's army. After seeing to his cattle, visiting some friends, and looking about for three weeks, Dodd began his journey back. But he took a wrong road, and his cutting through the woods to gain the correct one engaged the attention of a Federal patrol. When one soldier noticed that his shoes did not match, he was searched, and in one of the shoes were found papers filled with accurate details about Steele's army in Little Rock. Steele did not think that a child could have managed such an assignment and believed that the fear of death would make the boy divulge other names. But young Dodd did not talk. When the drop fell, his body was so light that his neck did not break, and soldiers

had to pull and jerk on the boy until his neck broke (Parham, "David O. Dodd").

4. Theophilus Holmes was relieved from his command of the District of Arkansas on March 16, 1864, and was succeeded on the same day by Sterling Price.

5. Prairie D'Ane is due east of Washington and about halfway between Murfreesboro and Camden in what is now Nevada County.

6. Perhaps because of their unusual but somewhat similar first names, Merrell confuses Generals Leonidas Polk (1806–64), who was killed at the battle of Pine Mountain in Georgia, and Lucius M. Walker (1829–63), who was killed September 6, 1863, in a duel with Marmaduke that was caused by Marmaduke's questioning the latter's courage at the battle of Helena on July 4. See *O.R.*, vol. 22, pt. 1, pp. 433, 436–37, 525–26.

CHAPTER IX

1. Steele left Little Rock on March 23, 1864. There were skirmishes almost daily as he moved southwest toward Washington.

2. James Gillpatrick Blunt (1826–81) had been transferred from Arkansas to command the District of the Frontier in June of 1863. He was ordered to relinquish command of the Indian Territory and Fort Smith on April 17, 1864 (*O.R.*, vol. 34, pt. 3, p. 225). Perhaps Merrell means General John Milton Thayer (1820–1906), who was to have led his Frontier Division from Fort Smith to join with Steele at Arkadelphia, but who was eight days late when he finally joined Steele on the Prairie D'Ane after taking a wrong road and encountering some foul weather. The delay exhausted Union supplies that might have lasted to Shreveport and caused Steele to turn to Camden in hopes of finding more. See Steele's reports, *O.R.*, vol. 34, pt. 1, p. 661, and pt. 3, p. 78; Britton, *Civil War on the Border* 2:254–57.

3. The battle of Poison Springs was fought on April 18, 1864.

4. A skirmish between Rice's and Shelby's brigades took place here on April 2, 1864. On the same day there were skirmishes at nearby Antoine and on Wolf Creek.

5. Mr. Sam Dickinson, who chaired the Arkansas Civil War Centennial Commission, informs me that the crossing place was not "Nacatoch Ford" (at Natchitoches Bluff) but was actually several miles upstream at Elkins' Ferry (see *O.R.*, vol. 34, pt. 1, pp. 661, 780, 822–23). I am indebted to Mr. Dickinson for reading Merrell's pages and my notes on the Camden Expedition and for making suggestions.

6. Brigadier General Samuel A. Rice (1828–64) was then in command of the First Brigade of Salomon's Third Division. At Jenkins' Ferry on March 30, a spur on his right boot was hit by a bullet, and the fragments entered his ankle. He died on July 6, 1864.

7. No Carnahan is listed as a resident of any county in southwest Arkansas in the 1860 census. The only Carnahans in the state are listed as living in Washington, Franklin, and Marion counties, all in the northern part of the state. In the margin of his manuscript Merrell has the note "Widow Carnahan," and Mr. Sam Dickinson informs me that General Steele camped at the plantation of a "Widow

Cornelius" at what was formerly called Nobbin Hill but which is now known as Missionary Grove in Nevada County, Arkansas.

8. Nathaniel Prentiss Banks (1816–94) had been Speaker of the U.S. House of Representatives (1856–57) and governor of Massachusetts (1858–60). A clearly political appointee to the rank of major general, Banks was frequently criticized for his performance, and even Lincoln's favor could not save him after the failure of the Red River Campaign.

9. The Federal objective was Shreveport, where Steele and Banks were to combine by May 1, 1864. Shreveport would then have become the staging area for further moves into Texas. The commander of the Red River Expedition, Nathaniel Prentiss Banks, wrote Sherman on January 24, 1864, that the occupation of Shreveport "will be as fatal to the troops west of the Mississippi as that of Chattanooga to the east" (*O.R.*, vol. 34, pt. 2, p. 145). On March 15, 1864, Ulysses S. Grant wrote to Steele and instructed him to move his force "in full co-operation with General N. R. Banks' attack on Shreveport" (*O.R.*, vol. 34, pt. 2, p. 616). See Britton, *Civil War on the Border* 2:253–54.

10. Although Steele was thinking in late February that he should try to turn the Rebel flank on the Red River and make them run to Texas, Sherman ordered him to push straight for Shreveport (*O.R.*, vol. 34, pt. 2, p. 449). Steele's eight-day delay was caused by the tardiness of Thayer in joining him from Fort Smith. Steele crossed the Little Missouri River at Elkins' Ferry on April 5, 1864, and Thayer joined him on the Prairie D'Ane, a few miles to the south, on April 8. Steele wrote from Elkins' Ferry on April 7, "Leaving here, I shall proceed directly to Camden with my whole force" (*O.R.*, vol. 34, pt. 1, p. 660), indicating that his decision to take Camden had nothing to do with Banks's repulse in Louisiana. In an attempt to gain needed supplies, Steele turned to take heavily fortified Camden, which Price had left after removing all its stores and leaving only a small guard (*O.R.*, vol. 34, pt. 1, pp. 661, 780). Steele entered Camden on the evening of April 15 and found it, like the countryside around it, barren of what his large army required (*O.R.*, vol. 34, pt. 1, p. 661). See the excellent description of the depleted state of Steele's supplies in Britton, *Civil War on the Border* 2:279.

Steele learned in Camden on April 18 that Banks had been repulsed in Louisiana on the eighth and ninth (*O.R.*, vol. 34, pt. 1, p. 662). But a letter that Steele wrote to Banks from Camden on April 23 shows clearly that their objective was still Shreveport: "I desire to co-operate with you in the best manner possible, at the same time covering Arkansas until Shreveport shall be ours" (*O.R.*, vol. 34, pt. 3, p. 267).

11. Merrell's estimates of troop strength again seem high. Although the numbers of both sides had been reduced by the preceding day's struggle at Mansfield, there were 12,647 Federals engaged at the battle of Pleasant Hill on April 9, 1864. They were opposed by 14,300 Confederates (Livermore, *Numbers and Losses in the Civil War*, 109–10).

12. Richard Taylor (1826–79) was the son of former president Zachary Taylor.

His skill and daring won the days at Mansfield and Pleasant Hill, but he clashed with Kirby Smith over strategy following these battles, thinking that Banks should have been hounded and destroyed after his defeats. Instead, Kirby Smith turned the department's forces back toward Camden to eliminate Steele.

13. The battles took place on April 8 and 9, 1864.

CHAPTER X

1. Taylor had about eleven thousand Confederate effectives at Mansfield to confront thirty thousand Union effectives (*O.R.*, vol. 34, pt. 1, p. 484).

2. Merrell would naturally record this brilliant feat of engineering, conceived by an engineer officer who was a former Wisconsin lumberjack. See pages 619–20 of Faust, *Historical Times Illustrated Encyclopedia of the Civil War*, for a concise account of this and other actions in the Red River Campaign.

3. Thomas James Churchill (1824–1905) was in 1864 in command of the First Arkansas Infantry Division of Magruder's Second Army Corps.

4. Steele wrote from Camden on April 17: "An immense amount of labor has been expended in fortifying Camden and cutting away forests. There are nine forts on eminences, and they seem to be well located. Strategically and commercially, I regard this as the first town in Arkansas" (*O.R.*, vol. 34, pt. 1, p. 661). I am indebted to Mr. Sam Dickinson for informing me that Tate's Bluff was north of Camden, where the Little Missouri River emptied into the Ouachita River, and that the Confederates had a small fort there which survives to this day.

5. In his diary Merrell noted: "Fri., Apr. 15: The engagement commenced at the forks of the road 15 miles west of Camden near Lee's house & continued until evening" (Smith Papers, Receipts book, box 103; copies at the Arkansas History Commission, Little Rock, and the Southwest Arkansas Regional Archives, Washington, Ark.).

6. His diary notes on April 15 that there were Confederate skirmishers firing opposite his house on Washington Street as the Union forces approached about five o'clock and that "the skirmishers' firing ceased not until the head of their columns was nearly opposite my house" (Smith Papers, Receipts book, box 103; copies at the Arkansas History Commission and the Southwest Arkansas Regional Archives).

7. Perhaps because he is writing these chapters after a ten years' residence in Camden, Merrell seems to be addressing an audience who would recognize the names, houses, and locations that he mentions. Except for some descriptions of Utica, he has not made this a practice in his memoirs.

8. Steele occupied Camden on the evening of April 15, 1864.

9. The figure given in the *Official Records* for Steele's aggregate strength present for the campaign was 13,754 (*O.R.*, vol. 34, pt. 1, p. 657).

10. Two entries in the diary that Merrell kept at the time will attest to the suffering of Steele's men in Camden: "Mon., Apr. 18, 1864: The men annoy us with applications & say they have had no bread but parched corn for four days"; "Sat.,

23d Apr. 1864: The divide among the troops was ¼ rations, which reduced them to foraging on their [   ], killing milch cows & calves & begging from door to door, sometimes in a very hostile manner" (Smith Papers, Receipts book, box 103; copies at the Arkansas History Commission, Little Rock, and the Southwest Arkansas Regional Archives, Washington, Ark.).

CHAPTER XI

1. The brigade of Richard Montgomery Gano (1830–1913) was at Poison Springs, but it was commanded by Colonel Charles De Morse (*O.R.*, vol. 34, pt. 1, pp. 846–48). Merrell may be confusing Gano with William Lewis Cabell (1827–1916), who commanded the center of the Confederate line in that battle and whose troops seem to have played the more active role that Merrell assigns to Gano's. The Confederate troops were made up of men picked from divisions commanded by Marmaduke, Fagan, Cabell, and Samuel Bell Maxey (1825–95), who outranked Marmaduke but who yielded to his plan of attack. The Indian force was Colonel Tandy Walker's Choctaw Brigade.

2. The Eighteenth Iowa Infantry Regiment.

3. There were 438 troops from the First Kansas Colored Volunteers engaged at Poison Springs. Of these men, 117 were killed and 65 were wounded under such circumstances as Merrell describes, although official reports do not single out Tandy Walker's Indians, who may have been bent on revenging the raids of these same Negro troops on their villages in Indian Territory. Colonel James M. Williams, the commander of the Federal escort of Poison Springs wrote, "Many wounded men belonging to the First Kansas Colored Volunteers fell into the hands of the enemy, and I have the most positive assurances from eye-witnesses that they were murdered on the spot." Major Richard G. Ward of the First Kansas Volunteers maintained that "the rebels were seen shooting those that fell into their hands" (*O.R.*, vol. 34, pt. 1, pp. 746, 754). Merrell notes in his diary on April 18, 1864: "It is alleged that no Negro prisoners were taken by the Confederates but all killed on the spot. Location Poison Spr." (Smith Papers, Receipts book, box 103; copies at Arkansas History Commission, Little Rock, and Southwest Arkansas Regional Archives, Washington, Ark.). See the grisly account of this battle in Britton, *Civil War on the Border* 2:278–91.

4. George H. Stinson (1827–99) lived across Washington Street from the Merrells in Camden. Stinson was a dealer in books, stationery, and jewelry in the town who, as a soldier, lost an eye at the battle of Shiloh in April 1862, then served in the quartermaster department until the close of the war (Goodspeed, *Biographical and Historical Memoirs of Southern Arkansas*, 694). Mr. Stinson's wife, Virginia McCollum Stinson, was Mrs. Merrell's good friend, and she watched over her in her final illness. Mrs. Stinson wrote an account of Steele's occupation, entitled "Yankees in Camden, Arkansas," which was published in *Heroines of Dixie*, edited by Katherine M. Jones. The Stinsons' descendants still operate Stinson's Jewelry on Washington Street in Camden.

516 Notes to Pages 368–371

5. I am indebted to Mr. Sam Dickinson of Prescott, Arkansas, for pointing out that "tolling" is an old Arkansas vernacular term for "enticing" or "luring." See Vance M. Randolph and George P. Wilson, *Down in the Holler: A Gallery of Arkansas Folk Speech* (Norman: University of Oklahoma Press, 1953), 83. It may be rooted in a rare old usage that means "to gather."

6. Generals John S. Marmaduke and James F. Fagan (1828–93) commanded cavalry divisions during the Camden Expedition, although Fagan's division earned most of the glory at Marks' Mills (April 25, 1864), capturing over two hundred wagons and inflicting sixteen hundred casualties.

7. Lieutenant Colonel Francis M. Drake commanded the Second Brigade of the Thirty-sixth Iowa Infantry at the Battle of Marks' Mills. See his report on the battle, during which he corroborates Merrell's statement about his wound, in *O.R.*, vol. 34, pt. 1, pp. 712–15.

8. General Fagan gives the following totals in his report of his division's action at Marks' Mills. "Many other prisoners were taken (in all over 1,300), 6 pieces of artillery (all they had), their entire train of 300 wagons, a large number of ambulances, very many small arms, and 150 negroes" (*O.R.*, vol. 34, pt. 1, p. 789).

9. Merrell kept records showing that the Confederate government paid him and Magill for the use of a brick office, a two-story brick warehouse, and a large cotton warehouse in Camden. These buildings and other Camden real estate were part of the payment that John Matlock made to Merrell for the Royston factory and site. The office was used by the inspector general, the storehouse by the post commissary, and the cotton warehouse as a military prison (Smith Papers, box 100, folder 6). This last building may have been the one known for years in Camden as "the old Star warehouse."

10. Merrell wrote in his diary on April 23, 1864: "Cannonading close at hand, at about sun-down" (Smith Papers, Receipts book, box 103; copies at Arkansas History Commission, Little Rock, and Southwest Arkansas Regional Archives, Washington, Ark.).

11. The battle of Marks' Mill occurred on April 25, 1864.

12. Merrell is correct about the length of the Federal occupation of Camden, but not correct about its dates. Steele occupied Camden from the evening of April 15, 1864, through the early morning hours of April 27. The diary that he kept at the time, had he consulted it, would have refreshed Merrell's memory on the events that he is now recounting in 1873.

13. "Genl. Steele shifted his Quarters from Mrs. Graham's house to Jas. Brooks, Genl. Salomon from J. T. Elliott's into the town" (Receipts book, Smith Papers, box 103; copies at Arkansas History Commission and Southwest Arkansas Regional Archives). The "Graham" house, later the T. J. Gaughan home, was across Washington Street from Merrell's own home (Gaughan, "Historic Camden," 250). Brigadier General Frederick Salomon (1826–97) was the commander of the Third Division of Steele's Army of Arkansas. Born in Prussia and a student of architecture, he fled to the United States following the revolutions of 1848. His troops

played key roles in the defense of Helena and in the battle of Jenkins' Ferry. Before and after the war Salomon was a surveyor and engineer (*O.R.*, vol. 22, pt. 2, p. 621).

CHAPTER XII

1. The Second Massachusetts Battery, commanded by Captain Ormand F. Nims, lost three pieces on the field, Nims said, "on account of the horses being disabled," and it lost the rest of the battery when the roads became clogged following the battle, "as well as the caissons, baggage wagons, battery wagon, and forge" (*O.R.*, vol. 34, pt. 1, pp. 462–63).

2. Merrell noted in his diary on April 18, 1864: "I believe the officers do their best to protect Citizens against depredations but without success. Our horses taken. Our Negroes set free & Munroe forced by threats of hanging to enlist in a Negro regt., but upon my reporting the same to Genl. Steele's Agt., he discharged Munroe from his obligation & indignantly inquired the name of the officer who had done the deed. Name not known. A guard promised me at my house" (Smith Papers, Receipts book, box 103; copies at Arkansas History Commission, Little Rock, and Southwest Arkansas Regional Archives, Washington, Ark.).

3. Richard Montgomery Gano (1830–1913), commander of "Gano's Brigade" of cavalry, was promoted to brigadier general in recognition of his performance during the Camden Expedition.

4. Fagan's division crossed Steele's route of evacuation from Camden only hours before him. "Being entirely without forage and subsistence," Fagan said later, "I moved out toward the Ouachita at the only point where anything of forage, etc., could be had between Princeton and Arkansas River." At midnight he received word that Steele was within eight miles of Jenkins' Ferry while he was thirty-four miles away. Although he moved out at dawn, Fagan found "on my arrival the fight had just closed" (*O.R.*, vol. 34, pt. 1, p. 790). Kirby Smith's chief of staff, William R. Boggs, later maintained that Fagan was sent to Little Rock and ordered to "*stop for nothing*," but that he had stopped, and the opportunity to surprise Little Rock was thus lost (*Military Reminiscences*, 78).

5. "That night Genl. Steele's army evacuated Camden with great skill & secrecy. So much so that a regiment of Infantry encamped opposite my house decamped while I was looking at them & expected it, yet I could not tell the precise time of their leaving. Genl. Steele certainly tried to prevent outrages by the rear guard stragglers, but without entire success. Several houses were sacked in spite of his patrol guard. At some houses he placed sentries, to others he refused. I guarded my own with a gun & was not molested" (Smith Papers, Receipts book, box 103; copies at Arkansas History Commission and Southwest Arkansas Regional Archives).

6. The fight began at daylight on April 30, 1864.

7. Brigadier General John B. Clark, Jr. (1831–1903), commanded the First Brigade of Mosby Parsons's Missouri Division during the Camden Expedition.

8. A prolonge is a rope with a hook and a toggle, used to drag a gun carriage or to attach it to a horse-drawn two-wheeled "limber."

9. The pronoun *this* refers to the Confederate flanking movement of the division of Texas infantry commanded by Major General John G. Walker (1822–93). See *O.R.*, vol. 34, pt. 1, pp. 782–83.

10. Incomplete returns show that 86 Confederates were killed and 356 were wounded at Jenkins' Ferry (*O.R.*, vol. 34, pt. 1, p. 788). Federal losses were 86 killed, 500 wounded, and 61 missing (Britton, *Civil War on the Border* 2:308) David Y. Thomas in *Arkansas in War and Reconstruction* says that Confederate losses totaled over 500 and that losses in the Union general Salomon's division alone totaled 63 killed, 413 wounded, and 45 missing (270).

11. A Confederate soldier in Walker's Texas Division gives an eyewitness account of Kirby Smith in battle at Jenkins' Ferry. "Seeing some of the Arkansas troops falling back, he rallied them by dismounting from his horse, and, taking a gun from one of the soldiers, he took his place in the ranks as a private. The troops, seeing him thus exposing his life, rallied to his support, and kept in line until the close of the battle. To see the commanding general of the Trans-Mississippi Department, wielding the destinies of a great fight, with its cares and responsibilities upon his shoulders, performing the duty of a private soldier, in the thickest of the conflict, is a picture worthy of an artist" (Blessington, *Campaigns of Walker's Texas Division*, 251).

12. The Merrells lived on the south side of Washington Street in Camden, just west of the town.

13. Merrell mentioned Judge George C. Watkins earlier in chapter VI (see note 6 of the chapter). Watkins was one of three judges listed for the district military court, the other two being W. P. Townsend and Presiding Judge Trusten Polk (Crute, *Confederate Staff Officers*, 90).

CHAPTER XIII

1. According to Kirby Smith's chief of staff, William R. Boggs, Governor Reynolds of Missouri and Sterling Price requested and were given permission "to make a demonstration into Missouri. They seemed to think that the people had suffered so severely at the hands of the Federals, that upon their appearance with an army a sufficient number of able bodied men would join them to enable them to regain possession of the State" (*Military Reminiscences*, 80).

2. Merrell may have intended to write a figure of 2,000 rather than 20,000 here. It is more likely that Price returned from his ill-fated expedition with about 3,500 men (Josephy, *Civil War on the Frontier*, 161). Only one-third of these 3,500 men were armed, and "over 10,000 men—killed, wounded, captured, or missing—who had followed Price's flags from Princeton or who had rallied to them en route, were left behind on—or under—Missouri's inhospitable soil" (Kerby, *Kirby Smith's Confederacy*, 352, 358).

3. For the breakdown in road transportation in the Trans-Mississippi, see Kerby, *Kirby Smith's Confederacy*, 383. Kirby Smith's General Order no. 19 of May 6, 1864, had given elaborate directions about the number of mules and wagons allo-

cated to various levels of headquarters and numbers of men. General Order no. 26 (May 21, 1864) placed further restrictions on their use (*General Orders. Head Quarters, Trans-Mississippi Department*, 11, 17). Merrell had so much trouble getting and keeping this ambulance that he preserved among his papers the orders, countermands, and reorders concerning it. Major W. H. Haynes, chief of Kirby Smith's Clothing Bureau, wrote Merrell from Shreveport on September 19, 1864, to see General Magruder, who had been placed in command of the District of Arkansas (on August 4 [*General Orders. Head Quarters, Trans-Mississippi Department*, 53]). "He has been directed to allow your use of the ambulance. I do not understand Lt. Wooten's meddlesome interference and doubt of my veracity." Lieutenant Thomas D. Wooten was a surgeon on Magruder's staff who must have given Merrell trouble (Crute, *Confederate Staff Officers*, 159). The same day, Haynes wrote Merrell, "Gen. Smith has directed the ambulance & mules turned over to you." This note was probably not in Merrell's hands in Camden when he wrote to a Major Moore, apparently Magruder's chief quartermaster, on September 20 that he had been delayed in reporting to Shreveport by "unreasonable persistence on the part of the Medical Department" and that he could not appeal to Magruder because Magruder had gone to the front. He adds that the ambulance was condemned when he received it and that he has worked on it daily. On September 21, S. H. Buck, assistant adjutant to Magruder, wrote an order that "Mr. Henry Merrell is permitted to retain the ambulance now in his possession to carry out instructions from Dept. Hdqtrs." Merrell made his journey to Shreveport, where he received his orders on September 27 to go to England. See Smith Papers, box 100, folder 6.

4. Merrell only hints that he was employed in "throwing up Earth-works," but it seems certain that he was employed in building up the several strong fortifications in and about Camden. His wife wrote to her sister Mrs. Smith in Roswell on July 3, 1864, that while awaiting orders from General Kirby Smith, "he is studying out all the time something for the good of the cause," that one of her husband's tasks has been to plan "the hasty breastworks which have helped Fagan and Marmaduke so much lately," and that "he has been to one of the battlegrounds since & is now improving upon them" (Smith Papers, box 100, folder 8). During the Camden campaign, a member of Walker's Texas Division, J. P. Blessington, feared that his division would have to attack Steele within the very fortifications that Holmes had constructed, perhaps with Merrell's help: "The fortifications at Camden, constructed by General Holmes, and improved by the enemy, were not inferior to any in the Trans-Mississippi Department, and from the appearance of the place, we should have had some difficulty in taking it, if the enemy had not left" (*Campaigns of Walker's Texas Division*, 247).

Work on these fortifications had begun shortly after the Merrells had arrived in Camden. Near the end of 1863, upon receiving instructions from Kirby Smith to fortify the town, Theophilus Holmes had ordered Brigadier General Alexander T. Hawthorne (1825–1899) to erect defensive works around Camden. But Hawthorne, a Camden attorney before the war, had "no previous experience in the field of engineering" (Shea, "Camden Fortifications," 319). This fact makes quite probable Merrell's employment on these defenses. Work on improving these fortifications was still incomplete in November of 1864, and the Trans-Mississippi Department considered their perfection "of the greatest importance," for Kirby Smith believed the line of the Ouachita and Little Missouri rivers to be "the true line of defense" (*O.R.*, vol. 41, pt. 4, pp. 1033, 1114, 1101).

5. From the 1840s through the early 1870s, Mound Prairie, Texas, was a large, thickly settled manufacturing community. During the Civil War, skillets, plows, iron singletrees, rifles, and bayonets were among the items manufactured from local iron ore. There was also a mill that wove cotton and woolen goods (*Palestine* [Texas] *Herald-Press*, Aug. 21, 1968, p. 16, cols. 1–3). From April through December of 1864, the Confederate government made three purchases of land in Mound Prairie, Texas. The first purchase was made on April 18 by Henry Day, the superintendent of the Government Iron Works in Texas; the second and third were made on August 10 and December 3 by J. J. Busby, major and quartermaster in the Confederate army, "for the use and benefit of the Southern Confederacy" (Anderson County, Texas, *Deed Book L*, 229, 260–62, 295). Although the deeds give no information of what was on the tracts or what use would be made of them, Busby's association with the purchases would indicate that the factories with which Merrell was concerned were built here, about nine miles north of Palestine, Texas. This long-abandoned industrial area has been subject to occasional rediscovery. See articles in the *Palestine Herald-Press*, Aug. 21, 1968, p. 16; Mar. 19, 1969, p. 7; Dec. 24, 1972, sec. 1, p. 14; May 13, 1977, p. 5; May 31, 1981, sec. B, p. 2; and June 3, 1981, p. 6.

6. D. W. Yandrell (Merrell spells the name Yandril) was appointed Chief Medical Director for the Department of the Trans-Mississippi in March 1864. He was released from these duties on October 7, 1864, shortly after the events that Merrell describes (*General Orders. Head Quarters, Trans-Mississippi Department*, 74). Before coming to the Trans-Mississippi, Yandrell had been Medical Inspector for Beauregard and Medical Director for Hardee (Crute, *Confederate Staff Officers*, 16, 79, 105, 178).

7. Henry Hopkins Sibley (1816–86) won some early successes in 1861 and 1862 in attempting to conquer for the Confederacy the territory that is now Arizona and New Mexico, capturing Santa Fe, Albuquerque, and other objectives. But he finally had to withdraw as far as San Antonio, Texas.

8. Colonel Richard Hanson Weightman (1816–61) commanded the First Brigade of the Second Division of the Missouri State Guard at the Battle of Oak Hills (Wilson's Creek) on August 10, 1861. He "fell mortally wounded at the head of his column" (*O.R.* 3:127–28).

9. On Mrs. Smith and her plantation see note 7 to chapter IV above.

10. Lieutenant Colonel Richard H. Musser of "Musser's Infantry Battalion," which was operating in the area during May and June of 1863 under John B. Clark's First Brigade of Frost's Division (*O.R.*, vol. 22, pt. 2, pp. 851, 866, 1157).

CHAPTER XIV

1. See note 5 in the preceding chapter concerning Mound Prairie, Texas.

2. Major W. H. Haynes, chief of the Clothing Bureau under Kirby Smith, wrote W. R. Boggs, Kirby Smith's chief of staff, on January 18, 1864, that he needed an efficient officer in Tyler, Texas, to put to work the machinery that we know to have arrived recently from Royston. "I respectfully suggest that Maj. J. J. Busby be ordered on that duty" (*O.R.*, vol. 22, pt. 2, p. 1135). Busby had previously been quartermaster under General John S. Roane (Crute, *Confederate Staff Officers*, 165). It seems clear that the remnants of Merrell's factory were first to be placed in Tyler but were later moved south to Mound Prairie.

3. Colonel Joseph W. Bocage (b. 1819) was one of the pioneers of the city of Pine Bluff, Arkansas. Born on the island of St. Lucia, he could speak only French when he arrived in America at the age of three. He was eighteen when his family came to Arkansas, where he was admitted to the bar in 1840. He eventually was a circuit court judge and mayor of Pine Bluff; he operated a foundry and manufactured steam engines. During the Civil War, he helped Hindman to raise the Second Arkansas Infantry Regiment, in which he served as colonel. See Goodspeed, *Biographical and Historical Memoirs of Central Arkansas*, 157–58; Hempstead, *Pictorial History of Arkansas*, 974.

4. Writing almost twenty-five years after the event, Judge J. W. Bocage said that the Confederate authorities took charge of the Pike County factory that Merrell had built and which now belonged to Matlock "early in 1863." This takeover could not have taken place until late 1863. By the end of the year, said Bocage, it "was hurriedly taken down, thrown promiscuously into wagons and transported over rivers, hills and dales to Mound Prairie, Anderson county, Texas nine miles north of Palestine, to be readjusted and operated by the government, for the benefit of the army of the trans-Mississippi department." He said that there was much disarray when the Merrell-Matlock machinery was originally delivered, "the parts of spinning and drawing frames, cards, railway heads, speeders, lappers, spoolers, and reels were badly mixed, many parts broken and many parts lost." To put everything together, he says, seemed impossible, especially because the blockade was rigid and no one in the South was manufacturing cotton machinery: "The ingenuity of the Confederate artisans was taxed to its utmost" (*Pine Bluff Daily Commercial*, July 16, 1887, p. 2, col. 3).

William H. Etter, the owner and editor of the *Washington Telegraph*, wrote an eyewitness account of the "Busby Cotton factory" to his children on November 16, 1864. "The cotton machinery is in its place in the building—but no Boiler or Engine up yet and no shafting nor did I find any hands at work on the machinery." He saw only a few hands "building the chimney stack" and "some hands working in the shops." Inquiring of someone there "at what time he expected the factory would be in operation," he received the answer of the first of January. He says, "My impression is it will be fully three months before they will be able to commence spinning." The main building "has the appearance of its having been put up with a view of its being a permanent institution for the benefit of the country after the war." But the most interesting feature of Mr. Etter's letter is this sentence: "Mr. Merrill who formerly owned the factory in Pike County started yesterday via Houston and Matamoros for England to purchase additional machinery for the factory, and they are framing another building for more machinery" (Private collection of William H. Etter III, of Washington, Arkansas).

5. It should be noted that it was Major W. H. Haynes of Kirby Smith's Clothing Bureau who was the major force behind these enterprises and the decision to send Merrell to England. His instructions to Merrell told him to get machinery "for providing Clothing & Camp & Garrison Equipage for the Trans-Mississippi Army" (Smith Papers, box 100, folder 6). How successful Haynes was in his efforts can be judged by a sentence from Kerby's *Kirby Smith's Confederacy:* "Haynes's various enterprises were so successful that, when it came time for the South to surrender, Kirby Smith's soldiers were probably the best-dressed troops in the Confederate army" (380). For more on Haynes, see Nichols, *Confederate Quartermaster in the Trans-Mississippi*, 14, 30–31, 33–38, 41–42.

6. Merrell's own records, as well as the Etter letter cited in note 4 above, show that he left Mound Prairie for Houston on November 15, 1864.

7. Records that Merrell kept show that he arrived in Houston on November 22, 1864, that Kirby Smith issued orders for him to depart on December 1, that there were further delays until December 25, and that he received his final instructions to depart on January 12, 1865 (Smith Papers, box 100, folder 6). The reader may wish to refer to the last part of the introduction to this section ("Arkansas") for a full explanation of Merrell's difficulties in getting off to England.

8. Matamoros is in Mexico, opposite Brownsville, Texas, on the Rio Grande. Mexico's neutrality prevented Union gunboats from interfering with shipping in its territorial waters. Matamoros, therefore, was a major port for Confederate blockade runners.

Colin J. McRae, the "Czar of purchasing in Europe, in charge of all Confederate agents," early in the Civil War received a contract from the Confederate government to erect a factory and cast cannon in Selma, Alabama (Eaton, *History of the Southern Confederacy*, 146, 138). Subsequently a Confederate general, he served as financial agent in Paris before returning to London in 1864 (*O.R.*, ser. 4, vol. 2, pp. 586, 824; ser. 4, vol. 3, pp. 296, 525–30). As "sole financial agent" for the Confederacy for the remainder of the war, McRae "made a remarkably successful record" (Coulter, *Confederate States of America*, 196). See Charles S. Davis, *Colin J. McRae*.

In a letter of October 25, 1864, Edmund Kirby Smith wrote Colin J. McRae a letter about Merrell that is printed in the *Official Records* of the Civil War. Kirby Smith tells McRae that his chief of the cotton office has been directed to transfer the sum of $100,000 to McRae's credit with the firm of Fraser, Trenholm & Company of Liverpool, "to be held for the purchase of machinery for the Trans-Mississippi Department, under special instructions from these headquarters." Kirby Smith describes Merrell as "a practical manufacturer of long standing and good social position at home. He is familiar with the wants of my department, and I have sent him to England to make all necessary purchases." He asks McRae to "advance him sufficient funds to defray his expenses and the cost of such assistance as he may require" (*O.R.*, vol. 41, pt. 4, pp. 1012–13).

9. These letters were not in the volume. A discolored rectangular space on two facing pages discloses where they may have been placed, but exhaustive searches of the Smith House have not led to their discovery.

10. According to the instructions that Major W. H. Haynes gave to Merrell, Lawson had been working previously for Major J. J. Busby at Mound Prairie, Texas. The order detailing Lawson to Merrell was Special Order 289 of the Trans-Mississippi Department, dated November 18, 1864 (Smith Papers, box 100, folder 6).

11. Major General Camille Armand Jules Marie, Prince de Polignac (1832–1913) served in the French army in Crimea and then retired to Central America. He offered his services to the Confederacy when the Civil War broke out, serving under Beauregard at Shiloh and Corinth and under Richard Taylor at Mansfield, where his gallantry won the day. He was promoted to major general on April 13, 1864, to date from April 8 (*General Orders. Head Quarters, Trans-Mississippi Department*, 7; *O.R.*, vol. 34, pt. 3, p. 764). He suggested to Kirby Smith that he might "do some good by conveying information abroad" and that he might be able "to enlist sympathy for the Southern Cause," whereupon Kirby Smith granted him a leave of six months. He took with him his chief of staff, Major T. C. Moncure, and Colonel Ernest Miltenberger, the aide-de-camp of H. W. Allen, the Confederate governor of Louisiana and close friend of Polignac's. Jefferson Davis knew nothing of this mission.

Polignac said that "at every stage of our journey" "through the breadth of Texas," he was received graciously by deputations of citizens and had not been allowed to settle any hotel bill. He "everywhere was received and considered as a guest of the state." He adds, "We travelled by stagecoach, and our progress was slow" (Polignac, "Polignac's Mission," 330). We may well imagine the effect that the adulation of a foreign prince, with whom he was sharing a slow stage, had upon Henry Merrell.

12. Yet the Trans-Mississippi Department's Niter and Mining Bureau of Thomas G. Clemson, for whom Clemson University is named, "never encountered any serious impediment to the production of adequate stores of lead, niter, saltpeter, and sulphur" (Kerby, *Kirby Smith's Confederacy*, 380).

13. Lee surrendered on April 9, 1865.

14. In this battle, which was fought on May 9, 1846, near Brownsville, Texas, the U.S. troops of Brigadier General Zachary Taylor routed a Mexican force commanded by General Mariano Arista.

15. Merrell's "Cortinas" is probably Juan Cortina, "the old nemesis of the border country," who had helped a bandit chieftain named Cobos seize Matamoros after Federal troops had expelled him from Brownsville. In a few days, Cortina

mounted a counterrevolution and shot Cobos (Kerby, *Kirby Smith's Confederacy*, 192). The Mexican general Santiago Vidaurri, a friend of the Confederacy and eventual supporter of Maximilian, held power in the town through most of the Civil War, although by its end the French were in control of Matamoros.

16. This picture is clearly of General Tomás Mejía, a conservative Indian chieftain, or *cacique*, from the Sierra Gordo, who had seized control in Querétaro in 1856. He was opposed to Benito Juárez, who was also an Indian. In his last days, Maximilian fled to Mejía in an attempt to escape capture. See Meyers and Sherman, *Course of Mexican History*, 79, 382, and Henry Bamford Parkes, *A History of Mexico*, 273.

17. Antonio López de Santa Anna (1794–1876) had retired from Mexican affairs and had moved to Jamaica in 1847, then to New Granada in 1853. He was not allowed to return to Mexico until two years before his death.

Postscript

1. Kirby Smith Papers, film no. M-404, reel 4.

2. Elizabeth Smith to her parents, August 15, 1866, and map, Smith Papers, box 100, folder 7, and box 9.

3. Elizabeth Merrell to her sister, Anne Magill Smith, July 8, 1865, Smith Papers, box 8.

4. "Case Files of Applications from Former Confederates for Presidential Pardons," roll 14, pp. 93, 95–97; Smith Papers, box 9.

5. "Case Files of Applications from Former Confederates for Presidential Pardons," roll 14, p. 94.

6. Oneida Historical Society, *Semi-Centennial History of the City of Utica*, 20.

7. Kirby Smith Papers, film no. M-404, reel 4.

8. Smith Papers, box 100, folder 6.

9. Conkling's letter states that he does not know Merrell personally but that he can "bear testimony to the high character of the relations of Mr. M. in this state" ("Case Files of Applications from Former Confederates for Presidential Pardons," roll 14, pp. 93, 95, 97).

10. Elizabeth Merrell to Anne Smith, May 2, 1866, Smith Papers, box 100, folder 8.

11. Major W. A. Broadwell was a quartermaster on Kirby Smith's staff from August 3, 1864 (Crute, *Confederate Staff Officers*, 176). One year earlier he had been appointed chief of the Trans-Mississippi Department's Cotton Bureau as a lieutenant colonel (*O.R.*, vol. 22, pt. 1, p. 953). Merrell's letter: Kirby Smith Papers, film no. M-404, reel 4.

12. Magill's partnership: *Camden Constitution Eagle*, January 13, 1866, in Sifford Scrapbooks, vol. 1. Magill to Helen Zubly Smith, January 11, 1867, Smith Papers, box 60, folder 10.

13. Thomas, *Arkansas and Its People* 2:452n.

14. The name "Merrell and Magill" to designate their joint business enterprises first appears in the Receipts book on November 30, 1863, a month after the two families moved from Pike County to Camden (Smith Papers, box 103); *Camden Daily Bulletin*, November 18, 1868, p. 1, col. 3.

15. Kellam Diaries, January 15, 1869.

16. *Camden Daily Bulletin*, November 18, 1868, p. 2, cols. 1–2.

17. Elizabeth Merrell to Archibald Smith, July 20, 1869, Smith Papers, box 100, folder 8.

18. Goodspeed, *Biographical and Historical Memoirs of Southern Arkansas*, 647.

19. *Camden Daily Bulletin*, November 18, 1868, p. 3, cols. 2–3.

20. Sifford Scrapbooks, vol. 1, clipping from the *Camden Beacon*, August 14, 1875.

21. First Presbyterian Church of Camden, Arkansas, "Minutes of Session" 1:26–28.

22. The council lasted from July 5 to July 10, 1877. Merrell's reports begin with an article on his departure and appear in the *South-Western Presbyterian*, June 21, August 2, 16, and 23, 1877.

23. Daniel, "The Late Major Henry Merrell."

24. E. M. Merrell, "Major Henry Merrell."

25. Diary of Archibald Smith, Jr., July 28–30, 1881, Smith Papers, box 62, folder 3. Merrell kept an account of his expenses on his rail trip from Camden to Roswell in May 1870. The trip from Camden via New Orleans to Chattanooga and Atlanta, including hotels and meals, cost him $58.30 (Slip in Merrell's handwriting, Smith Papers, box 100, folder 10).

26. John Merrell joined the Camden Presbyterian Church on October 3, 1872 (First Presbyterian Church of Camden, Arkansas, "Minutes of Session" 1:50). Other information on John Merrell courtesy of his grandson Chester Talcott Park of Oklahoma City, personal communication, January 9, 1989. Merrell's will did not survive the destruction of the Ouachita County courthouse by a tornado on December 13, 1931, but in a draft furnished by Mr. Park, dated July 3, 1882, Merrell gives "all that I may be possessed of at the time of my death" to his wife, with the provision that after her death, John Merrell should "inherit the same property or the proceeds & remainders of the same." These and other terms of this very complicated document, if it is Merrell's actual will, were apparently settled to everyone's satisfaction, as a group of documents on file under Mrs. Merrell's name in the Ouachita County Probate Clerk's Office can attest. Merrell's executors were his wife and H. G. Bunn, future chief justice of the state supreme court. Eventually most of Merrell's property came to the Smiths through Mrs. Merrell and most of Charles Arthur Magill's property came to the Smiths through his wife, Aurelia Isabella Bacon Magill.

27. Daniel, "The Late Major Henry Merrell."

28. E. M. Merrell, "Major Henry Merrell."

29. See notes 27 and 28 above.

30. Hull, *Patterns* 2:329; H. B. McKenzie, "Confederate Manufactures in Southwest Arkansas," 205; untitled editorial, *South-Western Presbyterian*, February 8, 1883, p. 4, col. 1.

31. Elizabeth Merrell to Anne Magill Smith, February 2, 1873, Smith Papers, box 100, folder 8.

32. This diary (in box 103), along with all of Merrell's personal papers that were found in the Smith House, is preserved in the Smith Papers.

33. Letters of Archibald Smith to P. Stotesbury, J. H. Johnston, and Woodward Barnwell, January 16, 24, and 25, 1883, Smith Papers, box 62, folder 1 (bound volume, p. 183). Diary entry of Archibald Smith, Jr., for December 28, 1882, Smith Papers, box 62, folder 3.

34. First Presbyterian Church of Camden, Arkansas, "Minutes of Session" 1:86–87.

35. Copy of will furnished by Mr. Chester Talcott Park of Oklahoma City, Oklahoma.

36. Goodspeed, *Biographical and Historical Memoirs of Southern Arkansas*, 313; Pike County Heritage Club, *Early History of Pike County*, 96.

37. McKenzie, "Confederate Manufactures in Southwest Arkansas," 205.

38. Pike County Heritage Club, *Early History of Pike County*, 96.

39. *Nashville News*, June 12, 1886, p. 5, col. 4.

40. Goodspeed, *Biographical and Historical Memoirs of Southern Arkansas*, 313.

41. *Southern Standard*, March 9, 1888, p. 3, col. 2.

42. *Nashville News*, June 2, 1888, p. 5, col. 5.

Bibliography

Standard biographical works such as the *Dictionary of American Biography* and *Who Was Who*, along with many older biographical sources, have been used to locate the people whom Henry Merrell mentions. If the information seems standard or can be found in several sources, no particular source for it is cited in the textual notes.

Many records that would have provided documentation for many of the people whom Merrell mentions, have been lost: the early records of Utica, New York, were destroyed in a fire in 1848; the courthouse of Cobb County, Georgia, was burned by Union troops in 1865; the Pike County, Arkansas, courthouse burned three times—in 1855, 1885, and 1895; and the Ouachita County, Arkansas, courthouse was destroyed by fire in 1875 and again by a tornado in 1931. Of all the areas where Henry Merrell lived and worked, Greene County, Georgia, has the most complete set of records. When these tricks of fate are added to the fact that only heads of households were listed in the U.S. Census until 1850, we are too often left with secondary sources for necessary background.

Public and Official Records, Archival Works, and Unpublished Materials

Acts of the General Assembly of the State of Georgia Passed in Milledgeville at a Biennial Session in November, December, and January, 1851–'2. Macon: Samuel J. Ray, 1852.

Acts of the General Assembly of the State of Georgia Passed in Milledgeville at an Annual Session in November and December, 1839. Milledgeville: Grieve and Orme, 1840.

Acts of the General Assembly of the State of Georgia Passed in Milledgeville at a Session of the Same in November and December, 1857. Columbus: Tennet Lomax, 1858.

Acts Passed at the Eleventh Session of the General Assembly of the State of Arkansas. Little Rock, 1857.

Anderson County, Texas. "Deed Book L (1864)." Palestine, Tex.

Bartovics, Albert F., and R. Bruce Council. "A Preliminary Site Report for Archaeological Salvage Undertaken at 9G37 (The Curtwright Factory Site)." University of Georgia Laboratory of Archaeology, Athens, 1978.

Belser, Thomas A., Jr. "Military Operations in Missouri and Arkansas, 1861–1865." Ph.D. diss., Vanderbilt University, 1958.

Berkhofer, Robert Frederick, Jr. "The Industrial History of Oneida County, New York, to 1850." Master's thesis, Cornell University, 1955.

"Burnt Records of Pike County." Abstract of Title Book Prior to 1900 owned by Guaranty Abstract and Title Co., Murfreesboro, Ark. Arkansas History Commission Microfilm, roll 14.

"Case Files of Applications from Former Confederates for Presidential Pardons

('Amnesty Papers'), 1865–1867." National Archives Microfilm Publication M1003. Washington, D.C.: National Archives and Records Service, General Services Administration, 1977.

"Cemetery, Church, and Town Records compiled by . . . Oneida Chapter, Daughters of the American Revolution, 1927–28." Vol. 3. Utica Public Library, Utica, N.Y. Typescript.

Chatham County, Georgia. *General Index to Wills, Estates, Administrations, Etc. in the Chatham County, Ga., Courthouse, Savannah, Georgia.* WPA Project No. 165-34-6999, 1937.

Clarke County, Georgia. "Deed Book S (1844–1847)." Athens, Ga.

——. "Deed Book T (1847–1850)." Athens, Ga.

——. "Deed Book U (1851–1854)." Athens, Ga.

——. "General Index to Deeds, 1801–1907 (L–Z and Reverse)." Athens, Ga.

——. "Receivers Book for 1845." Athens, Ga.

——. "Tax Book for 1846." Athens, Ga.

DePratter, Chester B., et. al. "The 1974–75 Archaeological Survey in the Wallace Reservoir, Greene, Hancock, Morgan and Putnam Counties, Georgia: Final Report." MS no. 193. University of Georgia Laboratory of Archaeology, Athens, 1976.

First Church of Whitestown (First Presbyterian Church of New Hartford), New York. "Bible, Cemetery, and Church Records Compiled by the Oneida Chapter, DAR, 1926–1927." Vols. 2 and 4. Utica Public Library, Utica, N.Y. Typescript.

First Presbyterian Church of Camden, Arkansas. "Minutes of Session, Vol. 1, 1852 to 1894."

General Orders. Head Quarters, Trans-Mississippi Department from March 6, 1863, to January 1, 1865. Houston: E. H. Cushing and Co., 1865.

Greene County, Georgia. "Deed Book NN (1839–1842)." Greensboro, Ga.

——. "Deed Book OO (1843–1847)." Greensboro, Ga.

——. "Deed Book PP (1847–1852)." Greensboro, Ga.

——. "Deed Book QQ (1852–1857)." Greensboro, Ga.

——. "Deed Book RR (1857–1862)." Greensboro, Ga.

——. "Marriage Licenses, White, 1852–1862." Greensboro, Ga.

——. "Mortgage Book A (1842–1863)." Greensboro, Ga.

——. "Tax Digest, 1853." Greensboro, Ga.

——. "Tax Record Book, 1854." Greensboro, Ga.

Griffin, M. L. "A Social History of Camden, Arkansas, 1824–1860." Master's thesis, Columbia University, 1932.

Jareckie, Stephen Barlow. "An Architectural Survey of New York Mills from 1808–1908." Master's thesis, Syracuse University, 1961.

Johnson, Boyd W. "The Civil War in Ouachita County." Camden and Ouachita County Public Library, Camden, Ark., 1960. Mimeographed.

Journal of the Congress of the Confederate States of America. 6 vols. Washington, D.C.: Government Printing Office, 1904–5.

Kellam, Robert F. Diaries of 1859–1861, 1868, 1869. Camden and Ouachita County Public Library, Camden, Ark.

Kirby Smith, Edmund. Papers. Southern Historical Collection. Manuscripts Department, Wilson Library, University of North Carolina, Chapel Hill.

Land Management Records. Record Group 049. Certificates 10237, 10306, 10333, 11496, 13055, 15478, and Land Warrant Certificates 43022, 43023. Washington, D.C.: National Archives and Records Administration.

Merrell, Henry. Papers and manuscripts. See Smith Papers.

Nichols, James Lynn. "Confederate Quartermaster Operations in the Trans-Mississippi Department." Master's thesis, University of Texas, 1947.

Otto, Rhea Cumming, comp. *1850 Census of Georgia (Chatham County)*. Savannah: Rhea Cumming Otto, 1975.

——. *1850 Census of Georgia (Cobb County)*. Savannah: Rhea Cumming Otto, 1975.

——. *1850 Census of Georgia (Greene County)*. Savannah: Rhea Cumming Otto, 1975.

——. *1850 Census of Georgia (Putnam County)*. Savannah: Rhea Cumming Otto, 1975.

Partain, Dorothy Lee, and William A. Cooley, comps. *1870 Federal Census. Pike County Arkansas. Complete Transcription.* Fort Smith, Ark.: Ancestor Shoppe, 1987.

Pike County, Arkansas. "Tax Records, 1834–1867." Arkansas History Commission, Little Rock.

Putnam County, Georgia. "Deed Book R (1847–1858)." Eatonton, Ga.

——. "General Index to Estate Records, M–Z." Eatonton, Ga.

——. "Record of Wills, B, 1822–1857." Eatonton, Ga.

"Records of the Paris Religious Society (A Congregational Church) in the town of Paris, Oneida County, N.Y., transcribed by the New York Genealogical and Bibliographical Society. Edited by Ryden Woodward Vosburgh. New York City, 1921." Copied by D.A.R., 1927. Vol. 3. Utica Public Library, Utica, N.Y. Typescript.

"Records of the Washington Presbyterian Church, 1849–1877." Vol. 1. Accession no. 2417. Washington, Ark.: Southwest Arkansas Regional Archives.

"Revolutionary Soldiers' Graves Listed by Oneida Chapter, D.A.R. by the Historic Records Research Committee, with the names of the wife when such name is found, 1926." Vol. 2. Utica Public Library, Utica, N.Y. Typescript.

Richardson, James D., comp. *A Compilation of the Messages and Papers of the Confederacy.* Vol. 1. Nashville: United States Publishing Co., 1905.

Roswell Manufacturing Company. Minutes. DeKalb College, Decatur, Ga.

Sifford, Dora Thomson. Scrapbooks. Camden and Ouachita County Public Library, Camden, Ark.

Smith Papers. Georgia Department of Archives and History, Atlanta. Papers include Henry Merrell's manuscript volumes (boxes 104, 105), other cited personal papers (boxes 100, 101), the 1847–1848 Letterbook (box 102), and the Receipts book and diary (box 103). Photocopies of Merrell's two manuscript volumes and the Receipts book are on file at the Arkansas History Commission, Little Rock.

"State of Arkansas Tract Book." Arkansas History Commission, Little Rock.

U.S. Bureau of the Census. *Population Schedules of the United States, 1820.* Microfilm. New York, roll 73, vol. 12. Washington, D.C.: National Archives and Records Service, General Services Administration.

——. *Sixth Census of the United States: 1840. Population.* Microfilm. Georgia, roll 39, vol. 2. Washington, D.C.: National Archives and Records Service, General Services Administration.

——. *Sixth Census of the United States: 1840. Schedules of Mines, Agriculture, Commerce, and Manufacturing in Georgia, 1840.* Microfilm. Georgia, roll 1, vol. 16. Washington, D.C.: National Archives and Records Service, General Services Administration.

——. *Seventh Census of the United States: 1850.* Compilations for Pike, Desha, and Ouachita counties, Ark. Little Rock: Arkansas History Commission.

——. *Eighth Census of the United States: 1860. Population.* Microfilm. Georgia, roll 125, vol. 7; Arkansas, roll 40, vol. 2; roll 41, vol. 3; roll 44, vol. 4; roll 47, vol. 6. Washington, D.C.: National Archives and Records Service, General Services Administration.

——. *Eighth Census of the United States: 1860. Population.* Compilations for Pike, Desha, and Ouachita counties, Ark. Little Rock: Arkansas History Commission.

——. *Eighth Census of the United States: 1860. Schedule 5. Products of Industry.* Microfilm. Pike County, Ark., Thompson Township, roll 8, p. 1. Washington, D.C.: National Archives and Records Service, General Services Administration.

——. *Eighth Census of the United States: 1860. Slave Schedules.* Microfilm. Arkansas, roll 54. Washington, D.C.: National Archives and Records Service, General Services Administration.

——. *Ninth Census of the United States: 1870. Population.* Microfilm. Arkansas, roll 59. Washington, D.C.: National Archives and Records Service, General Services Administration.

U.S. Naval War Records Office. *Official Records of the Union and Confederate Navies in the War of the Rebellion.* 30 vols., vol. 23. Washington, D.C.: U.S. Government Printing Office, 1894–1922.

U.S. Post Office Department. *Record of Appointment of Postmasters, 1832–Sept. 30, 1971.* Record Group 28. Microfilm Publication 841. Arkansas, roll 8, vols. 14, 25B, 40, 56; Georgia, roll 23, vols. 17, 26. Washington, D.C.: National Archives and Records Service, General Services Administration, 1973.

——. *Records of the Post Office Department. Geographical Site Location Reports, State of Arkansas, 1852–1945.* Record Group 28. Microfilm, roll 13. Washington, D.C.: National Archives and Records Service, General Services Administration, 1974.

U.S. War Department. *The War of the Rebellion: A Compilation of the Official Records of the Union and Confederate Armies.* 70 vols. in 128. Series 1, vols. 3, 8, 13, 17, 22, 34, 38, 41; Series 4, vols. 1–3; Washington, D.C.: Government Printing Office, 1880–1901.

Waldron, Carroll T. "A Hundred Years of Amusement in Utica, 1806–1906." Oneida County Historical Society, Utica, N.Y., n.d. Typescript.

Walsh, John J. "From Frontier Outpost to Modern City: A History of Utica, 1784–1920." Oneida County Historical Society, Utica, N.Y., 1978. Typescript.

——. "Trials and Tribulations: A Judicial History of Oneida County." Paper delivered before the Oneida Historical Society, Utica, N.Y., April 5, 1973. Typescript.

Wynd, Frances, comp. *Putnam County, Georgia, Records.* Albany, Ga.: Frances Wynd, n.d.

Books

Abstracts of Utica Sentinel and Gazette Newspapers, Oneida County, New York. 6 vols. N.p.: Hanson Publishing Co., n.d.

Allibone, S. Austin. *A Critical Dictionary of English Literature and British and American Authors.* 3 vols. Philadelphia: J. B. Lippincott and Co., 1870.

Anderson, John Q., ed. *Campaigning with Parsons' Texas Cavalry Division, CSA: The War Journals and Letters of Four Orr Brothers, 12th Texas Cavalry Regiment.* Hillsboro, Tex.: Hill Junior College Press, 1967.

Appleton's Cyclopedia of American Biography. New York: D. Appleton and Co., 1888–1931.

Armor, E. H. *The Cemeteries of Greene County, Georgia.* N.p.: Agee Publishers, Inc., 1987.

Ashmore, Harry S. *Arkansas: A Bicentennial History.* New York: W. W. Norton, 1978.

Avery, I. W. *History of Georgia.* New York: Brown and Derby, n.d.

Bagg, Moses M. *Memorial History of Utica, N.Y., from Its Settlement to the Present Times.* Syracuse: D. Mason and Co., 1892.

——. *The Pioneers of Utica from the Earliest Settlement to the Year 1825.* Utica, N.Y.: Curtiss and Childs, 1877.

Bailey, Anne J. *Between the Enemy and Texas: Parsons's Texas Cavalry in the Civil War.* Fort Worth: Texas Christian University Press, 1989.

Barkun, Michael. *Crucible of the Millennium: The Burned-over District of New York in the 1840's.* Syracuse: Syracuse University Press, 1986.

Bateman, Fred, and Thomas Weiss. *A Deplorable Scarcity: The Failure of Industrialization in the Slave Economy.* Chapel Hill: University of North Carolina Press, 1981.

Beaver, Patrick. *The Big Ship.* London: Bibliophile Books, 1969.

Bell, Malcolm, Jr. *Major Butler's Legacy: Five Generations of a Slaveholding Family.* Athens: University of Georgia Press, 1987.

Bielby, Isaac P. *Illustrated History of Utica.* N.p.: H.R. Page and Co., 1890.

Bishop, John Leander. *A History of American Manufactures from 1608 to 1860.* 2 vols. Philadelphia: Edward Young and Co., 1864.

Bless, Edwin Munsell. *A Concise History of Missions.* New York: Fleming H. Revell Co., 1897.

Blessington, Joseph Palmer. *The Campaigns of Walker's Texas Division.* Austin: Pemberton Press, 1968.

Bliss, Edwin Munsell. *A Concise History of Missions.* New York: Fleming H. Revell Co., 1897.

Boatner, Mark Mayo. *The Civil War Dictionary.* New York: David McKay Co., 1959.

Boggs, William Robertson. *Military Reminiscences of Gen. W. R. Boggs, C.S.A..* Durham, N.C.: Seeman Printery, 1913.

Britton, Wiley. *The Civil War on the Border.* 2 vols. New York: G. P. Putnam's Sons, 1899.

Bruner, David, et al. *An American Portrait: A History of the United States.* 2d ed. New York: Charles Scribner's Sons, 1985.

Buel, Clarence Clough, and Robert U. Johnson, eds. *Battles and Leaders of the Civil War.* 4 vols. New York: Century Co., 1887–1888.

Bulloch, James D. *The Secret Service of the Confederate States in Europe.* New York: Thomas Yoseloff, 1959.

Carroll, John M. *List of Staff Officers of the Confederate States Army.* Mattituck, N.Y., and Bryan, Tex.: J. M. Carroll and Company, 1983.

Catalogue of Books, Belonging to Merrell & Hastings' Circulating Library, Kept at Their Bookstore, No. 40 Genesee St. — Utica. Together with the Rules and Regulations. Utica, N.Y.: Merrell and Hastings, 1823.

Catton, Bruce. *Never Call Retreat.* New York: Washington Square Press, 1965.

Chappell, Absalom. *Miscellanies of Georgia.* Atlanta: James F. Meegan, 1874.

Clark, Mrs. Larry P. *Arkansas Pioneers and Allied Families.* N.p.: Mrs. Larry P. Clark, 1976.

Clark, Victor S. *History of Manufactures in the United States.* Vol. 1, 1607–1860. New York: Peter Smith, 1949.

Clarke, Thomas Wood. *Utica for a Century and a Half.* Utica, N.Y.: Widtman Press, 1952.

Cochran, Thomas C. *Frontiers of Change: Early Industrialism in America.* New York: Oxford University Press, 1981.

Coleman, Kenneth, and Charles Stephen Gurr, eds. *Dictionary of Georgia Biography.* 2 vols. Athens: University of Georgia Press, 1983.

Coleman, Richard G. *A Short History of the Roswell Manufacturing Company of Roswell, Georgia: Home of "Roswell Grey."* N.p.: Richard G. Coleman, 1982.

Cookinham, Henry J. *History of Oneida County.* 2 vols. Chicago: S. J. Clarke Publishing Co., 1912.

Coulter, E. Merton. *Auraria: The Story of a Georgia Gold-Mining Town.* Athens: University of Georgia Press, 1956.

———. *Travels in the Confederate States: A Bibliography.* Norman: University of Oklahoma Press, 1948.

Coulter, E. Merton, and Wendell Holmes Stephenson, eds. *The Confederate States of America, 1861–1865*. Vol. 7 of *A History of the South*. Baton Rouge: Louisiana State University Press, 1950.

Coulter, Merton, and Warren Grice, eds. *Georgia through Two Centuries*. New York: Lewis Historical Publishing Co., 1966.

Crave, Rev. Edgar Woods. *History of Albemarle County in Virginia*. Harrisonburg, Va.: C. J. Carrier Co., 1972.

Cross, Whitney. *The Burned-over District: The Social and Intellectual History of Enthusiastic Religion in Western New York*. Ithaca: Cornell University Press, 1950.

Crute, Joseph H., Jr. *Confederate Staff Officers, 1861–1865*. Powhatan, Va.: Derwent Books, 1982.

——. *Units of the Confederate States Army*. Midlothian, Va.: Derwent Books, 1987.

Davis, Charles S. *Colin J. McRae: Confederate Financial Agent*. Tuscaloosa, Ala.: Confederate Publishing Co., 1961.

Dodd, Donald B., and Wynelle S. Dodd. *Historical Statistics of the South, 1790–1970*. University: University of Alabama Press, 1973.

Donovan, Timothy P., and William B. Gatewood, Jr., eds. *The Governors of Arkansas: Essays in Political Biography*. Fayetteville: University of Arkansas Press, 1981.

Dunbar, Seymour. *A History of Travel in America*. 4 vols. Indianapolis: Bobbs-Merrill Co., 1925.

Durant, Samuel W. *History of Oneida County, New York*. Philadelphia: Everts and Fariss, 1878.

Eaton, Clement. *A History of the Southern Confederacy*. New York: Free Press, 1954.

Ellis, David M., et al. *A History of New York State*. Ithaca: Cornell University Press, 1957.

——. *The Upper Mohawk Country: An Illustrated History of Greater Utica*. Woodland Hills, Calif.: Windsor Publishing Co., 1982.

Evans, Clement A., ed. *Confederate Military History*. 13 vols. Atlanta: Confederate Publishing Co., 1899.

Faust, Patricia L., ed. *Historical Times Illustrated Encyclopedia of the Civil War*. New York: Harper and Row, 1986.

Ferguson, John L. *Arkansas and the Civil War*. Little Rock: Pioneer Press, 1957.

Ferguson, John L. and J. H. Atkinson. *Historic Arkansas*. Little Rock: Arkansas History Commission, 1966.

Filler, Louis. *The Crusade against Slavery*. New York: Harper Torchbooks, 1960.

Finney, Charles G. *The Memoirs of Rev. Charles G. Finney*. New York: A. S. Barnes, 1876.

——. *Revivals of Religion*. Virginia Beach, Va.: CBN Press, 1978.

Foote, Shelby. *The Civil War: A Narrative*. 3 vols. New York: Random House, 1958, 1963, 1974.

Fowler, Philemon H. *Historical Sketch of Presbyterianism in the Bounds of the Synod of New York*. Utica, N.Y.: Curtiss and Childs, 1877.

Frost, John, Moses Gillet, and Noah Cole. *A Narrative of the Revival of Religion, Particularly in the Bounds of the Presbytery of Oneida in the Year 1826*. Utica, N.Y., 1826.

Garrett, Franklin M. *Atlanta and Its Environs: A Chronicle of Its People and Events.* 2 vols. Athens: University of Georgia Press, 1954.

General Biographical Catalogue of Auburn Theological Seminary, 1818–1918. Auburn, N.Y.: Auburn Seminary Press, 1918.

General Catalogue of the Theological Seminary, Andover, Massachusetts, 1808–1908. Boston: Thomas Todd, n.d.

Gibb, George Sweet. *The Saco-Lowell Shops: Textile Machinery Building in New England, 1813–1949.* Cambridge: Harvard University Press, 1950.

Gillett, E. H. *History of the Presbyterian Church in the United States of America.* 2 vols. Philadelphia: Presbyterian Publishing Commission, 1864.

Gilmer, George R. *Sketches of Some of the First Settlers of Upper Georgia, of the Cherokees, and the Author.* Baltimore: Genealogical Publishing Co., 1965.

Goodspeed Publishing Company. *Biographical and Historical Memoirs of Central Arkansas.* Chicago: Goodspeed Publishing Company, 1889.

——. *Biographical and Historical Memoirs of Northwestern Arkansas.* Chicago: Goodspeed Publishing Company, 1889.

——. *Biographical and Historical Memoirs of Southern Arkansas.* Chicago: Goodspeed Publishing Company, 1889.

Hallum, John. *Biographical and Pictorial History of Arkansas.* Albany, N.Y.: Weed and Parsons, 1887.

Harrington, Elisha. *The Utica Directory.* Utica, N.Y.: Dauby and Maynard, 1828.

——. *The Utica City Directory for 1829, No. 2.* Utica, N.Y.: Dauby and Maynard, 1829.

——. *The Utica Directory No. 3 – 1832.* Utica, N.Y.: E. A. Maynard, 1832.

——. *The Utica Directory No. 4 – 1833.* Utica, N.Y.: E. A. Maynard, 1833.

——. *The Utica Directory No. 5 – 1834.* Utica, N.Y.: E. A. Maynard, 1834.

Hawke, David Freeman. *Nuts and Bolts of the Past: A History of American Technology, 1776–1860.* New York: Harper and Row, 1988.

Hayden, Rev. Horace Edwin. *Virginia Genealogies: A Genealogy of the Glassell Family of Scotland and Virginia.* Baltimore: Genealogical Publishing Co., 1979.

Heartsill, William Williston. *Fourteen Hundred and 91 Days in the Confederate Army: A Journal Kept by W. W. Heartsill for Four Years, One Month and One Day.* Edited by Bell Irvin Wiley. Wilmington, N.C.: Broadfoot Publishing Co., 1987.

Hempstead, Fay. *Historical Review of Arkansas.* Vol. 1. Chicago: Lewis Publishing Co., 1911.

——. *A Pictorial History of Arkansas from Earliest Times to the Year 1890.* St. Louis: N.D. Thompson Publishing Co., 1890.

Henderson, Harry McCorry. *Texas in the Confederacy.* San Antonio: Naylor Co., 1955.

Henry, Robert Selph. *The Story of the Confederacy.* Indianapolis: Bobbs-Merrill Co., Charter Books, 1964.

Herndon, Dallas T., ed. *Centennial History of Arkansas.* 3 vols. Chicago: S. J. Clarke Publishing Co., 1922.

——. *The High Lights of Arkansas History.* 2d ed. Little Rock: Arkansas History Commission, 1922.

Hotchkin, Rev. James H. *A History of the Purchase and Settlement of Western New York and of the Rise, Progress, and Present State of the Presbyterian Church in That Section.* New York: M. W. Dodd, 1848.

Howard, John Tasker. *Our Tradition in Music.* 3d ed. New York: Thomas Y. Crowell Co., 1946.

Howard, Joseph Parks. *General Edmund Kirby Smith, C.S.A.* Baton Rouge: Louisiana State University, 1954.

Hull, Henry. *Annals of Athens, Ga., 1801–1901.* Danielsville, Ga.: Heritage Papers, 1978.

Hull, John T. *Patterns: A Social History of Camden.* 2 vols. Little Rock: August House, 1987–88.

Hunt, Caroline C. *Oconee: Temporary Boundary.* Edited by Margaret Clayton Russell. Series Report No. 10. Athens: University of Georgia, Laboratory of Archaeology, 1973.

Hynds, Ernest C. *Antebellum Athens and Clarke County, Georgia.* Athens: University of Georgia Press, 1974.

Ingram, Henry L., comp. *Civil War Letters of George W. and Martha F. Ingram, 1861–1865.* College Station: Texas A&M University Library Miscellaneous Publication 9, 1973.

Johnson, Amanda. *Georgia as Colony and State.* Atlanta: Walter W. Brown Publishing Co., 1938.

Johnson, Boyd W. *The Arkansas Frontier.* N.p.: Boyd W. Johnson, 1957.

Johnson, Paul E. *A Shopkeeper's Millennium: Society and Revivals in Rochester, New York, 1815–1837.* New York: Hill and Wang, 1978.

Johnston, James Houston. *Western and Atlantic Railroad of the State of Georgia.* Atlanta: Georgia Public Service Commission, 1932.

Jones, Pomroy. *Annals and Recollections of Oneida County.* Rome, N.Y.: Jones, 1851.

Josephy, Alvin W. *The Civil War on the Frontier.* Alexandria, Va.: Time-Life Books, 1986.

Kane, Joseph Nathan. *Famous First Facts.* 4th ed. New York: H. W. Wilson Co., 1981.

Kerby, Robert Lee. *Kirby Smith's Confederacy: The Trans-Mississippi South, 1863–1865.* New York: Columbia University Press, 1972.

Knight, Lucian Lamar. *Georgia's Bi-Centennial Memoirs and Memories.* 4 vols. N.p.: L. L. Knight, 1932–33.

——. *A Standard History of Georgia and Georgians.* 6 vols. Chicago: Lewis Publishing Co., 1917.

Knox, Thomas W. *The Life and Work of Henry Ward Beecher.* New York: Wilson and Ellis, 1887.

Kouwenhoven, John A. *The Columbia Historical Portrait of New York City.* Garden City, N.Y.: Doubleday, 1953.

League of Women Voters of Fulton County, Roswell Unit. *Roswell.* 4th ed. Roswell, Ga., N.d.

Livermore, Thomas L. *Numbers and Losses in the Civil War in America, 1861–65.* Boston: Houghton-Mifflin Co., 1901.

Long, E. B., and Barbara Long. *The Civil War Day by Day: An Almanac, 1861–1865.* Garden City, N.Y.: Doubleday, 1971.

McCall, Hugh. *History of Georgia.* Atlanta: Cherokee Publishing Co., 1969.

McClendon, S. G. *History of the Public Domain of Georgia.* Atlanta: Foote and Davies, 1924.

McLoughlin, William G. *Modern Revivalism: Charles Grandison Finney to Billy Graham.* New York: Ronald Press, 1959.

McManus, Edgar J. *Black Bondage in the North.* Syracuse: Syracuse University Press, 1973.

McNutt, Walter Scott. *A History of Arkansas from Earliest Times to the Present.* Little Rock: Democrat Publishing and Lithograph Co., 1932.

McPherson, James M. *Battle Cry of Freedom: The Civil War Era.* Vol. 6 of *The Oxford History of the United States,* edited by C. Vann Woodward. New York: Oxford University Press, 1988.

Malone, Dumas. *Jefferson the President.* Vol. 5 of *Jefferson and His Time.* Boston: Little, Brown and Co., 1974.

Martin, Clarece. *A Glimpse of the Past: The History of Bulloch Hall and Roswell, Georgia.* Roswell, Ga.: Historic Roswell, 1973.

――――. *A History of Roswell Presbyterian Church.* Edited by Emmett R. Rushin. Dallas: Taylor Publishing Co., 1984.

Maynard, Theodore. *The Story of American Catholicism.* New York: Macmillan Co., 1941.

Meade, Bishop William. *Old Churches, Ministers, and Families of Virginia.* 2 vols. Philadelphia: J. B. Lippincott Co., 1959.

Medearis, Mary. *Washington, Arkansas: History of the Southwest Trail.* Hope, Ark.: Etter Printing Co., 1984.

Medearis, Mary, ed. *Sam Williams: Printer's Devil.* Hope, Ark.: Etter Printing Co., 1979.

Memoirs of Georgia, Containing Historical Accounts of the State's Civil, Military, Industrial and Personal Interests, and Personal Sketches of Many of its People. 2 vols. Atlanta: Southern Historical Association, 1895.

Meyers, Michael C., and William L. Sherman. *The Course of Mexican History.* New York: Oxford University Press, 1979.

Miller, Blandina Dudley. *A Sketch of Old Utica.* N.p., 1895.

Mitchell, Broadus. *The Rise of the Cotton Mills in the South.* Baltimore: Johns Hopkins University Press, 1921.

Morrison, John H. *History of Steam Navigation.* New York: Stephen Daye Press, 1958.

Murray County History Committee, comp. *Murray County Heritage.* Roswell, Ga.: W. H. Wolfe Associates, 1987.

Myers, Robert Mansen, ed. *The Children of Pride: A True Story of Georgia and the Civil War.* New Haven: Yale University Press, 1972.

The National Cyclopedia of American Biography during the History of the United States. Vols. 1–22. New York: James T. White Co., 1893–1932.

Navin, Thomas R. *The Whitin Machine Works Since 1831: A Textile Machinery Company in an Industrial Village.* New York: Russell and Russell, 1969.

Necrological Report Presented to the Alumni Association of Princeton Theological Seminary at Its Annual Meeting, May 10th, 1904. Princeton: C. S. Robinson and Co., 1904.

Nevin, Alfred. *Encyclopedia of the Presbyterian Church in the United States of America: Including the Northern and Southern Assemblies.* Philadelphia: Presbyterian Publishing Co., 1880.

Nevins, Allan. *The War for the Union.* 4 vols. New York: Charles Scribner's Sons, 1959–.

New Century Club. *Outline History of Utica and Vicinity.* Utica, N.Y.: L. C. Childs and Son, 1900.

Nichols, James L. *The Confederate Quartermaster in the Trans-Mississippi.* Austin: University of Texas Press, 1964.

Northen, William J., ed. *Men of Mark in Georgia.* 6 vols. Atlanta: A. B. Caldwell, 1907–12.

Oates, Stephen B. *Confederate Cavalry West of the River.* Austin: University of Texas Press, 1961.

O'Connell, Rev. Dr. J. J. *Catholocity in the Carolinas and Georgia: Leaves of Its History.* New York: D. & J. Sadlier and Co., 1879.

Oneida County. *The History of Oneida County.* Utica, N.Y.: Oneida County, 1977.

Oneida Historical Society, Half Century Club. *Semi-Centennial History of the City of Utica.* Utica, N.Y.: Curtiss and Childs, 1882.

Parkes, Henry Bamford. *A History of Mexico.* 3d ed. Boston: Houghton Mifflin Company, 1960.

Parsons Texas Cavalry Brigade Association. *A Brief and Condensed History of Parsons' Texas Cavalry Brigade.* 1892. Reprint. Waco, Tex.: W. M. Morrison, 1962.

Pike County Heritage Club. *Early History of Pike County, Arkansas: The First One Hundred Years.* Murfreesboro, Ark.: Pike County Heritage Club, 1978.

Prude, Jonathan. *The Coming of Industrial Order: Town and Factory Life in Rural Massachusetts, 1810–1860.* Cambridge: Cambridge University Press, 1983.

Randolph, Vance M. and George P. Wilson. *Down in the Holler: A Gallery of Arkansas Folk Speech.* Norman: University of Oklahoma Press, 1953.

Raper, Arthur Franklin. *Tenants of the Almighty.* New York: Macmillan Co., 1943.

Rawlings, Mary. *The Albemarle of Other Days.* Charlottesville, Va.: Michie Co., 1925.

Register, Alvaretta Kenan. *The Kenan Family and Some Allied Families.* Statesboro, Ga.: Kenan Print Shop, 1967.

Rice, C. Duncan. *The Rise and Fall of Black Slavery.* New York: Harper and Row, 1975.

Rice, Thaddeus Brockett, and Carolyn White Williams. *History of Greene County, Georgia, 1786–1886.* Macon, Ga.: J. W. Burke Co., 1961.

Richards, William, comp. *The Utica Directory: 1840–'41.* Utica, N.Y.: John P. Bush, 1840.

——. *The Utica Directory: 1842–'43.* Utica, N.Y.: John P. Bush, 1842.

Roberts, Edward Howell, comp. *Biographical Catalogue of the Princeton Theological Seminary, 1815–1932.* Princeton: Trustees of the Theological Seminary of the Presbyterian Church, 1933.

Rogers, Henry C. *History of the Town of Paris and the Valley of the Sauquoit.* Utica, N.Y.: White and Floyd, 1881.

Rohman, D. Gordon. *Here's Whitesboro: An Informal History.* New York: Stratford House, 1949.

Roller, David C., and Robert W. Twyman, eds. *Encyclopedia of Southern History.* Baton Rouge: Louisiana State University Press, 1979.

Ryan, Mary P. *Cradle of the Middle Class: The Family in Oneida County, New York, 1790–1865.* Cambridge: Cambridge University Press, 1981.

Savage, James. *A Genealogical Dictionary of the First Settlers of New England.* 4 vols. Boston: Little, Brown and Co., 1861.

Schott, Thomas E. *Alexander H. Stephens of Georgia: A Biography.* Baton Rouge: Louisiana State University Press, 1988.

Schwab, John C. *The Confederate States, 1861–1865: A Financial and Industrial History of the South During the Civil War.* New York: Charles Scribner's Sons, 1901.

Scott, Rev. E. C., comp. *Ministerial Directory of the Presbyterian Church, U.S., 1861–1941.* Austin, Tex.: Von Boeckmann-Jones Co., 1942.

Sernett, Milton C. *Abolition's Axe: Beriah Green, the Oneida Institute, and the Black Freedom Struggle.* New York: Syracuse University Press, 1986.

Seward, William H. *Autobiography of William H. Seward.* New York: D. Appleton and Co., 1877.

Sherwood, Adiel. *A Gazetteer of the State of Georgia.* Charleston: W. Riley, 1827.

——. *A Gazetteer of the State of Georgia.* 2d ed. Philadelphia: J. W. Martin and W. K. Boden, 1829.

——. *A Gazetteer of the State of Georgia.* 3d ed. Washington: P. Force, 1837.

——. *A Gazetteer of Georgia.* 4th ed. Macon: S. Boykin; Griffin: Brawner and Putnam; Atlanta: J. Richards, 1860.

Shriner, Charles H. *History of Murray County.* Murray County History Committee, 1911.

Skinner, Constance Lindsey. *Pioneers of the Old Southwest.* New Haven: Yale University Press, 1919.

Smith, George Gillman. *The Story of Georgia and the Georgia People, 1732 to 1860.* Macon, Ga.: Smith and Franklin Printing and Publishing Co., 1900.

Smith, George H. *Rambling Tale of a Rambling Town.* New Hartford, N.Y.: New Hartford Central School, 1955.

Sorin, Gerald. *The New York Abolitionists: A Case Study in Political Radicalism.* Westport, Conn.: Greenwood Publishing Co., 1971.

Sperry, Claire C. and Charles. *Families of Old Whitesborough, 1784–1824.* Whitesboro, N.Y. N.p., 1984.

Steadman, Erich. *A Brief Treatise on Manufacturing in the South.* Clarksville, Tenn.: C. O. Faxon, 1851.

——. *The Southern Manufacturer: Showing the Advantages of Manufacturing the Cotton in the Fields Where it is Grown.* Gallatin, Tenn.: Gray and Boyers, 1858.

Stevens, William Bacon. *History of Georgia.* 2 vols. Philadelphia: E. H. Butler, 1859.

Storsberg, Betty Peling. *Whitestown, New York, Celebrates America Bicentennial.* Whitestown: Recreational Committee of Greater Whitestown, 1977.

Temple, Sarah Blackwell Gober. *The First Hundred Years: A Short History of Cobb County, in Georgia.* Atlanta: Walter W. Brown Publishing Co., 1935.

Thomas, David Y. *Arkansas and Its People.* 4 vols. New York: American Historical Society, 1930.

——. *Arkansas in War and Reconstruction, 1861–1874.* Little Rock: Arkansas Division, United Daughters of the Confederacy, 1926.

Thomas, Emory M. *The Confederate Nation, 1861–1865.* New York: Harper and Row, 1979.

——. *The Confederacy as a Revolutionary Experience.* Englewood Cliffs, N.J.: Prentice-Hall, 1971.

Thomas, Joseph. *Universal Pronouncing Dictionary of Biography and Mythology.* Philadelphia: J. B. Lippincott Co., 1897.

Thompson, Ernest Trice. *Presbyterianism in the South.* Vol. 1, *1607–1861.* Richmond, Va.: John Knox Press, 1963.

Tucker, Barbara M. *Samuel Slater and the Origins of the American Textile Industry, 1790–1860.* Ithaca: Cornell University Press, 1984.

Tyler, Alice Felt. *Freedom's Ferment: Phases of American Social History from the Colonial Period to the Outbreak of the Civil War.* New York: Harper Torchbooks, 1961.

Utica Public Library, comp. *A Bibliography of the History and Life of Utica: A Centennial Contribution.* Utica, N.Y.: Goodenow Printing Co., 1932.

Wager, Daniel E., ed. *Our County and Its People: A Descriptive Work on Oneida County, New York.* Boston: Boston History Company, 1896.

Wallace, Anthony F. C. *Rockdale: The Growth of an American Village in the Early Industrial Revolution.* New York: Alfred A. Knopf, 1978.

Walsh, John J. *Vignettes of Old Utica.* Utica, N.Y.: Utica Public Library, 1982.

Walton, Perry. *The Story of Textiles.* New York: Tudor Publishing Co., 1936.

Warner, Ezra J. *Generals in Blue.* Baton Rouge: Louisiana State University Press, 1964.

——. *Generals in Gray.* Baton Rouge: Louisiana State University Press, 1959.

Whitcher, Martha L. *A Few Stray Leaves in the History of Whitesboro, by a Villager.* Utica, N.Y.: T. J. Griffiths, 1884.

White, George A. *Historical Collections of Georgia.* 3d ed. New York: Pudney and Russell, 1855.

——. *Statistics of Georgia.* Savannah: W. Thorne Williams, 1849.

White, Owen P. *Texas: An Informal Biography.* New York: G. P. Putnam's Sons, 1945.

Who Was Who in America: Historical Volume, 1607–1897. Chicago: A. N. Marquis, 1963.

Williams, C. Fred, et al. *A Documentary History of Arkansas.* Fayetteville: University of Arkansas Press, 1964.

Williams, Charlean Moss. *The Old Town Speaks: Recollections of Washington, Hempstead County, Arkansas.* Houston, Tex.: Anson Jones Press, 1961.

Williams, Emily. *Stagecoach Country: Utica to Sacketts Harbor.* Utica, N.Y.: Widtman and the Brodock Press, 1976.

Williams, Oscar, ed. *The Silver Treasury of Light Verse.* New York: Mentor Books, 1957.

Williams, William. *Utica Directory for the Year 1817 Combining the Village Census of 1816.* Utica, N.Y.: William Williams, 1920.

Wood, Karen G. *An Archaeological Survey of the Presumed Location of the First Roswell Factory.* Athens, Ga.: Southeastern Archaeological Services, 1989.

Woods, Rev. Edgar. *History of Albemarle County in Virginia.* Harrisonburg, Va.: C. J. Carrier Co., 1972.

Woods, James M. *Rebellion and Realignment: Arkansas' Road to Secession.* Fayetteville: University of Arkansas Press, 1987.

Wright, Marcus J. *General Officers of the Confederate Army.* New York: Neale Publishing Co., 1911.

Yates, A. P., comp. *The Utica Directory and City Advertiser, Arranged in Five Parts for 1839–40.* Utica, N.Y.: R. Northway, Jr., 1839.

Essays and Articles in Books, Periodicals, and Newspapers

Bagg, Moses M. "The Earliest Factories of Oneida and Their Projectors." In *Oneida Historical Society Transactions*, 112–24. Utica, N.Y.: Ellis H. Roberts Co., 1881.

Blicksilver, Jack. "Cotton Manufacturing in the Southeast: An Historical Analysis," Bulletin no. 5, *Studies in Business and Economics.* Atlanta: Bureau of Business and Economic Research, School of Business Administration, Georgia State College of Business Administration, 1959.

Bocage, J. W. "The Merrell Factory: History of Cotton Manufactures in Arkansas." *Pine Bluff Daily Commercial*, July 16, 1887, p. 2, col. 3.

Boney, F. N. "Part Three: 1820–1865." In *A History of Georgia*, edited by Kenneth Coleman, 129–204. Athens: University of Georgia Press, 1977.

Bonner, James C. "Cotton." In *Encyclopedia of Southern History*, edited by David C. Roller and Robert W. Twyman, 300–302. Baton Rouge: Louisiana State University, 1979.

Brough, Charles Hillman. "The Industrial History of Arkansas." *Publications of the Arkansas Historical Association* 1 (1906): 191–229.

Carolus. "Arkansas Manufacturing Company." *True Democrat*, May 19, 1857, p. 2, col. 8.

Clark, Victor S. "Manufactures during the Ante-Bellum and War Periods." In *The South in the Building of a Nation* 5:313–34. Richmond: Southern Publication Historical Society, 1909.

"The Cotton Mills." *Arkadelphia* (Ark.) *Southern Standard*, March 9, 1888, p. 3, col. 2.

Daniel, Eugene. "The Late Major Henry Merrell." *South-Western Presbyterian*, February 22, 1883, p. 1, cols. 1–2.

DeBow, J. D. B. "Arkansas." *DeBow's Review* 23 (1857): 209–11.

——. "Industry of the Southern and Western States." *DeBow's Review* 6 (1848): 285–304.

Dickinson, Sam D. "State's First Textile Mill Once Stood Near Narrows Dam on Turbulent Little Missouri River." *Arkansas Gazette*, April 9, 1950, p. 2B.

Dorow, James B. "Trenton Falls." In *The History of Oneida County*, 194. Utica, N.Y.: Oneida County, 1977.

Dimity, John. "Confederate Military History of Louisiana." Pt. 1, vol. 10, of *Confederate Military History*, edited by Clement A. Evans. Atlanta: Confederate Publishing Co., 1899.

"Dots from Murfreesboro." *Nashville* (Ark.) *News*, June 12, 1886, p. 5, col. 4.

Dougan, Michael B. "Life in Confederate Arkansas." *Arkansas Historical Quarterly* 31, no. 1 (1972): 15–35.

Ellis, David M. "Military Developments during Colonial and Revolutionary Era." In *The History of Oneida County*, 37–44. Utica, N.Y.: Oneida County, 1977.

Ely, A. W. "Cotton and Cotton Manufacturers." *DeBow's Review* 12 (1852): 356–61.

Fish, Paul R., and David J. Hally. "The Wallace Reservoir Archaeological Project: An Overview." *Early Georgia* 11, no. 1 (1983): 1–18.

Gaughan, J. E. "Historic Camden." *Arkansas Historical Quarterly* 20 (1961): 245–55.

"Georgia Manufacturers." *Savannah Daily Republican*, November 25, 1846, p. 2, col. 4.

"Georgia Manufactures." *Milledgeville (Southern) Recorder* July 7, 1846, p. 3, col. 2.

Gregg, William. "Domestic Industry — Manufacturers at the South." *DeBow's Review* 8 (1850): 134–46.

——. "Southern Patronage to Southern Imports and Domestic Industry." *DeBow's Review* 29 (1860): 77–83, 226–32, 494–500, 623–31, 771–78.

Griffin, Richard W. "The Origins of the Industrial Revolution in Georgia: Cotton Textiles, 1810–1865." *Georgia Historical Quarterly* 42 (1958): 355–75.

——. "Pro-Industrial Sentiment and Cotton Factories in Arkansas, 1820–1863." *Arkansas Historical Quarterly* 15, no. 2 (1956): 125–39.

——. "The Textile Industry in Greene County, Georgia, Before 1860." *Georgia Historical Quarterly* 43, no. 1 (1964): 81–84.

——. "Textile Industry." In *Encyclopedia of Southern History*, edited by David C. Roller and Robert W. Twyman, 1226–29. Baton Rouge: Louisiana State University Press, 1979.

Hall, M. R. "Utilization of Southern Water Powers." In *The South in the Building of a Nation* 5:580–86. Richmond: Southern Publication Society, 1909.

Harrell, John. "Confederate Military History of Arkansas." Pt. 2, vol. 10, of *Confederate Military History*, edited by Clement A. Evans. Atlanta: Confederate Publishing Co., 1899.

Hogan, George H. "Parsons's Brigade of Texas Cavalry." *Confederate Veteran* 33 (January 1925): 17–20.

Holladay, Florence Elizabeth. "The Powers of the Commander of the Confederate Trans-Mississippi Department, 1863–1865." *Southwestern Historical Quarterly* 21, nos. 3–4 (1918): 279–97, 333–59.

"Important Manufactory." *Washington* (Ark.) *Telegraph*, May 21, 1862, p. 2, col. 1.

Johnson, J. G. "Notes on Manufacturing in Ante-Bellum Georgia." *Georgia Historical Quarterly* 16 (1932): 214–31.

Jones, Ernest. "Mound Prairie Gave Community Its Name." *Palestine* (Tex.) *Herald-Press*, December 24, 1972, sec. 1, p. 14, cols. 1–5.

——. "Plenitude, Lost Industrial Ghost Town, Rediscovered." *Palestine* (Tex.) *Herald-Press*, March 19, 1969, p. 7, cols. 1–8.

J.T.S. "Campaign in Arkansas. Battle of Cotton Plant." *Tri-Weekly Telegraph* (Houston, Tex.), August 6, 1862, p. 1, cols. 3–4.

Larkin, F. Daniel. "Three Centuries of Transportation." In *The History of Oneida County*, 31–36. Utica, N.Y.: Oneida County, 1977.

Lewis, Elsie M. "Economic Conditions in Ante-Bellum Arkansas: 1850–1861." *Arkansas Historical Quarterly* 6, no. 3 (1947): 256–74.

McKenzie, H. N. "Confederate Manufactures in Southwest Arkansas." *Publications of the Arkansas Historical Association* 2 (1908): 199–210.

"Manufacturing in Georgia." *Savannah Republican*, April 20, 1849, p. 2, col. 3.

Manzelmann, Richard L. "Revivalism and Reform." In *The History of Oneida County*, 53–58. Utica, N.Y.: Oneida County, 1977.

"Marker to Be Dedicated at Site of Mound Prairie." *Palestine* (Tex.) *Herald-Press*, August 21, 1968, p. 16, cols. 1–3.

Marsh, Bryan. "The Confederate Letters of Bryan Marsh." *Chronicles of Smith County, Texas* 14 (Winter 1975): 9–53.

"Mass Meeting in Pike County." *True Democrat*, January 12, 1861, p. 1, col. 3.

Merrell, Elizabeth Magill. "Major Henry Merrell." *South-Western Presbyterian*, March 15, 1883, p. 1, cols. 1–2.

Merrell, Henry. "The Last of the Great Original Abolitionists." *South-Western Presbyterian*, December 23, 1875, p. 2, cols. 3–4.

——. "Manufacturing in Sober Earnest." *Milledgeville (Southern) Recorder*, March 30, 1847, p. 3, col. 4; April 13, 1847, p. 3, col. 2; April 20, 1847, p. 3, col. 4; April 27, 1847, p. 3, cols. 2–3.

——. ["Profit and Loss," pseud.] "Cotton Manufacturing in Georgia." *New York Journal of Commerce*, August 31, 1855, p. 3, col. 3; September 6, 1855, p. 1, col. 1; September 8, 1855, p. 3, cols. 4–5; September 17, 1855, p. 3, col. 3.

"Mr. Merrell and the Cotton Factory." *Washington* (Ark.) *Telegraph*, June 4, 1862, p. 2, col. 3.

Moore, Waddy William, "Arkansas." In *Encyclopedia of Southern History*, edited by David C. Roller and Robert W. Twyman, 61–76. Baton Rouge: Louisiana State University Press, 1979.

Morrison, Howard Alexander. "The Finney Takeover of the Second Great Awakening during the Oneida Revivals of 1825–1826." *New York History* 59 (January 1978): 27–54.

———. "Gentlemen of Proper Understanding: A Closer Look at Utica's Anti-Abolitionist Mob." *New York History* 62 (January 1981): 61–82.

"Murfreesboro Items." *Nashville* (Ark.) *News*, June 2, 1888, p. 5, col. 5.

"A New and Laudible Enterprise." *True Democrat*, September 9, 1856, p. 2, col. 2.

Nolan, Eugene A. "Four Unpublished Letters from Augustus Garland." *Arkansas Historical Quarterly* 18, no. 2 (1959): 78–109.

Parham, W. C. "David O. Dodd: The Nathan Hale of Arkansas." *Publications of the Arkansas Historical Association* 1 (1906): 531–35.

"Pioneer Cotton Factory." *Pine Bluff Daily Commercial*, July 13, 1887, p. 2, col. 1.

"The Planters Awakening." *Savannah Daily Republican*, January 9, 1845, p. 2, col. 3.

Polignac, Prince de Camille Armand Jules Marie. "Polignac's Mission." *Southern Historical Society Papers* 35 (1907): 326–34.

Preston, Douglas M., and David M. Ellis. "The Ethnic Dimension." In *The History of Oneida County*, 59–66. Utica, N.Y.: Oneida County, 1977.

Raper, Arthur. "Greene's Goin' Great." *Greensboro* (Ga.) *Herald-Journal*, February 20, 1942, p. 6, col. 6.

"Rattling around with Bones Jones." *Palestine* (Tex.) *Herald-Press*, May 31, 1981, sec. B, p. 2, cols. 1–2.

———. *Palestine* (Tex.) *Herald-Press*, June 3, 1981, p. 6, cols. 1–2.

Ray, Johnette Highsmith, ed. "Civil War Letters from Parsons' Texas Cavalry Brigade." *Southwestern Historical Quarterly* 69 (October 1965): 210–23.

Rice, Thaddeus B. "An Ex-Slave's Appeal." *Greensboro* (Ga.) *Herald-Journal*, March 7, 1941, p. 3, cols. 3–4.

———. "A Former Greensboro School Teacher." *Greensboro* (Ga.) *Herald-Journal*, October 7, 1938, p. 6, cols. 2–3.

———. "General Andrew Jackson's Last Visit to Georgia." *Greensboro* (Ga.) *Herald-Journal*, October 3, 1941, p. 7, cols. 2–3.

———. "Greene County's Vanished Villages." *Greensboro* (Ga.) *Herald-Journal*, July 18, 1941, p. 3, cols. 4–5.

———. "Towns, Villages, and Post Offices in Greene County." *Greensboro* (Ga.) *Herald-Journal*, February 17, 1939, p. 3, cols. 3–4.

———. "Why Sherman's Army Showed Mercy to Two Greene County Mills." *Greensboro* (Ga.) *Herald-Journal*, July 29, 1938, p. 3, cols. 4–5.

Roberts, O. M. "Confederate Military History of Texas." Pt. 1, vol. 11, of *Confederate Military History*, edited by Clement A. Evans. Atlanta: Confederate Publishing Co., 1899.

Scroggs, Jack B. "Arkansas in the Secession Crisis." *Arkansas Historical Quarterly* 12, no. 3 (1953): 179–224.

Shea, William L. "The Camden Fortifications." *Arkansas Historical Quarterly* 41 (1982): 318–26.

Shryock, R. H. "The Early Industrial Revolution in the Empire State." *Georgia Historical Quarterly* 11, no. 2 (June 1927): 109–28.

Smith, Henry M. Untitled editorial on Merrell's death. In *South-Western Presbyterian*, February 18, 1883, p. 4, col. 1.

Smith, Jodie A. "Battle-Grounds and Soldiers of Arkansas, 1861–1865." *Arkansas Historical Quarterly* 6 (1947): 180–85.

Snead, Thomas L. "The Conquest of Arkansas." In *Battles and Leaders of the Civil War*, edited by Clarence Clough Buel and Robert U. Johnson, 3:441–59. New York: Century Co., 1887.

Stinson, Virginia McCollum. "Yankees in Camden, Arkansas." In *Heroines of Dixie*, edited by Katherine M. Jones, 227–85. New York: Bobbs-Merrill Co., 1955.

Wager, Daniel E. "Whitesboro's Golden Age." In *Transactions of the Oneida Historical Society at Utica, 1881–1884*, 65–144. Utica, N.Y.: Ellis H. Roberts and Co., 1885.

White, Lonnie J. ed. "A Bluecoat's Account of the Camden Expedition." *Arkansas Historical Quarterly* 24 (1965): 82–89.

"Woman Locates Site of Town." *Palestine* (Tex.) *Herald-Press,* May 13, 1977, p. 5, cols. 1–2.

Index

References to illustrations are printed in italic.

Guns, 12, 48–49, 94, 146, 207–9, 266–67, 270, 276, 321–22, 332

Hackett, James Henry, 50
Hackett, Mrs. James Henry, 50
Hagg (millwright), 152
Haiti: Merrell's trip by, 388
Hale, David, 19
Hale, Lucretia Irvine, 17
Hale, Nathan, 19
Hale family: connections to Merrell family, 17, 19
Hamilton, Col., 112
Hand, Ira, 80, 149
Hardee, Isabella, 137, 140
Hardee, Gen. William Joseph, 137
Hartford, Conn., 16, 20
Harvey, Sylvanus, 68
Hastings, Thomas, 31–32
Havana, Cuba: Merrell's trip through, xxv, xxxiii, 233–34, 384–85, 386, 388, 392
Haydn, Franz Joseph, 31
Haynes, Maj. W. H., 232–33
Hayti (section of Utica), 7, 37, 61
Helena, Ark., 101, 234–35, 313, 314, 315, 328, 331. *See also* Civil War: battles and skirmishes
Hempstead County, Ark., 245. *See also* Washington, Ark.
Henderson (assault victim), 320
Herkimer, Gen. Nicholas, 12
Hill (millowner), 120
Hindman, Gen. Thomas Carmichael, xxxi; uses dictatorial methods, 298, 301, 308; assumes command of Trans-Mississippi, 299, 300; increases troops and supplies, 301; issues general order, 302; suppresses speculators, 304, 308; discourages private enterprise, 308; selects poor subordinates, 308–9; is relieved, 309, 315; accomplishments, 309–10;

commands at Prairie Grove, 315, 324–35
Hinman, John E., 42, 46
Hitchcock, Alfred, 125
Hobart, Bishop John Henry, 10
Holm, Maj., 386
Holmes, Gen. Theophilus Hunter, xxii, xxxi, xxxii; commissions Merrell, 227, 230; assumes command of Trans-Mississippi, 315; resources, 324, 325; responsibilities, 326; character, 327; repelled by Capt. Mackey, 328; employs Merrell as chief engineer, 329, 330; attacks Helena, 338–40; is ill after Helena, 342; reassumes command, 346; orders attack on Pine Bluff, 347; is relieved of Trans-Mississippi, 349; commands District of Arkansas, 349, 352; ordered to Richmond, 354; given farewell, 354; Merrell's opinion of, 355
Holt's Hotel (New York City), 104
Homestead Exemption Law, 250
Hooker, Mary, 43
Hooker, Sam, 42
Hopewell Presbytery, 206
Hopkins, Samuel, 59
Hotel Faranti (Mexico), 388
Houston, Tex., 232, 233, 384
Hovey, Gen. Alvin P., 314
Howell, David, 161, 165, 198, 201, 202
Hugh's Mill, 217, 238–39
Hulbert, Zelinda Merrell, 32
Hull, Amos G., 42
Hunt, Montgomery, 35
Hunt, Montgomery (son), 35
Huntsville, Tex.: textile factory at state penitentiary, 232, 306, 384
Hurlbert, Charles, 71

Immigrant Aid Society, 197
Indians, 6–7, 13, 20, 32, 41–42, 43–44,